GPU Pro 360
Guide to Rendering

GPU Pro 360

Guide to Rendering

Edited by Wolfgang Engel

CRC Press
Taylor & Francis Group
Boca Raton London New York

CRC Press is an imprint of the
Taylor & Francis Group, an **informa** business
AN A K PETERS BOOK

CRC Press
Taylor & Francis Group
6000 Broken Sound Parkway NW, Suite 300
Boca Raton, FL 33487-2742

Printed on acid-free paper

Printed and bound in India by Replika Press Pvt. Ltd.

International Standard Book Number-13: 978-0-8153-6550-1 (Paperback)
International Standard Book Number-13: 978-0-8153-6551-8 (Hardback)

Library of Congress Cataloging-in-Publication Data

Names: Engel, Wolfgang F., editor.
Title: GPU pro 360 guide to rendering / [edited by] Wolfgang Engel.
Description: Boca Raton : Taylor & Francis, CRC Press, 2018 | Includes bibliographical references.
Identifiers: LCCN 2017060380| ISBN ISBN 9780815365518 (hardback : acid-free paper)
   | ISBN 9780815365501 (pbk. : acid-free paper)
Subjects: LCSH: Computer graphics. | Rendering (Computer graphics) | Graphics processing
   units--Programming. | Pocket computers--Programming. | Mobile computing.
Classification: LCC T385 .G68887 2018 | DDC 006.6--dc23
LC record available at https://lccn.loc.gov/2017060380

Visit the eResources: www.crcpress.com/9780815365501

Visit the Taylor & Francis Web site at
http://www.taylorandfrancis.com

and the CRC Press Web site at
http://www.crcpress.com

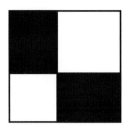

Contents

4   Virtual Texture Mapping 101   69
Matthäus G. Chajdas, Christian Eisenacher, Marc Stamminger, and
Sylvain Lefebvre

5   Pre-Integrated Skin Shading   81
Eric Penner and George Borshukov

6   Implementing Fur Using Deferred Shading   97
Donald Revie

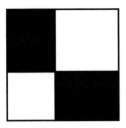

Introduction

This book is a reflection of some of the latest developments in the field of real-time rendering. Thanks to the flexibility of today's GPUs, we have witnessed an explosion in the number of methods and techniques used to sample real-world phenomenon or to model special effects from our own minds. It is great to see that almost every new game today holds a number of rendering recipes that gives it its unique look and feel. But it is even much greater that the makers of those products actually share their work with the entire community.

The chapters in this book cover a wide selection of topics, from surface rendering to stylization to post-processing to rendering systems.

We start with the chapter, "Quadtree Displacement Mapping with Height Blending," by Michał Drobot. This is a complete production-proof surface rendering solution with a multitude of powerful capabilities. The technique provides an accelerated approach to render displaced surfaces via smart use of a quad-tree structure during height-field ray tracing. The author covers the details of rendering dynamic displaced surfaces with multiple layers, soft-shadowing, ambient occlusion, and LOD support. This entire combination is achievable on current-generation hardware and consoles with a small memory footprint in comparison to basic normal mapping.

The next chapter is "NPR Effects Using the Geometry Shader," by Pedro Hermosilla and Pere-Pau Vázquez. This is a new real-time implementation of non-photorealistic rendering effects by relying on the geometry shader stage in recent GPUs. The authors show how to calculate proper textured silhouettes, which gives the capability to specify stylized outline ink types. A special discussion on pencil shading is also included.

The chapter, "Alpha Blending as a Post-Process," by Benjamin Hathaway introduces a novel and inspiring technique to render correct alpha-blended geometry without the need for depth sorting. It is a multi-pass approach that relies on a separate buffer for alpha-blending accumulation, which is then combined with the scene's render target in a single post-processing step.

The fourth chapter in the book is "Virtual Texture Mapping 101," written by Matthäus G. Chajdas, Christian Eisenacher, Marc Stamminger, and Sylvain Lefebvre. In this introductory chapter, the authors show the basics of a rendering system that supports rendering with a virtually unlimited set of textures while still utilizing a fixed amount of texture memory on the graphics card. The system manages streaming and paging textures into the GPU based on visible scene contents. The chapter discusses the system's implementation details, including texture filtering issues and other important considerations.

The chapter "Pre-Integrated Skin Shading," by Eric Penner and George Borshukov, presents an interesting and very efficient shading model for rendering realistic skin. It can be evaluated entirely in a pixel shader and does not require extra rendering passes for blurring, thus making it a very scalable skin-rendering technique.

Our next chapter is "Implementing Fur Using Deferred Shading," by Donald Revie. The popularity of deferred shading has increased dramatically in recent years. One of the limitations of working in a deferred-rendering engine is that techniques involving alpha blending, such as fur rendering, become difficult to implement. In this chapter we learn a number of tricks that enable fur to be rendered in a deferred-shading environment.

The chapter "Large-Scale Terrain Rendering for Outdoor Games," by Ferenc Pintér, presents a host of production-proven techniques that allow for large, high-quality terrains to be rendered on resource-constrained platforms such as current-generation consoles. This chapter provides practical tips for all areas of real-time terrain rendering, from the content-creation pipeline to final rendering.

The next chapter is "Practical Morphological Antialiasing," by Jorge Jimenez, Belen Masia, Jose I. Echevarria, Fernando Navarro, and Diego Gutierrez. The authors take a new, high-quality, antialiasing algorithm and demonstrate a highly optimized GPU implementation. This implementation is so efficient that it competes quite successfully with hardware-based antialiasing schemes in both performance and quality. This technique is particularly powerful because it provides a natural way to add antialiasing to a deferred-shading engine.

Emil Persson's "Volume Decals" is a practical technique to render surface decals without the need to generate special geometry for every decal. Instead, the GPU performs the entire projection operation. The author shows how to use volume textures to render decals on arbitrary surfaces while avoiding texture stretching and shearing artifacts.

The chapter "Practical Elliptical Texture Filtering on the GPU," by Pavlos Mavridis and Georgios Papaioannou, presents a useful technique for achieving high-quality, shader-based texture filtering on the GPU. The authors provide a reference implementation that can easily be integrated into an existing renderer.

The next chapter is "An Approximation to the Chapman Grazing-Incidence Function for Atmospheric Scattering," by Christian Schüler. This chapter describes an inexpensive approximation to atmospheric scattering and will be of particular interest to those interested in physically based, fully dynamic, virtual environments in which both visual realism and computational efficiency are of high importance.

The next chapter is "Volumetric Real-Time Water and Foam Rendering," by Daniel Scherzer, Florian Bagar, and Oliver Mattausch. This chapter presents a dynamic, multilayered approach for rendering fluids and foam. This technique is presented in the context of a GPU-based fluid simulation, but it is compatible with other forms of fluid simulation as well.

The chapter "Inexpensive Antialiasing of Simple Objects," by Mikkel Gjøl and Mark Gjøl, explores the use of discontinuity edge overdraw for antialiasing simple objects on mobile phones. The essence of this technique is to render a "smooth" line on top of aliasing primitive edges to cover the aliasing edge.

The chapter "Practical Planar Reflections Using Cubemaps and Image Proxies," by Sébastien Lagarde and Antoine Zanuttini, discusses a very fast and efficient system for approximating dynamic glossy and specular reflections on planar surfaces. The authors discuss the art tools, strategies, and runtime requirements for the their system and provide code snippets to help readers integrate a similar system into their own engine. The authors also provide a video of their techniques in the accompanying web material.

Our next chapter is "Real-Time Ptex and Vector Displacement," by Karl Hillesland. This chapter discusses a technique for overcoming issues introduced by texture seams particularly in the application of displacement maps where small texturing errors can result in very noticeable surface artifacts and cracks. An additional benefit of this system is that it eliminates the need for an explicit UV space.

In "Decoupled Deferred Shading on the GPU," Gábor Liktor and Carsten Dachsbacher describe a technique that leverages a unique G-Buffer structure to reduce the amount of shading computation and memory footprint of an antialiasing deferred renderer that matches the quality of hardware multisample antialiasing (MSAA). The authors discuss an implementation that includes a stochastic rasterization framework.

Our next chapter, "Tiled Forward Shading," is by Markus Billeter, Ola Olsson, and Ulf Assarsson. The authors describe a new and powerful rendering system that combines the flexibility of forward shading with the efficiency of deferred rendering. In addition to greater flexibility, this system also natively supports hardware MSAA, transparency, and heterogeneous materials. The authors provide a detailed description of their implementation (full demo source code available in the web material) as well as a very thorough performance analysis.

Next is "Forward+: A Step Toward Film-Style Shading in Real Time," by Takahiro Harada, Jay McKee, and Jason C. Yang. This chapter builds on the previous chapter by discussing an advanced tiled forward renderer that was used in a full production environment. The authors go on to describe many extensions to tiled forward rendering such as exploiting the latest GPU hardware features, indirect lighting, advanced tile culling, and hybrid raytraced shadows.

"Progressive Screen-Space Multichannel Surface Voxelization," by Athanasios Gaitatzes and Georgios Papaioannou, describes a new technique for computing scene voxelizations that can be used for real-time global illumination computation. The key idea of their chapter is that a voxelization is built incrementally across frames from geometry present in the depth buffer, combining the performance of screen-space approaches with improved volume coverage comparable to full-scene voxelization.

"Rasterized Voxel-Based Dynamic Global Illumination," by Hawar Doghramachi, presents an approximate global illumination technique, again building on a voxel representation: the scene is rendered into a 3D read-write buffer using atomic functions. Next, the illumination of each voxel is computed and it is then treated as an indirect (virtual) light source. After propagating its contribution through the grid (similar to light propagation volumes (LDVs)), the scene can be indirectly lit.

The next chapter is "Per-Pixel Lists for Single Pass A-Buffer," by Sylvain Lefebvre, Samuel Hornus, and Anass Lasram. Identifying all the surfaces projecting into a pixel has many important applications in computer graphics, such as computing transparency. They often also require ordering of the fragments in each pixel. This chapter discusses a very fast and efficient approach for recording and simultaneously sorting of all fragments that fall within a pixel in a single geometry pass.

Next is "Reducing Texture Memory Usage by 2-Channel Color Encoding," by Krzysztof Kluczek. This chapter discusses a technique for compactly encoding and efficiently decoding color images using only 2-channel textures. The chapter details the estimation of the respective 2D color space and provides example shaders ready for use.

"Particle-Based Simulation of Material Aging," by Tobias Günther, Kai Rohmer, and Thorsten Grosch, describes a GPU-based, interactive simulation of material aging processes. Their approach enables artists to interactively control the aging process and outputs textures encoding surface properties such as precipitate, normals, and height directly usable during content creation.

"Simple Rasterization-Based Liquids," by Martin Guay, describes a powerful yet simple way of simulating particle-based liquids on the GPU. These simulations typically involve sorting the particles into spatial acceleration structures to resolve inter-particle interactions. In this chapter, the author details how this costly step can be sidestepped with splatting particles onto textures, i.e., making use of the rasterization pipeline, instead of sorting them.

In "Next-Generation Rendering in Thief" by Peter Sikachev, Samuel Delmont, Uriel Doyon, and Jean-Normand Bucci, a number of advanced rendering techniques, specifically designed for the new generation of gaming consoles, are presented. The authors discuss real-time reflections, contact shadows, and compute-shader-based postprocessing techniques.

Next is "Grass Rendering and Simulation with LOD" by Dongsoo Han and Hongwei Li. In this chapter, the authors present a GPU-based system for grass simulation and rendering. This system is capable of simulating and rendering more than 100,000 blades of grass, entirely on the GPU, and is based on earlier work related to character hair simulation.

"Hybrid Reconstruction Antialiasing" by Michał Drobot provides the reader with a full framework of antialiasing techniques specially designed to work efficiently with AMD's GCN hardware architecture. The author presents both spatial and temporal antialiasing techniques and weighs the pros and cons of many different implementation strategies.

Egor Yusov's "Real-Time Rendering of Physically Based Clouds Using Precomputed Scattering" provides a physically based method for rendering highly realistic and efficient clouds. Cloud rendering is typically very expensive, but here the author makes clever use of lookup tables and other optimizations to simulate scattered light within a cloud in real time.

In "Sparse Procedural Volume Rendering" by Doug McNabb, a powerful technique for volumetric rendering is presented. Hierarchical data structures are used to efficiently light and render complex volumetric effects in real time. The author also discusses methods in which artists can control volumetric forms and thus provide strong direction on the ultimate look of volumetric effects.

The chapter "Adaptive Virtual Textures," by Ka Chen, presents a technique for large, open world texturing. This technique is able to achieve very high resolution textures and also supports dynamically composited decals that help create unique and complex-looking surfaces.

Next, we have "Deferred Coarse Pixel Shading" by Rahul P. Sathe and Tomasz Janczak. In this chapter the authors present an optimization technique in which regions of low visual complexity may be shaded at less than the pixel frequency. The performance benefits demonstrated by the authors are quite impressive!

Finally, we have "Progressive Rendering Using Multi-frame Sampling" by Daniel Limberger, Karsten Tausche, Johannes Linke, and Jürgen Döllner. In this chapter the authors present a framework for achieving very high quality rendered results by distributing sampling work across multiple frames. The authors demonstrate their framework in the context of antialiasing, depth of field, screen-space ambient occlusion, and order-independent transparency.

I would like to thank all our authors for sharing their exciting new work with the graphics community. We hope that these ideas encourage readers to further extend the state of the art in real-time rendering, and we look forward to the new advances that these ideas inspire!

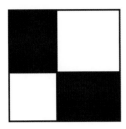

Web Materials

Example programs and source code to accompany some of the chapters are available on the CRC Press website: go to https://www.crcpress.com/9780815365501 and click on the "Downloads" tab.

The directory structure follows the book structure by using the chapter numbers as the name of the subdirectory.

General System Requirements

The material presented in this book was originally published between 2010 and 2016, and the most recent developments have the following system requirements:

- The DirectX June 2010 SDK (the latest SDK is installed with Visual Studio 2012).

- DirectX 11 or DirectX 12 capable GPUs are required to run the examples. The chapter will mention the exact requirement.

- The OS should be Microsoft Windows 10, following the requirement of DirectX 11 or 12 capable GPUs.

- Visual Studio C++ 2012 (some examples might require older versions).

- 2GB RAM or more.

- The latest GPU driver.

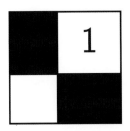

Quadtree Displacement Mapping
with Height Blending
Michał Drobot

1.1   Overview

This article presents an overview and comparison of current surface rendering techniques, and introduces a novel approach outperforming existing solutions in terms of performance, memory usage, and multilayer blending. Algorithms and ideas researched during *Two Worlds 2* development are shared, and the article proposes strategies for tackling problems of realistic terrain, surface and decal visualization considering limited memory, and computational power on current-generation consoles. Moreover, problems of functionality, performance, and aesthetics are discussed, providing guidelines for choosing the proper technique, content creation, and authoring pipeline.

We focus on various view and light-dependant visual clues important for correct surface rendering such as displacement mapping, self-shadowing with approximate penumbra shadows, ambient occlusion, and surface correct texture blending, while allowing real-time surface changes. Moreover, all presented techniques are valid for high quality real-time rendering on current generation hardware as well as consoles (as Xbox 360 was the main target platform during research).

First, existing parallax mapping techniques are compared and contrasted with real-life demands and possibilities. Then we present a state-of-the-art algorithm yielding higher accuracy with very good performance, scaling well with large height fields. It makes use of empty space skipping techniques and utilizes texture MIP levels for height quadtree storage, which can be prepared at render time. Second, a soft shadows computation method is proposed, which takes advantage of the quadtree. We expand upon this to calculate an ambient-occlusion term. Next, we introduce an LOD technique which allows higher performance and

Figure 1.1. Normal mapped environment.

Figure 1.2. Fully featured surface rendering using the methods proposed in this article.

quality for minification. Then we focus on surface blending methods, proposing a new method that exhibits better resemblance to real life and allows aggressive optimization during blended height-field displacement mapping. The proposed methods—depending on combinations and implementation—guarantee fast, scalable, and accurate displacement mapping of blended surfaces, including visually pleasing ambient occlusion and soft penumbra soft shadowing (compare Figures 1.1 and 1.2). Specific attention will be given to the various implementations and the proper choice of rendering method and asset authoring pipeline.

1.2 Introduction

During the last change of console generation we have seen a dramatic improvement in graphics rendering quality. With modern GPUs pushing millions of triangles per second, we are looking for more fidelity in areas that are still being impractical for performance reasons. One of those is surface rendering, which is one of the most fundamental building blocks of believable virtual world.

Each surface at its geometric level has a number of complex properties such as volume, depth, and various frequency details that together model further visual clues like depth parallax, self-shadowing, self-occlusion, and light reactivity. The topic of light interactions depending on surface microstructure is well researched and so many widely used solutions are provided (such as Cook-Torrance's lighting model and its optimizations). However, correct geometry rendering is still problematic. The brute force approach of rendering every geometry detail as a triangle mesh is still impractical because it would have to consist of millions of vertices, thus requiring too much memory and computations. Moreover, surface blending such as widely seen on terrain (i.e., sand mixing with rocks) only complicate the situation in terms of blend quality and additional performance impact. Last but not least, we would like to manipulate surface geometric properties at render time (i.e., dynamic water erosion simulation, craters forming after meteor strike).

To sum up, we would like our surface rendering method to support:

- accurate depth at all angles (depth parallax effect);
- self-shadowing;
- ambient occlusion;
- fast blending;
- dynamic geometric properties;
- current-generation hardware (taking console performance into account);
- minimal memory footprint compared to common normal mapping.

Common normal mapping techniques (those which create the illusion of detailed surface by performing light computation on precalculated normal data set) fail to meet our demands, as they do not model visual geometry clues. However, we still find it useful in light interaction calculations, thus complementing more sophisticated rendering solutions.

The only rendering method class that is able to suit all our needs are height-field-based ray-tracing algorithms. The idea behind those algorithms is to walk along a ray that entered the surface volume, finding the correct intersection of the ray with the surface. They operate on grayscale images representing height values of surfaces, thus exchanging vertex for pixel transformations, which suits our hardware better in terms of performance and memory usage. Moreover, they mix well with existing normal mapping and are performing better as GPUs become more general processing units. However, none of them are aimed at high performance surface blending or ambient occlusion calculation.

During our research we were seeking for the best possible rendering method meeting our demands, being robust, functional and fast as we were aiming for Xbox360-class hardware. As our scenario involved fully-featured rendering of outdoor terrain with many objects and indoor cave systems, we were forced to take special care for an automatic LOD system. Several methods were compared and evaluated, finally ending with the introduction of a new solution that proved to be suiting all our needs. We describe our research and the motivation behind it, going in detail with each building block of the Quadtree Displacement Mapping with Height Blending technique.

1.3 Overview of Ray-Tracing Algorithms

Every height-field-based ray-tracing algorithm is working with additional displacement data, commonly encoded in height map format (grayscale image scaled to $[0; 1]$ range). Calculations are done in tangent space to allow computations for arbitrary surfaces. Correct surface depth is calculated by finding the intersection between viewing ray and height field. That ensures correct parallax offset for further color and lighting calculations.

Figure 1.3 illustrates the depth parallax effect and presents the general intersection calculation.

General height-field ray-tracing algorithms can be summarized as follows:

1. Calculate tangent-space normalized view vector V per-vertex, and interpolate for pixel shader.

2. Ray cast the view ray to compute intersection with the height field, acquiring the texture coordinate offset required for arriving at the correct

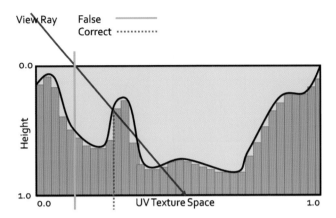

Figure 1.3. Height-field ray-trace scheme.

surface point. We start at texture input T1 coordinates, sampling along the surface's profile, finally computing new texture coordinates T2.

3. Compute the normal lighting equation using surface attributes sampled at the new texture coordinates T2.

The following algorithms implement various methods for intersection computation, varying in speed, accuracy and use of additional precomputed data.

1.3.1 Online Algorithms

Relief mapping. Relief mapping [Policarpo 2005] performs intersection calculation by linear search in two-dimensional height-field space followed by binary search.

We want to find the intersection point (p, r). We start by calculating point (u, v), which is the two-dimensional texture coordinate of the surface point where the viewing ray reaches a depth $= 1.0$. The point (u, v) is computed based on initial texture coordinates (x, y) on the transformed view direction with scaling factor applied. Then we search for (p, r) by sampling the height field between (x, y) and (u, v). We check for intersections by comparing ray depth with the stored depth at the current sampling point. When the latter is smaller, we have found the intersection and we can refine it using binary search. Figure 1.4 illustrates the process.

Binary search is taking advantage of texture filtering and operates in minimized space around the found intersection point. That ensures fast convergence and high accuracy. However, using that kind of search utilizes dependant reads on the GPU, thus vastly affecting performance. While a linear- and binary-search

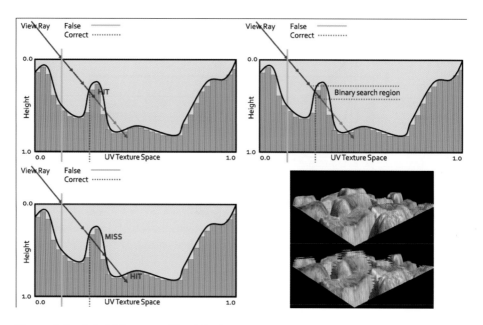

Figure 1.4. Relief Mapping. Top left: linear search. Top right: binary search around point found in linear search. Bottom left: possible miss of linear search. Bottom right: resulting aliasing artifacts as opposed to correct rendering.

combo is a known and proven solution, its linear part is prone to aliasing due to under sampling. During the search, when there are not enough search steps (step length is too big), we might miss important surface features as shown in Figure 1.4. Increasing search steps potentially minimizes the problem but severely affects performance, making this algorithm highly unreliable when sampling large height fields or surfaces exhibiting very large displacement scales. Nonetheless, it is still very effective in simple scenarios that do not require high sampling count, as the performance is saved on ALU instructions.

Parallax occlusion mapping. Several researchers tried to optimize this algorithm by omitting the expensive binary search. *Parallax occlusion mapping* [Tatarchuk 2006] relies on accurate high-precision intersection calculation (see Figure 1.5). A normal linear search is performed finding point (p, r) and last step point (k, l). Then the ray is tested against a line made of (p, r) and (k, l), effectively approximating the height profile as a piecewise linear curve. Moreover, solutions for additional LOD and soft shadows were proposed. POM, while being accurate enough and faster than relief mapping, is still prone to aliasing and so exhibits the same negative traits of linear search (Listing 1.1).

```
float Size = 1.0 / LinearSearchSteps;
float Depth = 1.0;
int StepIndex = 0;
float CurrD = 0.0;
float PrevD = 1.0;
float2 p1 = 0.0;
float2 p2 = 0.0;

while(StepIndex < LinearSearchSteps)
{
    Depth -= Size; //move the ray
    float4 TCoord = float2(p+(v*Depth)); // new sampling pos
    CurrD = tex2D(texSMP, TCoord).a; //new height
    if (CurrD > Depth) //check for intersection
    {
        p1 = float2(Depth, CurrD);
        p2 = float2(Depth + Size, PrevD); //store last step
        StepIndex = LinearSearchSteps; //break the loop
    }
    StepIndex++;
    PrevD = CurrD;
}

//Linear approximation using current and last step
//instead of binary search, opposed to relief mapping.
float d2 = p2.x - p2.y;
float d1 = p1.x - p1.y;

return (p1.x * d2 - p2.x * d1) / (d2 - d1);
```

Listing 1.1. POM code.

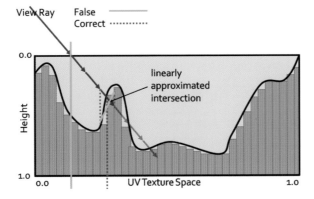

Figure 1.5. POM.

1.3.2   Algorithms Using Precomputed Data

In response to the arising problem of performance and accuracy, several solutions were proposed that make use of additional data to ensure skipping of empty space and prohibit missing surface features. However, additional memory footprint or preprocessing computation time limits their usefulness.

Per-pixel displacement with distance function. *Per-pixel displacement with distance function* [Donelly 2005] uses precalculated three-dimensional texture representation of the surface's profile. Each texel represents a sphere whose radius is equal to the nearest surface point. We are exchanging the well-known linear search for sphere tracing. With each sample taken we know how far we can march our ray without missing any possible intersection. Traversing that kind of structure allows skipping large space areas and ensures that we will not miss the intersection point. Moreover, the intersection search part is very efficient. However, memory requirements and precomputation time for this method make it impractical for real-time game environments. As stated in [Donelly 2005], even simple surfaces may require a three-dimensional texture size of $256 \times 256 \times 16$ with dimensions rising fast for more complex and accurate rendering. That increase in memory footprint is unacceptable for the limited memory of current consoles and PC hardware, not to mention the prohibitive preprocessing time.

Cone step mapping (CSM). CSM [Dummer 2006] is based on a similar idea. It uses a cone map that associates a circular cone with each texel of the height-field texture. The cone angle is calculated so that the cone is the largest one not intersecting the height field (see Figure 1.6). This information allows us

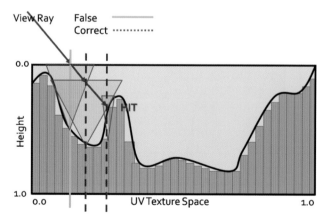

Figure 1.6. CSM. Ray traversal by cone radius distance.

to calculate a safe distance during sampling, as in per-pixel displacement with distance function. Consequently, the ray may skip empty spaces and never miss the correct intersection. Due to its conservative nature, the algorithm may require too many steps to actually converge. For performance reasons, it is required to set a maximum number of steps, which often results in stopping the ray trace too early and returning incorrect texture coordinates for further rendering.

Cone step mapping performance varies widely depending on the spatial coherency of the height field. Generally, it outperforms linear search algorithms while guaranteeing less noticeable errors. Its memory footprint is quite bearable as it requires only one additional 8-bit texture for cone maps. However, its preprocessing time makes it impossible to alter the height field at render time, as this would require recompilation of the cone map with every change. The precomputation algorithm is of complexity $O(n^2)$, where n denotes number of height-field texels, making it impractical on current GPUs. Moreover, properties of the cone map prohibit correct and easy surface blending.

Relaxed cone step mapping (RCSM). RCSM [Policarpo 2007] takes CSM one step further, making it less conservative. The idea is to use larger cones that intersect the height field only once. The search is performed the same way as in CSM. When the intersection is found, the correct point is searched, using binary search in space restricted by the last cone radius, therefore converging very quickly. The combination leads to more efficient space leaping, while remaining accurate, due to final refinement. Furthermore, an LOD scheme is proposed which, while it lacks accuracy, provides performance gains. In practice, RCSM is currently the fastest ray-tracing algorithm available, making it very useful in scenarios where neither long preprocessing times, disability of efficient blending, and dynamic height-field alteration are irrelevant.

1.4 Quadtree Displacement Mapping

We introduce a GPU-optimized version of the classic [Cohen and Shaked 1993] hierarchical ray-tracing algorithm for terrain rendering on CPU, using height-field pyramid, with bounding information stored in mipmap chain. It was presented on recent hardware by [OH 2006], yielding good accuracy and performance, but at the same time was less adequate for game scenario use. We describe our implementation, optimized for current GPUs, with an automatic LOD solution and accurate filtering. Moreover, we expand it for optimized surface blending, soft shadowing and ambient occlusion calculation.

QDM uses the mipmap structure for resembling a dense quadtree, storing maximum heights above the base plane of the height field (it is worth noting that our implementation is actually using depth maps as 0 value representing maximum displacement, as we are storing depth measured under the reference plane. In consequence, maximum heights are minimum depths, stored in our data structure). We traverse it to skip empty space and not to miss any detail. During traversal we are moving the ray from cell boundary to cell boundary, until level 0 is reached—hence valid intersection region. While moving through the hierarchy, we compute the proper hierarchy level change. Finally, we use refinement search in the region of intersection to find the accurate solution when needed.

Gf 8800	256^2	512^2	1024^2	2048^2
Quad tree	0.15ms	0.25ms	1.15ms	2.09ms
CSM	< 2min	< 14min	< 8h	/

Table 1.1. Data preprocessing time.

1.4.1 Quadtree Construction

The quadtree is represented by a hierarchical collection of images in a mipmap. The construction is simple, as it requires generating mipmaps with the min operator instead of average as during normal mipmapping. As a result, MIP level 0 (2^n) represents the original height field with the following levels 1 (2^{n-1}), 2 (2^{n-2}), ... containing the minimum value of the four nearest texels from levels above. The entire process can be run on the GPU. Due to hardware optimization, quadtree construction is very fast. The timings in Table 1.1 were obtained on a PC equipped with Intel Core 2 Duo 2.4 GHz and GeForce 8800. For comparison, timings for RCSM are given. The quadtree was computed on the GPU, while the cone map was on the CPU due to algorithm requirements.

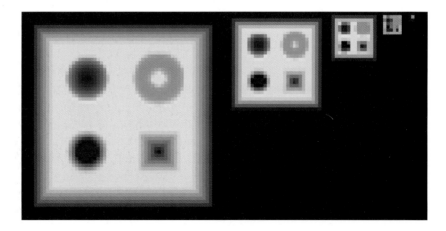

Figure 1.7. Generated QDM on mipmaps.

As we can see, quadtree computation time is negligible, even for on-the-fly generation, whereas cone maps could even be problematic for off-line rendering during texture authoring (see Figure 1.7).

1.4.2 Quadtree Traversal

The general steps of intersection search are shown by the pseudocode in Listing 1.2. We start the computation at the highest mipmap level. The stopping condition of the main loop is to reach the lowest hierarchy level, which effectively means finding the intersection region where the linear approximation can be performed. At each step, we determine if we can move the ray further or if there is a need for further refinement. We algebraically perform the intersection test between the ray and the cell bounding planes and the minimum depth plane.

In case the ray does not intersect the minimum plane, then the current cell is blocking our trace. We have to refine the search by descending in the hierarchy by one level. In the other case, we have to find the first intersection of the ray with the minimum plane or the cell boundary. When the right intersection is computed, we move the ray to the newly acquired point. In case we have to cross the cell boundary, then we choose the next cell via the nearest-neighbor method, thus minimizing error. At this point, we perform hierarchy level update for optimization (see the optimization section).

Figure 1.8 presents step-by-step ray traversal in QDM: Step (a) shows a ray coming from the initial geometry plane and stopping at the maximum level or minimum plane. Steps (b) and (c) illustrate further refinement while the search descends to lower hierarchy levels. Step (d) presents where the ray must cross the cell in order to progress. While the minimum plane of the current cell is not blocking the way, we have to move the ray to the nearest cell boundary. Steps (e) and (f) show further ray traversal while refining the search while (g) presents the main loop's stopping condition, as the ray has reached level 0. Therefore, we can proceed to linear interpolation between the nearest texels in Step (h).

```
While (hierarchy_level > 0)
    depth=get_maximum_depth(position, hierarchy level)
    If(ray_depth < depth)
        move_ray_to_cell_boundry_or_minimum_depth_plane
    else
        descend_one_hierarchy_level
    end
    find_intersection_using_linear_interpolation
```

Listing 1.2. General QDM search steps.

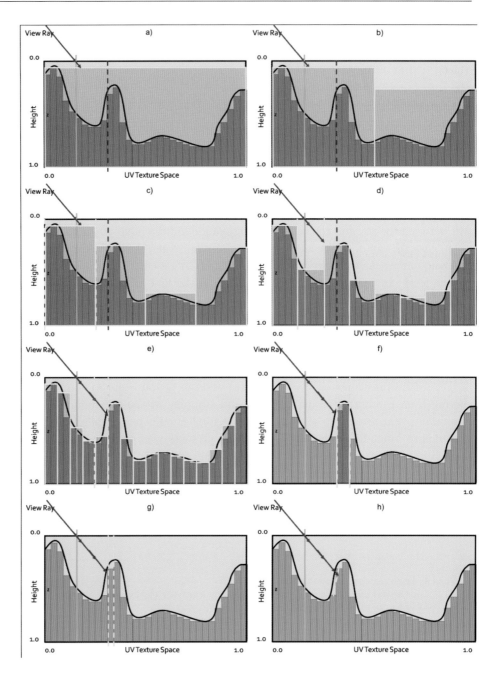

Figure 1.8. QDM traversal.

It is important to correctly calculate sampling positions since we are working with a discrete data structure. For correct results, we should use point-filtering on the GPU and integer math. However, if we cannot afford an additional sampler for the same texture using POINT and LINEAR, it is possible to use linear filtering with enough care taken for correct calculations. As SM 3.0 only emulates integer operations, we have to account for possible errors in calculations (using SM 4.0 is preferable, due to the presence of real integer math).

Listing 1.3 is heavily commented to explain the algorithm's steps in detail.

```
const int MaxLevel = MaxMipLvl;
const int NodeCount = pow(2.0, MaxLevel);
const float HalfTexel = 1.0 / NodeCount / 2.0;
float d;
float3 p2 = p;
int Level = MaxLevel;

//We calculate ray movement vector in inter-cell numbers.
int2 DirSign = sign(v.xy);

//Main loop
while (Level >= 0)
{
    //We get current cell minimum plane using tex2Dlod.
    d = tex2Dlod(HeightTexture, float4(p2.xy, 0.0 , Level)).w;

    //If we are not blocked by the cell we move the ray.
    if (d > p2.z)
    {
        //We calculate predictive new ray position.
        float3 tmpP2 = p + v * d;

        //We compute current and predictive position.
        //Calculations are performed in cell integer numbers.
        int NodeCount = pow(2, (MaxLevel - Level));
        int4 NodeID = int4((p2.xy , tmpP2.xy) * NodeCount);

        //We test if both positions are still in the same cell.
        //If not, we have to move the ray to nearest cell
        //boundary.
        if (NodeID.x != NodeID.z || NodeID.y != NodeID.w)
        {
            //We compute the distance to current cell boundary.
            //We perform the calculations in continuous space.
            float2 a = (p2.xy - p.xy);
            float2 p3 = (NodeID.xy + DirSign) / NodeCount;
            float2 b = (p3.xy - p.xy);
```

```
                    //We are choosing the nearest cell
                    //by choosing smaller distance.
                    float2 dNC = abs(p2.z * b / a);
                    d = min(d, min(dNC.x, dNC.y));

                    //During cell crossing we ascend in hierarchy.
                    Level+=2;

                    //Predictive refinement
                    tmpP2 = p + v * d;
            }

            //Final ray movement
            p2 = tmpP2;
        }

        //Default descent in hierarchy
        //nullified by ascend in case of cell crossing
        Level--;
    }
    return p2;
```

Listing 1.3. QDM search steps.

1.4.3   Optimizations

Convergence speed-up. It is worth noting that during traversal, the ray can only descend in the hierarchy. Therefore, we are not taking full advantage of the quadtree. The worst-case scenario occurs when the ray descends to lower levels and passes by an obstacle really close, consequently degenerating further traversal to the linear search. To avoid that problem, we should optimally compute the correct level higher in the hierarchy during cell crossing. However, current hardware is not optimized for such dynamic flow. A simple one step up move in the hierarchy should be enough. For more complicated surfaces which require many iterations, we discovered that this optimization increases performance by 30% (tested on a case requiring >64 iterations).

Fixed search step count. While the algorithm tends to converge really quickly, it may considerably slow down at grazing angles on complex high-resolution height fields. Therefore, an upper bound on iterations speeds up rendering without very noticeable artifacts. The number of iterations should be exposed to technical artists to find optimal values.

Linear filtering step. Depending on surface magnification and the need for accurate results, final refinement may be used. One can utilize the well-know binary search which would converge quickly (five sampling points is enough for most purposes) due to the tight search range. However, we propose linear interpolation for piecewise surface approximation, similar to the one proposed in POM. This approach proves to be accurate on par with binary search (considering limited search range), while being optimal for current hardware.

After finding the correct cell of intersection (at hierarchy level 0), we sample the height field in direction of the ray cast, one texel before and one texel after the cell. Then we find the intersection point between the ray and linearly approximated curve created by sampled points.

LOD scheme. Here we propose a mixed automatic level of detail scheme. First, we dynamically compute the number of iterations based on the simple observation that parallax is larger at grazing angles, thus requiring more samples, so we can express the correct value as a function of the angle between the view vector and the geometric normal. Notice that the minimum sampling number should not be less than the total number of hierarchy levels, otherwise the algorithm will not be able to finish traversal even without any cell crossing. Moreover, we observed that with diminishing pixel size on screen, parallax depth details become less visible. Thus, we can stop our quadtree traversal at a fixed hierarchy level without significant loss of detail. We determine the right level by computing the mipmap level per pixel scaled by an artist-directed factor. For correct blending between levels, we linearly interpolate between depth values from the nearest hierarchy level by the fractional part of the calculated mipmap level. After an artist-specified distance we blend parallax mapping to normal mapping.

This combined solution guarantees high accuracy via a dynamic sampling rate, and it guarantees high performance due to quadtree pruning, thus giving a stable solution overall. For performance and quality comparisons, see the results section.

Storage. For precision reasons, it is required that the stored quadtree is accurate. A problem arises when we want to store it with textures. Generally, textures compressed with DXT compression result in a significant speedup and memory footprint reduction. DXT is a lossy compression scheme; thus it is not recommended for accurate data storage (as opposed to, e.g., diffuse textures). However, we noticed that in the general case, storing the quadtree in the alpha channel of a DXT5-compressed texture results in minor artifacts (it highly depends on the surface's profile, so it must be done with care). Still, the preferable solution is to take the memory hit and store the additional data in 1-channel 8-bit lossless textures.

Comparison. Performance tests were conducted on a test machine equipped with Intel quad core 2.8Ghz CPU and GeForce 260 GTX in full HD, using three various levels from early beta of TW2. The results can be seen in Tables 1.2, 1.3, and 1.4.

Scenarios contained fully featured levels, using various height fields of resolution 512^2 to 1024^2. Each scene pushed around one million triangles, with the

Depth Scale	POM	QDM
1.0	5ms	5.7ms
1.5	6.65ms	6.7ms
5.0	18.9ms	9ms

Relief	CSM	QDM
$\sqrt{n}$	$\leq \sqrt{n}$	$\log n$

Table 1.2. Analytical performance.   **Table 1.3.** General scenario performance.

POM	QDM
73ms	14ms

Table 1.4. Extreme high detail performance.

parallax displacement method of choice, covering the entire screen. Depth scale dependence was measured, and iteration count was set for close quality match between methods. Table 1.4 shows the timing for ultra-high resolution and complexity case of the height field. Figures 1.9 and 1.10 show results for various implementations of ray- and height-field-intersection algorithms.

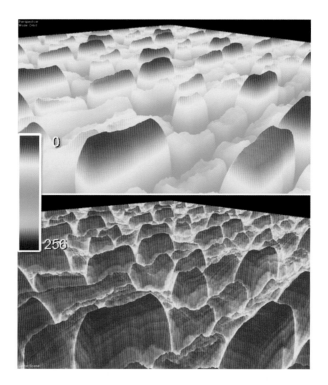

Figure 1.9. Convergence comparison.

Figure 1.10. Quality comparison. Left POM. Right QDM. Depth Scale: 1.0, 1.5, 5.0. From depth scale 1.5 and above artifacts are visible while using POM.

As we can see, QDM is converging in a pace similar to RCSM, but results in worse performance due to higher ALU cost and less efficient texture cache usage (as many dependant samples, from various MIP levels tend to cause cache misses). However, it is still comparably fast compared to linear search algorithms, outperforming them when the height-field's complexity, depth, or resolution increases. After further research we discovered that QDM is a faster solution onwards from 512×512 high-complexity textures or for any 1024×1024 and larger sizes. Moreover, an additional advantage is visible with depth scale increase. We do not take into consideration RCSM for resolutions higher than 1024×1024 as the preprocessing time becomes impractical.

1.5   Self-Shadowing

1.5.1   General Self-Shadowing

The general algorithm for self-shadowing [Policarpo 2005] involves ray tracing along the vector from L (light source) to P (calculated parallax offset position), then finding its intersection PL with the height field. Then we simply compare PL with P to determine whether the light is visible from P or not. If not, then that means we are in shadow. See Figure 1.11 for illustration.

This method generates hard shadows using any intersection search method, thus suffering from the same disadvantages as the chosen algorithm (i.e., aliasing with linear search). Moreover, the cost is the same as view and height-field

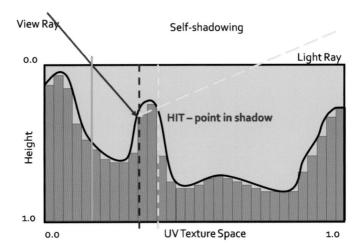

Figure 1.11. Shadow test.

intersection computations. When we are looking for soft shadows, we would have to perform several ray casts of the light vector, which is impractical for performance reasons.

A good approximation for soft shadow calculation was proposed in POM. We can cast a ray towards the light source from point P and perform horizon visibility queries of the height profile along the light direction. We sample the height profile at a fixed number of steps to determine the occlusion coefficient by subtracting sampled depth from original point P depth. This allows us to determine the penumbra coefficient by calculating blocker-to-receiver ratio (the closer the blocker is to the surface, the smaller the resulting penumbra). We scale each sample's contribution by the distance from P and use the maximum value, then we use the visibility coefficient in the lighting equation for smooth shadow generation. The algorithm makes use of linear sampling and produces well-behaving soft shadows. However, the alias-free shadow range is limited by the fixed sampling rate, so real shadows cannot be generated without searching through the entire height field, which effectively degenerates the algorithm to a linear search.

1.5.2   Quadtree Soft Shadowing

Fast horizon approximation. We propose a new algorithm based on POM soft shadowing. This algorithm makes use of the quadtree used in QDM.

First we introduce the algorithm for fast horizon visibility approximation. We use a method similar to POM by performing horizon visibility queries along a

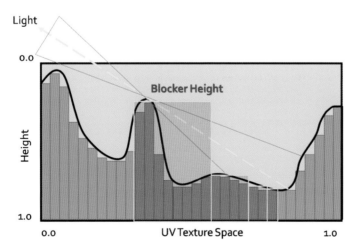

Figure 1.12. QDM horizon approximation.

given direction. The maximum height is taken from the calculated samples and is subtracted from the initial starting point P, thus giving the horizon visibility coefficient. See Figure 1.12 for illustration.

We use the observation that small scale details at distance have negligible impact on the result (especially during any lighting calculations). Thus we can approximate further lying profile features by using the maximum height data from higher levels of the quadtree. That way we can calculate the approximated horizon angle with a minimized number of queries. The full profile can be obtained in $\log n$ steps as opposed to n steps in POM, where n is the number of height-field texels along a given direction D. In all further solutions, we are using a slightly modified version of this algorithm, which is weighting each sample by a distance function. That makes it more suitable for penumbra light calculation as samples far away from P are less important.

QDM shadowing. For shadowing, we use a fast horizon visibility approximation using the parallax offset point P and the normalized light vector L. Accuracy and performance is fine-tuned by technical artists setting the plausible number of iterations ($\log n$ is the maximum number, where n is the height-field's largest dimension) and light vector scale coefficient as shown in Listing 1.4.

```
//Light direction
float2 lDir = (float2(l.x, -l.y)) * dScale;

//Initial displaced point
float h0 = tex2Dlod(heightTexture, float4(P,0,0)).w;
float h = h0;

//Horizon visibility samples
//w1..w5---distance weights
h = min(1,w1 * tex2Dlod(height, float4(P + 1.0 * lDir,0,3.66)).w);
h = min(h,w2 * tex2Dlod(height, float4(P + 0.8 * lDir,0,3.00)).w);
h = min(h,w3 * tex2Dlod(height, float4(P + 0.6 * lDir,0,2.33)).w);
h = min(h,w4 * tex2Dlod(height, float4(P + 0.4 * lDir,0,1.66)).w);
h = min(h,w5 * tex2Dlod(height, float4(P + 0.2 * lDir,0,1.00)).w);

//Visibility approximation
float shadow = 1.0 - saturate((h0 - h) * selfShadowStrength);

return shadow;
```

Listing 1.4. QDM soft shadows, fast, hard-coded solution.

Results. As we can see in Table 1.5, plausible soft shadows using the quadtree are significantly faster than traditional methods while delivering similar quality (see Figure 1.13). For further optimization we calculate shadows only when $N \cdot L \geq 0$.

POM Shadows	QDM Shadows
1.6ms	0.5ms

Table 1.5. One light shadows calculation time for the test scene.

Figure 1.13. Soft shadows ON/OFF.

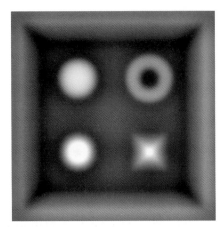

Figure 1.14. Generated high quality AO.

1.6   Ambient Occlusion

Ambient occlusion is computed by integrating the visibility function over the hemisphere H with respect to a projected solid angle:

$$A_0 = \frac{1}{\pi} \sum_H V_{p,\omega} (N \cdot \omega) d\omega,$$

where $V_{p,\omega}$ is the visibility function at p, such as $V_{p,\omega}$ is 0 when occluded in direction ω and 1 otherwise.

Ambient occlusion adds a great deal of lighting detail to rendered images (see Figure 1.14). It is especially useful for large-scale terrain scenarios, where objects can take the occlusion value from the terrain (i.e., darkening buildings lying in a valley).

1.6.1   QDM Ambient Occlusion

Dynamically calculating ambient occlusion for surfaces was thought to be impractical for performance reasons, as the visibility function and the integration were too slow to be useful. Now with fast horizon visibility approximation we can tackle that problem in a better way.

We approximate the true integral by integrating the visibility function in several fixed directions. We discovered that for performance reasons integration in four to eight directions lying in the same angle intervals yields acceptable results. Moreover, we can increase quality by jittering and/or rotating the directions by a random value for every pixel.

Accuracy	AO
4 directions	2.1ms
8 directions	6.3ms
4 jittered	2.6ms

Table 1.6. AO calculation time.

1.6.2 Performance

As we can see from Table 1.6, the algorithm requires substantial processing power, being even less efficient with randomized directions (as it is hurting GPU parallelism, but it is still faster than integrating more directions). However, it is used only when the surface height field is changing. Moreover, it can be accumulated throughout several frames, amortizing the cost.

1.7 Surface Blending

1.7.1 Alpha Blending

Blending is commonly used for surface composites, such as terrain, where several varied textures have to mix together (e.g., rocky coast with sand).

Typically, surface blends are done using the alpha-blending algorithm given by the following equation:

$$\text{Blend} = \frac{(v_1, \ldots, v_n) \cdot (w_1, \ldots, w_n)}{(1, \ldots, 1) \cdot (w_1, \ldots, w_n)},$$

where $(w_1, \ldots, w_n)$ is the blend weight vector and $(v_1, \ldots, v_n)$ denotes the value vector.

Commonly, the blend vector for a given texel is supplied by vertex interpolation, stored at vertex attributes (thus being low frequency). During pixel shading, interpolated values are used to perform the blending.

1.7.2 Raytracing Blended Surfaces

Any height-field intersection algorithm can be used in such a scenario. We should compute the parallax offset for each surface and finally blend them together using the blend vector. However, it is worth noting that the computational cost for such blending would be n-times higher than one surface, where n is the total number of surfaces. Moreover, using vertex-interpolated values results in view-dependant surfaces floating near blend zones. Figure 1.15 illustrates the problem. However,

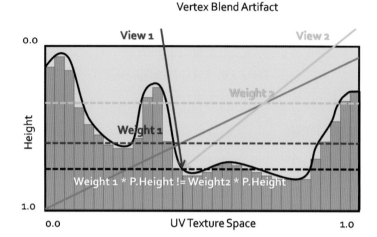

Figure 1.15. Depth floating artifact using vertex blend.

with enough care taken to minimize depth scale near blend zones, it should not be too distracting.

One possible solution is to use per-pixel blend weights that would modify the surface on-the-fly during intersection search. However, this would require sampling an additional weight texture with every iteration, thus doubling the sample count.

Let us consider four surface blends. Optimally, we can encode up to four blend weights in one RGBA 32-bit texture, so with each sample we get four weights. The blend texture can be fairly low-resolution, as generally it should resemble per-vertex blending (it can be even generated on the fly from vertex weights). Having a four-scalar blend vector, we can perform the intersection search on the dynamically modified height field simply by sampling all four height fields with each step and blending them by the blend vector. Moreover, we can compose all four height fields into one RGBA 32-bit texture, thus finally optimizing the blend intersection search.

The pseudocode in Listing 1.5 shows the modification for the intersection search method of choice.

```
d = tex2D(HeightTexture,p.xy).xyzw;
b = tex2D(BlendTexture,p.xy).xyzw;
d = dot(d,b);
```

Listing 1.5. Height profile blend code.

Modification requires only one additional sample and one dot product. However, we are sampling four channels twice instead of one channel (as in the single surface algorithm).

This solution is therefore very fast but lacks robustness, as it would require us to preprocess height-field composites, creating possibly dozens of new textures containing all possible height profiles composites. We can of course try sampling the data without composites, but that would result in additional sampling cost and cache misses (as four samplers would have to be used simultaneously, which would most probably result in a bandwidth bottleneck).

Another problem is that we cannot use this method for algorithms using precomputed distance data, as it would require us to recompute the distance fields (i.e., cone maps) for blend modified height fields, which effectively prohibits using advanced ray-casting algorithms.

1.7.3   Height Blending

To overcome the aforementioned problems, we introduce a new method for surface blending, which seems to fit the task more naturally, and it guarantees faster convergence.

First, let us consider typical alpha blending for surface mixing. In real life, surfaces do not blend. What we see is actually the highest material (the material on the top of the surface).

Therefore, we propose to use height information as an additional blend coefficient, thus adding more variety to blend regions and a more natural look as shown in Listing 1.6.

This method is not computationally expensive, and it can add much more detail as opposed to vertex-blended surfaces (as can be seen in Figure 1.16).

The most important feature is that we pick the highest surface, so during the intersection search phase, we need only to find the highest point.

Therefore, the new height field is produced by the new blend equation:

$$\text{Blend} = \max(h_1, \dots, h_n).$$

Using this blend equation we are interested only in finding the intersection point with the highest surface profile modified by its blend weight. That effectively means taking a minimal number of steps, as we will stop the ray cast at

Relief Mapping	POM	POM with HB
3ms	2.5ms	1.25ms

Table 1.7. Surface blend performance comparison.

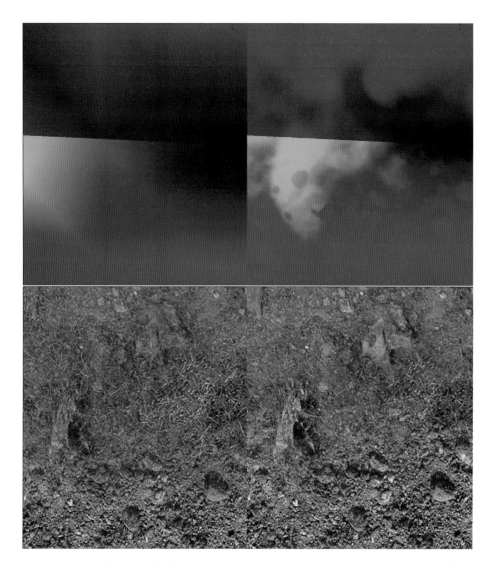

Figure 1.16. Vertex blend and height blend comparison.

```
float4 FinalH;
float4 f1, f2, f3, f4;

//Get surface sample.
f1 = tex2D(Tex0Sampler,TEXUV.xy).rgba;

//Get height weight.
FinalH.a = 1.0 - f1.a;
f2 = tex2D(Tex1Sampler,TEXUV.xy).rgba;
FinalH.b = 1.0 - f2.a;
f3 = tex2D(Tex2Sampler,TEXUV.xy).rgba;
FinalH.g = 1.0 - f3.a;
f4 = tex2D(Tex3Sampler,TEXUV.xy).rgba;
FinalH.r = 1.0 - f4.a;

//Modify height weights by blend weights.
//Per-vertex blend weights stored in IN.AlphaBlends
FinalH*= IN.AlphaBlends;

//Normalize.
float Blend = dot(FinalH, 1.0) + epsilon;
FinalH /= Blend;

//Get final blend.
FinalTex = FinalH.a * f1 + FinalH.b * f2 + FinalH.g * f3 +
          FinalH.r * f4;
```

Listing 1.6. Surface blend code.

the first intersection with highest blend weight modified height profile, which—by definition—is the first one to be pierced by the ray.

With each intersection search step, we reconstruct the height-field profile using the new blend operator as shown in Listing 1.7.

As can be seen in Table 1.7, this method proved to minimize the convergence rate by 25% on average in our scenario without sacrificing visual quality (see Figure 1.17, and is more plausible for our new height blend solution. It can be used with blend textures or vertex blending, as well as every intersection search algorithm.

```
d = tex2D(HeightTexture,p.xy).xyzw;
b = tex2D(BlendTexture,p.xy).xyzw;
d *= b;
d = max(d.x,max(d.y,max(d.z,d.w)));}
```

Listing 1.7. Surface height blend code.

Figure 1.17. Surface blend quality comparison. Top: relief. Bottom: POM with height blending.

1.7.4 QDM with Height Blending

We still cannot use the height blend operator directly for algorithms based on precomputed data. However, QDM is based on depth data, so it is relatively easy to obtain new correct data structure. Note that

$$\max(x_1, x_2, \ldots, x_n) \cdot \max(w_1, w_2, \ldots, w_n) \geq$$
$$\max([(x_1, x_2, \ldots, x_n) \cdot (w_1, w_2, \ldots, w_n)]).$$

Thus multiplying one min/max quadtree by another gives us a conservative quadtree, and that is exactly what we need for correct surface blending. We can pack up to four blend quadtrees in one RGBA 32-bit texture with mipmaps containing blend vector quadtrees. Then in QDM, to reconstruct the blended surface quadtree, we simply sample and blend it at the correct position and level, and compute the dot product between it and the height-field vector sampled from the height-field composite.

The blend texture should map quadtree texels as close as possible. However, we discovered that while using hardware linear sampling and accepting small artifacts we can use sizes as small as 32^2 (while blending 1024^2 height fields) when the weight gradients are close to linear. Such blended quadtrees can be constructed on the fly in negligible time, allowing dynamic surface alterations.

Effectively, we can use QDM with all its benefits while blending surfaces for artifact-free rendering (see Figure 1.18). Convergence will be slower, due to the conservative quadtree, and more iterations may be needed depending on the height-field's complexity. In practice, the conservative approach needs <10% more iterations than what should be really used. This method proves to be the fastest method for dynamic accurate surface rendering of high complexity height fields.

In our implementation we decided to use vertex blending to avoid high texture cache misses. However, we were forced to accept small depth-floating artifacts.

As QDM is converging really fast in empty space regions, the algorithm can make the best use of faster convergence, due to height blending.

1.7.5 Self-Shadowing and Ambient Occlusion for Blended Surfaces

Self shadowing and ambient occlusion can be done while rendering blended surfaces. However, a naïve approach of calculating shadowing terms for each surface and blending the results is simply impractical for current generation hardware. We propose to use QDM and the height blend and perform computations for the highest modified height profile only. Proper height-field selection requires additional dynamic branching, further restricting GPU parallelism. Consequently, self shadowing and/or ambient occlusion are viable only for high-end hardware.

Figure 1.18. QDM height blend surface.

1.8   General Advice

In this article we proposed and discussed several battle-proven surface rendering methods, varying in ALU/Texture sampling performance, accuracy, and flexibility. Most solutions were introduced as general building blocks from which, depending on requirements, an optimal solution can be built.

1.8.1   Case Study

During *Two Worlds 2* production we decided to settle on several solutions used under specific circumstances. We present a case study of each method used:

General terrain blend. Our terrain exhibits small-scale height features such as cracks, small rocks, etc. The maximum number of blending surfaces was capped at four to allow texture packing. We are using linear search with linear piecewise approximation, automatic LOD, and height blend optimization. Blending is done on a per-vertex basis. Depending on texture configuration, parallax can be switched off for each surface individually. The specular term and normal vectors are generated on-the-fly due to the Xbox360's memory restrictions.

Special terrain features. Several extreme detail terrain paths were excluded as additional decal planes. We are rendering them at ultra-high quality (high resolution, high accuracy) and alpha-blending them with existing terrain. Decal planes may present roads, paths, muddy ponds, and craters, etc. For rendering, we are using QDM with automatic LOD and soft shadows. Where needed, QDM per-pixel height blending is used. Blend-based decals are for PC only.

General object surface. For general surface rendering, we are using linear search with linear piecewise approximation and automatic LOD. Soft shadows are used at the artist's preference. Surfaces with extreme complexity, depth scale, or resolutions over 1024^2 are checked, and using QDM is optimal. The same method is used on Xbox360 and PC.

1.8.2 Surface Rendering Pipeline

During asset finalization, technical artists optimized height-field-based textures, checking whether high resolution or additional details (such as soft shadows) are really needed. It is worth noting that low frequency textures tend to converge faster during the intersection search, so blurring height fields when possible is better for performance and accuracy reasons when using linear search-based methods.

One important feature of our surface rendering pipeline is the preference for generation of additional surface properties on-the-fly, as it allows us to save memory and performance on texture-fetch-hungry shaders.

Texture-heavy locations (such as cities) are using mostly two 24-bit RGB compressed textures per object. The specular term is generated from the diffuse color and is modified by an artist on a per-material-specified function such as inversion, power, or scale. The generated coefficient generally exhibits high quality.

Data generation is taken to the extreme during terrain rendering as individual terrain texture is using only 32-bit RGBA DXT5 textures, from which per-pixel normal vectors, specular roughness, and intensities (as the default lighting model is a simplified Cook-Torrance BRDF) are generated.

1.9 Conclusion

We have discussed and presented various surface rendering techniques with several novel improvements for industry proven approaches. Combinations of parallax mapping, soft shadowing, ambient occlusion, and surface blending methods were proposed to be in specific scenarios aiming for maximum quality/performance/memory usage ratio. Furthermore, a novel solution—Quadtree Displacement Mapping with Height Blending—was presented. Our approach proves to be significantly faster for ultra-high quality surfaces that use complex, high resolution height fields. Moreover, we proposed solutions for efficient surface blending, soft shadowing, ambient occlusion, and automatic LOD schemes using the introduced quadtree structures. In practice, our techniques tend to produce higher quality results with less iterations and texture samples. This is an advantage, as we are trading iteration ALU cost for texture fetches, making it more useful for GPU generations to come, as computation performance scales faster than bandwidth.

Surface rendering techniques research allowed us to make vast graphic improvements in our next-gen engine, thus increasing quality and performance. We hope to see the techniques described herein being used in more upcoming titles.

Bibliography

[Cohen and Shaked 1993] D. Cohen and A. Shaked. "Photo-Realistic Imaging of Digital Terrains." *Computer Graphics Forum* 12:3 (1993), 363–373.

[Donelly 2005] W. Donelly. "Per-Pixel Displacement Mapping with Distance Functions." In *GPU Gems 2*, edited by Matt Pharr, pp. 123–36. Reading, MA: Addison-Wesley, 2005.

[Dummer 2006] J. Dummer. "Cone Step Mapping: An Iterative Ray-Heightfield Intersection Algorithm." 2006. Available at http://www.lonesock.net/files/ConeStepMapping.pdf.

[OH 2006] K. Oh, H. Ki, and C. H. Lee. "Pyramidal Displacement Mapping: a GPU based Artifacts-Free Ray Tracing through Image Pyramid." *In VRST '06: Proceedings of the ACM symposium on Virtual Reality Software and Technology* (2006), 75–82.

[Policarpo 2005] F. Policarpo, M. M. Oliveira, and J. L. D. Comba. "Real Time Relief Mapping on Arbitrary Polygonal Surfaces." *In Proceedings of I3D'05* (2005), 155–162.

[Policarpo 2007] F. Policarpo and M. M. Oliveira. "Relaxed Cone Step Mapping for Relief Mapping." In *GPU Gems 3*, edited by Hubert Nguyen, pp. 409–428. Reading, MA: Addison-Wesley Professional, 2007.

[Tatarchuk 2006] N. Tatarchuk. "Practical Parallax Occlusion Mapping with Approximate Soft Shadow." In *ShaderX5*. Brookline, MA: Charles River Media, 2006.

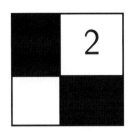

NPR Effects Using the Geometry Shader

Pedro Hermosilla and Pere-Pau Vázquez

2.1 Introduction

Non-photorrealistic rendering (NPR) techniques [Achorn et al. 03, Gooch and Gooch 01] have been here for quite a while [Saito and Takahashi 90]. In contrast to traditional rendering, these techniques deal with geometric entities such as silhouettes, which makes them not easily amenable to GPU algorithms, although some papers already address some NPR algorithms in hardware [Dietrich 00, Mitchell et al. 02, Everitt 02, Card and Mitchell 02]. With the arrival of more modern graphics hardware that includes the geometry shader stage, some of these techniques can be implemented in hardware, making them real time in many cases [McGuire and Hughes 04, Dyken et al. 08, Doss 08]. In this chapter we present a set of techniques that can be implemented using the GPU by taking advantage of the geometry shader pipeline stage. Concretely, we show how to make use of the geometry shader in order to render objects and their silhouettes in a single pass, and to imitate pencil drawing.

2.2 Previous Work

Silhouette rendering has been studied extensively. Two major groups of algorithms require the extraction of silhouettes in real time: shadow volume-based approaches and non-photorealistic rendering [Gooch and Gooch 01].

From the literature, we may extract two different approaches: object-space and image-space algorithms. However, most modern algorithms work in either image space or hybrid space. For the purposes of this chapter, we are interested in GPU-based algorithms, and these are the ones we will present. We refer the interested reader to the works of [Isenberg et al. 03] and [Hartner et al. 03] for overviews and deep comparisons on CPU-based silhouette extraction algorithms.

GPU-assisted algorithms may compute the silhouette either using multiple rendering passes [Mitchell et al. 02] or in a single pass. Single pass methods usually use some sort of precomputation in order to store adjacency information into the vertices [Card and Mitchell 02], or make use of the geometry shader feature [Doss 08], as this may query adjacency information. These algorithms generate the silhouette in a single rendering pass, though still a first geometry pass is required for the object itself.

One of the first attempts to extract silhouettes using hardware is due to [Raskar 01], where a new stage at the rendering pipeline is introduced: the primitive shader. At this stage, polygons are treated as single primitives, similar to the way actual geometric shaders do. Raskar's proposal also requires modification of the incoming geometry. For instance, extending back faces to render silhouettes, and adding polygons in order to render ridges and valleys.

[Card and Mitchell 02] pack adjacent normals into the texture coordinates of vertices and render edges as degenerated quads, which expand if they are detected to belong to a silhouette edge in the vertex processor. This is a single pass algorithm that requires rendering extra geometry for the silhouette extraction. This approach is also used by [Achorn et al. 03]. [McGuire and Hughes 04] extend this technique to store the four vertices of the two faces adjacent to each edge, instead of explicit face normals. This allows the authors to construct correct face normals under animation and add textures to generate artistic strokes.

In [Ashikhmin 04], silhouettes are generated without managing adjacency information through a multiple rendering passes algorithm that reads back the frame buffer in order to determine face visibility. More recently, [Dyken et al. 08] extract silhouettes from a triangle mesh and perform an adaptive tessellation in order to visualize the silhouette with smooth curvature. However, this system neither textures the silhouettes nor extrudes the silhouette geometry. [Doss 08] develops an algorithm similar to the one presented here: he extrudes the silhouettes, but with no guarantee of continuity between the extrusions generated from different edges; consequently, gaps are easily noticeable as the silhouette width grows.

A completely different approach is used by [Gooch et al. 99], as they note that environment maps can be used to darken the contour edges of a model but, as a result, the rendered lines have uncontrolled variable thickness. The same idea was refined by [Dietrich 00], who took advantage of the GPU hardware available at that moment (GeForce 256). [Everitt 02] used MIP-maps to achieve similar effects. In all of these cases, it is difficult to fine-tune an artistic style because there is no support geometry underlying the silhouette.

The approach presented here is conceptually similar to [Raskar 01], but takes advantage of modern hardware. We also borrow ideas from [Doss 08] and [McGuire and Hughes 04] for silhouette geometry generation. In contrast to these approaches, we generate both the silhouette and the object in a single pass, and we present an algorithm for correct texturing with coherent and continuous texture coordinates along the entire silhouette.

2.3 Silhouette Rendering

Silhouette rendering is a fundamental element in most NPR effects, as it plays an important role in object shape understanding. In this section we present a novel approach for the detection, generation, and texturing of a model in a single rendering pass. First we will present an overview of our algorithm, and then we will detail how each of the steps is implemented.

2.3.1 Algorithm Overview

In order to carry out the entire process in a single step, we will take advantage of some of the modern features of GPUs; concretely, we will make an extensive use of the geometry shader. This stage permits triangle operations, with knowledge of adjacent triangles, and the generation of new triangles to the geometry.

Our process for silhouette rendering performs the following steps at the different stages of the pipeline (Figure 2.1):

- *Vertex shader.* Vertices are transformed in the usual way to camera space.

- *Geometry shader.* In this stage, edges that belong to the silhouette are detected by using the information of the current triangle and its adjacency, and the corresponding geometry is generated.

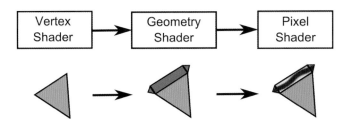

Figure 2.1. Pipeline overview: the vertex shader (left) transforms the vertex coordinates of the incoming geometry; the second step (geometry shader) generates new geometry for the silhouette of the object. Finally, the fragment shader generates correct texture coordinates.

- *Pixel shader.* For each rasterized fragment, its texture coordinates are generated and pixels are shaded according to the color obtained from the texture.

Before we may send a mesh throughout the pipeline, we first perform a special reordering of the indices of the triangles. This will make the adjacency information available at the geometry shader level. In order to access such information, we send six indices per triangle (instead of the normal three), ordered as depicted in Figure 2.2. The central triangle, identified by indices 0, 4, and 2 is the one to be analyzed. The remaining adjacent triangles are needed to show if any of the edges of the central triangle belong to the silhouette.

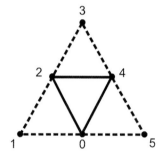

Figure 2.2. Index sort.

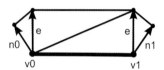

Figure 2.3. Edge geometry.

2.3.2 Silhouette Detection and Geometry Generation

We consider a closed triangle mesh with consistently oriented triangles. The set of triangles is denoted, $T_1 \ldots T_N$. The set of vertices is $v_1 \ldots v_n$ in $\Re^3$, and normals are given by triangles: n_t is the normal of a triangle $T_t = [v_i, v_j, v_k]$, using the notation by [Dyken et al. 08]. This triangle normal is defined as the normalization of the vector $(v_j - v_i) \times (v_k - v_i)$. Given an observer at position $x \in \Re^3$, we may say a triangle is *front facing* in v if $(v - x) \cdot n \leq 0$, otherwise it is *back facing*. The silhouette of a triangle mesh is the set of edges where one of the adjacent triangles is front facing while the other is back facing. In order to detect a silhouette in a triangulated mesh we need to process any triangle, together with the triangles that share an edge with it. This test is performed at the geometry shader level for each edge of the triangle being processed. In order to avoid duplicate silhouettes when processing both the front facing and the back facing triangles, we only generate silhouettes for the front-facing triangles. The code in Listing 2.1 shows how to detect a silhouette edge at the geometry shader level.

As shown in Figure 2.3, once an edge (indicated by $\overline{v0v1}$) has been determined as a silhouette one, we generate the geometry that will act as the silhouette by

```
[maxvertexcount(21)]
void main( triangleadj VERTEXin input[6],
          inout TriangleStream<VERTEXout> TriStream )
{

 //Calculate the triangle normal and view direction.
 float3 normalTrian = getNormal( input[0].Pos.xyz,
   input[2].Pos.xyz, input[4].Pos.xyz );
 float3 viewDirect = normalize(-input[0].Pos.xyz
   - input[2].Pos.xyz - input[4].Pos.xyz);

 //If the triangle is frontfacing
 [branch]if(dot(normalTrian,viewDirect) > 0.0f)
 {

  [loop]for(uint i = 0; i < 6; i+=2)
  {

   //Calculate the normal for this triangle.
   float auxIndex = (i+2)%6;
   float3 auxNormal = getNormal( input[i].Pos.xyz,
     input[i+1].Pos.xyz, input[auxIndex].Pos.xyz );
   float3 auxDirect = normalize(- input[i].Pos.xyz
     - input[i+1].Pos.xyz - input[auxIndex].Pos.xyz);

   //If the triangle is backfacing
   [branch]if(dot(auxNormal,auxDirect) <= 0.0f)
   {

    //Here we have a silhouette edge.

   }
  }
 }
}
```

Listing 2.1. Geometry shader silhouette detection code.

applying the algorithm in [McGuire and Hughes 04]. It consists of four triangles. The central triangles forming the quad are generated by extruding the edges' vertices using as the extrusion direction of a vector orthogonal to the edge and view directions. The remaining triangles are generated by extruding the vertices from the edge in the direction of the vertex normal as projected on screen. The generation of such geometry can be done either in world space or in screen space. We usually use screen space because this way is easier to obtain a silhouette geometry of constant size in screen. The code needed to generate this geometry appears in Listing 2.2.

```
//Transform the positions to screen space.
float4 transPos1 = mul(input[i].Pos,projMatrix);
transPos1 = transPos1/transPos1.w;
float4 transPos2 = mul(input[auxIndex].Pos,projMatrix);
transPos2 = transPos2/transPos2.w;

//Calculate the edge direction in screen space.
float2 edgeDirection = normalize(transPos2.xy - transPos1.xy);

//Calculate the extrude vector in screen space.
float4 extrudeDirection = float4(normalize(
  float2(-edgeDirection.y,edgeDirection.x)),0.0f,0.0f);

//Calculate the extrude vector along the vertex
//normal in screen space.
float4 normExtrude1 = mul(input[i].Pos + input[i].Normal
  ,projMatrix);
normExtrude1 = normExtrude1 / normExtrude1.w;
normExtrude1 = normExtrude1 - transPos1;
normExtrude1 = float4(normalize(normExtrude1.xy),0.0f,0.0f);
float4 normExtrude2 = mul(input[auxIndex].Pos
  + input[auxIndex].Normal,projMatrix);
normExtrude2 = normExtrude2 / normExtrude2.w;
normExtrude2 = normExtrude2 - transPos2;
normExtrude2 = float4(normalize(normExtrude2.xy),0.0f,0.0f);

//Scale the extrude directions with the edge size.
normExtrude1 = normExtrude1 * edgeSize;
normExtrude2 = normExtrude2 * edgeSize;
extrudeDirection = extrudeDirection * edgeSize;

//Calculate the extruded vertices.
float4 normVertex1 = transPos1 + normExtrude1;
float4 extruVertex1 = transPos1 + extrudeDirection;
float4 normVertex2 = transPos2 + normExtrude2;
float4 extruVertex2 = transPos2 + extrudeDirection;

//Create the output polygons.
VERTEXout outVert;

outVert.Pos = float4(normVertex1.xyz,1.0f);
TriStream.Append(outVert);
outVert.Pos = float4(extruVertex1.xyz,1.0f);
TriStream.Append(outVert);
outVert.Pos = float4(transPos1.xyz,1.0f);
TriStream.Append(outVert);
outVert.Pos = float4(extruVertex2.xyz,1.0f);
TriStream.Append(outVert);
outVert.Pos = float4(transPos2.xyz,1.0f);
TriStream.Append(outVert);
outVert.Pos = float4(normVertex2.xyz,1.0f);
```

```
TriStream.Append(outVert);

TriStream.RestartStrip();
```

Listing 2.2. Geometry shader silhouette generation.

In some cases, this solution may produce an error when the extrusion direction has a different direction than the projected normal version. There are several ways to solve this. One of the simplest ones consists of changing the direction of the projected normal, as commented in [Hermosilla and Vázquez 09]. Some cases also might require different silhouette geometry (see [McGuire and Hughes 04] for more details).

2.3.3 Silhouette Texturing

Once the silhouette geometry has been generated, it becomes obvious that texturing this geometry will increase the number of effects that can be achieved. In order to properly texture the silhouette geometry, we need to generate texture coordinates. Texture coordinates generation is a bit tricky, as we need to generate continuous coordinates along the entire silhouette. Therefore we may not simply assign coordinates from 0 to 1 for each edge, as this would cause irregular coordinate distribution if the edges are not created all with the same length. Instead we need a global strategy for coordinate generation because each triangle of the silhouette will not be aware of the neighbor triangles' coordinates.

From the two texture coordinates u and v, coordinate v can be simply defined, because it changes from zero to one as long as we go away from the object, as depicted in Figure 2.4.

Coordinate u has to be generated in such a way that its value is continuous along the silhouette of the object. In order to make sure that two adjacent edges will generate coherent texture coordinates, we will build a function that depends on the position of the projection of the vertices on screen. As a consequence, the coordinates will be continuous because neighbor edges share a vertex.

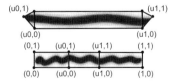

Figure 2.4. The v-coordinate has a value of 0 for the edge vertex and 1 for the extruded vertices.

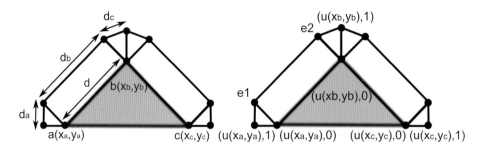

Figure 2.5. The u-coordinates are generated from the edge vertex coordinates in screen space. The first vertex of the edge and the vertex extruded from the first vertex normal gets the u-coordinate from the coordinates of the first vertex (a) The other edge endpoint, and the vertex extruded from the second vertex normal gets the u-coordinate from the coordinates of the second vertex (b) The vertices extruded from the extrusion vector ($e1$ & $e2$) obtain their u-coordinates by interpolation, as show in Equation (2.1).

This is achieved when the geometry shader sends the x- and y-coordinates of the generated vertices in screen, together with v-coordinate. The pixel shader will receive such coordinates as interpolated values, and will generate the corresponding u value. Figure 2.5 shows how this information is used.

Vertices e receive their coordinates from linear interpolation as shown in the following equations:

$$e1.ux = x_a + (|\vec{ab}| * ((d * d_a)/(d_a + d_b + d_c)))$$
$$e1.uy = y_a + (|\vec{ab}| * ((d * d_a)/(d_a + d_b + dc)))$$
$$e1.v = 0$$

(2.1)

$$e2.ux = x_b + (|\vec{ba}| * ((d * d_a)/(d_a + d_b + d_c)))$$
$$e2.uy = x_b + (|\vec{ba}| * ((d * d_a)/(d_a + d_b + d_c)))$$
$$e2.v = 0.$$

The pixel shader will receive those coordinates interpolated and will use them to compute the final texture coordinates.

In order to compute the final u component, we will transform components x and y into polar coordinates. The reference system will be the screen space position of the center of the bounding box of the object, and the x- and y- axes will be those of the viewport. Therefore, we will have polar coordinates computed as

- Polar angle: α will be the angle between the x-axis, and the vector with initial point at the origin of the coordinates system, and final point at (x, y).

- Distance: d is the distance from (x, y) to the origin of the coordinates system.

```
float4 main(PIXELin inPut):SV_Target
{
  //Initial texture coordinate.
  float2 coord = float2(0.0f,inPut.UV.z);

  //Vector from the projected center bounding box to
  //the location.
  float2 vect = inPut.UV.xy - aabbPos;

  //Calculate the polar coordinate.
  float angle = atan(vect.y/vect.x);
  angle = (vect.x < 0.0f)?angle+PI:
    (vect.y < 0.0f)?angle+(2*PI):angle;

  //Assign the angle plus distance to the u texture coordinate.
  coord.x = ((angle/(2*PI)) + (length(vect)*lengthPer))*scale;

  //Get the texture color.
  float4 col = texureDiff.Sample(samLinear,coord);

  //Alpha test.
  if(col.a < 0.1f)
    discard;

  //Return color.
  return col;
}
```

Listing 2.3. Silhouette texturing.

Finally, we compute u as indicated in the following equation:

$$u = (\frac{\alpha}{2 * \pi}) + (k * d).$$

As we may see, the polar angle is divided by 2π in order to transform it into a value in the $[0..1]$ range. The distance is weighted by a factor k that may be changed interactively. For objects of a sphere-like shape, k value can be set to close to 0, but for objects with edges that roughly point to the origin of coordinates, the value k must be different from 0. Otherwise, texture coordinates at both ends of those edges would be similar. The code that implements this is shown in Listing 2.3.

This algorithm may produce small artifacts in edges that are projected on the screen close to the center of the bounding box. However, these are not visible in most of the models we tested.

2.3.4 Single Pass Geometry and Silhouette Rendering

Most silhouette rendering algorithms perform two passes, one for the geometry, and another one for the silhouettes. This means that the geometry is sent two times into the rendering pipeline. We can avoid this by taking further advantage of the geometry shader with little modifications to the original code. This is achieved by simply rendering the triangle being analyzed by the geometry shader, even if it does not have any edge belonging to the silhouette. This can be done thanks to the fact that the geometry shader may output more than a single triangle.

So far, the pixel shader code deals only with edges and textures them accordingly. In order to render the triangles belonging to the geometry in a single pass, we must inform the pixel shader of the sort of triangle that originated the rasterized fragment: silhouette or geometry. We encode this information in the texture coordinates. As we are passing three coordinates, we will use one of them—in this case the v-coordinate—to encode this information. For triangles belonging to this geometry, we assign the value 2. This way, the pixel shader can easily distinguish between both kinds of triangles, and shade them accordingly.

2.3.5 Results

We can see some results of our algorithm in Figure 2.6. The algorithm presented here achieves real-time performance, as can be seen in Table 2.1. These results were obtained on a 6 GB Quad Core PC equipped with a GeForce 9800 GX2 GPU. The viewport resolution (key for image space algorithms) was 1680×1050. Note that even complex objects (such as the Buddha model), with more than 1M polygons, achieve interactive framerates.

Models	Triangles	FPS
Buddha	1087716	8.50
Armadillo	345944	21.07
Asian Dragon	225588	25.75
Dragon	100000	60.07
Bunny	69666	110.78
Atenea	15014	337.59

Table 2.1. Framerates obtained with the textured silhouette algorithm on a GeForce 9800 GX2 GPU with a viewport resolution of 1680×1050.

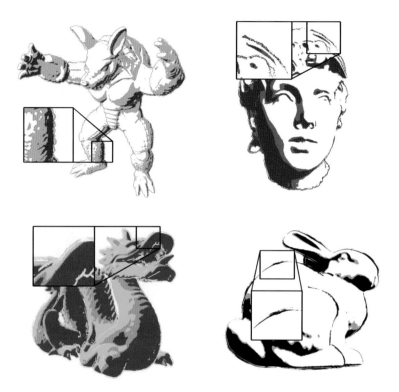

Figure 2.6. Images showing the algorithm in action. Silhouettes have been generated and textured in real time.

2.4 Pencil Rendering

In this section we will present how to implement pencil rendering in the geometry shader. This is based on the technique presented by [Lee et al. 06].

2.4.1 Algorithm Overview

The original technique by [Lee et al. 06] works in the following way. First, the minimal curvature at each vertex is computed. Then, triangles are sent through the pipeline with this value as a texture coordinate for each vertex. In order to shade the interior of a triangle, the curvatures at the vertices are used to rotate a pencil texture in screen space. This texture is rotated three times in screen space, one for each curvature, and the result is combined with blending. Several textures with different tones are used at the same time, stored in an array of textures. The correct one is selected according to illumination.

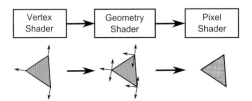

Figure 2.7. Pipeline overview: the vertex shader transforms the vertices to screen space; the geometry shader assigns the vertex curvatures of the triangle to the three vertices. Finally, the pixel shader generates texture coordinates for the three curvatures and calculates the final color.

We may implement this algorithm using the GPU pipeline in the following way (Figure 2.7):

- *Vertex shader.* Vertices are transformed to screen coordinates. Vertex curvature is transformed too, and only x- and y-components are passed through as a two-dimensional vector.

- *Geometry shader.* The curvature values are assigned to each vertex as texture coordinates.

- *Pixel shader.* Final color is computed.

2.4.2 Geometry Shader Optimization

This technique has an important shortcoming: It is necessary to make a copy of each vertex for each triangle that shares it. This is because each pixel receives the interpolated curvature by using each vertex, and the three curvatures are required unchanged. Each duplicated vertex is assigned the three curvatures of the vertices of the triangle in order to make each fragment get the three exact curvatures.

In order to avoid vertex duplication, we will use the geometry shader. At the geometry shader level, we receive the three vertices of a triangle, with its corresponding curvatures. These curvatures are assigned as three texture coordinates to the vertices of the output triangle in the same order. Thus, the fragment shader will receive the three values without interpolation. The code corresponding to the geometry shader appears in Listing 2.4.

2.4.3 Pixel Texturing

The final color composition is performed in the following way: the fragment shader receives the coordinates of the fragment, together with the curvatures. We will use components x and y of the fragment in screen space as texture coordinates. These coordinates are scaled to the range $[0..1]$.

```
[maxvertexcount(3)]
void main( triangle VERTEXin input[3],
    inout TriangleStream<VERTEXout> TriStream )
{
  //Assign triangle curvatures to the three vertices.
  VERTEXout outVert;
  outVert.Pos = input[0].Pos;
  outVert.norm = input[0].norm;
  outVert.curv1 = input[0].curv;
  outVert.curv2 = input[1].curv;
  outVert.curv3 = input[2].curv;
  TriStream.Append(outVert);

  outVert.Pos = input[1].Pos;
  outVert.norm = input[1].norm;
  outVert.curv1 = input[0].curv;
  outVert.curv2 = input[1].curv;
  outVert.curv3 = input[2].curv;
  TriStream.Append(outVert);

  outVert.Pos = input[2].Pos;
  outVert.norm = input[2].norm;
  outVert.curv1 = input[0].curv;
  outVert.curv2 = input[1].curv;
  outVert.curv3 = input[2].curv;
  TriStream.Append(outVert);

  TriStream.RestartStrip();
}
```

Listing 2.4. Pencil geometry shader.

In order to orient the texture according to the surface curvature, and to avoid deformations inside large triangles, the paper texture is oriented by using the three curvatures at the vertices, and blending them with equal weights. The implementation has three steps: First, the angles between curvatures and the x-axis are computed. Then, three two-dimensional rotation matrices are built using these angles. Finally, these matrices are used to transform the texture coordinates obtained from the fragment coordinates, and this yields three new texture coordinates. These are the ones used for final texturing.

The model may be shaded by using the dot product between the light direction and the surface normal in order to access a texture array of different tones. We use a single texture but modified with a function that changes brightness and contrast according to the incident illumination at each point. We use the following function:

```
p = 1.0 - {max}({dot}(light,normal),0.0)
colorDest = {pow}(colorSrc,p*S + O).
```

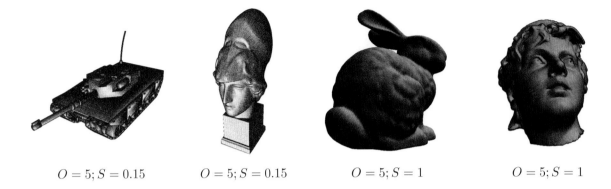

$O = 5; S = 0.15$ $O = 5; S = 0.15$ $O = 5; S = 1$ $O = 5; S = 1$

Figure 2.8. Pencil rendering results.

The resulting color of texture mapping is powered to a value in the range $[O..S + O]$. This value is determined from the dot product between the light and normal vectors. This will darken dark regions and lighten lighter regions, as can be seen in Figure 2.8 where we show the comparison using different values of O and S. The code corresponding to the geometry shader is shown in Listing 2.5.

```
float4 main(PIXELin inPut):SV_Target
{
 float2 xdir = float2(1.0f,0.0f);
 float2x2 rotMat;
 //Calculate the pixel coordinates.
 float2 uv = float2(inPut.Pos.x/width,inPut.Pos.y/height);

 //Calculate the rotated coordinates.
 float2 uvDir = normalize(inPut.curv1);
 float angle = atan(uvDir.y/uvDir.x);
 angle = (uvDir.x < 0.0f)?angle+PI:
  (uvDir.y < 0.0f)?angle+(2*PI):angle;
 float cosVal = cos(angle);
 float sinVal = sin(angle);
 rotMat[0][0] = cosVal;
 rotMat[1][0] = -sinVal;
 rotMat[0][1] = sinVal;
 rotMat[1][1] = cosVal;
 float2 uv1 = mul(uv,rotMat);

 uvDir = normalize(inPut.curv2);
 angle = atan(uvDir.y/uvDir.x);
 angle = (uvDir.x < 0.0f)?angle+PI:
  (uvDir.y < 0.0f)?angle+(2*PI):angle;
```

```
cosVal = cos(angle);
sinVal = sin(angle);
rotMat[0][0] = cosVal;
rotMat[1][0] = -sinVal;
rotMat[0][1] = sinVal;
rotMat[1][1] = cosVal;
float2 uv2 = mul(uv,rotMat);

uvDir = normalize(inPut.curv3);
angle = atan(uvDir.y/uvDir.x);
angle = (uvDir.x < 0.0f)?angle+PI:
  (uvDir.y < 0.0f)?angle+(2*PI):angle;
cosVal = cos(angle);
sinVal = sin(angle);
rotMat[0][0] = cosVal;
rotMat[1][0] = -sinVal;
rotMat[0][1] = sinVal;
rotMat[1][1] = cosVal;
float2 uv3 = mul(uv,rotMat);

//Calculate the light incident at this pixel.
float percen = 1.0f - max(dot(normalize(inPut.norm),
  lightDir),0.0);

//Combine the three colors.
float4 color = (texPencil.Sample(samLinear,uv1)*0.333f)
  +(texPencil.Sample(samLinear,uv2)*0.333f)
  +(texPencil.Sample(samLinear,uv3)*0.333f);

//Calculate the final color.
percen = (percen*S) + O;
color.xyz = pow(color.xyz,float3(percen,percen,percen));
return color;
}
```

Listing 2.5. Pencil pixel shader.

Models	Triangles	FPS
Buddha	1087716	87.71
Armadillo	345944	117.22
Asian Dragon	225588	199.20
Dragon	100000	344.28
Bunny	69666	422.20
Atenea	15014	553.55

Table 2.2. Framerates obtained with our implementation of the pencil rendering algorithm on a GeForce 9800 GX2 GPU graphics card and a viewport resolution of 1680×1050.

2.4.4   Results

Table 2.2 shows the framerates obtained with the pencil rendering technique. Note that we obtain high framerates because the implementation is relatively cheap, and that from the numbers we can deduce that the timings depend strongly on vertex count rather than rasterized fragments count.

2.5   Acknowledgments

The authors want to thank the reviewers for their valuable comments. This work has been supported by project TIN2007-67982-C02-01 of the Spanish Government.

Bibliography

[Achorn et al. 03] Brett Achorn, Daniel Teece, M. Sheelagh T. Carpendale, Mario Costa Sousa, David Ebert, Bruce Gooch, Victoria Interrante, Lisa M. Streit, and Oleg Veryovka. "Theory and Practice of Non-Photorealistic Graphics: Algorithms, Methods, and Production Systems." In *SIGGRAPH 2003*. ACM Press, 2003.

[Ashikhmin 04] Michael Ashikhmin. "Image-Space Silhouettes for Unprocessed Models." In *GI '04: Proceedings of Graphics Interface 2004*, pp. 195–202. School of Computer Science, University of Waterloo, Waterloo, Ontario, Canada: Canadian Human-Computer Communications Society, 2004.

[Card and Mitchell 02] Drew Card and Jason L. Mitchell. "Non-Photorealistic Rendering with Pixel and Vertex Shaders." In *Direct3D ShaderX: Vertex and Pixel Shader Tips and Tricks*, edited by Wolfgang Engel. Plano, Texas: Wordware, 2002.

[Dietrich 00] Sim Dietrich. "Cartoon Rendering and Advanced Texture Features of the GeForce 256 Texture Matrix, Projective Textures, Cube Maps, Texture Coordinate Generation and Dotproduct3 Texture Blending." Technical report, NVIDIA, 2000.

[Doss 08] Joshua Doss. "Inking the Cube: Edge Detection with Direct3D 10." http://www.gamasutra.com/visualcomputing/archive, 2008.

[Dyken et al. 08] Christopher Dyken, Martin Reimers, and Johan Seland. "Real-Time GPU Silhouette Refinement Using Adaptively Blended Bézier Patches." *Computer Graphics Forum* 27:1 (2008), 1–12.

[Everitt 02] Cass Everitt. "One-Pass Silhouette Rendering with GeForce and GeForce2." White paper, NVIDIA Corporation, 2002.

[Gooch and Gooch 01] Amy A. Gooch and Bruce Gooch. *Non-Photorealistic Rendering*. A K Peters, 2001. ISBN: 1568811330, 250 pages.

[Gooch et al. 99] Bruce Gooch, Peter-Pike J. Sloan, Amy A. Gooch, Peter Shirley, and Richard Riesenfeld. "Interactive Technical Illustration." In *1999 ACM Symposium on Interactive 3D Graphics*, pp. 31–38, 1999.

[Hartner et al. 03] Ashley Hartner, Mark Hartner, Elaine Cohen, and Bruce Gooch. "Object Space Silhouette Algorithms.", 2003. Unpublished.

[Hermosilla and Vázquez 09] Pedro Hermosilla and Pere-Pau Vázquez. "Single Pass GPU Stylized Edges." In *Proceedings of IV Iberoamerican Symposium in Computer Graphics*, pp. 47–54, 2009.

[Isenberg et al. 03] Tobias Isenberg, Bert Freudenberg, Nick Halper, Stefan Schlechtweg, and Thomas Strothotte. "A Developer's Guide to Silhouette Algorithms for Polygonal Models." *IEEE Comput. Graph. Appl.* 23:4 (2003), 28–37.

[Lee et al. 06] Hyunjun Lee, Sungtae Kwon, and Seungyong Lee. "Real-Time Pencil Rendering." In *NPAR '06: Proceedings of the 4th International Symposium on Non-photorealistic Animation and Rendering*, pp. 37–45. New York: ACM, 2006.

[McGuire and Hughes 04] Morgan McGuire and John F. Hughes. "Hardware-Determined Feature Edges." In *NPAR '04: Proceedings of the 3rd International Symposium on Non-photorealistic Animation and Rendering*, pp. 35–47. New York: ACM, 2004.

[Mitchell et al. 02] Jason L. Mitchell, Chris Brennan, and Drew Card. "Real-Time Image-Space Outlining for Non-Photorealistic Rendering." In *Siggraph 02*, 2002.

[Raskar 01] Ramesh Raskar. "Hardware Support for Non-photorealistic Rendering." In *2001 SIGGRAPH / Eurographics Workshop on Graphics Hardware*, pp. 41–46. ACM Press, 2001.

[Saito and Takahashi 90] Takafumi Saito and Tokiichiro Takahashi. "Comprehensible Rendering of 3-D Shapes." *SIGGRAPH90* 24:3 (1990), 197–206.

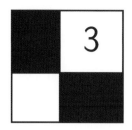

3

Alpha Blending as a Post-Process
Benjamin Hathaway

3.1 Introduction

In this article we will present a novel alpha-blending technique that was developed for the off-road racing game *Pure* (see Figure 3.1). *Pure* was released in the summer of 2008 for the Xbox360, PS3, and PC platforms and featured races that subjected the player to extreme elevations, revealing detailed vistas stretching out to a distance of over 30 kilometers. With the art direction set on a photo-realistic look and locations taken from around the globe—some would require a high degree of foliage cover to be at all believable, or even recognizable.

Figure 3.1. A typical scene from *Pure* (post tone mapping & bloom effects).

During development it became apparent that we were going to need alpha blending, and lots of it! Unfortunately, alpha blending is one aspect of computer graphics that is difficult to get right, and trade-offs between performance and visual quality are often made; indeed, reluctance to risk performance has led to some game titles avoiding the use of alpha blending altogether. For a thorough introduction to the issues posed by alpha blended rendering, the reader is referred to the [Thibieroz 08] paper on advanced rendering techniques and the seminal work [Porter and Duff 84].

3.2 The Alternatives

Pure was destined to run on several platforms, each being equipped with at least one Dx9 class GPU (supporting shader model 3). This immediately presented us with several (hardware assisted) options for rendering our foliage geometry.

Alpha blending. Alpha blending uses a scalar value output by the pixel shader (alpha-value) to blend a rendered fragment with the destination pixel data.

When rendering layers of foliage with alpha blending, z-buffering artifacts are common. This can largely be resolved if the rendered primitives are sorted to draw furthest from the camera first. Sorting primitives before rendering is usually a prohibitive CPU cost for game rendering, and in the case of intersecting primitives there may indeed be no single correct draw order.

Alpha testing. Alpha testing uses a binary value output by the pixel shader to determine if the output fragment is visible or not. Alpha testing is usually combined with z-buffering techniques, which can either negate the need for geometric depth sorting or provide fill-rate optimizations (by way of z-rejection) when the scene is sorted in a front-to-back order.

Alpha testing is one of the most commonly used solutions to date; however the technique is prone to aliasing at the alpha edges.

Alpha-to-coverage. Alpha-to-coverage converts the alpha value output by the pixel shader into a coverage mask. This coverage mask is combined with the standard multisample coverage mask to determine which samples should be updated.

When alpha-to-coverage is combined with alpha testing, softer edges can be rendered whilst maintaining all the technical benefits afforded by alpha test rendering, i.e., sort independence and z-rejection opportunities. Although this is an improvement on simple alpha testing, the resulting alpha gradients can be of a poor quality compared to those obtained in alpha blending. This is particularly true when using a low number of samples or on hardware that does not support flexible coverage masks.

3.3 The Source Artwork

To try and emulate the richness of natural foliage, each tree and bush was constructed from a multitude of polygonal planes. The planes were oriented as randomly as possible, thus increasing the perceived density of foliage.

As can be seen in Figure 3.2, this leads to a great deal of primitive intersection, which raises two issues:

1. How are we to correctly sort all the intersecting primitives?

2. How are we going to deal with the high degree of depth complexity present within a single foliage model?

Figure 3.2. Geometric structure of a typical tree model rendered in *Pure* (shown from the front and side).

To correctly depth sort the primitives would require that we split the primitives along all the intersections. However, this would have increased the vertex count substantially and put a heavy burden on our memory budget, while also increasing memory bandwidth usage.

These issues are further exacerbated when the foliage is allowed to react to dynamic influences such as the wind, or physical collisions. Such influences may even cause neighboring foliage models to overlap rather unpredictably, and would therefore be impossible to optimize off-line, instead requiring a more costly, real-time solution.

3.4   Initial Attempts

Due to the high levels of primitive interpenetration within the artwork, we initially implemented our foliage renderer in the simplest manner possible, by using a combination of z-buffering and alpha-test techniques. After auditioning a number of variations of the alpha-reference value, we managed to achieve some reasonable results, although the overall look of the foliage tended to appear a little harsh, or synthetic, at times.

The most objectionable effect occurred when the camera performed slow translational motions from side-to-side (for example, during the pre-race camera sequences). As the camera moved, the alpha-channeled holes & edges within the foliage would begin to *sparkle* (due to the binary nature of alpha testing) and would often be exaggerated by the high degree of depth complexity present within each foliage model.

Next, we turned our attention towards the alpha-to-coverage feature. Alpha-to-coverage rendering integrates alpha-testing techniques with multi-sample rendering; it produces softer edges while maintaining all the technical benefits of alpha-test rendering. While initial results were favorable and the sparkling artifacts were indeed attenuated, we struggled to reproduce consistent results across all of our platforms. We also suffered from the increased fill-rate and bandwidth costs incurred by rendering the foliage at MSAA resolutions.

Neither approach seemed to deliver a high enough visual quality and it seemed a shame to quantize all those beautiful alpha-textures so heavily. Something new was needed—and we felt the answer was hiding in the silhouette of the foliage.

3.5   The Screen-Space Alpha Mask

The solution we devised—screen-space alpha masking (SSAM)—is a multi-pass approach (see the overview in Figure 3.3) implemented with rendering techniques that negate the need for any depth sorting or geometry splitting. Our solution can

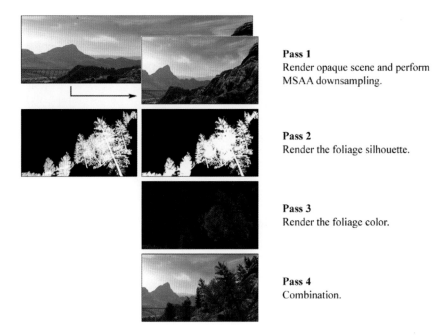

Pass 1
Render opaque scene and perform
MSAA downsampling.

Pass 2
Render the foliage silhouette.

Pass 3
Render the foliage color.

Pass 4
Combination.

Figure 3.3. Diagram showing an overview of screen-space alpha masking.

yield results on par with alpha blending while correctly resolving internal overlaps
(and depth intersections) on a per-pixel basis, using alpha-testing techniques.

We effectively performed *deferred alpha blending* using a full-screen post-
process that resembles frame-buffer blending with the blend-operation set to
ADD; the source and destination arguments are set to SRCALPHA and INVSRCALPHA,
respectively. The inputs to the *blend* are rendered into three separate render targets and are then bound to texture samplers, referenced by the *final combination*
post-process pixel shader (see Listing 3.2 in Section 3.11).

In terms of memory resources, we need at least three screen-resolution render-
targets, two having at least three color channels (rtOpaque & rtFoliage), one
with a minimum of two channels (rtMask), and a single depth buffer (rtDepth).

Note: this is *in addition* to any MSAA render-target memory requirements.

3.5.1 The Opaque Pass

During the first pass we rendered all our opaque scene elements into the color
render target: rtOpaque (see Figure 3.4); the depth information generated was
also kept and stored in the depth buffer: rtDepth (see Figure 3.5).

Figure 3.4. The opaque scene (color) written to `rtOpaque`.

For *Pure*, we rendered the opaque scene at 2× MSAA resolution and both the color and depth buffers were down sampled into screen-resolution render targets. Care had to be taken when down sampling the depth information, as incorrect samples were obtained when filtering was applied.

Figure 3.5. The opaque scene (depth) written to `rtDepth`.

Instead, we read a number of samples from the depth buffer (two, in the case of 2× MSAA), compared them, and simply retained the sample that was closest to the observer. For a more complete description of the solution adopted for *Pure*, the reader is referred to the work of [Iain Cantlay 04].

From this point onwards, we continued to render at non-MSAA resolutions, as it was observed that MSAA contributed little or nothing towards the quality of alpha generated edges—only those of a geometric nature. At this point, and depending on platform architecture, it may be necessary to copy the down sampled images back in to VRAM (repopulation) before further rendering can continue.

Additionally, at this point steps may need to be taken to update any hierarchical-z (hi-z) information that might be associated with `rtDepth`, and potentially optimize any subsequent draw calls that are depth occluded.

Note: Detailed information regarding the repopulation of depth information and restoration of Hi-Z can be obtained from the platform vendors and is unfortunately outside the scope of this article.

3.5.2   The Mask Generation Pass

In the second pass we generated a *silhouette*, or *mask*, of the foliage we wanted to render (see Figure 3.6). The silhouette image was rendered into our second render-target, `rtFoliage`, and we used the previously generated depth buffer, `rtDepth`, to correctly resolve any depth occlusions caused by the opaque scene.

Figure 3.6. Additively accumulated foliage alpha mask.

The mask is a monochromatic image of the alpha-channel values that would normally be used during regular alpha blending. The alpha-values are additively blended onto a black background, during which, we enabled depth testing, and disabled both back-face culling and depth writes.

As the additive blending of two primitives produces the same result regardless of the draw order, it seemed to be the ideal option for efficient mask generation. However, some artifacts were evident when the mask was used: *as-is*, (as the blend factor) due to the limited bit depth of the render-targets being used, during the *final combination* pass, the additively accumulated values would quickly saturate towards white—even at a modest depth complexity. The saturation was most evident when foliage close to the observer was expected to possess low-order opacity, but is rendered in an area of high foliage depth complexity.

To generate as high quality a mask as possible, we needed to obtain as much detail from our silhouette as we could; we therefore set the alpha-reference render-state to zero during this pass, to avoid the rejection low opacity alpha-values.

A refinement on additive blending was the use of the max-blending mode. In this case we built up an image of the single highest alpha-value to have been written to each pixel, in effect acting as an *alpha-z-buffer*. As with additive blending, we set the source and destination blend arguments to D3DBLEND_ONE, but change the blend operation to D3DBLENDOP_MAX.

As can be seen in Figure 3.7, the max-blended mask contains a higher degree of structural information (than the additively blended mask) while still retaining the subtle alpha gradients located towards the outer edges of the foliage.

Figure 3.7. MAX blended foliage alpha mask.

Despite these attractive qualities, when the max-blended mask was used as the blend factor during the final combination pass, the foliage took on a wholly transparent look. We were left feeling that perhaps the solution lay somewhere in between the two approaches. And it did—quite literally.

The thought was that perhaps some linear combination of both masks would be the answer. Perhaps the saturation of the additive blending would compensate for the transparency of the max blending? And correspondingly, would the subtle alpha-gradients of the max-blended image reduce the saturation evident in the low-opacity, high-depth-complexity areas of the additive mask?

Fortunately the answer proved to be yes in both cases, and luckily for us all the platforms we were working with provided a method that could generate both of our masks in a single pass!

Separate alpha blend enable. Most DX9 class hardware supports the ability to specify separate blend operations and arguments for both the color *and* alpha channels, independently.

By enabling `D3DRS_SEPARATEALPHABLENDENABLE` and setting the correct series of operation and arguments, it is possible to simultaneously write the max-blended mask to the rgb channels (as a monochromatic image), and the additively-blended mask to the alpha channel (see Table 3.1).

Note: Both masks are combined at a later stage, prior to their use as the blend-factor in the final composition pass.

In order to send the alpha values to both blending units, we needed to replicate the alpha values across to all the color channels. This required a small modification to the end of the foliage shaders that resembled

```
Out.Color.xyzw = Out.Color.wwww;
```

Render State	Value
D3DRS_ALPHABLENDENABLE	TRUE
D3DRS_SEPERATEALPHABLENDENABLE	TRUE
D3DRS_BLENDOP	D3DBLENDOP_MAX
D3DRS_BLENDOPALPHA	D3DBLENDOP_ADD
D3DRS_SRCBLEND	D3DBLEND_ONE
D3DRS_SRCBLENDALPHA	D3DBLEND_ONE
D3DRS_DESTBLEND	D3DBLEND_ONE
D3DRS_DESTBLENDALPHA	D3DBLEND_ONE

Table 3.1. The blend-related render states used during mask generation.

The modification not only performed the replication, but also had the added benefit of optimizing the foliage-alpha rendering shader without us needing any prior knowledge of how the alpha value was generated. For example: to what sampler stage the alpha-texture-source was bound, etc.

All of the optimizing shader compilers we tested performed some form of *dead-code stripping*, see: ["Dead Code" 09]. This optimization removed any code that did not directly contribute to the output value, substantially increasing fill-rate efficiency, in this case, removing all of the color-related lighting equations and texture-fetch instructions that were not common to the generation of the alpha value.

HLSL source code for a typical mask rendering shader is provided in Listing 3.1 in Section 3.11.

3.5.3   The Color Pass

For the third rendering pass, we rendered an image of the foliage color into our final render-target: `rtFoliage` (see Figure 3.8), and again we use the depth buffer obtained during the opaque pass, stored in `rtDepth` (see Figure 3.9).

In order to maintain correct depth ordering (as is necessary in the case of the color image), we disabled both back-face culling and alpha blending, while enabling alpha test rendering, depth testing, and depth writes. Enabling depth writes during this pass also ensured that any subsequently rendered transparencies would be correctly depth sorted with the foliage.

When rendering the foliage color with alpha testing enabled, a suitable alpha reference value had to be chosen and we exposed the color-pass alpha reference value to the artists for tweaking.

The final value ended up being a trade-off between two values. First was a value high enough to produce visually pleasing alpha-test edges—for *Pure*, a value of ≈ 128. Second was a value low enough to minimize certain blending artifacts (that will be covered in Section 3.6), which for *Pure*, ended up being a value of ≈ 64.

3.5.4   The Final Composition Pass

In the fourth and final pass, we rendered a full screen post-process that essentially performed a linear interpolation of our opaque and foliage-color images, using the mask image as the blend-factor (see Figure 3.10).

The final composition blend equation resembled

```
finalColor = rtOpaque + (rtFoliage - rtOpaque) * rtMask;
```

Application of the post-process consisted of the rendering of an orthographically projected, quadrilateral polygon mapped over the entire screen onto which

Figure 3.8. The foliage-color image written to `rtFoliage`.

Figure 3.9. The foliage-depth (alpha-tested) written into `rtDepth`.

Figure 3.10. The image produced by the final-combination pixel shader.

we applied a pixel shader to actually perform the blending work. To ensure that we only sampled one texel per screen pixel, we took the platform's texture-sampling center into account and adjusted texture coordinates accordingly.

We now had two mask images to process, the max and additively blended masks, which needed to be combined in some way into a scalar blend-factor. For our implementation we chose to combine the masks using linear interpolation (or in HLSL, the *lerp* operation).

The final-composition blend equation, with linearly blended masks resembled

```
mask = rtMask.a + (rtMask.r - rtMask.a) * maskLerp;
```

```
rtResult = rtOpaque + (rtFoliage - rtOpaque) * mask;
```

The interpolation of the two masks introduced the value `maskLerp`, for which a value must be selected. Like the alpha-reference value, this is chosen on purely artistic grounds and was also exposed to the art team for experimentation. The final value for *Pure* was 0.85 (which produces a blend-factor composed of: 85% additive mask and 15% max-blended mask).

With `maskLerp` equal to 0.85, just enough max-blended mask is brought in to reduce the saturation artifacts without making the foliage too transparent.

In fact, it should be noted that some degree of transparency was found to be desirable. The slight transparency of the max contribution revealed distant structure (such as trunks and branches) belonging to foliage that would have otherwise have been completely occluded by near foliage (adding a certain richness to the forest scenes).

The full HLSL source for the final composition pixel shader is given in Listing 3.2 in Section 3.11.

3.6   Alpha Reference Issues

As alpha test rendering was employed during the foliage color pass, an alpha-reference value was chosen—one that was high enough to stop overlapping edges from appearing too chunky (as mentioned, for *Pure* a value was chosen somewhere between ≈64 and ≈128). As a consequence, halo-like blending artifacts are sometimes visible where the foliage blended into the opaque image (see Figure 3.11).

3.6.1   The Clear-Screen Color Fix

Due to the alpha-reference value being set to a higher value during the color pass than that set during the mask-generation pass (for which the alpha-reference value was actually zero), moving outwards along an alpha gradient (from a value of one to zero), you can actually run out of foliage-color pixels before the mask-intensity reaches zero. This would reveal a proportion of the color-pass background color

Figure 3.11. Image showing blending artifacts caused by a non-zero alpha reference value during the foliage-color pass.

Figure 3.12. The effect of different clear screen colors (from top to bottom): too dark, too light, and just right.

in pixels whose mask intensity fell below the color-pass alpha reference value. The solution employed for *Pure* was to expose the foliage color passes' clear screen color to the artists, the idea being that by adjusting the color, you could lighten the artifact until it was hardly visible (see Figure 3.12).

The technique worked well but felt less than optimum, especially as the artists could only choose one color per level. The color also tended to affect the overall color balance of the scene and would have to work for foliage rendered in both the lightest and darkest of conditions—very much a compromise.

3.6.2 The Squared Alpha Trick

A small modification made to the last line of the final composition pixel shader substantially improved the quality of the blending, almost entirely compensating for the aforementioned alpha-reference artifacts (see Figure 3.13). If the final

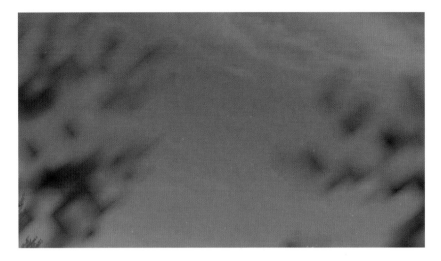

Figure 3.13. A close-up of the just-right clear screen color fix and the squared-alpha modification applied together.

mask value is numerically squared, the foliage alpha will roll off to black a little quicker while correctly maintaining areas of solid opacity.

```
return lerp(opaquePixel, foliagePixel, mask * mask);
```

It should be noted that while squaring the alpha channel does contract the foliage silhouette a little, a slight reduction in the foliage-color pass alpha-reference value should compensate for this.

3.7 Rendering Pipeline Integration

Foliage rendering is by no means the final step in rendering a game. There are many other alpha-blended elements to be integrated into the scene: grass, light shafts, and particle effects, to name but a few. Integration with these other stages is actually pretty straightforward, largely due to the fact that depth writing was enabled during the foliage-color pass.

This ensured that any subsequent depth testing would correctly resolve any depth-wise occlusions caused by the foliage (and/or opaque) scene elements.

3.8 Conclusion

In this article we have presented a novel (cross-platform) solution to the alpha blending of foliage, a solution that increases the quality of a wide range of alpha-test-class renderings, giving them the appearance of true alpha blending.

The use of SSAM within the game *Pure* had a profound effect on the overall perceived quality of the environments. The effect yielded a soft natural look without sacrificing any of the detail and contrast present in the source artwork. Below we list a few of the pros & cons to using SSAM:

Pros:

- Foliage edges are blended smoothly with the surrounding environment.

- Internally overlapping and interpenetrating primitives are sorted on a per-pixel basis using alpha testing techniques.

- The effect is implemented using simple, low-cost rendering techniques that do not require any geometric sorting or splitting (only consistency in primitive dispatch order is required).

- The final blending operations are performed at a linear cost (once per pixel) regardless of scene complexity and over-draw.

- The effect integrates well with other alpha-blending stages in the rendering pipeline (Particles, etc).

- When combined with other optimizations such as moving lighting to the vertex shader, and optimizing the shaders for each pass, overall performance can be higher than that of MSAA-based techniques.

Cons:

- The overhead of rendering the extra passes.

- Memory requirements are higher, as we need to store three images.

- The technique cannot be used to sort large collections of semi-transparent, glass-like surfaces (or soft alpha gradients that span large portions of the screen) without potentially exhibiting visual artifacts.[1]

3.9   Demo

A RenderMonkey scene, as well as several instructional .PSD files, are available in the book's web materials on the CRC Press website.

---

[1]There are occasional opacity-related artifacts visible within overlapping alpha-gradients (when the alpha-foliage-mask is either: > 0 or, < 1). Fortunately, the foliage-color pass always yields the nearest, and therefore the most visually correct, surface color.

3.10   Acknowledgments

I would like to say a big thank you to everyone at Black Rock Studio who contributed to this article, particularly: Jeremy Moore and Tom Williams (for pushing me to write the article in the first place), and Damyan Pepper and James Callin for being there to bounce ideas off during the initial development.

An extra special thank you goes to Caroline Hathaway, Nicole Ancel, and Wessam Bahnassi for proofreading and editing the article.

3.11   Source Code

```
sampler2D foliageTexture : register(s0);

struct PS_INPUT
{
    half2 TexCoord : TEXCOORD0;
};

half4 main(PS_INPUT In) : COLOR
{
    return tex2D(foliageTexture, In.TexCoord).wwww;
}
```

Listing 3.1. HLSL source code for a typical mask rendering pixel shader.

```
sampler2D rtMask : register(s0);
sampler2D rtOpaque : register(s1);
sampler2D rtFoliage : register(s2);
half maskLerp : register(c0); // 0.85h

half4 main(float2 texCoord: TEXCOORD0) : COLOR
{
    half4 maskPixel = tex2D( rtMask, texCoord);
    half4 opaquePixel = tex2D( rtOpaque, texCoord);
    half4 foliagePixel = tex2D(rtFoliage, texCoord);
    half mask = lerp(maskPixel.x, maskPixel.w, maskLerp);

    return lerp(opaquePixel, foliagePixel, mask * mask);
}
```

Listing 3.2. HLSL source code for the final composition pixel shader.

Bibliography

["Dead Code" 09] "Dead Code Elimination." *Wikipedia*. Available at http://en. wikipedia.org/wiki/Dead_code_elimination, 2009.

[Iain Cantlay 04] Iain Cantlay. "High-Speed, Off-Screen Particles." In *GPU Gems 3*, edited by Hubert Nguyen. Reading, MA: Addison-Wesley Professional, 2007.

[Thibieroz 08] Nicolas Thibieroz. "Robust Order-Independent Transparency via Reverse Depth Peeling in DirectX10." In *ShaderX6: Advanced Rendering Techniques* (2008).

[Porter and Duff 84] Thomas Porter and Tom Duff. "Compositing Digital Images." *Computer Graphics* 18:3 (1984): 253–59.

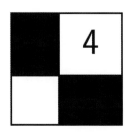

4

Virtual Texture Mapping 101
Matthäus G. Chajdas, Christian Eisenacher, Marc Stamminger, and Sylvain Lefebvre

4.1 Introduction

Modern games and applications use large amounts of texture data; the number and the resolution of textures also continues to grow quickly. However, the amount of available graphics memory is not growing at the same pace and, in addition to textures, GPU memory is also used for complex post-processing effects and lighting calculations. *Virtual texture mapping* (VTM) is a technique to reduce the amount of graphics memory required for textures to a point where it is only dependent on the screen resolution: for a given viewpoint we only keep the visible parts of the textures in graphics memory, at the appropriate MIP map level (see Figure 4.1).

In this chapter, we will investigate how to implement a fully functional VTM system. Readers already familiar with VTM might want to skip right to Section 4.3, which covers several non-obvious implementation aspects. Our tutorial implementation follows this article very closely, so we encourage you to look at the relevant code for each section.

4.2 Virtual Texture Mapping

While early texture management schemes were designed for a single large texture [Tanner et al. 98], recent VTM systems are more flexible and mimic the virtual memory management of the OS: textures are divided into small *tiles*, or pages [Kraus and Ertl 02, Lefebvre et al. 04]. Those are automatically cached and loaded onto the GPU as required for rendering the current viewpoint. However, it is necessary to redirect accesses to missing data to a fallback texture. This

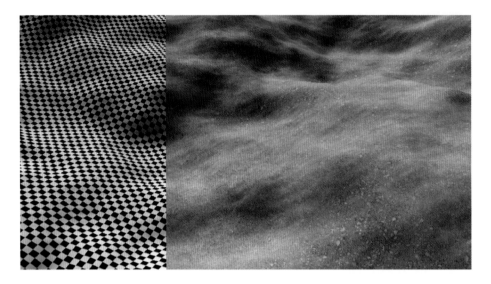

Figure 4.1. Uniquely textured terrain rendering using a single virtual texture.

prevents "holes" from appearing in the rendering, or blocking and waiting until the load request finishes.

Our implementation is inspired by the GDC talk of Sean Barrett [Barret 08] and we suggest watching the video of his presentation while reading this section. As illustrated in Figure 4.2, we begin each frame by determining which tiles are visible. We identify the ones not cached and request them from disk. After the tiles have been uploaded into the tile cache on the GPU, we update an *indirection texture*, or page table. Eventually, we render the scene, performing an initial lookup into the indirection texture to determine where to sample in the tile cache.

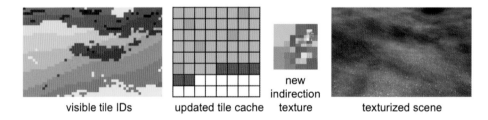

visible tile IDs   updated tile cache   new indirection texture   texturized scene

Figure 4.2. We render tile IDs, then identify and upload newly visible tiles into the tile cache (red), possibly overwriting ones that are no longer visible (blue). We update the indirection texture and render the texturized surfaces.

The indirection texture is a scaled down version of the complete virtual texture, where each texel points to a tile in the tile cache. In our case, the tile cache is simply one large texture on the GPU, containing small, square tiles of identical resolution. This means tiles from different MIP map levels cover differently sized areas of the virtual texture, but simplifies the management of the tile cache considerably.

4.2.1 Page Fault Generation

For each frame we determine the visible tiles, identify the ones not yet loaded onto the GPU, and request them from disk. Future hardware might simplify this with native page faults [Seiler et al. 08], but we still need to determine visible tiles, substitute data and redirect memory accesses.

A simple approach is to render the complete scene with a special shader that translates the virtual texture coordinates into a tile ID. By rendering the actual geometry of the scene, we trivially handle occlusion. The framebuffer is then read back and processed on the CPU along with other management tasks. As tiles typically cover several pixels, it is possible to render tile IDs at a lower resolution to reduce bandwidth and processing costs. Also, in order to pre-fetch tiles that will be visible "soon," the field of view can be slightly increased. The corresponding shader code can be found in Section 4.5.2.

4.2.2 Page Handler

The page handler loads requested tiles from disk, uploads them onto the GPU, and updates the indirection texture. Depending on disk latency and camera movement, loading the tiles might become a bottleneck. To illustrate this we fly over a large terrain covered by a single virtual texture and graph the time per frame in Figure 4.3. Given a reasonably large tile cache, very few tiles are requested and on average we need less than ten ms per frame for I/O and rendering. However, in frame 512 we turn the camera 180 degrees and continue backwards. This u-turn requests over 100 tiles, taking 350 ms to load.

To ensure smooth rendering we simply limit the number of updated tiles per frame. For requests not served in the same frame we adjust the indirection texture and redirect texture access to the finest parent tile available in the tile cache. The coarsest level is always present, and this distributes load spikes over several frames. If the update limit is larger than the average number of requested tiles, we are guaranteed to catch up with the requests eventually. For our example we request fewer than five tiles in 95% of the frames, and set the upload limit to a very conservative 20 tiles.

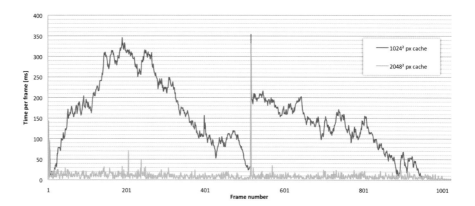

Figure 4.3. We fly over a terrain with one large virtual texture and record the time per frame. In frame 512 we turn the camera 180 ° and continue backwards. This turn is a worst case scenario for VTM: many new tiles—which are no longer in the cache— become visible and have to be loaded. While sufficiently large caches prevent thrashing, they help little in this challenging event.

Of course the missing tiles reduce visual quality. Therefore we upload the requested tiles with all their ancestors, prioritized from coarse to fine. This increases the total number of cache updates, but as Figure 4.4 shows, image quality is restored in a more balanced fashion—very similar to progressive JPEG. As more ancestors are present in the cache, this also improves quality in less challenging situations and reduces artifacts when rendering tile IDs with a very low resolution.

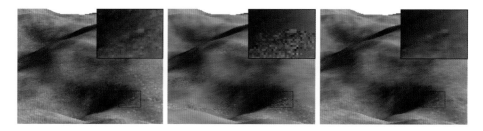

Figure 4.4. Half a second after the u-turn. Left: waiting for all tiles provides superior image quality but stalls for 330 ms. Middle: limiting the uploads per frame and using coarser MIP map levels as fallback provides smooth frame rates, but MIP levels vary strongly. Right: using prioritized loading of ancestors improves fallback, and image quality is much more balanced after the same time.

4.2.3 Rendering

When texturing the surface we perform a fast unfiltered lookup into the indirection texture, using the uv-coordinate of the fragment in virtual texture space. This provides the position of the target tile in the cache and the actual resolution of its MIP map level in the pyramid of the indirection texture. The latter might be different from the resolution computed from the fragment's MIP map level due to our tile upload limit. We add the offset inside the tile to the tile position and sample from the tile cache. The offset is simply the fractional part of the uv-coordinate scaled by the actual resolution:

$$\text{offset} := \text{frac}(uv \times \text{actualResolution}) = \text{frac}(uv \times 2^{\text{indTexEntry.z}}).$$

Note that storing the actual resolution as $\log_2(\text{actualResolution})$ allows us to use 8-bit textures. The complete shader code including the computation of correct texture gradients (see Section 4.3.3) can be found in Section 4.5.3.

4.3 Implementation Details

In this section we will investigate various implementation issues with a strong emphasis on texture filtering. Again we will follow the processing of one frame, from page fault generation over page handling to rendering.

4.3.1 Page Fault Generation

MIP map level. To compute the tile ID in the tile shader we need the virtual texture coordinates and the current MIP map level. The former are directly the interpolated uvs used for texturing, but on DX 9 and 10 hardware, we have to compute the latter manually using gradient instructions [Ewins et al. 98, Wu 98]: let $ddx = (\frac{\delta u}{\delta x}, \frac{\delta v}{\delta x})$ and $ddy = (\frac{\delta u}{\delta y}, \frac{\delta v}{\delta y})$ be the uv gradients in x- and y-direction. Using their maximal length we compute the MIP map level as

$$\text{MIP} = \log_2(\max(|ddx|, |ddy|)).$$

The corresponding shader code can be found in Section 4.5.1.

DX 10.1 provides the HLSL function `CalculateLevelOfDetail()`. Further DX 11 gives access to coarse gradients (`dd{x|y}_coarse()`) which might provide an even faster alternative to the level of detail function.

4.3.2 Page Handler

Compressed tiles. For efficient rendering it is desirable to have a DXTC compressed tile cache. It requires less memory on the GPU and reduces the upload and rendering bandwidth. However, as the compression ratio of DXTC is fixed and quite low, we store the tiles using JPEG and transcode them to DXTC before we upload them. This also allows us to reduce quality selectively and e.g., compress tiles of inaccessible areas stronger.

Disk I/O. For our tutorial implementation we store tiles as individual JPEG files for the sake of simplicity. However, reading many small files requires slow seeks and wastes bandwidth. Packing the tiles into a single file is thus very important, especially for slow devices with large sectors like DVDs.

It is possible to cut down the storage requirements by storing only every second MIP map level and computing two additional MIP maps for each tile: if an intermediate level is requested, we load the corresponding four pages from the finer level instead. More ideas about storage and loading can be found in [van Waveren 08].

Cache saturation. Unused tiles are overwritten with newly requested tiles using an LRU policy. However, the current working set might still not fit into the cache. In this case we remove tiles that promise low impact on visual quality. We replace the tiles with the finest resolution with their lower-resolution ancestors. This plays nicely with our progressive update strategy and quickly frees the tile cache. Other good candidates for removal are tiles with low variance or small screen space area.

Tile upload. Uploading the tiles to the GPU should be fast, with minimum stalling. Using DX 9, we create a managed texture and let the driver handle the upload to the GPU. Other approaches for DX 9 are described in detail by [Mittring 08]. For DX 10 and 11, we create a set of intermediate textures and update these in turn. The textures are copied individually into the tile cache [Thibieroz 08]. DX 11 adds the possibility to update the tiles concurrently, which further increases performance.

Indirection texture update. After the tiles have been uploaded, we update the indirection texture by recreating it from scratch. We start by initializing the top

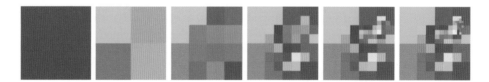

Figure 4.5. Creating the indirection texture for a camera looking over a large terrain: initializing the top level with the lowest resolution tile, we copy parent entries into the next finer level and add entries for tiles present in the cache.

of its MIP map pyramid with an entry for the tile with the lowest resolution, so each fragment has a valid fallback. For each finer level we copy the entries of the parent texels, but replace the copy with entries for tiles from that level, should they reside in the cache. We continue this process until the complete indirection texture pyramid is filled (see Figure 4.5).

If tiles are usually seen at a single resolution, we can upload only the finest level to the GPU. This reduces the required upload bandwidth, simplifies the lookup, and improves performance. This is sufficient when every object uses an unique texture, in particular for terrain rendering.

4.3.3 Rendering

While rendering with a virtual texture is straight forward, correct filtering, especially at tile edges, is less obvious. Neighboring tiles in texture space are very likely not adjacent to each other in the tile cache. Filtering is especially challenging if the hardware filtering units should be used, as those rely on having MIP maps and correct gradients available. The following paragraphs describe how to use HW filtering with an anisotropy of up to 4:1 as shown in Figure 4.6. The corresponding shader code can be found in Section 4.5.3.

Texture gradients. When two adjacent tiles in texture space are not adjacent in the tile cache, as shown in Figure 4.7, the *uv*-coordinates for the final texture lookup will vary a great deal between neighboring fragments. This results in large texture gradients and the graphics hardware will use a very wide filter for sampling, producing blurry seams. To address this, we manually compute the

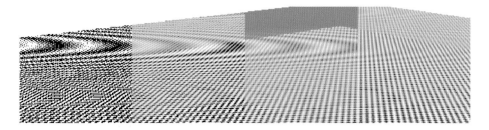

Figure 4.6. From left to right: Hardware point (175 fps), bilinear (170 fps), trilinear (170 fps), and 4:1 anisotropic filtering (165 fps) on an NVIDIA 9700M GT. The transition between tiles is especially pronounced with trilinear filtering. A single tile has to serve several MIP map levels in this example, but only one additional MIP map level is available for filtering per tile. All other methods seem to not use MIP maps at all with the tested driver version.

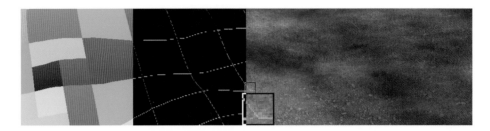

Figure 4.7. Even though the surface has a continuous mapping, the arrangement of the tiles in the cache causes discontinuities. From left to right: direct visualization of the lookup position into the tile cache; *uv* gradients, wrong across tile edges; blurry seams resulting from too wide filters when sampling. Manually scaled gradients fix this artifact.

gradients from the original virtual texture coordinates, scale them depending on the MIP map level of the tile and pass them on to the texture sampler.

Tile borders. Even with correct texture gradients, we still have to filter into neighboring pages, which very likely contain a completely different part of the virtual texture. To avoid the resulting color bleeding we need to add borders. Depending on what constraints we want to place on the size of the tile, we can use *inner* or *outer* borders.

We use the latter and surround our 128^2 tiles with a four-pixel border, making them 136^2. This keeps the resolution a multiple of four, allowing us to compress them using DXTC and perform 4:1 anisotropic filtering in hardware.

DXTC border blocks. As Figure 4.8 illustrates, adding a border to tiles might lead to different DXTC blocks at the edges of tiles. As the different blocks will be compressed differently, texels that represent the same points in virtual texture space will not have the same values in both tiles. This leads to color bleeding across tile edges, despite the border. By using a four-pixel outer border, these compression related artifacts vanish.

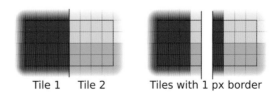

Tile 1   Tile 2   Tiles with 1 px border

Figure 4.8. Adding a one-pixel border around a tile creates different DXTC blocks for neighboring tiles. Depending on the texture they might be compressed differently, leading to visible seams in the virtual texture despite having borders.

4.4 Conclusion

In this chapter, we described a basic virtual texture mapping system. It is simple and fast, even on older hardware. We gave a few pointers on how to further improve performance, should your application or game require it. Even with newer hardware that might natively support page faults, strategies for loading, compressing and filtering textures will still be required. We hope this article and our tutorial implementation will help you to get started with VTM. You can integrate it into your own application or just play with different parameters and strategies.

4.5 Shader Code

4.5.1 MIP Map Calculation

```
float ComputeMipMapLevel(float2 UV_pixels, float scale)
{
    float2 x_deriv = ddx(UV_pixels);
    float2 y_deriv = ddy(UV_pixels);

    float d = max(length(x_deriv), length(y_deriv));

    return max(log2(d) - log2(scale), 0);
}
```

4.5.2 Tile ID Shader

```
float2 UV_pixels = In.UV * VTMResolution,

float mipLevel = ComputeMipMapLevel(UV_pixels, subSampleFactor);
mipLevel = floor(min (mipLevel, MaxMipMapLevel));

float4 tileID;
tileID.rg = floor(UV_pixels / (TileRes * exp2(mipLevel)));
tileID.b  = mipLevel;
tileID.a  = TextureID;

return tileID;
```

4.5.3 Virtual Texture Lookup

```
float3 tileEntry = IndTex.Sample(PointSampler, In.UV);
float actualResolution = exp2(tileEntry.z);

float2 offset = frac(In.UV * actualResolution) * TileRes;

float scale = actualResolution * TileRes;
float2 ddx_correct = ddx(In.UV) * scale;
float2 ddy_correct = ddy(In.UV) * scale;

return TileCache.SampleGrad(TextureSampler,
                           tileEntry.xy + offset,
                           ddx_correct,
                           ddy_correct);
```

4.6 Acknowledgments

We'd like to thank J.M.P van Waveren for generously sharing his insights on virtual texture mapping.

Bibliography

[Barret 08] Sean Barret. "Sparse Virtual Textures." 2008. http://silverspaceship.com/src/svt/.

[Ewins et al. 98] JP Ewins, MD Waller, M. White, and PF Lister. "MIP-Map Level Selection For Texture Mapping." *Visualization and Computer Graphics, IEEE Transactions on* 4:4 (1998), 317–329.

[Kraus and Ertl 02] Martin Kraus and Thomas Ertl. "Adaptive Texture Maps." In *HWWS '02: Proceedings of the ACM SIGGRAPH/EUROGRAPHICS Conference on Graphics Hardware*, pp. 7–15. Aire-la-Ville, Switzerland, Switzerland: Eurographics Association, 2002.

[Lefebvre et al. 04] Sylvain Lefebvre, Jerome Darbon, and Fabrice Neyret. "Unified Texture Management for Arbitrary Meshes." Technical Report RR5210, INRIA, 2004. Available online (http://www-evasion.imag.fr/Publications/2004/LDN04).

[Mittring 08] Martin Mittring. "Advanced Virtual Texture Topics." 2008. http://ati.amd.com/developer/SIGGRAPH08/Chapter02-Mittring-Advanced_Virtual_Texture_Topics.pdf.

[Seiler et al. 08] Larry Seiler, Doug Carmean, Eric Sprangle, Tom Forsyth, Michael Abrash, Pradeep Dubey, Stephen Junkins, Adam Lake, Jeremy Sugerman, Robert Cavin, Roger Espasa, Ed Grochowski, Toni Juan, and Pat Hanrahan. "Larrabee: A Many-Core x86 Architecture for Visual Computing." *ACM Trans. Graph.* 27:3 (2008), 1–15.

[Tanner et al. 98] C.C. Tanner, C.J. Migdal, and M.T. Jones. "The Clipmap: A Virtual Mipmap." In *Proceedings of the 25th Annual Conference on Computer Graphics and Interactive Techniques*, pp. 151–158. ACM New York, 1998.

[Thibieroz 08] Nicolas Thibieroz. "Ultimate Graphics Performance for DirectX 10 Hardware." GDC Presentation, 2008.

[van Waveren 08] J. M. P. van Waveren. "Geospatial Texture Streaming from Slow Storage Devices." 2008. http://software.intel.com/en-us/articles/geospatial-texture-streaming-from-slow-storage-devices/.

[Wu 98] Kevin Wu. "Direct Calculation of MIP-Map Level for Faster Texture Mapping." Hewlett-Packard Laboratories, 1998. http://www.hpl.hp.com/techreports/98/HPL-98-112.html.

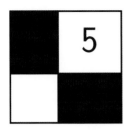

5

Pre-Integrated Skin Shading
Eric Penner and George Borshukov

5.1 Introduction

Rendering realistic skin has always been a challenge in computer graphics. Human observers are particularly sensitive to the appearance of faces and skin, and skin exhibits several complex visual characteristics that are difficult to capture with simple shading models. One of the defining characteristics of skin is the way light bounces around in the dermis and epidermis layers. When rendering using a simple diffuse model, the light is assumed to immediately bounce equally in all directions after striking the surface. While this is very fast to compute, it gives surfaces a very "thin" and "hard" appearance. In order to make skin look more "soft" it is necessary to take into account the way light bounces around inside a surface. This phenomenon is known as *subsurface scattering*, and substantial recent effort has been spent on the problem of realistic, real-time rendering with accurate subsurface scattering.

Current skin-shading techniques usually simulate subsurface scattering during rendering by either simulating light as it travels through skin, or by gathering incident light from neighboring locations. In this chapter we discuss a different approach to skin shading: rather than gathering neighboring light, we pre-integrate the effects of scattered light. Pre-integrating allows us to achieve the nonlocal effects of subsurface scattering using only locally stored information and a custom shading model. What this means is that our skin shader becomes just that: a simple pixel shader. No extra passes are required and no blurring is required, in texture space nor screen space. Therefore, the cost of our algorithm scales directly with the number of pixels shaded, just like simple shading models such as Blinn-Phong, and it can be implemented on any hardware, with minimal programmable shading support.

5.2   Background and Previous Work

Several offline and real-time approaches have been based on an approach, taken from film, called *texture-space diffusion* (TSD). TSD stores incoming light in texture space and uses a blurring step to simulate diffusion. The first use of this technique was by [Borshukov and Lewis 03, Borshukov and Lewis 05] in the *Matrix* sequels. They rendered light into a texture-space map and then used a custom blur kernel to gather scattered light from all directions. Based on extensive reference to real skin, they used different blur kernels for the red, green, and blue color channels, since different wavelengths of light scatter differently through skin. Since the texture-space diffusion approach used texture-blur operations, it was a very good fit for graphics hardware and was adopted for use in real-time rendering [Green 04, Gosselin et al. 04]. While TSD approaches achieved much more realistic results, the simple blurring operations performed in real time couldn't initially achieve the same level of quality of the expensive, original, nonseparable blurs used in film.

A concept that accurately describes how light diffuses in skin and other translucent materials is known as the *diffusion profile*. For a highly scattering translucent material it is assumed that light scatters equally in all directions as soon as it hits the surface. A diffusion profile can be thought of as a simple plot of how much of this diffused light exits the surface as a function of the distance from the point of entry. Diffusion profiles can be calculated using measured scattering parameters via mathematical models known as *dipole* [Jensen et al. 01] or *multipole* [Donner and Jensen 05] diffusion models. The dipole model works for simpler materials, while the multipole model can simulate the effect of several layers, each with different scattering parameters.

The work by [d'Eon and Luebke 07] sets the current high bar in real-time skin rendering, combining the concept of fast Gaussian texture-space diffusion with the rigor of physically based diffusion profiles. Their approach uses a sum of Gaussians to approximate a multipole diffusion profile for skin, allowing a very large diffusion profile to be simulated using several separable Gaussian blurs. More recent approaches have achieved marked performance improvements. For example, [Hable et al. 09] have presented an optimized texture-space blur kernel, while [Jimenez et al. 09] have applied the technique in screen space.

5.3   Pre-Integrating the Effects of Scattering

We have taken a different approach to the problem of subsurface scattering in skin and have departed from texture-space diffusion (see Figure 5.1). Instead, we wished to see how far we could push realistic skin rendering while maintaining the benefits of a local shading model. Local shading models have the advantage of not requiring additional rendering passes for each object, and scale linearly with the number of pixels shaded. Therefore, rather than trying to achieve subsur-

Figure 5.1. Our pre-integrated skin-shading approach uses the same diffusion profiles as texture-space diffusion, but uses a local shading model. Note how light bleeds over lighting boundaries and into shadows. (Mesh and textures courtesy of XYZRGB.)

face scattering by gathering incoming light from nearby locations (performing an integration during runtime), we instead seek to pre-integrate the effects of sub-surface scattering in skin. Pre-integration is used in many domains and simply refers to integrating a function in advance, such that calculations that rely on the function's integral can be accelerated later. Image convolution and blurring are just a form of numerical integration.

The obvious caveat of pre-integration is that in order to pre-integrate a function, we need to know that it won't change in the future. Since the incident light on skin can conceivably be almost arbitrary, it seems as though precomputing this effect will prove difficult, especially for changing surfaces. However, by focusing only on skin rather than arbitrary materials, and choosing specifically where and what to pre-integrate, we found what we believe is a happy medium. In total, we pre-integrate the effect of scattering in three special steps: on the lighting model, on small surface details, and on occluded light (shadows). By applying all of these in tandem, we achieve similar results to texture-space diffusion approaches in a completely local pixel shader, with few additional constraints.

To understand the reasoning behind our approach, it first helps to picture a completely flat piece of skin under uniform directional light. In this particular case, no visible scattering will occur because the incident light is the same everywhere. The only three things that introduce visible scattering are changes in the surrounding mesh curvature, bumps in the normal map, and occluded light (shadows). We deal with each of these phenomena separately.

5.4   Scattering and Diffuse Light

If we take our previously flat surface with no visible scattering and start to make it a smooth and curvy surface, like skin (we will keep it smooth for now), scattering will start to become visible. This occurs due to the changes in incident light across the surface. The Lambert diffuse-lighting model assumes that diffuse light scatters equally in all directions, and the amount of incident light is proportional to the cosine of the angle between the surface normal and light direction ($N \cdot L$).

Since $N \cdot L$ falloff is a primary cause of changing incident light, and thus visible scattering, there have been several rendering tricks that attempt to add the look of scattering by altering the $N \cdot L$ fall-off itself. This involves making the falloff wrap around the back of objects, or by letting each wavelength of light (r, g, and b) fall off differently as $N \cdot L$ approaches zero. What we found to be the big problem with such approaches is that they aren't based on physical measurements of real skin-like diffusion profiles; and if you tune them to look nice for highly curved surfaces, then there will be a massive falloff for almost-flat surfaces (and vice versa).

To address both issues, we precompute the effect of diffuse light scattering. We do this in a fashion similar to measured *bidirectional reflectance distribution functions* (BRDFs). Measured BRDFs use physically measured data from real surfaces to map incoming to outgoing light. This is as opposed to analytical BRDFs such as Blinn-Phong that are analytical approximations for an assumed micro-facet structure. Typical measured BRDFs don't incorporate $N \cdot L$ since $N \cdot L$ just represents the amount of incoming light and isn't part of the surface's reflectance. We are concerned *only* with $N \cdot L$ (diffuse light), as this is the light that contributes to subsurface scattering.

One approach we considered to precompute the effect of scattered light at any point on a surface, was to simulate lighting from all directions and compress that data using spherical harmonics. Unfortunately, spherical harmonics can efficiently represent only very low frequency changes or would require too many coefficients. Thus, instead of precomputing the effect of scattering at all locations, we chose to precompute the scattering falloff for a subset of surface shapes and determine the best falloff during forward rendering. As discussed above, one characteristic that we can calculate in a shader is surface curvature, which largely determines the effect of scattering on smooth surfaces.

To measure the effect of surface curvature on scattering, we add curvature as the second parameter to our measured diffuse falloff. The skin diffusion profiles from [d'Eon and Luebke 07] on flat skin can be used to simulate the effect of scattering on different curvatures. We simply light a spherical surface of a given curvature from one direction and measure the accumulated light at each angle with respect to the light (see Figures 5.2 and 5.3). This results in a two-dimensional lookup texture that we can use at runtime. More formally, for each skin curvature and for all angles θ between N and L, we perform the integration in Equation (5.1):

$$D(\theta, r) = \frac{\int_{-\pi}^{\pi} \cos(\theta + x) \cdot R(2r \sin(x/2)) dx}{\int_{-\pi}^{\pi} R(2 \sin(x/2)) dx} \tag{5.1}$$

The first thing to note is that we have approximated a spherical integration with integration on a ring. We found the difference was negligible and the ring integration fits nicely into a shader that is used to compute the lookup texture. The variable $R()$ refers to the diffusion profile, for which we used the sum of Gaussians from [d'Eon and Luebke 07] (see Table 5.1). Rather than performing an expensive arccos() operation in our shader to calculate the angle, we push this into the lookup, so our lookup is indexed by $N \cdot L$ directly. This is fine in our case, as the area where scattering occurs has plenty of space in the lookup. Figures 5.2 and 5.3 illustrate how to compute and use the diffuse lookup texture.

While this measured skin model can provide some interesting results on its own, it still has a few major flaws. Primarily, it assumes that all skin resembles a sphere, when, in fact, skin can have fairly arbitrary topology. Stated another way, it assumes that scattered light arriving at a given point depends on the curvature of that point itself. In actuality it depends on the curvature of all of the surrounding points on the surface. Thus, this approximation will work very well on smooth surfaces without fast changes in curvature, but breaks down when curvature changes too quickly. Thankfully, most models of skin are broken up into two detail levels: smooth surfaces represented using geometry, and surface

Variance	Red	Green	Blue
0.0064	0.233	0.455	0.649
0.0484	0.100	0.366	0.344
0.187	0.118	0.198	0.0
0.567	0.113	0.007	0.007
1.99	0.358	0.004	0.0
7.41	0.078	0	0.0

Table 5.1. The weights used by [d'Eon and Luebke 07] for texture-space diffusion. Although we aren't limited to the sum of Gaussians approximations, we use the same profile for comparison.

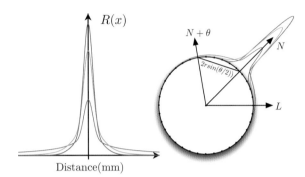

Figure 5.2. The graph (left) illustrates the diffusion profile of red, green, and blue light in skin, using the sum of Gaussians from Table 5.1. The diagram (right) illustrates how we pre-integrate the effect of scattering into a diffuse BRDF lookup. The diffusion profile for skin (overlaid radially for one angle) is used to blur a simple diffuse BRDF for all curvatures of skin.

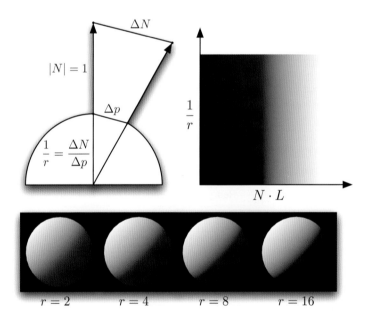

Figure 5.3. The diagram (top left) illustrates how we calculate curvature while rendering using two derivatives. The diffuse BRDF lookup, indexed by curvature (sphere radius) and $N \cdot L$ (top right). Spheres of different sized renderings using the new BRDF lookup (bottom).

details represented in a normal map. We take advantage of this and let the measured diffuse falloff be chosen at the smooth geometry level, while adding another approach to deal with creases and small bumps in normal maps, which are responsible for quick changes in curvature.

5.5   Scattering and Normal Maps

We now turn to the effect of scattering on small wrinkles and pores that are usually represented with a normal map. Since the normal from a small crease always returns to the dominant surface normal, the reflected scattered light coming from that crease will look very similar to light reflected from a nonscattering surface with a physically broader (or blurred-out) crease. Coincidentally, one way of approximating the look of scattered-over small creases and bumps is to simply blur the creases and bumps themselves! Most important however, this effect will be different for each wavelength of light, because of their different diffusion profiles.

Interestingly, the inverse of this phenomenon was noted when capturing normals from a real subject, using image-based lighting. Ma et al. [Ma et al. 07] noted that, when captured using spherical gradient lighting, normals become bent toward the dominant-surface normal, depending on the wavelength of light used to capture them (red was more bent than green, etc.). They also noted that a local skin-shading model was improved by using all the normals they captured instead of only one. In this case the image-based normal capture was physically integrating all the scattered light when determining the best normal to fit the data. Since we have only one set of normal maps to begin with, we essentially work in reverse. We assume that our original normal map is the accurate surface normal map and blur it several times for each wavelength, resulting in a separate normal map for each color, and for specular reflection. As mentioned by previous authors [d'Eon and Luebke 07, Hable et al. 09, Jimenez et al. 09], care should be taken to make sure the original normal map has not been blurred already in an attempt to get a smoother look.

While it might seem to make sense to simply blur the normal map using the diffusion profile of skin, this approach is not completely valid since lighting is not a linear process with regard to the surface normal. What we really want to have is a representation of the normal which can be linearly filtered, much in the same way that shadow maps can be filtered linearly using a technique like variance shadow mapping. Interestingly, there has been some very recent work in linear normal map filtering. *Linear efficient antialiased normal* (LEAN) mapping [Olano and Baker 10] represents the first and second moments of bumps in surface-tangent space. Olano and Baker focused primarily on representing specular light but also suggest a diffuse-filtering approximation from [Kilgard 00] which simply uses the linearly filtered unnormalized normal and standard diffuse lighting. It is noteworthy that the unnormalized normal is actually a valid approximation when a bump self-shadowing and incident/scattered lighting term is constant over the normal-map filtering region. In that case,

$$\frac{1}{n}\Sigma_{i=1}^{n}(K_{\text{diffuse}}L \cdot N_i) = K_{\text{diffuse}}L \cdot (\frac{1}{n}\Sigma_{i=1}^{n}N_i).$$

The reason this isn't always the case is that diffuse lighting incorporates a self-shadowing term $\max(0, N \cdot L)$ instead of simply $N \cdot L$. This means back-facing bumps will actually contribute negative light when linearly filtered. Nonetheless, using the unnormalized normal will still be valid when all bumps are unshadowed or completely shadowed, and provides a better approximation than the normalized normal in all situations, according to [Kilgard 00].

Although we would prefer a completely robust method of pre-integrating normal maps that supports even changes in incident/scattered light over the filtering region, we found that blurring, using diffusion profiles, provided surprisingly good results (whether or not we renormalize). In addition, since using four normals would require four transformations into tangent space and four times the memory, we investigated an approximation using only one mipmapped normal map. When using this optimization, we sample the specular normal as usual, but also sample a red normal clamped below a tunable miplevel in another sampler. We then transform those two normals into tangent space and blend between them to get green and blue normals. The resulting diffuse-lighting calculations must then be performed three times instead of once. The geometry normal can even be used in place of the second normal map sample, if the normal map contains small details exclusively. If larger curves are present, blue/green artifacts will appear where the normal map and geometry normal deviate, thus the second mipmapped sample is required.

We found that this approach to handling normal maps complements our custom diffuse falloff very well. Since the red normal becomes more heavily blurred, the surface represented by the blurred normal becomes much more smooth, which is the primary assumption made in our custom diffuse falloff. Unfortunately, there is one caveat to using these two approaches together. Since we have separate normals for each color, we need to perform three diffuse lookups resulting in three texture fetches per light. We discuss a few approaches to optimizing this in Section 5.7.

5.6   Shadow Scattering

Although we can now represent scattering due to small- and large-scale features, we are still missing scattering over occluded light boundaries (shadows). The effect of light scattering into shadows is one of the most noticeable features of realistically rendered skin. One would think that scattering from shadows is much more difficult since they are inherently nonlocal to the surface. However, by using

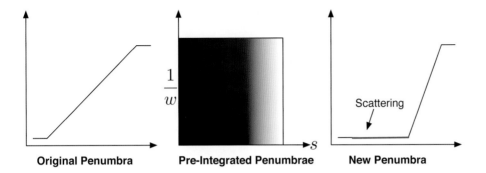

Figure 5.4. Illustration of pre-integrated scattering falloff from shadows. A typical shadow falloff from a box-filtered shadow map (left). A smaller penumbra that we pre-integrate against the diffusion profile of skin (right). The lookup maps the first penumbra into the second but also stores additional scattered light. The lookup is parameterized by the original shadow value and the width of the penumbra in world space (center).

a small trick, we found we could pre-integrate the effect of scattering over shadow boundaries in the same way we represent scattering in our lighting model.

The trick we use for shadows is to think of the results of our shadow mapping algorithm as a falloff function rather than directly as a penumbra. When the falloff is completely black or white, we know we are completely occluded or unoccluded, respectively. However, we can choose to reinterpret what happens between those two values. Specifically, if we ensure the penumbra size created by our shadow map filter is of adequate width to contain most of the diffusion profile, we can choose a different (smaller) size for the penumbra and use the rest of the falloff to represent scattering according to the diffusion profile (see Figure 5.4).

To calculate an accurate falloff, we begin by using the knowledge of the shape of our shadow mapping blur kernel to pre-integrate a representative shadow penumbra against the diffusion profile for skin. We define the representative shadow penumbra $P()$ as a one-dimensional falloff from filtering a straight shadow edge (a step function) against the shadow mapping blur kernel. Assuming a monotonically decreasing shadow mapping kernel, the representative shadow falloff is also a monotonically decreasing function and is thus *invertible* within the penumbra. Thus, for a given shadow value we can find the position within the representative penumbra using the inverse $P^{-1}()$. As an example, for the simple case of a box filter, the shadow will be a linear ramp, for which the inverse is also a linear ramp. More complicated filters have more complicated inverses and need to be derived by hand or by using software like Mathematica. Using the inverse, we can create a lookup texture that maps the original falloff back to its location

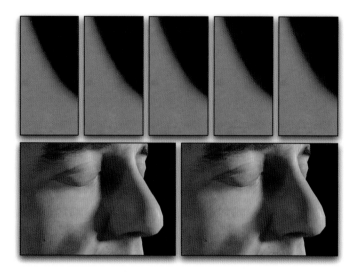

Figure 5.5. Illustration of pre-integrated scattering falloff from shadows. Controlled scattering based on increased penumbra width, such as a penumbra cast onto a highly slanted surface (top). Comparison with and without shadow scattering (bottom).

in the penumbra and then to a completely different falloff. Specifically, we can make the new shadow falloff smaller and use the remainder to represent subsurface scattering from the new penumbra. In the end, we are left with a simple integration to perform that we can use as a lookup during rendering, exactly like our diffuse falloff.

We should note at this point that we could run into problems if our assumptions from above are invalidated. We found that a two-dimensional shadow falloff was not noticeably different from a one-dimensional one, but we have also assumed that all shadow transitions are sharp. For example, if something like a screen door were to cast a shadow, it might result in a constant penumbra value between zero and one. In that case, we would assume there is scattering from a falloff that isn't there. Additionally, we have assumed projection onto a flat surface. If the surface is highly slanted, then the true penumbra size will be much larger than the one we used during pre-integration. For this reason we add a second dimension to our shadow falloff texture, which represents the size of the penumbra in world space. This is similar to the way we pre-integrate lighting against all sphere sizes. In the end, our two-dimensional shadow-lookup integration is a simple convolution:

$$P_S(s, w) = \frac{\int_{-\infty}^{\infty} P'(P^{-1}(s) + x)R(x/w)dx}{\int_{-\infty}^{\infty} R(x/w)dx},$$

where $P^{-1}()$ is the inverse of our representative falloff, $P'()$ is the new, smaller penumbra, $R()$ is the diffusion profile, and s and w are the shadow value and penumbra width in world space, respectively. Penumbra width can be detected using either the angle of the surface with respect to the light, or potentially the derivative of the shadow value itself. Since creating a large penumbra is expensive using conventional shadow filtering (although, see the *Pixel Quad Amortization* chapter), having the penumbra stretched over a slanted surface provides a larger space for scattering falloff and thus can actually be desirable if the initial shadow penumbra isn't wide enough. In this case the lookup can be clamped to insure that the falloff fits into the space provided.

5.7 Conclusion and Future Work

We have presented a new local skin-shading approach based on pre-integration that approximates the same effects found in more expensive TSD-based approaches. Our approach can be implemented by adding our custom diffuse- and shadow-falloff textures to a typical skin shader (see Figure 5.6).

Although we found that our approach worked on a large variety of models, there are still a few drawbacks that should be mentioned. When approximating curvature using pixel shader derivatives, triangle edges may become visible where curvature changes quickly. Depending on how the model was created we also found that curvature could change rapidly or unnaturally in some cases. We are looking into better approaches to approximating curvature in these cases. This is much more easily done with geometry shaders that can utilize surface topology.

Pre-Integration   Texture Space Diffusion

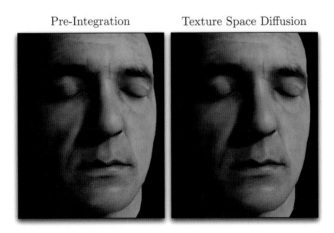

Figure 5.6. Comparison of our approach with texture-space diffusion using an optimized blur kernel from [Hable et al. 09]. (Mesh and textures courtesy of XYZRGB.)

We would also like to look at the effect of using more than one principal axis of curvature. For models where curvature discontinuities occur, we generate a curvature map that can be blurred and further edited by hand, similar to a stretch map in TSD.

Another challenge we would like to meet is to efficiently combine our normal map and diffuse-lighting approaches. When using three diffuse normals, we currently need three diffuse-texture lookups. We found we could use fewer lookups depending on the number of lights and the importance of each light. We have also found it promising to approximate the diffuse and shadow falloffs using analytical approximations that can be evaluated without texture lookups.

We would also like to apply our technique to environment mapping. It should be straightforward to support diffuse-environment mapping via an array of diffuse-environment maps that are blurred based on curvature, in the same manner as our diffuse-falloff texture.

5.8   Appendix A: Lookup Textures

```
float   Gaussian (float   v, float r)
{
    return 1.0/sqrt(2.0*PI*v) * exp(-(r*r)/(2*v));
}


float3 Scatter(float  r)
{
    //Coefficients from GPU Gems 3 - ``Advanced Skin Rendering
        .''
    return Gaussian(0.0064 * 1.414,r) * float3
        (0.233,0.455,0.649) +
            Gaussian(0.0484 * 1.414,r) * float3
                (0.100,0.336,0.344) +
            Gaussian(0.1870 * 1.414,r) * float3
                (0.118,0.198,0.000) +
            Gaussian(0.5670 * 1.414,r) * float3
                (0.113,0.007,0.007) +
            Gaussian(1.9900 * 1.414,r) * float3
                (0.358,0.004,0.000) +
            Gaussian(7.4100 * 1.414,r) * float3
                (0.078,0.000,0.000);
}


float3 integrateShadowScattering(float  penumbraLocation,
                                 float  penumbraWidth)
{
    float3 totalWeights = 0;
    float3 totalLight = 0;
```

```
    float a= -PROFILE_WIDTH;
    while( a<=PROFILE_WIDTH )
    while( a<=PROFILE_WIDTH )
    {
        float light = newPenumbra(penumbraLocation + a/
            penumbraWidth);
        float sampleDist = abs(a);
        float3 weights = Scatter(sampleDist);
        totalWeights += weights;
        totalLight += light * weights;
        a+=inc;
    }

    return totalLight / totalWeights;
}

float3 integrateDiffuseScatteringOnRing(float cosTheta,float
    skinRadius)
{
    // Angle from lighting direction.
    float  theta = acos(cosTheta);
    float3 totalWeights = 0;
    float3 totalLight = 0;

    float a= -(PI/2);
    while( a<=(PI/2) )
    while( a<=(PI/2) )
    {
        float sampleAngle = theta + a;
        float diffuse = saturate( cos(sampleAngle) );
        float sampleDist = abs(2.0*skinRadius*sin(a*0.5));
            // Distance.
        float3 weights = Scatter(sampleDist);
            // Profile Weight.
        totalWeights += weights;
        totalLight += diffuse * weights;
        a+=inc;
    }
    return totalLight / totalWeights;
}
```

Listing 5.1. Shader code to precompute skin falloff textures.

5.9 Appendix B: Simplified Skin Shader

```
float3 SkinDiffuse( float curv, float3 NdotL )
{
    float3 lookup = NdotL * 0.5 + 0.5;
    float3 diffuse;
```

```
        diffuse.r = tex2D(SkinDiffuseSampler, float2(lookup.r, curv
            ) ).r;
        diffuse.g = tex2D(SkinDiffuseSampler, float2(lookup.g, curv
            ) ).g;
        diffuse.b = tex2D(SkinDiffuseSampler, float2(lookup.b, curv
            ) ).b;
        return diffuse;
}

float3 SkinShadow( float shad, float width )
{
        return tex2D(SkinShadowSampler, float2(shad, width) ).rgb;
}
...
//Simple curvature calculation.
float curvature = saturate(length(fwidth(Normal)) /
                    length(fwidth(WorldPos)) * tuneCurvature ) ;
...
//Specular/Diffuse Normals.
float4 normMapHigh    = tex2D(NormalSamplerHigh, Uv) * 2.0 -
    1.0;
float4 normMapLow     = tex2D(NormalSamplerLow , Uv) * 2.0 -
    1.0;
float3 N_high = mul(normMapHigh.xyz,TangentToWorld);
float3 N_low  = mul(normMapLow.xyz,TangentToWorld);
float3 rS = N_high;
float3 rN = lerp(N_high,N_low,tuneNormalBlur.r);
float3 gN = lerp(N_high,N_low,tuneNormalBlur.g);
float3 bN = lerp(N_high,N_low,tuneNormalBlur.b);
...
//Diffuse lighting
float3 NdotL = float3( dot(rN,L), dot(gN,L), dot(bN,L) );
float3 diffuse = SkinDiffuse( curvature, NdotL ) * LightColor *
                SkinShadow( SampleShadowMap(ShadowUV) );
```

Listing 5.2. Skin shader example.

Bibliography

[Borshukov and Lewis 03] George Borshukov and J.P. Lewis. "Realistic Human Face Rendering for The Matrix Reloaded." In *ACM Siggraph Sketches and Applications*. New York: ACM, 2003.

[Borshukov and Lewis 05] George Borshukov and J.P. Lewis. "Fast Subsurface Scattering." In *ACM Siggraph Course on Digital Face Cloning*. New York: ACM, 2005.

[d'Eon and Luebke 07] E. d'Eon and D. Luebke. "Advanced Techniques for Realistic Real-Time Skin Rendering." In *GPU Gems 3*, Chapter 14. Reading, MA: Addison Wesley, 2007.

[Donner and Jensen 05] Craig Donner and Henrik Wann Jensen. "Light Diffusion in Multi-Layered Translucent Materials." *ACM Trans. Graph.* 24 (2005), 1032–1039.

[Gosselin et al. 04] D. Gosselin, P.V. Sander, and J.L. Mitchell. "Real-Time Texture-Space Skin Rendering." In *ShaderX³: Advanced Rendering with DirectX and OpenGl*. Hingham, MA: Charles River Media, 2004.

[Green 04] Simon Green. "Real-Time Approximations to Subsurface Scattering." In *GPU Gems*, pp. 263–278. Reading, MA: Addison-Wesley, 2004.

[Hable et al. 09] John Hable, George Borshukov, and Jim Hejl. "Fast Skin Shading." In *ShaderX⁷: Advanced Rendering Techniques*, Chapter II.4. Hingham, MA: Charles River Media, 2009.

[Jensen et al. 01] Henrik Jensen, Stephen Marschner, Mark Levoy, and Pat Hanrahan. "A Practical Model for Subsurface Light Transport." In *Proceedings of the 28th Annual Conference on Computer Graphics and Interactive Techniques, SIGGRAPH '01*, pp. 511–518. New York: ACM, 2001.

[Jimenez et al. 09] Jorge Jimenez, Veronica Sundstedt, and Diego Gutierrez. "Screen-Space Perceptual Rendering of Human Skin." *ACM Transactions on Applied Perception* 6:4 (2009), 23:1–23:15.

[Kilgard 00] Mark J. Kilgard. "A Practical and Robust Bump-Mapping Technique for Today's GPUs." In *GDC 2000*, 2000.

[Ma et al. 07] W.C. Ma, T. Hawkins, P. Peers, C.F. Chabert, M. Weiss, and P. Debevec. "Rapid Acquisition of Specular and Diffuse Normal Maps from Polarized Spherical Gradient Illumination." In *Eurographics Symposium on Rendering*. Aire-la-Ville, Switzerland: Eurographics Association, 2007.

[Olano and Baker 10] Marc Olano and Dan Baker. "LEAN mapping." In *ACM Siggraph Symposium on Interactive 3D Graphics and Games*, pp. 181–188. New York: ACM, 2010.

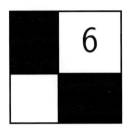

6

Implementing Fur Using Deferred Shading
Donald Revie

This chapter is concerned with implementing a visually pleasing approximation of fur using deferred shading rather than attempting to create an accurate physical simulation. The techniques presented can also be used to create a number of materials that are traditionally difficult to render in deferred shading.

6.1   Deferred Rendering

For the purposes of this chapter, the term *deferred rendering* can be extended to any one of a group of techniques characterized by the separation of lighting calculations from the rendering of light-receiving objects within the scene, including deferred shading [Valient 07], deferred lighting [Mittring 09], inferred lighting [Kircher 09], and light-prepass rendering [Engel 09]. The fur-rendering technique being presented has been implemented in deferred shading but should be applicable to any rendering solution based on one of these techniques.

This separation of light-receiving objects from light sources is achieved by storing all relevant information about light-receiving objects in the scene as texture data, collectively referred to as a *geometry buffer* or G-buffer because it represents the geometric scene.

When rendering the lights, we can treat the G-buffer as a screen-aligned quad with per-pixel lighting information. Rendering the G-buffer discards all occluded geometry, effectively reducing the three-dimensional scene into a continuous screen-facing surface (Figure 6.1). By using the two-dimensional screen position, depth, and normal information, a pixel shader can reconstruct any visible point in the scene from its corresponding pixel. It is this surface information that is used to calculate lighting values per pixel rather than the original scene geometry.

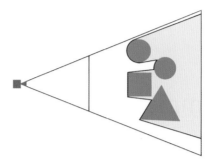

Figure 6.1. G-buffer surface.

In deferred rendering the format of the G-buffer (Figure 6.2) defines a standard interface between all light-receiving materials and all light sources. Each object assigned a light-receiving material writes a uniform set of data into the G-buffer, which is then interpreted by each light source with no direct information regarding the original object. One key advantage to maintaining this interface is that geometric complexity is decoupled from lighting complexity.

This creates a defined pipeline (Figure 6.3) in which we render all geometry to the G-buffer, removing the connection between the geometric data and individual objects, unless we store this information in the G-buffer. We then calculate lighting from all sources in the scene using this information, creating a light-accumulation buffer that again discards all information about individual lights. We can revisit this information in a material pass, rendering individual meshes again and using the screen-space coordinates to identify the area of the light-accumulation buffer and G-buffer representing a specific object. This material phase is required in deferred lighting, inferred lighting, and light pre-pass rendering to complete the lighting process since the G-buffer for these techniques

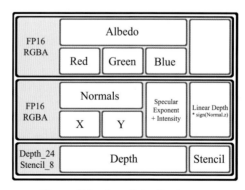

Figure 6.2. Our G-buffer format.

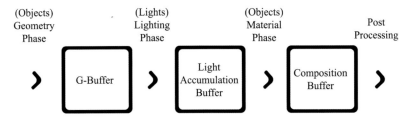

Figure 6.3. General deferred rendering pipeline.

does not include surface color. After this, a post-processing phase acts upon the contents of the composition buffer, again without direct knowledge of individual lights or objects.

This stratification of the deferred rendering pipeline allows for easy extensibility in the combination of different materials and lights. However, adherence to the interfaces involved also imposes strict limitations on the types of materials and lights that can be represented. In particular, deferred rendering solutions have difficulty representing transparent materials, because information regarding surfaces seen through the material would be discarded. Solutions may also struggle with materials that reflect light in a nontypical manner, potentially increasing the complexity of all lighting calculations and the amount of information required within the G-buffer. Choosing the right phases and buffer formats are key to maximizing the power of deferred rendering solutions.

We describe techniques that address the limitations of rendering such materials while continuing to respect the interfaces imposed by deferred rendering. To illustrate these techniques and demonstrate ways in which they might be combined to form complex materials, we outline in detail a solution for implementing fur in deferred shading.

6.2 Fur

Fur has a number of characteristics that make it difficult to represent using the same information format commonly used to represent geometry in deferred rendering solutions.

Fur is a structured material composed of many fine strands forming a complex volume rather than a single continuous surface. This structure is far too fine to describe each strand within the G-buffer on current hardware; the resolution required would be prohibitive in both video memory and fragment processing. As this volumetric information cannot be stored in the G-buffer, the fur must be approximated as a continuous surface when receiving light. We achieve this by ensuring that the surface exhibits the observed lighting properties that would normally be created by the structure.

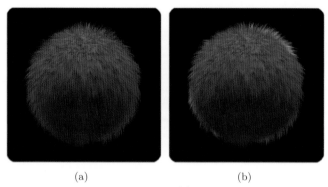

(a)   (b)

Figure 6.4. Fur receiving light from behind (a) without scattering and (b) with scattering approximation.

The diffuse nature of fur causes subsurface scattering; light passing into the volume of the fur is reflected and partially absorbed before leaving the medium at a different point. Individual strands are also transparent, allowing light to pass through them. This is often seen as a halo effect; fur is silhouetted against a light source that illuminates the fur layer from within, effectively bending light around the horizon of the surface toward the viewer. This is best seen in fur with a loose, "fluffy" structure (see Figure 6.4).

The often-uniform, directional nature of fur in combination with the structure of individual strands creates a natural grain to the surface being lit. The reflectance properties of the surface are anisotropic, dependent on the grain direction. Anisotropy occurs on surfaces characterized by fine ridges following the grain of the surface, such as brushed metal, and causes light to reflect according to the direction of the grain. This anisotropy is most apparent in fur that is "sleek" with a strong direction and a relatively unbroken surface (see Figure 6.5).

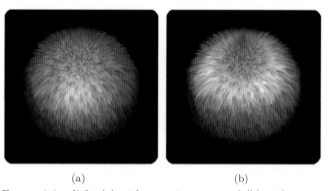

(a)   (b)

Figure 6.5. Fur receiving light (a) without anisotropy and (b) with anisotropy approximation.

6.3   Techniques

We look at each of the characteristics of fur separately so that the solutions discussed can be reused to represent other materials that share these characteristics and difficulties when implemented within deferred rendering.

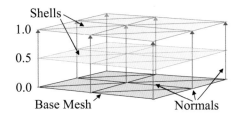

Figure 6.6. Concentric shells.

6.3.1   Volumetric Fur Rendering Using Concentric Shells

It is common to render volumetric structures in real time by rendering discrete slices of volumetric texture data into the scene and using alpha blending to combine the results, such as light interacting with dust particles in the air [Mitchell 04]. Provided enough slices are rendered, the cumulative result gives the appearance of a continuous volume featuring correct perspective, parallax, and occlusion.

The concentric shells method of rendering fur [Lengyel 01] represents the volumetric layer of fur as a series of concentric shells around the base mesh; each shell is a slice through the layer of fur parallel to the surface. These shells are constructed by rendering the base mesh again and pushing the vertices out along the normal of the vertex by a fraction of the fur layer depth; the structure of the fur is represented by a volume texture containing a repeating section of fur (see Figure 6.6). By applying an offset parallel to the mesh surface in addition to the normal we can comb the fur volume (see Figure 6.7, Listing 6.1).

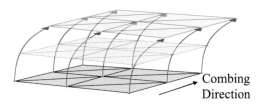

Figure 6.7. Combing.

```
// Get shell depth as normalized distance between base and
// outer surface.
float shellDepth = shellIndex * (1.f/numShells);

// Get offset direction vector
float3 dir = IN.normal.xyz + (IN.direction.xyz * _shellDepth);
dir.xyz = normalize(dir.xyz);

// Offset vertex position along fur direction.
OUT.position = IN.position;
OUT.position.xyz = (dir.xyz * _ shellDepth * furDepth
    * IN.furLength);
OUT.position = mul(worldViewProjection, OUT.position);
```

Listing 6.1. Vertex offsetting.

This method of fur rendering can be further augmented with the addition of
fins, slices perpendicular to the surface of the mesh, which improve the quality of
silhouette edges. However, fin geometry cannot be generated from the base mesh
as part of a vertex program and is therefore omitted here (details on generating
fin geometry can be found in [Lengyel 01]).

This technique cannot be applied in the geometry phase because the structure
of fur is constructed from a large amount of subpixel detail that cannot be stored
in the G-buffer where each pixel must contain values for a discrete surface point.
Therefore, in deferred shading we must apply the concentric shell method in the
material phase, sampling the lighting and color information for each hair from a
single point in the light-accumulation buffer. The coordinates for this point can
be found by transforming the vertex position of the base mesh into screen space
in the same way it was transformed originally in the geometry phase (Listing 6.2).

```
// Vertex shader.
// See (Listing 3.1.1) for omitted content.
// Output screen position of base mesh vertex.
OUT.screenPos = mul(worldViewProjection, IN.position);

// ---------------------------
// Pixel shader.
IN.screenPos /= IN.screenPos.w;

// Bring values into range (0,1) from (-1,1).
float2 screenCoord = (IN.screenPos.xy + 1.f.xx) * 0.5f.xx;

// Sample lit mesh color
color = tex2D(lightAccumulationTexture, screenCoord).
```

Listing 6.2. Sampling lit objects.

This sampling of lighting values can cause an issue specific to rendering the fur. As fur pixels are offset from the surface being sampled, it is possible for the original point to have been occluded by other geometry and thus be missing from the G-buffer. In this case the occluding geometry, rather than the base mesh, would contribute to the coloring of the fur leading to visual artifacts in the fur (Figure 6.8). We explore a solution to this in Sections 6.3.4 and 6.4.4 of this article.

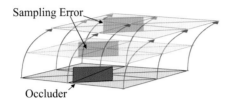

Figure 6.8. Occlusion error.

6.3.2 Subsurface Scattering

Scattering occurs in materials wherein light enters the surface at one point, is transmitted through the medium beneath the surface being reflected and refracted by internal structures and is partially absorbed, before exiting the surface at a different point (Figure 6.9). This light exiting the surface softens the appearance of lighting on the surface by creating a subtle glow.

Much work has been done on the approximation of subsurface scattering properties in skin that is constructed of discrete layers, each with unique reflectance properties. One such solution is to apply a weighted blur to the light accumulated on the surface [Hable 09, Green 04]. In existing forward shaded solutions, this blurring is typically applied in texture space.

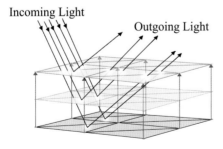

Figure 6.9. Simple subsurface scattering.

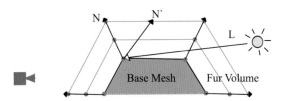

Figure 6.10. Rim glow (N.L $<$ 0) (N'.L $>$ 0).

In deferred rendering, this technique can be applied in both the geometry phase and the material phase. In the geometry phase the scattering can be approximated by blurring the surface normals written into the G-buffer or by recalculating the mesh normals as a weighted sum of neighboring vertex normals [Patro 07].

Blurring can be performed in the material phase, in texture space, by sampling the accumulated lighting in the same manner as that used for the fur rendering. The texture coordinates of the mesh would then be used as vertex positions to write those values into the mesh's texture space before applying a blur. Once blurred, these values are written back into the light-accumulation buffer by reversing the process. Alternatively, the material-phase blurring could be performed in screen space by orienting the blur kernel to the local surface, using the normals stored in the G-buffer at each pixel.

One issue with this solution is that scattering beneath a surface will also allow light entering the back faces of an object to be transmitted through the medium and exit the surface facing the viewer. In materials such as skin and fur, which form a scattering layer over a more solid structure, this transfer of light appears most often around the silhouette edges of the object. We can adjust for this by bending normals at the silhouette edge of the mesh to point away from the viewer and sample lighting from behind the object (see Figure 6.10 and Listing 6.3). In doing so, these pixels will no longer receive direct lighting correctly; this must then be accounted for during the blur phase (see Sections 6.3.4 and 6.4.4 for details of our solution).

```
// Get normal based for back face samples.
// Glow strength and falloff are supplied by material values.

half NdotV = saturate(dot(normal.xyz, -view));
half rimWeight = glowStrenth * pow(1.f - NdotV), glowFalloff);
normal.xyz += view.xyz * rimWeight;
normal.xyz = normalize(normal.xyz);
```

Listing 6.3. Pushing edge pixels around edges.

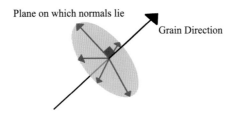

Figure 6.11. Strand normals.

6.3.3 Anisotropy

Anisotropic light reflection occurs on surfaces where the distribution of surface normals is dependent on the surface direction; such surfaces are often characterized by fine ridges running in a uniform direction across the surface, forming a "grain." The individual strands in fur and hair can create a surface that exhibits this type of lighting [Scheuermann 04].

This distinctive lighting is created because in anisotropic surfaces the ridges or, in this case, the strands are considered to be infinitely fine lines running parallel to the grain. These lines do not have a defined surface normal but instead have an infinite number of possible normals radiating out perpendicularly to their direction (see Figure 6.11). Therefore, the lighting calculation at any point on the surface must integrate the lighting for all the normals around the strand. This is not practical in a pixel shader; the best solution is to choose a single normal that best represents the lighting at this point [Wyatt 07].

In forward shading, anisotropy is often implemented using a different lighting calculation from those used to describe other surfaces (Listing 6.4) [Heidrich 98]. This algorithm calculates lighting based on the grain direction of the surface rather than the normal.

```
Diffuse  =  sqrt(1 - (< L,T >)^2)
Specular = sqrt(1 - (< L,T >)^2) sqrt(1 - (< V, T > )^2)
    - < L, T >  < V, T >
```

Listing 6.4. Anisotropic light calculation.

In deferred shading we cannot know in the geometry phase the nature of any light sources that might contribute to the lighting on the surface and are bound by the interface of the G-buffer to provide a surface normal. Therefore, we define

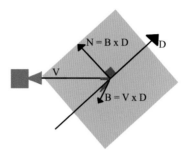

Figure 6.12. Normal as tangent to plane.

the most significant normal as the normal that is coplanar with the grain direction and the eye vector at that point (see Figure 6.12). We calculate the normal of this plane as the cross product of the eye vector and the grain direction, the normal for lighting is then the cross product of the plane's normal and the grain direction (see Listing 6.5).

```
// Generate normal from fur direction.
IN.direction = IN.direction-(dot(IN.direction, normal) * normal);
IN.direction.xyz = normalize(IN.direction.xyz);
half3 binorm = cross(IN.eyeVector, IN.direction);
half3 grainNorm = cross(binorm, IN.direction);
normalize(grainNorm);
```

Listing 6.5. Anisotropic normal calculation.

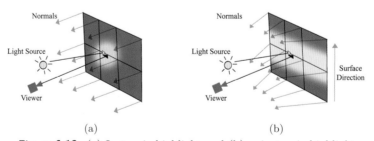

Figure 6.13. (a) Isotropic highlight and (b) anisotropic highlight.

By calculating surface normals in this way we create the effect of curving the surface around the view position, resulting in the lighting being stretched perpendicular to the surface grain (Figure 6.13). While this method does not perfectly emulate the results of the forward-shading solution, it is able to generate this characteristic of stretched lighting for all light sources, including image-based lights.

6.3.4 Stippled Rendering

Stippled rendering is a technique in which only some pixels of an image are written into the frame buffer, leaving other pixels with their original values. This technique was originally inspired by the stippled alpha transparencies used in games before the widespread availability of hardware alpha blending, also referred to as screen-door transparency [Mulder 98]. The values for the transparent object are written to only some of the pixels covered by the object so as not to completely obscure the scene behind it (see Figure 6.14 and Listing 6.6).

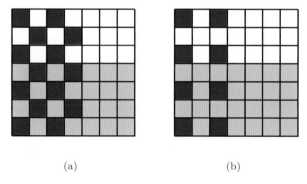

(a)   (b)

Figure 6.14. Stipple patterns (a) 1 in 2 and (b) 1 in 4.

```
// Get screen coordinates in range (0, 1).
float2 screenCoord = ((IN.screenPos.xy/IN.screenPos.w)
   + 1.f.xx) * 0.5h.xx;
// Convert coordinates into pixels.
int2 sample = screenCoord.xy * float2(1280.f, 720.f);

// If pixel is not the top left in a 2x2 tile discard it.
int2 tileIndices = int2(sample.x \% 2,  sample.y \% 2);
if((tileIndices.x != 0) || (tileIndices.y != 0))
discard;
```

Listing 6.6. One in four Stipple pattern generation.

In deferred shading, transparent objects are written into the G-buffer using a stipple pattern. During the material phase, the values of pixels containing data for the transparent surface are blended with neighboring pixels containing information on the scene behind. By varying the density of the stipple pattern, different resolutions of data can be interleaved, allowing for multiple layers of transparency. This technique is similar to various interlaced rendering methods for transparent surfaces [Pangerl 09, Kircher 09].

The concept of stippled rendering can be extended further to blend multiple definitions of a single surface together. By rendering the same mesh multiple times but writing distinctly different data in alternating pixels, we can assign multiple lighting values for each point on the object at a reduced resolution. During the material phase the object is rendered again, and this information is deinterlaced and combined to allow for more complex lighting models. For example, a skin material could write separate values for a subsurface scattering pass and a specular layer, as interleaved samples. The material pass would then additively blend the specular values over the blurred result of the diffuse lighting values.

6.4 Fur Implementation Details

Ease of use and speed of implementation were key considerations when developing the fur solution. We found that to enable artists to easily apply the fur material to meshes, it was important to provide flexibility through a fine degree of control, coupled with real-time feedback. We also wished to ensure minimal changes to existing assets and work methods. It was also important that the technique have minimal impact on our rendering framework, and that it work well with our existing asset-creation pipeline.

To this end, the solution has been implemented with minimal code support; all shader code is implemented within a single effect file with multiple passes for the geometry and material phases of rendering. Annotations provide the renderer with information on when and where to render passes. For real-time feedback, a separate technique is provided within the effect file that renders the fur in a forward-shaded fashion suitable for use within various asset-creation packages.

6.4.1 Asset Preparation

Combing direction. The fur solution is applicable to any closed mesh with per-vertex position, normal, tangent, binormal, and a single set of two-dimensional texture coordinates. This is a fairly standard vertex format for most asset-creation packages.

In addition, we require an RGBA color per vertex to define the combing direction and length of fur at a given vertex (see Figure 6.15). The RGB components encode combing direction as a three-component vector in the object's local space compressing a range of $[-1, 1]$ to $[0, 1]$; this vector is also used to describe the surface direction when generating the anisotropic surface normals. The alpha channel of the color is used to scale the global fur length locally at each vertex.

Figure 6.15. Fur length (left) and direction (right) encoded as color.

A color set was chosen to encode this data for a number of reasons. First, many asset-creation tools allow for easy "painting" of vertex colors while viewing the shaded mesh in real time. This effectively allows the author to choose a direction represented as a color and then comb sections of the fur appropriately using the tool, setting an alpha component to the color trims the length of the fur locally. Second, the approach of encoding direction as color is already familiar to most authors through the process of generating world- and tangent-space normal maps. The process has proven to be quite intuitive and easy to use.

As part of the loading process, we transform the vectors encoded in this color channel from the local space of the mesh into its tangent space and at the same time orthonormalize them, making them tangential to the mesh surface. Thus when the mesh is deformed during animation, the combing direction of the fur will remain constant in relation to the surface orientation. This is the only engine side code that was required to fully support the fur-rendering technique (see Listing 6.7).

```
// Build local to tangent space matrix.
Matrix tangentSpace;
tangentSpace.LoadIdentity();
tangentSpace.SetCol(0, tangent);
tangentSpace.SetCol(1, binormal);
tangentSpace.SetCol(2, normal);
tangentSpace.Transpose();

// Convert color into vector.
```

```
Vector3 dir(pColour[0], pColour[1], pColour[2]);
dir = (dir * 2.f) - Vector3(1.f);

// Gram Schmidt orthonormalization.
dir = dir - (dot(dir, normal) * normal); dir.Normalise();

// Transform vector into tangent space.
tangentSpace.TransformInPlace(dir);

// Convert vector into color.
dir = (dir + Vector3(1.f)) * 0.5;
pColour[0] = dir.getX();
pColour[1] = dir.getY();
pColour[2] = dir.getZ();
```

Listing 6.7. Processing of fur directions.

Texture data. To provide the G-buffer with the necessary surface information, the material is assigned an RGB albedo map and a lighting map containing per pixel normal information and specular intensity and exponent at any given pixel. In addition to this, a second albedo map is provided to describe the changes applied to lighting as it passes deeper into the fur; over the length of the strands, the albedo color that is used is blended from this map to the surface color. This gives the author a high degree of control over how the ambient occlusion term is applied to fur across the whole surface, allowing for a greater variation.

To represent the fur volume required for the concentric shell rendering, a heightfield was chosen as an alternative to generating a volumetric data set. While this solution restricts the types of volume that can be described, it requires considerably less texture information to be stored and accessed in order to render the shells. It is more flexible in that it can be sampled using an arbitrary number of slices without the need to composite slices when undersampling the volume, and it is far simpler to generate with general-image authoring tools.

6.4.2   Geometry Phase

The geometry phase is split into two passes for the purpose of this technique. The first pass renders the base mesh to the G-buffer. In the vertex shader the position, tangent, and normal are transformed into view space and the combing direction is brought into local space in the range [-1, 1]. The pixel shader generates a new normal, which is coplanar to the eye and combing vectors to achieve anisotropic highlights (Figure 6.16).

The second pass renders the top layer of the fur in a stipple pattern, rendering to one in every four pixels on screen. The vertex shader is identical to the first pass, but pushes the vertex positions out along the vertex normals offset by the

Figure 6.16. Geometry pass 1 (depth/normals/albedo).

global fur length scaled by the vertex color alpha. The pixel shader identifies likely silhouette edges using the dot product of the view vector and the surface normals; the normals at these points are adjusted by adding the view vector scaled by this weight value. The unmodified normals are recalculated to use the anisotropic normals like those of the first pass (Figure 6.17).

This second pass solves the occlusion issue when constructing concentric fur shells from the light-accumulation buffer, since both samples are unlikely to be occluded simultaneously while any part of the strand is still visible. The second pass allows light calculations to be performed for both the surface of the mesh and also the back faces where light entering the reverse faces may be visible.

In order to avoid incorrect results from *screen-space ambient occlusion* (SSAO), edge detection, and similar techniques that rely on discontinuities in the G-buffer, these should be calculated before the second pass since the stipple pattern will create artifacts.

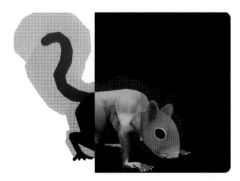

Figure 6.17. Geometry pass 2 (depth/normals/albedo).

6.4.3 Light Phase

During the light phase both the base and stipple samples within the G-buffer receive lighting in the same manner as all other values in the G-buffer, adherence to a common interface allows the fur to receive lighting from a wide range of sources.

Figure 6.18. Light-accumulation buffer.

6.4.4 Material Phase

The material phase of rendering involves reading the values from the light-accumulation buffer and interpreting these based on specific qualities of the material, in this case by constructing shells of fur. In deferred shading, since the majority of the lighting values are already correct in the light-accumulation buffer, a copy of these values is required onto which the material phase of the fur can be composited (see Figure 6.18).

The stipple values, being distributed on the outermost shell of the fur, will occlude the layers of fur beneath. To correct this, all fur surfaces must be rendered again using the outermost shell, while sampling color values from the light-accumulation buffer and depth values from the linear depth stored in the G-buffer (see Figure 6.19). For most pixels, these color and depth values are written directly into the composition buffer, however, where a stipple value would be sampled the neighboring pixel is used instead, effectively erasing all stipple values from the light-accumulation and depth buffers.

The buffer now contains the base mesh of the object only, providing a basis on which to composite the volumetric layer of fur. Rendering of the fur is performed by a series of passes, each pass rendering a concentric shell by offsetting the vertex positions. The pass also constructs positions in screen space, from which both the sample corresponding to the base mesh and the stipple sample corresponding to the outermost shell can be obtained.

Figure 6.19. Stipple obliteration pass.

In the pixel shader these two samples are retrieved from the light-accumulation buffer, their respective linear depths in the G-buffer are also sampled to compare against the depth of the sample coordinates and thus correct for occlusion errors. If both samples are valid, the maximum of the two is chosen to allow for the halo effect of scattering around the edges of the object without darkening edges where there is no back lighting. The contribution of the albedo map to the accumulated light values is removed by division and then reapplied as a linear interpolation of the base and top albedo maps to account for ambient occlusion by the fur. The heightfield for the fur volume is sampled at a high frequency by applying an arbitrary scale to the mesh UVs in the material. The smoothstep function is used to fade out pixels in the current shell as the interpolation factor equals and exceeds the values stored in the heightfield, thus individual strands of fur fade out at different rates, creating the impression of subpixel detail (see Figure 6.20).

Figure 6.20. Shell pass (16 shells).

Figure 6.21. Final image.

6.5   Conclusion

This article has described a series of techniques used to extend the range of materials that can be presented in a deferred rendering environment, particularly a combination of these techniques that can be used to render aesthetically pleasing fur at real-time speeds.

6.6   Acknowledgments

Thanks to everyone at Cohort Studios for showing their support, interest, and enthusiasm during the development of this technique, especially Bruce McNeish and Gordon Bell, without whom there would be no article.

Special thanks to Steve Ions for patiently providing excellent artwork and feedback while this technique was still very much in development, to Baldur Karlsson and Gordon McLean for integrating the fur, helping track down the (often humorous) bugs, and bringing everything to life, and to Shaun Simpson for all the sanity checks.

Bibliography

[Engel 09] W. Engel. "The Light Pre-Pass Renderer." In *ShaderX*[7], pp. 655–666. Hingham, MA: Charles River Media, 2009.

[Green 04] S. Green. "Real-Time Approximations to Sub-Surface Scattering." In *GPU Gems*, pp. 263–278. Reading, MA: Addison Wesley, 2004.

[Hable 09] J. Hable, G. Borshakov, and J. Heil. "Fast Skin Shading." In *ShaderX*[7], pp. 161–173. Hingham, MA: Charles River Media, 2009.

[Heidrich 98] W. Heidrich and Hans-Peter Seidel. "Efficient Rendering of Anisotropic Surfaces Using Computer Graphics Hardware." In Proceedings of Image and Multi-Dimensional Digital Signal Processing Workshop,Washington, DC: IEEE, 1998.

[Kircher 09] S. Kircher and A Lawrance. "Inferred Lighting: Fast Dynamic Lighting and Shadows for Opaque and Translucent Objects." In *Proceedings of the 2009 ACM SIGGRAPH Symposium on Video Games*, Sandbox '09, pp. 39–45. New York: ACM, 2009.

[Lengyel 01] J. Lengyel, E. Praun, A. Finkelstein, and H. Hoppe. "Real-Time Fur Over Arbitrary Surfaces." In *I3D '01 Proceedings of the 2001 Symposium on Interactive 3D Graphics*, pp. 227–232. New York, ACM Press, 2001.

[Mitchell 04] J. Mitchell. "Light Shafts: Rendering Shadows in Participating Media." Game Developers Conference, 2004. Availablwe online at http://developer.amd.com/media/gpu_assets/Mitchell_LightShafts.pdf.

[Mittring 09] M. Mittring. "A Bit More Deferred - CryEngine3." Triangle Game Conference, 2009.

[Mulder 98] J. D. Mulder, F. C. A. Groen, and J. J. van Wijk. "Pixel Masks for Screen-Door Transparency." In *Proceedings of the Conference on Visualization '98*, pp. 351–358. Los Alamitos, CA: IEEE Computer Society Press, 1998.

[Pangerl 09] D. Pangerl. "Deferred Rendering Transparency," In *ShaderX^7*, pp. 217–224. Hingham, MA: Charles River Media, 2009.

[Patro 07] R. Patro, "Real-Time Approximate Subsurface Scattering," Available at http://www.cs.umd.edu/\simrob/Documents/sss.pdf, 2007.

[Scheuermann 04] T. Scheuermann, "Hair Rendering and Shading." Game Developer's Conference, 2004.

[Wyatt 07] R. Wyatt, "Custom Shaders and Effects." Available at http://www.insomniacgames.com/research_dev/, 2007.

[Valient 07] M. Valient. "Deferred Rendering in Killzone 2." Develop Conference, July 2007.

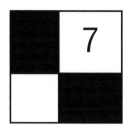

7
Large-Scale Terrain Rendering for Outdoor Games

Ferenc Pintér

7.1 Introduction

Visualizing large scale (above 10 km^2) landscapes on current generation consoles is a challenging task, because of the restricted amount of memory and processing power compared with high-end PCs. This article describes in detail how we approach both limitations and deal with the different content creation, rendering, and performance issues. After a short explanation of the decisions and trade-offs we made, terrain-content generation and rendering methods will follow. We conclude by listing the pros and cons of our technique, measured implementation performance, as well as possible extensions.

Figure 7.1. In-game screenshot of a 10 km^2 canyon area. (© 2010 Digital Reality.)

A variety of industry solutions exist for both representing terrain geometry
and texturing its surface. Our choices were made with regard to our requirements,
which were: a small memory footprint (<20 MB), good rendering performance
(<6 ms), easy in-editor (re)painting without UV distortions, and large view distances (>10km), as in Figure 7.1.

7.1.1 Geometry Choice

We opted for mesh-based terrain, which allows for steep, distortion-free slopes and
vastly different resolution levels, with complete artist control (as compared with
heightfields with vertex-texture fetching, or *render to vertex buffer* (R2VB) [An-
dersson 07]-heightfields, which, however, can provide in-editor/runtime modifi-
able geometry). We also chose to store the compressed vertex and triangle data
instead of performing on-the-fly mesh construction and the caching, which is
sometimes found in planetary rendering engines [Brebion 08, Kemen 08]. Our
scale is smaller, and once again we opted for greater artist flexibility.

7.1.2 Texturing Choice

Our solution is based on per-pixel splatting from tiling atlas texture elements,
thus it reuses texels over the entire surface of the terrain. This is similar to techniques implemented in other games (*Battlestations: Pacific* [Eidos 08], Figure 7.2,
and *Infinity* [Brebion 08]), but instead of using just height- and slope-based rules
with additional noise to determine the terrain type at any given pixel, it also relies on precomputed data. This way our artists can paint over the entire terrain,
even on uniquely modeled mesh objects. Since the terrain's UVs are unique and
relaxed, no distortion appears, even on vertical or slightly overhanging walls.

This method has two main advantages over streaming ultrahigh resolution
maps [van Waveren 09, Mittring 08, Barrett 08, van Rossen 08]. First, the required storage space is very low (<15 MB). Second, it does not saturate streaming
or *bus transfer bandwidth*. Instant switching between cameras located far from
each other is also solved due to the runtime evaluation of shading and texturing.
Another advantage is complete artist control of the texturing, which might be
more difficult when relying only on procedural or fractal-based methods [Bre-
bion 08, Kemen 08, Eidos 08]. On the other hand, not using unique texture data
does result in less variance, though we did not find this to be noticeable.

Extending our asset creation and rendering by using procedural techniques
proved to be invaluable. The techniques helped create the basis for various outdoor art assets (foliage, detail object, and terrain texturing) through subtle parameter changes, thus saving time. They also cut memory and bandwidth usage
too, emphasizing the fact that GPUs are much faster at doing math than fetching
from memory.

Figure 7.2. Screenshot from *Battlestations: Pacific*, released on XBOX 360 and PC. (© 2008 Square Enix Europe.)

7.2 Content Creation and Editing

7.2.1 Workflow

Our terrain assets originate from multiple DCC tools. Artists create the base terrain layout and simple mesh objects with which designers can test level functionality. After this first phase is complete, the base terrain model gets greater morphological and soil-type detail using erosion tools. Artists can iteratively retouch the detailed models if needed, and can also bake *ambient occlusion* (AO) values to the mesh vertices. Parallel to advancing in geometry, textures representing different soil-types get authored and used by the terrain shader. The following steps happen in our in-game editor, after the meshes have been imported from COLLADA format. During this import step, the base terrain gets split into smaller chunks, and *level-of-detail* (LOD) levels are generated. We also use smaller, paintable, and reuseable objects for rock formations, referred to as mesh objects later on. The next step in content creation is additional manual painting for both the base terrain and the mesh objects in the game editor. The finest detail in soil-type information and color tinting is determined in this phase. Finally, mesh and texture assets go through different compression paths for each platform. The complete process is illustrated in Figure 7.3.

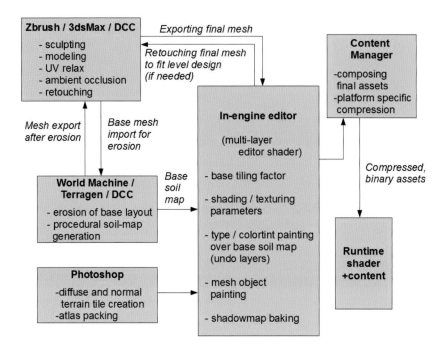

Figure 7.3. Terrain content pipeline/art workflow. (© 2010 Digital Reality.)

7.2.2   Determining Soil Type

Multiple approaches may be used to decide which soil type to apply to a given region of the terrain. Since this information does not change during gameplay it may be precomputed and stored offline.

7.2.3   Procedural Rules Stored in a Lookup Table

A *lookup table* (LUT) may be used to determine which terrain type shall occur at different terrain slope and height values. The LUT can be stored as a two-dimensional texture parameterized by terrain slope and height along the u and v axes. Addressing the table at runtime requires using slope-height pairs, interpolated data coming from the vertex shader [Eidos 08, Brebion 08]. Its advantage is fast iteration times, and simple implementation, though it has its drawbacks too. Because the LUT is applied globally to the terrain, it does not allow the artists to have local control over the terrain's texturing. Moreover, because the LUT is completely decoupled from the position of terrain in the game world, we cannot store local shading or color-tint information such as local soil types in it.

We found these drawbacks too restricting, and chose to go with the approaches listed below.

7.2.4 Procedural and Manual Painting Stored in a UV-Space Tilemap

Alternatively, we can use tile-index texture that covers the entire terrain and can be sampled using the unique, relaxed UV. In our case, we used a 4-channel map, encoding a color-tint value in three channels (to break repetitive patterns), and the terrain-type index in the fourth (see Figure 7.4). This method has multiple advantages over the first: it can be locally controlled by art needs, separate regions within the map can be edited concurrently by multiple artists, and it can also use procedural methods as its basis. The only drawback is that is uses a fixed resolution for terrain-type data, but this never proved to be a problem for us.

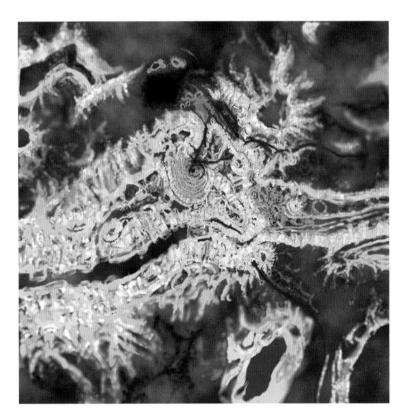

Figure 7.4. Alpha channel of the painted 512^2 tilemap, containing terrain-type info. (© 2010 Digital Reality.)

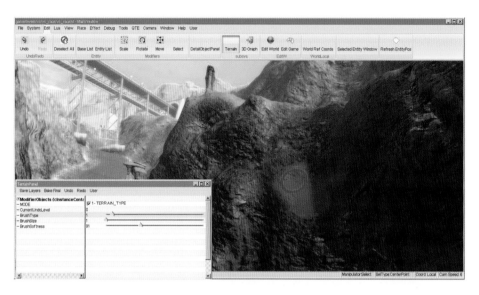

Figure 7.5. Editor-artist interface for painting the tilemap, red ring indicating brush position. (© 2010 Digital Reality.)

Creating the tilemap is very intuitive. Its terrain-index part can be based on either soil-type maps exported from many commercial terrain-generation/erosion software programs (though you might need to convert the world-space type values to relaxed UV space), or global terrain height- and slope-based rules, enhanced by noise.

The base for the color part can again originate from DCC tools, from shadow maps, or can be simply desaturated color noise. Over this base, artists can easily paint or modify the chosen terrain-type values using simple brushes, and temporary layers. Ray casting is used to determine which tilemap texels the brush touches. The editor interface (see Figure 7.5) can also support multiple undo-levels (by caching paint commands), soft brushes, or paint limitations (to allow painting only over regions within desired height/slope limits).

At runtime, hardware bilinear filtering of the tilemap indices automatically solves type-blending problems present in the LUT method, and different nearby tile-index values will get smoothly interpolated over the terrain pixels. We can also compress the tilemap using DXT5 texture compression. Since this format compresses the three color channels independently from the alpha channel, we can keep most of the index resolution while shrinking memory usage.

Note: Suppose we have sand encoded as tile-index value 0, grass as 1, and rock as 2. Now, due to filtering, rock can never be visible near sand, but only through an intermediate grass area. This can be avoided by duplicating types with different neighbors in the atlas, backed by a bit more complex atlas-sampling math. We did not need this, however.

7.2.5 Procedural and Manual Painting Stored in Mesh Vertices

We can also detach geometry containing holes, overhangs, twists, or other hard-to-relax regions from the general terrain mesh, or create any geometry and use it as a paintable terrain-mesh object. Apart from better fitting into the base terrain, we can spare quite a lot of texture memory by using shared atlases and a slightly modified terrain shader here too, instead of unique maps. Artists can UV-map the meshes using arbitrary methods and DCC tools, producing a nonoverlapping unique UV, with seams and connections moved to less noticeable areas.

DCC tools do not have direct view of relative asset extents and spatial proportions inside the game. To help artists with UV mapping and proper tiling factors, we multiply the base UV during editor import with a constant value. This value is determined by the total geometrical surface of the object divided by its total UV-space surface. This way, tiling matches perfectly on all objects and the terrain, no matter how much UV space is used inside the $0 \ldots 1$ region for the given object in the DCC tool. Another feature implemented to help artists is that which allows already-painted mesh objects to reuse their respective paintings if their geometry gets modified again in the DCC tools. This functionality stores the painting of every object also as a texture that gets saved from the editor automatically, along with mesh data. It is used only in the editor, and its texels contain UV and soil-type information, one texel for every vertex. Reapplying paintings is merely finding a UV match between the vertices of the modified mesh, and the saved texels. If the majority of vertices kept their original UVs after the DCC mesh modification, most painting information can be reused.

After geometry authoring is done for a mesh, its procedural and manual painting follows in the editor. Manual painting works similarly to painting the base terrain (illustrated in Figure 7.6). By using ray casting, we can figure out which object, thus which shared-mesh vertex buffer to modify, and with a simple vertex-distance-based spherical three-dimensional brush, artists can encode soil-type information into the mesh vertices. (This can sometimes be hidden for free in an unused byte of a compressed vertex, like in the w component of position or normal data.)

Soil-type continuity where the mesh objects meet the terrain is almost as important as matching normals near the connection region. Because mesh paintings are shared between instances of the same object, and terrain painting is unique due to the tilemap, the latter can be easily retrofitted to match the objects at the connection region. Also, by using a second pair of diffuse/normal atlases for the mesh objects, (containing only a few redundant tiles from the main terrain atlas for connections) greater soil variance can be achieved. Because of complete UV control, we can use tiles that have dominant directional features too.

Figure 7.6. Editor-artist interface for painting mesh objects, red sphere indicating brush volume. (© 2010 Digital Reality.)

On the base terrain, UV relaxing causes tiles to be mapped in different directions based on which side of a hill they are on—UV derivatives change directions with respect to world-space coordinates—thus tiles with heavy direction dependency might be used properly on only one side of a hill, or by putting multiple rotated versions in the atlas.

If required, color-tint or luminance information such as AO can also be painted (or computed in-editor) and baked into mesh vertices.

7.3 Runtime Shading

The base of the runtime rendering solution is texture splatting on a per-pixel level. Using some per-pixel input data, and a unique, relaxed UV channel, the shader can sample different tiling-terrain textures, and blend among them.

To reduce the count of textures the shader needs to sample from, these tiling textures—corresponding to different soil types—can be packed into textures atlases (see Figure 7.7), or texture arrays on XBOX 360 and DX10/11 architectures [Brebion 08, Wloka 03]. Care shall be taken when generating miplevels for the atlas though, as the individual tile-mipmap texels must not get mixed with their neighbors. Creating the compressed and mipmapped tiles first, and then packing them to an atlas is one solution. Anisotropic filtering also becomes more complex when using atlases [van Waveren 09].

If we choose the atlas method, we want the tiling to wrap around in a smaller UV region (hence this is sometimes referred to as subtiling), say $0 \ldots 0.25$ if

Figure 7.7. A packed 2048^2 diffuse-texture atlas, containing 16 different terrain types. (© 2010 Digital Reality.)

we have a 4×4 atlas. This also means that we cannot rely on hardware texture wrapping; this must be performed manually in the shader. As we will see, this causes problems in hardware miplevel selection (texture arrays do not need these corrections, however). For this to work correctly, one must know how the hardware calculates which mip levels to use. GPUs use the first derivatives of screen-space texture coordinates in any given 2×2 pixel block and the dimensions of the texture itself to determine the pixel-to-texel projection ratio, and thus find the appropriate miplevel to use. To access a tile from the atlas for any pixel, we need to emulate the hardware wrapping for the tile. By using the `frac()` hlsl

intrinsic, we break the screenspace UV derivative continuity for the pixel quads
at tile borders. Since the derivatives will be very large, the hardware will pick the
largest miplevel from the chain, which in turn results in a one-pixel-wide seam
whenever the subtiling wraps around. Fortunately, we have many options here:
we can balance the GPU load between texture filtering, *arithmetic logic unit*
(ALU) cost, shader thread counts, texture stalls, and overall artifact visibility.

The safest but slowest option is to calculate the mip level manually in the
shader, right before sampling from the atlas [Wloka 03, Brebion 08]. This produces the correct result, but the extra ALU cost is high since we need to issue
gradient instructions that require extra GPU cycles, and textures need to be sampled with manually specified mip levels, which reduces the sampling rate on many
architectures. As a side effect, texture stalls begin to appear in the pipeline. We
can use multiple methods to shorten these stalls. Some compilers and platforms
allow for explicitly setting the maximum number of general purpose *GPU registers* (GPRs) a compiled shader can use. (They try to optimize the shader code
to meet the specified limit, sometimes by issuing more ALUs to move temporary
shader data around with fewer registers.) If a shader uses fewer GPRs, more
shading cores can run it in parallel, thus the number of simultaneous threads
increases. Using more threads means that stalling all of them is less probable.
On systems using unified shader architectures, one can also increase pixel shader
GPR count by reducing the available GPRs for the vertex shader. Some platforms
also have shader instructions that explicitly return the mip level the hardware
would use at a given pixel, thus saving you from having to compute it yourself in
a shader. Using dynamic branching and regular hardware mipmapping on pixel
quads far from the `frac()` `region` as speedup might also prove useful.

Branch performance might degrade for faraway fragments though, where tiling
UV values and derivatives vary fast, and pixels in the same GPU-pixel-processing
vector must take different branches. Branching might be disabled for distant
fragments, since stall problems are also most relevant on up close terrain, which
fills most screen area and uses the first few mip levels.

One option for estimating the correct mip level is to construct a texture that
encodes the mip index in the texture itself (for example, the first mip level encodes
"0" in all its texels, the second mip level encodes "1" in all its texels, etc.). This
texture should have the same dimensions as the atlas tile. You can then use a
normal texture fetch to sample this texture and allow the hardware to choose the
appropriate mip level. The value of the texel that is fetched will indicate which
mip level was chosen by the hardware and then can be used to issue a `tex2dlod`
instruction on the atlas tile. Dynamic branching is a viable option here too.

We chose to go with a third option, which is the fastest, but does result
in some minor artifacts which we deemed acceptable. We simply sample using
regular `tex2D`, but we generate only the first four mipmaps of the mip chain. This
means that the GPU has to filter a bit more, but our measurements have shown
that only 7–10% of texels fall into the larger miplevels, thus the performance

Figure 7.8. Screenshot from the canyon, with 100x UV tiling factor (note the lack of UV distortions on walls). (© 2010 Digital Reality.)

impact is considered to be minimal compared to using reduced-speed `tex2Dlods`. The visual artifacts are minimized because the seam will always use the fourth mip level, and colors differ much less between the first and last levels. We also switched to texture atlases of 1×16 dimensions instead of 4×4, thus we can use hardware texture wrapping for one direction, halving mip level errors arising from using `frac()`, while also using fewer ALU operations to address the atlases.

At this point, we have diffuse and normal atlases ready to be sampled in the shader. To improve quality, we blend between two nearby tiles—using the fractional part of the interpolated tile index—by reading twice from the same atlas, with respective UV offsets. Shading the terrain and the painted meshes is identical, and is based on simple per-pixel lambertian diffuse, and hemispherical ambient terms. Shadow contribution is composed of a lookup into a precomputed and blurred static-shadow map, cross-fading with a cascaded dynamic and blurred *exponential shadow map* (ESM), and AO baked into vertices. There are many ways to experiment with more complex lighting models, however, correctly set atmospheric settings, fog, *high dynamic range* (HDR), fake scattering [Quilez 09], and soil-type maps can provide a solid impression already. See Figure 7.8 for reference.

For your convenience, the runtime per-pixel, texture-splatting shader code is listed in Listing 3.1. Note that editor-mode paint layers, brush-ring-overlay paint functionality, vertex unpacking, shadows, and fog calculations are omitted for clarity.

```
//Runtime terrain shader with tilemap-based per-pixel
//splatting using atlases (tangent-space lighting).

static const float TILEMAP_SIZE= 512.0f;
static const float TILES_IN_ROW= 4.0f;
static const float MAX_TILE_VALUE= TILES_IN_ROW*TILES_IN_ROW-1;

struct sVSInput
{
    float4 Position : POSITION;
    float3 Normal   : NORMAL;
    float2 UV       : TEXCOORD0;
    float3 Tangent  : TEXCOORD1;
};

struct sVSOutput
{
    float4 ProjPos     : POSITION;
    float2 UV          : TEXCOORD0;
    float3 Normal      : TEXCOORD1;
    float3 TgLightVec  : TEXCOORD2;
};

float4x3 cWorldMatrix;
float4x4 cViewProjMatrix;
float cUVmultiplier; //Terrain-texture tiling factor.
float3 cCameraPos;
float3 cSunDirection;
float3 cSunColor;

//Lighting is in tangent space.
float3x3 MakeWorldToTangent(float3 iTangent, float3 iNormal)
{
    float3x3 TangentToLocal=
        float3x3(iTangent, cross(iNormal,iTangent), iNormal);
    float3x3 TangentToWorld=
        mul(TangentToLocal,(float3x3)cWorldMatrix);
    float3x3 WorldToTangent = transpose(TangentToWorld);

    return WorldToTangent;
}

sVSOutput vpmain(sVSInput In)
{
    sVSOutput Out;

    float3 WorldPos= mul(In.Position, cWorldMatrix);
    Out.ProjPos= mul(float4(WorldPos,1), cViewProjMatrix);

    Out.Normal= mul(In.Normal.xyz, (float3x3)cWorldMatrix);

    Out.UV= In.UV * cUVmultiplier;
```

```
    float3x3 WorldToTangent=
        MakeWorldToTangent(In.Tangent, In.Normal);

    Out.TgLightVec= mul(cSunDirection.xyz, WorldToTangent);

    return Out;
}

sampler2D DiffAtlas;
sampler2D NormAtlas;
sampler2D TileTable;

float GetMipLevel(float2 iUV, float2 iTextureSize)
{
    float2 dx= ddx(iUV * iTextureSize.x);
    float2 dy= ddy(iUV * iTextureSize.y);
    float d= max( dot(dx, dx), dot(dy, dy) );
    return 0.5 * log2(d);
}

float4 fpmain(sVSOutput In) : COLOR
{
    float4 TileMapTex= tex2D(TileTable, In.UV/cUVmultiplier);
    float3 ColorTint= TileMapTex.xyz;
    float TileIndex= TileMapTex.w * MAX_TILE_VALUE;

    float MIP= GetMipLevel(In.UV, TILEMAP_SIZE.xx);

    float2 fracUV = frac(In.UV);
    float2 DiffCorrectUV= fracUV/4.0f;

    //Blend types and blend ratio.
    float type_A = floor(TileIndex);
    float type_B = ceil(TileIndex);
    float factor = TileIndex - type_A;

    float tmp = floor(type_A/4);
    float2 UV_A = DiffCorrectUV + float2(type_A-tmp*4,tmp)/4;
    tmp = floor(type_B/4);
    float2 UV_B = DiffCorrectUV + float2(type_B-tmp*4,tmp)/4;

    // 2 Lookups needed, for blending between layers.
    float4 colA= tex2Dlod(DiffAtlas, float4(UV_A,0,MIP));
    float4 colB= tex2Dlod(DiffAtlas, float4(UV_B,0,MIP));

    float4 DiffuseColor= lerp(colA, colB, factor);

    float4 normA= tex2Dlod(NormAtlas, float4(UV_A,0,MIP));
    float4 normB= tex2Dlod(NormAtlas, float4(UV_B,0,MIP));

    float4 normtex= lerp(normA, normB, factor);

    //Extract normal map.
    float3 norm= 2*(normtex.rgb-0.5);
```

```
    float3 tgnormal= normalize(norm);

    float NdotL=
        saturate(dot(tgnormal, normalize(In.TgLightVec)));
    float3 SunDiffuseColor= NdotL * cSunColor;
    float3 Albedo= DiffuseColor.xyz * ColorTint * 2;
    float3 AmbientColor= 0.5;

    float3 LitAlbedo= Albedo * (AmbientColor + SunDiffuseColor);
    return float4(LitAlbedo,1);
}
```

Listing 7.1. Simplified runtime shaders including manual mipmap computation.

7.4 Performance

The system load for rendering the base terrain mesh spanning a 10 km^2 area, and consisting of 600 k triangles is 14 MB memory, and 6 ms frame time, on XBOX 360. This includes geometry vertex and index data, LODs, diffuse, normal, shadow, and terrain type maps, while not using any streaming bandwidth. To reach the desired rendering time and memory footprint, a couple of optimizations are required.

To allow using 16-bit indices in the triangle list, the terrain had to be sliced into blocks no larger than 65 k vertices, during COLLADA import. Using blocks with <1 km^2 area also helps our static KD-tree based culling. Balancing between better culling and fewer draw calls can be done by adjusting block count and block size. LODs are also generated at import time, since they are essential to reduce vertex load, and also keep the pixel quad efficiency high. If the LODs are generated by skipping vertices, only index data needs to be extended by a small amount (say, 33%, if each consecutive level contains a quarter of the previous version, with regard to triangle count), and each new LOD can refer to the original, untouched vertex buffer. Keeping silhouettes and vertices at block boundaries regardless of LOD are important in order to prevent holes from appearing in places where differed LODs meet. To help pre- and post-transform vertex and index caches, vertex and index reordering is also done at the import phase.

Vertex compression is also heavily used to reduce the required amount of memory and transfer bandwidth. We can store additional information in the vertices. AO and soil-type indices are valid choices, but color-tint values, shadow terms, or bent normals for better shading are still possible.

Texture atlases are also compressed. We found atlases of 4×4 512^2 tiles to contain enough variation and resolution too. The diffuse atlas can use the DXT1 format, while the normal atlas can use better, platform-specific 2-channel compressed formats where available. The tilemap can also be compressed to DXT5, keeping most information of the tile indices in the alpha channel, while heavily compressing color-tint data. The static shadow map can also be compressed to DXT1, or luminance of multiple shadow texels can be packed into one texel of a two-channel map. (ATI1N (BC4/DXT5A), ATI2N (BC5/3Dc), DXN, and CTX1 formats are easy choices.) Using floating-point depth buffers and depth pre-pass for rejecting pixels, and occlusion queries or conditional rendering to entirely skip draw calls can also prove to be helpful.

7.5 Possible Extensions

Many aspects of the described system can be improved or extended. Some of the methods listed below are general improvements, some are platform specific, while some trade flexibility for faster rendering or less resource usage.

Heightmap-based geometry can provide a more compact, though computationally more expensive representation of the terrain. Representing steep slopes without texture distortions might be possible if we store three component-position offsets of vertices of relaxed UV space grid, like mesh textures. More aggressive vertex compression is also still possible, even without using heightmaps. Using more blocks of terrain with smaller block sizes, or using triplanar mapping [Geiss 07] might yield better compression opportunities.

Texturing can be enhanced in multiple ways, though most of them put more texture fetch and filtering burden on the GPU. Using a large tiling factor can either result in visible tiling of soil types, or not having the ability to visualize larger terrain features, originating from the atlas. A solution is to sample the atlases twice, with two very different tiling factors, and cross fade their color and normal data. This enhances large details in the far regions, lending unique character to the terrain, while it provides detail up close where tiling is less visible. Large details dissolve as the camera moves close, but this is barely noticeable. Figure 7.9 illustrates the concept.

Another option is reducing the tiling factor, and blending in desaturated detail textures up close. This allows a choice among different detail maps, based on the general terrain soil-type. Using noise (defined by interpolated height and slope data) to perturb the soil-type on per-pixel level in the shader with ALU instructions is also a possibility to reduce tiling or add up close detail. The inverse of this method is also viable, and has been the de facto standard for terrain texturing for many years. We can stream a large, unique, diffuse, and normal map for far details, and blend in the per-pixel splatting as close-up or mid-range detail. Transition regions between different soil types can also be enhanced by using blend maps, which can be efficiently packed into the alpha channel of the diffuse atlas [Hardy 09]]. Yet another option is to use more soil-type textures in the atlas to give more variance. Soil-type information can also

Figure 7.9. Screenshot of a canyon wall, with distance-dependant atlas tiling factor. (© 2010 Digital Reality.)

drive collision-particle generation, or procedural placement of detail object and foliage [Andersson 07].

We can use ambient aperture lighting to give bump maps some shadowing [Persson 06], and image-based ambient and diffuse lighting using bent normals. Specular reflections can also be added where surfaces are wet, for example, riverbanks [Geiss 07]. Atmospheric scattering with volumetric light/fog (or faking it [Quilez 09]) is also an option to enhance realism of the rendered terrain. Enhancing normal mapping by using more complex parallax effects might also be feasible.

Finally, caching previously computed fragment data (composed albedo or final normal data), either in screen space, or around the camera in relaxed UV space can speed up rendering [Herzog et al. 10].

7.6 Acknowledgments

First, I would like to thank Balázs Török, my friend and colleague, for his helpful suggestions and for the initial idea of contributing to the book. I would also like to thank the art team at Digital Reality for their excellent work, on which I based my illustrations. Also, special thanks to my love Tímea Kapui for her endless patience and support.

Bibliography

[Andersson 07] Johan Andersson. "Terrain Rendering in Frostbite Using Procedural Shader Splatting." In *ACM SIGGRAPH 2007 courses.* New York: ACM, 2007. Available online (http://ati.amd.com/developer/SIGGRAPH07/Chapter5-Andersson-Terrain_Rendering_in_Frostbite.pdf).

[Barrett 08] Sean Barrett. "Sparse Virtual Textures blog." 2008. Available online (http://www.silverspaceship.com/src/svt/).

[Brebion 08] Flavien Brebion. "Journal of Ysaneya, gamedev.net." 2008. Available online (http://www.gamedev.net/community/forums/mod/journal/journal.asp?jn=263350).

[Dudash 07] Bryan Dudash. "DX10 Texture Arrays, nVidia SDK." 2007. Available online (http://developer.download.nvidia.com/SDK/10/Samples/TextureArrayTerrain.zip).

[Eidos 08] Eidos, Square Enix Europe. "Battlestations: Pacific." 2008. Available online (http://www.battlestations.net).

[Geiss 07] Ryan Geiss. "Generating Complex Procedural Terrains Using the GPU." In *GPU Gems 3.* Reading, MA: Addison Wesley, 2007. Available online (http://http.developer.nvidia.com/GPUGems3/gpugems3_ch01.html).

[Hardy 09] Alexandre Hardy. "Blend Maps: Enhanced Terrain Texturing." 2009. Available online (http://www.ahardy.za.net/Home/blendmaps).

[Herzog et al. 10] Robert Herzog, Elmar Eisemann, Karol Myszkowski, and H-P. Seidel. "Spatio-Temporal Upsampling on the GPU." In *Proceedings of the 2010 ACM SIGGRAPH symposium on Interactive 3D Graphics and Games, I3D '10*, pp. 91–98. New York: ACM, 2010.

[Kemen 08] Brano Kemen. "Journal of Lethargic Programming, Cameni's gamedev.net blog, July 2008." 2008. Available online (http://www.gamedev.net/community/forums/mod/journal/journal.asp?jn=503094&cmonth=7&cyear=2008).

[Mittring 08] Martin Mittring. "Advanced Virtual Texturing Topics." In *ACM SIGGRAPH 2008 Classes SIGGRAPH '08*, pp. 23–51. New York, NY, USA: ACM, 2008.

[Pangilinan and Ruppel 10] Erick Pangilinan and Robh Ruppel. "Uncharted 2 Art direction." *GDC 2010.* Available online (http://www.gdcvault.com/free/category/280/conference/).

[Persson 06] Emil Persson. "Humus, Ambient Aperture Lighting." 2006. Available online (http://www.humus.name/index.php?page=3D&ID=71).

[Quilez 09] Inigo Quilez. "Behind Elevated." *Function 2009.* Available online (http://www.iquilezles.org/www/material/function2009/function2009.pdf).

[Schueler 06] Christian Schueler. "Normal Mapping without Pre-Computed Tangents." In *ShaderX⁵: Advanced Rendering Techniques*, Chapter II.6. Hingham, MA: Charles River Media, 2006. Available online (http://www.shaderx5.com/TOC.html).

[van Rossen 08] Sander van Rossen. "Sander's Blog on Virtual Texturing." 2008. Available online (http://sandervanrossen.blogspot.com/2009/08/virtual-texturing-part-1.html).

[van Waveren 09] J. M. P. van Waveren. "idTech5 Challeges: From Texture Virtualization to Massive Parallelization." *Siggraph 2009.* Available online (http://s09.idav.ucdavis.edu/talks/05-JP_id_Tech_5_Challenges.pdf).

[Wetzel 07] Mikey Wetzel. "Under The Hood: Revving Up Shader Performance." *Microsoft Gamefest Unplugged Europe, 2007.* Available online (http://www.microsoft.com/downloads/details.aspx?FamilyId=74DB343E-E8FF-44E9-A43E-6F1615D9FCE0&displaylang=en).

[Wloka 03] Matthias Wloka. "Improved Batching Via Texture Atlases." In *ShaderX³*. Hingham, MA: Charles River Media, 2003. Available online (http://www.shaderx3.com/Tables%20of%20Content.htm).

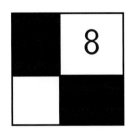

Practical Morphological Antialiasing

Jorge Jimenez, Belen Masia, Jose I. Echevarria,
Fernando Navarro, and Diego Gutierrez

The use of antialiasing techniques is crucial when producing high quality graphics. Up to now, *multisampling antialiasing* (MSAA) has remained the most advanced solution, offering superior results in real time. However, there are important drawbacks to the use of MSAA in certain scenarios. First, the increase in processing time it consumes is not negligible at all. Further, limitations of MSAA include the impossibility, in a wide range of platforms, of activating multisampling when using *multiple render targets* (MRT), on which fundamental techniques such as deferred shading [Shishkovtsov 05, Koonce 07] rely. Even on platforms where MRT and MSAA can be simultaneously activated (i.e., DirectX 10), implementation of MSAA is neither trivial nor cost free [Thibieroz 09]. Additionally, MSAA poses a problem for the current generation of consoles. In the case of the Xbox 360, memory constraints force the use of CPU-based tiling techniques in case high-resolution frame buffers need to be used in conjunction with MSAA; whereas on the PS3 multisampling is usually not even applied. Another drawback of MSAA is its inability to smooth nongeometric edges, such as those resulting from the use of alpha testing, frequent when rendering vegetation. As a result, when using MSAA, vegetation can be antialiased only if alpha to coverage is used. Finally, multisampling requires extra memory, which is always a valuable resource, especially on consoles.

In response to the limitations described above, a series of techniques have implemented antialiasing solutions in shader units, the vast majority of them being based on edge detection and blurring. In *S.T.A.L.K.E.R.* [Shishkovtsov 05], edge detection is performed by calculating differences in the eight-neighborhood depth values and the four-neighborhood normal angles; then, edges are blurred using a cross-shaped sampling pattern. A similar, improved scheme is used in *Tabula Rasa* [Koonce 07], where edge detection uses threshold values that are resolution independent, and the full eight-neighborhood of the pixel is considered for differences in the normal angles. In *Crysis* [Sousa 07], edges are detected by using depth values, and rotated triangle samples are used to perform texture lookups using bilinear filtering. These solutions alleviate the aliasing problem but do not mitigate it completely. Finally, in *Killzone 2*, samples are rendered into a double horizontal resolution G-buffer. Then, in the lighting pass, two samples of the G-buffer are queried for each pixel of the final buffer. The resulting samples are then averaged and stored in the final buffer. However, this necessitates executing the lighting shader twice per final pixel.

In this article we present an alternative technique that avoids most of the problems described above. The quality of our results lies between $4x$ and $8x$ MSAA at a fraction of the time and memory consumption. It is based on morphological antialiasing [Reshetov 09], which relies on detecting certain image patterns to reduce aliasing. However, the original implementation is designed to be run in a CPU and requires the use of list structures that are not GPU-amenable.

Since our goal is to achieve real-time practicality in games with current mainstream hardware, our algorithm implements aggressive optimizations that provide an optimal trade-off between quality and execution times. Reshetov searches for specific patterns (U-shaped, Z-shaped, and L-shaped patterns), which are then decomposed into simpler ones, an approach that would be impractical on a GPU. We realize that the pattern type, and thus the antialiasing to be performed, depends on only four values, which can be obtained for each edge pixel (*edgel*) with only two memory accesses. This way, the original algorithm is transformed so that it uses texture structures instead of lists (see Figure 8.1). Furthermore, this approach allows handling of all pattern types in a symmetric way, thus avoiding the need to decompose them into simpler ones. In addition, precomputation of

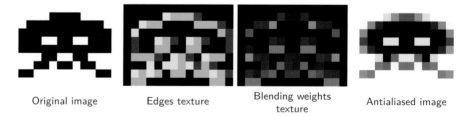

Original image   Edges texture   Blending weights texture   Antialiased image

Figure 8.1. Starting from an aliased image (left), edges are detected and stored in the edges texture (center left). The color of each pixel depicts where edges are: green pixels have an edge at their top boundary, red pixels at their left boundary, and yellow pixels have edges at both boundaries. The edges texture is then used in conjunction with the precomputed area texture to produce the blending weights texture (center right) in the second pass. This texture stores the weights for the pixels at each side of an edgel in the RGBA channels. In the third pass, blending is performed to obtain the final antialiased image (right).

certain values into textures allows for an even faster implementation. Finally, in order to accelerate calculations, we make extensive use of hardware bilinear interpolation for smartly fetching multiple values in a single query and provide means of decoding the fetched values into the original unfiltered values. As a result, our algorithm can be efficiently executed by a GPU, has a moderate memory footprint, and can be integrated as part of the standard rendering pipeline of any game architecture.

Some of the optimizations presented in this work may seem to add complexity at a conceptual level, but as our results show, their overall contribution makes them worth including. Our technique yields image quality between $4x$ and $8x$ MSAA, with a typical execution time of 3.79 ms on Xbox 360 and 0.44 ms on a NVIDIA GeForce 9800 GTX+, for a resolution of 720p. Memory footprint is $2x$ the size of the backbuffer on Xbox 360 and $1.5x$ on the 9800 GTX+. According to our measurements, $8x$ MSAA takes an average of 5 ms per image on the same GPU at the same resolution, that is, our algorithm is $11.80x$ faster.

In order to show the versatility of our algorithm, we have implemented the shader both for Xbox 360 and PC, using DirectX 9 and 10 respectively. The code presented in this article is that of the DirectX 10 version.

8.1 Overview

The algorithm searches for patterns in edges which then allow us to reconstruct the antialiased lines. This can, in general terms, be seen as a revectorization of edges. In the following we give a brief overview of our algorithm.

First, edge detection is performed using depth values (alternatively, luminances can be used to detect edges; this will be further discussed in Section 8.2.1). We then compute, for each pixel belonging to an edge, the distances in pixels from it to both ends of the edge to which the edgel belongs. These distances define the position of the pixel with respect to the line. Depending on the location of the edgel within the line, it will or will not be affected by the antialiasing process. In those edges which have to be modified (those which contain yellow or green areas in Figure 8.2 (left)) a blending operation is performed according to Equation (8.1):

$$c_{\text{new}} = (1 - a) \cdot c_{\text{old}} + a \cdot c_{\text{opp}}, \tag{8.1}$$

where c_{old} is the original color of the pixel, c_{opp} is the color of the pixel on the other side of the line, c_{new} is the new color of the pixel, and a is the area shown in yellow in Figure 8.2 (left). The value of a is a function of both the pattern type of the line and the distances to both ends of the line. The pattern type is defined by the *crossing edges* of the line, i.e., edges which are perpendicular to the line and thus define the ends of it (vertical green lines in Figure 8.2). In order to save processing time, we precompute this area and store it as a two-channel texture that can be seen in Figure 8.2 (right) (see Section 8.3.3 for details).

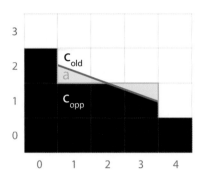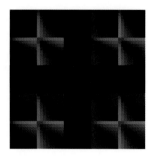

Figure 8.2. Antialiasing process (left). Color c_{opp} bleeds into c_{old} according to the area a below the blue line. Texture containing the precomputed areas (right). The texture uses two channels to store areas at each side of the edge, i.e., for a pixel and its opposite (pixels $(1,1)$ and $(1,2)$ on the left). Each 9×9 subtexture corresponds to a pattern type. Inside each of these subtextures, (u, v) coordinates encode distances to the left and to the right, respectively.

The algorithm is implemented in three passes, which are explained in detail in the following sections. In the first pass, edge detection is performed, yielding a texture containing edges (see Figure 8.1 (center left)). In the second pass the corresponding blending weight[1] (that is, value a) for each pixel adjacent to the edge being smoothed is obtained (see Figure 8.1 (center right)). To do this, we first detect the pattern types for each line passing through the north and west boundaries of the pixel and then calculate the distances of each pixel to the *crossing edges*; these are then used to query the precomputed area texture. The third and final pass involves blending each pixel with its four-neighborhood using the blending weights texture obtained in the previous pass.

The last two passes are performed separately to spare calculations, taking advantage of the fact that two adjacent pixels share the same edgel. To do this, in the second pass, pattern detection and the subsequent area calculation are performed on a per-edgel basis. Finally, in the third pass, the two adjacent pixels will fetch the same information.

Additionally, using the *stencil buffer* allows us to perform the second and third passes only for the pixels which contain an edge, considerably reducing processing times.

8.2 Detecting Edges

We perform edge detection using the depth buffer (or luminance values if depth information is not available). For each pixel, the difference in depth with respect to the pixel on top and on the left is obtained. We can efficiently store the edges

---

[1] Throughout the article *blending weight* and *area* will be used interchangeably.

for all the pixels in the image this way, given the fact that two adjacent pixels have a common boundary. This difference is thresholded to obtain a binary value, which indicates whether an edge exists in a pixel boundary. This threshold, which varies with resolution, can be made resolution independent [Koonce 07]. Then, the left and top edges are stored, respectively, in the red and green channels of the edges texture, which will be used as input for the next pass.

Whenever using depth-based edge detection, a problem may arise in places where two planes at different angles meet: the edge will not be detected because of samples having the same depth. A common solution to this is the addition of information from normals. However, in our case we found that the improvement in quality obtained when using normals was not worth the increase in execution time it implied.

8.2.1 Using Luminance Values for Edge Detection

An alternative to depth-based edge detection is the use of luminance information to detect image discontinuities. Luminance values are derived from the CIE XYZ (color space) standard:

$$L = 0.2126 \cdot R + 0.7152 \cdot G + 0.0722 \cdot B.$$

Then, for each pixel, the difference in luminance with respect to the pixel on top and on the left is obtained, the implementation being equivalent to that of depth-based detection. When thresholding to obtain a binary value, we found 0.1 to be an adequate threshold for most cases. It is important to note that using either luminance- or depth-based edge detection does not affect the following passes.

Although qualitywise both methods offer similar results, depth-based detection is more robust, yielding a more reliable edges texture. And, our technique takes, on average, 10% less time when using depth than when using luminance values. Luminance values are useful when depth information cannot be accessed and thus offer a more universal approach. Further, when depth-based detection is performed, edges in shading will not be detected, whereas luminance-based detection allows for antialias shading and specular highlights. In general terms, one could say that luminance-based detection works in a more perceptual way because it smoothes *visible* edges. As an example, when dense vegetation is present, using luminance values is faster than using depth values (around 12% faster for the particular case shown in Figure 8.5 (bottom row)), since a greater number of edges are detected when using depth values. Optimal results in terms of quality, at the cost of a higher execution time, can be obtained by combining luminance, depth, and normal values.

Listing 8.1 shows the source code of this pass, using depth-based edge detection. Figure 8.1 (center left) is the resulting image of the edge-detection pass, in this particular case, using luminance-based detection, as depth information is not available.

```
float4 EdgeDetectionPS(float4 position: SV_POSITION,
                       float2 texcoord: TEXCOORD0): SV_TARGET {

  float D = depthTex.SampleLevel(PointSampler,
                                 texcoord, 0);
  float Dleft = depthTex.SampleLevel(PointSampler,
                                     texcoord, 0, -int2(1, 0));
  float Dtop  = depthTex.SampleLevel(PointSampler,
                                     texcoord, 0, -int2(0, 1));

  // We need these for updating the stencil buffer.
  float Dright  = depthTex.SampleLevel(PointSampler,
                                       texcoord, 0, int2(1, 0));
  float Dbottom = depthTex.SampleLevel(PointSampler,
                                       texcoord, 0, int2(0, 1));

  float4 delta = abs(D.xxxx -
                     float4(Dleft, Dtop, Dright, Dbottom));
  float4 edges = step(threshold.xxxx, delta);

  if (dot(edges, 1.0) == 0.0) {
    discard;
  }

  return edges;
}
```

Listing 8.1. Edge detection shader.

8.3   Obtaining Blending Weights

In order to calculate the blending weights we first search for the distances to the ends of the line the edgel belongs to, using the edges texture obtained in the previous pass (see Section 8.3.1). Once these distances are known, we can use them to fetch the crossing edges at both ends of the line (see Section 8.3.2). These crossing edges indicate the type of pattern we are dealing with. The distances to the ends of the line and the type of pattern are used to access the precalculated texture (see Section 8.3.3) in which we store the areas that are used as blending weights for the final pass.

As mentioned before, to share calculations between adjacent pixels, we take advantage of the fact that two adjacent pixels share the same boundary, and

```
float4 BlendingWeightCalculationPS(
        float4 position: SV_POSITION,
        float2 texcoord: TEXCOORD0): SV_TARGET {
  float4 weights = 0.0;

  float2 e = edgesTex.SampleLevel(PointSampler,
                                  texcoord, 0).rg;

  [branch]
  if (e.g) { // Edge at north.
    float2 d = float2(SearchXLeft(texcoord),
                      SearchXRight(texcoord));

    // Instead of sampling between edges, we sample at -0.25,
    // to be able to discern what value each edgel has.
    float4 coords = mad(float4(d.x, -0.25, d.y + 1.0, -0.25),
                        PIXEL_SIZE.xyxy, texcoord.xyxy);
    float e1 = edgesTex.SampleLevel(LinearSampler,
                                    coords.xy, 0).r;
    float e2 = edgesTex.SampleLevel(LinearSampler,
                                    coords.zw, 0).r;
    weights.rg = Area(abs(d), e1, e2);
  }

  [branch]
  if (e.r) { // Edge at west.
    float2 d = float2(SearchYUp(texcoord),
                      SearchYDown(texcoord));

    float4 coords = mad(float4(-0.25, d.x, -0.25, d.y + 1.0),
                        PIXEL_SIZE.xyxy, texcoord.xyxy);
    float e1 = edgesTex.SampleLevel(LinearSampler,
                                    coords.xy, 0).g;
    float e2 = edgesTex.SampleLevel(LinearSampler,
                                    coords.zw, 0).g;
    weights.ba = Area(abs(d), e1, e2);
  }

  return weights;
}
```

Listing 8.2. Blending weights calculation shader.

we perform area calculation on a per-edgel basis. However, even though two adjacent pixels share the same calculation, the resulting a value is different for each of them: only one has a blending weight a, whereas for the opposite one, a equals zero (pixels $(1, 2)$ and $(1, 1)$, respectively, in Figure 8.2). The one exception to this is the case in which the pixel lies at the middle of a line of odd length (as pixel $(2, 1)$ in Figure 8.2); in this case both the actual pixel and its opposite have a nonzero value for a. As a consequence, the output of this pass is a texture which, for each pixel, stores the areas at each side of its corresponding edges (by *the areas at each side* we refer to those of the actual pixel and its opposite). This yields two values for north edges and two values for west edges in the final blending weights texture. Finally, the weights stored in this texture will be used in the third pass to perform the final blending. Listing 8.2 shows the source code of this pass; Figure 8.1 (center right) is the resulting image.

8.3.1   Searching for Distances

The search for distances to the ends of the line is performed using an iterative algorithm, which in each iteration checks whether the end of the line has been reached. To accelerate this search, we leverage the fact that the information stored in the edges texture is binary—it simply encodes whether an edgel exists—and query from positions between pixels using bilinear filtering for fetching two pixels at a time (see Figure 8.3). The result of the query can be: a) 0.0, which means that neither pixel contains an edgel, b) 1.0, which implies an edgel exists in both pixels, or c) 0.5, which is returned when just one of the two pixels contains an edgel. We stop the search if the returned value is lower than one.[2] By using a simple approach like this, we are introducing two sources of inaccuracy:

1. We do not stop the search when encountering an edgel perpendicular to the line we are following, but when the line comes to an end;

2. When the returned value is 0.5 we cannot distinguish which of the two pixels contains an edgel.

Although an error is introduced in some cases, it is unnoticeable in practice—the speed-up is considerable since it is possible to jump two pixels per iteration. Listing 8.3 shows one of the distance search functions.

In order to make the algorithm practical in a game environment, we limit the search to a certain distance. As expected, the greater the maximum length, the better the quality of the antialiasing. However, we have found that, for the majority of cases, distance values between 8 and 12 pixels give a good trade-off between quality and performance.

---

[2]In practice we use 0.9 due to bilinear filtering precision issues.

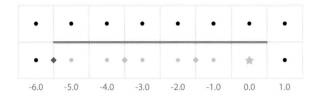

Figure 8.3. Hardware bilinear filtering is used when searching for distances from each pixel to the end of the line. The color of the dot at the center of each pixel represents the value of that pixel in the edges texture. In the case shown here, distance search of the left end of the line is performed for the pixel marked with a star. Positions where the edges texture is accessed, fetching pairs of pixels, are marked with rhombuses. This allows us to travel twice the distance with the same number of accesses.

In the particular case of the Xbox 360 implementation, we make use of the `tfetch2D` assembler instruction, which allows us to specify an offset in pixel units with respect to the original texture coordinates of the query. This instruction is limited to offsets of -8 and 7.5, which constrains the maximum distance that can be searched. When searching for distances greater than eight pixels, we cannot use the hardware as efficiently and the performance is affected negatively.

```
float SearchXLeft(float2 texcoord) {
  texcoord -= float2(1.5, 0.0) * PIXEL_SIZE;
  float e = 0.0;
  // We offset by 0.5 to sample between edges, thus fetching
  // two in a row.
  for (int i = 0; i < maxSearchSteps; i++) {
    e = edgesTex.SampleLevel(LinearSampler, texcoord, 0).g;
    // We compare with 0.9 to prevent bilinear access precision
    // problems.
    [flatten] if (e < 0.9) break;
    texcoord -= float2(2.0, 0.0) * PIXEL_SIZE;
  }
  // When we exit the loop without finding the end, we return
  // -2 * maxSearchSteps.
  return max(-2.0 * i - 2.0 * e, -2.0 * maxSearchSteps);
}
```

Listing 8.3. Distance search function (search in the left direction case).

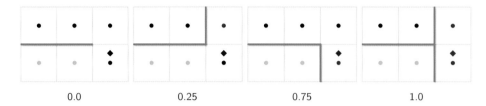

0.0   0.25   0.75   1.0

Figure 8.4.   Examples of the four possible types of crossing edge and corresponding value returned by the bilinear query of the edges texture. The color of the dot at the center of each pixel represents the value of that pixel in the edges texture. The rhombuses, at a distance of 0.25 from the center of the pixel, indicate the sampling position, while their color represents the value returned by the bilinear access.

8.3.2   Fetching Crossing Edges

Once the distances to the ends of the line are calculated, they are used to obtain the crossing edges. A naive approach for fetching the crossing edge of an end of a line would be to query two edges. A more efficient approach is to use bilinear filtering for fetching both edges at one time, in a manner similar to the way the distance search is done. However, in this case we must be able to distinguish the actual value of each edgel, so we query with an offset of 0.25, allowing us to distinguish which edgel is equal to 1.0 when only one of the edges is present. Figure 8.4 shows the crossing edge that corresponds to each of the different values returned by the bilinear query.

8.3.3   The Precomputed Area Texture

With distance and crossing edges information at hand, we now have all the required inputs to calculate the area corresponding to the current pixel. As this is an expensive operation, we opt to precompute it in a four-dimensional table which is stored in a conventional two-dimensional texture (see Figure 8.2 (right)).[3] This texture is divided into subtextures of size 9×9, each of them corresponding to a pattern type (codified by the fetched *crossing edges* $e1$ and $e2$ at each end of the line). Inside each of these subtextures, (u, v) coordinates correspond to distances to the ends of the line, eight being the maximum distance reachable. Resolution can be increased if a higher maximum distance is required. See Listing 8.4 for details on how the precomputed area texture is accessed.

To query the texture, we first convert the bilinear filtered values $e1$ and $e2$ to an integer value in the range 0..4. Value 2 (which would correspond to value 0.5 for $e1$ or $e2$) cannot occur in practice, which is why the corresponding row and column in the texture are empty. Maintaining those empty spaces in the texture

---

[3]The code to generate this texture is available in the web material.

```
#define NUM_DISTANCES 9
#define AREA_SIZE (NUM_DISTANCES * 5)

float2 Area(float2 distance, float e1, float e2) {
    // * By dividing by AREA_SIZE - 1.0 below we are
    //   implicitely offsetting to always fall inside a pixel.
    // * Rounding prevents bilinear access precision problems.
    float2 pixcoord = NUM_DISTANCES *
                      round(4.0 * float2(e1, e2)) + distance;
    float2 texcoord = pixcoord / (AREA_SIZE - 1.0);
    return areaTex.SampleLevel(PointSampler, texcoord, 0).rg;
}
```

Listing 8.4. Precomputed area texture access function.

allows for a simpler and faster indexing. The `round` instruction is used to avoid possible precision problems caused by the bilinear filtering.

Following the same reasoning (explained at the beginning of the section) by which we store area values for two adjacent pixels in the same pixel of the final blending weights texture, the precomputed area texture needs to be built on a per-edgel basis. Thus, each pixel of the texture stores two a values, one for a pixel and one for its opposite. (Again, a will be zero for one of them in all cases with the exception of those pixels centered on lines of odd length.)

8.4 Blending with the Four-Neighborhood

In this last pass, the final color of each pixel is obtained by blending the actual color with its four neighbors, according to the area values stored in the weights texture obtained in the previous pass. This is achieved by accessing three positions of the blending weights texture:

1. the current pixel, which gives us the north and west blending weights;

2. the pixel at the south;

3. the pixel at the east.

Once more, to exploit hardware capabilities, we use four bilinear filtered accesses to blend the current pixel with each of its four neighbors. Finally, as one pixel can belong to four different lines, we find an average of the contributing lines. Listing 8.5 shows the source code of this pass; Figure 8.1 (right) shows the resulting image.

```
float4 NeighborhoodBlendingPS(
        float4 position: SV_POSITION,
        float2 texcoord: TEXCOORD0): SV_TARGET {
  float4 topLeft = blendTex.SampleLevel(PointSampler,
                                        texcoord, 0);
  float right    = blendTex.SampleLevel(PointSampler,
                                        texcoord, 0,
                                        int2(0, 1)).g;
  float bottom   = blendTex.SampleLevel(PointSampler,
                                        texcoord, 0,
                                        int2(1, 0)).a;
  float4 a = float4(topLeft.r, right, topLeft.b, bottom);

  float sum = dot(a, 1.0);

  [branch]
  if (sum > 0.0) {
    float4 o = a * PIXEL_SIZE.yyxx;
    float4 color = 0.0;
    color = mad(colorTex.SampleLevel(LinearSampler,
                texcoord + float2( 0.0, -o.r), 0), a.r, color);
    color = mad(colorTex.SampleLevel(LinearSampler,
                texcoord + float2( 0.0,  o.g), 0), a.g, color);
    color = mad(colorTex.SampleLevel(LinearSampler,
                texcoord + float2(-o.b,  0.0), 0), a.b, color);
    color = mad(colorTex.SampleLevel(LinearSampler,
                texcoord + float2( o.a,  0.0), 0), a.a, color);
    return color / sum;
  } else {
    return colorTex.SampleLevel(LinearSampler, texcoord, 0);
  }
}
```

Listing 8.5. Four-neighborhood blending shader.

8.5   Results

Qualitywise, our algorithm lies between $4x$ and $8x$ MSAA, requiring a memory consumption of only $1.5x$ the size of the backbuffer on a PC and of $2x$ on Xbox 360.[4] Figure 8.5 shows a comparison between our algorithm, $8x$ MSAA, and no antialiasing at all on images from Unigine Heaven Benchmark. A limitation of our algorithm with respect to MSAA is the impossibility of recovering subpixel

---

[4]The increased memory cost in the Xbox 360 is due to the fact that two-channel render targets with 8-bit precision cannot be created in the framework we used for that platform, forcing the usage of a four-channel render target for storing the edges texture.

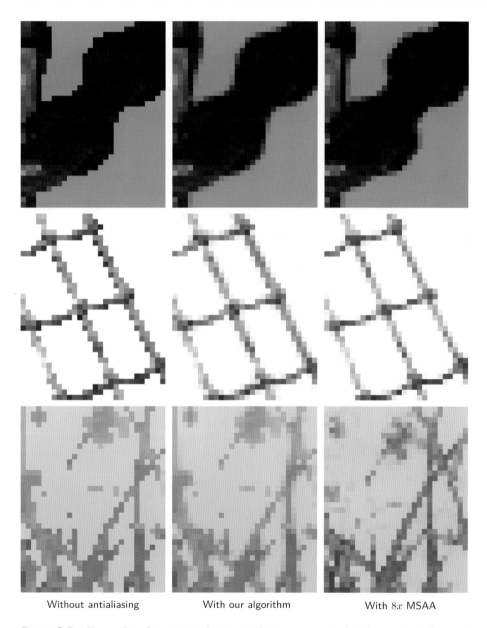

Without antialiasing   With our algorithm   With $8x$ MSAA

Figure 8.5. Examples of images without antialiasing, processed with our algorithm, and with $8x$ MSAA. Our algorithm offers similar results to those of $8x$ MSAA. A special case is the handling of alpha textures (bottom row). Note that in the grass shown here, alpha to coverage is used when MSAA is activated, which provides additional detail, hence the different look. As the scene is animated, there might be slight changes in appearance from one image to another. (Images from Unigine Heaven Benchmark courtesy of Unigine Corporation.)

Figure 8.6.   Images obtained with our algorithm. Insets show close-ups with no antialiasing at all (left) and processed with our technique (right). (Images from *Fable III* courtesy of Lionhead Studios.)

Figure 8.7. More images showing our technique in action. Insets show close-ups with no antialiasing at all (left) and processed with our technique (right). (Images from *Fable III* courtesy of Lionhead Studios.)

| | Xbox 360 | | GeForce 9800 GTX+ | | |
	Avg.	Std. Dev.	Avg.	Std. Dev.	Speed-up
Assassin's Creed	4.37 ms	0.61 ms	0.55 ms	0.13 ms	$6.31x^\star$
Bioshock	3.44 ms	0.09 ms	0.37 ms	0.00 ms	n/a
Crysis	3.92 ms	0.10 ms	0.44 ms	0.02 ms	$14.80x$
Dead Space	3.65 ms	0.45 ms	0.39 ms	0.03 ms	n/a
Devil May Cry 4	3.46 ms	0.34 ms	0.39 ms	0.04 ms	$5.75x$
GTA IV	4.11 ms	0.23 ms	0.47 ms	0.04 ms	n/a
Modern Warfare 2	4.38 ms	0.80 ms	0.57 ms	0.17 ms	$2.48x^\star$
NFS Shift	3.54 ms	0.35 ms	0.42 ms	0.04 ms	$14.84x$
Split/Second	3.85 ms	0.27 ms	0.46 ms	0.05 ms	n/a
S.T.A.L.K.E.R.	3.18 ms	0.05 ms	0.36 ms	0.01 ms	n/a
Grand Average	3.79 ms	0.33 ms	0.44 ms	0.05 ms	$11.80x$

Table 8.1. Average times and standard deviations for a set of well-known commercial games. A column showing the speed-up factor of our algorithm with respect to $8x$ MSAA is also included for the PC/DirectX 10 implementation. Values marked with * indicate $4x$ MSAA, since $8x$ was not available, and the grand average of these includes values only for $8x$ MSAA.

features. Further results of our technique, on images from *Fable III*, are shown in Figures 8.6 and 8.7. Results of our algorithm in-game are available in the web material.

As our algorithm works as a post-process, we have run it on a batch of screenshots of several commercial games in order to gain insight about its performance in different scenarios. Given the dependency of the edge detection on image content, processing times are variable. We have noticed that each game has a more or less unique "look-and-feel," so we have taken a representative sample of five screenshots per game. Screenshots were taken at 1280×720 as the typical case in the current generation of games. We used the slightly more expensive luminance-based edge detection, since we did not have access to depth information. Table 8.1 shows the average time and standard deviation of our algorithm on different games and platforms (Xbox 360/DirectX 9 and PC/DirectX 10), as well as the speed-up factor with respect to MSAA. On average, our method implies a speed-up factor of $11.80x$ with respect to $8x$ MSAA.

8.6   Discussion

This section includes a brief compilation of possible alternatives that we tried, in the hope that it would be useful for programmers employing this algorithm in the future.

Edges texture compression. This is perhaps the most obvious possible optimization, saving memory consumption and bandwidth. We tried two different alternatives: a) using 1 bit per edgel, and b) separating the algorithm into a vertical and a horizontal pass and storing the edges of four consecutive pixels in the RGBA channels of each pixel of the edges texture (vertical and horizontal edges separately). This has two advantages: first, the texture uses less memory; second, the number of texture accesses is lower since several edges are fetched in each query. However, storing the values and—to a greater extent—querying them later, becomes much more complex and time consuming, given that bitwise operations are not available in all platforms. Nevertheless, the use of bitwise operations in conjunction with edges texture compression could further optimize our technique in platforms where they are available, such as DirectX 10.

Storing crossing edges in the edges texture. Instead of storing just the north and west edges of the actual pixel, we tried storing the crossing edges situated at the left and at the top of the pixel. The main reason for doing this was that we could spare one texture access when detecting patterns; but we realized that by using bilinear filtering we could also spare the access, without the need to store those additional edges. The other reason for storing the crossing edges was that, by doing so, when we searched for distances to the ends of the line, we could stop the search when we encountered a line perpendicular to the one we were following, which is an inaccuracy of our approach. However, the current solution yields similar results, requires less memory, and processing time is lower.

Two-pass implementation. As mentioned in Section 8.1, a two-pass implementation is also possible, joining the last two passes into a single pass. However, this would be more inefficient because of the repetition of calculations.

Storing distances instead of areas. Our first implementation calculated and stored only the distances to the ends of the line in the second pass, and they were then used in the final pass to calculate the corresponding blending weights. However, directly storing areas in the intermediate pass allows us to spare calculations, reducing execution time.

8.7   Conclusion

In this chapter, we have presented an algorithm crafted for the computation of antialiasing. Our method is based on three passes that detect edges, determine the position of each pixel inside those image features, and produce an antialiased result that selectively blends the pixel with its neighborhood according to its relative position within the line it belongs to. We also take advantage of hardware texture filtering, which allows us to reduce the number of texture fetches by half.

Our technique features execution times that make it usable in actual game environments, and that are far shorter than those needed for MSAA. The method presented has a minimal impact on existing rendering pipelines and is entirely implemented as an image post-process. Resulting images are between $4x$ and

$8x$ MSAA in quality, while requiring a fraction of their time and memory consumption. Furthermore, it can antialias transparent textures such as the ones used in alpha testing for rendering vegetation, whereas MSAA can smooth vegetation only when using alpha to coverage. Finally, when using luminance values to detect edges, our technique can also handle aliasing belonging to shading and specular highlights.

The method we are presenting solves most of the drawbacks of MSAA, which is currently the most widely used solution to the problem of aliasing; the processing time of our method is one order of magnitude below that of $8x$ MSAA. We believe that the quality of the images produced by our algorithm, its speed, efficiency, and pluggability, make it a good choice for rendering high quality images in today's game architectures, including platforms where benefiting from antialiasing, together with outstanding techniques like deferred shading, was difficult to achieve. In summary, we present an algorithm which challenges the current gold standard for solving the aliasing problem in real time.

8.8   Acknowledgments

Jorge would like to dedicate this work to his eternal and most loyal friend Kazán. The authors would like to thank the colleagues at the lab for their valuable comments, and Christopher Oat and Wolfgang Engel for their editing efforts and help in obtaining images. Thanks also to Lionhead Studios and Microsoft Games Studios for granting permission to use images from *Fable III*. We are very grateful for the support and useful suggestions provided by the Fable team during the production of this work. We would also like to express our gratitude to Unigine Corporation, and Denis Shergin in particular, for providing us with images and material for the video (available in the web material) from their Unigine Heaven Benchmark. This research has been funded by a Marie Curie grant from the 7th Framework Programme (grant agreement no.: 251415), the Spanish Ministry of Science and Technology (TIN2010-21543) and the Gobierno de Aragón (projects OTRI 2009/0411 and CTPP05/09). Jorge Jimenez and Belen Masia are also funded by grants from the Gobierno de Aragón.

Bibliography

[Koonce 07] Rusty Koonce. "Deferred Shading in Tabula Rasa." In *GPU Gems 3*, pp. 429–457. Reading, MA: Addison Wesley, 2007.

[Reshetov 09] Alexander Reshetov. "Morphological Antialiasing." In *HPG '09: Proceedings of the Conference on High Performance Graphics 2009*, pp. 109–116. New York: ACM, 2009. Available online (http://visual-computing.intel-research.net/publications/papers/2009/mlaa/mlaa.pdf).

[Shishkovtsov 05] Oles Shishkovtsov. "Deferred Shading in S.T.A.L.K.E.R." In *GPU Gems 2*, pp. 143–166. Reading, MA: Addison Wesley, 2005.

[Sousa 07] Tiago Sousa. "Vegetation Procedural Animation and Shading in Crysis." In
     GPU Gems 3, pp. 373–385. Reading, MA: Addison Wesley, 2007.

[Thibieroz 09] Nicolas Thibieroz. "Deferred Shading with Multisampling Anti-Aliasing
     in DirectX 10." In *ShaderX^7*, pp. 225–242. Hingham, MA: Charles River Media,
     2009.

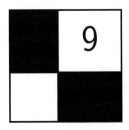

9

Volume Decals

Emil Persson

9.1 Introduction

Decals are often implemented as textured quads that are placed on top of the scene geometry. While this implementation works well enough in many cases, it can also provide some challenges. Using decals as textured quads can cause Z-fighting problems. The underlying geometry may not be flat, causing the decal to cut into the geometry below it. The decal may also overhang an edge, completely ruining its effect. Dealing with this problem often involves clipping the decal to the geometry or discarding it entirely upon detecting the issue. Alternatively, very complex code is needed to properly wrap the decal around arbitrary meshes, and access to vertex data is required. On a PC this could mean that system-memory copies of geometry are needed to maintain good performance. Furthermore, disturbing discontinuities can occur, as in the typical case of shooting a rocket into a corner and finding that only one of the walls got a decal or that the decals do not match up across the corner. This article proposes a technique that overcomes all of these challenges by projecting a decal volume onto the underlying scene geometry, using the depth buffer.

9.2 Decals as Volumes

9.2.1 Finding the Scene Position

The idea behind this technique is to render the decal as a volume around the selected area. Any convex volume shape can be used, but typical cases would be spheres and boxes. The fragment shader computes the position of the underlying geometry by sampling the depth buffer. This can be accomplished as follows:

```
// texCoord is the pixel's normalized screen position
float depth = DepthTex.Sample(Filter, texCoord);
float4 scrPos = float4(texCoord, depth, 1.0f);
float4 wPos = mul(scrPos, ScreenToWorld);
```

Figure 9.1. Example decal rendering.

```
float3 pos = wPos.xyz / wPos.w;
// pos now contains pixel position in world space
```

The `ScreenToWorld` matrix is a composite matrix of two transformations: namely the transformation from screen coordinates to clip space and then from clip space to world space. Transforming from world space to clip space is done with the regular `ViewProjection` matrix, so transforming in the other direction is done with the inverse of this matrix. Clip space ranges from -1 to 1 in x and y, whereas the provided texture coordinates are in the range of 0 to 1, so we also need an initial scale-bias operation baked into the matrix. The matrix construction code could look something like this:

```
float4 ScaleToWorld = Scale(2, -2, 1) *
    Translate(-1, 1, 0) * Inverse(ViewProj);
```

What we are really interested in, though, is the local position relative to the decal volume. The local position is used as a texture coordinate used to sample a volume texture containing a volumetric decal (see Figure 9.1). Since the decal is a volumetric texture, it properly wraps around nontrivial geometry with no discontinuities (see Figure 9.2). To give each decal a unique appearance, a random rotation can also be baked into the matrix for each decal. Since we do a matrix transformation we do not need to change the shader code other than to name the matrix more appropriately as `ScreenToLocal`, which is then constructed as follows:

Figure 9.2. Proper decal wrapping around nontrivial geometry.

```
float4 ScreenToLocal = Scale(2, -2, 1) *
    Translate(-1, 1, 0) * Inverse(ViewProj) *
    DecalTranslation * DecalScale * DecalRotation;
```

The full fragment shader for this technique is listed below and a sample with full source code is available in the web materials.

```
Texture2D <float> DepthTex;
SamplerState DepthFilter;

Texture3D <float4> DecalTex;
SamplerState DecalFilter;

cbuffer Constants
{
    float4x4 ScreenToLocal;
    float2 PixelSize;
};

float4 main(PsIn In) : SV_Target
{

    // Compute normalized screen position
    float2 texCoord = In.Position.xy * PixelSize;
```

```
    // Compute local position of scene geometry
    float depth = DepthTex.Sample(DepthFilter, texCoord);
    float4 scrPos = float4(texCoord, depth, 1.0f);
    float4 wPos = mul(scrPos, ScreenToLocal);

    // Sample decal
    float3 coord = wPos.xyz / wPos.w;
    return DecalTex.Sample(DecalFilter, coord);
}
```

Listing 9.1. The full fragment shader.

9.2.2 Implementation and Issues

In a deferred-rendering system [Thibieroz 04] this technique fits perfectly. The decals can be applied after the *geometry buffer* (G-buffer) pass and the relevant attributes, such as diffuse color and specularity, can simply be updated, and then lighting can be applied as usual. This technique also works well with a light prepass renderer [Engel 09], in which case lighting information is readily available for use in the decal pass.

In a forward rendering system the decals will be applied after lighting. In many cases this is effective also, for instance, for burn marks after explosions, in which case the decals can simply be modulated with the destination buffer. With more complicated situations, such as blending with alpha, as is typically the case for bullet holes, for instance, the decal application may have to take lighting into account. One solution is to store the overall lighting brightness into alpha while rendering the scene; the decal can then pre-multiply source color with alpha in the shader and multiply with destination alpha in the blender to get reasonable lighting. This will not take light color into account, but may look reasonable if lighting generally is fairly white. Another solution is to simply go by the attenuation of the closest light and not take any normal into account. Alternatively, a normal can be computed from the depth buffer, although this is typically slow and has issues of robustness [Persson 09].

One issue with this technique is that it applies the decal on everything within the decal volume. This is not a problem for static objects, but if you have a large decal volume and dynamic objects move into it they will get the decal smeared onto them, for instance, if you previously blew a bomb in the middle of the road and a car is passing through at a later time. This problem can be solved by drawing dynamic objects after the decal pass. A more elaborate solution is to render decals and dynamic objects in chronological order so that objects that are moved after the decal is added to the scene will not be affected by the decal. This will allow dynamic objects to be affected by decals as well. Another solution is to use object IDs. The decal can store the IDs of objects that intersected the decal volume at the time it was added to the scene and cull for discarded pixels that do not belong to any of those objects.

9.2.3 Optimizations

On platforms where the depth-bounds test is supported, the depth-bounds test can be used to improve performance. On other platforms, dynamic branching can be used to emulate this functionality by comparing the sample depth to the depth bounds. However, given that the shader is relatively short and typically a fairly large number of fragments survive the test, it is recommended to benchmark to verify that it actually improves performance. In some cases it may in fact be faster to not attempt to cull anything.

9.2.4 Variations

In some cases it is desirable to use a two-dimensional texture instead of a volume decal. Volume textures are difficult to author and consume more memory. Not all cases translate well from a two-dimensional case to three dimensions. A bullet hole decal can be swept around to a spherical shape in the three-dimensional case and can then be used in any orientation, but this is not possible for many kinds of decals; an obvious example is a decal containing text, such as a logo or graffiti tag.

An alternate technique is to sample a two-dimensional texture using just the x, y components of the final coordinates. The z component can be used for fading. When a volume texture is used, you can get an automatic fade in all directions by letting the texture alpha fade to zero toward the edges and using a border color with an alpha of zero. In the 2D case you will have to handle the z direction yourself.

Two-dimensional decals are not rotation invariant so when placing them in the scene they must be oriented such that they are projected sensibly over the underlying geometry. The simplest approach would be to just align the decal plane with the normal of the geometry at the decal's center point. Some problematic cases exist though, such as when wrapping over a corner of a wall. If it is placed flat against the wall you will get a perpendicular projection on the other side of the corner with undesirable texture-stretching as a result.

An interesting use of the two-dimensional case is to simulate a blast in a certain direction. This can be accomplished by using a pyramid or frustum shape from the point of the blast. When the game hero shoots a monster you place a frustum from the bullet-impact point on the monster to the wall behind it in the direction of the bullet and you will get the effect of blood and slime smearing onto the wall. The projection matrix of this frustum will have to be baked into the `ScreenToLocal` matrix to get the proper projection of the texture coordinates.

The blast technique can also be varied for a cube decal scenario. This would better simulate the effect of a grenade blast. In this case a cube or sphere would be rendered around the site of the blast and a cubemap lookup is performed with the final coordinates. Fading can be effected using the length of the coordinate vector.

To improve the blast effect you can use the normals of underlying geometry to eliminate the decal on back-facing geometry. For the best results, a shadowmapesque technique can be used to make sure only the surfaces closest to the front get smeared with the decal. This "blast-shadow map" typically has to be generated only once at the time of the blast and can then be used for the rest of the life of the decal. Using the blast-shadow map can ensure splatter happens only in the blast shadow of monsters and other explodable figures, whereas areas in the blast-shadow map that contain static geometry only get scorched. This requires storing a tag in the shadow buffer for pixels belonging to monsters, however. Creative use of the shadow map information also can be used to vary the blood-splatter intensity over the distance from the blast to the monster and from the monster to the smeared wall.

9.3   Conclusions

An alternate approach for decal rendering has been shown that suggests solutions to many problems of traditional decal-rendering techniques. Using volumes instead of flat decal geometry allows for continal decals across nontrivial geometry. It also eliminates potentially expensive buffer locks or the need for system-memory buffer copies.

Bibliography

[Thibieroz 04] Nicolas Thibieroz. "Deferred Shading with Multiple Render Targets." In *ShaderX^2: Shader Programming Tips and Tricks with DirectX 9*, edited by Wolfgang Engel, pp. 251–269. Plano, TX: Wordware Publishing, 2004.

[Engel 09] Wolfgang Engel. "Designing a Renderer for Multiple Lights - The Light Pre-Pass Renderer." In *ShaderX^7: Advanced Rendering Techniques*, edited by Wolfgang Engel, pp. 655–666. Hingham, MA: Charles River Media, 2009.

[Persson 09] Emil Persson. "Making It Large, Beautiful, Fast and Consistent: Lessons Learned Developing Just Cause 2." in *GPU Pro: Advanced Rendering Techniques*, pp. 571–596. Natick, MA: A K Peters, 2010.

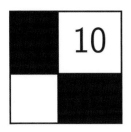

10

Practical Elliptical Texture
Filtering on the GPU

Pavlos Mavridis and Georgios Papaioannou

10.1 Introduction

Hardware texture filtering, even on state-of-the-art graphics hardware, suffers from several aliasing artifacts, in both the spatial and temporal domain. These artifacts are mostly evident in extreme conditions, such as grazing viewing angles, highly warped texture coordinates, or extreme perspective, and become especially annoying when animation is involved. Poor texture filtering is evident as excessive blurring or moiré patterns in the spatial domain and as pixel flickering in the temporal domain, as can be seen in Figure 10.1 and the accompanying demo application.

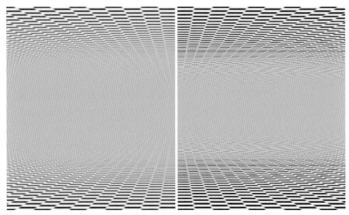

Figure 10.1. A benchmark scene consisting of two infinite planes demonstrating the improvement of elliptical filtering (left) over the native hardware texture filtering (right).

In this chapter, we present a series of simple and effective methods to perform high quality texture filtering on modern GPUs. We base our methods on the theory behind the elliptical weighted average (EWA) filter [Greene and Heckbert 86]. EWA is regarded as one of the highest quality texture filtering algorithms and is used as a benchmark to test the quality of other algorithms. It is often used in offline rendering to eliminate texture aliasing in the extreme conditions mentioned above, but due to the high computational cost it is not widely adopted in real-time graphics.

We first present an exact implementation of the EWA filter that smartly uses the underlying bilinear filtering hardware to gain a significant speedup. We then proceed with an approximation of the EWA filter that uses the underlying anisotropic filtering hardware of the GPU to construct a filter that closely matches the shape and the properties of the EWA filter, offering vast improvements in the quality of the texture mapping. To further accelerate the method, we also introduce a spatial and temporal sample distribution scheme that reduces the number of required texture fetches and the memory bandwidth consumption, without reducing the perceived image quality. We believe that those characteristics make our method practical for use in games and other interactive applications, as well as applications that require increased fidelity in texture mapping, like GPU renderers and image manipulation programs. We first described these methods at the 2011 Symposium on Interactive 3D Graphics and Games [Mavridis and Papaioannou 11]. This chapter reviews the main ideas of that paper with an emphasis on small, yet important implementation details.

10.2   Elliptical Filtering

This section provides an overview of the theory behind texture filtering and the elliptical weighted average (EWA) filter.

In computer graphics the pixels are point samples. The pixels do not have an actual shape, since they are points, but we often assign an area to them. This area is the footprint (the nonzero areas) of the filter that is used to reconstruct the final continuous image from these point samples, according to the sampling theorem. As discussed in [Smith 95], high quality reconstruction filters, like a truncated sinc or Gaussian, have a circular footprint, so a high quality texture filtering method should assume circular overlapping pixels.

The projection of a pixel with circular footprint to texture space is an ellipse with arbitrary orientation, as illustrated in Figure 10.2. In degenerate cases, like extreme grazing viewing angles, the projection is actually an arbitrary conic section, but for our purposes an elliptical approximation suffices, since, for these cases, any visible surface detail is lost anyway. A texture filtering algorithm should return a convolution of the texels (texture point samples) inside the projected area S of the pixel with the projection of the reconstruction filter H in

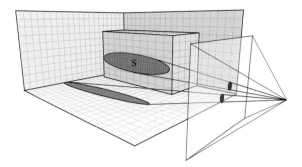

Figure 10.2. The projection of a pixel with circular footprint on a surface covers an elliptical region.

texture space. In particular, it should compute the following equation:

$$C_f(s,t) = \sum_{u,v \in S} H(u,v)C(u,v),$$

where $C(u,v)$ is the color of the texel at the (u,v) texture coordinates and $C_f(s,t)$ is the filtered texture color. In the above equation H is normalized.

The EWA algorithm approximates the projected pixel footprint with an elliptical region, defined by the following equation [Heckbert 89]:

$$d^2(u,v) = Au^2 + Buv + Cv^2,$$

where the center of the pixel is assumed to be at $(0,0)$ in texture space and

$$A = A_{nn}/F,$$
$$B = B_{nn}/F,$$
$$C = C_{nn}/F,$$
$$F = A_{nn}C_{nn} - B_{nn}^2/4,$$
$$A_{nn} = (\partial v/\partial x)^2 + (\partial v/\partial y)^2,$$
$$B_{nn} = -2 * (\partial u/\partial x * \partial v/\partial x + \partial u/\partial y * \partial v/\partial y),$$
$$C_{nn} = (\partial u/\partial x)^2 + (\partial u/\partial y)^2.$$

The partial derivatives $(\partial u/\partial x, \partial u/\partial y, \partial v/\partial x, \partial v/\partial y)$ represent the rate of change of the texture coordinates relative to changes in screen space. The quantity d^2 denotes the squared distance of the texel (u,v) from the pixel center when projected back into screen space. The algorithm scans the bounding box of the elliptical region in texture space and determines which texels reside inside the ellipse $(d^2 \leq 1)$. These samples contribute to the convolution sum, with weights

```
// Computes the Elliptical Weighted Average filter
// p are the sampling coordinates
// du/dv are the derivatives of the texture coordinates
vec4 ewaFilter(sampler2D tex, vec2 p, vec2 du, vec2 dv)
{
  // compute ellipse coefficients A, B, C, F:
  float A,B,C,F;
  A = du.t*du.t+dv.t*dv.t+1;
  ...

  // Compute the ellipse's bounding box in texture space
  int u_min, u_max, v_min, v_max;
  u_min = int(floor(p.s - 2. / (-B*B+4.0*C*A)*
          sqrt((-B*B+4.0*C*A)*C*F)));
  ...

  // Iterate over the ellipse's bounding box and
  // calculate Ax^2+Bxy*Cy^2; when this value
  // is less than F, we're inside the ellipse.
  vec4 color = 0;
  float den = 0;
  for (int v = v_min; v <= v_max; ++v)
  {
    float q = A*u*u+B*u*v*C*v*v;
    for (int u = u_min; u <= u_max; ++u)
      if (q < F)
      {
        float d = q / F;
        float weight = Filter(d);
        color += weight* texture2D(tex, vec2(u+0.5,v+0.5)/size);
        den += weight;
      }
  }

  return color*(1./den);
}
```

Listing 10.1. Pseudocode implementation of the EWA filter.

proportional to the distance d. Listing 10.1 outlines this idea. `Filter(d)` denotes the reconstruction filter. [Greene and Heckbert 86] propose the usage of a Gaussian filter, but in practice any reconstruction filter can be used.

10.2.1 Bounding the Runtime Cost

The runtime of the brute-force algorithm is directly proportional to the area of the ellipse in texture space and the number of texels it includes. To reduce the number of the texture samples in this area, a mip-map pyramid is used and sampling is performed from the mip-map level in which the minor ellipse radius is between one and three pixels, depending on the required quality and performance. Even when using mip-maps, the area of a highly eccentric ellipse can be arbitrarily

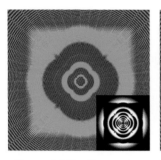 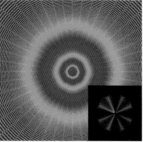 

Figure 10.3. Comparison of the lod calculation of an Nvidia Fermi card when using the lowest quality settings in the drivers (left), the highest possible quality settings (middle), and the optimal lod calculations (right).

high, resulting in unacceptably long running times. To avoid this, the maximum eccentricity of the ellipse is clamped to a predefined maximum. Taking these two measures ensures a bounded runtime for the algorithm.

Computing the mip-map level (lod) and clamping ellipses with high eccentricity requires the computation of the minor (R_{minor}) and major (R_{major}) radius of the ellipse

$$r = \sqrt{(A - C)^2 + B^2},$$
$$R_{\mathrm{major}} = \sqrt{2/(A + C - r)},$$
$$R_{\mathrm{minor}} = \sqrt{2/(A + C + r)},$$
$$\mathrm{lod} = \log_2(R_{\mathrm{minor}}/\text{texels-per-pixel.}) \tag{10.1}$$

Instead of computing the lod level based on the minor ellipse radius, we have investigated the option to use the lod values calculated explicitly by the hardware. On newer hardware this can be done using the appropriate shading language function (`textureQueryLOD()` in GLSL), or in older hardware by fetching a texel from a texture with color-coded lod levels. Figure 10.3 visualizes the lod selection on the latest Nvidia graphics cards and compares it with the ideal lod selection based on the ellipse minor radius. We observe that Nvidia's hardware, at the highest quality settings, performs a piecewise approximation of the optimal calculations, resulting in suboptimal lod selection on pixels depending on their angle and that the measured deviation (shown in the insets of Figure 10.3) peaks at intervals of 45 degrees. An overestimation of the lod level will result in excessive blurriness, while underestimation will result in longer runtimes. In practice, we have observed that using the hardware lod calculations does not result in visible quality degradation, while the performance of the method is increased.

Hardware trilinear filtering interpolates between the closest two lod levels, in order to avoid discontinuities. We have found that it is much more preferable to perform better filtering in the high detail lod level (by using more samples), than to compute two inferior estimates and interpolate between them. In that case, discontinuities from the lod selection can only be observed in very extreme cases, and even then can be dealt with using more projected texels in each pixel (Equation (10.1)).

10.2.2   Filtering sRGB Textures

A very important implementation detail that is often omitted, is that all the texture filtering and antialiasing operations should be done in linear color space. On the other hand, 8 bits-per-component textures are usually stored in sRGB color space, in order to better take advantage of the available precision, by taking into account the characteristics of human vision. Therefore, the texture data should be first converted to a linear color space before the filtering operations. And, after the shading operations, colors should be converted back to sRGB for display in the output device. Fortunately, the latest graphics hardware can do this conversion using specialized fixed-function hardware, without any additional overhead. In OpenGL in particular, this can be done by using the `GL_EXT_texture_sRGB` and `GL_EXT_framebuffer_sRGB` extensions, while Direct3D provides similar mechanisms. Furthermore, all the prefiltered mip-maps should also be computed in linear color space. The importance of filtering in the proper color space is demonstrated in Figure 10.4. (All the images in this chapter were produced with filtering in linear color space.)

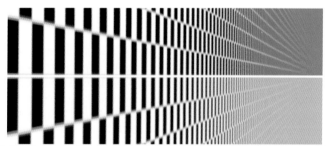

Figure 10.4. Texture filtering using mip-maps computed in sRGB color space (top). Proper filtering in linear color space (bottom). Filtering in nonlinear color space leads to incorrect darkening when the lowest mip-map levels are used.

10.2.3   GPU Optimizations

A naïve direct implementation of the EWA filter on the GPU would read every texel in the bounding box of the elliptical region, and if it were located inside the ellipse, it would be weighted and accumulated. A much better approach is to use the linear filtering of the graphics hardware to reduce the number of fetches to one half, by smartly fetching two texels at a time using one bilinear fetch. For two neighboring texels C_i and C_{i+1}, with weights w_i and w_{i+1}, respectively, the following weighted sum can be replaced by a single bilinear texture fetch operation at position x between the two texel centers:

$$w_i C_i + w_{i+1} C_{i+1} = C_x (w_i + w_{i+1}),$$
$$x = i + \frac{w_{i+1}}{w_i + w_{i+1}},$$
$$0 \le \frac{w_{i+1}}{w_i + w_{i+1}} \le 1.$$

The last inequality is always true for reconstruction filters with positive weights, like the Gaussian one. In our case, the texel weight w_i is derived from the reconstruction filter (`Filter(d)` in Listing 10.1) and the distance d of the texel to the filter center, as explained in Section 10.2. The for loop in Listing 10.1 should be adjusted to process two texels at a time. An important implementation detail is that when using this technique, we should take into account the exact coordinates of the texel centers. In the case of OpenGL, texel centers are assumed to be at the centers of a grid (meaning that texels are located at coordinates integer$+0.5$).

This technique assumes that the cost of one texture fetch with bilinear filtering is less than the cost of two fetches with point sampling plus the time to combine them. Our experiments confirm that this assumption is true. The results from this method should be identical with the ones from the reference implementation, but slight deviations may occur due to the difference in the precision in which operations are performed by the shader units and by the fixed-function bilinear filtering units.

Extending the same principle in two dimensions, we can replace four weighted texture fetches with a single fetch from the appropriate position. While it is trivial to find this position in the case of a box filter, in the case of a Gaussian filter the weights can only be approximated. In other words, we can calculate the position that best approximates the Gaussian weights and perform a single texture fetch from that position. In practice we did not observe any significant performance gain from this method, while on the other hand it imposes significant constraints on the nature of the reconstruction filters that can be used.

10.3 Elliptical Footprint Approximation

In the same spirit as the Feline algorithm [McCormack et al. 99], we present a method that uses simpler shapes to closely match the shape of the ideal elliptical filter. Instead of using simple trilinear probes like in the Feline algorithm, we propose the usage of the anisotropic probes provided by the graphics hardware.

We place the probes on a line along the major axis of the ellipse, as shown in Figure 10.5. The length of the line L and the number of probes N_{probes} are given

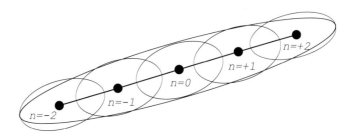

Figure 10.5. The basic idea of our method: approximating a highly eccentric ellipse with many ellipses of low eccentricity. This way we can overcome the limits imposed by the hardware and better filter elliptical footprints with high degrees of anisotropy.

by the following equations

$$N_{\text{probes}} = 2 * (R_{\text{major}}/(\alpha * R_{\text{minor}})) - 1,$$
$$L = 2 * (R_{\text{major}} - \alpha * R_{\text{minor}}), \tag{10.2}$$

where α is the degree of anisotropy of the underlying hardware probes. For $\alpha = 1$ our algorithm is equivalent to Feline. For simplicity, an odd number of probes is considered. Similar to Feline, probes are placed around the midpoint (u_m, v_m) of the filter, as follows:

$$\theta = \text{atan}(B/(A - C))/2,$$
$$du = \cos(\theta) * L/(N_{\text{probes}} - 1),$$
$$dv = \sin(\theta) * L/(N_{\text{probes}} - 1),$$
$$(u_n, v_n) = (u_m, v_m) + n/2 * (du, dv), \quad n = 0, \pm 2, \pm 4 \ldots, \tag{10.3}$$

where (u_n, v_n) is the position of n-th probe. To better match the shape of the EWA filter, the probes are weighted proportionally to their distance from the center of the footprint, according to a Gaussian function. The shape of the filter in texture space compared to an exact EWA filter is shown in Figure 10.6.

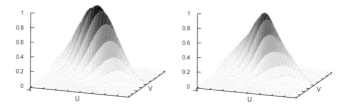

Figure 10.6. Comparison of the exact EWA filter (left) with our approximation using three elliptical probes (right).

We don't have any strong guarantees about the quality or the shape of those probes, since the OpenGL specification does not explicitly enforce any particular method for anisotropic filtering. The only hint given by the hardware implementation is that the probes approximate an anisotropic area with maximum anisotropy of N. In the above analysis, we have assumed that the hardware anisotropic probes are elliptical, but in practice, to compensate for their potential imperfections in shape and to better cover the area of the elliptical filter, we just increase the number of probes depending on the desired quality. Using an adaptive number of probes creates an irregular workload per pixel for the graphics hardware scheduler, which should be avoided. In practice, setting the number of probes to a constant number gives better performance. In our tests, using five probes eliminated all the visible artifacts on the Nvidia hardware (with high quality texture filtering enabled). For more than five probes, no significant improvement in image quality could be measured.

If the probes fail to cover the ellipse, then aliasing will occur. On the other hand, if the probes exceed the extents of the ellipse (e.g., by placing them beyond half the length of the central line in each direction) then blurring will occur. Our method always avoids the second case, but the first case can still happen in extreme cases, since we have clamped the maximum number of probes. Still, our method always provides an improvement over hardware texture filtering.

10.3.1 Spatial Filter

After some investigation of the benchmark scenes, we have observed that the regions where the hardware filtering fails are limited. For the majority of a scene, the quality of the image is free of any aliasing artifacts. As expected, the problematic regions are regions with high anisotropy, and, in particular, on the

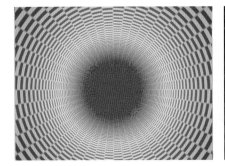

Figure 10.7. Regions in red denote areas with anisotropy greater than 16, the limit in current hardware implementations. An infinite tunnel benchmark scene (left). A typical game scene (right).

Nvidia hardware, regions with anisotropy greater than 16, which is the advertised maximum anisotropy of the hardware unit. Figure 10.7 highlights the problematic regions on the benchmark scene and one typical game scene.

After this observation, we perform high-quality filtering only in the regions highlighted with red, and for the rest of the scene we use hardware filtering. The anisotropy of a pixel is accurately measured using Equations (10.1). To eliminate any visible seams between the two regions, areas close to the threshold level use a blend of hardware and software filtering. This approach creates exactly two different workloads for the hardware, one high and one low. In the majority of cases, the two different sampling methods are used in spatially coherent pixel clusters within a frame. Therefore, compared to a completely adaptive sample selection, our tests indicate that this case is handled more efficiently by the GPU hardware scheduler and results in a sizable performance gain.

10.3.2 Temporal Sample Distribution

In order to further improve the runtime performance of our filtering algorithm in games and other real-time applications that display many rendered images at high frame rates, we present a temporal sample distribution scheme, where texture filtering samples are distributed among successive frames.

In particular, the n anisotropic samples (probes) of Equation (10.3) are distributed in two successive frames. The first frame uses samples $0, \pm 4, \pm 8 \ldots$ and the next one $0, \pm 2, \pm 6 \ldots$. The sample at the center of the filter (sample 0) is included in both frames to minimize the variance between the two. When the frames are displayed in quick succession, the human eye perceives the average of the two frames.

For this technique to work, the application should maintain a stable and vertical sync-locked frame rate of 60 Hz or more. The usage of vertical sync is mandatory; otherwise the rate of the rendered frames will not match the rate at which they are displayed and are perceived by the human eye, and the method naturally fails. This is a shortcoming, but we should note that in the era of high-performing graphics hardware, rendering without vertical sync makes little sense, since it introduces visible tearing. Obviously the method can be extended to distribute samples in more than two frames when the refresh rate of the application and the output device is high enough.

Using this method, the quality of texture filtering is enhanced considerably for static or distant objects, but fast-moving objects receive fewer samples. This is hardly objectionable, since in that case potential aliasing artifacts are difficult to notice. In our tests, the usage of temporal sample distribution always improved the perceived image quality for a given number of samples.

Overall, this temporal method is very simple to implement, does not require additional memory, and always provides a constant speedup. The obvious shortcoming is that the application should maintain a high frame rate. The success of the method is also highly dependent on the ability of the output device to be synchronized with the graphics hardware. We had great success when using PC monitors, but some projection equipment might fail in the synchronization with the graphics hardware.

10.4 Results

Figure 10.8 demonstrates the improvement our method produces in a benchmark scene consisting of an infinite tunnel with a checkerboard texture. To better assess the extent of the improvement, the reader is highly encouraged to run the accompanying demo application, since the aliasing artifacts are highly objectionable in motion. The same figure also shows the resulting filtering from all the filtering methods we have presented in this chapter.

Figure 10.9 demonstrates the improvement from increasing the maximum degrees of anisotropy. A higher maximum degree of anisotropy offers more detail at grazing angles. We observe that direct convolution filtering with an anisotropic ratio of 64:1 preserves more detail at the center of the tunnel. An ideal filtering algorithm would show the lines to converge at the center of the left image,

Figure 10.8. Top: A benchmark scene consisting of an infinite tunnel demonstrating the improvement of elliptical filtering (left) over the native hardware texture filtering (right). Close-up comparisons of the various texture filtering methods (bottom). From left to right: hardware filtering, elliptical, approximated filter, spatial filter, temporal filter (average of two frames).

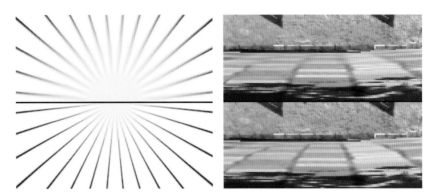

Figure 10.9. Close-ups demonstrating the improved clarity when increasing the maximum degrees of anisotropy from 16 (up) to 64 (down).

but in practice this is very difficult because an infinite anisotropy level would be required. Apart from the increased clarity, in practice we also observe that the elliptical filtering eliminates the occasional pixel flickering (temporal aliasing) of the hardware implementation.

10.4.1 Performance Measurements

Figure 10.10 presents comprehensive performance and quality measurements for all the methods presented in this chapter. The spatial and temporal sample distribution schemes can be used to accelerate both the direct convolution methods and the ellipse approximation method, but since we are interested in the highest possible performance, we only present results when distributing the samples of the ellipse approximation method. The performance of the method was mea-

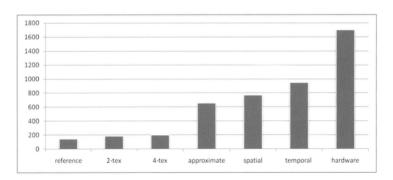

Figure 10.10. The performance of the methods presented in this chapter measured in Mtexes/sec on an Nvidia GTX460.

sured on the tunnel scene of the accompanying demo application on a middle range graphics card. We observe that the direct convolution methods (reference, 2-tex, 4-tex) are an order of magnitude slower than the approximating ones, making their applicability for real-time applications rather limited.

10.4.2 Integration with Game Engines

The proposed texture filtering algorithms can be implemented as a direct replacement to the built-in texture lookup functions, making the integration with game engines trivial. In the accompanying material of this book, we provide our proof-of-concept implementation in GLSL. In the case of temporal filtering, the current frame number should be exposed inside the shaders. One integration option is to globally replace all the texturing function calls with the enhanced ones, but this method is probably an overkill. Alternatively, at content-creation time, the enhanced texture filtering could selectively be applied only on certain problematic surfaces. The second option can lead to better runtime performance, but at the cost of increased authoring time.

10.5 Conclusions

We have shown that high-quality elliptical filtering is practical on today's GPUs, by employing several methods to speed up the reference algorithm. Texture filtering quality is one issue that separates the offline production rendering from the real-time one, and this work can provide a viable texture filtering improvement for hardware-accelerated rendering applications.

10.6 Acknowledgments

The authors would like to thank Matt Pharr for providing a sample CPU implementation of the EWA filter on his website, which was a starting point for this project, and Inigo Quilez for providing the GLSL code to ray-trace the infinite plane and tunnel test scenes, as part of Shader Toy.

Bibliography

[Greene and Heckbert 86] Ned Greene and Paul S. Heckbert. "Creating Raster Omnimax Images from Multiple Perspective Views Using the Elliptical Weighted Average Filter." *IEEE Comput. Graph. Appl.* 6:6 (1986), 21–27.

[Heckbert 89] Paul S. Heckbert. "Fundamentals of texture mapping and image warping." Technical Report UCB/CSD-89-516, EECS Department, University of California, Berkeley, 1989.

[Mavridis and Papaioannou 11] Pavlos Mavridis and Georgios Papaioannou. "High Quality Elliptical Texture Filtering on GPU." In *Symposium on Interactive 3D Graphics and Games, I3D '11*, pp. 23–30. New York: ACM Press, 2011.

[McCormack et al. 99] Joel McCormack, Ronald Perry, Keith I. Farkas, and Norman P. Jouppi. "Feline: Fast Elliptical Lines for Anisotropic Texture Mapping." In *Proceedings of SIGGRAPH '99, Proceedings, Annual Conference Series*, edited by Alyn Rockwood, pp. 243–250. Reading, MA: ACM Press/Addison-Wesley Publishing, 1999.

[Smith 95] Alvy Ray Smith. "A pixel is not a little square, a pixel is not a little square, a pixel is not a little square! (And a voxel is not a little cube)." Technical report, Technical Memo 6, Microsoft Research, 1995.

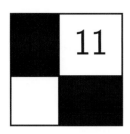

11

An Approximation to the Chapman Grazing-Incidence Function for Atmospheric Scattering

Christian Schüler

11.1 Introduction

Atmospheric scattering for computer graphics is the treatment of the atmosphere as a participating medium, essentially "calculating the color of the sky." This is interesting for any application where the time of day, the season, or the properties of the atmosphere are not known in advance, or the viewpoint may not be restricted to a point on the earth's surface. It is a historically difficult effect to render, especially at planetary scale.

Early attempts at atmospheric scattering can be found in [Klassen 87] and [Nishita et al. 93]. Recent implementations with an emphasis on real time are [Hoffmann and Preetham 02], [O'Neil 05], and [Bruneton and Neyret 08]. A common theme of all these approaches is finding ways to efficiently evaluate or precompute the Chapman function, $\mathrm{Ch}(x, \chi)$. This is the density integral for a ray in a spherically symmetric, exponentially decreasing atmosphere.

The Chapman function has been subject to extensive treatment in the physics literature. Approximations and tabulations have been published, most of it with a focus on precision. This article explores a different direction for its evaluation: an approximation so cheap that $\mathrm{Ch}(x, \chi)$ can be considered a commodity, while still being accurate enough for our graphics needs.

11.2 Atmospheric Scattering

This section is a brief review of atmospheric scattering and a definition of terms.

When light travels through air, it will be partly absorbed and partly scattered into other directions. This gives rise to the phenomenon of *aerial perspective*. The

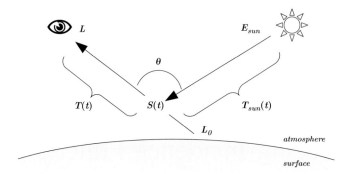

Figure 11.1. Atmospheric scattering 101. See the text for an explanation of the symbols.

fraction of light that is unimpeded along a path is the transmittance T, and the amount that is added into the path due to scattering is the in-scatter S (see Figure 11.1). Thus, the aerial perspective of a distant source of radiance L_0 is seen by an observer as the radiance L:

$$L \;=\; L_0\,T + S.$$

To arrive at the total in-scatter S, in general one would have to integrate it along the path. Then, the in-scatter at a particular point $S(t)$ would have to be calculated from the local irradiance field E over the entire sphere of directions Ω with an atmosphere-dependent phase function $f(\theta)$:

$$S \;=\; \int S(t)\,T(t)\,dt,$$
$$S(t) \;=\; \int_\Omega E(t)\,f(\theta)\,d\Omega.$$

The irradiance is usually discretized as a sum of individual contributions. Especially during the day, the single most important contributor is the sun, which can be simplified to a directional point source E_{sun}, for the irradiance arriving at the outer atmosphere boundary; E_{sun} is attenuated by the transmittance T_{sun} for the path from the atmosphere boundary towards point $S(t)$:

$$S(t) \;=\; E_{\text{sun}}\,T_{\text{sun}}(t)\,f(\theta).$$

The transmittance itself is an exponentially decreasing function of the airmass m times an extinction coefficient β. The latter is a property of the scattering medium, possibly wavelength dependent. The airmass is an integral of the air density $\rho(t)$ along the path:

$$T = \exp\left(-\beta m\right),$$
$$m = \int \rho(t)dt.$$

To complete the calculation, we need a physical model for β and f. There exists Rayleigh theory and Mie theory, which have been discussed in depth in previous publications, e.g., [Nishita et al. 93] and [Hoffmann and Preetham 02]. It is beyond the scope of this article to provide more detail here.

11.3   The Chapman Function

In order to reduce the algorithmic complexity, it would be nice to have an efficient way to calculate transmittances along rays. It turns out that this reduces to an evaluation of the Chapman function.

Without loss of generality, let's start a ray at an observer inside the atmosphere and extend it to infinity (see Figure 11.2). The ray can be traced back to a point of lowest altitude r_0. We take the liberty to call this point the *periapsis* even though the path is not an orbit. Here we define $t = 0$, and the altitude for any point along the ray as follows:

$$r(t) = \sqrt{r_0^2 + t^2}.$$

Let's further assume a spherically symmetric atmosphere with an exponentially decreasing density, characterized by a scale height H. We normalize the

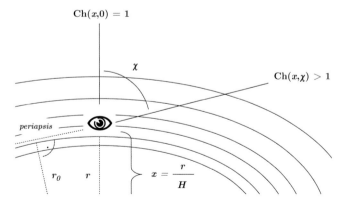

Figure 11.2. The Chapman function. Relative airmass in an exponentially decreasing atmosphere with scale height H, normalized observer altitude x and incidence angle χ. The lowest altitude is at r_0.

density to a reference density ρ_0 at reference altitude R. The density at any altitude is then

$$\rho(r) \;=\; \rho_0 \, \exp\left(\frac{R-r}{H}\right).$$

Combining these expressions yields an integral for the airmass along the entire ray. The integration boundary is trigonometrically related to the observer altitude r and the incidence angle χ:

$$m \;=\; \rho_0 \int_{r\cos\chi}^{\infty} \exp\left(\frac{R-\sqrt{r_0^2+t^2}}{H}\right) dt,$$

$$r_0 \;=\; r\sin\chi.$$

This integral does not have a simple solution, except when looking straight upwards into the zenith ($\chi = 0$). In this case, the mass along the ray is just the mass of the air column above the observer. This is, by the definition of the density distribution, one scale height times the density at the observer. Let's call that mass $m_\perp$:

$$m_\perp \;=\; \rho_0 \, H \exp\left(\frac{R-r}{H}\right).$$

Can we possibly have a function that relates $m_\perp$ to m? We can, for this is the Chapman function $\mathrm{Ch}(x,\chi)$, named after the physicist who was the first to formulate this problem [Chapman 31]. We write the Chapman function as follows:

$$m \;=\; m_\perp \, \mathrm{Ch}(x,\chi),$$

with

$$x \;=\; \frac{r}{H}.$$

The arguments are historically named x for normalized altitude and the Greek letter chi for incidence angle (don't blame me for that). The function is independent of scale and is usually tabulated or approximated numerically. For convenience, an analytic expression is given below. This has been stripped down from a more general solution found in [Kocifaj 96]:

$$\mathrm{Ch}(x,\chi) = \frac{1}{2}\left[\cos(\chi)+\right.$$

$$\left. + \exp\left(\frac{x\cos^2\chi}{2}\right) \mathrm{erfc}\left(\sqrt{\frac{x\cos^2\chi}{2}}\right)\left(\frac{1}{x}+2-\cos^2\chi\right)\sqrt{\frac{\pi x}{2}}\right].$$

The above expression is not practical for real-time evaluation, for several reasons: it contains the complementary error function, erfc, which needs a numerical approximation for itself. It has bad numerical behavior for large x and small χ, where the exp-term becomes very large and the erfc-term virtually zero. We use this expression, however, as our ground-truth standard, evaluated with arbitrary precision math software.

11.4 Towards a Real-Time Approximation

To better understand the Chapman function, we will plot a graph of it (see Figure 11.3) and observe a number of important properties:

$$\text{The function is even wrt. } \chi; \qquad \text{Ch}(x,\chi) = \text{Ch}(x,-\chi).$$
$$\text{There is unity at } \chi = 0; \qquad \text{Ch}(x,0) = 1.$$
$$\text{There is a limit for large } x; \qquad \lim_{x \to \infty} \text{Ch}(x,\chi) = \frac{1}{\cos \chi}.$$

These properties are easily explained. The even symmetry follows from the problem specification. Only the cosine of the incidence angle appears in the expression. This allows us to reduce the covered range to $0 < \chi < 180°$. Second, since $\text{Ch}(x,\chi)$ relates $m_\perp$ to m, its value must approach unity for small incidence angles. And finally, in the limit of a flat earth, the Chapman function must approach the secant function.

These properties can be used to engineer our approximation, Ch'. The limit for large x suggests a rational approximation, as we are going to cope with a pole. Runtime efficiency demands the lowest possible order. So we are going to

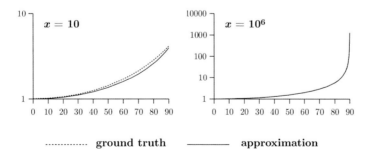

Figure 11.3. Graph of the Chapman function. $\text{Ch}(x,\chi)$ is plotted on a logarithmic scale as a function of incidence angle χ, for two extreme cases of x. An observer on the earth's surface with an atmosphere scale height of 8.4 km would correspond to an x of $r_\oplus/8.4 \simeq 760$.

look for a first-order rational function of $\cos \chi$, approaching unity on the left and the value of $\mathrm{Ch}_{\parallel}(x)$ on the right, where $\mathrm{Ch}_{\parallel}(x)$ is used as a shorthand for the Chapman function evaluated at $\chi = 90°$. There is only one possibility for such a rational function:

$$\mathrm{Ch}'(c, \chi) \quad = \quad \frac{c}{(c-1)\cos(\chi)+1} \qquad \Big| \; |\chi| < 90°,$$

with

$$c \quad = \quad \mathrm{Ch}_{\parallel}(x).$$

As it turns out, this low-order function is a pretty good approximation. The useful range for χ is, however, limited to below $90°$. Beyond that angle, the approximation grows hyperbolically to a pole at infinity, while the exact Chapman function grows exponentially, and always stays finite. We will look for ways to handle $\chi > 90°$, but we must first turn our attention to the coefficient c.

11.4.1 At the Horizon

If the observer altitude is fixed, we could precalculate a value for c. However, for a moving observer, and in the absence of a Chapman function to fall back on, we need an approximation for c itself. Let's take a look at $\mathrm{Ch}_{\parallel}(x)$:

$$\mathrm{Ch}_{\parallel}(x) \quad = \quad \left(\frac{1}{2x}+1\right)\sqrt{\frac{\pi x}{2}}.$$

This is already a lot simpler than the full Chapman function, but still requires a square root and a division. To simplify it further, we assume that x is usually large and neglect the term $1/2x$ to get a function that is purely proportional to $\sqrt{x}$. Using the value $\sqrt{\pi/2} \simeq 1.2533$ as a coefficient results in

$$\mathrm{Ch}_{\parallel}(x) \quad \simeq \quad 1.2533\sqrt{x} \qquad \big| \; x > 10.$$

11.4.2 Beyond the Horizon

Consider Figure 11.4. The airmass m_L along an entire line is the airmass along the forward ray plus the airmass along the backward ray:

$$m_L \quad = \quad \rho\Big[\mathrm{Ch}(x, \chi) + \mathrm{Ch}(x, 180° - \chi)\Big].$$

The above equation must be true for any point along the line. We can move the observer to the periapsis, where both the forward and the backward ray are horizontal. Using trigonometry, the altitude at the periapsis is $x_0 = x \sin \chi$ and density follows as $\rho \exp(x - x_0)$. Another way of expressing m_L is therefore

$$m_L \quad = \quad 2\rho \exp(x - x_0)\,\mathrm{Ch}_{\parallel}(x_0).$$

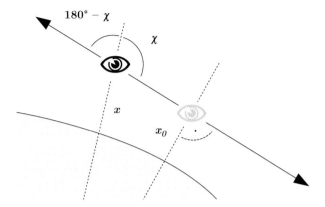

Figure 11.4. Airmass along an entire line. A virtual observer is placed at the periapsis.

Combining the above equations, it is possible to arrive at an identity that expresses the Chapman function in terms of itself with a reflected incidence angle:

$$\text{Ch}(x, \chi) = 2 \exp(x - x \sin \chi) \, \text{Ch}_{\parallel}(x \sin \chi) - \text{Ch}(x, 180° - \chi).$$

If the Chapman function is known for $0 < \chi < 90°$, it is therefore known for all χ.

11.5 Implementation

See Listing 11.1 for an implementation of the approximate Chapman function in C. It consists of a branch on the value of χ, either applying the identity or not. The code differs from the mathematical formulae in three aspects, which are discussed in Sections 11.5.1–11.5.3.

11.5.1 Numeric Range

First, a numeric range problem must be resolved, which happens when x is large and x_0 is small. The identity formula contains the exponential $\exp(x - x_0)$, which overflows. To remedy this situation, we introduce a modified function $\text{Ch}_{\text{h}}(X, h, \chi)$:

$$\text{Ch}_{\text{h}}(X, h, \chi) = \text{Ch}(X + h, \chi) \exp(-h).$$

This function takes a reference altitude X and the corresponding observer height h, and includes the factor $\exp(-h)$. This factor would have to be applied anyway to calculate the airmass. By including it in the function, the range problem cancels out, since $\exp(x - x_0) \exp(-h) = \exp(X - x_0)$.

```
float chapman_h( float X, float h, float coschi )
{
    // The approximate Chapman function
    // Ch(X+h,chi) times exp2(-h)
    // X - altitude of unit density
    // h - observer altitude relative to X
    // coschi - cosine of incidence angle chi
    // X and h are given units of the 50%-height

    float c = sqrt( X + h );
    if( coschi >= 0. )
    {
        // chi above horizon
        return c / ( c * coschi + 1. ) * exp2( -h );
    }
    else
    {
        // chi below horizon, must use identity
        float x0 = sqrt( 1. - coschi * coschi ) * ( X + h );
        float c0 = sqrt( x0 );
        return
            2. * c0 * exp2( X - x0 ) -
            c / ( 1. - c * coschi ) * exp2( -h );
    }
}
```

Listing 11.1. The approximate Chapman function in C, with modifications discussed in the text.

11.5.2   Distance Differences

The second modification relates to the ability of the approximation to stay faithful to sums and differences of path lengths. Special attention is drawn to the case of an observer who is close above a reflective surface. Consider Figure 11.5. Assuming near-horizontal angles, the airmasses m_A, m_B, and m_C for the three segments can be simplified to

$$
\begin{aligned}
m_A &\sim \text{Ch}(x, \chi), \\
m_B &\sim \text{Ch}(x, 180° - \chi) - \text{Ch}(x', 180° - \chi), \\
m_C &\sim \text{Ch}(x', \chi).
\end{aligned}
$$

The question is now, does the approximation satisfy $m_A = m_B + m_C$? This would be required for an exact color match at the horizon above a water surface. The short answer is that the original approximation does not hold for this property. The form of the denominator in the rational function, as well as the factor 1.2533, stand in the way. The approximation must be rigged to enable this

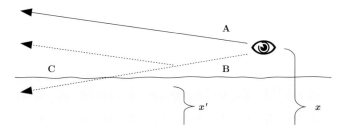

Figure 11.5. The Chapman function on a reflected ray. Is the approximation going to stay true to sums and differences of path lengths?

property; this new approximation is even simpler:

$$\mathrm{Ch}'(c, \chi) = \frac{c}{c\cos(\chi) + 1},$$

with

$$c = \sqrt{x}.$$

Dropping the factor of 1.2533 hardly makes a difference in the visual result. The change in the denominator is more severe, causing the approximation to fall below unity for small incidence angles. However, for typical uses with x well in the hundreds, the visual impact is again negligible. If needed, the loss can be compensated by an increase of the β-coefficients.

11.5.3 Using exp2

The code will make exclusive use of the dual exponential 2^x instead of the natural exponential e^x. We will therefore need all scales converted to the dual logarithm. We need a 50%-height H_{50} instead of the scale height H; we need 50%-extinction coefficients, and so on:

$$H_{50} = H \ln 2,$$
$$\beta_{50} = \beta \ln 2,$$
$$\dots$$

The reason for this change is that exp2 is usually the more efficient function to compute. To optimize even more, an implementation can employ a fast exp2 function for all scattering calculations. An example of such a fast exp2 function is presented in the appendix (Section 11.8). It is a definitive win when the calculation is CPU-based, especially if it is vectorized with SIMD, calculating four values at once. On the GPU, there have been assembly instructions for a fast version (called exp2pp for "partial precision") or the shader compiler takes it as a hint if a call to exp2 has both a low-precision argument and a low-precision result.

```
vec3 transmittance( vec3 r, vec3 viewdir )
{
    // calculate the transmittance along a ray
    // from point r towards infinity

    float rsq = dot(r,r);
    float invrl = inversesqrt( rsq );
    float len = rsq * invrl;
    float x = len * invH50;
    float h = x - X50;
    float coschi = dot( r, viewdir ) * invrl;
    return exp2( -beta50 * H50 * chapman_h( X50, h, coschi ) );
}
```

Listing 11.2. Function for the transmittance along a ray.

11.6   Putting the Chapman Function to Use

Finally, in this section we are going to explore the ways in which we can use our shiny new tool. You should consult the example code on the website since not all listings are shown here.

11.6.1   Airmass and Transmittance

The airmass is calculated easily with the modified Chapman function. You need to know the observer height against some reference altitude (conveniently, this is the planet radius, or mean sea level), and the scale height of the atmosphere:

$$m \quad = \quad H\,Ch_h(X, h, \chi).$$

It is a small step from the airmass to the transmittance, since $T = \exp(-\beta m)$. See Listing 11.2 for a function to calculate the transmittance along a straight line through the atmosphere. The scale height and the extinction coefficients must be available globally. In the complete fragment program, this function is used to calculate the local sun color for surface shading.

11.6.2   Aerial Perspective

The full aerial perspective function has two colors as a result: the transmittance and the in-scatter. The function is too long to be listed here, but is included in the fragment program on the website. The signature is as follows:

```
void aerial_perspective( out vec3 T, out vec3 S,
    in vec3 r0, in vec3 r1, in bool infinite );
```

The function calculates the aerial perspective from point r0 to point r1, or alternatively, from point r0 along the ray through r1 to infinity. The resulting transmittance is written to argument T and the in-scatter is written to argument S.

Here is a short explanation of the algorithm: In a first step, the function intersects the ray with the atmosphere boundary to get the integration interval, which is subdivided into a fixed number of segments. It then iterates over all segments in reverse order (back to front). For each segment, the Chapman function is called to calculate airmass, transmittance, and in-scatter. The in-scatter is then propagated along the ray in a way similar to alpha-blending.

11.6.3   The Example Raytracer

The accompanying online material for this article contains a shader (fragment- and vertex program) that implements a fully ray-traced, atmospheric single-scattering solution in real time. See the color images in Figure 11.6. You should be able to load the shader into a shader authoring tool (RenderMonkey, FX-Composer) and apply it on a unit sphere. If you are on the Mac, there is a ShaderBuilder project that you can simply double click.

The code assumes a planet centered at the origin of variable radius, with a Rayleigh atmosphere. For each pixel that hits the atmosphere, `aerial_perspective` is called once to get the in-scatter against the black background of space. The transmittance is not needed. For each pixel that hits the surface, the `aerial_perspective` function is called twice, one time for the view ray, and a second time for the ocean reflection.

To give a realistic appearance, the β-values were calculated for a situation similar to Earth. A little bit of orange absorption was added to account for the effect of atmospheric ozone, which is significant at twilight (see [Nielsen 03]). The landmass is shaded according to the Lommel-Seeliger law, which is a good model for rough surfaces, avoiding the typical Lambertian limb darkening. The specular reflection of the sun in the ocean is shaded with an approximate microfacet model (see [Schüler 09]). The final color is then tone mapped with an exponential soft saturation and 2.2 display gamma.

11.7   Conclusion

This article shows a way to accelerate atmospheric scattering calculations, by making the Chapman function an efficient commodity. This allows a strength reduction of the numerical integration, up to the point where the full single-scattering solution can be run in real time in a shader program.

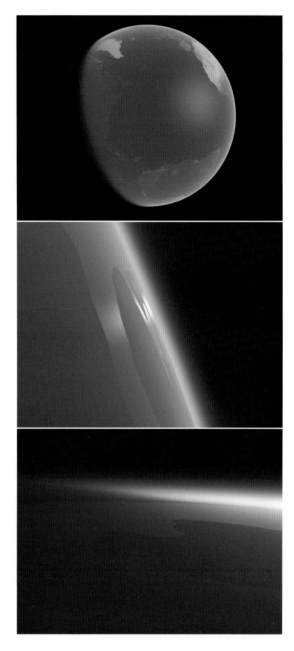

Figure 11.6. Color images from the example ray tracer. View of the Atlantic Ocean (top). Sun reflection, which is yellow due to transmittance (middle). Earth shadow, which is implicit in the solution (bottom).

```
float exp2pp( float x )
{
    // partial precision exp2, accurate to 12 bits

    const float c[3] = { 5.79525, 12.52461, -2.88611 };
    int e = round(x);
    float t = x - e;
    float m = ( t*t + c[0]*t + c[1] ) / ( c[2]*t + c[1] );
    return ldexp( m, e );
}
```

Listing 11.3. An example of a fast `exp2` function.

11.8   Appendix

11.8.1   A Fast exp2 Function

Listing 11.3 shows an example for a fast `exp2` function for use in atmospheric-scattering calculations. It is a low-order rational function in the range $-1/2$ to $+1/2$ together with the usual range reduction and scaling. Although it is an approximation, it does preserve the property that $1 - \exp(-x)$ is strictly positive if $x > 0$, which is important for the scattering calculations. The function is dependent on an efficient way to assemble a floating point number from a mantissa and an exponent. For the sake of brevity, this part is expressed here in terms of the standard C-function `ldexp`. The optimal method would be a direct bit-manipulation, using language-specific constructs.

Bibliography

[Bruneton and Neyret 08] Éric Bruneton and Fabrice Neyret. "Precomputed Atmospheric Scattering." *Comput. Graph. Forum. Proceedings of the 19th Eurographics Symposium on Rendering 2008* 27:4 (2008), 1079–1086. Special Issue.

[Chapman 31] Sydney Chapman. "The Absorption and Dissociative or Ionizing Effect of Monochromatic Radiation in an Atmosphere on a Rotating Earth." *Proceedings of the Physical Society* 43:1 (1931), 26. Available online (http://stacks.iop.org/0959-5309/43/i=1/a=305).

[Hoffmann and Preetham 02] Naty Hoffmann and Arcot J. Preetham. "Rendering outdoor light scattering in real time." Technical report, ATI Technologies, Inc., 2002. Available online (http://www.ati.com/developer).

[Klassen 87] R. Victor Klassen. "Modeling the Effect of the Atmosphere on Light." *ACM Trans. Graph.* 6 (1987), 215–237. Available online (http://doi.acm.org/10.1145/35068.35071).

[Kocifaj 96] M. Kocifaj. "Optical Air Mass and Refraction in a Rayleigh Atmosphere." *Contributions of the Astronomical Observatory Skalnate Pleso* 26:1 (1996), 23–30. Available online (http://www.ta3.sk/caosp/Eedition/Abstracts/1996/Vol_26/No_1/pp23-30_abstract.html).

[Nielsen 03] R. S. Nielsen. "Real Time Rendering of Atmospheric Scattering Effects for Flight Simulators." Master's thesis, Informatics and Mathematical Modelling, Technical University of Denmark, 2003. Available online (http://www2.imm.dtu.dk/pubdb/p.php?2554).

[Nishita et al. 93] Tomoyuki Nishita, Takao Sirai, Katsumi Tadamura, and Eihachiro Nakamae. "Display of the Earth Taking into Account Atmospheric Scattering." In *Proceedings of SIGGRAPH '93, Proceedings, Annual Conference Series*, edited by James T. Kajiya, pp. 175–182. New York: ACM Press, 1993. Available online (http://doi.acm.org/10.1145/166117.166140).

[O'Neil 05] Sean O'Neil. "Accurate Atmospheric Scattering." In *GPU Gems 2*, edited by Matt Pharr and Randima Fernando, pp. 253–268. Reading, MA: Addison-Wesley, 2005.

[Schüler 09] Christian Schüler. "An Efficient and Physically Plausible Real-Time Shading Model." In *ShaderX^7: Advanced Rendering Techniques*, edited by Wolfgang Engel, Chapter 2.5, pp. 175 187. Hingham, MA: Charles River Media, 2009.

12

Volumetric Real-Time Water and Foam Rendering

Daniel Scherzer, Florian Bagar, and Oliver Mattausch

12.1 Introduction

Over the last decade, simulation and rendering of complex natural phenomena such as fire, smoke, clouds, and fluids have been an active and most diverse research area in computer graphics. Among these phenomena, water may be the most fascinating and challenging problem, due to the familiarity that even a

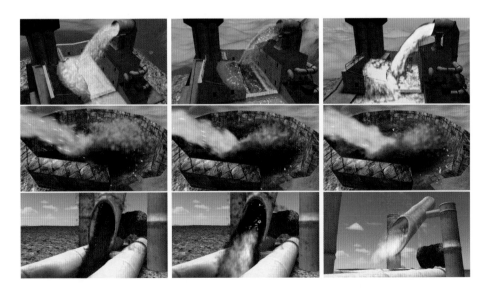

Figure 12.1. The proposed algorithm allows water to be rendered in many ways.

casual observer has with the phenomenon. Although the visual quality of water rendering is continually improving, we are still a long way from capturing all the physical properties of real water, like the forming of foam and droplets and their interaction with the environment.

In this chapter we present a method for creating a fully dynamic multilayered real-time water rendering approach. This approach can represent the volumetric properties of water and the physical formation of volumetric foam, thereby creating much higher visual fidelity than previous real-time approaches. It is based on a very fast particle-based fluid simulation that is fully hardware-accelerated using Nvidia PhysX and rendering in OpenGL, and therefore easily runs at real-time frame rates. The algorithm has a small memory footprint and is simple to implement and integrate into existing rendering engines. Additionally, our method is highly configurable from an artistic point of view, and thus can produce a multiplicity of visual appearances to help to create the desired atmosphere for a scene (see Figure 12.1).

12.2   Simulation

In order to render believable water, we first have to simulate its behavior. The dynamics of water as an incompressible fluid can be described by a version of the Navier–Stokes equations, which apply Newton's second law (conservation of momentum) and conservation of mass to fluid motion. These equations relate the body forces (gravity) and the contact forces (pressure and stress) that act on a fluid. This results in nonlinear partial differential equations that are very hard to solve (assuming that an exact solution for a given case even exists). As we do not need an exact solution, but are mainly concerned with speed, we are fine with an approximate numerical solution. Approximations in this problem domain mainly use Euler integration. (There are more accurate methods, such as Runge-Kutta or midpoint, but these take more time to evaluate.)

12.2.1   Smoothed-Particle Hydrodynamics

Smoothed-particle hydrodynamics (SPH) is a robust and fast way for simulating the behavior of water [Desbrun and Gascuel 96]. The main idea here is to approximate a fluid by a particle system (a division of the fluid into discrete elements) to calculate its dynamic behavior. Each particle has a mass and additional properties, such as position, density, velocity, and lifetime. In classic particle systems, each particle is updated based only on its properties, disregarding particle-particle interaction for the sake of speed. For the simulation of fluids this will not suffice because of the contact forces. Each particle can potentially affect all other particles, which results in a computational complexity in the order of $O(n^2)$—too slow for practical purposes if we use tens of thousands of particles.

```
struct FluidParticle
{
    Vector3        position;
    float          density;
    Vector3        velocity;
    float          lifetime;
    unsigned int   id;        // unique number identifying the particle
    float          foam;
};
```

Listing 12.1. Structure representing the properties of a single particle.

In practice, particles influence each other depending on the distance between them. So it makes sense to define an interaction cut-off distance, inside which a kernel function is applied to weight the influence of the individual particles on each other. This effectively reduces calculation complexity to $O(n)$. Note that this cut-off distance is also called the *smoothing length* because it gives the volume over which properties are "smoothed" by the kernel function (hence the name smoothed-particle hydrodynamics).

All major physics engines already include a solver for SPH. We have used PhysX [Nvidia 11] because of its hardware acceleration, but any other physics engine would do as well.

The fluid simulation is created by passing a fluid description structure to the physics engine, which defines the behavior of the SPH simulation. The simulation data is a nonsorted 3D point cloud and each of the particles has the properties as shown in Listing 12.1. Note that for our use the particle structure also includes a foam parameter that is updated as described in Section 12.2.2. The physics engine updates and returns this point cloud by applying the SPH simulation.

12.2.2 Foam

We want to be able to simulate not only water particles, but also foam. Foam is a substance that is formed by trapping air bubbles inside a liquid (see Figure 12.4). Note that this can be as spray or bubbles above the surface of the fluid, but also deep inside a fluid, as in the case of a waterfall. The formation of foam can be described by the Weber number. It is defined as the ratio of the kinetic energy to the surface energy:

$$We = \frac{\rho v^2 l}{\sigma},$$

where ρ is the density, v is the relative velocity between the liquid and the surrounding gas, l is the droplet diameter, and σ is the surface tension. If We is large, the kinetic energy is greater than the surface energy, which causes water to mix with the surrounding gas (air), and the result is foam. For our purposes, we use the particle size as the droplet diameter and use a constant value for the surface tension. We also assume that the air is not moving, and that therefore the relative velocity is equal to the velocity of the liquid at this point.

The Weber number for each particle can now be calculated by using each particle's ρ and v from the physics engine. This number is then compared to a user-defined threshold that describes how easily this fluid forms foam. Thus, particles can be separated into water particles and foam particles. Thus, foam (from the viewpoint of the simulation) is not a totally different phenomenon, but is just a state of water particles [Bagar et al. 10].

With all these simulation parts in place we now have to tackle the problem of how to render the water.

12.3 Rendering

Rendering water with a scanline renderer in an efficient manner is a twofold problem: first, a water surface has to be extracted from the simulation data and second, the shading of this surface has to take into account the volumetric properties of water. Due to the fact that real-time physics engines are often limited to 64 K particles, while offline systems, as used in movies, often use hundreds of millions of particles, our particle sizes will be much larger; we therefore must take extra care to render believable water surfaces.

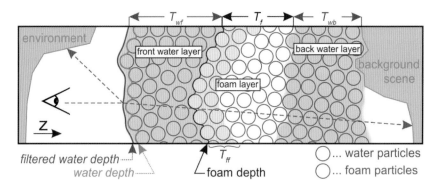

Figure 12.2. A cross section of our layered water model: the volumetric appearance of the result is achieved by accounting for water thickness T_{wb}, foam thickness T_f, and the thickness of water in front of the foam T_{wf} at each pixel. We also partition foam into two differently colored layers (T_{ff}) to achieve more interesting foam. See also Figure 12.5 for renderings of the individual layers.

12.3.1 Splatting

One method for extracting surfaces from particles is to use a marching cubes method. This has a number of disadvantages: First, as the surface of the water is expected to change continually, the surface may exhibit temporal aliasing. Second, marching cubes is very computationally expensive, and third, the resulting geometry will likely be very complex, especially when incorporating foam effects.

A method that avoids these disadvantages and works well on current hardware is splatting: the idea is to splat each particle by using a certain kernel shape (for instance, a sphere) into a depth (and thickness) buffer (see Figures 12.2 and 12.6). By using a 3D kernel, we create volumetric particles. Splatting particles into a depth buffer (with depth test on) results in a screen-space approximation of the water surface (see Listing 12.2). While additively splatting (adding up sphere radii, see Listing 12.3) into a thickness buffer creates an approximation of the water thickness for each pixel (which we will later use for shading the surface). Accumulating water thickness this way is an acceptable approximation because the particles from the physics simulation can be assumed to be largely nonoverlapping.

```
 1 FragShaderOutput FluidSplattingFP(  float2 texCoord : TEXCOORD0,
 2                                      float4 eyeSpace : TEXCOORD1)
 3 {
 4      FragShaderOutput OUT;
 5      // calculate eye-space normal from texture coordinates
 6      float3 n;
 7      n.xy = texCoord.xy * float2(2.0f, -2.0f) + float2(-1.0f, 1.0f);
 8      float r2 = dot(n.xy, n.xy);
 9      // kill pixels outside circle
10      if (r2 > 1.0f) discard;
11      //calculate radius
12      n.z = sqrt(1.0f - r2);
13      // position of this pixel on sphere in eye space
14      float4 eyeSpacePos = float4(eyeSpace.xyz + n*eyeSpace.w, 1.0f);
15      float4 clipSpacePos = mul(glstate.matrix.projection, eyeSpacePos);
16      // output eye-space depth
17      OUT.color = float4(eyeSpacePos.z, 0.0f, 0.0f, 0.0f);
18      OUT.depth = (clipSpacePos.z / clipSpacePos.w) * 0.5f + 0.5f;
19      return OUT;
20 }
```

Listing 12.2. Pixel shader for splatting the particle data as spheres into the depth texture.

```
        // calculate thickness with exponential falloff based on radius
        float thickness = n.z * particleSize * 2.0f * exp(-r2 * 2.0f);
        OUT.color = float4(thickness, 0.0f, 0.0f, 0.0f);
```

Listing 12.3. Splatting the particle data into the thickness texture. (Note: This shader is based on the shader shown in Listing 12.2 and replaces lines 13–18.)

12.3.2   Adaptive Screen-Space Curvature Flow Filtering

If we use a sphere-shaped kernel to splat the particles, the result of directly rendering is often unconvincing (see Figure 12.3, upper-left image). The sphere geometry of the individual particles is clearly visible due to the large particle size. Making particles smaller and thereby requiring more particles for adequate simulation of these scenes is not an option because we already operate near the maximum of 64 K particles, and more particles also make the simulation and the rendering slower. Another solution is to smooth the depth buffer that contains the splatted particles in a way that avoids high curvature. This is the idea behind curvature flow filtering [van der Laan et al. 09]. Here, a surface is shifted along its normal vector depending on the mean curvature of the surface:

$$\frac{\partial z}{\partial t} = H,$$

where z is the depth (as found in the depth buffer), t is a smoothing time step, and H is the mean curvature. For a surface in 3D space, the mean curvature is defined as follows:

$$2H = \nabla \cdot \hat{n}, \tag{12.1}$$

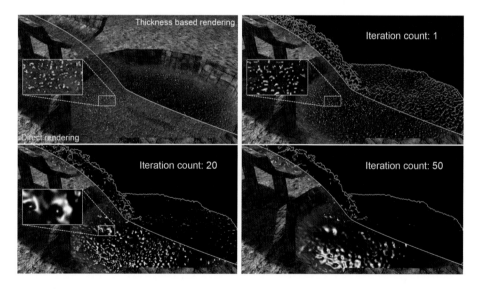

Figure 12.3. Directly rendering the particles from the simulation as spheres results in jelly-like water. Shading of the water can be improved by using the thickness of the water to attenuate the water color (upper-left). Iteratively smoothing the depth buffer by applying screen-space curvature flow filtering reduces the curvature of the water and leads to more convincing results.

where $\hat{n}$ is the unit normal of the surface. The normal is calculated by taking the cross product between the derivatives of the viewspace position P in x- and y-directions, resulting in a representation of the unit normal [van der Laan et al. 09]:

$$\hat{n}(x,y) = \frac{n(x,y)}{|n(x,y)|} = \frac{(-C_y \frac{\partial z}{\partial x}, -C_x \frac{\partial z}{\partial y}, C_y z)^T}{\sqrt{D}}, \tag{12.2}$$

where

$$D = C_y^2 \left(\frac{\partial z}{\partial x}\right)^2 + C_x^2 \left(\frac{\partial z}{\partial y}\right)^2 + C_x^2 C_y^2 z^2.$$

Finite differencing is used to calculate the spatial derivatives, and C_x and C_y are the viewpoint parameters in the x- and y-directions, respectively. They are computed from the field of view and the size of the viewport V_x and V_y, as shown in Equations (12.3) and (12.4):

$$C_x = \frac{2}{V_x \tan\left(\frac{FOV}{2}\right)}, \tag{12.3}$$

$$C_y = \frac{2}{V_y \tan\left(\frac{FOV}{2}\right)}. \tag{12.4}$$

The unit normal $\hat{n}$ from Equation (12.2) is substituted into Equation (12.1), which enables the derivation of H, leading to

$$2H = \frac{\partial \hat{n}_x}{\partial x} + \frac{\partial \hat{n}_y}{\partial y} = \frac{C_y E_x + C_x E_y}{D^{\frac{3}{2}}},$$

in which

$$E_x = \frac{1}{2} \frac{\partial z}{\partial x} \frac{\partial D}{\partial x} - \frac{\partial^2 z}{\partial x^2} D,$$

$$E_y = \frac{1}{2} \frac{\partial z}{\partial y} \frac{\partial D}{\partial y} - \frac{\partial^2 z}{\partial y^2} D.$$

The GLSL shader in Listing 12.4 performs this operation in screen space.

The effect of applying this filter repeatedly is shown in Figure 12.3. Iterative filtering leads to a greater smoothing effect. If we want to maintain a certain level of smoothness for water that is at the same time near and distant to the viewer, the number of iterations has to be adjusted adaptively for each pixel. We found that the number of iterations is indirectly proportional to the eye-space distance—water nearby needs more iterations—far-away water needs fewer iterations. Details regarding this derivation can be found in our paper [Bagar et al. 10].

```
// samples for finite differencing (vsp = view space position)
float depth   = texRECT(depthMap, vsp.xy).x;
float depth_d = texRECT(depthMap, vsp.xy + float2( 0.0f,-1.0f)).x;
float depth_l = texRECT(depthMap, vsp.xy + float2(-1.0f, 0.0f)).x;
float depth_r = texRECT(depthMap, vsp.xy + float2( 1.0f, 0.0f)).x;
float depth_u = texRECT(depthMap, vsp.xy + float2( 0.0f, 1.0f)).x;
// derivatives (finite differencing)
float dx = (0.5f * (depth_r - depth_l));
float dy = (0.5f * (depth_u - depth_d));
// second derivatives
float dxx = (depth_l - 2.0f * depth + depth_r);
float dyy = (depth_d - 2.0f * depth + depth_u);
// constants
const float dx2 = dx*dx; const float dy2 = dy*dy;
const float Cx2 = Cx*Cx; const float Cy2 = Cy*Cy;
// calculate curvature
float D = Cy2*dx2 + Cx2*dy2 + Cx2*Cy2*depth*depth;
float H =  Cy*dxx*D - Cy*dx*(Cy2*dx*dxx + Cx2*Cy2*depth*dx)
    + Cx*dyy*D - Cx*dy*(Cx2*dy*dyy + Cx2*Cy2*depth*dy);
H /= pow(D, 3.0f/2.0f);
// curvature dependent shift
OUT.color = depth + epsilon * H;
```

Listing 12.4. This pixel shader code performs one step in the iterative process of screen-space curvature flow filtering.

12.3.3 Foam and Layers

Up to now we have discussed the problem of how to create a surface for our water. What remains is to provide this surface with realistic shading and to add foam effects.

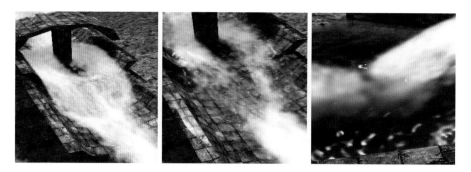

Figure 12.4. The three cases of foam formation that are handled by our rendering model: foam without water (left), foam on water (middle), and foam inside water (right).

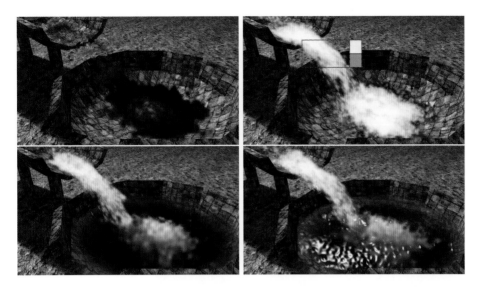

Figure 12.5. The individual layers of our water model: back water layer (upper-left), foam layer with the two user-defined colors that define the look of the foam as inlay (upper-right), front water layer (lower-left), and reflections and specular highlights (lower-right).

We have investigated the different scenarios where foam occurs and have found three main cases for a single pixel: foam without water, foam in front with water behind, and foam inside water (see Figure 12.4). We disregard more complex scenarios, like multiple layers of foam, because in practice the visual difference compared with a single foam layer will be negligible. These cases can be cast into a three-layered model (see Figures 12.2 and 12.5).

12.3.4   Steps of the Algorithm

To put this model into practice, our algorithm separates water and foam particles and splats them into different buffers. The complete algorithm performs the following steps in each frame (see Figure 12.6):

- Update the physics simulation.
- Render the background scene into a depth and color buffer.
- Calculate foam depth by splatting foam particles into a depth buffer.
- Calculate the front water depth by splatting water particles that are in front of the foam.
- Calculate the filtered front water depth by applying adaptive curvature flow filtering.

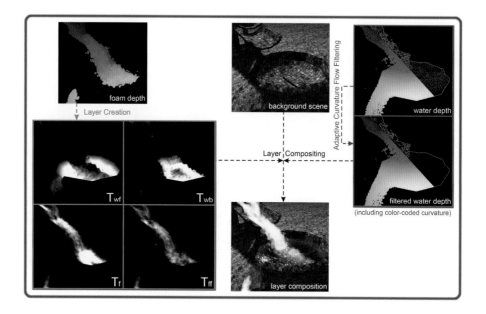

Figure 12.6. Overview of the buffers used in our method. T_{wf} denotes the thickness of the water in front of the foam, T_{wb} denotes the thickness of the water behind the foam, T_f denotes the foam thickness, and T_{ff} denotes the thickness of the front foam layer.

- Calculate the thickness of
  - the foam T_f,
  - the water in front of the foam T_{wf},
  - the water behind the foam T_{wb},
  - the front foam layer T_{ff}.

- Perform volumetric compositing

We use a sphere kernel for water particles and multiply the sphere kernel with a Perlin noise texture for foam particles to get more details. Smoothing is only applied to the front-most water layer, because the surface of water behind a layer of foam will be obfuscated anyway. The front foam layer thickness T_{ff} is an artificial construct that accumulates only foam particles within a user-defined distance behind the foam depth. We found this to create more interesting looking foam.

We have already discussed the basics behind each of the steps, except for the final one, volumetric compositing, that builds on top of all the other steps.

12.3.5 Volumetric Compositing

The difference between the usual compositing of layers and volumetric compositing is that we take the thickness of each layer into account to attenuate a viewing ray. Compositing along a viewing ray back to front, we have (see Figure 12.2):

$$
\begin{aligned}
C_{wb} &= \text{lerp}(c_{\text{fluid}}, C_{\text{background}}, e^{-T_{wb}}), \\
C_{\text{foam}} &= \text{lerp}(c_{fb},\ c_{ff}, e^{-T_{ff}}), \\
C_{f} &= \text{lerp}(C_{\text{foam}}, C_{wb}, e^{-T_{f}}), \\
C_{wf} &= \text{lerp}(c_{\text{fluid}}, C_{f}, e^{-T_{wf}}),
\end{aligned}
$$

where c_{fluid} is the water color and c_{ff} and c_{fb} are two user-defined colors that are blended together to create more freedom in designing the look of the foam.

After attenuation, we calculate highlights at the front water surface, as well as reflection and refraction (including the Fresnel Term). Here, refraction considers the whole water (front and back water layer) as one volume, so $C_{\text{background}}$ is sampled from the scene background texture perturbed along the normal vector, scaled using $T_{wb} + T_{wf}$ [van der Laan et al. 09].

Figures 12.5 and 12.7 show the individual steps and colors used in the compositing, and Listing 12.5 shows the GLSL pixel shader.

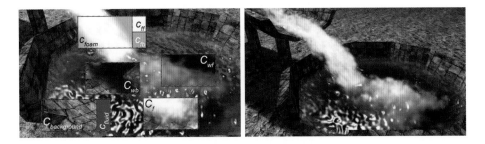

Figure 12.7. User-defined colors (c_{fluid}, c_{ff}, c_{fb}), and resulting colors from the compositing steps ($C_{\text{background}}$, C_{wb}, C_{foam}, C_{f}, C_{wf}) (left) and final shading results (right).

12.4 Artist Control

We have introduced a number of user-controllable parameters into our algorithm to allow artists to produce a multiplicity of visual appearances (see Figure 12.1).

The visual appearance of water is controlled by the fluid/water color (c_{fluid}), which is combined during the composition depending on the different water thicknesses (t_{wb}, t_{wf}) and a user-defined falloff scale. Additionally, the specular color and specular shininess, as well as the Fresnel bias, scale, and power, which are

```
1  // surface properties (v = view vector, h = half angle vector)
2  float specular = pow(max(0.0, dot(normal, h)), fluidShininess);
3  // bias, scale, and power = user-defined parameters to tune
4  // the Fresnel Term
5  float fresnelTerm = bias + scale * pow(1.0 + dot(v, normal), power);
6  float3 c_reflect = texCUBE(cubeMap, mul((float3x3)invView,
7     reflect(-v, normal)));
8  ...
9  // attenuation factors (incl. user-defined falloff scales)
10 float att_wb = saturate(exp(-t_wb * falloffScale));
11 float att_foam = saturate(exp(-t_f * foamFalloffScale));
12 float att_ff = saturate(exp(-t_ff * foamScale));
13 float att_wf = saturate(exp(-t_wf * falloffScale));
14 // composition (frag = fragment position in screen space
15 float3 c_background = texRECT(scene, frag.xy+normal.xy*(t_wb+t_wf));
16 float3 c_wb = lerp(c_fluid, c_background, att_wb);
17 float3 c_foam = lerp(c_fb, c_ff, att_ff);
18 float3 c_f = lerp(c_foam, c_wb, att_foam);
19 float3 c_wf = lerp(c_fluid, c_f, att_wf);
20 // calculate factor to suppress specular highlights if
21 // foam is the frontmost visual element
22 float spw = saturate(1.0f - att_wf + att_foam) * (1.0f - att_wf);
23 // combine with fresnel and specular highlight
24 float3 surfaceColor = lerp(c_wf, c_reflect, min(fresnelTerm, spw))
25    + fluidSpecularColor * specular * spw;
```

Listing 12.5. Pixel shader for compositing along a viewing ray: lighting (lines 2–7), thickness dependent attenuation (lines 9–19), and final color (lines 20–25).

used to control the approximation of the Fresnel equations, are exposed to be used by artists. The approximation of the Fresnel equations is then used to combine the reflection and the thickness-dependent attenuation of our algorithm (see Listing 12.5).

The reflection itself can be influenced by an artist by modifying or replacing the cubic environment map (cubeMap) of the corresponding scene. Note that the cubic environment map has a large influence on the visual appearance of our algorithm because it is blended directly with the thickness-dependent attenuation and furthermore, it describes the static illumination of the scene.

The visual appearance of the foam is composed of a foam back color (c_{fb}) and a foam front color (c_{ff}), which are blended depending on the thickness of the front foam layer (t_{ff}) (see Figure 12.7) and a user-defined scale factor. Again, as for the water, a user-defined falloff scale is used to control the overall opacity of the foam. The final parameter that should be exposed to artists is the Weber number threshold. As mentioned earlier, this user-defined threshold controls how easily the simulated fluid forms foam.

12.5 Conclusion

We have presented a physically based water (fluid) and foam rendering algorithm that can handle arbitrary dynamic scenes where water is allowed to freely interact and flow everywhere, but which also allows artists to fine-tune the look of the result. This algorithm runs easily in real time (on average 16 ms rendering time) on modern hardware and integrates well with rendering engines (especially with deferred shading).

For more theoretical details and exhaustive benchmarks for the presented method, please refer to the paper [Bagar et al. 10] and the thesis [Bagar 10] on which this work is based.

Bibliography

[Bagar et al. 10] Florian Bagar, Daniel Scherzer, and Michael Wimmer. "A Layered Particle-Based Fluid Model for Real-Time Rendering of Water." *Computer Graphics Forum (Proceedings EGSR 2010)* 29:4 (2010), 1383–1389.

[Bagar 10] Florian Bagar. "A Layered Particle-Based Fluid Model for Real-Time Rendering of Water." Master's thesis (Diplomarbeit), Vienna University of Technology, Austria, 2010.

[Desbrun and Gascuel 96] Mathieu Desbrun and Marie-Paule Gascuel. "Smoothed Particles: A New Paradigm for Animating Highly Deformable Bodies." In *Proceedings of the Eurographics Workshop on Computer Animation and Simulation '96*, pp. 61–76. New York: Springer-Verlag New York, 1996. Available online (http://dl.acm.org/citation.cfm?id=274976.274981).

[Nvidia 11] Nvidia. "NVIDIA PhysX." http://developer.nvidia.com/physx, 2011.

[van der Laan et al. 09] Wladimir J. van der Laan, Simon Green, and Miguel Sainz. "Screen Space Fluid Rendering with Curvature Flow." In *I3D '09: Proceedings of the 2009 Symposium on Interactive 3D Graphics and Games*, pp. 91–98. New York: ACM Press, 2009.

13

Inexpensive Antialiasing of Simple Objects
Mikkel Gjøl and Mark Gjøl

13.1 Introduction

In the age of mobile devices, every algorithm gets a second chance. This article explores a use of discontinuity edge overdraw [Sander et al. 01] for antialiasing simple objects on 3D-capable mobile devices. The essence of this technique is to render a "smooth" line on top of aliasing primitive edges in order to cover the aliasing edge.

The method is trivially useful for rendering objects whose outline is geometrically defined or easily derived. This applies to everything from GUI-elements to 2D objects positioned in 3D, or even simple 3D-objects—anything where the outline is defined by geometry. For textured 2D-elements, the usual way to deal with antialiasing is to use textures with a translucent edge, relying on texture-sampling to produce a smooth transition at the boundary. While this is a good solution, it requires careful construction of the mip-chain to avoid artifacts during scaling or when viewed at steep angles.

13.2 Antialiasing via Smoothed Lines

The founding observation of [Sander et al. 01] was that aliasing in 3D scenes appears mostly at geometric silhouette edges and crease edges, and so only pixels along these lines require antialiasing. As these boundaries can be described as lines, and since line smoothing is widely available in hardware, aliasing can be reduced by rendering smooth lines on top of the aliasing edges. The main contribution of [Sander et al. 01] was an algorithm to find the aliasing edges. For some applications, the potentially aliasing edges are trivially available, allowing us to use this method easily. It is worth noting that the resulting algorithm does not work for translucent objects, and does nothing to improve upon texture-aliasing,

203

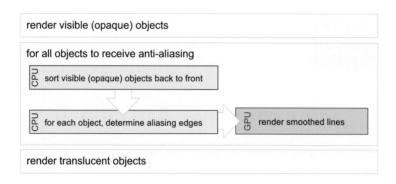

Figure 13.1. Basic rendering setup.

including aliasing when rendering 2D sprites. Hardware texture filtering mostly solves this issue however, and is available on the majority of modern mobile GPUs.

Applying the algorithm consists of just two steps (see Figure 13.1):

1. Determine the geometric edges that are causing aliasing.

2. Render aliasing edges as smooth lines.

In the general case it is not trivial to determine which edges cause aliasing, and we refer readers to the exhaustive discussion in [Sander et al. 01]. In summary, three sets of geometric edges should be considered for any visible object:

- silhouette edges,

- discontinuous edges, e.g., "hard" edges or texture seams,

- intersection-edges between geometric objects.

While discontinuous edges are typically static for a triangle mesh and can be precomputed, silhouette edges change with the viewer. Dealing with scenes constructed entirely of triangles, a geometric approach to finding silhouette edges is to locate all edges where one of the adjacent triangles faces towards the viewer and the other faces away. Computing exact intersections between geometric objects is computationally expensive, and a solution was not presented in [Sander et al. 01].

When rendering lines to cover the detected aliasing edges, "over" alpha-blending is applied (`src_alpha,one_minus_src_alpha`), and depth buffering is used to achieve correct occlusion. While the rendered lines are potentially subject to z-fighting, the fighting pixels have the same color as the object on which they are rendered. Since the main contribution of the smooth lines is outside the aliasing object, z-fighting causes minimal issues. Rendering multiple layers of alpha-blended pixels necessitates composition in a back-to-front manner. This is an issue only at the few pixels where the smooth lines overlap, making the errors caused by incorrect depth sorting mostly unnoticeable. Doing only an approximate per-object sort is sufficient for most purposes, and skipping sorting altogether could be considered.

Shading of the lines should be done identically to the aliasing edges, applying lighting and texturing as for the underlying object. The same vertex program and fragment program should similarly be applied during rendering of smoothed lines (see also Section 1.3.3). Since the aliasing edge is an edge in the rendered mesh, the original vertex data can be used for the smooth line. For ambiguous cases where multiple sets of vertex data are associated with an edge, one set must be selected. Again, we refer to [Sander et al. 01] for treatment of the general case, but in summary, blending between two versions of the edge data is needed in all but the trivial case in order to alleviate popping.

13.3 Rendering Lines

Lines and triangles are rasterized fundamentally differently: while triangles generate fragments where a fragment center is contained within the triangle, lines generate fragments where they pass through a "diamond" centered around the fragment center (see Figure 13.2). In the case of triangles, vertex values are linearly interpolated to the fragment center, while line-generated fragments always receive the value at the rasterized point projected onto the center of the line.

OpenGL|ES defines the coverage of a fragment to be the exact area of overlap between the fragment and the rectangle centered around the line. Rendered lines thus give perfect coverage values for the affected fragments, making them ideal for antialiasing purposes. It is worth noting that the specification does allow variations in the implementation, so the exact outcome may vary.

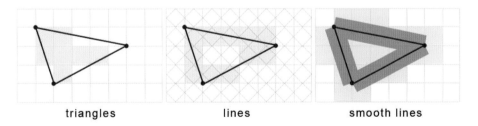

triangles   lines   smooth lines

Figure 13.2. Rasterization rules for various primitives.

13.3.1 OpenGL|ES 1.x

The OpenGL|ES 1.x specification includes the functionality of rendering smoothed points and lines, as also available in "regular" OpenGL (see Listing 13.1).

```
gl.glLineWidth(1.0f);
gl.glEnable(GL10.GL_LINE_SMOOTH);
gl.glBlendFunc(GL10.GL_SRC_ALPHA,GL10.GL_ONE_MINUS_SRC_ALPHA);
gl.glEnable(GL10.GL_BLEND);
```

Listing 13.1. Enabling line smoothing in OpenGL|ES 1.x.

Implementations are not required to provide line widths beyond one pixel, however for this method wider lines are not required. While line smoothing is present on most phones exclusively supporting OpenGL|ES1.x, some phones supporting OpenGL|ES 1.x, as well as OpenGL|ES 2.x, did not provide line-smoothing functionality. The emulator for the iPhone provides smoothed lines, but alas the device itself does not [Flaherty 10].

13.3.2   OpenGL|ES 2.x

For OpenGL|ES 2.0, point- and line-smoothing were removed from the specification, and multisample-antialiasing (MSAA) was introduced, to allow for antialiasing of all primitives.[1] Not all OpenGL|ES2.x hardware supports MSAA, but where it is supported, it should be easily implemented and provides a very flexible solution.

Using multisampling does, however, significantly increase the number of processed fragments, while also increasing the memory used by depth and color buffers to store the multisampled buffers.[2] This overhead might not be acceptable for all applications, for reasons related to memory and performance, as well as to battery-life.

13.3.3   General Solution to Smoothed Line Rendering

Rather than rely on specific hardware capabilities, there are several methods available for manual rendering of antialiased lines [Bærentzen et al. 08, Texture 04]. The following three are of particular interest (see Figure 13.3):

1. Render an extra band of geometry along an edge, setting vertex alpha to 0 along the border.

2. Render with a masking alpha texture to smooth edges (optionally using a distance-field).

3. Analytically calculate the distance to a line segment in the pixel shader and use the mapped distance as an alpha-mask.

---

[1]MSAA is supported on the iPhone via the extension `APPLE_framebuffer_multisample`, while on Android `EGL_SAMPLE_BUFFERS` is passed to `eglChooseConfig` to determine the number of samples.

[2]Note that on some architectures, there is no memory overhead [IMG 11].

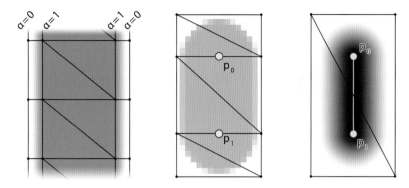

Figure 13.3. Vertex-alpha (left), texture-alpha (middle), and analytical distance (right).

For rendering lines with a width of only a few pixels like the ones sought here, rendering an extra strip of translucent vertices is impractical as it generates numerous small, thin triangles. First, it is not guaranteed that any fragment centers are contained within the triangles, requiring wide falloffs to guarantee smoothness. Second, because hardware often shades pixels in quads of 2×2 pixels, processing may be wasted on nonvisible fragments. Additionally, the method does not deal correctly with endpoints. At best, adding an end segment would produce bi-linearly interpolated areas, causing unsightly artifacts.

Using a simple alpha texture as a mask relies on the texture filtering and pre-filtered mip-maps to produce a smooth result. Using a texture easily allows us to specify a custom falloff for the line, allowing increased control over the smoothness. As the texture can be very small, e.g., a grayscale 32×32 pixels, memory is not a concern. In order to produce properly filtered lines at all scales, it is important to provide a mip-map for the texture. Applying the alpha texture can be done using either shaders or register combiners—having the final texture combiner replace the alpha for the masked texture alpha.

The third option for analytically calculating the distance provides the most accurate result, but can only be easily implemented using shaders. While the per-fragment distance calculations require more ALU instructions than using a texture lookup, it is still a viable option, as only a few fragments are touched using this shader. If the base shader is bandwidth bound, it may even be the preferred option. A hybrid of the second and third methods is possible, sampling a distance texture and mapping it to an alpha value, potentially providing yet more control over the falloff.

It is worth noting the importance of generating lines with a constant screen-space antialiasing footprint. Also, the rendered lines should have valid depths to be useful for depth culling. The following options are available for producing the needed geometry:

1. Project all points to screen space, extrude line geometry, and project back to world space.

2. Directly render collapsed triangles in world space, and do the expansion after projection within the vertex-shader.

3. For hardware with geometry-shaders, render line segments and expand vertices in the geometry shader.

Depending on hardware and the specific case, any of these methods could be preferable. The second method requires access to shaders, and results in only a small memory overhead to store vertex IDs. Geometry shaders, while not currently available on mobile hardware, would provide the most flexible solution, requiring very few changes compared to ordinary line rendering. In order to maintain backwards compatibility, we opted for generating all line geometry directly in world space, on the CPU. The downside to this is the overhead of creating new positions and texture coordinates whenever the view changes.

The method for generating line geometry is fairly straight forward, but is provided here for completeness (see Figure 13.4):

For each aliasing line segment $\{p_0, p_1\}$

1. Project $\{p_0, p_1\}$ to the near plane $\{p_0^{np}, p_1^{np}\}$.

2. Expand $\{p_0, p_1\}$ to eight vertices v_{n0-n7} forming lines on the near plane.

3. Generate plane P from the three points p_0, p_1, and $p_0 + \vec{v} \times (p_0 - p_1)$, where $\vec{v}$ is the view vector in world coordinates.

4. Project v_{n0-n7} on to P, thus obtaining world-space vertices.

Recalling that triangle rasterization only affects fragments whose center lies within the triangle, it is necessary to render lines wider than the targeted width, in order to affect the same fragments touched by smooth line rendering. The minimum line width required to affect the same fragments as a 1-pixel antialiased

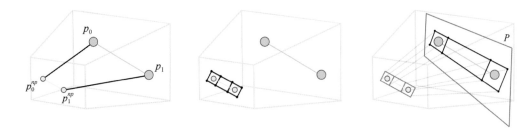

Figure 13.4. Generating world-space line geometry in three stages.

line depends on angle and offset. To cover the worst case, a width of $2\sqrt{2} = 2.8$ pixels can be used. If desired, a bias towards a smoother result can be introduced by artificially increasing the width of the lines.

During rendering, we want the alpha mask texture interpolation to happen in screen space. In other words, we want to do screen-space linear interpolation of the texture coordinates. OpenGL|ES does not currently support `noperspective` interpolation, but the same result is achievable using shaders, by negating the perspective transform as follows, see [Bærentzen et al. 08]: in the vertex shader, multiply the `texcoords` with the w-component of the clip space vertex position— then in the fragment shader, multiply the interpolated texture coordinates by the interpolated $1/w$.

Recalling that the lines should be rendered with the same lighting and textures as the object itself, it is generally sufficient to bind an extra vertex stream supplying the texture coordinates for the masking texture. If using shaders, specific variants of the vertex and fragment programs should be created that apply the extra alpha mask.

13.4 Discussion

Manual rendering of smooth lines was implemented in the Android application *Floating Image*. The application renders simple photos in a gallery-type manner. All potentially aliasing edges are static, and thus this application lends itself well to this particular method of antialiasing. It is a very simple application, and several other methods of antialiasing could also have been used—the simplest

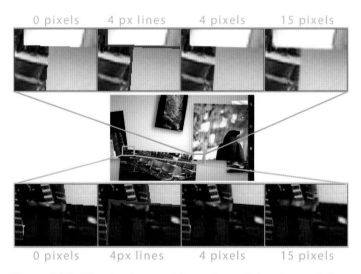

Figure 13.5. Floating image with varying widths of smooth lines.

	9 photos(no AA)	9 photos+AA (36 lines)	AA Cost
HTC Magic (320x480)	56Hz	22Hz	27.59ms
Nexus One (480x800)	52Hz	49Hz	1.17ms
Samsung Galaxy S (480x800)	56Hz	56Hz	"0ms"
	27 photos (no AA)	27 photos+AA (108 lines)	AA Cost
HTC Magic (480x320)	25Hz	9Hz	71ms
Nexus One (480x800)	34Hz	32Hz	1.8ms
Samsung Galaxy S (480x800)	56Hz	56Hz	"0ms"

Table 13.1. Performance timings on various Android devices. MSAA was not supported on these devices for comparison.

being to introduce a band of one translucent pixel around the edge of every mip-level in the photo texture. While occlusions could, and normally should, be handled using the depth buffer, *Floating Image* does manual compositing via the painter's algorithm for device-compatibility reasons, rendering all objects back-to-front.

The implementation uses an alpha texture to render smooth lines, and slightly biases towards blurriness by using a texture with a large falloff and oversized lines. Figure 13.5 shows the result achieved, along with a much over-blurred version. It is worth noting that the method always slightly expands the silhouette of objects: whereas a lot of FSAA techniques blend with a background pixel of a color assumed identical to one of the pixel neighbors, discontinuity edge overdraw always adds occluding pixels on top.

Due to the choice between generating lines directly in world space and rendering via a texture alpha mask, vertex-buffer data needs to be regenerated per frame. Opting for performance over compatibility, vertex-shader expansion of the lines could be used for line expansion, similar to what is often done for billboards.

We have tested the implementation on several devices with varying capabilities. None of the devices were capable of MSAA, and only the Nexus One supported GL_LINE_SMOOTH. Using the smooth lines method we were able to achieve antialiasing on all the devices. The performance has only been tested naïvely, by varying the number of photos displayed and noting the framerate (see Table 13.1). Adding smooth edges hardly impacts performance of the Nexus One, while the HTC is likely CPU-bound due to the line-expansion. The fastest of the devices remains capped at refresh-rate.

13.5   Conclusion

The main drawback of the algorithm is that it depends on the geometric complexity of the rendered scene. Traversing all geometry very quickly becomes impractical, thus limiting use of the method to reasonably simple setups. Furthermore, the need to track aliasing lines per frame makes it necessary to keep all geometry accessible to the CPU. Even though many modern mobile GPUs use a shared memory architecture, the APIs make it difficult to get around duplicating data.

While the algorithm is not complicated to set up, and is arguably trivial if line smoothing is available in hardware, it is challenging to make it scale with increasing geometric complexity. Any object where outlines are trivially found, or as in our example, are entirely static, is an obvious candidate. In general, 2D elements lend themselves well to the technique, whether in screen space or positioned in a 3D scene. For complex 3D scenes, other solutions will likely yield better results.

13.6 Acknowledgments

We would like to thank José Esteve, Romain Toutain, and Andreas Bærentzen for their feedback on this chapter.

Floating Image is available on the Android Market at https://market.android.com/details?id=dk.nindroid.rss and source code is available under GPL at http://code.google.com/p/floatingimage/.

Bibliography

[Bærentzen et al. 08] Jakob Andreas Bærentzen, Steen Munk-Lund, Mikkel Gjøl, and Bent Dalgaard Larsen. "Two Methods for Antialiased Wireframe Drawing with Hidden Line Removal." *Proceedings of the Spring Conference in Computer Graphics*, edited by Karol Myszkowski, pp. 171–177. Bratislava, Slovakia: Comenius University, 2008.

[Flaherty 10] Adam Flaherty. "How to Render Anti-Aliased Lines with Textures in iOS 4." O'Reilly Answers. June 24, 2010. Available at http://answers.oreilly.com/topic/1669-how-to-render-anti-aliased-lines-with-textures-in-ios-4/.

[IMG 11] "POWERVR Series5 Graphics: SGX Architecture Guide for Developers." Imagination Technologies. July 5, 2011. Available at http://www.imgtec.com/powervr/insider.

[OpenGL 08] "OpenGL ES Common/Common-Lite Profile Specification: Version 1.1.12." Edited by David Blythe, Aaftab Munshi, and Jon Leech. The Khronos Group and Silicon Graphics. April 24, 2008. Available at http://www.khronos.org/registry/gles/specs/1.1/es_full_spec_1.1.12.pdf.

[OpenGL 10] "OpenGL ES Common Profile Specification: Version 2.0.25." Edited by Aaftab Munshi and Jon Leech. The Khronos Group. November 2, 2010. Available at http://www.khronos.org/registry/gles/specs/2.0/es_full_spec_2.0.25.pdf.

[Rasterization 11] "Rasterization Rules (Direct3D 10)." *msdn*. Microsoft. 2011. Available at http://msdn.microsoft.com/en-us/library/cc627092(v=vs.85).aspx.

[Sander et al. 01] P. Sander, H. Hoppe, J. Snyder, and S. Gortler. "Discontinuity Edge Overdraw." In *I3D '01 Proceedings of the 2001 Symposium on Interactive 3D Graphics*, pp. 167–174. New York: ACM Press, 2001.

[Texture 04] "Texture AntiAliasing." Apple. 2004. Available at http://homepage.mac.com/arekkusu/bugs/invariance/TexAA.html.

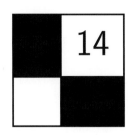

14

Practical Planar Reflections Using Cubemaps and Image Proxies

Sébastien Lagarde and Antoine Zanuttini

14.1 Introduction

Rendering scenes with glossy and specular reflections has always been a challenge in the field of real-time rendering. Due to their importance in assessing image quality, many techniques have been developed to simulate reflections. These techniques can be classified in four categories:

1. Real-time techniques, such as dynamic environment mapping, with all kinds of parameterization: cubemaps, 2D mirror planes, dual paraboloid. Dynamic reflections of this type are accurate but costly because they require resending the whole scene to the graphics pipeline. Many optimizations have been devised to speed up the process, such as mesh or shader simplifications, but it still induces a significant overhead.

2. Precomputed techniques, such as static environment mapping with all kinds of parameterization: cube maps, sphere maps, dual paraboloid, etc. Static reflections lack the accuracy of dynamic reflection but are far cheaper to use.

3. Screen-space techniques, such as screen-space local reflection [Tiago et al. 12], often come at a manageable cost for pleasant localized results, but fail where on-screen information is missing.

4. Real-time ray-tracing techniques such as the image-based reflections found in Epic's Samaritan demo [Mittring and Dudash 11] are promising techniques, but they require support for features not available on older graphics hardware.

For our game *Remember Me*, targeting current generation console hardware (DX9/PS3/Xbox 360), we tried to find a reflection technique similar in cost to precomputed techniques, but with improved accuracy and realism.

This chapter introduces a new algorithm with a set of artist tools that allow simulating planar glossy/specular reflections. The goal of our method is to replace the accurate but costly real-time planar reflection with a cheaper approximation that does not require re-rendering the scene geometry. In our game, we mostly use these tools for ground reflections.

The principle of the algorithm is to render an approximation of the reflected scene into a 2D reflection texture, then use this texture during the scene rendering. In order to build the approximated reflected scene, we provide our artists with several tools that let them combine the reflected scene with offline-generated elements: environment maps and image proxies. To increase quality, we parallax-correct elements of the reflected scene for the current view when they are rendered in the reflection texture. In order to update the parallax-correction, the reflection texture is updated for each frame.

We will start the description of our algorithm and tools with the generation of the reflection texture. We will describe how our algorithm fits within a local image-based lighting (IBL) strategy, following the work we presented in [Lagarde and Zanuttini 12]. We will conclude with the processing and usage of this 2D reflection texture for the scene rendering.

14.2   Generating Reflection Textures

14.2.1   Cubemap Reflection Environment

Our algorithm begins by generating an approximation of the reflected scene. We are trying to avoid the cost of re-rendering the scene geometry at runtime. In this case, the common technique for approximating reflections is to create an environment map, such as a cubemap, that is the parameterization of choice due to its hardware efficiency. However, the reflection stored in the cubemap is correct only from a single point in space. Applying a cubemap onto a planar geometry such as a ground surface creates visual issues in part due to lack of parallax (Figure 14.3). The graphics literature proposes several algorithms to fix this problem. All these algorithms share the requirement of a geometry proxy to represent the reflection environment: simple sphere volumes [Bjorke 04], box volumes [Czuba 10] or cube depth buffers [Szirmay-Kalos et al. 05]. The reflected view vector by the surface normal is used to intersect the proxy geometry. A corrected reflected view vector is created from the pixel's world position, which can then be used to fetch the right cubemap sample. Cost and quality increase with the geometry proxy's complexity. For completeness, we note that other cheap parallax correction methods without a geometry proxy are available [Geiss 05, Brennan 02], but they require manual tuning for each object. Our solution to

Figure 14.1. Cubemap with a box volume (white) and reflection plane (red) matching a rectangular room environment.

the parallax problem is unique in that we don't use the scene's geometry since we cannot access the pixel's world position when we render into the 2D reflection texture. Moreover, we limit ourselves to planar reflections.

We developed tools for our artists to allow placing cubemaps in levels and associating them with a geometry proxy: a convex volume approximating the reflection environment. For example, in a rectangular room an artist can place a cubemap in the center of the room and define a box volume to approximate the room boundaries. The center of the box volume doesn't need to match the position of the cubemap. As we target planar reflections, we also require having a reflection plane for the cubemap (Figure 14.1). The reflection plane could be specified as a distance from the cubemap position and oriented by the cubemap's up axis or extracted from a game's entity.

In order to correct for parallax, we make the following observation (see Figure 14.2):

Consider a scene with a ground surface (hashed line), a reflection environment (yellow) approximated by a proxy geometry (box volume in green) and a camera. The camera looks at a position on the ground. The reflected view vector $\vec{R}$ is used to get the intersection P with the proxy geometry. P is then used with the cubemap that was captured at center C to recover the cubemap's sample direction $\vec{D}$. If we reflect the camera about the reflection plane, the new view vector $\vec{V}$ of the reflected camera matches the previous $\vec{R}$ vector and intersects the same point P. From this observation, we deduce that in order to fix the parallax issue we could simply project the cubemap onto its geometry proxy, and then render the geometry from the point of view of the reflected camera.

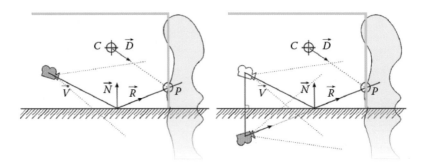

Figure 14.2. The view vector of the reflected camera equals the reflected view vector of the camera.

The rendering process is similar to standard real-time planar reflection rendering. We build a ViewProjection matrix by mirroring the View matrix by the reflection plane and compose it with an oblique near clipping plane matrix [Lengyel 07]. We then render the back face of the geometry proxy with this ViewProjection matrix. As we reflect the camera, we must inverse the winding order. C++ pseudocode and shader code are provided in Listing 14.1.

```
// C++ pseudocode
Matrix Mirror = CreateMirrorMatrix(ReflectionPlaneWS);
Matrix ReflectView = Mirror * View;
Matrix ClipProjection = NearObliqueMatrix(ReflectionPlaneVS);
Matrix ViewProjection = View * ClipProjection;
// Render back face but remember to inverse culling order
SetInverseFrontFaceCulling();
DrawConvexVolume();


// Shader code
float4x4 LocalToWorld;
float4x4 ViewProjection;

VertexMain() {

  float4 PositionWS = mul(LocalToWorld, InPositionOS);
  float4 PositionSS = mul(ViewProjection, PositionWS);
  OutPosition = PositionSS;
  // Current direction sampling direction
  OutDirection = PositionWS.xyz - CubeCenterWS.xyz;
}

PixelMain() {
  OutColor = texCUBE(CubeTexture, OutDirection);
}
```

Listing 14.1. Pseudocode of parallax-corrected cubemap.

Figure 14.3. Box (top) and convex (bottom) room with a specular ground reflecting the environment with a cubemap. With parallax issue (left) and with correction (right).

Our algorithm allows for the rendering of accurate reflections for any space matching the convex volume used as a geometry proxy (Figure 14.3). It is possible to use concave volumes as geometry proxies but it will result in artifacts because we don't use the Z-buffer during the drawing. Additionally, some information will not be captured in the cubemap. In the next section, we will present a technique to add information into the 2D reflection texture to complete the cubemap that can be used to hide these artifacts.

14.2.2   Image Proxies

The previous section described the projection of a parallax-corrected cubemap onto a 2D reflection texture to approximate the reflected scene. This kind of rendering has its limits because it can miss or lose information: dynamic elements may disappear, the 2D texture resolution can be too low, causing flickering or the disappearance of bright small elements, and concave volumes used as geometry proxies will occlude details. It is possible to enhance the cubemap's contribution to the rendering of the reflected scene with image proxies in the spirit of the light cards used in the AMD's Whiteout demo [Wiley and Scheuermann 07] or the billboards from Epic's Samaritan demo [Mittring and Dudash 11]. The addition of image proxies to our algorithm is easy. We use a quad as a geometry proxy for an image representing a part of the reflected scene, then we render the quad as in the previous section. A detailed description of the creation, rendering and usage of image proxies follows.

Figure 14.4. Editor view showing the link between an image proxy and a cubemap (left) and the orthogonal frustum for a 2D scene capture (right).

Creating image proxies. An image proxy is a quad textured with an authored image or a 2D capture from the scene. The quad is used as a geometric approximation of the reflection environment a.k.a. the geometry proxy.

We developed tools for our artists to allow placing image proxies in levels, customizing the quad size, customizing the texture resolution and performing 2D scene captures (Figure 14.4). The 2D capture is done with an orthogonal frustum set up inside our game editor. The capture considers empty areas (pixels that have not been touched during rendering) as transparent.

Image proxies are very similar to sprite particles and they can share many properties. We decided to take a subset of sprite particles functionality. Image proxies can

- always face the camera, resulting in a spherical billboard;

- define a constraint axis and try to face the camera but rotate along that axis, resulting in a cylindrical billboard;

- use different blending modes (interpolative, additive).

Note that we restrict ourselves to quad image proxies for efficiency, but other plane shapes could apply here.

Rendering image proxies. All image proxies are transparent objects (this choice will be explained later in this section) and thus need to be sorted back to front before rendering since we do not use a Z-buffer. We use the distance from the camera to the image proxies as a criterion for sorting. For an accurate rendering, particularly in the case of overlapping image proxies, we should perform a binary space partitioning (BSP) of the quads but we found out that using a priority system to force the rendering order was sufficient in our case. Rendering image proxies is similar to cubemap rendering. We also allow image proxies to be two sided. C++ pseudocode and shader code are provided in Listing 14.2.

```
// C++ pseudocode
Matrix Mirror = CreateMirrorMatrix(ReflectionPlaneWS);
Matrix ReflectView = Mirror * View;
Matrix ClipProjection = NearObliqueMatrix(ReflectionPlaneVS);
Matrix ViewProjection = View * ClipProjection;

// Image proxy specific
Vector ReflectViewOrigin = Mirror * ViewOrigin;
Matrix InverseReflectView = ReflectView.Inverse();
Vector ViewUp = -InverseReflectView * Vector(0,1,0);

// Following is done for each IP (Image proxy)
// Calc X and Y sprite vector based on option.
Vector YVector = IP ->LocalToWorld * Vector (0, 1, 0);
if(IP->bCameraFacing) {
  float ScaleFactor = YVector.Length();
  YVector = CameraUp.Normalize() * ScaleFactor;
}

Vector CameraDirWS = (CameraWS - IP->Location).Normalize();

Vector XVector = IP->LocalToWorld * Vector(1, 0, 0);
if(IP->bCameraFacing || IP->bCameraFacingReflectionAxis) {
  float ScaleFactor = XVector.Lenght();
  XVector = CameraDir ^ YVector;
  XVector = XVector.Normalize() * ScaleFactor;
}


// Shader code
float4x4 LocalToWorld;
float4x4 ViewProjection;
float3 IPPosition;

VertexMain() {
  float3 VPosition = IPPosition + InPosition.x * XVector -
InPosition.y * YVector;
  float4 PositionSS = mul(ViewProjection, float4(VPosition, 1));
  OutPosition = PositionSS;
  UVOut = UV;
}

float4 IPColor ;

PixelMain() {}
  OutColor = IPColor * tex2D(SpriteTexture, InUV);
}
```

Listing 14.2. Pseudocode for parallax-corrected rendering of image proxies.

A disturbing problem of naively rendering image proxies as presented here is
temporal aliasing. The low resolution of our textures (both 2D reflection textures
and image proxy textures) causes severe aliasing along the edges of image proxies,
especially when the camera moves near the boundaries of the geometry proxy.
To minimize aliasing we set the alpha value of image proxy texture borders to be
fully translucent, forcing us to render the image proxies as transparent objects
(Figure 14.5). It would also be possible to set this value from within the shader.

Figure 14.5. An image proxy of a door rendered with aliasing (left). The floor is flat and specular to highlight the aliasing issue. The same with fully transparent texture borders (right).

It should be noted that the choice of a quad geometry simplifies this step: a more complex geometry would require more efforts in order to deal with aliasing.

Using image proxies for dynamic reflections. An image proxy is not restricted to a static quad. By dynamically updating its position (for instance by attaching it to a game entity), it is possible to handle gameplay events such as an opening door (Figure 14.6). In this case the cubemap must not contain the scene geometry represented by the image proxies, i.e., the door must not be present when generating the cubemap. We provide flags to our artists to specify the scene object visibility based on the type of rendering (2D capture, cubemap, or scene).

We also use dynamic updates of image proxies to simulate character reflections. Character image proxies are just image proxies linked to the character's main bones with a constraint along each bone's axis. In this case we use an authored texture that consists in just a white sphere that can be tinted by characters. During gameplay we update the character's image proxies based on the transformation of their attached bones and link them to the current cubemap (Figure 14.7).

Figure 14.6. Image proxies can be moved in real-time to match the action.

Best practices. Image proxies are powerful tools, but they require production time from the artists. There are plenty of creative ways to use them to enhance reflections and we present some best practices here. Figure 14.8 shows screenshots of typical use cases with only the cubemap applied and with the contribution of the image proxies:

Figure 14.7. Character proxies (left), the texture used for the main bones (center), and the character proxies on a flat mirror, highlighting the coarse approximation (right).

1. Rendering small light sources inside small resolution cubemap is problematic. They can flicker or completely drop out. Image proxies can compensate for the low resolution.

2. Control the brightness strength of the cubemap: As a cubemap is a single texture generated in the engine, it is painful to boost the brightness in only a part of it. Image proxies can control their brightness individually.

3. Enhance lights: in order to emulate a stretch highlight on a wet ground similar to the Blinn-Phong lighting model, artists can create a cylinder billboard image proxy with an authored texture instead of a capture of that part of the scene.

4. Hide undesirable reflections: by placing a 2D scene capture proxy at the appropriate position, it is possible to hide reflection elements either in the cubemap or in another image proxy.

5. Handle multiple reflection planes: Standard real-time reflection can only reflect for one plane at a time. By settings image proxies at different height with their quad geometries parallel to the reflection plane, we could simulate multiple plane reflections inside one texture.

6. Hide concave geometry proxy artifacts: if the cubemap captures a corner corridor, image proxies can be used to hide the missing information caused by occlusions.

Another useful property of image proxies arises when dealing with multiple cubemaps at the same time, as will be shown in the next section.

14.2.3   Local Image-Based Lighting

Our game uses a local image-based lighting (IBL) system. Our local IBL provides accurate environment lighting information that can be used for glossy and/or specular reflections and has the additional advantage of smooth lighting transitions between objects. The system has been covered in detail in the authors' SIGGRAPH 2012 talk [Lagarde and Zanuttini 12] and personal blog [Lagarde 12]. It consists of blending multiple cubemaps in the neighborhood of a point of interest (the camera, the player...) and using the blended cubemap for indirect lighting on scene objects. The blending weights are authored by artists as influence regions around a cubemap. We extend the previous work by blending cubemaps inside a 2D reflection texture instead of a cubemap and by adding image proxies to the mix. The move from a cubemap to a 2D texture is motivated by performance requirements since we need to handle only one view instead of six.

Figure 14.8. Examples of best practices. Top to bottom: cases 2, 3, and 4. On the left, the scene with only the cubemap reflection and the image proxy capture frustum (red box). on the right, the enhancement resulting from image proxy use.

Rendering multiple cubemaps and image proxies. In order to render multiple cube-maps correctly, we should render each cubemap and its linked image proxy sep-arately and then blend the result. This is because of the reflection plane, the sorting order and the blending mode of the image proxies. This has both a mem-ory and a computational cost. As a performance optimization, we chose to first render all cubemaps sorted by increasing blend weight with additive blending, then render all sorted image proxies. This can cause trouble when mixing cube-maps with different reflection planes but we let artists manage this case. Other artifacts are less noticeable.

Extra care needs to be taken for character image proxies as these are dynami-cally linked to the cubemaps. In the blending case, they must be linked to all the gathered cubemaps in order to be fully visible (the sum of their blending weights will equal 100%). We render them in each cubemap rather than at the end to get smoother transitions when a cubemap with a different reflection plane comes into the mix.

Similarly to character proxies, other image proxies may be shared by multiple cubemaps. If the image proxy uses interpolative blending, this could result in a final image intensity that is lower than expected because of repeated interpolation. This can be fixed in the shader by tweaking the alpha value according to the blending weight.

Image proxy best practices with local IBL. Our local IBL approach provides seam-less transitions between lighting environments represented by cubemaps. A sim-ple example of a corridor environment has been presented in our SIGGRAPH talk. This still applies to our planar reflection. We set up three cubemaps in the corridor with overlapping influence regions and identical geometry proxies. For clarity, only the geometry proxies (the box volumes in red, green, and blue) are shown, with a small scale so that they are all visible. This setup and our planar reflection technique provide detailed reflections and smooth transitions (Figure 14.9). There is a video in the web material accompanying this article showing the result when the camera moves.

Image proxies are of great help in more complex cases. Again, artists must be creative, and we help by presenting some best practices. Figure 14.9 shows the setup of geometry proxies and screenshots of typical usage (refer to the video for better visualization). Purple lines are image proxies; red, green and blue boxes are geometry proxies of cubemaps:

1. Corner corridor: The set of geometry proxies include a concave volume. Artists use image proxies to hide the artifacts. The image proxies are captures of the walls.

2. Two successive rooms, separated by an opening door: The geometry proxies overlap and include the two rooms. The image proxies are captures of the separating walls. Walls should not be included in the cubemap generation.

Figure 14.9. Top view of the scene's cubemap setup (left) and the resulting rendition (right). From top to bottom: corridor case from the SIGGRAPH talk, best case 1, and best case 2.

14.3 Using Reflection Textures

14.3.1 Glossy Material Support

We saw how to generate a 2D reflection texture to approximate a reflected scene. This texture is better suited for specular materials like perfect mirrors. In order to support glossy material we store preconvolved versions of the base texture in the mipmaps (Figure 14.10). This is similar to a preconvolved cubemap [Kautz et al. 00]. Each mipmap level maps to a different glossiness. A highly glossy reflection (more detailed) will look up a lower mipmap level, a less glossy reflection (more blurred) will look up the average of a large number of pixels. We experimented with two ways of generating the mipmaps: by rendering the reflected scene for each mipmap, and by successively blurring base mipmaps.

Rendering the reflected scene in each mipmap. We first try to re-render the approximated reflected scene for each mipmap. For better results, we should use both preconvolved cubemaps and preconvolved image proxies. At rendering time, the current mipmap level to render is used to sample the current mipmap level of the texture applied on the cubemap or image proxies. The difficulty of this

Figure 14.10. Different mipmap levels matching different roughness strengths.

approach lies in the generation of accurate preconvolved image proxies, which is impossible because of the lack of information outside of the 2D texture. The low resolution of the mipmap is also problematic: small image proxies will contribute too few pixels. Finally, if there are several characters in a scene then the number of draw calls can increase significantly. Since we know we cannot achieve sufficient accuracy anyway, we choose a cheaper approach.

Convolving base mipmaps. A simpler approach consists of recursively blurring mipmap textures. Each mipmap stores the result of convolving the previous lower mipmap level with a specified blurring kernel. We use a Gaussian blur that we found to be sufficient for our needs.

Aliasing. Aliasing is an important issue that our method must address. The reader may notice that in Listing 14.1 a texCUBE instruction is used instead of texCUBElod that would force a fetch from the base cubemap. This reduces aliasing even if mipmaps are generated in a subsequent step. For completeness, it should be added that a better way would be to use the texCUBElod instruction and, at scene rendering time, compute the required hardware mipmap level and the desired mipmap level based on roughness, then chose the larger of the two values [Scheuermann and Isidoro 05]. We decided against this approach for performance reasons.

14.3.2   Applying the 2D Reflection Texture

The preconvolved 2D reflection texture can now be used on any planar objects lying at the same height as the reflection plane used to generate the texture. The rendering process for our texture is similar to the mirror surface case. We use the texture to provide the reflection value by performing a texture lookup with the actual screen coordinates as the texture coordinates. We approximate rough surfaces by offsetting the texture coordinates along the XY components of the surface normal with an artist-controlled parameter for the distortion strength. We also use the glossiness of the surface to select the right mipmap level to use (Listing 14.3). It is possible to divide the distortion value by the post-perspective Z-coordinate. The distortion will vary with distance but we did not find it to

```
float2 ScreenUV = ScreenPosition.xy / ScreenPosition.w *
float2(0.5f, -0.5f) + 0.5f;
float2 R = ScreenUV + TangentNormal.xy * DistortionStrenght;
return tex2Dlod ( ReflectionTexture, float4(R, 0.0f, ScaleBias.x *
Glossiness + ScaleBias.y)).rgb;
```

Listing 14.3. High-level shading language (HLSL) pseudocode to use a 2D reflection texture.

improve the final quality in our case. Note that for performance reasons, we do not transform the normal to view-space but keep it in tangent space, implying that we could not distort in the correct direction. In practice the result is good enough and the correct result would still be an approximation anyway (Figure 14.11).

14.3.3 Cost

We provide some performance measurements of our implementation with a $128 \times 128 \times 6$ cubemap stored using DXT1 compression, 128×128 image proxies using DXT5, and a 256×256 2D reflection texture. Image proxies use DXT5 to support the alpha pixel border we add for antialiasing. We provide our performance measurements as ranges since timings vary with the number of cubemaps, image proxies and pixels clipped by the reflection plane. The typical case includes two cubemaps and 10 to 15 image proxies. The whole process is in HDR format.

Figure 14.11. The influence of the distortion strength on the reflection.

On the PlayStation 3, we generate the reflection texture in the RGBA half16 format. The texture generation costs between 0.10 ms and 0.33 ms, with an average of 0.17 ms. The mipmap generation costs 0.16 ms. The process is render-output-bound due to the use of RGBA half16.

On the Xbox 360 we use the 10-bit float 7e3 format. The texture generation costs between 0.06 ms and 0.24 ms with an average of 0.1 ms. The mipmap generation costs 0.09 ms.

14.4   Conclusion and Future Work

We have presented a good alternative to real-time 2D reflections applied to planar objects to simulate specular and/or glossy materials. Our approach is fast and practical and can be used in conjunction with other techniques such as local IBL. It has been used in production in our game targeting current generation consoles. A video showing various best practices and use cases of our technique is available in the accompanying web material.

The technique is satisfying but could be improved in a number of ways:

First, using a cubemap reflection texture instead of a 2D reflection texture will improve the accuracy of the reflection distortion with rough surfaces at the cost of doing the process six times and requiring more time to generate mipmap. It should be highlighted that this still does not provide the correct result because we are generating the cubemap reflection texture only for normals perpendicular to the reflection plane. Using it for shifted normals introduces a distortion that increases with the angle between the normal and the plane normal (Figure 14.12) [Lagarde and Zanuttini 12]. Another parameterization, more efficient but with the same benefits, could be a dual paraboloid map [Scherzer et al. 12]. This will require tessellating our geometry proxies to limit the projection warping artifacts and rotating the lighting to local space aligned on the reflection plane's normal.

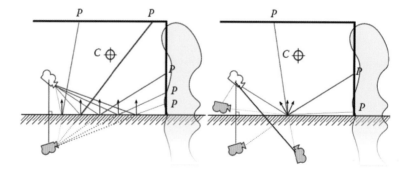

Figure 14.12. Our cubemap reflection is only valid for pixels with a normal vector perpendicular to the ground (left). For perturbed normals, the intersection requires moving the reflected camera's position (right).

Second, anisotropic reflections could be emulated by stretching image proxies based on some physical properties. A more physically based approach could be developed for the mipmap generation step.

Finally image reflections as used in Epic's Samaritan demo [Mittring and Dudash 11] also are an interesting future development.

14.5 Acknowledgments

The screenshots in Figures 14.1, 14.4, 14.5, 14.6, 14.8, and 14.11 are *Remember Me* gameplay images from the game demo at Gamescom 2012. Images courtesy of Capcom U.S.A., Inc., © Capcom Co. Ltd. 2013, all rights reserved.

Bibliography

[Bjorke 04] Kevin Bjorke. "Image base lighting." In *GPU Gems*, edited by Randima Fernando, pp. 307–321. Reading, MA: Addison-Wesley, 2004.

[Brennan 02] Chris Brennan. "Accurate Environment Mapped Reflections and Refractions by Adjusting for Object Distance." In *ShaderX*, edited by Wolfgang Engel, pp. 290–294. Plano, TX: Wordware Inc., 2002.

[Czuba 10] Bartosz Czuba. "Box Projected Cubemap Environment Mapping." *Gamedev.net*. http://www.gamedev.net/topic/568829-box-projected-cubemap-environment-mapping/, April 20, 2010.

[Geiss 05] Ryan Geiss. "The Naked Truth Behind NVIDIA's Demos." Exhibitor Tech Talk, ACM SIGGRAPH 2005, Los Angeles, CA, 2005.

[Kautz et al. 00] Jan Kautz, Pere-Pau Vázquez, Wolfgang Heidrich, and Hans-Peter Seidel. "Unified Approach to Prefiltered Environment Maps." In *Proceedings of the Eurographics Workshop on Rendering Techniques 2000*, pp. 185–196. London: Springer-Verlag, 2000.

[Lagarde 12] Sébastien Lagarde. "Image-Based Lighting Approaches and Parallax-Corrected Cubemap." *Random Thoughts about Graphics in Games*. http://seblagarde.wordpress.com/2012/09/29/image-based-lighting-approaches-and-parallax-corrected-cubemap/, September 29, 2012.

[Lagarde and Zanuttini 12] Sébastien Lagarde and Antoine Zanuttini. "Local Image-Based Lighting with Parallax-Corrected Cubemap." In *ACM SIGGRAPH 2012 Talks*, article no. 36. New York: ACM, 2012.

[Lengyel 07] Eric Lengyel. "Projection Matrix Tricks." Presentation, Game Developers Conference 2007, San Francisco, CA, 2007.

[Mittring and Dudash 11] Martin Mittring and Bryan Dudash. "The Technology Behind the DirectX 11 Unreal Engine 'Samaritan' Demo." Presentation, Game Developers Coneference 2001, San Francisco, CA, 2011.

[Scherzer et al. 12] Daniel Scherzer, Chuong H. Nguyen, Tobias Ritschel, and Hans-Peter Seidel. "Pre-convolved Radiance Caching." Eurographics Symposium on Rendering: *Computer Graphics Forum* 31:4 (2012), 1391–1397.

[Scheuermann and Isidoro 05] Thorsten Scheuermann and John Isidoro. "Cubemap filtering with CubeMapGen." Presentation, Game Developers Conference, San Francisco, CA, 2005.

[Szirmay-Kalos et al. 05] László Szirmay-Kalos, Barnabás Aszódi, István Lazányi, and Mátyás Premecz. "Approximate Ray-Tracing on the GPU with Distance Impostors." *Computer Graphics Forum* 24:3 (2005), 695–704.

[Tiago et al. 12] Tiago Sousa, Nickolay Kasyan, and Nicolas Schulz. "CryENGINE 3: Three Years of Work in Review." In *GPU Pro 3*, edited by Wolfgang Engel, pp. 133–168. Boca Raton, FL: CRC Press, 2012.

[Wiley and Scheuermann 07] Abe Wiley and Thorsten Scheuermann. "The Art and Technology of Whiteout." Presentation, ACM SIGGRAPH 2007, San Diego, CA, 2007.

15

Real-Time Ptex and
Vector Displacement
Karl Hillesland

15.1   Introduction

A fundamental texture authoring problem is that it's difficult to unwrap a mesh with arbitrary topology onto a continuous 2D rectangular texture domain. Meshes are broken into pieces that are unwrapped into "charts" and packed into a rectangular texture domain as an "atlas" as shown in Figure 15.4(b). Artists spend time setting up UVs to minimize distortion and wasted space in the texture when they should ideally be focusing on the actual painting and modeling.

Another problem is that edges of each chart in the atlas introduce seam artifacts. This seam problem becomes much worse when the texture is a displacement map used for hardware tessellation, as any discrepancy manifests as a crack in the surface.

This chapter describes an implicit texture parametrization system to solve these problems that we call *packed Ptex*. It builds on the Ptex method developed by Disney Animation Studios for production rendering [Burley and Lacewell 08]. Ptex associates a small independent texture map with each face of the mesh. Each texture map has its own mip chain. In the original Ptex method, adjacency information is used for filtering across the edge of one face texture and into the next.

There are two main advantages of Ptex relative to conventional texture atlasing. First, there is no need for explicit UV. Second, there are no seaming issues arising from unwrapping a complete mesh of arbitrary topology onto a single-texture domain. These are the two main advantages of the original Ptex method that we preserve in our adaptation.

The drawbacks of packed Ptex relative to conventional texture atlasing are additional runtime computation, additional texture filtering expense, and changes in asset production. The main change in asset production is that our method currently targets meshes consisting of quads. There can either be additional memory cost or savings relative to conventional texture atlasing methods depending on the particular circumstances.

Although this approach works for many texture types, it works particularly well for vector displacement mapping. The lack of seam issues is particularly valuable for this application, while many of the drawbacks of the approach are irrelevant.

There are two barriers to real-time performance in the original Ptex method. First, it's typically not practical to have an individual texture for each primitive. Second, the indirection required when a filter kernel crosses from one face to another is costly in performance, and precludes the use of any hardware texture filtering. The next section describes the offline process to address these issues. Then we follow up with how to use this at runtime and some details related to displacement mapping. We finish by discussing the tradeoffs of this method as well as some possible alternatives.

15.2   Packed Ptex

To reduce the number of textures required, we pack all face textures and their mip chains into a single texture atlas (Figure 15.1). The atlas is divided into blocks of the same resolution. Within the block, the face textures are packed one after another in rows. Because the atlas width generally is not a multiple of the face-texture width, there will be unused texels at the end of each row. There will be additional empty space at the end of the last row, because it generally will not be filled to capacity.

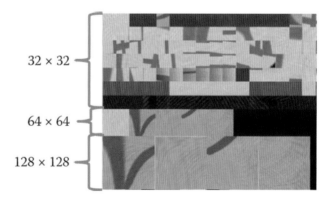

Figure 15.1. This is a portion of a packed Ptex atlas. There are four faces that have 128×128 base (level 0) resolution and one with 64×64 base resolution. The block of 64×64 contains both the one level 0 for the 64×64 face texture, and the four level 1 mips from the 128×128 face textures.

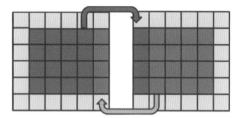

Figure 15.2. Faces that are adjacent in model space are not generally adjacent in texture space. A filter kernel that spills over the edge of a face must pick up texels from the adjacent face, which will generally be somewhere else in the texture atlas. We copy border texels from adjacent face textures to handle this case.

Just as in the original Ptex system, each face texture has its own mip chain. We sort the faces by their base (level 0) resolution to create the packing we describe here, and for runtime as described in Section 15.3.2. Since we are including face textures with different base resolutions, a given block will include different mip levels (Figure 15.1).

15.2.1 Borders for Filtering

Texture filtering hardware assumes that neighbors in texture space are also neighbors in model space. Generally, this is not true either for conventional texture atlasing methods nor for Ptex. It's the reason conventional texture atlasing methods often come with seam artifacts.

For our method, we copy texels from the border of a neighboring face to solve this problem (Figure 15.2). That way, there will be data available when the texture filter crosses the edge of the face texture. The padding on each side will be equal to at least half the filter width. This is a common solution to the problem, particularly for situations like tile-based textures for terrain. However, the memory overhead for this solution is generally much higher for Ptex than for conventional texture atlasing methods. This is one disadvantage in using Ptex; anisotropic filtering quickly becomes too expensive in terms of memory cost.

15.2.2 Texture Compression

Current GPUs have hardware support for texture compression. The compression relies on coherency within 4×4 texel blocks. For this reason, it is best not to have a 4×4 block span face textures. We have already discussed adding a single-texel border to support hardware bilinear filtering. To get good results with compression, we add an additional border to get to a multiple of 4×4. Generally, this means two-texel borders for compressed textures.

15.3　Runtime Implementation

In the original Ptex system, texture lookups were done by first finding which face you are in and then finding where you are within the face. The real-time version essentially starts with the same steps, but with an additional mapping into the texture atlas space. This section walks through each of these steps in detail. For trilinear filtered lookups, the basic outline is the following:

1. Select the texture level of detail (LOD) (Section 15.3.1).

2. Compute the location within atlas for each LOD level and perform a hardware, bilinear lookup for each (Section 15.3.2).

3. Lerp in the shader for a final trilinear value.

For nonfiltered lookups, the sequence is easier; all that's required is to find the location in the atlas and do a single lookup. We will discuss the first two steps in detail.

15.3.1　Texture LOD Selection

The first step in a trilinear filtered, packed Ptex lookup is to determine which resolution of face texture is desired. In conventional hardware trilinear filtering, this is done for you automatically by the GPU. However, hardware trilinear filtering assumes the derivative of texture space with respect to screen space is continuous everywhere. This is not the case for a texture atlas in general, although it's often "good enough" for conventional texture atlasing with some tweaking. However, tiled textures like real-time Ptex often require manual texture LOD selection. The code for this is given in Listing 15.1.

15.3.2　Packed Ptex Lookup

Once we know which resolution we want, we clamp it to the maximum resolution available for that face (i.e., mip level 0). Table 15.1 demonstrates how to look up the maximum resolution for a face texture without having to resort to any per-face information. The method uses a sorted ordering according to face texture resolution and prefix sums.

The next step is to find the location of the resolution block within the atlas. This is possible by lookup into a table indexed by resolution.

The sorted ordering and prefix sum are used again to find the index of the face within the block. In general, not all faces will have a representation in the resolution block, as some face-texture base resolutions will be higher than others. Again, Table 15.1 describes the procedure.

We can find the face texture origin within the block using the index of the face within the resolution block. If the texture width is W and the face texture

```
float ComputeLOD( float2 vUV,   float nMipLevels )
{
   float2 vDx = ddx(vUV);
   float2 vDy = ddy(vUV);

   // Compute du and dv magnitude across quad
   float2 vDCoords;
   vDCoords = vDx * vDx;
   vDCoords += vDy * vDy;

   // Standard mip mapping uses max here
   float fMaxTexCoordDelta = max(vDCoords.x, vDCoords.y);
   float fMipLevelPower;

   if (fMaxTexCoordDelta == 0)
       fMipLevelPower = nMipLevels -1;
   else
   {
      // 0.5 is for the square root
      fMipLevelPower = 0.5 * log2(1.0 / fMaxTexCoordDelta);
   }

   float mipLevel = clamp(fMipLevelPower, 0, nMipLevels -1);
   return nMipLevels - 1 - mipLevel;
}
```

Listing 15.1. Texture LOD Selection. Allowing for nonsquare textures simply requires a scale by aspect ratio on one of the directions.

width including borders is w, then the number of faces in a row is $n = \lfloor W/w \rfloor$. Using i as the index within the block, we can compute the row as $\lfloor i/n \rfloor$ and the column as $i \% n$.

Each face has its own implicit UV parametrization. We adopt a convention with respect to the order of the vertices in the quad. For example, we choose the first index to be (0,0), the next is (1,0) and the last as (0,1). These can be assigned in the hull-shader stage. The pixel shader will receive the interpolated coordinate, which we call the "face UV." We also need the primitive ID, which is also defined in the hull-shader stage.

Max Resolution	Face Count	Prefix Sum
16×16	5	5
32×32	5	10
64×64	3	13

Table 15.1. If faces are sorted by resolution, and you have the prefix sum of face count for each resolution bin, you can look up the resolution for any given face from the index in the sorting. In this example, a face of index 7 would have a maximum resolution of 32×32 because it is greater than 5 and less than 10. If we want the index of that face within that bin, it is $7 - 5 = 2$.

```
float2 ComputeUV (
    uint faceID , // From SV_PrimitiveID
    float2 faceUV , // Position within the face
    uint nLog2 , // Log2 of the resolution we want
    int texWidth , // Atlas texture width
    int resOffset , // Prefix sum for this resolution
    int rowOffset , // Start of resolution block in atlas
    int borderSize ) // Texel thickness of border on each face
{
    // Here we assume a square aspect ratio.
    // A non-square aspect would simply scale the height
    // relative to width accordingly.
    float faceWidth = 1 << nLog2;
    float faceHeight = faceWidth;
    float borderedFaceWidth = faceWidth + 2*borderSize;
    float borderedFaceHeight = borderedFaceWidth;

    int nFacesEachRow = (int)texWidth / (int)borderedFaceWidth;
    int iFaceWithinBlock = faceID - resOffset;

    float2 faceOrigin = float2(
        (iFaceWithinBlock % nFacesEachRow) * borderedFaceWidth ,
        (iFaceWithinBlock / nFacesEachRow) * borderedFaceHeight
        + rowOffset );


    // Take face UV into account.
    // Still in texel units , but generally not
    // an integer value for bilinear filtering purposes.
    float2 uv = float2(faceWidth , faceHeight) * faceUV;
    uv += float2(nBorderSize , nBorderSize);
    uv += faceOrigin;

    // Finally scale by texture width and height to get
    // value in [0 ,1].
    return float2(uv) / float2(texWidth , texHeight);
}
```

Listing 15.2. Go from face UV to atlas UV.

Scale and offsets are applied to get the face UV range of [0,1] mapped into the atlas UV, including an offset to get to the right resolution block and another to put the face texture origin (0,0) inside the face border. Listing 15.2 details the process of computing a UV within the packed Ptex atlas.

The last steps are to do the bilinear filtered lookup for each LOD we need, and the final trilinear lerp between them.

15.3.3 Resolution Discrepancies

There are discrepancies in resolution that translate to discontinuities when approaching a polygon edge from either side. This is illustrated in Figure 15.3. This can happen when the gradient used for mip selection changes as the edge of a polygon is crossed. However, this is not particular to packed Ptex and is fur-

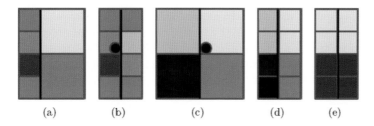

Figure 15.3. (a) Resolution discrepency (b) Bilinear lookup into border from view of left face. (c) Bilinear lookup into border from view of right face. (d) Changing the border on the left face to resolve resolution discrepancy by downsampling. (e) The solution for displacement when values must match exactly is to replicate at the lower resolution.

ther mitigated by the final lerp of trilinear filtering. In cases when we have used packed Ptex with trilinear filtering we have not seen any problems yet; therefore we have not pursued more sophisticated solutions.

The second cause for resolution discrepancy is capping to different resolutions due to different maximum (mip level 0) resolutions. The problem of max resolution discrepancy is mitigated by effectively clamping borders to the lower resolution when padding (Figure 15.3).

15.4 Adding Displacement

Displacement mapping adds geometric detail to a coarser mesh. Each polygon of the coarse mesh is tessellated further at runtime, and the vertices are displaced according to values stored in a displacement texture map. Displacement mapping provides a method of geometric LOD. The model can be rendered without the displacement for the lowest poly model, and different tessellations can be applied for higher quality models.

In classical displacement mapping, there is just a single scalar per texel. However, we have pursued vector displacement, which uses a 3D vector to specify displacement. This technique is much more expressive, but at greater memory cost on a per texel basis.

Authoring displacement maps in a conventional texture atlas without cracks can be quite difficult. If a shirt, for example, is unwrapped onto a texture, the edges where the charts meet on the model must match in value at every location. This is why games typically only apply displacement maps to flat objects like terrain, and why even Pixar's RenderMan, which is considered well engineered for displacement mapping, still performs a messy procedural crack-fill step during rendering [Apodaca and Gritz 99]. By contrast, you can export Ptex vector displacement maps from Autodesk Mudbox, and apply them without the need for manual fixup or runtime crack patching.

For displacement maps, we treat the borders and corners a little differently than described in Section 15.2.1. First of all, we do not need an extra border for filtering, as we use point sampling. However, adjacent faces must have identical values along their shared border to avoid cracks when using hardware tessellation. So instead of copying in a border from an adjacent face, we change the original borders by averaging them as shown in Figure 15.3.

Corners of a face texture correspond to a vertex in the model. Similar to how we handle borders, we walk the mesh around the vertex, gathering all corner values and average them. This value is then written back to all corners that share this vertex so that they are consistent and do not produce cracks. Note that it's necessary that this value is exactly the same. If you recompute this average for each quad, remember you are using floating-point math, and therefore must accumulate in the same order for each quad.

Displacement mapping is done in object space in the domain shader. In our implementation, we point sample from the highest resolution displacement map regardless of tessellation level. Becauseweare not filtering, the filter-related issues of packed Ptex are not relevant, and there is both less compute and bandwidth cost than for the typical texture map application in a pixel shader.

15.5   Performance Costs

To give a general idea of the cost difference between packed Ptex and conventional texturing, we measured the difference between a packed-Ptex and a conventionally textured version of the character shown in Figure 15.4(a). The AO, specular, albedo, normal and displacement maps are packed Ptex. GPU render time is 3.6 ms on an AMD Radeon HD 7970. If we change the AO, specular, albedo and normal maps to conventional texture lookups (all but displacement) we find the time goes down by an average of 0.6 ms.

The main cost is the search for maximum resolution in this implementation, for which there are plenty of opportunities for optimization we have not yet explored. We could, for example, move the computation as far up as the hull constant shader. There is also a cost due to reduced texture cache efficiency, as packed Ptex will generally not have as good locality of reference relative to conventional texturing. The entire UV computation was repeated for each texture, which should also not generally be necessary in practice.

Given the difficulty in authoring a valid displacement map for a model like the character in Figure 15.4(a) we measured packed Ptex displacement mapping against no displacement mapping at all. This model is made from 5,504 quads and tessellated up to 99,072 triangles. The cost of vector displacement with packed Ptex on this model is 0.14 ms. This is with 16-bit floats for each component, which is on the high end of what should normally be necessary in practice.

(a)

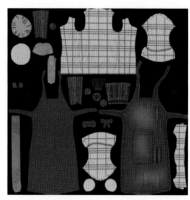

(b) Conventional atlas: 37% black.

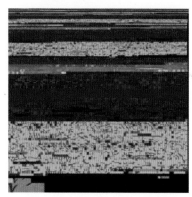

(c) Packed Ptex atlas: 7% black

Figure 15.4. All textures for the model in (a) are in the packed Ptex format: Albedo, AO, specular, normal, and vector displacement: (b) an example of a conventional texture map and (c) an equivalent packed Ptex texture map.

We have a second model, shown in Figure 15.5, that uses packed Ptex only for vector displacement. It has a total of 86,954 quads in the base mesh and is animated with both skinning and blend shapes. When tessellated up to 1.6 million triangles, the cost of displacement lookup is 2.7 ms out of a total of 14.2 ms with our current implementation.

Figure 15.5. Model with vector displacement.

15.6 Memory Costs

Conventional texture atlases are often difficult to author without wasting texture space between the charts. In Figure 15.4(b) we see a typical example where 37% of the space is wasted. Ptex, by contrast, is built completely from rectangular pieces and is therefore much easier to pack into a rectangular domain. We make no special effort to find the optimal resolution to pack the face textures into, and yet the waste in our experience has been only around 7% (Figure 15.4(c)).

The greater memory overhead for packed Ptex is in the use of borders. Fundamentally, the border cost goes up proportional to the square root of the area. Here we give some formulas and concrete numbers to give an idea of what the overhead is. Each face of square resolution r and border size n_B wastes $(2n_B + r)^2 - r^2$ texels. Table 15.2 shows example costs as a percentage of waste due to borders in packed Ptex. Two items are worth mentioning here. First, we can see more concretely how high the per-face resolution should be to keep memory overhead down. Second, we also see why borders beyond a couple texels, as would be required for anisotropic filtering, is too expensive in memory cost.

	Border Size		
Resolution	1	2	4
4×4	56/56%	75/75%	89/89%
8×8	36/41%	56/62%	75/80%
16×16	21/24%	36/41%	56/62%
32×32	11/13%	21/23%	36/40%
64×64	6.0/6.4%	11/12%	21/23%
128×128	3.1/3.2%	6.0/6.2%	11/12%

Table 15.2. This table shows memory overhead for borders. The first percentage in each pair is for a single resolution, and the second is for mip chains down to 4×4. These values should be weighed against the waste inherent in a conventional texture atlas, such as the 37% illustrated in Figure 15.4(b).

15.7 Alternatives and Future Work

One way to avoid having a separate texture per face is to put each per-face texture in its own texture array slice [McDonald and Burley 11, McDonald 12]. This simplifies the texture addressing to some extent. However, there are limitations in the number of texture array slices, and resolutions cannot be mixed within a single texture array. Therefore, what would be a single texture in the conventional or packed Ptex approach would be split into multiple textures, one for each resolution, with further splitting as required for texture array limits. The amount of texture data used in the shader does not increase, excepting perhaps due to alignment or other per-texture costs, but the amount of conditional reads is significantly higher.

Rather than computing per-face texture information, we could store it in a resource indexed by face ID, and possibly by mip level [McDonald and Burley 11, McDonald 12].

Ptex takes the extreme approach of assigning an individual texture map to each primitive. The paper by B. Purnomo, et al. describes similar solutions to what is described here, but they group multiple primitives into rectangular patches in texture space for packing and handling seams [Purnomo et al. 04]. This reduces the overhead for borders, which would make larger filter kernels feasible. A next step might be to integrate some of the ideas from that paper.

15.8 Conclusion

Packed Ptex enables the main advantages of the original Ptex method while enabling real-time use. Authoring effort is saved first by eliminating the need for explicit UV assignment and second by naturally avoiding seaming issues that normally arise when trying to unwrap a 3D surface into at 2D rectangular domain. It does, however, require modeling with quads in its current implementation.

Packed Ptex also incurs higher runtime cost than conventional texture mapping. Memory costs can actually be lower relative to conventional texturing, depending primarily on the per-face texture resolution, filter kernel width, and the savings relative to the waste inherent with conventional texture atlases. Although packed Ptex can be applied to many different texture types, the most promising is probably displacement mapping, where the relative overhead is lower and the benefit of seamlessness is greatest.

15.9   Acknowledgments

The techniques described here were developed in collaboration with Sujeong Kim and Justin Hensley. Tim Heath, Abe Wiley, Exigent and Zoic helped on the art side. This work was done under the management and support of Jason Yang and David Hoff. Sujeong Kim, Takahiro Harada and Christopher Oat all provided valuable feedback in writing this article.

Bibliography

[Apodaca and Gritz 99] Anthony A. Apodaca and Larry Gritz. *Advanced RenderMan: Creating CGI for Motion Picture*, First edition. San Francisco: Morgan Kaufmann Publishers Inc., 1999.

[Burley and Lacewell 08] Brent Burley and Dylan Lacewell. "Ptex: Per-Face Texture Mapping for Production Rendering." In *Proceedings of the Nineteenth Eurographics conference on Rendering*, pp. 1155–1164. Aire-la-Ville, Switzerland: Eurographics Association, 2008.

[McDonald 12] John McDonald. "Practical Ptex for Games." *Game Developer Magazine* 19:1 (2012), 39–44.

[McDonald and Burley 11] John McDonald, Jr and Brent Burley. "Per-face Texture Mapping for Real-Time Rendering." In *ACM SIGGRAPH 2011 Talks*, article no. 10. New York: ACM, 2011.

[Purnomo et al. 04] Budirijanto Purnomo, Jonathan D. Cohen, and Subodh Kumar. "Seamless Texture Atlases." In *Proceedings of the 2004 Eurographics/ACM SIGGRAPH Symposium on Geometry Processing*, pp. 65–74. New York: ACM, 2004.

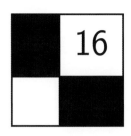

16

Decoupled Deferred Shading
on the GPU

Gábor Liktor and Carsten Dachsbacher

Deferred shading provides an efficient solution to reduce the complexity of image synthesis by separating the shading process itself from the visibility computations. This technique is widely used in real-time rendering pipelines to evaluate complex lighting, and recently gained increasing focus of research with the advent of computational rendering.

The core idea of the technique is to presample visible surfaces into a *G-buffer* prior to shading. However, antialiasing is complicated with deferred shading, as supersampling the G-buffer leads to tremendous growth in memory bandwidth and shading cost. There are several post-processing methods that are mostly based on smoothing discontinuities in the G-buffer [Reshetov 09, Chajdas et al. 11], but these result in inferior antialiasing quality compared to forward rendering with multisample antialiasing (MSAA) or do not address the problem of memory requirements.

16.1 Introduction

In this article we discuss decoupled deferred shading, a technique that uses a novel G-buffer structure to reduce the number of shading computations while keeping the antialiasing quality high. Our edge antialiasing is an exact match of hardware MSAA, while shading is evaluated at a per-pixel (or application-controlled) frequency, as shown in Figure 16.1.

Our G-buffer implementation stores visibility samples and shading samples in independent memory locations, where a visibility sample corresponds to a subsample tested by the rasterizer, while shading samples contain surface information, which has been previously stored on a subsample level. Using decoupled sampling, several visibility samples can refer to a single shading sample. We do not seek to skip the shading of G-buffer samples in order to reduce shading costs,

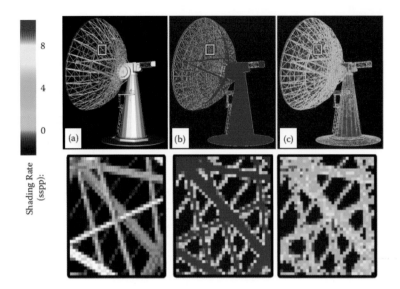

Figure 16.1. In this example our deferred shading method (a) achieves equivalent antialiasing quality to 8× MSAA, but (c) significantly reduces the number of shader evaluations. (b) To the same antialiasing quality, classic deferred shading needs a super-sampled G-buffer.

instead we *deduplicate* the data itself, ensuring that a visible surface is shaded only once, regardless of the number of subsamples it covers.

This article is based on our recent research paper, presented at the 2012 ACM Symposium on Interactive 3D Graphics and Games [Liktor and Dachsbacher 12]. We cover the basic theory of decoupled sampling, and then focus on the implementation details of our new G-buffer in the OpenGL pipeline.

16.2   Decoupled Sampling in a Rasterization Pipeline

16.2.1   The Nature of Aliasing

To understand the motivation of decoupled sampling, let us consider the rendering of a 2D image as a signal-processing problem. Rasterization uses point sampling to capture visible surfaces that causes problems if the sampled signal is not band-limited: frequencies higher than the sampling frequency lead to aliasing in the rendered image. Antialiasing methods can prefilter the signal to eliminate frequencies above the sampling limit, increase the frequency of sampling, or alternatively apply reconstruction filters to supress aliasing artifacts.

Any rendering method using point sampling must first solve the *visibility problem* to find the surface points that determine the colors at each sample.

Discontinuities, such as surface silhouettes, are the primary sources of aliasing. The second type of aliasing is the possible undersampling of surface shading. Unlike visibility, shading is often treated as a continuous signal on a given surface, thus it can be prefiltered (e.g., by using texture mipmaps). It is therefore a tempting idea to save computations by sampling visibility and shading information at different granularities.

16.2.2   Decoupled Sampling

In a modern rasterization pipeline this problem is addressed by MSAA. The rasterizer invokes a single fragment shader for each covered pixel; however, there are multiple subsample locations per pixel, which are tested for primitive coverage. Shading results are then copied into covered locations. This is an elegant solution for supersampling visibility without increasing the shading cost.

Decoupled sampling [Ragan-Kelley et al. 11] is a generalization of this idea. Shading and visibility are sampled in separate domains. In rasterization, the *visibility domain* is equivalent to subsamples used for coverage testing, while the *shading domain* can be any parameterization over the sampled primitive itself, such as screen-space coordinates, 2D patch-parameters, or even texture coordinates. A *decoupling map* assigns each visibility sample to a coordinate in the shading domain. If this mapping is a many-to-one projection, the shading can be reused over visibility samples.

Case study: stochastic rasterization. Using stochastic sampling, rasterization can be extended to accurately render effects such as depth of field and motion blur. Each coverage sample is augmented with temporal and lens parameters. Defocused or motion blurred triangles are bounded in screen space according to their maximum circle of confusion and motion vectors. A deeper introduction of this method is outside the scope of this article, but we would like to refer the interested reader to [McGuire et al. 10] for implementation details. In short, the geometry shader is used to determine the potentially covered screen region, the fragment shader then generates a ray corresponding to each stochastic sample, and intersects the triangle.

We now illustrate decoupled sampling using the example of motion blur: if the camera samples over a finite shutter interval, a moving surface is visible at several different locations on the screen. A naïve rendering algorithm would first determine the barycentics of each stochastic sample covered by a triangle, and evaluate the shading accordingly. In many cases, we can assume that the observed color of a surface does not change significantly over time (even offline renderers often do this). MSAA or post-processing methods cannot solve this issue, as corresponding coverage samples might be scattered over several pixels of the noisy image. We can, however, rasterize a sharp image of the triangle at a fixed *shading time*, and we can find corresponding shading for each visibility sample by projecting them into the pixels of this image.

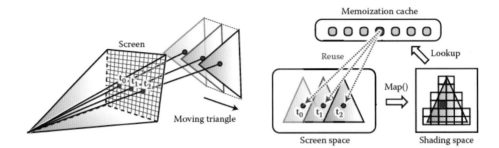

Figure 16.2. The idea of the memoization cache. Decoupled sampling uses visibility and shading samples in separate domains. Assuming constant shading over a short exposure time, multiple visibility samples can refer to the identical shading sample. Recently computed shading samples are cached during rasterization, to avoid redundant shader execution.

Memoization cache. This concept is illustrated in Figure 16.2. Note that the second rasterization step mentioned above does not actually happen, it is only used to define a *shading grid* on the triangle, a discretization of the shading domain. A shading sample corresponds to one cell of the shading grid, and we can then assign a linear index to each shading sample. Using this indexing, Ragan-Kelley et al. augmented the conventional rasterization pipeline with a *memoization cache* [Ragan-Kelley et al. 11]. In their extended pipeline, each visibility sample requests its shading sample from the cache using the decoupling map, and fragment shaders are only executed on a cache miss. Unfortunately, this method is not directly applicable to the current hardware architecture.

16.3   Shading Reuse for Deferred Shading

Conventional deferred shading methods couple visibility and surface data in the G-buffer. After the geometry sampling pass it is no longer trivial to determine which samples in the G-buffer belong to the same surface. Stochastic rasterization further increases the complexity of the problem by adding significant noise to visibility samples, preventing the use of any edge-based reconstruction.

The memory footprint is one of the most severe problems of deferred shading. As all shading data must be stored for each subsample in the G-buffer, even if one could save computation by reusing shading among these samples, the supersampling quality would still be bounded by memory limitations. Current real-time applications typically limit their deferred multisampling resolution to $2\times/4\times$ MSAA, then apply reconstruction filters. It has been demonstrated that accurate rendering of motion blur or depth of field would require an order of magnitude larger sample count with stochastic sampling [McGuire et al. 10].

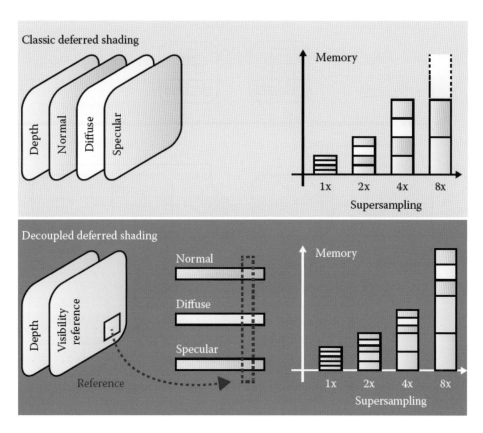

Figure 16.3. The G-buffer stores shading data at full supersampled resolution before shading and resolving. We introduce a visibility buffer that references shading data in compact linear buffers. Due to our shading reuse scheme, the size of the compact buffers does not scale with the supersampling density.

Compact geometry buffer. Instead of trying to use reconstruction filters or sparse shading of the supersampled G-buffer, we can avoid any shading and memory consumption overhead by not storing redundant shading data in the first place. We address this problem with a novel data structure, the *compact G-buffer*, a decoupled storage for deferred shading. It has the same functionality as the G-buffer, storing the inputs of shaders for delayed evaluation. However, instead of storing this information in the framebuffer, we collect *shading samples* in compact linear buffers. The contents of the framebuffer are purely *visibility samples*, each sample storing its depth value and a reference to a shading sample in the linear buffers. We compare this data layout to the conventional G-buffer in Figure 16.3. Akin to classic deferred shading, our methods can render images in three main stages.

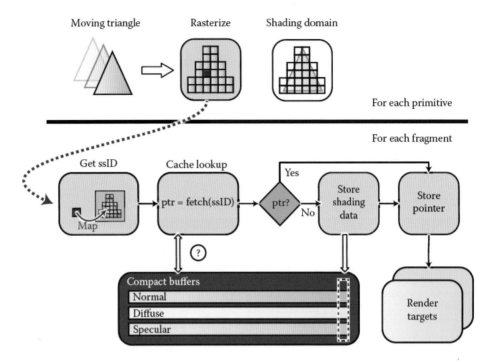

Figure 16.4. The outline of decoupled deferred shading in a rasterization pipeline. Prior to rasterization, each primitive is bound and projected to a shading grid. During fragment processing, the fragments are mapped to their corresponding cells on the shading grid. Shading reuse is implemented by referencing the same data from multiple samples in the render targets.

16.3.1   Algorithm Outline

Sampling stage. We rasterize all surfaces into the compact geometry buffer (*CG-buffer*). Figure 16.4 shows the outline of this sampling stage. During rasterization each fragment is assigned to a shading sample ID (*ssID*), which is searched in the cache. If the shading data was found, we only store a pointer to its address in the memory. In case of a miss, we also need to allocate a new slot in the compact buffers and store the data in addition to referencing it.

In Section 16.2.2 we have already introduced the concept of a shading grid. In our pipeline, we use this grid to allocate an ssID range for each primitive. This virtual address space ensures that shading sample keys of concurrently rasterized primitives do not overlap, and the sampler can use these ssIDs to uniquely reference a cached shading sample entry.

We provide further implementation details in the next section. In fact, we only made a small modification in the decoupled sampling pipeline. While the

CG-buffer itself could be directly used as a global memoization cache, it would be very inefficient to search for shading samples directly in it, especially that a cached entry is only relevant for the currently rasterized primitives in flight.

Shading and resolving stages. The collected samples in the compact buffers are then shaded using GPU compute kernels. These kernels only execute for shading samples that are marked visible (see the next section). Finally each visibility sample can gather its final color value in a full-screen pass. This method trivially extends to an arbitrary number of render targets, supporting efficient shading reuse for multiview rasterization as well.

16.4 Implementation

In this section we focus on how to implement decoupled deferred shading on a modern GPU. In our examples we provide OpenGL Shading Language (GLSL) source code snippets. We use global atomics and scatter operations, therefore a minimum version of OpenGL 4.2 is required for our application. The implementation could also be done in DirectX 11.1, which supports unordered access binding to all shader stages.

The primary problem for our example is the lack of hardware support for decoupled shading reuse, which is an architectural limitation. The hardware version of the memoization cache, as described in Section 16.2.2, is a fast on-chip least recently used (LRU) cache assigned to each rasterizer unit. Of course, every component of the pipeline (ultimately even rasterization) can be implemented in software, but only with reduced performance compared to dedicated hardware. From now on we assume that our renderer still uses the hardware rasterizer, though this technique could be also integrated into a full software implementation, such as [Laine and Karras 11].

16.4.1 Architectural Considerations

Note that the implementation of decoupled sampling for a forward renderer would be very inefficient on current GPUs. First, using hardware rasterization, we can only simulate the caching behavior from fragment shaders. Unfortunately we cannot prevent the execution of redundant shaders, like the proposed architecture of [Ragan-Kelley et al. 11] does. The rasterizer will launch fragment shaders for each covered pixel or subsample and we can only terminate redundant instances afterwards. This introduces at least one new code path into the shading code, breaking its coherency.

The second problem is how to avoid redundant shading. Shading reuse can be regarded as an *election problem*: shader instances corresponding to the same shading sample must elect one instance that will evaluate the shading, the others need to wait for the result. This can only be solved using global synchronization, as current hardware does not allow local on-chip memory usage in rasterization mode, and the execution of fragment shaders is nondeterministic. Furthermore, waiting for the result would mean a significant delay for a complex shader.

With our modification we can move the shader evaluation into a deferred stage, which results in a more coherent fragment shader execution. While we cannot avoid using the global memory to simulate the memoization cache, the overhead of decoupled sampling is independent from the shading complexity. This is the key difference that makes our algorithm feasible even for current GPUs: if the shading computation is "expensive enough," the constant overhead of our caching implementation will be less than the performance gain of reduced shading. Furthermore, we can utilize our CG-buffer to keep the memory footprint of the shading data minimal.

16.4.2 Decoupling Shading Samples

We now discuss a method that implements the sampling stage of decoupled deferred shading in a single rasterization pass. The first problem we need to solve is how to assign shading samples to fragments. Prior to rasterization, each primitive needs to be processed to determine its shading domain (see Section 16.3.1

```
in vec2 in_scrPos[]; // screen-space positions
flat out ivec4 domain; // shading grid of the triangle
flat out uint startID; // ID of the first sample in the sh. grid

uniform float shadingRate;

// global SSID counter array
layout(size1x32) uniform uimageBuffer uCtrSSID;

void main(){
    // project screen position to the shading grid
    vec2 gridPos0 = scrPos[0] * shadingRate; [...]

    vec2 minCorner = min(gridPos0, min(gridPos1, gridPos2));
    vec2 maxCorner = max(gridPos0, max(gridPos1, gridPos2));

    // shading grid: xy-top left corner, zw-grid size
    domain.x = int(minCorner.x) - 1;
    domain.y = int(minCorner.y) - 1;
    domain.z = int((maxCorner.x)) - domain.x + 1;
    domain.w = int((maxCorner.y)) - domain.y + 1;

    // we allocate the ssID range with an atomic counter.
    uint reserved = uint((domain.z) * (domain.w));
    startID = imageAtomicAdd(uCtrSSID, 0, reserved);
}
```

Listing 16.1. The geometry shader generates a shading grid for each triangle, and ensures globally unique ssIDs using an atomic counter.

for details). As we only consider triangles, we can conveniently implement this
functionality in a geometry shader.

Listing 16.1 is an extract from the geometry shader code that assigns a shading
grid for each rasterized triangle. In our implementation, the geometry shader
might also set up conservative bounds for stochastically rasterized triangles.

Listing 16.2 shows the pseudocode of the fragment shader, implementing the
remainder of our pipeline. As we described before, the output of this shader
is only a pointer to the corresponding shader data. Note that due to driver
limitations on integer multisampling, we need to store the references in floating
point, using the `intBitsToFloat` GLSL function. The shading samples are stored
using image buffers.

We omit the details of visibility testing, which might be standard multi-
sampled rasterization, or the implementation of stochastic rasterization, which
casts randomly distributed rays inside the conservative screen space bounds of the
triangles. We only assume that the visibility method returned the barycentrics of
the intersection point. The visibility sample is then assigned to a shading sample,
using the grid provided by the geometry shader.

```
layout(location = 0, index = 0) out float FragPtr;

// shader inputs: position, normal, texcoords
flat in vec3 vpos0...

// packed CG-buffer data
layout(rg32ui) uniform uimageBuffer uColorNormalBuffer;
layout(rgba32f) uniform uimageBuffer uViewPosBuffer;

void main(){
    // hw-interpolation or stochastic ray casting...
    vec3 baryCoords = getViewSamplePos();

    // get nearest shading sample
    uint localID = projectToGrid(baryCoords, shadingRate);
    uint globalID = startID + localID;
    bool needStore = false;

    int address = getCachedAddress(globalID, needStore);
    FragPtr = intBitsToFloat(address);

    if(needStore){
        // for each texture...
        textureGradsInShadingSpace(localID, dx, dy);
        vec4 diffuse = textureGrad(texDiffuse, texCoord, dx, dy);
        [...]
        // pack color, normal, view positions into the CGbuffer
        imageStore(uColorNormalBuffer, address, ...);
    }
}
```

Listing 16.2. The fragment shader implements the decoupling map and the chaching
mechanism for shading samples.

```
uint projectToGrid(vec3 baryCoords, float shadingRate){
    vec3 vpos = coords.x * vpos0 + coords.y * vpos1 + coords.z * vpos2;
    vec2 screenPos = projToScreen(vpos);
    ivec2 gridPos = ivec2(screenPos * shadingRate + vec2(0.5f)) - domain
        .xy;
    return uint(domain.z * gridPos.y + gridPos.x);
}
```

Listing 16.3. The decoupling map is a simple projection to a regular grid. The density of this grid is determined by the shading rate.

The method `projectToGrid` assigns the fragment to a shading sample, as we show in Listing 16.3. The local index of the shading sample is the linearized index of the closest shading grid cell to the visibility sample. Later, when the shading data is interpolated, some shading samples might fall outside the triangle. These are snapped to the edges (by clamping the barycentrics to 0 or 1, respectively), otherwise some shading values would be extrapolated.

The computation of the texture mip levels also needs special attention. Normally, this is done by the hardware, generating texture gradients of 2×2 fragment blocks. Depending on the shading rate, the shading space gradients can be different. For example, a shading rate of 0.5 would mean that 2×2 fragments might use the same shading sample, which would be detected (incorrectly) as the most detailed mip level by the hardware. Therefore we manually compute the mip level, using the `textureGrad` function.

In Listing 16.2 we have also tried to minimize the divergence of fragment shader threads. The method `getCachedAddress` returns the location of a shading sample in the global memory. In case of a cache miss, a new slot is reserved in the CG-buffer (see below), but the shading data is only written later, if the `needStore` boolean was set.

16.4.3   Global Shading Cache

For a moment let us consider the cache as a "black box" and focus on the implementation of the CG-buffer. If a shading sample is not found in the cache, we need to append a new entry to the compact linear buffers, as shown in Figure 16.4. The CG-buffer linearly grows as more samples are being stored. We can implement this behavior using an atomic counter that references the last shading data element:

```
address = int(atomicCounterIncrement(bufferTail));
```

The streaming nature of the GPU suggests that even a simple first-in, first-out (FIFO) cache could be quite efficient as only the recently touched shading samples are "interesting" for the fragments. We therefore did not attempt to simulate an LRU cache, as suggested by Ragan-Kelley et al. On a current GPU there can be several thousand fragments rasterized in parallel, thus the global cache should also be able to hold a similar magnitude of samples to achieve a good hit rate. In a naïve implementation, a thread could query the buffer tail, and check the last N items in the CG-buffer. Of course the latency of the iterative memory accesses would be prohibitively high. We now show a cache implementation that performs cache lookups *with only one buffer load* and an atomic lock.

The concept of the shading grid already creates indices for shading samples that are growing approximately linearly with the rasterized fragments. Thus the FIFO cache could also be implemented by simply storing the last N *ssID* values. Consequently, instead of linearly searching in a global buffer, we could introduce a bucketed hash array. The full implementation of our optimized algorithm is shown in Listing 16.4.

The hash function (hashSSID) is a simple modulo operation with the number of buckets. This evenly distributes queries from rasterized fragments over the buckets, which is important to minimize cache collisions (when threads with different ssIDs compete for the same bucket). In case of a cache miss, multiple threads compete for storing the shading samples in the same bucket, therefore we use a per-bucket locking mechanism (uBucketLocks). Note that we try to minimize the number of instructions between obtaining and releasing a lock: the computation of a shading sample does not happen inside the critical section, but we only set the needStore flag to perform the storage later.

As the execution order of fragments is nondeterministic, there is no guarantee that all threads obtain the lock in a given number of steps. In practice we have very rarely experienced cases when the fragment shader execution froze for starving fragment shaders. While we hope this will change on future architectures, we have limited the spinlock iterations, and in case of failure the fragment shader falls back to storing the shading sample without shading reuse. In our experiments this only happened to a negligible fraction of fragments.

One other interesting observation was that if the number of cache buckets is high enough, we can really severely limit the bucket size. As the reader can see in the source code, a bucket stores only a single uvec4 element, which corresponds to two shading samples: a cache entry is a tuple of an ssID and a memory address. This is a very important optimization, because instead of searching inside the cache, we can look up any shading sample with a single load operation using its hash value.

In our first implementation, each bucket in the cache has been stored as a linked list of shading sample addresses, similarly to the per-pixel linked list algorithm of [Yang et al. 10]. When we have made experiments to measure the necessary length of this list, we have found that in most cases even a single element per bucket is sufficient, and we did not have any cache misses when we considered only two elements per bucket. This is why we could discard the expensive linked

```
layout(rgba32ui) uniform uimageBuffer uShaderCache;
layout(r32ui) uniform volatile uimageBuffer uBucketLocks;

int getCachedAddress(uint ssID, inout bool needStore){
    int hash = hashSSID (ssID);
    uvec4 bucket = imageLoad(uShaderCache, hash);
    int address = searchBucket(ssID, bucket);

    // cache miss
    while(address < 0 && iAttempt++ < MAX_ATTEMPTS){
        // this thread is competing for storing a sample
        uint lock = imageAtomicCompSwap(uBucketLocks, hash, FREE, LOCKED
            );
        if(lock == FREE){
            address = int(atomicCounterIncrement(bufferTail));

            // update the cache
            bucket = storeBucket(ssID, hash, bucket);
            imageStore(uShaderCache, hash, bucket);
            needStore = true;

            memoryBarrier(); // release the lock
            imageStore(uBucketLocks, hash, FREE);
        }

        if(lock == LOCKED){
            while(lock == LOCKED && lockAttempt++ < MAX_LOCK_ATTEMPTS)
                lock = imageLoad(uBucketLocks, hash).x;

            // now try to get the address again
            bucket = imageLoad(uShaderCache, hash);
            address = searchBucket(ssID, bucket);
        }

        // if everything failed, store a the data redundantly
        if(address < 0){
            address = int(atomicCounterIncrement(bufferTail));
            needStore = true;
        }
    }
}
```

Listing 16.4. Implementation of the global shading cache.

list behavior and pack all buffers in a single vector. However, this optimization only works if the hash function uniformly distributes cache requests (like ours), and the number of buckets is high. In our examples we use a bucket count of 32,768.

16.4.4 Shading and Resolving

While the sampling stage described above successfully eliminates all duplicate shading samples, the resulting CG-buffer might still hold redundant information. Depending on the rasterization order of triangles, several samples in the compact buffers might not belong to any visible surfaces. Even filling up the z-buffer in a depth prepass might not solve the problem: if early z-testing is disabled a z-culled fragment can still write data into a uniform image buffer. We therefore execute another pass that marks visible shading samples, and optionally removes invisible data from the CG-buffer.

Visibility. Marking visible samples is surprisingly easy. After the sampling stage is finished, we render a full-screen quad with subsample fragment shader execution, and each fragment shader stores a visibility flag corresponding to its shading sample. There is no synchronization needed, as each thread stores the same value. To evaluate the quality of shading reuse, we used a variant of this technique, which counts visibility samples per-shading sample. In the diagnostics code we atomically increment a per-shading sample counter for each subsample in the framebuffer. The heatmap visualizations in this article were generated using this method.

Compaction. Because of the rasterization order, there is no explicit bound on the size of the compact buffers. Using the visibility flags, we can perform a stream compaction on the shading data before shading. Besides efficient memory footprint this also increases the execution coherence during the shading process.

In this article we do not provide implementation details for shading, as it is orthogonal to our decoupling method. The final pixel colors are evaluated by rendering a full-screen quad and gathering all shaded colors for each visibility sample. This is the same behavior as the resolve pass of a standard multisampled framebuffer, except for the location of subsample colors.

16.5   Results

In this section we discuss possible application of our method in deferred rendering. While current GPU architectures do not have hardware support for decoupled sampling, the overhead of our global cache management can be amortized by the reduction of shader evaluations. We focus on stochastic sampling, a rendering problem especially challenging for deferred shading.

While the software overhead of decoupled sampling makes our method rather interactive than real time, we demonstrate significant speedup for scenes with complex shading. All images in this article were rendered at 1280×720 pixels on an Nvidia GTX580 GPU and Intel Core i7 920 CPU.

Adaptive shading. We have computed the average shading rate of these images, to roughly estimate the shading speedup compared to supersampled deferred shading. We save further computation by reducing the density of the shading grid of blurry surfaces. Our adaptive shading rate implementation is only a proof-of-concept based entirely on empirically chosen factors. For better quality,

Figure 16.5. Focusing from the background (left column) to a foreground object (right column), our adaptive method concentrates shading samples on sharp surfaces. The motivation is to prefilter shading more agressively, as defocus is similar to a low-pass filter over the image. The middle row visualizes the shading rate. In the bottom row we show how the same surface shading would appear from a pinhole camera. The texture filtering matches the shading resolution.

our method could be easily extended with the recent results of [Vaidyanathan et al. 12], who presented a novel anisotropic sampling algorithm, based on image space frequency analysis.

Depth of field. Figure 16.5 shows two renderings of the Crytek Sponza Atrium scene from the same viewing angle, but different focusing distance. In this example the most expensive component of rendering is the computation of the single-bounce global illumination, using 256 virtual point lights (VPLs), generated from a reflective shadow map (RSM) [Dachsbacher and Stamminger 05].

　　We do not only avoid supersampling the G-buffer, but also reduce the shading frequency of surfaces using the minimum circle of confusion inside each primitive. This approach prefilters shading of defocused triangles, causing slight overblurring of textures, however, we found this effect even desirable if the number of visibility

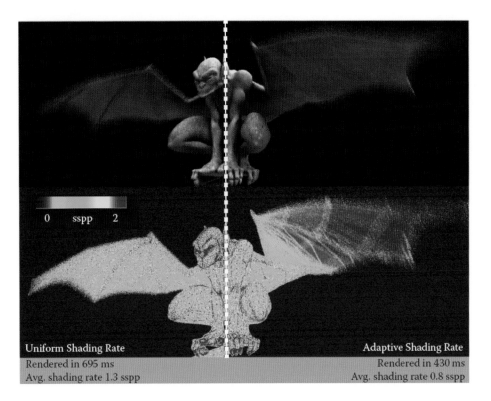

Figure 16.6. A motion blurred character rendered with eight times stochastic supersampling. Deferred shading is computed using 36 ambient occlusion samples per shading sample. The shading rate stays close to one shading sample per pixel (sspp) despite the supersampling density (left side). We can save further ∼30% of the rendering time by adaptively reducing sampling of fast-moving surfaces (right side).

samples is small (it effectively reduces the apparent noise of surfaces). The images were rendered using four times supersampling, the stochastic sampling stage took 90 ms, and the shading with 256 VPLs took 160 ms.

Motion blur. Figure 16.6 presents an animated character, rendered with motion blur. This example features ray-traced ambient occlusion and image-based lighting, using the Nvidia OptiX raytracing engine. When using hardware rasterization, high-performance ray tracing is only possible in a deferred computational shading pass. Here we demonstrate adaptive shading again, by reducing the shading rate of fast-moving triangles. We scale the shading grid based on the x and y component of the triangle motion vectors. Our results (and the reduction of shading) can be significantly improved by using the anisotropic shading grid of [Vaidyanathan et al. 12].

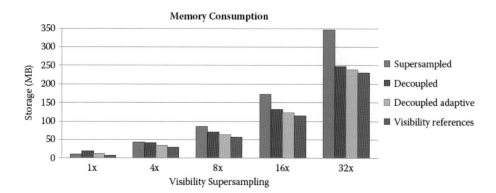

Figure 16.7. Storage requirements of the CG-buffer compared to a standard deferred G-buffer. Only the size of the visibility data grows with supersampling. We rendered the Sponza scene at $1,280 \times 720$ pixels.

16.5.1 Memory Consumption

We have analyzed the memory consumption of our method, compared to supersampled deferred shading. We save storage by essentially deduplicating shading data in the G-buffer. However, as a shading sample might not coincide with any visibility samples on the surface, we cannot reconstruct the surface positions based on a subpixel depth value. While other solutions are possible, we assume that we are forced to store the view space position of each shading sample.

We assume that the ground truth deferred method uses 12 bytes per subsample in the G-buffer: 32 bits for depth-stencil and two RGBA8 textures for normals and material information. In fact, most modern deferred renderers use typically more bytes per subsample. The memory footprint of our CG-buffer can be divided into per-visibility and per-shading sample costs. In the former we need to store an integer pointer besides the 32-bit depth-stencil. We need 16 bytes per shading sample: the view positions are packed into 8 bytes (16 bits for $x - y$ and 32 bits for z), and we store the same normal and material information.

If the shading rate is one and there is no multisampling, our method uses twice as much memory as conventional techniques. However, the number of shading samples does not scale with the supersampling resolution. At $4\times$ MSAA, our memory consumption matches the supersampled G-buffer's, and we save significant storage above this sample count. Our measurements on the Sponza scene are summarized in Figure 16.7.

16.5.2 Conclusion

In this chapter we presented a decoupled deferred shading method for high-quality antialiased rendering. To our knowledge this is the first deferred shading method designed for stochastic rasterization. Unfortunately on current GPUs we need to implement stochastic rasterization and the shading cache using shaders, to overcome the limitations of the hardware pipeline. We consider our results beneficial for interactive applications, where shading cost dominates the rendering, however, the overhead of the global cache implementation is generally too high for real-time rendering.

We expect that the major synchronization bottleneck will disappear in future rendering architectures. While we cannot predict whether future GPUs would have a hardware-accelerated version of the memoization cache, some way of local synchronization among fragment shaders would already remove most of the overhead. Using a tile-based rendering architecture instead of sort-last-fragment would allow us to use a more efficient, per-tile on-chip shading cache.

In our examples we have assumed that the visible color of surfaces remains constant in a single frame, and shading can be prefiltered. This might cause artifacts on fast-moving surfaces, therefore we could extend our method to support interpolation among temporal shading samples. In the future it will be interesting to separate the frequency content of shading itself: a hard shadow edge in fact cannot be prefiltered, but there are low-frequency components of shading, e.g., diffuse indirect illumination, where sparse shading can bring relevant speedup.

16.6   Acknowledgments

We would like to thank Anton Kaplanyan and Bal'azs T'oth for the helpful discussions during the development of this project. Gábor Liktor is funded by Crytek GmbH.

Bibliography

[Chajdas et al. 11] Matthäus G. Chajdas, Morgan McGuire, and David Luebke. "Subpixel Reconstruction Antialiasing for Deferred Shading." In *Proceedings of Symposium on Interactive 3D Graphics and Games*, pp. 15–22. New York: ACM, 2011.

[Dachsbacher and Stamminger 05] Carsten Dachsbacher and Marc Stamminger. "Reflective Shadow Maps." In *Proceedings of the 2005 Symposium on Interactive 3D Graphics and Games*, pp. 203–231. New York: ACM, 2005.

[Laine and Karras 11] Samuli Laine and Tero Karras. "High-Performance Software Rasterization on GPUs." In *Proceedings of the ACM SIGGRAPH Symposium on High Performance Graphics*, pp. 79–88. New York: ACM, 2011.

[Liktor and Dachsbacher 12] Gábor Liktor and Carsten Dachsbacher. "Decoupled Deferred Shading for Hardware Rasterization." In *Proceedings of the*

ACM Symposium on Interactive 3D Graphics and Games, pp. 143–150. New York: ACM, 2012.

[McGuire et al. 10] M. McGuire, E. Enderton, P. Shirley, and D. Luebke. "Real-Time Stochastic Rasterization on Conventional GPU Architectures." In *Proceedings of the Conference on High Performance Graphics*, pp. 173–182. Aire-la-Ville, Switzerland: Eurographics Association, 2010.

[Ragan-Kelley et al. 11] J. Ragan-Kelley, J. Lehtinen, J. Chen, M. Doggett, and F. Durand. "Decoupled Sampling for Graphics Pipelines." *ACM Transactions on Graphics* 30:3 (2011), article no. 17.

[Reshetov 09] Alexander Reshetov. "Morphological Antialiasing." In *Proceedings of the Conference on High Performance Graphics 2009*, pp. 109–116. New York: ACM, 2009.

[Vaidyanathan et al. 12] Karthik Vaidyanathan, Robert Toth, Marco Salvi, Solomon Boulos, and Aaron E. Lefohn. "Adaptive Image Space Shading for Motion and Defocus Blur." In *Proceedings of the Fourth ACM SIGGRAPH/Eurographics Conference on High Performance Graphics*, pp. 13–21. Aire-la-Ville, Switzerland: Eurographics Association, 2012.

[Yang et al. 10] Jason C. Yang, Justin Hensley, Holger Grün, and Nicolas Thibieroz. "Real-Time Concurrent Linked List Construction on the GPU." *Computer Graphics Forum* 29:4 (2010), 1297–1304.

Tiled Forward Shading

Markus Billeter, Ola Olsson, and Ulf Assarsson

17.1 Introduction

We will explore the *tiled forward shading* algorithm in this chapter. Tiled forward shading is an extension or modification of *tiled deferred shading* [Balestra and Engstad 08, Swoboda 09, Andersson 09, Lauritzen 10, Olsson and Assarsson 11], which itself improves upon traditional deferred shading methods [Hargreaves and Harris 04, Engel 09].

Deferred shading has two main features: decoupling of lighting and shading from geometry management and minimization of the number of lighting computations performed [Hargreaves and Harris 04]. The former allows for more efficient geometry submission and management [Shishkovtsov 05] and simplifies shaders and management of shader resources. However the latter is becoming less of an issue on modern GPUs, which allow complex flow control in shaders, and support uniform buffers and more complex data structures in GPU memory.

Traditional forward pipelines typically render objects one by one and consider each light for each rasterized fragment. In deferred shading, one would instead render a representation of the geometry into a screen-sized G-buffer [Saito and Takahashi 90], which contains shading data for each pixel, such as normal and depth/position. Then, in a separate pass, the lighting and shading is computed by, for example, rendering light sources one by one (where each light source is represented by a bounding volume enclosing the light's influence region). For each generated fragment during this pass, data for the corresponding pixel is fetched from the G-buffer, shading is computed, and the results are blended into an output buffer. The number of lighting computations performed comes very close to the optimum of one per light per visible sample (somewhat depending on the bounding volumes used to represent light sources).

Deferred shading thereby succeeds in reducing the amount of computations needed for lighting, but at the cost of increased memory requirements (the G-buffer is much larger than a color buffer) and much higher memory bandwidth usage. Tiled deferred shading fixes the latter (Section 17.2), but still requires large G-buffers.

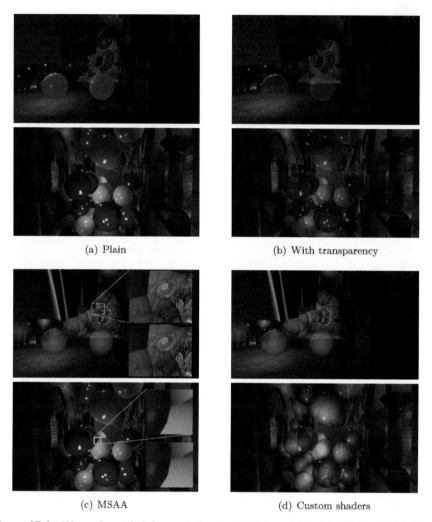

(a) Plain

(b) With transparency

(c) MSAA

(d) Custom shaders

Figure 17.1. We explore tiled forward shading in this article. (a) While tiled deferred shading outperforms tiled forward shading in the plain (no transparency, no multisample antialiasing (MSAA)) case by approximately 25%, (b) tiled forward shading enables use of transparency. Additionally, (c) we can use hardware supported MSAA, which, when emulated in deferred shading requires large amounts of memory. Furthermore, at 4× MSAA, tiled forward shading outperforms deferred with equal quality by 1.5 to 2 times. The image shows 8× MSAA, which we were unable to emulate for deferred rendering due to memory constraints. (d) Finally, we discuss custom shaders. As with standard forward rendering, shaders can be attached to geometry chunks. The scene contains 1,024 randomly placed lights, and the demo is run on an NVIDIA GTX480 GPU.

Tiled forward shading attempts to combine one of the main advantages of (tiled) deferred rendering, i.e., the reduced amount of lighting computations done, with the advantages of forward rendering. Besides reduced memory requirements (forward rendering does not need a large G-buffer), it also enables transparency [Kircher and Lawrance 09,Enderton et al. 10] (Section 17.5), enables multisampling schemes [Swoboda 09, Lauritzen 10] (Section 17.6), and does not force the use of übershaders if different shading models must be supported (Section 17.7). See the images in Figure 17.1 for a demonstration of these different aspects.

17.2   Recap: Forward, Deferred, and Tiled Shading

The terms *forward, deferred,* and *tiled shading* will be appearing quite frequently in this chapter. Therefore, let us define what we mean, since usage of these terms sometimes varies slightly in the community. The definitions we show here are identical to the ones used by [Olsson and Assarsson 11].

With *forward shading*, we refer to the process of rendering where lighting and shading computations are performed in the same pass as the geometry is rasterized. This corresponds to the standard setup consisting of a vertex shader that transforms geometry and a fragment shader that computes a resulting color for each rasterized fragment.

Deferred shading splits this process into two passes. First, geometry is rasterized, but, in contrast to forward shading, geometry attributes are output into a set of geometry buffers (G-buffers). After all geometry has been processed this way, an additional pass that computes the lighting or full shading is performed using the data stored in the G-buffers.

In its very simplest form, the second pass (the lighting pass) may look something like following:

```
for each G-buffer sample {
  sample_attr = load attributes from G-buffer

  for each light {
    color += shade(sample_attr, light)
  }

  output pixel color;
}
```

Sometimes, the order of the loops is reversed. The deferred algorithm described in Section 17.1 is an example of this.

The light pass shown above requires $\mathcal{O}(N_{\text{lights}} \cdot N_{\text{samples}})$ lighting computations. If we somehow know which lights were affecting what samples, we could reduce this number significantly [Trebilco 09].

Tiled deferred shading does this by dividing samples into tiles of $N \times N$ samples. (We have had particularly good successes with $N = 32$, but this should be somewhat hardware and application dependent.) Lights are then assigned to these tiles. We may optionally compute the minimum and maximum Z-bounds of each tile, which allows us to further reduce the number of lights affecting each tile (more discussion on this in Section 17.4).

Benefits of tiled deferred shading [Olsson and Assarsson 11] are the following:

- The G-buffers are read only once for each lit sample.

- The framebuffer is written to once.

- Common terms of the rendering equation can be factored out and computed once instead of recomputing them for each light.

- The work becomes coherent within each tile; i.e., each sample in a tile requires the same amount of work (iterates over the same lights), which allows for efficient implementation on SIMD-like architectures (unless, of course, the shader code contains many branches).

For tiled deferred shading (and most deferred techniques) to be worthwhile, most lights must have a limited range. If all lights potentially affect all of the scene, there is obviously no benefit to the tiling (Figure 17.2(a)).

Tiled deferred shading can be generalized into *Tiled Shading*, which includes both the deferred and forward variants. The basic tiled shading algorithm looks like the following:

1. Subdivide screen into tiles.

2. Optional: find minimum and maximum Z-bounds for each tile.

3. Assign lights to each tile.

4. For each sample: process all lights affecting the current sample's tile.

Step 1 is basically free; if we use regular $N \times N$ tiles, the subdivision is implicit. Finding minimum and maximum Z-bounds for each tile is optional (Step 2). For instance, a top-down view on a scene with low depth complexity may not allow for additional culling of lights in the Z-direction. Other cases, however, can benefit from tighter tile Z-bounds, since fewer lights are found to influence that tile (Figure 17.2(b)).

In tiled *deferred* shading, the samples in Step 4 are fetched from the G-buffers. In tiled *forward* shading, the samples are generated during rasterization. We will explore the latter in the rest of the article.

We recently presented an extension to tiled shading, called *clustered shading* [Olsson et al. 12b]. Clustered shading is an extension of tiled shading that

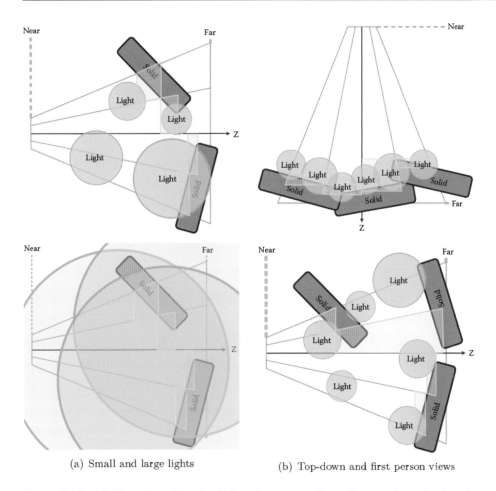

(a) Small and large lights (b) Top-down and first person views

Figure 17.2. (a) The effect of having lights that are too large (bottom image): there is no gain from the tiling, as all light sources affect all tiles (drawn in yellow), compared to the top image, where there is one light per tile on average. (b) Comparison of a top-down view and a first-person view. In the top-down view (top), all lights are close to the ground, which has only small variations in the Z-direction. In this case, not much is gained from computing minimum and maximum Z-bounds. In the first-person view (bottom), the bounds help (three lights in the image affect no tiles at all).

handles complex light and geometry configurations more robustly with respect to performance. However, tiled forward shading is significantly simpler to implement, and works on a much broader range of hardware. We will discuss the clustered shading extension and how it interacts with the tiled forward shading presented here in Section 17.8.

17.3 Tiled Forward Shading: Why?

The main strength of deferred techniques, including tiled deferred shading, is that over-shading due to over-draw is eliminated. However, most deferred techniques suffer from the following weaknesses when compared to forward rendering:

- Transparency/blending is tricky, since traditional G-buffers only allow storage of a single sample at each position in the buffer.

- The memory storage and bandwidth requirements are higher and become even worse with MSAA and related techniques (Section 17.6).

Forward rendering, on the other hand, has good support for

- transparency via alpha blending,

- MSAA and related techniques through hardware features (much less memory storage is required).

In addition, forward rendering trivially supports different shaders and materials for different geometries. Deferred techniques would generally need to fall back to übershaders (or perform multiple shading passes).

A special advantage for tiled forward shading is its low requirements on GPU hardware. It is possible to implement a tiled forward renderer without compute shaders and other (relatively) recent hardware features. In fact, it is possible to implement a tiled forward renderer on any hardware that supports dependent texture lookups in the fragment shader. On the other hand, if compute shaders are available, we can take advantage of this during, say, light assignment (Section 17.4).

In the following sections, we first present a tiled forward shading renderer to which we add support for transparency, MSAA and finally experiment with having a few different shaders for different objects. We compare performance and resource consumption to a reference tiled deferred shading renderer and show where the tiled forward renderer wins.

17.4 Basic Tiled Forward Shading

We listed the basic algorithm for all tiled shading variants in Section 17.2. For clarity, it is repeated here including any specifics for the forward variant.

1. Subdivide screen into tiles

2. Optional: pre-Z pass—render geometry and store depth values for each sample in the standard Z-buffer.

3. Optional: find minimum and/or maximum Z-bounds for each tile.

4. Assign lights to each tile.

5. Render geometry and compute shading for each generated fragment.

Subdivision of screen. We use regular $N \times N$ pixel tiles (e.g., $N = 32$). Having very large tiles creates a worse light assignment; each tile will be affected by more light sources that affect a smaller subset of samples in the tile. Creating very small tiles makes the light assignment more expensive and increases the required memory storage—especially when the tiles are small enough that many adjacent tiles are found to be affected by the same light sources.

Optional pre-Z pass. An optional pre-Z pass can help in two ways. First, it is required if we wish to find the Z-bounds for each tile in the next step. Secondly, in the final rendering pass it can reduce the number of samples that need to be shaded through early-Z tests and similar hardware features.

The pre-Z pass should, of course, only include opaque geometry. Transparent geometry is discussed in Section 17.5.

Though a pre-Z pass is scene and view dependent, in our tests we have found that adding it improves performance significantly. For instance, for the images in Figure 17.1(a), rendering time is reduced from 22.4 ms (upper view) and 37.9 ms (lower view) to 15.6 ms and 18.7 ms, respectively.

Optional minimum or maximum Z-bounds. If a depth buffer exists, e.g., from the pre-Z pass described above, we can use this information to find (reduce) the extents of each tile in the Z-direction (depth). This yields smaller per-tile bounding volumes, reducing the number of lights that affect a tile during light assignment.

Depending on the application, finding only either the minimum or the maximum bounds can be sufficient (if bounds are required at all). Again, transparency (Section 17.5) interacts with this, as do various multisampling schemes (Section 17.6).

In conjunction with the pre-Z test above, the minimum or maximum reduction yields a further significant improvement for the views in Figure 17.1(a). Rendering time with both pre-Z and minimum or maximum reduction is 10.9 ms (upper) and 13.8 ms (lower), respectively—which is quite comparable to the performance of tiled deferred shading (8.5 ms and 10.9 ms). The reduction itself is implemented using a loop in a fragment shader (for simplicity) and currently takes about 0.75 ms (for $1,920 \times 1,080$ resolution).

Light assignment. Next, we must assign lights to tiles. Basically, we want to efficiently find which lights affect samples in which tiles. This requires a few choices and considerations.

In tiled shading, where the number of tiles is relatively small (for instance, a resolution of $1,920 \times 1,080$ with 32×32 tiles yields just about 2,040 tiles), it can be feasible to do the assignment on the CPU. This is especially true if the number of lights is relatively small (e.g., a few thousand). On the CPU, a simple implementation is to find the screen-space axis-aligned bounding boxes (AABBs) for each light source and loop over all the tiles that are contained in the 2D region of the AABB. If we have computed the minimum and maximum depths for each tile, we need to perform an additional test to discard lights that are outside of the tile in the Z-direction.

On the GPU, a simple brute-force variant works for moderate amounts of lights (up to around 10,000 lights). In the brute-force variant, each tile is checked against all light sources. If each tile gets its own thread group, the implementation is fairly simple and performs relatively well. Obviously, the brute-force algorithm does not scale very well. In our clustered shading implementation [Olsson et al. 12b], we build a simple light hierarchy (a BVH) each frame and test the tiles (clusters) against this hierarchy. We show that this approach can scale up to at least one million lights in real time. The same approach is applicable for tiled shading as well.

Rendering and shading. The final step is to render all geometry. The pipeline for this looks almost like a standard forward rendering pipeline; different shaders and related resources may be attached to different chunks of geometry. There are no changes to the stages other than the fragment shader.

The fragment shader will, for each generated sample, look up which lights affect that sample by checking what lights are assigned to the sample's tile (Listing 17.1).

17.5   Supporting Transparency

As mentioned in the beginning of this article, deferred techniques have some difficulty dealing with transparency since traditional G-buffers only can store attributes from a single sample at each buffer location [Thibieroz and Grün 10]. However, with forward rendering, we never need to store attributes for samples. Instead we can simply blend the resulting colors using standard alpha-blending.

Note that we are not solving the order-dependent transparency problem. Rather, we support, unlike many deferred techniques, standard alpha-blending where each layer is lit correctly. The application must, however, ensure that transparent objects are drawn in the correct back-to-front order.

We need to make the following changes, compared to the basic tiled forward shading algorithm (Section 17.4).

Optional minimum or maximum Z-bounds. We need to consider transparent geometry here, as nonoccluded transparent objects will affect a tile's bounds inasmuch that it moves a tile's minimum Z-bound ("near plane") closer to the camera.

We ended up using two different sets of tiles for opaque and transparent geometries, rather than extending a single set of tiles to include both opaque and

```glsl
// 1D texture holding per-tile light lists
uniform isampleBuffer tex_tileLightLists;

// uniform buffer holding each tile's light count and
// start offset of the tile's light list (in
// tex_tileLightIndices)
uniform TileLightListRanges
{
  ivec2 u_lightListRange[MAX_NUM_TILES];
}

void shading_function( inout FragmentData aFragData )
{
  // ...

  // find fragment's tile using gl_FragCoord
  ivec2 tileCoord = ivec2(gl_FragCoord.xy)
    / ivec2(TILE_SIZE_X, TILE_SIZE_Y);
  int tileIdx = tileCoord.x
    + tileCoord.y * LIGHT_GRID_SIZE_X;

  // fetch tile's light data start offset (.y) and
  // number of lights (.x)
  ivec2 lightListRange = u_lightListRange[tileIdx].xy;

  // iterate over lights affecting this tile
  for( int i = 0; i < lightListRange.x; ++i )
  {
    int lightIndex = lightListRange.y + i;

    // fetch global light ID
    int globalLightId = texelFetch(
      tex_tileLightLists, lightIndex ).x;

    // get the light's data (position, colors, ...)
    LightData lightData;
    light_get_data( lightData, globalLightId );

    // compute shading from the light
    shade( aFragData, lightData );
  }

  // ...
}
```

Listing 17.1. GLSL pseudocode that demonstrates how lights affecting a given sample are fetched. First, we find the fragment's associated tile (`tileIdx`) based on its position in the framebuffer. For each tile we store two integers (`u_lightListRange` array), one indicating the number of lights affecting the tile, and the other describes the offset into the global per-tile light list buffer (`tex_tileLightLists`). The light list buffer stores a number of integers per tile, each integer identifying a globally unique light that is affecting the tile.

transparent geometries. The Z-bounds for tiles used with opaque geometry are computed as described in Section 17.4, which gives a good light assignment for the opaque geometry (Figure 17.3(a)).

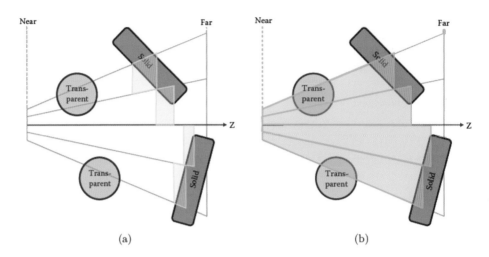

Figure 17.3. Z-bounds used for (a) opaque and (b) transparent geometries.

For transparent geometry, we would like to find the transparent objects' minimum Z-value and the minimum of the transparent objects' and opaque objects' respective maximum Z-values. However, this is somewhat cumbersome, requiring several passes over the transparent geometry; therefore, we simply use the maximum Z-value from the opaque geometry to cap the tiles in the far direction. This discards lights that are hidden by opaque geometry. In the near direction, we extend the tiles to the camera's near plane, as shown in Figure 17.3(b).

Using separate bounds turned out to be slightly faster than using the same tile bounds for both opaque and transparent geometry; in Figure 17.1(b), when using separate bounds, rendering takes 15.1 ms (upper) and 21.9 ms (lower), compared to 16.1 ms and 23.5 ms when using the extended bounds for both opaque and transparent geometries.

We would like to note that this is, again, scene dependent. Regardless of whether we use the approximate variant or the exact one, we can still use the depth buffer from the opaque geometry during the final render in order to enable early-Z and similar optimizations. If we do not use the minimum or maximum reduction to learn a tile's actual bounds, no modifications are required to support transparency.

Light assignment. If separate sets of tiles are used, light assignment must be done twice. In our case, a special optimization is possible: we can first assign lights in two dimensions and then discard lights that lie behind opaque geometry (use the maximum Z-bound from the tiles only). This yields the light lists for transparent geometry. For opaque geometry, we additionally discard lights based on the minimum Z-bound information (Listing 17.2).

```
// assign lights to 2D tiles
tiles2D = build_2d_tiles();
lightLists2D = assign_lights_to_2d_tiles( tiles2D );

// draw opaque geometry in pre-Z pass and find tiles'
// extents in the Z-direction
depthBuffer = render_preZ_pass();
tileZBounds = reduce_z_bounds( tiles2D, depthBuffer );

// for transparent geometry, prune lights against maximum Z-direction
lightListsTrans
  = prune_lights_max( lightLists2D, tileZBounds );

// for opaque geometry additionally prune lights against
// minimum Z-direction
lightListsOpaque
  = prune_lights_min( lightListsTrans, tileZBounds );

// ...

// later: rendering
draw( opaque geometry, lightListsOpaque );
draw( trasparent geometry, lightListsTrans );
```

Listing 17.2. Pseudocode describing the rendering algorithm used to support transparency, as shown in Figure 17.1(b). We perform the additional optimization where we first prune lights based on the maximum Z-direction, which gives the light assignment for transparent geometry. Then, we prune lights in the minimum Z-direction, which gives us light lists for opaque geometry.

Rendering and shading. No special modifications are required here, other than using the appropriate set of light lists for opaque and transparent geometries, respectively. First, all opaque geometry should be rendered. Then the transparent geometry is rendered back to front.[1]

17.6 Support for MSAA

Supporting MSAA and similar schemes is very simple with tiled forward shading. We mainly need to ensure that all render targets are created with MSAA enabled. Additionally we need to consider all (multi)samples during the optional minimum or maximum Z-reduction step.

We show the effect of MSAA on render time in Figure 17.4. As we compare to tiled deferred shading, which does not support transparency, Figure 17.4 includes timings for tiled forward both with (Figure 17.1(b)) and without (Figure 17.1(a)) transparency. Additionally, we compare memory usage between our forward and deferred implementations.

---

[1]In our demo, we sort on a per-object basis, which obviously causes some artifacts when transparent objects overlap. This is not a limitation in the technique but rather one in our implementation.

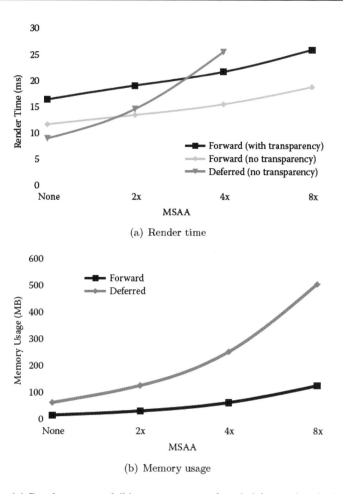

(a) Render time

(b) Memory usage

Figure 17.4. (a) Render time and (b) memory usage for tiled forward and tiled deferred shading with varying MSAA settings. We were unable to allocate the 8× MSAA framebuffer for deferred, which is why no timing results are available for that configuration. Memory usage estimates are based on a G-buffer with 32-bit depth, 32-bit ambient, and 64-bit normal, diffuse, and specular components (using the `RGBA16F` format).

One interesting note is that our unoptimized Z-reduction scales almost linearly with the number of samples: from 0.75 ms when using one sample to 5.1 ms with 8× MSAA. At that point, the contribution of the Z-reduction is quite significant with respect to the total frame time. However, it still provides a speedup in our tests. It is also likely possible to optimize the Z-reduction step further, for instance, by using compute shaders instead of a fragment shader.

17.7 Supporting Different Shaders

Like all forward rendering, we can attach different shaders and resources (textures, uniforms, etc.) to different chunks of geometry. Of course, if desired, we can still use the übershader approach in the forward rendering.

We have implemented three different shader types to test this, as seen in Figure 17.1(d): a default diffuse-specular shader, a shader emulating two-color car paint (see transparent bubbles and lion), and a rim-light shader (see large fabric in the middle of the scene).

The forward renderer uses the different shaders, compiled as different shader programs, with different chunks of geometry. For comparison, we implemented this as an übershader for deferred rendering. An integer identifying which shader should be used is stored in the G-buffer for each sample. (There were some unused bits available in the G-buffer, so we did not have to allocate additional storage.) The deferred shading code selects the appropriate shader at runtime using runtime branches in GLSL.

Performance degradation for using different shaders seems to be slightly smaller for the forward renderer; switching from diffuse-specular shading only to using the different shaders described above caused performance to drop by 1.4 ms on average. For the deferred shader, the drop was around 2.2 ms. However, the variations in rendering time for different views are in the same order of magnitude.

17.8 Conclusion and Further Improvements

We have explored *tiled forward shading* in this chapter. Tiled forward shading combines advantages from both tiled deferred shading and standard forward rendering. It is quite adaptable to different conditions, by, for instance, omitting steps in the algorithm made unnecessary by application-specific knowledge. An example is the optional computation of minimum and/or maximum Z-bounds for top-down views.

An extension that we have been exploring recently is *clustered shading*. Tiled shading (both forward and deferred) mainly considers 2D groupings of samples, which, while simple, cause performance and robustness issues in some scene and view configurations. One example of this is in scenes with first-person-like cameras where many discontinuities occur in the Z-direction (Figure 17.5). In clustered shading, we instead consider 3D groupings of samples, which handle this case much more gracefully.

Clustered shading's main advantage is a much lower view dependency, delivering more predictable performance in scenes with high or unpredictable complexity in the Z-direction. The disadvantages are increased complexity, requirements on hardware (we rely heavily on compute shaders/CUDA), and several new constant costs. For instance, with tiled shading, the subdivision of the screen into tiles is basically free. In clustered shading, this step becomes much more expensive—in

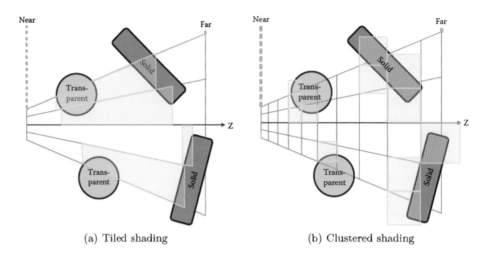

(a) Tiled shading   (b) Clustered shading

Figure 17.5. Comparison between volumes created by (a) the tiling explored in this article and (b) clustering, as described in [Olsson et al. 12b]. Finding the tiled volumes is relatively simple and can be done in standard fragment shaders. Clustering is implemented with compute shaders, as is the light assignment to clusters.

fact, in some cases it offsets time won in the shading from the better light-to-sample mapping offered by clustering (Figure 17.6). We are also further exploring clustered forward shading [Olsson et al. 12a], which shows good promise on modern high-end GPUs with compute shader capabilities. Tiled forward shading, on the other hand, is implementable on a much wider range of hardware.

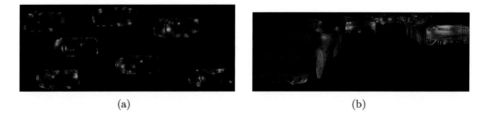

(a)   (b)

Figure 17.6. Comparison between tiled forward shading and clustered forward shading. (a) In the top-down view, tiled forward outperforms our current clustered forward implementation (6.6 ms versus 9.3 ms). (b) In the first-person-like view, tiled forward becomes slightly slower (9.4 ms versus 9.1 ms). While somewhat slower in the first view, one of the main features of clustered shading is its robust performance. There are 1,024 randomly placed light sources.

Bibliography

[Andersson 09] Johan Andersson. "Parallel Graphics in Frostbite - Current & Future." SIGGRAPH Course: Beyond Programmable Shading, New Orleans, LA, August 6, 2009. (Available at http://s09.idav.ucdavis.edu/talks/04-JAndersson-ParallelFrostbite-Siggraph09.pdf.)

[Balestra and Engstad 08] Christophe Balestra and Pål-Kristian Engstad. "The Technology of Uncharted: Drake's Fortune." Presentation, Game Developer Conference, San Francisco, CA, 2008. (Available at http://www.naughtydog.com/docs/Naughty-Dog-GDC08-UNCHARTED-Tech.pdf.)

[Enderton et al. 10] Eric Enderton, Erik Sintorn, Peter Shirley, and David Luebke. "Stochastic Transparency." In *I3D 10: Proceedings of the 2010 ACM SIGGRAPH Symposium on Interactive 3D Graphics and Games*, pp. 157–164. New York: ACM, 2010.

[Engel 09] Wolfgang Engel. "The Light Pre-Pass Renderer: Renderer Design for Efficient Support of Multiple Lights." SIGGRAPH Course: Advances in Real-Time Rendering in 3D Graphics and Games, New Orleans, LA, August 3, 2009. (Available at http://www.bungie.net/News/content.aspx?type=opnews&link=Siggraph_09.)

[Hargreaves and Harris 04] Shawn Hargreaves and Mark Harris. "Deferred Shading." Presentation, NVIDIA Developer Conference: 6800 Leagues Under the Sea, London, UK, June 29, 2004. (Available at http://http.download.nvidia.com/developer/presentations/2004/6800_Leagues/6800_Leagues_Deferred_Shading.pdf.)

[Kircher and Lawrance 09] Scott Kircher and Alan Lawrance. "Inferred Lighting: Fast Dynamic Lighting and Shadows for Opaque and Translucent Objects." In *Sandbox '09: Proceedings of the 2009 ACM SIGGRAPH Symposium on Video Games*, pp. 39–45. New York: ACM, 2009.

[Lauritzen 10] Andrew Lauritzen. "Deferred Rendering for Current and Future Rendering Pipelines." SIGGRAPH Course: Beyond Programmable Shading, Los Angeles, CA, July 29, 2010. (Available at http://bps10.idav.ucdavis.edu/talks/12-lauritzen_DeferredShading_BPS_SIGGRAPH2010.pdf.)

[Olsson and Assarsson 11] Ola Olsson and Ulf Assarsson. "Tiled Shading." *Journal of Graphics, GPU, and Game Tools* 15:4 (2011), 235–251. (Available at http://www.tandfonline.com/doi/abs/10.1080/2151237X.2011.621761.)

[Olsson et al. 12a] Ola Olsson, Markus Billeter, and Ulf Assarsson. "Clustered and Tiled Forward Shading: Supporting Transparency and MSAA." In *SIGGRAPH '12: ACM SIGGRAPH 2012 Talks*, article no. 37. New York: ACM, 2012.

[Olsson et al. 12b] Ola Olsson, Markus Billeter, and Ulf Assarsson. "Clustered Deferred and Forward Shading." In *HPG '12: Proceedings of the Fourth ACD SIGGRPAH/Eurographics Conference on High Performance Graphics*, pp. 87–96. Aire-la-Ville, Switzerland: Eurogaphics, 2012.

[Saito and Takahashi 90] Takafumi Saito and Tokiichiro Takahashi. "Comprehensible Rendering of 3D Shapes." *SIGGRAPH Comput. Graph.* 24:4 (1990), 197-206.

[Shishkovtsov 05] Oles Shishkovtsov. "Deferred Shading in S.T.A.L.K.E.R." In *GPU Gems 2*, edited by Matt Pharr and Randima Fernando, pp. 143–166. Reading, MA: Addison-Wesley, 2005.

[Swoboda 09] Matt Swoboda. "Deferred Lighting and Post Processing on PLAYSTATION 3." Presentation, Game Developer Conference, San Francisco, 2009. (Available at http://www.technology.scee.net/files/presentations/gdc2009/DeferredLightingandPostProcessingonPS3.ppt.)

[Thibieroz and Grün 10] Nick Thibieroz and Holger Grün. "OIT and GI Using DX11 Linked Lists." Presentation, Game Developer Conference, San Francisco, CA, 2010. (Available at http://developer.amd.com/gpu_assets/OIT%20and%20Indirect%20Illumination%20using%20DX11%20Linked%20Lists_forweb.ppsx.)

[Trebilco 09] Damian Trebilco. "Light Indexed Deferred Rendering." In *ShaderX7: Advanced Rendering Techniques*, edited by Wolfgang Engel, pp. 243–256. Hingham, MA: Charles River Media, 2009.

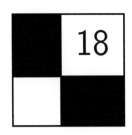

18

Forward+: A Step Toward Film-Style Shading in Real Time

Takahiro Harada, Jay McKee, and Jason C. Yang

18.1 Introduction

Modern GPU hardware along with the feature set provided by the DirectX 11 API provides developers more flexibility to choose among a variety of rendering pipelines. In order to exploit the performance of modern GPUs, we believe it is important to choose a pipeline that takes advantage of GPU hardware features, scales well, and provides flexibility for artists, tech artists, and programmers to achieve high-quality rendering with unique visuals. The ability to differentiate a game's visual look from today's games, which modern computer-generated (CG) films are extremely good at doing, likely will be a key for game graphics in the future. However, the ability to produce high-quality renderings that approach the styling in CG films will require great flexibility to support arbitrary data formats and shaders for more sophisticated rendering of surface materials and special effects.

Our goal was to find a rendering pipeline that would best meet these objectives. We boiled things down to a few specific requirements:

- Materials may need to be both physically and nonphysically based. Tech artists will want to build large trees of materials made of arbitrary complexity. Material types will likely be similar to those found in offline renderers such as RenderMan, mental ray, and Maxwell Render shading systems.

- Artists want complete freedom regarding the number of lights that can be placed in a scene at once.

- Rendering data should be decoupled from the underlying rendering engine. Artists and programmers should be able to write shaders and new materials freely at runtime for quick turnaround—going from concept to seeing results

277

should be fast and easy. The architecture should be simple and not get in the way of creative expression.

We have devised a rendering pipeline that we believe meets these objectives well and is a good match for modern GPU hardware going into the foreseeable future. We refer to it as the Forward+ rendering pipeline [Harada et al. 11].

18.2 Forward+

The Forward+ rendering pipeline requires three stages:

- **Z prepass**. Z prepass is an option for forward rendering, but it is essential for Forward+ to reduce the pixel overdraws of the final shading step. This is especially expensive for Forward+ due to the possible traversal of many lights per pixel, which we will detail later in this section.

- **Light culling**. Light culling is a stage that calculates the list of lights affecting a pixel.

- **Final shading**. Final shading, which is an extension to the shading pass in forward rendering, shades the entire surface. A required change is the way to pass lights to shaders. In Forward+, any lights in a scene have to be accessible from shaders rather than binding some subset of lights for each objects as is typical of traditional forward rendering.

18.2.1 Light Culling

The light-culling stage is similar to the light-accumulation step of deferred lighting. Instead of calculating lighting components, light culling calculates a list of light indices overlapping a pixel. The list of lights can be calculated for each pixel, which is a better choice for final shading.

However, storing a per-pixel light list requires a large memory footprint and significant computation at the light-culling stage. Instead, the screen is split into tiles and light indices are calculated on a per-tile basis (Figure 18.1). Although tiling can add false positives to the list for a pixel in a tile, it reduces the overall memory footprint and computation time necessary for generating the light lists. Thus we are making a tradeoff between light-index buffer memory and final shader efficiency.

By utilizing the computing capability of modern GPUs, light culling can be implemented entirely on the GPU as detailed in Section 18.3. Therefore, the whole lighting pipeline can be executed entirely on the GPU.

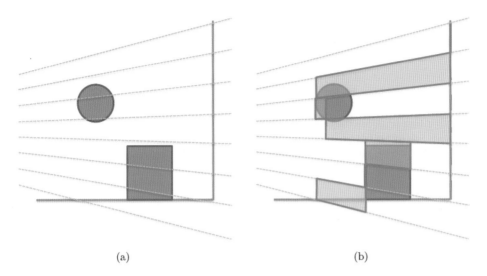

(a)   (b)

Figure 18.1. Illustration of light culling in 2D. (a) A camera is placed on the left, and green lines indicate tile borders. (b) Light culling creates a frustum for each tile bounded by minimum and maximum depth of pixels in a tile.

18.2.2 Shading

Whereas light culling creates the list of lights overlapping each pixel, final shading loops through the list of lights and evaluates materials using material parameters describing the surface properties of the rendered object along with information stored for each light. With unordered access view (UAV) support, per-material instance information can be stored and accessed in linear structured buffers passed to material shaders. Therefore, at least in theory, the full render equation can be satisfied without limitation because light accumulation and shading happen simultaneously in one place with complete material and light information.

Use of complex materials and more accurate lighting models to improve visual quality is not constrained other than by the GPU computational cost, which is largely determined by the average number of overlapping lights on each pixel multiplied by the average cost for material calculation.

With this method, high pixel overdraw can kill performance; therefore, a Z prepass is critical to minimize the cost of final shading.

18.3 Implementation and Optimization

A standard forward rendering pipeline can be converted to a Forward+ rendering pipeline by adding the light-culling stage and modifying existing pixel shaders to make them implement Forward+'s final shading stage as described in Section 18.2. No modification is necessary for the Z prepass, so we do not describe its implementation. The light-culling stage can be implemented in several ways thanks to the flexibility of current GPUs. Specifically, direct compute and read-writable structure data buffers or UAVs are the key features to utilizing Forward+. In this section, we first describe which features of DirectX 11 are essential to making Forward+ work well on modern GPUs. Then we explain a light-culling implementation that works well for a scene with thousands of lights. If there are more lights, we might be better off considering other implementations such as those described in [Harada et al. 11]. This section concludes by describing modifications for final shading.

18.3.1 Gather-Based Light Culling

During light culling, the computation is done on a by-tile basis. Therefore, it is natural to execute a thread group for a tile. A thread group can share data using thread group shared memory (called shared memory from now on), which can reduce a lot of redundant computation in a thread group. The computation is identical for each tile; therefore, we explain the computation for a single tile.

The compute shader for light culling is executed as a two-dimensional (2D) work group. A thread group is assigned a unique 2D index, and a thread in a thread group is assigned a unique 2D index in the group.

In the pseudocode in this subsection, the following macros are used for these variables:

- GET_GROUP_IDX: thread group index in X direction (SV_GroupID);

- GET_GROUP_IDY: thread group index in Y direction (SV_GroupID);

- GET_GLOBAL_IDX: global thread index in X direction (SV_DispatchThreadID);

- GET_GLOBAL_IDY: global thread index in Y direction (SV_DispatchThreadID);

- GET_LOCAL_IDX: local thread index in X direction (SV_GroupThreadID);

- GET_LOCAL_IDY: local thread index in Y direction (SV_GroupThreadID).

The first step is computation of the frustum of a tile in view space. To reconstruct four side faces, we need to calculate the view-space coordinates of the four corner points of the tile. With these four points and the origin, four side planes can be constructed.

```
float4 frustum [4];
{  //   construct frustum
  float4 v[4];
  v[0]=projToView(8*GET_GROUP_IDX , 8*GET_GROUP_IDY ,1.f) );
  v[1]=projToView(8*(GET_GROUP_IDX+1), 8*GET_GROUP_IDY ,1.f) );
  v[2]=projToView(8*(GET_GROUP_IDX+1) ,8*(GET_GROUP_IDY+1) ,1.f));
```

```
    v[3]=projToView(8*GET_GROUP_IDX, 8*(GET_GROUP_IDY+1),1.f) );
    float4 o = make_float4(0.f,0.f,0.f,0.f);
    for(int i=0; i<4; i++)
        frustum[i] = createEquation( o, v[i], v[(i+1)&3] );
}
```

`projToView()` is a function that takes screen-space pixel indices and depth value and returns coordinates in view space. `createEquation()` creates a plane equation from three vertex positions.

The frustum at this point has infinite length in the depth direction; however, we can clip the frustum by using the maximum and minimum depth values of the pixels in the tile. To obtain the depth extent, a thread first reads the depth value of the assigned pixel from the depth buffer, which is created in the depth prepass. Then it is converted to the coordinate in view space. To select the maximum and minimum values among threads in a group, we used atomic operations to shared memory. We cannot use this feature if we do not launch a thread group for computation of a tile.

```
float depth = depthIn.Load(
uint3(GET_GLOBAL_IDX,GET_GLOBAL_IDY,0) );

float4 viewPos = projToView(GET_GLOBAL_IDX, GET_GLOBAL_IDY,
depth);

int lIdx = GET_LOCAL_IDX + GET_LOCAL_IDY*8;
{// calculate bound
    if( lIdx == 0 )// initialize
    {
        ldsZMax = 0;
        ldsZMin = 0 xffffffff;
    }
    GroupMemoryBarrierWithGroupSync();
    u32 z = asuint( viewPos.z );
    if( depth != 1.f )
    {
        AtomMax( ldsZMax, z );
        AtomMin( ldsZMin, z );
    }
    GroupMemoryBarrierWithGroupSync();
    maxZ = asfloat( ldsZMax );
    minZ = asfloat( ldsZMin );
}
```

`ldsZMax` and `ldsZMin` store maximum and minimum z coordinates, which are bounds of a frustum in the z direction, in shared memory. Once a frustum is constructed, we are ready to go through all the lights in the scene. Because there are several threads executed per tile, we can cull several lights at the same time. We used 8×8 for the size of a thread group; thus, 64 lights are processed in parallel. The code for the test is as follows:

```
for(int i=0; i<nBodies; i+=64)
{
  int il = lIdx + i;
  if( il < nBodies )
  {
    if(overlaps (frustum, gLightGeometry[il]))
    {
      appendLightToList(il);
    }
  }
}
```

In `overlaps()`, a light-geometry overlap is checked against a frustum using the separating axis theorem [Ericson 04]. If a light is overlapping the frustum, the light index is stored to the list of the overlapping lights in `appendLightToList()`. There are several data structures we can use to store the light list. The obvious way would be to build a linked list using a few atomic operations [Yang et al. 10].

However, this approach is relatively expensive: we need to use a few global atomic operations to insert a light, and a global memory write is necessary whenever an overlapping light is found. Therefore, we took another approach in which a memory write is performed in two steps. A tile is computed by a thread group, and so we can use shared memory for the first level storage. Light index storage and counter for the storage is allocated as follows:

```
groupshared u32 ldsLightIdx[LIGHT_CAPACITY];
groupshared u32 ldsLightIdxCounter;
```

In our implementation, we set `LIGHT_CAPACITY` to 256. The `appendLightToList()` is implemented as follows:

```
void appendLightToList( int i )
{
  u32 dstIdx = 0;
  InterlockedAdd( ldsLightIdxCounter, 1, dstIdx );
  if( dstIdx < LIGHT_CAPACITY )
    ldsLightIdx[dstIdx] = i;
}
```

With this implementation, no global memory write is necessary until all the lights are tested.

After testing all the lights against a frustum, indices of lights overlapping that frustum are collected in the shared memory. The last step of the kernel is to write these to the global memory.

For the storage of light indices in the global memory, we allocated two buffers: `gLightIdx`, which is a memory pool for the indices, and `gLightIdxCounter`, which is a memory counter for the memory pool. Memory sections for light indices for a tile are not allocated in advance. Thus, we first need to reserve memory in `gLightIdx`. This is done by an atomic operation to `gLightIdxCounter` using a thread in the thread group.

Once a memory offset is obtained, we just fill the light indices to the assigned contiguous memory of `gLightIdx` using all the threads in a thread group. The code for doing this memory write is as follows:

```
{  //  write back
  u32 startOffset = 0;
  if( lIdx == 0 )
  {// reserve memory
    if( ldsLightIdxCounter != 0 )
      InterlockedAdd( gLightIdxCounter, ldsLightIdxCounter,
startOffset );

    ptLowerBound[tileIdx] = startOffset;
    ldsLightIdxStart = startOffset;
  }
  GroupMemoryBarrierWithGroupSync();
  startOffset = ldsLightIdxStart;

  for(int i=lIdx; i<ldsLightIdxCounter; i+=64)
  {
    gLightIdx[startOffset+i] = ldsLightIdx[i];
  }
}
```

This light-culling kernel reads light geometry (for spherical lights, that includes the location of the light and its radius). There are several options for the structure of the light buffer. Of course, we can pack light geometry and lighting properties, such as intensity and falloff, to a single structure. However, this is not a good idea for our light-culling approach because all the necessary data for the light culling is padded with light properties, which are not used in the light culling. A GPU usually reads data by page. Therefore, it is likely to transfer lighting properties as well as light geometry although they are not read by the kernel when this data structure is employed for the lights.

A better choice for the data structure is to separate the light geometry and lighting properties into two separate buffers. The light-culling kernel only touches the light geometry buffer, increasing the performance because we do not have to read unnecessary data.

18.3.2 Final Shading

For final shading, all objects in the camera frustum are rendered with their authored materials. This is different than forward rendering because we need to iterate through the lights overlapping each tile.

To write a pixel shader, we created "building blocks" of common operations for different shaders. This design makes it easy to write shaders, as we will show now. The most important building blocks are the following two, implemented as macros:

```
#define LIGHT_LOOP_BEGIN
  int tileIndex = GetTileIndex(screenPos);
  uint startIndex, endIndex;
  GetTileOffsets( tileIndex, startIndex, endIndex );

  for( uint lightListIdx = startIdx;
       lightListIdx < endIdx;
       lightListIdx++ )
  {
    int lightIdx = LightIndexBuffer[lightListIdx];
    LightParams directLight;
    LightParams indirectLight;

    if( isIndirectLight( lightIdx ) )
    {
      FetchIndirectLight(lightIdx , indirectLight);
    }
    else
    {
      FetchDirectLight( lightIndex, directLight );
    }
#define LIGHT_LOOP_END
  }
```

LIGHT_LOOP_BEGIN first calculates the tile index of the pixel using its screen-space position. Then it opens a loop to iterate all the lights overlapping the tile and fills light parameters for direct and indirect light. LIGHT_LOOP_END is a macro to close the loop.

By using these building blocks, an implementation of a pixel shader is simple and looks almost the same as a pixel shader used in forward rendering. For example, a shader for a microfacet surface is implemented as follows:

```
float4 PS ( PSInput i ) : SV_TARGET
{
    float3 colorOut = 0;
#LIGHT_LOOP_BEGIN
    colorOut += EvaluateMicrofacet ( directLight, indirectLight );
#LIGHT_LOOP_END
    return float4(colorOut, 1.f );
}
```

Other shaders can be implemented by just changing the lines between the two macros. This building block also allows us to change the implementation easily based on performance needs. For instance, we can change `LIGHT_LOOP_BEGIN` to iterate a few lights on a slower platform.

An optimization we can do for the host side is to sort all render draw calls by material type and render all triangles that belong to each unique material at the same time. This reduces GPU state change and makes good use of the cache because all pixels needing the same data will be rendered together.

18.4 Results

We implemented Forward+ using DirectX 11 and benchmarked using the scene shown in Figure 18.2 to compare the performance of Forward+ to compute-based deferred lighting [Andersson 11].

In short, Forward+ was faster on both the AMD Radeon HD 6970 and HD 7970 (Figure 18.3). Once we compare the memory transfer size and the amount of computing, it makes sense. Three timers are placed in a frame of the benchmark to measure time for prepass, light processing, and final shading. In Forward+, these three are depth prepass, light culling, and final shading. In compute-based deferred, they are geometry pass (or G-pass), which exports geometry information to full screen buffers, light culling, screen-space light accumulation, and final shading.

Prepass. Forward+ writes a screen-sized depth buffer while deferred writes a depth buffer and another float4 buffer that packs the normal vector of the visible pixel. The specular coefficient can be stored in the W component of the buffer, too. Therefore, Forward+ writes less than deferred and is faster on prepass.

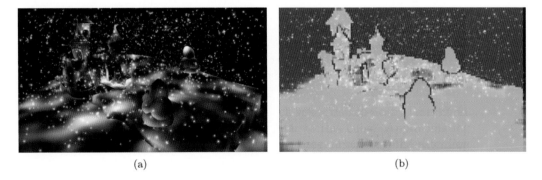

(a)   (b)

Figure 18.2. A scene with 3,072 dynamic lights rendered in 1,280 × 720 resolution. (a) Using diffuse lighting. (b) Visualization of number of lights overlapping each tile. Blue, green and red tiles have 0, 25, and 50 lights, respectively. The numbers in between are shown as interpolated colors. The maximum number is clamped to 50.

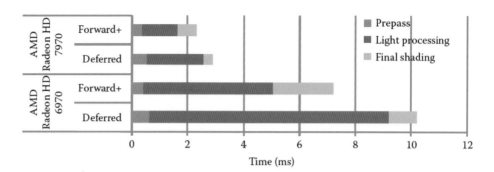

Figure 18.3. Breakdown of the computation time for three stages of Forward+ and deferred on an AMD Radeon HD 6970 GPU and an AMD Radeon HD 7970 GPU.

Light processing. Forward+ reads the depth and light geometry buffers. Deferred also reads them, but the `float4` buffer storing normal vectors and lighting properties has to be read as well because lighting is done at this stage. Therefore, Forward+ has less memory read compared to deferred.

As for the amount of the computation, Forward+ culls lights. On the other hand, deferred not only culls lights but also performs lighting computation. Forward+ has less computation.

For the memory write, Forward+ writes light indices, the sizes of which depend on the scene and tile size. If 8×8 tiles are used, deferred has to write $8 \times 8 \times 4$ bytes if a `float4` data is written for each pixel. With this data size, Forward+ can write 256 ($8 \times 8 \times 4$) light indices for a tile; if the number of lights is less than 256 per tile, Forward+ writes less. In our test scene, there was no tile overlapped with more than 256 lights.

To summarize this stage, Forward+ is reading, computing, and writing less than deferred. This is why Forward+ is so fast at this stage.

Final shading. It is obvious that Forward+ takes more time compared to deferred at shading because it has to iterate through all the lights in the pixel shader. This is a disadvantage in terms of the performance, but it is designed this way to get more freedom.

18.5   Forward+ in the AMD Leo Demo

We created the AMD Leo demo to show an implementation of Forward+ in real-time in a real-world setting. A screenshot from the demo is shown in Figure 18.4. We chose scene geometry on the order of what can be found in current PC-based video games (one to two million polygons). We also had the objective of rendering with a unique stylized look that could be characterized as "CGish" in that it uses material types that resemble those found in an offline renderer. There are more

Figure 18.4. A screenshot from the AMD Leo Demo.

than 150 lights in the scenes. Artists created about 50 lights by hand. Other lights are dynamically spawned at runtime for one-bounce indirect illumination lighting using the technique described in this section. Although Forward+ is capable of using thousands of dynamic lights, a few hundred lights were more than enough for our artists to achieve their lighting goals, especially for a single-room indoor scene.

We use a material system in which a material consists of N layers where each layer can have M weighted BRDF models along with other physically based constants like those involving transmission, absorption, refraction, and reflections of incoming light.

Material parameters for a single layer include physical properties for lighting such as coefficients for a microfacet surface and a refractive index as well as many modifiers for standard lighting parameters. We deliberately allow numeric ranges to go beyond the "physically correct" values to give artists freedom to bend the rules for a given desired effect.

For lighting, artists can dynamically create and place any number of omnidirectional lights and spotlights into a scene. The light data structure contains a material index mask. This variable is used to filter lights to only effect specific material types. While not physically correct, this greatly helps artists fine-tune lighting without unwanted side effects.

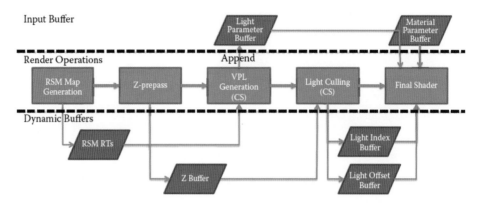

Figure 18.5. Forward+ render passes and GPU buffers in the AMD Leo Demo.

18.5.1   One-Bounce Indirect Illumination

As a unique extension of the light-culling system, lights can be used as what we call an indirect light to generate one-bounce indirect illumination in the scene. If a given light is tagged to be an indirect light, the following will occur for that light before any rendering passes at runtime:

- Generate a reflective shadow map (RSM) of the scene from the point of view of the light [Dachsbacher and Stamminger 05]. Normal buffer, color buffer, and world-space buffers are generated.

- A compute shader is executed to create spotlights at the location captured in the RSM. The generated spotlights are appended to the main light list. The direction of the spotlight will be the reflection of the vector from the world position to the original indirect light around the normal. Set other parameters for the new spotlight that conforms to the settings for the indirect light. We added art-driven parameters to control the effect of indirect lighting.

This new "indirect" light type is used by artists to spawn virtual spotlights that represent one-bounce lighting from the environment. This method seems to give artists good control over all aspects of lighting without requiring them to hand-place thousands or millions of lights or prebake lightmaps. Each indirect light can spawn $N \times N$ virtual spotlights, so it takes only a handful to create a nice indirect lighting effect. Once virtual lights are spawned in the compute shader, they go through the same light-culling process as all the other lights in the system. Thus, we could keep the entire rendering pipeline simple. Figure 18.5 illustrates the rendering pipeline used in the AMD Leo demo.

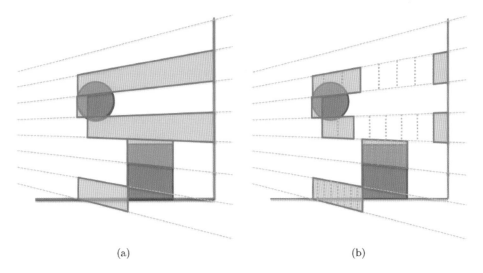

(a)   (b)

Figure 18.6. Illustration of 2.5D culling. (a) Frustum culling creates a long frustum for a tile with foreground and background. (b) 2.5D culling—splitting depth into eight cells—does not capture lights falling between foreground and background.

18.6   Extensions

18.6.1   2.5D Culling

At the light-culling stage of Forward+, light geometries are tested against a frustum of each tile that is clipped by the maximum and minimum depth values of a tile. This light culling works well if there is little variance in the depth in a tile. Otherwise, it can create a long frustum for a tile. This results in capturing a lot of lights for a tile, as we can see at the edge of geometries in Figure 18.3(b), although some lights have no influence on any of the pixels in a tile if they fall at the void space in the frustum.

As the number of lights reported for a tile increases, the computational cost of final shading increases. This is critical especially when the shading computation for a light is expensive. This is often the case because one of the motivations of employing Forward+ is its ability to use sophisticated BRDFs for shading.

One obvious way to improve the efficiency of culling is to cull the lights using a 3D grid. However, this increases the computation as well as the size of the data to be exported. It is possible to develop sophisticated and expensive culling, but it shouldn't be overkill. Our proposed 2.5D culling constructs a nonuniform 3D grid without adding a lot of computation or stressing the memory bandwidth.

The idea is illustrated in Figure 18.6. This approach first constructs a frustum for a tile in the same way as the screen-space culling described in Section 18.3.

Then the extent of a frustum is split into cells; for each pixel in a tile, we flag a cell to which the pixel belongs. We call the data we construct for a tile a frustum and an array of occupancy flags a depth mask.

To check overlap of light geometry on the tile, the light geometry first is checked against the frustum. If the light overlaps, a depth mask is created for the light. This is done by calculating the extent of the light geometry in the depth direction of the frustum and flagging the cells to that extent. By comparing the depth mask for a light to the depth mask for the tile, we can cull the light in the depth direction. Overlap of the light is reported only if there is at least one cell flagged by both depth masks.

If a tile has a foreground and background, the 2.5D culling can detect and drop lights that fall between these two surfaces, thus reducing the number of lights to be processed at the final shading.

Implementation. The 2.5D culling splits a frustum into 32 cells, and so the occupancy information is stored in a 32-bit value. This cell data is allocated in shared memory to make it available to all threads in a group. The first modification to the light-culling kernel is the construction of an occupancy mask of the surface. This is performed after calculating the frustum extent in the depth direction. The pitch of a cell is calculated from the extent.

Once the pitch and the minimum depth value are obtained, any depth value can be converted to a cell index. To create the depth mask for a tile, we iterate through all the pixels in the tile and calculate a cell index for each pixel. Then a flag for the occupied cell is created by a bit shift, which is used to mark the depth mask in shared memory using an atomic logical-or operation.

Once we find a light overlapping the frustum, a depth mask is created for the light. The minimum and maximum depth values of the geometry are calculated and converted to cell indices. Once the cell indices are calculated, two bit-shift operations and a bit-and operation are necessary to create the depth mask for the light. If the light and surface occupy the same cell, both have the same flag at the cell. Thus taking logical and operation between these two masks is enough to check the overlap.

Results. We took several scenes and counted the number of lights per tile with the original Forward+ and Forward+ with our proposed 2.5D culling. The first benchmark is performed against the scene in Figure 18.7(a), which has a large variance in the depth. Figures 18.7(b) and 18.7(c) visualize the number of lights overlapping each tile using Forward+ with frustum culling and the proposed 2.5D culling.

Figure 18.7(b) makes clear that tiles that contain an object's edge capture a large number of lights. The number of overlapping lights is reduced dramatically when 2.5D culling is used (Figure 18.7(c)). We also counted the number of lights overlapping each tile and quantitatively compared these two culling methods

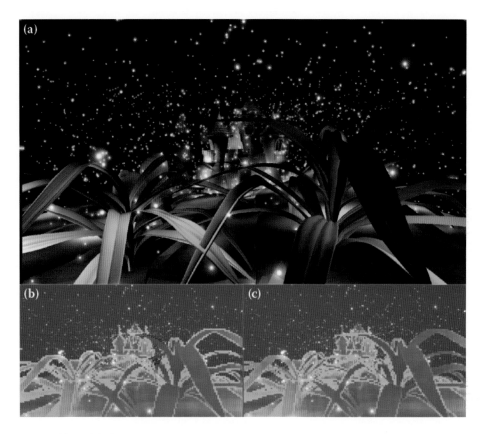

Figure 18.7. (a) A scene with a large depth variance that the original Forward+ could not process efficiently. (b) Visualization of the number of lights per tile using frustum culled with maximum and minimum depth values in a tile. (c) Visualization of the number of lights per tile using the proposed 2.5D culling.

(Figure 18.9(a)). Without the proposed method, there are a lot of tiles with more than 200 lights overlapping. However, by using the 2.5D culling, a tile has at most 120 overlapping lights. The benefit we can get from final shading depends on the implementation of shader, but culling eliminates a lot of unnecessary memory reads and computation for the final shader.

We also performed a test on the scene shown in Figure 18.8(a), which does not have as much depth variance as the scene in Figure 18.7(a). Because the depth difference is not large in these scenes, the number of lights overlapping a tile, including an edge of an object, is less than in the previous scene. However, color temperature is low when the 2.5D culling is used. A quantitative comparison is shown in Figure 18.9(b). Although the improvement is not as large as the

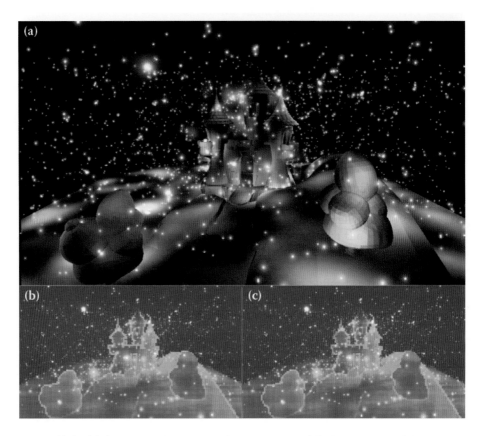

Figure 18.8. (a) A scene without a large depth variance. (b) Visualization of the number of lights per tile using frustum culled with maximum and minimum depth values in a tile. (c) Visualization of the number of lights per tile using the proposed 2.5D culling.

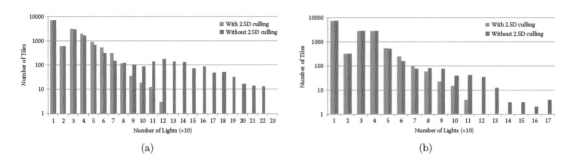

Figure 18.9. The count of tiles in terms of the number of lights for the scenes shown in Figures 18.7(a) and 18.8(a), respectively.

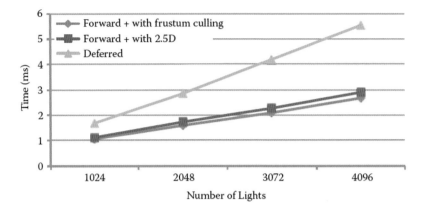

Figure 18.10. Comparison of computation time for the light-culling stage of Forward+ using frustum culling only and frustum culling plus 2.5D culling by changing the number of lights in the scene shown in Figure 18.7(a). Computation time for the light accumulation in compute-based deferred lighting is also shown.

previous scene, the proposed method could reduce the number of overlapping lights on tiles.

Figure 18.10 compares the computation time for the light-culling stage for the scene of Figure 18.1(a) as measured on an AMD Radeon HD 7970 GPU. This comparison indicates the overhead of additional computation in 2.5D culling is less than 10% of the time without the culling; when there are 1,024 lights, the overhead is about 5%. The 2.5D culling is effective regardless of the number of the light in the scene.

Figure 18.10 also contains the light accumulation time of the compute-based deferred lighting. We can see that the light-culling stage with the 2.5D culling in Forward+ is much faster than its counterpart in deferred lighting.

18.6.2   Shadowing from Many Lights

Shadows from a light can be calculated by a shadow map, with which we can get occlusion from the light in the pixel shader when the forward-rendering pipeline is used. We can calculate shadows in the same way for Forward+.

Because Forward+ is capable of using hundreds of lights for lighting, it is natural to wonder how we can use all of those lights in the scene as shadow-casting lights. One option is use a shadow map for each light. This solution is not practical because shadow map creation—the cost of which is linear to scene complexity—can be prohibitively expensive.

We can reduce the shadow map resolution, but this results in low-quality shadows.

Another option relies on rasterization and also borrows an idea from ray tracing. To check the visibility to a light, we can cast a ray to the light. If the light is local, the length of the ray is short. This means we do not have to traverse much in the scene; the cost is not as high as the cost of ray casting a long ray in full ray tracing.

In this subsection, we describe how ray casting can be integrated in Forward+ to add shadows from hundreds of lights and show that a perfect shadow from hundreds of lights can be obtained in real time. After adding this feature, Forward+ is not just an extension of forward-rendering pipeline but a hybrid of forward, deferred-rendering pipelines and ray tracing.

Implementation. To ray cast against the scene, we need the position and normal vector of a primary ray hit and the acceleration data structure for ray casting. The position of a primary ray hit can be reconstructed from the depth buffer by applying inverse projection. The normal vector of the entire visible surface, which is used to avoid casting rays to a light that is at the back of the surface and to offset the ray origin, can be written at the depth prepass. The prepass is no longer writing only the depth value, and so it is essentially identical to a G-pass in the deferred-rendering pipeline. The acceleration structure has to be updated every frame for a dynamic scene; however, this is a more extensive research topic and we do not explore it in this chapter. Instead, we just assume that the data structure is built already.

After the prepass, implementing a ray-cast shadow is straightforward. In a pixel shader, we have access to all the information about lights, which includes light position. A shadow ray can be created by the light position and surface location. Then we can cast the ray against the acceleration structure for an intersection test. If the ray is intersecting, contribution from the light is masked.

Although this naive implementation is easy to implement, it is far from practical in terms of performance. The issue is a legacy of the forward-rendering pipeline. The number of rays to be cast for each pixel is not constant, which means the computational load or time can vary considerably among pixels even if they belong to the same surface. This results in a poor utilization of the GPU.

An alternative is to separate ray casting from pixel shading for better performance. After separating ray casting from pixel shading, the pipeline looks like this:

- G-pass,

- light culling,

- ray-cast job creation,

- ray casting,

- final shading.

After indices of lights overlapping each tile are calculated in the light-culling stage, ray-cast jobs are created and accumulated in a job buffer by iterating through all the screen pixels. This is a screen-space computation in which a thread is executed for a pixel and goes through the list of lights. If a pixel overlaps a light, a ray-cast job is created. To create a ray in the ray-casting stage, we need a pixel index to obtain surface position and normal, and a light index against which the ray is cast. These two indices are packed into a 32-bit value and stored in the job buffer.

After creating all the ray-cast jobs in a buffer, we dispatch a thread for each ray-cast job. Then it does not have the issue of uneven load balancing we experience when rays are cast in a pixel shader. Each thread is casting a ray. After identifying whether a shadow ray is blocked, the information has to be stored somewhere to pass to a pixel shader. We focused only on a hard shadow, which means the output from a ray cast is a binary value. Therefore, we have packed results from 32 rays into one 32-bit value.

But in a scene with hundreds of lights, storing a mask for all of them takes too much space even after the compression. We took advantage of the fact that we have a list of lights per tile; masks for lights in the list of a tile are only stored. We limit the number of rays to be cast per pixel to 128, which means the mask can be encoded as an int4 value. At the ray-casting stage, the result is written to the mask of the pixel using an atomic OR operation to flip the assigned bit.

After separating ray casting from pixel shading, we can keep the final shading almost the same in Forward+. We only need to read the shadow mask for each pixel; whenever a light is processed, the mask is read to get the occlusion.

Results. Figure 18.11 is a screenshot of a scene with 512 shadow-casting lights. We can see legs of chairs are casting shadows from many dynamic lights in the scene. The screen resolution was $1,280 \times 720$. The number of rays cast for this scene was more than 7 million. A frame computation time is about 32 ms on an AMD Radeon HD 7970 GPU. G-pass and light culling took negligible time compared to ray-cast job creation and ray casting, each of which took 11.57 ms and 19.91 ms for this frame. This is another example of hybrid ray-traced and rasterized graphics.

18.7 Conclusion

We have presented Forward+, a rendering pipeline that adds a GPU compute-based light-culling stage to the traditional forward-rendering pipeline to handle many lights while keeping the flexibility for material usage. We also presented the implementation detail of Forward+ using DirectX 11, and its performance. We described how the Forward+ rendering pipeline is extended to use an indirect illumination technique in the AMD Leo Demo.

Figure 18.11. Dynamic shadowing from 512 lights in a scene with 282,755 triangles.

Because of its simplicity and flexibility, there are many avenues to extend Forward+. We have described two extensions in this chapter: a 2.5D culling, which improves the light-culling efficiency, and dynamic shadowing from many lights.

18.8   Acknowledgments

We would like to thank to members of AMD GPU Tech initiatives and other people who worked on the AMD Leo demo.

Bibliography

[Andersson 11] J. Andersson. "DirectX 11 Rendering in Battlefield 3." Presentation, Game Developers Conference, San Francisco, CA, 2011.

[Dachsbacher and Stamminger 05] C. Dachsbacher and M. Stamminger. "Reflective Shadow Maps." In *Symposium on Interactive 3D Graphics and Games (I3D)*, pp. 203–231. New York: ACM, 2005.

[Ericson 04] C. Ericson. *Real-Time Collision Detection*. San Francisco: Morgan Kaufmann, 2004.

[Harada et al. 11] T. Harada, J. McKee, and J. C. Yang. "Forward+: Bringing Deferred Lighting to the Next Level," Eurographics Short Paper, Cagliari, Italy, May 15, 2012.

[Yang et al. 10] J. C. Yang, J. Hensley, H. Grun, and N. Thibieroz. "Real-Time Concurrent Linked List Construction on the GPU." *Computer Graphics Forum* 29:4 (2010), 1297–1304.

19

Progressive Screen-Space Multichannel Surface Voxelization

Athanasios Gaitatzes and Georgios Papaioannou

19.1 Introduction

An increasing number of techniques for real-time global illumination effects rely on volume data. Such representations allow the fast, out-of-order access to spatial data from any deferred shading graphics pipeline stage as in [Thiedemann et al. 11, Mavridis and Papaioannou 11, Kaplanyan and Dachsbacher 10]. For dynamic environments where both the geometry of the scene and the illumination can arbitrarily change between frames, these calculations must be performed in real time. However, when the per frame time budget is limited due to other, more important operations that must take place while maintaining a high frame rate, the fidelity of full-scene voxelization has to be traded for less accurate but faster techniques. This is especially true for video games, where many hundreds of thousands of triangles must be processed in less than 2–3 ms. In this chapter we present the novel concept of *progressive voxelization*, an incremental image-based volume generation scheme for fully dynamic scenes that addresses the view-dependency issues of image-based voxelization within the above time constraints.

Screen-space volume generation methods provide very fast and guaranteed response times compared to geometry-based techniques but suffer from view-dependency. More specifically, any technique that is performed entirely in screen space (as in deferred shading) considers only geometry that has been rendered into the depth buffer and thus has the following strong limitations: First, it ignores geometry located outside the field of view. Second, it ignores geometry that is inside the view frustum but occluded by other objects. Yet these geometry parts may have a significant influence on the desired final result (see our indirect illumination case study in this article).

In single-frame screen-space voxelization, volume attributes already available as fragment data in view-dependent image buffers are transformed and rasterized (*injected*) into the volume buffer to form a partial volume of the observed space. These commonly include the view camera G-buffers like depth, albedo, normals, and the light sources' *reflective shadow maps* (RSMs) [Dachsbacher and Stamminger 05]. The injection procedure is explained in more detail in [Kaplanyan 09] and Section 19.2.2 Since the only volume samples that can be produced in each frame are the ones that are visible in at least one of the images available in the rendering pipeline, each time the (camera or light) view changes, a new set of sample points becomes available and the corresponding voxels are generated from scratch to reflect the newly available image samples. Thus the generated volume will never contain a complete voxelization of the scene. This leads to significant frame-to-frame inconsistencies and potentially inadequate volume representations for the desired volume-based effect, especially when the coverage of the scene in the available image buffers is limited.

To alleviate the problems of screen-space voxelization techniques, but maintain their benefit of predictable, controllable, and bound execution time relative to full-scene volume generation methods, we introduce the concept of *progressive voxelization* (PV). The volume representation is incrementally updated to include the newly discovered voxels and discard the set of invalid voxels, which are not present in any of the current image buffers. Using the already available camera and light source buffers, a combination of volume injection and voxel-to-depth-buffer reprojection scheme continuously updates the volume buffer and discards invalid voxels, progressively constructing the final voxelization.

The algorithm is lightweight and operates on complex dynamic environments where geometry, materials, and lighting can change arbitrarily. Compared to single-frame screen-space voxelization, our method provides improved volume coverage (completeness) over nonprogressive methods while maintaining its high performance merits.

We demonstrate our technique by applying it as an alternative voxelization scheme for the *light propagation volumes* (LPV) diffuse global illumination method of [Kaplanyan and Dachsbacher 10]. However, being a generic multiattribute scalar voxelization method, it can be used in any other real-time volume generation problem.

19.2   Overview of Voxelization Method

Our progressive voxelization scheme is able to produce stable and valid volume data in a geometry-independent manner. As the user interacts with the environment and dynamic objects move or light information changes, new voxel data are accumulated into the initial volume and old voxels are invalidated or updated if their projection in any of the image buffers (camera or light) proves inconsistent with the respective available recorded depth. For a schematic overview see Figure 19.1, and for a resulting voxelization see Figures 19.4 and 19.5.

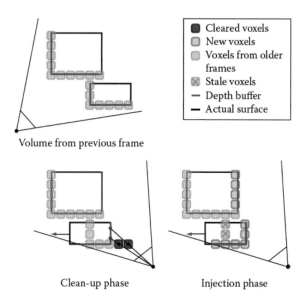

Figure 19.1. Schematic overview of the algorithm. During the cleanup phase each voxel is tested against the available depth images. If the projected voxel center lies in front of the recorded depth, it is cleared; otherwise it is retained. During the injection phase, voxels are "turned-on" based on the RSM-buffers and the camera-based depth buffer.

In each frame, two steps are performed: First, in a *cleanup* stage, the volume is swept voxel-by-voxel and the center of each voxel is transformed to the eye-space coordinate system of the buffer and tested against the available depth image value, which is also projected to eye-space coordinates. If the voxel lies closer to the image buffer viewpoint than the recorded depth, the voxel is invalidated and removed. Otherwise, the current voxel attributes are maintained. The update of the volume is performed by writing the cleared or retained values into a separate volume in order to avoid any atomic write operations and thus make the method fast and a very broadly applicable one. At the end of each cleanup cycle, the two volume buffers are swapped. After the cleanup phase, samples from all the available image buffers are injected into the volume (similar to the LPV method [Kaplanyan 09]).

When multiple image buffers are available, the cleanup stage is repeated for each image buffer, using the corresponding depth buffer as input for voxel invalidation. Each time, the currently updated (read) and output (written) buffers are swapped. The current image buffer attributes are then successively injected in the currently updated volume. The whole process is summarized in Figure 19.1.

```
in vec3 voxel_position, voxel_tex_coord;
uniform float voxel_r; // voxel radius
uniform sampler3D vol_shR, vol_shG, vol_shB, vol_normals;

void main (void)
{
  vec4 voxel_pos_wcs = vec4 (voxel_position, 1.0);
  vec3 voxel_pos_css = PointWCS2CSS (voxel_pos_wcs.xyz);
  vec3 voxel_pos_ecs = PointWCS2ECS (voxel_pos_wcs.xyz);
  vec3 zbuffer_ss = MAP_-1To1_0To1 (voxel_pos_css);
  float depth = SampleBuf (zbuffer, zbuffer_ss.xy).x;
  vec3 zbuffer_css = vec3 (voxel_pos_css.xy, 2.0*depth-1.0);
  vec3 zbuffer_ecs = PointCSS2ECS (zbuffer_css);

  vec3 voxel_mf_wcs = voxel_pos_wcs.xyz + voxel_r * vec3(1.0);
  voxel_mf_wcs = max (voxel_mf_wcs,
                      voxel_pos_wcs.xyz + voxel_half_size);
  vec3 voxel_mb_wcs = voxel_pos_wcs.xyz + voxel_r * vec3(-1.0);
  voxel_mb_wcs = min (voxel_mb_wcs,
                      voxel_pos_wcs.xyz - voxel_half_size);
  vec3 voxel_mf_ecs = PointWCS2ECS (voxel_mf_wcs);
  vec3 voxel_mb_ecs = PointWCS2ECS (voxel_mb_wcs);
  float bias = distance (voxel_mf_ecs, voxel_mb_ecs);

  vec4 shR_value = SampleBuf (vol_shR, voxel_tex_coord);
  vec4 shG_value = SampleBuf (vol_shG, voxel_tex_coord);
  vec4 shB_value = SampleBuf (vol_shB, voxel_tex_coord);
  vec4 normal_value = SampleBuf (vol_normals, voxel_tex_coord);

  if (voxel_pos_ecs.z > zbuffer_ecs.z + bias) { // discard
    normal_value = vec4 (0,0,0,0);
    shR_value = shG_value = shB_value = vec4 (0,0,0,0);
  }

  // keep
  gl_FragData[0] = normal_value;
  gl_FragData[1] = shR_value;
  gl_FragData[2] = shG_value;
  gl_FragData[3] = shB_value;
}
```

Listing 19.1. Cleanup phase fragment shader.

19.2.1 Cleanup Phase

Throughout the entire voxelization process, each voxel goes through three state transitions: "turn-on," "turn-off," and "keep" (see Listing 19.1). The "turn-on" state change is determined during the injection phase. During the cleanup stage we need to be able to determine if the state of the voxel will be retained or turned off (cleared). For each one of the available depth buffers, each voxel center $\mathbf{p}_v$ is transformed to eye-space coordinates $\mathbf{p}'_v$; accordingly the corresponding image buffer depth $Z(\mathbf{p}')$ is transformed to eye-space coordinates z_e.

Expressing the coordinates in the eye reference frame (Figure 19.2), if $\mathbf{p}'_{v,z} > z_e$ the voxel must be cleared, as it lies in front of the recorded depth boundary in the

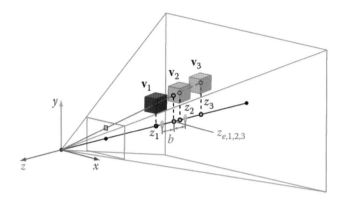

Figure 19.2. Cleanup stage: Voxels beyond the boundary depth zone are retained (orange), while voxels closer to the buffer center of projection are rejected (red). Voxels that correspond to the depth value registered in the buffer must be updated (green).

image buffer. However, the spatial data are quantized according to the volume resolution and therefore a bias b has to be introduced in order to avoid rejecting boundary samples. Since the depth comparison is performed in eye-space, b is equal to the voxel's $\mathbf{p}_v$ radius (half diagonal) clamped by the voxel boundaries in each direction. Therefore the rejection condition becomes

$$\mathbf{P}'_{v,z} > ze + b.$$

The example in Figure 19.2 explains the cleanup and update state changes of a voxel with respect to the available depth information in an image buffer. All voxels in the figure correspond to the same image buffer sample with eye-space value $z_{e,1,2,3}$. Voxel $\mathbf{v}_1$ is rejected (cleared) because z_1 is greater than $z_{e,1,2,3} + b$. Voxel $\mathbf{v}_2$ must be updated since it lies within the boundary depth zone $[z_{e,1,2,3} - b, z_{e,1,2,3} + b]$. Finally, voxel $\mathbf{v}_3$ is retained, since it lies beyond the registered depth value.

19.2.2 Injection Phase

In the injection phase, a rectangular grid of point primitives corresponding to each depth image buffer is sent to a vertex shader that offsets the points according to the stored depth. The points are subsequently transformed to world space and finally to volume-clip space. If world-space or volume clip-space coordinates are already available in the buffers, they are directly assigned to the corresponding injected points. The volume clip-space depth is finally used to determine the slice in the volume where the point sample attributes are accumulated (see Listing 19.2). At the end of this stage, the previous version of the scene's voxel representation has been updated to include a partial voxelization

```
// Vertex-Shader Stage

flat out vec2 tex_coord;
uniform sampler2D zbuffer;

void main (void)
{
  tex_coord = gl_Vertex.xy;
  float depth = SampleBuf (zbuffer, tex_coord).x;

  // screen space --> canonical screen space
  vec3 pos_css = MAP_0To1_-1To1 (vec3 (gl_Vertex.xy, depth));

  // canonical screen space --> object space
  vec3 pos_wcs = PointCSS2WCS (zbuffer_css);

  // world space --> clip space
  gl_Position = gl_ModelViewProjectionMatrix *
                vec4 (pos_wcs, 1.0);
}

// Geometry-Shader Stage

layout(points) in;
layout(points, max_vertices = 1) out;

uniform int vol_depth;
flat in vec2 tex_coord[];
flat out vec2 gtex_coord;

void main (void)
{
  gtex_coord = tex_coord[0];
  gl_Position = gl_PositionIn[0];
  gl_Layer = int (vol_depth * MAP_-1To1_0To1 (gl_Position.z));

  EmitVertex();
}
```

Listing 19.2. Injection phase using a geometry shader to select the destination slice of the volume for the point samples.

of the scene based on the newly injected point samples. The resolution of the grid of 2D points determines how much detail of the surfaces represented by the depth buffer is transferred into the volume and whether or not the geometry is sparsely sampled. If too few points are injected, the resulting volume will have gaps. This may be undesirable for certain application cases, such as the LPV method [Kaplanyan 09] or algorithms based on ray marching.

19.2.3   Single-Pass Progressive Algorithm

In order to transfer the geometric detail present in the G-buffers to the volume representation and ensure a dense population of the resulting volume, a large resolution for the grid of injected points must be used. However, the injection stage involves rendering the point grid using an equal number of texture lookups and, in some implementations, a geometry shader. This has a potentially serious impact on performance (see Figure 19.8), especially for multiple injection viewpoints.

We can totally forgo the injection phase of the algorithm and do both operations in one stage. Using the same notation as before, the logic of the algorithm remains practically the same. If the projected voxel center lies in front of the recorded depth (i.e., $\mathbf{p}'_{v,z} > z_e + b$), it is still cleared. If the projected voxel center lies behind the recorded depth (i.e., $\mathbf{p}'_{v,z} < z_e - b$), the voxel is retained; otherwise it is turned-on (or updated) using the attribute buffers information. The last operation practically replaces the injection stage.

As we are effectively sampling the geometry at the volume resolution instead of doing so at higher, image-size-dependent rate and then down-sampling to volume resolution, the resulting voxelization is expected to degrade. However, since usually depth buffers are recorded from multiple views, missing details are gradually added. A comparison of the method variations and analysis of their respective running times is given in Section 19.5.

19.3 Progressive Voxelization for Lighting

As a case study, we applied progressive voxelization to the problem of computing indirect illumination for real-time rendering. When using the technique for lighting effects, as in the case of the LPV algorithm of [Kaplanyan 09] or the ray marching techniques of [Thiedemann et al. 11, Mavridis and Papaioannou 11], the volume attributes must include occlusion information (referred to as *geometry volume* in [Kaplanyan 09]), sampled normal vectors, direct lighting (VPLs), and optionally surface albedo in the case of secondary indirect light bounces. Direct illumination and other accumulated directional data are usually encoded and stored as low-frequency spherical harmonic coefficients (see [Sloan et al. 02]).

Virtual point lights (VPLs) are points in space that act as light sources and encapsulate light reflected off a surface at a given location. In order to correctly accumulate VPLs in the volume, during the injection phase, a separate volume buffer is used that is cleared in every frame in order to avoid erroneous accumulation of lighting. For each RSM, all VPLs are injected and additively blended. Finally, the camera attribute buffers are injected to provide view-dependent dense samples of the volume. If lighting from the camera is also exploited (as in our implementation), the injected VPLs must replace the corresponding values in the volume, since the camera direct lighting buffer provides cumulative illumination. After the cleanup has been performed on the previous version of the attribute volume V_{prev}, nonempty voxels from the separate injection buffer replace corresponding values in V_{curr}. This ensures that potentially stale illumination on valid volume cells from previous frames is not retained in the final volume buffer. In Figure 19.3 we can see the results of progressive voxelization and its application to diffuse indirect lighting.

Figure 19.3. (a–f) As the camera moves left to right, we observe correct indirect illumination. (g) Final rendering of the room.

19.4 Implementation

The progressive voxelization method runs entirely on the GPU and has been implemented in a deferred shading renderer using basic OpenGL 3.0 operations on a NVIDIA GTX 285 card with 1 GB of memory. We have implemented two versions of the buffer storage mechanism in order to test their respective speed. The first uses 3D volume textures along with a geometry shader that sorts injected fragments to the correct volume slice. The second unwraps the volume buffers into 2D textures and dispenses with the expensive geometry processing (respective performance can be seen in Figure 19.8).

The texture requirements are two volume buffers for ping-pong rendering (V_{prev}, V_{curr}). Each volume buffer stores N-dimensional attribute vectors $\mathbf{a}$ and corresponds to a number of textures (2D or 3D) equal to $\lceil N/4 \rceil$, for 4-channel textures. For the reasons explained in Section 19.3 an additional N-dimensional volume buffer is required for lighting applications. In our implementation we need to store surface normals and full color spherical harmonics coefficients for incident flux in each volume buffer, which translates to 3×4 textures in total.

In terms of volume generation engine design, the user has the option to request several attributes to be computed and stored into floating-point buffers for later use. Among them are surface attributes like albedo and normals, but also dynamic lighting information and radiance values in the form of low-order spherical harmonics (SH) coefficients representation (either monochrome radiance or full color encoding, i.e., separate radiance values per color band). In our implementation the radiance of the corresponding scene location is calculated and stored as a second-order spherical harmonic representation for each voxel. For each color band, four SH coefficients are computed and encoded as RGBA float values.

19.5 Performance and Evaluation

In terms of voxelization robustness, our algorithm complements single-frame screen-space voxelization and supports both moving image viewpoints and fully dynamic geometry and lighting. This is demonstrated in Figures 19.4 and 19.5. In addition, in Figure 19.6, a partial volume representation of the Crytek Sponza II Atrium model is generated at a 64^3 resolution and a 128^2-point injection grid using single-frame and progressive voxelization. Figures 19.6(a) and (b) are the single-frame volumes from two distinct viewpoints. Figure 19.6(c) is the progressive voxelization after the viewpoint moves across several frames. Using the partial single-frame volumes for global illumination calculation, we observe abrupt changes in lighting as the camera reveals more occluding geometry (e.g., left arcade wall and floor in Figures 19.6(d) and (e)). However, the situation is gradually remedied in the case of progressive voxelization, since newly discovered volume data are retained for use in following frames (Figures 19.6(f) and (g)).

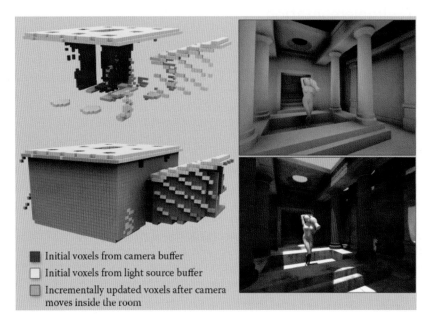

Figure 19.4. Left: Screen-space voxelization after one step of the process having injected the camera and light buffers (top), and voxelization of the scene after the camera has moved for several frames (bottom). Right: Example of resulting indirect illumination (top) and final illumination (bottom).

Figure 19.5. Progressive voxelization of a scene. Red voxels correspond to screen-space voxelization using image buffers from the current frame only, while other colors refer to voxels generated during previous frames using PV. On the right, volume-based global illumination results using the corresponding volumes. PV (top) achieves more correct occlusion and stable lighting.

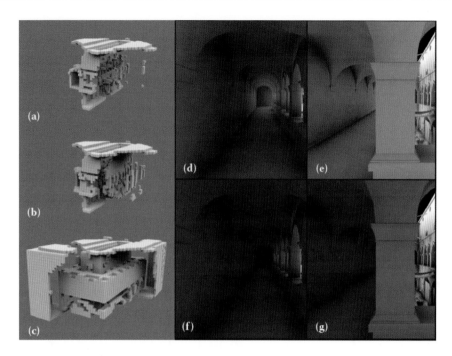

Figure 19.6. Comparison of the voxelization of the Crytek Sponza II Atrium. (a, b) Single-frame screen-space voxelization from two distinct viewpoints where it is not possible to capture all environment details as no information exists in the buffers. (c) Progressive voxelization produced over several frames. (d, e) Indirect lighting buffers corresponding to the single frame voxelization of (a) and (b). (f, g) PV indirect lighting buffers (of the voxelization in (c)).

Figure 19.7 demonstrates progressive voxelization in a dynamic environment in real time. In particular, it shows an animated sequence of a scene with moving and deformable objects, as well as the corresponding voxelization from the camera viewpoint. Observe how the wall behind the closed door is not initially present in the volume, but after the door opens, it is gradually added to the volume and remains there even after the door swings back. The same holds true for the geometry behind the character. Notice also how the voxels representing the articulated figure correctly change state as the figure moves.

Figure 19.8 shows a decomposition of the total algorithm running time into the cleanup and injection stage times respectively versus different volume buffer resolutions for three different injection grid sizes using the 3D volume textures implementation (left) and the 2D textures implementation (center). For fixed injection grid resolutions, we have observed that injection times are not monotonically increasing with respect to volume size as one would expect. The performance also decreases when the buffer viewpoint moves close to geometry.

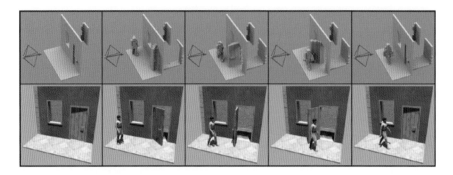

Figure 19.7. Screen-space voxelization of a dynamic scene containing an articulated object using only camera-based injection.

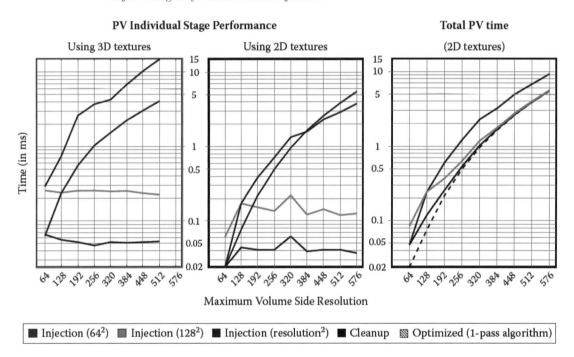

Figure 19.8. Running time (in ms) for the cleanup and injection stages against different volume resolutions for the Crytek Sponza II Atrium model using the 3D volume textures implementation (left) and the 2D textures implementation (center). We used a single G-buffer (camera) as input and one multiple render target (four floats) as output. Injection is measured for three different grid sizes, one being proportional to the volume side. We also show the total progressive voxelization times (right). Note that the performance of the optimized progressive voxelization is identical to that of the cleanup stage.

We attribute this to the common denominator of both cases, namely the fact that pixel overdraw is induced, as points are rasterized in the same voxel locations. This is particularly evident in the blue curve of the 64^2 injection stage graph of Figure 19.8 (left). Note that this behavior is an inherent attribute of injection techniques in general; screen-space voxelization methods depend heavily on the sampling rate used. When this rate is incompatible with the voxel space resolution, holes might appear (undersampling). To ensure adequate coverage of the voxel grid, dense screen-space point samples are drawn, which in turn leads to overdraw problems in many cases. One can use an injection grid proportional to the volume resolution, which partially alleviates the overdraw issue but in turn decreases performance as can be seen in the red curve of the injection graph of Figure 19.8 (left and center).

The time required for a single-frame screen-space voxelization (one G-buffer) equals the time of our injection stage plus a very small overhead to clear the volume buffer, since the two operations are equivalent. Thus, the only difference in the execution time of progressive voxelization is the cleanup stage time. With regard to the quality of the two methods, PV offers more stable and accurate results as new viewpoints gradually improve the volume.

The total voxelization time (Figure 19.8, right) is the sum of the cleanup and injection stages. As the cleanup stage performance depends only on the volume resolution and not on the injection grid size, it vastly improves the voxelization quality compared to using only screen-space injection from isolated frames, at a constant overhead per frame. Especially when applied to global illumination calculations, where small volumes are typically used, the version of the algorithm that uses 2D textures (Figure 19.8, center) has a significantly lower execution footprint. This is because it is not influenced by the geometry shader execution of the 3D textures version (Figure 19.8, left), though both methods are affected by pixel overdraw during injection.

The performance of the optimized progressive voxelization is identical to that of the cleanup stage as expected, since it is essentially a modified cleanup stage. It follows that the dual stage version performance will always be slower than the optimized one.

The maximum volume resolution reported is due to hardware resource limitations on the number and size of the allocated buffers and not algorithm bounds.

In Table 19.1 we report the voxelization performance results for several scenes using our method and the geometry-based multichannel full scene voxelization method of [Gaitatzes et al. 11], which, as ours, is based on the rendering pipeline (GPU). We show a big speed improvement even when adding to the whole process the G-buffers creation time.

In Table 19.2 we report on the quality of our voxelization method. The camera was moved around the mesh for several frames, in order for the algorithm to *progressively* compute the best possible voxelization. For several models and resolutions we show the Hausdorff distance between the original mesh and the

Scene	Grid	GS	G-buffers	PV
	Size	4-floats	Creation	4-floats
Conference	128^3	31.73		0.28
(282K tris)	512^3	64.67	3.2	4.93
Dragon	128^3	198.33		0.18
(871K tris)	512^3	–	59	6.98
Turbine Blade	128^3	265.7		0.14
(1.76M tris)	512^3	–	121	5.37
Hairball	128^3	436.2		0.33
(2.88M tris)	320^3	–	–	4.04

Table 19.1. Voxelization timings (in ms) of various scenes using progressive voxelization (PV) and the geometry slicing (GS) method of [Gaitatzes et al. 11] with 11 output vertices. We present the total (injection + cleanup) performance values of our 2D textures implementation using an injection grid proportional to the volume size, which is our algorithm's worst case as can be seen from the red plot of Figure 19.8.

Scene	Grid	Hausdorff	
	Size	% d_H	(X, Y)
Bunny	64^3	0.3289	0.2168
	128^3	0.1694	0.1091
(69.5K tris)	256^3	0.1064	–
Dragon	64^3	0.3621	0.2565
	128^3	0.1878	0.1289
(871K tris)	256^3	0.1256	0.0645
Turbine Blade	64^3	0.3457	0.2763
	128^3	0.1821	0.1424
(1.76M tris)	256^3	0.1232	0.0697

Table 19.2. Comparison of a full voxelization. We record the normalized (with respect to the mesh bounding box diagonal) average Hausdorff distance (percent). Mesh X is the original mesh to be voxelized and Y is the point cloud consisting of the voxel centers of the voxelization using PV (column 3) and a geometry-based full scene voxelization (column 4).

resulting voxelization using the PV method (see column 3). We notice that our voxelized object (voxel centers) is on average 0.1% different from the original mesh. In addition, we report the Hausdorff distance between the original mesh and the geometry-based full scene voxelization of [Gaitatzes et al. 11] (see col-

Figure 19.9. A series of voxelizations of the dragon model at 128^3 resolution showing the normal vectors. The voxelization is incrementally updated over several frames as the camera moves around the model.

umn 4). We observe that the difference between the corresponding volumes is in the 0.01% range.

In Figure 19.9 we show a series of voxelizations of the dragon model using only the camera G-buffers. In addition, we show the respective Hausdorff distance between the original dragon model and the computed voxel centers (see plot in Figure 19.10). The voxelization is incrementally updated and improved over

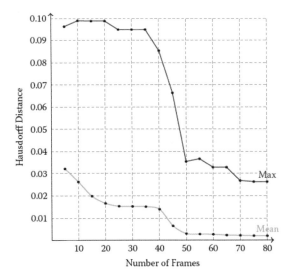

Figure 19.10. The decreasing Hausdorff distance between the original dragon model and the computed progressive voxelizations of Figure 19.9.

several frames as the camera does a complete rotation around each of the principal axis for an equal amount of frames. As the animation progresses, we observe that the Hausdorff distance decreases as the process converges to a full voxelization.

19.6   Limitations

One limitation of our method is that the cleanup phase will only remove invalid voxels that are visible in any of the current image buffers (camera multiple render targets and light RSMs). The visible invalid voxels will be removed from the voxelization the next time they appear in the image buffers. However, the correctness of the voxelization cannot be guaranteed for existing voxels that are not visible in any buffer. For moving geometry, some progressively generated voxels may become stale, as shown in the case of the bottom right of Figure 19.1. Nevertheless, in typical dynamic scenes, the stale voxels are often eliminated either in subsequent frames due to their invalidation in the moving camera buffer or due to their invalidation in other views in the same frame (see Figure 19.11).

Another limitation is that the extents of the voxelization region must remain constant throughout volume updates; otherwise computations are performed with stale buffer boundaries. When the bounding box of the scene is modified or the scene changes abruptly or it is reloaded, the attribute volumes must be deleted and progressively populated again. This is also the reason why the cascaded light propagation volumes method of [Kaplanyan and Dachsbacher 10] could not take advantage of progressive voxelization for the cascades near the user, as the method assumes that they follow the user around, constantly modifying the current volume extents.

Figure 19.11. Correct indirect shadowing effects and color bleeding: Stale voxels from one view (behind the tank) are effectively invalidated in other views (reflective shadow map).

19.7 Conclusion

We have presented a novel screen-space method to progressively build a voxelization data structure on the GPU. Our method achieves improved quality over nonprogressive methods, while it maintains the high performance merits of screen-space techniques.

19.8 Acknowledgments

The Atrium Sponza II Palace in Dubrovnik model was remodeled by Frank Meinl at Crytek. The original Sponza model was created by Marko Dabrovic in early 2002. The Bunny and Dragon models are provided courtesy of the Stanford University Computer Graphics Laboratory.

Bibliography

[Dachsbacher and Stamminger 05] Carsten Dachsbacher and Marc Stamminger. "Reflective Shadow Maps." In *Symposium on Interactive 3D Graphics and Games (I3D)*, pp. 203–231. New York: ACM, 2005.

[Gaitatzes et al. 11] Athanasios Gaitatzes, Pavlos Mavridis, and Georgios Papaioannou. "Two Simple Single-Pass GPU Methods for Multi-channel Surface Voxelization of Dynamic Scenes." In *Pacific Conference on Computer Graphics and Applications—Short Papers (PG)*, pp. 31–36. Aire-la-Ville, Switzerland: Eurographics Association, 2011.

[Kaplanyan 09] Anton Kaplanyan. "Light Propagation Volumes in CryEngine 3." SIGGRAPH Course: Advances in Real-Time Rendering in 3D Graphics and Games, SIGGRAPH 2009, New Orleans, LA, August 3, 2009.

[Kaplanyan and Dachsbacher 10] Anton Kaplanyan and Carsten Dachsbacher. "Cascaded Light Propagation Volumes for Real-Time Indirect Illumination." In *Symposium on Interactive 3D Graphics and Games (I3D)*, pp. 99–107. New York: ACM, 2010.

[Mavridis and Papaioannou 11] Pavlos Mavridis and Georgios Papaioannou. "Global Illumination Using Imperfect Volumes." Presentation, International Conference on Computer Graphics Theory and Applications (GRAPP), Algarve, Portugal, 2011.

[Sloan et al. 02] Peter-Pike Sloan, Jan Kautz, and John Snyder. "Precomputed Radiance Transfer for Real-Time Rendering in Dynamic, Low-Frequency Lighting Environments." In *29th Conference on Computer Graphics and Interactive Techniques (SIGGRAPH)*, pp. 527–536. New York: ACM, 2002.

[Thiedemann et al. 11] Sinje Thiedemann, Niklas Henrich, Thorsten Grosch, and Stefan Müller. "Voxel-Based Global Illumination." In *Symposium on Interactive 3D Graphics and Games (I3D)*, pp. 103–110. New York: ACM, 2011.

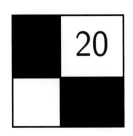

20

Rasterized Voxel-Based Dynamic Global Illumination
Hawar Doghramachi

20.1 Introduction

For modern games it becomes more and more important to offer a realistic environment, where a convincing illumination plays a central role. Therefor, not only direct illumination but also indirect illumination has to be taken into account. At the same time modern games increasingly offer the player the possibility to interact with the game world, i.e., move objects around, destroy buildings, or change the lighting dynamically. This is where *dynamic global illumination* comes into play; in contrast to static precalculated solutions, it does account for highly dynamic environments.

Rasterized voxel-based dynamic global illumination takes into consideration that scenes, especially indoor, can contain a large number of light sources of different types (e.g., point, spot, and directional lights). At the same time it produces visually good and stable results while maintaining high interactive frame rates.

20.2 Overview

This technique efficiently utilizes features, which were introduced by DirectX 11 hardware, to accomplish the above stated results.

In the first step a voxel grid representation is created for the scene by using the hardware rasterizer. Here the scene is rendered without depth testing into a small 2D render-target, but instead of outputting the results into the bound render-target, the rasterized pixels are written into a 3D read-write buffer by using atomic functions. In this way the rasterizer is turned into a "voxelizer," creating efficiently a highly populated 3D grid representation of the scene. This voxel grid contains the diffuse albedo and normal information of the geometry

317

and is used later to generate the indirect illumination and to test for geometry occlusion. Since the voxel grid is recreated each frame, the proposed technique is fully dynamic and does not rely on any precalculations.

In the second step, the voxels inside the grid are illuminated by each light source. The illumination is then converted into virtual point lights (VPLs), stored as second-order spherical harmonics coefficients (SH-coefficients). The graphics hardware is utilized again by using the built in blending stage, in order to combine the results of each light source. Later the generated VPLs are propagated within the grid, in order to generate the indirect illumination. In contrast to the light propagation volume (LPV) technique, as proposed by [Kaplanyan and Dachsbacher 10], it is required neither to create a reflective shadow map for each light source nor to inject VPLs into a grid afterwards. Furthermore, there is no need to generate occlusion information separately. Yet the obtained information will be more precise than, e.g., information obtained from depth peeling.

20.3   Implementation

The proposed technique can be subdivided into five distinct steps.

20.3.1   Create Voxel Grid Representation of the Scene

We first need to define the properties of a cubic voxel grid, i.e., its extents, position, and view-/projection-matrices. The grid is moved synchronously with the viewer camera and snapped permanently to the grid cell boundaries to avoid flickering due to the discrete voxel grid representation of the scene. To correctly map our scene to a voxel grid, we need to use an orthographic projection; thus, we will use three view-matrices to get a higher coverage of the scene: one matrix for the back-to-front view, one matrix for the right-to-left view, and one for the top-to-down view. All other calculations will be done entirely on the GPU.

Next we render the scene geometry that is located inside the grid boundaries with disabled color writing and without depth testing into a small 2D render-target. We will use a $32 \times 32 \times 32$ grid; for this it is entirely enough to use a 64×64 pixel render-target with the smallest available pixel format, since we will output the results into a read-write buffer anyway. Basically we pass the triangle vertices through the vertex shader to the geometry shader. In the geometry shader the view-matrix is chosen at which the triangle is most visible, in order to achieve the highest number of rasterized pixels for the primitive. Additionally the triangle size in normalized device coordinates is increased by the texel size of the currently bound render-target. In this way, pixels that would have been discarded due to the low resolution of the currently bound render-target will still be rasterized. The rasterized pixels are written atomically into a 3D read-write structured buffer in the pixel shader. In this way, in contrast to [Mavridis and Papaioannou 11], there is no need to amplify geometry within the geometry shader in order to obtain a highly populated 3D grid representation of the scene. Listing 20.1 shows how this is done for DirectX 11 in HLSL.

```
// vertex shader

VS_OUTPUT main(VS_INPUT input)
{
  VS_OUTPUT output;
  output. position = float4(input.position,1.0f);
  output.texCoords = input.texCoords;
  output.normal = input.normal;
  return output;
}

// geometry shader

static float3 viewDirections[3] =
{
  float3(0.0f,0.0f,-1.0f), // back to front
  float3(-1.0f,0.0f,0.0f), // right to left
  float3(0.0f,-1.0f,0.0f) // top to down
};

int GetViewIndex(in float3 normal)
{
  float3x3 directionMatrix;
  directionMatrix[0] = -viewDirections[0];
  directionMatrix[1] = -viewDirections[1];
  directionMatrix[2] = -viewDirections[2];
  float3 dotProducts = abs(mul(directionMatrix,normal));
  float maximum = max (max(dotProducts.x,dotProducts.y), dotProducts.z);
  int index;
  if(maximum == dotProducts.x)
    index = 0;
  else if(maximum == dotProducts.y)
    index = 1;
  else
    index = 2;
  return index;
}

[maxvertexcount(3)]
void main(triangle VS_OUTPUT input[3],inout TriangleStream<GS_OUTPUT>
         outputStream)
{
  float3 faceNormal = normalize(input[0].normal+input[1].normal+
                                input[2].normal);
  // Get view, at which the current triangle is most visible, in order to
  // achieve highest possible rasterization of the primitive.
  int viewIndex = GetViewIndex(faceNormal);

  GS_OUTPUT output[3];
  [unroll]
  for(int i=0;i<3;i++)
  {
    output[i].position = mul(constBuffer.gridViewProjMatrices[viewIndex],
                             input[i].position);
    output[i].positionWS = input[i].position.xyz; // world-space position
    output[i].texCoords = input[i].texCoords;
    output[i].normal = input[i].normal;
  }
```

```
  // Increase size of triangle in normalized device coordinates by the
  // texel size of the currently bound render-target.
  float2 side0N = normalize(output[1].position.xy-output[0].position.xy);
  float2 side1N = normalize(output[2].position.xy-output[1].position.xy);
  float2 side2N = normalize(output[0].position.xy-output[2].position.xy);
  float texelSize = 1.0f/64.0f;
  output[0].position.xy += normalize(-side0N+side2N)*texelSize;
  output[1].position.xy += normalize(side0N-side1N)*texelSize;
  output[2].position.xy += normalize(side1N-side2N)*texelSize;

  [unroll
  for(int j=0;j<3;j++)
    outputStream.Append(output[j]);

  outputStream.RestartStrip();
}

// pixel shader
struct VOXEL
{
  uint colorMask; // encoded color
  uint4 normalMasks; // encoded normals
  uint occlusion; // voxel only contains geometry info if occlusion > 0
};
RWStructuredBuffer<VOXEL> gridBuffer: register(u1);

// normalized directions of four faces of a tetrahedron
static float3 faceVectors[4] =
{
  float3(0.0f,-0.57735026f,0.81649661f),
  float3(0.0f,-0.57735026f,-0.81649661f),
  float3(-0.81649661f,0.57735026f,0.0f),
  float3(0.81649661f,0.57735026f,0.0f)
};

int GetNormalIndex(in float3 normal,out float dotProduct)
{
  float4x3 faceMatrix;
  faceMatrix[0] = faceVectors[0];
  faceMatrix[1] = faceVectors[1];
  faceMatrix[2] = faceVectors[2];
  faceMatrix[3] = faceVectors[3];
  float4 dotProducts = mul(faceMatrix,normal);
  float maximum = max (max(dotProducts.x,dotProducts.y),
                       max(dotProducts.z,dotProducts.w));
  int index;
  if(maximum == dotProducts.x)
    index = 0;
  else if(maximum == dotProducts.y)
    index = 1;
  else if(maximum == dotProducts.z)
    index = 2;
  else
    index = 3;

  dotProduct = dotProducts[index ];
  return index;
}

void main(GS_OUTPUT input)
{
  float3 base = colorMap.Sample(colorMapSampler,input.texCoords).rgb;
```

```
// Encode color into the lower 24 bit of an unsigned integer, using
// 8 bit for each color channel.
uint colorMask = EncodeColor(base.rgb);

// Calculate color-channel contrast of color and write value into the
// highest 8 bit of the color mask.
float contrast = length(base.rrg-base.gbb)/
                 (sqrt(2.0f)+base.r+base.g+base.b);
int iContrast = int(contrast*255.0f);
colorMask |= iContrast<<24;

// Encode normal into the lower 27 bit of an unsigned integer, using
// for each axis 8 bit for the value and 1 bit for the sign.
float3 normal = normalize(input.normal);
uint normalMask = EncodeNormal(normal.xyz);

// Calculate to which face of a tetrahedron current normal is closest
// and write corresponding dot product into the highest 5 bit of the
// normal mask.
float dotProduct;
int normalIndex = GetNormalIndex(normal,dotProduct);
int iDotProduct = int(saturate(dotProduct)*31.0f);
normalMask |= iDotProduct<<27;

// Get offset into voxel grid.
float3 offset = (input.positionWS-constBuffer.snappedGridCenter)*
                constBuffer.invGridCellSize;
offset = round(offset);

// Get position in voxel grid.
int3 voxelPos = int3(16,16,16)+int3(offset);

// Only output voxels that are inside the boundaries of the grid.
if((voxelPos.x>-1)&&(voxelPos.x<32)&&(voxelPos.y>-1)&&
   (voxelPos.y<32)&&(voxelPos.z>-1)&&(voxelPos.z<32))
{
  // Get index into voxel grid.
  int gridIndex = (voxelPos.z*1024)+(voxelPos.y*32)+voxelPos.x;

  // Output color.
  InterlockedMax(gridBuffer[gridIndex].colorMask,colorMask);

  // Output normal according to normal index.
  InterlockedMax(gridBuffer[gridIndex].normalMasks[normalIndex],
                 normalMask);

  // Mark voxel that contains geometry information.
  InterlockedMax(gridBuffer[gridIndex].occlusion,1);
}
}
```

Listing 20.1. Generation of the voxel grid.

   To avoid race conditions between multiple threads that write into the same
location, atomic functions have to be used. Since atomic operations are only
supported in DirectX 11 for integer types, all values have to be converted into
integers. Among the variety of DirectX 11 buffers, the RWStructuredBuffer is
chosen, since this is the only way to hold multiple integer variables in one single
buffer and at the same time perform atomic operations on them.

Since voxels are a simplified representation of the actual scene, detailed geometric information is lost. In order to amplify color bleeding in the final global illumination output, colors with high difference in their color channels ("contrast") are preferred. By writing the contrast value into the highest 8 bit of the integer color mask, colors with the highest contrast will dominate automatically, since we write the results with an `InterlockedMax()` into the voxel grid. Since, e.g., thin geometry can have opposite normals in one single voxel, not only the color but also the normal has to be carefully written into the voxels. Therefore it is determined to which face of a tetrahedron the current normal is closest. By writing the corresponding dot product into the highest 5 bit of the integer normal mask, the closest normal to each tetrahedron face is selected automatically since we again write the results with an `InterlockedMax()`. According to the retrieved tetrahedron face, the normal is written into the corresponding normal channel of the voxel. Later on, when the voxels are illuminated, the closest normal to the light vector is chosen so that the best illumination can be obtained. In this way sometimes it is possible that the normal is taken from a different geometry face as the color. However, since voxels condense information from the actual geometry within its boundaries, this is completely fine and will not have any negative impact on the global illumination result.

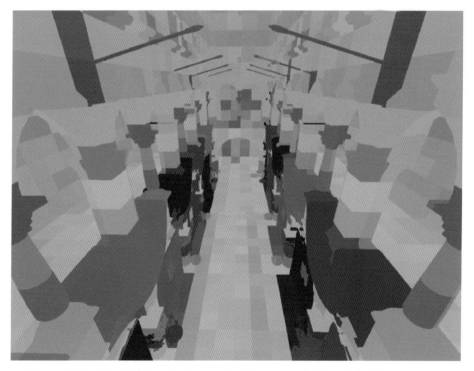

Figure 20.1. Visualization for the voxel grid representation of the Sponza scene.

Since all operations are performed using a very small render-target (64×64 pixels), this generation step is surprisingly fast. Figure 20.1 shows a screenshot in which the voxel grid representation of the Sponza scene is visualized. To create this image for each visible pixel of the rendered scene, the word-space position is reconstructed. With the help of the reconstructed position, we can determine the location of the corresponding voxel inside the grid. Finally, each visible pixel will be colored with the diffuse albedo information that is stored inside the corresponding voxel. In order to cover the entire scene, two nested voxel grids have been used: a fine-resolution grid for the area near to the viewer and a coarse-resolution grid for the distant area.

20.3.2 Create VPLs in Voxel Space

In this step we create VPLs entirely from the previously generated voxel grid. For each light source that is located inside the boundaries of the grid, we render a small quad of 32×32 pixels. By using hardware instancing, for each quad we are able to render 32 instances with a single draw call. After passing the vertices through the vertex shader, the geometry shader will choose the corresponding render-target slice in the currently bound 2D texture arrays. The pixel shader will then illuminate all voxels that contain geometry information according to the type of the current light source. Finally, the illuminated voxels are converted into a second-order spherical harmonic representation of VPLs. By using additive hardware blending, the results of all light sources are automatically combined. Listing 20.2 generically shows how this is done for DirectX 11 in HLSL.

```
// vertex shader

VS_OUTPUT main(VS_INPUT input,uint instanceID: SV_InstanceID)
{
  VS_OUTPUT output;
  output.position = float4(input.position,1.0f);
  output.instanceID = instanceID;
  return output ;
}

// geometry shader

struct GS_OUTPUT

{

  float4 position: SV_POSITION;
  uint rtIndex: SV_RenderTargetArrayIndex;
};

[maxvertexcount(4)]
void main(line VS_OUTPUT input[2],inout TriangleStream<GS_OUTPUT>
          outputStream)
{
  // Generate a quad from two corner vertices.
  GS_OUTPUT output[4];
```

```
    // lower-left vertex
    output[0].position = float4(input[0].position.x,input[0].position.y,
                                input[0].position.z,1.0f);

    // lower-right vertex
    output[1].position = float4(input[1].position.x,input[0].position.y,
                                input[0].position.z,1.0f);

    // upper-left vertex
    output[2].position = float4(input[0].position.x,input[1].position.y,
                                input[0].position.z,1.0f);

    // upper-right vertex
    output[3].position = float4(input[1].position.x,input[1].position.y,
                                input[0].position.z,1.0f);
    // By using hardware instancing, the geometry shader will be invoked 32
    // times with the corresponding instance ID. For each invocation the
    // instance ID is used to determine into which slice of a 2D texture
    // array the current quad should be rasterized.
    [unroll]
    for(int i=0;i<4;i++)
    {
      output[i].rtIndex = input[0].instanceID;
      outputStream.Append(output[i]);
    }
      outputStream.RestartStrip();
}

// pixel shader

StructuredBuffer<VOXEL> gridBuffer: register(t0);

struct FS_OUTPUT
{
  float4 fragColor0: SV_TARGET0; // red SH-coefficients
  float4 fragColor1: SV_TARGET1; // blue SH-coefficients
  float4 fragColor2: SV_TARGET2; // green SH-coefficients
};
// Calculate second-order SH-coefficients for clamped cosine lobe function.
float4 ClampedCosineSHCoeffs(in float3 dir)
{
  float4 coeffs;
  coeffs.x = PI/(2.0f*sqrt(PI));
  coeffs.y = -((2.0f*PI)/3.0f)*sqrt(3.0f/(4.0f*PI));
  coeffs.z = ((2.0f*PI)/3.0f)*sqrt(3.0f/(4.0f*PI));
  coeffs.w = -((2.0f*PI)/3.0f)*sqrt(3.0f/(4.0f*PI));
  coeffs.wyz *= dir;
  return coeffs;
}
// Determine which of the four specified normals is closest to the
// specified direction. The function returns the closest normal and as
// output parameter the corresponding dot product.
float3 GetClosestNormal(in uint4 normalMasks,in float3 direction,out float
                        dotProduct)
{
  float4x3 normalMatrix;
  normalMatrix[0] = DecodeNormal(normalMasks.x);
  normalMatrix[1] = DecodeNormal(normalMasks.y);
  normalMatrix[2] = DecodeNormal(normalMasks.z);
  normalMatrix[3] = DecodeNormal(normalMasks.w);
  float4 dotProducts = mul(normalMatrix,direction);

  float maximum = max (max(dotProducts.x,dotProducts.y),
                       max(dotProducts.z,dotProducts.w));
```

```
    int index;
    if(maximum==dotProducts.x)
        index = 0;
    else if(maximum==dotProducts.y)
        index = 1;
    else if(maximum==dotProducts.z)
        index = 2;
    else
        index = 3;

    dotProduct = dotProducts[index];
    return normalMatrix[index];
}

PS_OUTPUT main(GS_OUTPUT input)
{
    PS_OUTPUT output;

    // Get index of current voxel.
    int3 voxelPos = int3(input.position.xy,input.rtIndex);
    int gridIndex = (voxelPos.z*1024)+(voxelPos.y*32)+voxelPos.x;

    // Get voxel data and early out, if voxel has no geometry information.
    VOXEL voxel = gridBuffer[gridIndex];
    if(voxel.occlusion==0)
        discard;

    // Get world-space position of voxel.
    int3 offset = samplePos-int3(16,16,16);
    float3 position = (float3(offset)*constBuffer.gridCellSize)+
                        constBuffer.snappedGridCenter;

    // Decode color of voxel.
    float3 albedo = DecodeColor(voxel.colorMask);

    // Get normal of voxel that is closest to the light direction.
    float nDotL;
    float3 normal = GetClosestNormal(voxel.normalMasks,lightVecN,nDotL);

    // Calculate diffuse lighting according to current light type.
    float3 diffuse = CalcDiffuseLighting(albedo,nDotL);

#ifdef USE_SHADOWS

    // Calculate shadow term according to current light type with the help
    // of a shadow map.
    float shadowTerm = ComputeShadowTerm(position);
    diffuse *= shadowTerm;
#endif

    // Calculate clamped cosine lobe SH-coefficients for VPL.
    float4 coeffs = ClampedCosineSHCoeffs(normal);

    // Output SH-coefficients for each color channel.
    output.fragColor0 = coeffs*diffues.r;
    output.fragColor1 = coeffs*diffuse.g;
    output.fragColor2 = coeffs*diffuse.b;

    return output;
}
```

Listing 20.2. VPL creation.

To output the second-order SH-coefficients for all three color channels, we render this time into three 2D texture arrays with half floating-point precision. Since all calculations are done entirely in voxel space and are limited to voxels, which actually contain geometry information, this technique scales very well with an increasing number of light sources of all different types.

In many situations we can even abandon the use of shadow maps for point lights and spotlights without noticeably affecting the final render output. However, for large point lights, spotlights, and directional lights, we do need to use shadow maps to avoid light leaking. Here we can simply reuse the shadow maps that have already been created for the direct illumination step.

20.3.3   Propagate VPLs

In this step the previously created VPLs are propagated iteratively across the grid according to the LPV technique proposed by [Kaplanyan and Dachsbacher 10]. Basically each VPL cell propagates its light along the three axes of a Cartesian coordinate system to its surrounding six neighbor cells. While doing this propagation, the voxel grid from the first step is used to determine how strongly the light transport to the neighbor cells is occluded. The results from the first propagation step are then used to perform a second propagation step. This is done iteratively until we get a visually satisfying light distribution. In the first iteration no occlusion is used, in order to initially let the light distribute; from the second iteration on, we use the geometry occlusion in order to avoid light leaking.

The iterative propagation is performed in DirectX 11 by utilizing a compute shader since we do not need the rasterization pipeline for this job. Listing 20.3 demonstrates this.

```
// compute shader
Texture2DArray inputRedSHTexture: register(t0);
Texture2DArray inputGreenSHTexture: register(t1);
Texture2DArray inputBlueSHTexture: register(t2);
StructuredBuffer<VOXEL> gridBuffer: register(t3);
RWTexture2DArray<float4> outputRedSHTexture: register(u0);
RWTexture2DArray<float4> outputGreenSHTexture: register(u1);
RWTexture2DArray<float4> outputBlueSHTexture: register(u2);

// directions to six neighbor cell centers
static float3 directions[6] =
{
  float3(0.0f,0.0f,1.0f), float3(1.0f,0.0f,0.0f), float3(0.0f,0.0f,-1.0f),
  float3(-1.0f,0.0f,0.0f), float3(0.0f,1.0f,0.0f), float3(0.0f,-1.0f,0.0f)
};

// SH-coefficients for six faces (ClampedCosineSHCoeffs(directions[0-5])
static float4 faceCoeffs[6] =
{
  float4(PI/(2*sqrt(PI)),0.0f,((2*PI)/3.0f)*sqrt(3.0f/(4*PI)),0.0f),
  float4(PI/(2*sqrt(PI)),0.0f,0.0f,-((2*PI)/3.0f)*sqrt(3.0f/(4*PI))),
  float4(PI/(2*sqrt(PI)),0.0f,-((2*PI)/3.0f)*sqrt(3.0f/(4*PI)),0.0f),
  float4(PI/(2*sqrt(PI)),0.0f,0.0f,((2*PI)/3.0f)*sqrt(3.0f/(4*PI))),
```

```
    float4(PI/(2*sqrt(PI)),-((2*PI)/3.0f)*sqrt(3.0f/(4*PI)),0.0f,0.0f),
    float4(PI/(2*sqrt(PI)),((2*PI)/3.0f)*sqrt(3.0f/(4*PI)),0.0f,0.0f)
};

// offsets to six neighbor cell centers
static int3 offsets[6] =
{
  int3(0,0,1), int3(1,0,0), int3(0,0,-1),
  int3(-1,0,0), int3(0,1,0), int3(0,-1,0)
};

[numthreads(8,8,8)]
void main(uint3 GroupID: SV_GroupID,uint3 DispatchThreadID:
          SV_DispatchThreadID,uint3 GroupThreadID: SV_GroupThreadID ,
          uint GroupIndex: SV_GroupIndex)
{
    // Get grid position of current cell.
    int3 elementPos = DispatchThreadID.xyz;

    // Initialize SH-coefficients with values from current cell.
    float4 sumRedSHCoeffs = inputRedSHTexture.Load(int4(elementPos,0));
    float4 sumGreenSHCoeffs = inputGreenSHTexture.Load(int4(elementPos,0));
    float4 sumBlueSHCoeffs = inputBlueSHTexture.Load(int4(elementPos,0));

    [unroll]
    for(int i=0;i<6;i++)
    {
        // Get grid position of six neighbor cells.
        int3 samplePos = elementPos+offsets[i];
        // continue, if cell is out of bounds
        if((samplePos.x<0)||(samplePos.x>31)||(samplePos.y<0)||
           (samplePos.y>31)||(samplePos.z<0)||(samplePos.z>31))
            continue;

        // Load SH-coefficients for neighbor cell.
        float4 redSHCoeffs = inputRedSHTexture.Load(int4(samplePos,0));
        float4 greenSHCoeffs = inputGreenSHTexture.Load(int4(samplePos,0));
        float4 blueSHCoeffs = inputBlueSHTexture.Load(int4(samplePos,0));

#ifdef USE_OCCLUSION
        float4 occlusionCoeffs = float4(0.0f,0.0f,0.0f,0.0f);

        // Get index of corresponding voxel.
        int gridIndex = (samplePos.z*1024)+(samplePos.y*32)+samplePos.x;
        VOXEL voxel = gridBuffer[gridIndex];

        // If voxel contains geometry information, find closest normal to
        // current direction. In this way the highest occlusion can be
        // generated. Then calculate SH-coefficients for retrieved normal.
        if(voxel.occlusion > 0)
        {
            float dotProduct;
            float3 occlusionNormal = GetClosestNormal(voxel.normalMasks,
                                    -directions[i],dotProduct);
            occlusionCoeffs = ClampedCosineSHCoeffs(occlusionNormal);
        }
#endif

        [unroll]
        for(int j=0;j<6;j++)
        {
            // Get direction for face of current cell to current neighbor
            // cell center.
            float3 neighborCellCenter = directions[i];
```

```
                float3 facePosition = directions[j]*0.5f;
                float3 dir = facePosition-neighborCellCenter;
                float fLength = length(dir);
                dir /= fLength;

                // Get corresponding solid angle.
                float solidAngle = 0.0f;
                if(fLength>0.5f)
                  solidAngle = (fLength>=1.5f) ? (22.95668f/(4*180.0f)) :
                                                 (24.26083f/(4*180.0f));
                // Calculate SH-coefficients for direction.
                float4 dirSH;
                result.x = 1.0f/(2*sqrt(PI));
                result.y = -sqrt(3.0f/(4*PI));
                result.z = sqrt(3.0f/(4*PI));
                result.w = -sqrt(3.0f/(4*PI));
                result.wyz *= dir;

                // Calculate flux from neighbor cell to face of current cell.
                float3 flux;
                flux.r = dot(redSHCoeffs,dirSH);
                flux.g = dot(greenSHCoeffs,dirSH);
                flux.b = dot(blueSHCoeffs,dirSH);
                flux = max(0.0f,flux)*solidAngle;
#ifdef USE_OCCLUSION
                // apply occlusion
                float occlusion = 1.0f-saturate(dot(occlusionCoeffs,dirSH));
                flux *= occlusion;
#endif
                // Add contribution to SH-coefficients sums.
                float4 coeffs = faceCoeffs[j];
                sumRedSHCoeffs += coeffs*flux.r;
                sumGreenSHCoeffs += coeffs*flux.g;
                sumBlueSHCoeffs += coeffs*flux.b;
            }
        }
        // Write out generated red, green, and blue SH-coefficients.
        outputRedSHTexture[elementPos] = sumRedSHCoeffs;
        outputGreenSHTexture[elementPos] = sumGreenSHCoeffs;
        outputBlueSHTexture[elementPos] = sumBlueSHCoeffs;
    }
```

Listing 20.3. Propagation of VPLs.

For each propagation step the compute shader is dispatched with $4 \times 4 \times 4$ thread groups so that altogether $32 \times 32 \times 32$ threads are utilized, which corresponds to the total cell count of the grid.

20.3.4 Apply Indirect Lighting

In this step the previously propagated VPLs are finally applied to the scene. For this we need a depth buffer from which the world-space position of the visible pixels can be reconstructed, as well as a normal buffer that contains the perturbed normal information for each pixel. Obviously, deferred rendering as a direct illumination approach is perfectly fitted for our case since both pieces of information are already available and no extra work has to be done.

While rendering a full-screen quad, the pixel shader reconstructs the world-space position and the normal for each pixel. According to the world-space position, the previously generated grid (in the form of three 2D texture arrays) is sampled with linear hardware filtering. Therefore we manually only have to perform a filtering in the third dimension so that we retrieve smooth results. With the help of the sampled SH-coefficients and the surface normal, we can perform an SH-lighting for each pixel. See Listing 20.4 for details.

```
// pixel shader

Texture2DArray inputRedSHTexture: register(t0);
Texture2DArray inputGreenSHTexture: register(t1);
Texture2DArray inputBlueSHTexture: register(t2);

PS_OUTPUT main(GS_OUTPUT input)
{
  PS_OUTPUT output;
  float depth = depthBuffer.Sample(depthBufferSampler,input.texCoords).r;
  float4 position = ReconstructPositionFromDepth(depth);


  float3 albedo = colorMap.Sample(colorMapSampler,input.texCoords).rgb;
  float3 normal =
    normalBuffer.Sample(normalBufferSampler,input.texCoords).xyz;

  // Get offset into grid.
  float3 offset = (position.xyz-constBuffer.snappedGridCenter)*
                  constBuffer.invGridCellSize;

  // Get texCoords into Texture2DArray.
  float3 texCoords = float3(16.5f,16.5f,16.0f)+offset;
  texCoords.xy /= 32.0f;

  // Get texCoords for trilinear sampling.
  int lowZ = floor(texCoords.z);
  int highZ = min(lowZ+1,32-1);
  float highZWeight = texCoords.z-lowZ;
  float lowZWeight = 1.0f-highZWeight;
  float3 tcLow = float3(texCoords.xy,lowZ);
  float3 tcHigh = float3(texCoords.xy,highZ);

  // Perform trilinear sampling of red, green, and blue SH-coefficients
  // from Texture2DArray.
  float4 redSHCoeffs =
    lowZWeight*inputRedSHTexture.Sample(linearSampler,tcLow)+
    highZWeight*inputRedSHTexture.Sample(linearSampler,tcHigh);
  float4 greenSHCoeffs =
    lowZWeight*inputGreenSHTexture.Sample(linearSampler,tcLow)+
    highZWeight*inputGreenSHTexture.Sample(linearSampler,tcHigh);
  float4 blueSHCoeffs =
    lowZWeight*inputBlueSHTexture.Sample(linearSampler,tcLow)+
    highZWeight* inputBlueSHTexture.Sample(linearSampler,tcHigh);

  // Calculate clamped cosine lobe SH-coefficients for surface normal.
  float4 surfaceNormalLobe = ClampedCosineSHCoeffs(normal);

  // Perform diffuse SH-lighting.
  float3 diffuseGlobalIllum;
  diffuseGlobalIllum.r = dot(redSHCoeffs,surfaceNormalLobe);
```

```
        diffuseGlobalIllum.g = dot(greenSHCoeffs,surfaceNormalLobe);
        diffuseGlobalIllum.b = dot(blueSHCoeffs,surfaceNormalLobe);
        diffuseIllum = max(diffuseIllum,float3(0.0f,0.0f,0.0f));
        diffuseGlobalIllum /= PI;

        output.fragColor = float4(diffuseGlobalIllum*albedo,1.0f);
        return output;
    }
}
```

Listing 20.4. Indirect lighting.

As can be seen in the above listing, only the diffuse indirect illumination is calculated. However there is the possibility to extract a dominant light source from SH-coefficients [Sloan 08]. With the help of this extracted light source, a conventional specular lighting can be performed. This gives us the possibility to add a fast, but coarse, approximation of specular indirect lighting.

20.3.5   Clear the Voxel Grid

In this final step the `RWStructuredBuffer` used for the voxel grid is cleared by using a simple compute shader. Just like for the propagation step, the compute shader is dispatched with $4 \times 4 \times 4$ thread groups, whereby each thread group runs $8 \times 8 \times 8$ threads, so that $32 \times 32 \times 32$ threads are utilized, which corresponds to the total voxel count of the grid.

20.4   Handling Large Environments

Since we are using a $32 \times 32 \times 32$ voxel grid, it is quite obvious that this alone cannot deal with realistic large game environments. According to the use of multiple cascades in the LPV technique proposed by [Kaplanyan and Dachsbacher 10], several nested voxel grids can be used. Each grid will have the same number of cells, but the size of the grid cells will increase. In this way detailed indirect lighting can be maintained in the vicinity of the viewer, while in the distance still sufficient coarse indirect lighting is used. However, a linear interpolation should be performed between the grids to avoid a harsh transition at the borders between them. This can be done in the step when indirect lighting is applied to each visible pixel. Therefor across the border area the global illumination value is calculated for both adjoining grids. The distance of the world-space position of the current pixel to the center of the higher-resolution grid can be used to linearly interpolate between both global illumination values.

20.5   Results

Table 20.1 shows the performance results using the proposed technique in the Sponza scene. All lights were fully dynamic and contributed to the indirect illumination.

	Min fps	Max fps	Average fps
1 directional light	63	90	71
1 directional light + 12 medium-sized moving point lights	61	89	70

Table 20.1. Performance results in the Sponza scene (~280,000 triangles) using two grid cascades (on a Nvidia Geforce 485 GTX Mobile with 1,280 × 720 resolution).

Figure 20.2. Sponza scene with direct illumination only.

Figures 20.2–20.4 show how this technique can improve the appearance of a scene. For the screenshots the same Sponza scene has been used as for the previous performance results.

20.6 Conclusion

By utilizing new DirectX 11 features, this technique is capable of producing visually good and stable results for a high number of light sources contained in realistic game environments while maintaining high interactive frame rates. Moreover the video memory consumption is kept at a low level.

Figure 20.3. Sponza scene with indirect illumination only.

Figure 20.4. Final combined output of the Sponza scene.

However, besides the fact that this approach will only run on DirectX 11 or higher hardware, it requires also a depth and a normal buffer for reconstructing the position and normal of the visible pixels. Therefore it is best fitted for direct illumination approaches such as deferred rendering.

Bibliography

[Kaplanyan and Dachsbacher 10] Anton Kaplanyan and Carsten Dachsbacher. "Cascaded Light Propagation Volumes for Real-Time Indirect Illumination." In *Symposium on Interactive 3D Graphics and Games (I3D)*, pp. 99–107. New York: ACM, 2010.

[Mavridis and Papaioannou 11] Pavlos Mavridis and Georgios Papaioannou. "Global Illumination Using Imperfect Volumes." Presentation, International Conference on Computer Graphics Theory and Applications (GRAPP), Algarve, Portugal, 2011.

[Sloan 08] Peter-Pike Sloan. "Stupid Spherical Harmonics (SH) Tricks." Companion to Game Developers Conference 2008 lecture, http://www.ppsloan.org/publications/StupidSH36.pdf, February 2008.

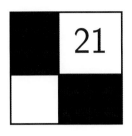

21

Per-Pixel Lists for Single Pass A-Buffer
Sylvain Lefebvre, Samuel Hornus, and Anass Lasram

21.1 Introduction

Real-time effects such as transparency strongly benefit interactive modeling and visualization. Some examples can be seen Figure 21.1. The rightmost image is a screenshot of our parametric Constructive Solid Geometry (CSG) modeler for 3D printing, IceSL [Lefebvre 13]. Modeled objects are rendered in real time with per-pixel boolean operations between primitives.

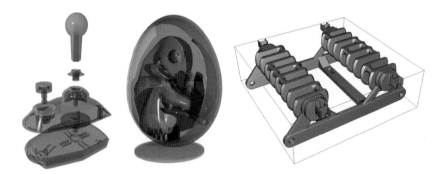

Figure 21.1. Left: Joystick model rendered with the PRE-OPEN A-buffer technique described in this chapter, on a GeForce Titan. 539236 fragments, max depth: 16, FPS: 490. Middle: Dinosaur in Egg, rendered with transparent surfaces and shadows using two A-buffers. Right: A robot body modeled with 193 solid primitives in boolean operations (CSG), rendered interactively with the PRE-OPEN A-buffer technique (modeler: IceSL). [Joystick by Srepmup (Thingiverse, 30198), Egg Dinosaur by XXRDESIGNS (Thingiverse, 38463), Spidrack by Sylefeb (Thingiverse, 103765).]

These effects have always been challenging for real-time rasterization. When the scene geometry is rasterized, each triangle generates a number of *fragments*. Each fragment corresponds to a screen pixel. It is a small surface element *potentially* visible through this pixel. In a classical rasterizer only the fragment closest to the viewer is kept: the rasterizer blindly rejects all fragments that are farther away than the current closest, using the Z-buffer algorithm. Instead, algorithms dealing with transparency or CSG have to produce ordered lists of all the fragments falling into each pixel. This is typically performed in two stages: First, a list of fragments is gathered for each pixel. Second, the lists are sorted by depth and rendering is performed by traversing the lists, either accumulating opacity and colors (for transparency effects), or applying boolean operations to determine which fragment is visible (for rendering a CSG model). The data structure is recreated at every frame, and therefore has to be extremely efficient and integrate well with the rasterizer.

A large body of work has been dedicated to this problem. Most techniques for fragment accumulation implement a form of A-buffer [Carpenter 84]. The A-buffer stores in each pixel the list of fragments that cover that pixel. The fragments are sorted by depth and the size of the list is called the *depth-complexity*, as visualized in Figure 21.3 (top-right). For a review of A-buffer techniques for transparency we refer the reader to the survey by Maule et al. [Maule et al. 11].

In this chapter we introduce and compare four different techniques to build and render from an A-buffer in real time. One of these techniques is well known while the others are, to the best of our knowledge, novel. We focus on scenes with moderate or sparse depth complexity; the techniques presented here will not scale well on extreme transparency scenarios. In exchange, their implementation is simple and they integrate directly in the graphics API; a compute API is not necessary. All our techniques build the A-buffer in a single geometry pass: the scene geometry is rasterized once per frame.

A drawback of storing the fragments first and sorting them later is that some fragments may in fact be unnecessary: in a transparency application the opacity of the fragments may accumulate up to a point where anything located behind makes no contribution to the final image. Two of the techniques proposed here afford for a conservative early-culling mechanism: inserted fragments are always sorted in memory, enabling detection of opaque accumulation.

The companion code includes a full implementation and benchmarking framework.

21.1.1   Overview

An A-buffer stores a list of fragments for each pixel. Sorting them by increasing or decreasing depth are both possible. However, the sorting technique that we describe in Section 21.3 is easier to explain and implement for decreasing values as we walk along the list. Adding to that, early culling of negligible fragments is possible for transparency rendering only when the fragments are sorted front-to-back. In order to meet both requirements for the described techniques, we consistently sort in decreasing order and obtain a front-to-back ordering by inverting the usual depth value of a fragment: if the depth z of a fragment is a `float` in the range $[-1, 1]$, we transform it in the pixel shader into the integer $\lfloor S(1-z)/2 \rfloor$, where S is a scaling factor (typically $2^{32} - 1$ or $2^{24} - 1$).

Our techniques rely on a buffer in which all the fragments are stored. We call it the *main buffer*. Each fragment is associated with a cell in the main buffer where its information is recorded. Our techniques comprise three passes: a CLEAR pass is used to initialize memory, then a BUILD pass assembles a list of fragments for each pixel and finally a RENDER pass accumulates the contribution of the fragments and writes colors to the framebuffer.

The four techniques differ along two axes. The first axis is the scheduling of the sort: when do we spend time on depth-sorting the fragments associated with each pixel? The second axis is the memory allocation strategy used for incrementally building the per-pixel lists of fragments. We now describe these two axes in more detail.

21.1.2 Sort Strategies

We examine two strategies for sorting the fragments according to their depth. The first one, POST-SORT, stores all the fragments during the BUILD pass and sorts them only just prior to accumulation in the RENDER pass: the GLSL shader copies the pixel fragments in local memory, sorts them in place, and performs in-order accumulation to obtain the final color.

The second strategy, PRE-SORT, implements an insertion-sort during the BUILD pass, as the geometric primitives are rasterized. At any time during the rasterization, it is possible to traverse the fragments associated with a given pixel in depth order.

Both strategies are summarized in Table 21.1.

Each has pros and cons: In the PRE-SORT method, insertion-sort is done in the slower global memory, but the method affords for early culling of almost invisible fragments. It is also faster when several RENDER passes are required on the same A-buffer, since the sort is done only once. This is for instance the case when CSG models are sliced for 3D printing [Lefebvre 13].

Pass	Rasterized geometry	POST-SORT	PRE-SORT
CLEAR	fullscreen quad	clear	clear
BUILD	scene triangles	insert	insertion-sort
RENDER	fullscreen quad	sort, accumulate	accumulate

Table 21.1. Summary of the POST-SORT and PRE-SORT sorting strategies.

In the POST-SORT method, sorting happens in local memory, which is faster but limits the maximum number of fragments associated with a pixel to a few hundred. Allocating more local memory for sorting more fragments increases register pressure and reduces parallelism and performance.

21.1.3   Allocation Strategies

In addition to the scheduling of the sort, we examine two strategies for allocating cells containing fragment information in the main buffer. The first one, LIN-ALLOC, stores fragments in per-pixel linked-lists and allocates fresh cells linearly from the start of the buffer to its end. Since many allocations are done concurrently, the address of a fresh cell is obtained by atomically incrementing a global counter. Additional memory is necessary to store the address of the first cell (head) of the list of fragments of each pixel. Section 21.2 details the LIN-ALLOC strategy.

The second strategy that we examine, OPEN-ALLOC, is randomized and somewhat more involved. To each pixel p we associate a pseudo-random sequence of cell positions in the main buffer: $(h(p, i))_{i \geq 1}$, for i ranging over the integers. In the spirit of the "open addressing" techniques for hash tables, the cells at positions $h(p, i)$ are examined by increasing value of i until an empty one is found. A non-empty cell in this sequence may store another fragment associated with pixel p or with a different pixel q. Such a *collision* between fragments must be detected and handled correctly. Section 21.3 details the OPEN-ALLOC strategy.

The combination of two allocation strategies (LIN-ALLOC and OPEN-ALLOC) with two schedules for sorting (POST-SORT and PRE-SORT) gives us four variations for building an A-buffer: POST-LIN (Sections 21.2.1 and 21.2.2), PRE-LIN (Section 21.2.3), POST-OPEN (Section 21.3.2) and PRE-OPEN (Section 21.3.3).

Section 21.4.1 details how fragments are sorted in local memory in the RENDER pass of the POST-SORT method. Some memory management issues, including buffer resizing, are addressed in Section 21.5, and information about our implementation is given in Section 21.6. In Section 21.7, we compare these four variations, as implemented on a GeForce 480 and a GeForce Titan.

21.2   Linked Lists with Pointers (LIN-ALLOC)

The first two approaches we describe construct linked lists in each pixel, allocating data for new fragments linearly in the main buffer. A single cell contains the depth of the fragment and the index of the next cell in the list. Since no cell is ever removed from a list, there is no need for managing a free list: allocating a new cell simply amounts to incrementing a global counter `firstFreeCell` that stores the index of the first free cell in the buffer. The counter `firstFreeCell` is initialized to zero. The increment is done atomically to guarantee that every thread allocating new cells concurrently does obtain a unique memory address. A second array, called `heads`, is necessary to store the address of the head cell of the linked list of each pixel.

Having a lot of threads increment a single global counter would be a bottleneck in a generic programing setting (compute API). Fortunately, GLSL fragment shaders feature dedicated counters for this task, via the `ARB_shader_atomic_counters` extension. If these are not available, it is possible to relieve some of the contention on the counter by allocating K cells at once for a list (typically $K = 4$). To obtain such a paged allocation scheme, the thread atomically increases the global counter by K and uses a single bit in each head pointer as a local mutex when inserting fragments in this page of K cells. The technique is described in full detail by Crassin [Crassin 10], and is implemented in the accompanying code (see `implementations.fp`, function `allocate_paged`). In our tests, the dedicated counters always outperformed the paging mechanism. However, if a generic atomic increment is used instead then the paging mechanism is faster. We use a single dedicated atomic counter in all our performance tests (Section 21.7).

We now describe the two techniques based on the LIN-ALLOC cell allocation strategy: POST-LIN and PRE-LIN.

21.2.1 Building Unsorted Lists (POST-LIN)

The simplest approach to building an unsorted list of fragments is to insert new fragments at the head of the pixel list. A sample implementation is provided in Listing 21.1.

In line 7, a cell position `fresh` is reserved and the counter is incremented. The operation must be done atomically so that no two threads reserve the same position in the buffer. It is then safe to fill the cell with relevant fragment data in lines 8 and 9. Finally, indices are exchanged so that the cell `buffer[fresh]` becomes the new head of the list.

Later, in Section 21.4.1, we describe how the fragments associated with each pixel are gathered in a thread's local memory and sorted before rendering.

```
1 const int gScreenSize    = gScreenW * gScreenH;
2 atomic_uint firstFreeCell = 0;
3 int heads[gScreenSize];
4 LinkedListCell_t buffer[gBufferSize];
5
6 void insertFront(x, y, float depth, Data data) {
7   const int fresh = atomicCounterIncrement(firstFreeCell);
8   buffer[fresh].depth = depth;
9   buffer[fresh].data  = data;
10  buffer[fresh].next  = atomicExchange(&heads[x+y*gScreenW], fresh);
11 }
```

Listing 21.1. Insertion at the head of a linked list.

```
1  atomic_uint firstFreeCell = gScreenSize;
2  Data     databuf[gBufferSize];
3  uint64_t buffer[gBufferSize + gScreenSize];
4
5  uint64_t pack(uint32_t depth, uint32_t next) {
6   return ((uint64_t)depth << 32) | next;
7  }
8
9  void insertFrontPack(x, y, uint32_t depth, data) {
10   const int fresh = atomicCounterIncrement(firstFreeCell);
11   databuf[fresh-gScreenSize] = data;
12   buffer[fresh] = atomicExchange(buffer+x+y*gScreenW,
13                                  pack(depth, fresh));
14  }
```

Listing 21.2. Insertion at the head of a linked list with packing.

21.2.2   Packing depth and next Together

In order to facilitate the understanding of later sections and render the exposition more uniform with Section 21.3, this section introduces specific changes to the buffer layout. We illustrate this new layout by describing an alternative way to build unsorted linked-lists.

The following changes are done: First, all fragment data except `depth` are segregated in a specific data buffer, that we call `databuf`. Second, the `depth` and the `next` fields are packed in a single 64-bits word. Third, the main buffer is enlarged with as many cells as pixels on screen. These additional cells at the beginning of the buffer are used just like the `heads` array in Listing 21.1.

Listing 21.2 shows the new insertion procedure. Two observations should be kept in mind:

- We must follow the `next` index $n - 1$ times to access the depth of the nth fragment, and n times to access its other data.

- Notice the new initial value of `firstFreeCell` and the offset needed when accessing the fragment data.

We keep this buffer layout throughout the remainder of the chapter.

The following diagram illustrates the position of four fragments $f_i, i = 1, 2, 3, 4$, inserted in this order, with depth z_i and data d_i, associated with a pixel with coordinates (x, y). Observe how each cell of the main buffer packs the depth z_i of a fragment and the index n_i of the next item in the list. Note that with this layout the index n_i of the fragment following f_i never changes.

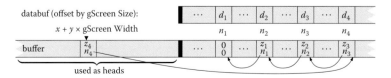

```
 1  uint_32_t getNext(uint64_t cell) {
 2    return cell; // extract least significant 32 bits
 3  }
 4
 5  void insertSorted(x, y, uint32_t depth, Data data) {
 6    const int fresh = atomicCounterIncrement(firstFreeCell);
 7    buffer[fresh]    = 0; // 64-bits zero
 8    memoryBarrier(); // make sure init is visible
 9    databuf[fresh]   = data;
10    uint64_t record = pack(depth,fresh), old, pos;
11    pos = gScreenW * y + x; // start of the search
12    while((old=atomicMax64(buffer+pos, record)) > 0) {
13      if( old > record ) { // go to next
14        pos = getNext(old);
15      } else { // inserted! update record itself
16        pos = getNext(record);
17        record = old;
18  } } }
```

Listing 21.3. Insertion-sort in a linked list.

21.2.3 Building Sorted Lists with Insertion-Sort (PRE-LIN)

It is also possible to perform parallel insertions at any position inside a linked list, and therefore, to implement a parallel version of "insertion-sort." General solutions to this problem have been proposed. In particular, our approach is inspired by that of Harris [Harris 01], albeit in a simplified setting since there is no deletion of single items. A sample implementation is provided in Listing 21.3.

The idea is to walk along the linked list until we find the proper place to insert the fragment. Contrary to the implementation of Harris, which relies on an atomic compare-and-swap, we use an atomic max operation on the cells of the main buffer at each step of the walk (line 12). Since the depth is packed in the most significant bits of a cell (line 10), the atomicMax operation will overwrite the fragment stored in the buffer if and only if the new fragment depth is larger. In all cases the value in the buffer prior to the max is returned in the variable old.

If the new fragment has smaller depth (line 13) then the buffer has not changed and the new fragment has to be inserted further down the list: we advance to the next cell (line 14).

If the new fragment has a larger depth (line 15) then it has been inserted by the atomicMax. At this point the new fragment has been inserted, but the remainder of the list has been cut out: the new fragment has no follower (line 7). We therefore restart the walk (line 16), this time trying to insert old as the next element of record (line 17). That walk will often succeed immediately: the atomicMax operation will be applied at the end of the first part of the list and will return zero (line 12). This single operation will merge back both parts of the list. However there is an exception: another thread may have concurrently inserted more elements, in which case the walk will continue until all elements

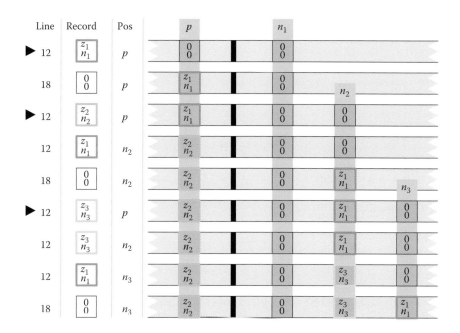

Figure 21.2. Insertion of three fragments into the list of pixel p. Their respective depths are z_1, z_2 and z_3 with $z_2 > z_3 > z_1$. The triangles on the left indicate the start of the insertion of a new fragment. Each line is a snapshot of the variables and main buffer state at each iteration of the **while** loop at lines 12 or 18 of Listing 21.3.

have been properly re-inserted. Figure 21.2 illustrates the insertion of three fragments associated with a single pixel p.

Compared to the approach of [Harris 01] based on a 32-bit atomic compare and swap, our technique has the advantage of compactness and does not require synchronization in the main loop. In particular the loop in Listing 21.3 can be rewritten as follows:

```
1   while((old=atomicMax64(buffer+pos, record)) > 0) {
2     pos    = getNext( max(old,record) );
3     record = min(old,record);
4   }
```

Please refer to the accompanying source code for an implementation of both approaches (file `implementations.fp`, functions `insert_prelin_max64` and `insert_prelin_cas32`).

21.3 Lists with Open Addressing (OPEN-ALLOC)

In the previous section, a cell was allocated by incrementing a global counter, and each cell in a list had to store the index of the next cell in that list. This is the traditional linked-list data structure.

In this section, we describe a different way to allocate cells in the main buffer and traverse the list of fragments associated with a given pixel. This technique frees us from storing the index of the next cell, allowing more fragments to fit in the same amount of memory. It does come with some disadvantages as well, in particular the inability to store more that 32 bits of data per fragment.

We start with a general introduction of this allocation strategy and then introduce the two techniques based on it, POST-OPEN and PRE-OPEN.

21.3.1 Insertion

For each pixel p, we fix a sequence of cell positions in the main buffer, $(h(p, i))_{i \geq 1}$ and call it a *probe sequence*. The function h is defined as

$$h(p, i) = p + o_i \mod H,$$

or, in C speak,   `(p + offsets[i]) % gBufferSize`.

where $H = $ `gBufferSize` is the size of the main buffer. The sequence $(o_i)_{i \geq 1}$ should ideally be a random permutation of the set of integers $[0..H - 1]$, so that the probe sequence $(h(p, i))_{i \geq 1}$ covers all the cells of the main buffer. We call $(o_i)_{i \geq 1}$ the *sequence of offsets*. In practice this sequence is represented with a fixed-length array of random integers, which we regenerate before each frame. The fragments associated with pixel p are stored in the main buffer at locations indicated by the probe sequence. When a fragment covering pixel p is stored at position $h(p, i)$, we say that it has *age i*, or that i is the age of this stored fragment.

There are two interesting consequences to using the probe sequence defined by function h. First, note that the sequence of offsets is independent of the pixel position p. This means that the probe sequence for pixel q is a translation of the probe sequence for pixel p by the vector $q - p$. During the rasterization, neighboring threads handle neighboring pixels and in turn access neighboring memory locations as each is traversing the probe sequence of its corresponding pixel. This *coherence* in the memory access pattern eases the stress of the GPU memory bus and increases memory bandwidth utilization. It was already exploited by García et al. for fast spatial hashing [García et al. 11].

Second, assuming that H is greater than the total number of screen pixels, then the function h becomes invertible in the sense that knowing $h(p, i)$ and i is enough to recover p as

$$p = h(p, i) - o_i \mod H,$$

or, in C speak,   (hVal + gBufferSize - offsets[i]) % gBufferSize.

Let us define $h^{-1}(v, i) = v - o_i \mod H$. The function h^{-1} lets us recover the pixel p, which is covered by a fragment of age i stored in cell v of the main buffer: $p = h^{-1}(v, i)$. In order to compute this inverse given v, the age of a fragment stored in the main buffer must be available. Hence, we reserve a few bits (typically 8) to store that age in the buffer, together with the depth and data of the fragment.

When inserting the fragments, we should strive to minimize the age of the oldest fragment, i.e., the fragment with the largest age. This is particularly important to ensure that when walking along lists of fragments for several pixels in parallel, the slowest thread—accessing old fragments—does not penalize the other threads too much. This maximal-age minimization is achieved during insertion: old fragments are inserted with a higher priority, while young fragments must continue the search of a cell in which to be written.

We define the *load-factor* of the main buffer as the ratio of the number of fragments inserted to the total size of the main buffer.

Collisions. A collision happens when a thread tries to insert a fragment in a cell that already contains a fragment. Collisions can happen since the probe sequence that we follow is essentially random. When the main buffer is almost empty (the load-factor is low), collisions rarely happen. But as the load-factor increases, the chance of collisions increases as well. The open addressing scheme that we have just described works remarkably well even when the load-factor is as high as 0.95.

A collision happens when a thread tries to insert a fragment f_p covering pixel p at position $h(p, i)$ for some i, but the cell at that position already contains a fragment f_q for some other pixel q. We then have $h(p, i) = h(q, j)$ and solve the collision depending on the value of i and j:

- If $j = i$, then $q = p$. The fragment f_q covers the same pixel p; we keep it there and try to insert fragment f_p at the next position $h(p, i+1)$. Alternatively, as in Section 21.3.3, we might compare the depths of both fragments to decide which one to keep at that position and which one to move.

- If $j \neq i$, then pixels p and q are different pixels. In that case, we store the fragment with the largest age in that cell and continue along the probe sequence of the other fragment. More precisely, if $i > j$ then the older fragment f_p replaces f_q in the main buffer and the insertion of the younger fragment f_q is restarted at age $j + 1$, i.e., at position $h(q, j + 1)$ in the main buffer. Note that the value q is not known in advance and must be computed as $q = h^{-1}(h(p, i), j)$. If $i < j$, then fragment f_q does not move and the search for a free cell for f_p proceeds at age $i + 1$ in the probe sequence of pixel p.

This *eviction* mechanism, whereby an "old" fragment evicts a younger fragment, has been demonstrated to effectively reduce the maximum age of the fragments stored in the main buffer, over all pixels. This property was discovered by Celis and Munro in their technique called *Robin Hood Hashing* [Celis et al. 85].

21.3.2 Building Unsorted Lists (POST-OPEN)

In this section, we give the full details of the construction of unsorted lists of fragments using the allocation scheme described above.

In the rest of this chapter, we assume that a cell of the main buffer occupies 64 bits, which lets us use atomic operations on a cell, and that the age of a fragment is stored in the most significant bits of the cell:

$$\text{MSB} \boxed{\text{age: 8 bits} \mid \text{empty: 24 bits} \mid \text{data: 32 bits}} \text{LSB}$$

In this way, the eviction mechanism described above can be safely accomplished using a single call to `atomicMax`.

We use an auxiliary 2D table A that stores, for each pixel p, the age of the oldest fragment associated with p in the main buffer. Thus, $A[p]$ indicates the end of the list of p's fragments; from which we can start the search for an empty cell for the new fragment f_p to be inserted.

The insertion procedure is shown in Listing 21.4. It increments a counter `age` starting from $A[p] + 1$ (line 2) until it finds an empty cell at position $h(p, \text{age})$

```
1 void insertBackOA(p, depth, data) {
2   uint      age   = A[p] + 1;
3   uint64_t record = OA_PACK(age,depth,data);
4   int       iter = 0;
5   while (iter++ < MAX_ITER) {
6     uvec2    h   = ( p + offsets[age] ) % gBufSz;
7     uint64_t old = atomicMax(&buffer[h], record);
8     if (old < record) {
9       atomicMax(&A[p], age);
10      if (old == 0) break;
11      uint32_t oage = OA_GET_AGE(old);
12      p    = (h + gBufSz - offsets[oage]) % gBufSz;
13      age  = A[p];
14      record = OA_WRITE_AGE(old, age);
15    }
16    ++age;
17    record = record + OA_INC_AGE;
18 } }
```

Listing 21.4. Insertion in a list with open addressing.

in which the `record` is successfully inserted (line 10). The `record` is tentatively inserted in the buffer at line 7. If the insertion fails, the insertion proceeds in the next cell along the probe sequence (lines 16 and 17). If it succeeds, the table A is updated and if another fragment f' was evicted (`old != 0`), the pixel q covered by f' is computed from the age of f' (line 11) and function h^{-1} (line 12). The insertion of f' continues from the end of the list of fragments for pixel q, given by $A[q] + 1$.

The macro `OA_PACK` packs the age, depth and data of a fragment in a 64-bits word. The age occupies the 8 most significant bits. The macro `OA_WRITE_AGE` updates the 8 most significant bits without touching the rest of the word. Finally, the constant `OA_INC_AGE = ((uint64_t)1<<56)` is used to increment the age in the packed `record`.

21.3.3   Building Sorted Lists with Insertion-Sort (Pre-Open)

In this section, we modify the construction algorithm above so as to keep the list of fragments sorted by depth, by transforming it into an insertion-sort algorithm.

Let f_p be the fragment, associated with pixel p, that we are inserting in the main buffer. When a collision occurs at age i with a stored fragment f'_p associated with the *same* pixel p, we know that both fragments currently have the same age. Therefore, the `atomicMax` operation will compare the cell bits that are lower than the bits used for storing the age. If the higher bits, among these lower bits, encode the depth of the fragment then we ensure that the fragment with largest depth is stored in the main buffer after the atomic operation:

MSB	age: 8 bits	depth: 24 bits	data: 32 bits	LSB

Further, it is possible to show that during the insertion of fragment f_p at age i, if a collision occurs with a fragment f_q with $h(q, j) = h(p, i)$, then $i \leq j$. Thus, the insertion procedure will skip over all stored fragments that are not associated with pixel p (since $i \neq j \Rightarrow q \neq p$) and will correctly keep the fragments associated with p sorted by decreasing depth along the probe sequence of p. The interested reader will find more detail and a proof of correctness of the insertion-sort with open addressing in our technical report [Lefebvre and Hornus 13].

Thus, we obtain an insertion-sort with open addressing simply by packing the depth of the fragment right after its age and always starting the insertion of a fragment at the beginning of the probe sequence. A sample implementation is given in Listing 21.5.

21.4   Post-sort and Pre-sort

In this section we discuss details depending on the choice of scheduling for the sort. We discuss the sort in local memory required for Post-Lin and Post-Open, as well as how to perform early culling with Pre-Lin and Pre-Open.

```
 1 void insertSortedOA(p, depth, data) {
 2   uint        age  = 1;
 3   uint64_t record = OA_PACK(age,depth,data);
 4   int        iter = 0;
 5   while (iter++ < MAX_ITER) {
 6     uvec2     h   = ( p + offsets[age] ) % gBufSz;
 7     uint64_t old = atomicMax(&buffer[h], record);
 8     if (old < record) {
 9       atomicMax(&A[p], age);
10       if (old == 0) break;
11       age = OA_GET_AGE(old);
12       p       = (h + gBufSz - offsets[age]) % gBufSz;
13       record = old;
14     }
15     ++age;
16     record = record + OA_INC_AGE;
17 } }
```

Listing 21.5. Insertion-sort with open addressing.

21.4.1 POST-SORT: Sorting in Local Memory

In the POST-SORT method, the BUILD pass accumulates the fragments of each pixel in a list, without sorting them. The RENDER pass should then sort the fragments prior to accumulating their contributions. This is done in a pixel shader invoked by rasterizing a fullscreen quad. The shader for a given pixel p first gathers all the fragments associated with p in a small array allocated in local memory. The array is then sorted using bubble-sort, in a manner similar to [Crassin 10]. Insertion-sort could also be used and benefit cases where the transparent fragments are rasterized roughly in back-to-front order.

In contrast to the POST-SORT techniques, the PRE-SORT approaches perform sorting during the BUILD pass. This allows for early culling of unnecessary fragments, as described in the next section.

21.4.2 PRE-SORT: Early Culling

The PRE-SORT method has the unique advantage of keeping the fragments sorted at all times. In a transparency application, when a fragment is inserted in a sorted list it is possible to accumulate the opacity of the fragments in front of it in the list. If this opacity reaches a given threshold, we know that the color of fragment f will contribute little to the final image and we can decide to simply discard it. This early culling mechanism is possible only when the lists of fragments are always sorted, and it provides an important performance improvement as illustrated in Section 21.7.

21.5   Memory Management

All four techniques use the main buffer for storing fragments. We discuss in Section 21.5.1 how to initialize the buffer at each new frame. All implementations assumed so far that the buffer is large enough to hold all incoming fragments. This may not be true depending on the selected viewpoint, and we therefore discuss how to manage memory and deal with an overflow of the main buffer in Section 21.5.2.

21.5.1   The CLEAR Pass

With the LIN-ALLOC strategy, the beginning of the main buffer that stores the heads of the lists has to be zeroed. This is implemented by rasterizing a fullscreen quad. The global counter for cell allocation has to be initially set to `gScreenSize`. In addition, when using the paged allocation scheme with the PRE-LIN method, an additional array containing for each pixel the free cell index in its last page has to be cleared as well.

With the OPEN-ALLOC strategy the entire main buffer has to be cleared: the correctness of the insertion algorithm relies on reading a zero value to recognize a free cell. The array A used to store the per-pixel maximal age has to be cleared as well.

Figure 21.3 shows a breakout of the timings of each pass. As can be seen, the CLEAR pass is only visible for the OPEN-ALLOC techniques, but remains a small percentage of the overall frame time.

21.5.2   Buffer Overflow

None of the techniques we have discussed require us to count the number of fragments before the BUILD pass. Therefore, it is possible for the main buffer to overflow when too many fragments are inserted within a frame. Our current strategy is to detect overflow *during* frame rendering, so that rendering can be interrupted. When the interruption is detected by the host application, the main buffer size is increased, following a typical size-doubling strategy, and the frame rendering is restarted from scratch.

When using linked lists we conveniently detect an overflow by testing if the global allocation counter exceeds the size of the main buffer. In such a case, the fragment shader discards all subsequent fragments.

The use of open addressing requires a slightly different strategy. We similarly keep track of the number of inserted fragments by incrementing a global counter. We increment this counter *at the end* of the insertion loop, which largely hides the cost of the atomic increment. With open addressing, the cost of the insertion grows very fast as the load-factor of the main buffer nears one (Figure 21.4). For this reason, we interrupt the BUILD pass when the load-factor gets higher than $10/16$.

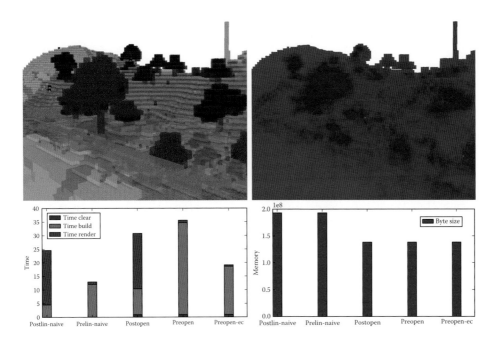

Figure 21.3. The lost empire scene, modeled with Minecraft by Morgan McGuire. The top row (left) shows the textured rendering, with 0.5 opacity (alpha from textures is ignored). The trees appear solid due to a large number of quads. The top row (right) shows a color coded image of the depth complexity. Full red corresponds to 64 fragments (average: 10.3, maximum: 46). The left chart gives the timing breakout for each pass and each technique. The CLEAR pass (red) is negligible for LIN-ALLOC techniques. POST-SORT techniques are characterized by a faster BUILD (green) but a significantly longer RENDER (blue) due to the sort. preopen-ec uses early culling, strongly reducing the cost of BUILD (threshold set to 0.95 cumulated opacity). The right chart shows the memory cost of each technique, assuming the most compact implementation. *Load-factor: 0.4.*

21.6 Implementation

We implement all techniques in GLSL fragment programs, using the extension `NV_shader_buffer_store` on NVIDIA hardware to access GPU memory via pointers. We tested our code on both a GeForce GTX 480 (Fermi) and a GeForce Titan (Kepler), using NVIDIA drivers 320.49. We designed our implementation to allow for easy swapping of techniques: each different approach is compiled as a separate DLL. Applications using the A-buffer use a common interface abstracting the A-buffer implementation (see `abuffer.h`).

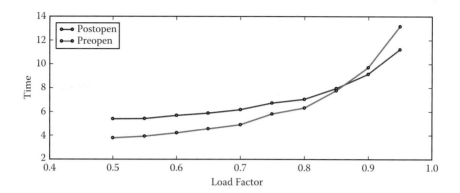

Figure 21.4. Frame time (ms) versus load-factor for open addressing techniques. Note the significant performance drop as the load-factor increases. *GeForce Titan, 320.49, 2.5M fragments, average depth complexity: 2.9.*

An important benefit of the techniques presented here is that they directly fit in the graphics pipeline, and do not require switching to a compute API. Therefore, the BUILD pass is the same as when rendering without an A-buffer, augmented with a call to the insertion code. This makes the techniques easy to integrate in existing pipelines. In addition all approaches require fewer than 30 lines of GLSL code.

Unfortunately implementation on current hardware is not as straightforward as it could be, for two reasons: First, the hardware available to us does not natively support `atomicMax` on 64 bits in GLSL (Kepler supports it natively on CUDA). Fortunately the `atomicMax` 64 bits can be emulated via an `atomicCompSwap` instruction in a loop. We estimated the performance impact to approximately 30% by emulating a 32 bits `atomicMax` with a 32 bits `atomicCompSwap` (on a GeForce GTX480). The second issue is related to the use of atomic operations in loops, inside GLSL shaders. The current compiler seems to generate code leading to race conditions that prevent the loops from operating properly. Our current implementation circumvents this by inserting additional atomic operations having no effect on the algorithm result. This, however, incurs in some algorithms a penalty that is difficult to quantify.

21.7   Experimental Comparisons

We now compare each of the four versions and discuss their performance.

21.7.1   3D Scene Rendering

We developed a first application for rendering transparent, textured scenes. It is included in the companion source code (`bin/seethrough.exe`). Figure 21.3 shows a 3D rendering of a large scene with textures and transparency. It gives the timings breakout for each pass and each technique, as well as their memory cost.

21.7.2   Benchmarking

For benchmarking we developed an application rendering transparent, front facing quads in orthographic projection. The position and depth of the quads are randomized and change every frame. All measures are averaged over six seconds of running time. We control the size and number of quads, as well as their opacity. We use the `ARB_timer_query` extension to measure the time to render a frame. This includes the CLEAR, BUILD, and RENDER passes as well as checking for the main buffer overflow. All tests are performed on a GeForce GTX480 and a GeForce Titan using drivers 320.49. We expect these performance numbers to change with future driver revisions due to issues mentioned in Section 21.6. Nevertheless, our current implementation exhibits performance levels consistent across all techniques as well as between Fermi and Kepler.

The benchmarking framework is included in the companion source code (`bin/benchmark.exe`). The python script `runall.py` launches all benchmarks.

Number of fragments. For a fixed depth complexity, the per-frame time is expected to be linear in the number of fragments. This is verified by all implementations as illustrated Figure 21.5. We measure this by rendering a number of quads perfectly aligned on top of each other, in randomized depth order. The number of quads controls the depth complexity. We adjust the size of the quads to vary the number of fragments only.

Depth complexity. In this experiment we compare the overall performance for a fixed number of fragments but a varying depth complexity. As the size of the per-pixel lists increases, we expect a quadratic increase in frame rendering time. This is verified Figure 21.6. The technique PRE-OPEN is the most severely impacted by the increase in depth complexity. The main reason is that the sort occurs in global memory, and each added fragment leads to a full traversal of the list via the eviction mechanism.

Early culling. In scenes with a mix of transparent and opaque objects, early culling fortunately limits the depth complexity per pixel. The techniques PRE-OPEN and PRE-LIN both afford for early culling (see Section 21.4.2). Figure 21.7 demonstrates the benefit of early culling. The threshold is set up to ignore all fragments after an opacity of 0.95 is reached (1 being fully opaque).

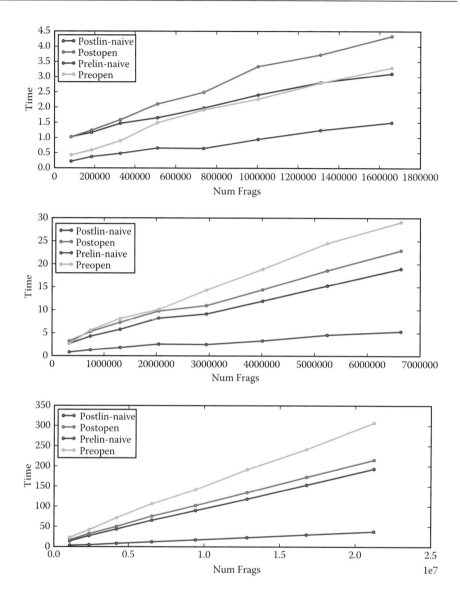

Figure 21.5. Frame time (ms) versus number of fragments. From top to bottom, the depth complexity is 5, 20, and 63 in all pixels covered by the quads. Increase in frame time is linear in number of fragments.

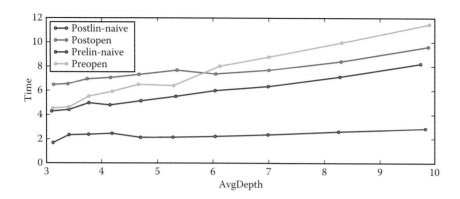

Figure 21.6. Frame time (ms) versus average depth complexity. *GeForce Titan, driver 320.49, load-factor: 0.5, 2.5M fragments.*

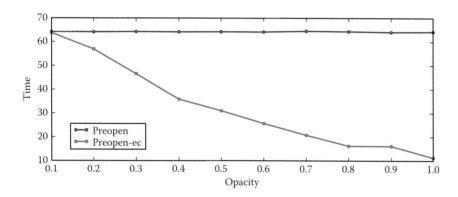

Figure 21.7. Frame time versus opacity for PRE-OPEN with and without early culling. Early culling (green) quickly improves performance when opacity increases. *GeForce Titan, driver 320.49, load-factor: 0.5, 9.8M fragments.*

21.8 Conclusion

Our tests indicate that PRE-LIN has a significant advantage over other techniques, while the OPEN-ALLOC cell allocation strategy falls behind. This is, however, not a strong conclusion. Indeed, all of these methods, with the exception of POST-LIN, are penalized by the emulation of the atomic max 64 bits. More importantly, the implementation of the OPEN-ALLOC techniques currently suffers from unnecessary atomic operations introduced to avoid race conditions.

The LIN-ALLOC cell allocation strategy strongly benefits from the dedicated increment atomic counters. Our tests indicate that without these, the BUILD performance is about three times slower (using paged allocation, which is then faster), making PRE-OPEN competitive again. This implies that in a non-GLSL setting the performance ratios are likely to differ.

Finally, the POST-SORT techniques could benefit from a smarter sort, bubble-sort having the advantage of fitting well in the RENDER pass due to its straight-forward execution pattern. Using a more complex algorithm would be especially beneficial for larger depth complexities. However, increasing the number of fragments per-pixel implies increasing the reserved temporary memory. This impedes performance: for the rendering of Figure 21.3, allocating a temporary array of size 64 gives a RENDER time of 20 ms, while using an array with 256 entries increases the RENDER time to 57 ms. This is for the exact same rendering: reserving more memory reduces parallelism. In contrast, the PRE-SORT techniques suffer no such limitations and support early fragment culling.

For updates on code and results please visit http://www.antexel.com/research/gpupro5.

21.9   Acknowledgments

We thank NVIDIA for hardware donation as well as Cyril Crassin for discussions and feedback on GPU programming. This work was funded by ERC ShapeForge (StG-2012-307877).

Bibliography

[Carpenter 84] Loren Carpenter. "The A-buffer, an Antialiased Hidden Surface Method." *SIGGRAPH* 18:3 (1984), 103–108.

[Celis et al. 85] Pedro Celis, Per-Åke Larson, and J. Ian Munro. "Robin Hood Hashing (Preliminary Report)." In *Proceedings of the 25th Annual Symposium on Foundations of Computer Science*, pp. 281–288. Washington, DC: IEEE, 1985.

[Crassin 10] Cyril Crassin. "OpenGL 4.0+ A-buffer V2.0: Linked lists of fragment pages." http://blog.icare3d.org/2010/07/opengl-40-abuffer-v20-linked-lists-of.html, 2010.

[García et al. 11] Ismael García, Sylvain Lefebvre, Samuel Hornus, and Anass Lasram. "Coherent Parallel Hashing." *ACM Transactions on Graphics* 30:6 (2011), Article no. 161.

[Harris 01] Timothy L. Harris. "A Pragmatic Implementation of Non-blocking Linked-Lists." In *Proceedings of the 15th International Conference on Distributed Computing, DISC '01*, pp. 300–314. London: Springer-Verlag, 2001.

[Lefebvre and Hornus 13] Sylvain Lefebvre and Samuel Hornus. "HA-Buffer: Coherent Hashing for Single-Pass A-buffer." Technical Report 8282, Inria, 2013.

[Lefebvre 13] Sylvain Lefebvre. "IceSL: A GPU Accelerated Modeler and Slicer." In *Distributed Computing: 15th International Conference, DISC 2001, Lisbon, Portugal, October 3–5, 2001, Proceedings, Lecture Notes in Computer Science 2180*, pp. 300–314. Berlin: Springer-Verlag, 2013.

[Maule et al. 11] Marilena Maule, João Luiz Dihl Comba, Rafael P. Torchelsen, and Rui Bastos. "A Survey of Raster-Based Transparency Techniques." *Computers & Graphics* 35:6 (2011), 1023–1034.

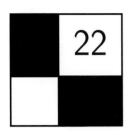

Reducing Texture Memory Usage
by 2-Channel Color Encoding
Krzysztof Kluczek

22.1 Introduction

In modern games, textures are the primary means of storing information about
the appearance of materials. While often a single texture is applied to an entire
3D mesh containing all materials, they equally often represent individual materials, e.g., textures of walls, terrain, vegetation, debris, and simple objects. These
single-material textures often do not exhibit large color variety and contain a limited range of hues, while using a full range of brightness resulting from highlights
and dark (e.g., shadowed), regions within the material surface. These observations, along with web articles noticing very limited color variety in Hollywood
movies [Miro 10] and next-gen games, coming as far as the proposal of using only
two color channels for the whole framebuffer [Mitton 09], were the motivation for
the technique presented in this chapter.

   The method presented here follows these observations and aims to encode any
given texture into two channels: one channel preserving full luminance information and the other one dedicated to hue/saturation encoding.

22.2 Texture Encoding Algorithm

Figure 22.1 presents the well-known RGB color space depicted as a unit cube.
Each source texel color corresponds to one point in this cube. Approximating
this space with two channels effectively means that we have to find a surface
(two-dimensional manifold) embedded within this unit cube that lies as close as
possible to the set of texels from the source texture. To simplify the decoding
algorithm, we can use a simple planar surface or, strictly speaking, the intersection of a plane with the RGB unit cube (right image of Figure 22.1). Because we
have already decided that *luminance* information should be *encoded losslessly* in
a separate channel, the color plane should pass through the RGB space's origin

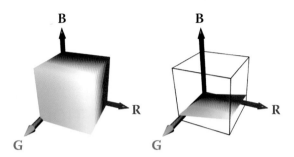

Figure 22.1. RGB color space as unit cube (left) and its intersection with a plane (right).

of zero luminance (black). Therefore, the simplified color space for the 2-channel compression is defined by a single three-dimensional vector—the plane normal.

22.2.1 Color Plane Estimation

Fitting a plane to approximate a set of 3D points is a common task and various algorithms exist. In order to find the best plane for color simplification we have to take the following preparatory steps.

First, we have to remember that RGB pixel color values in most image file formats do not represent linear base color contribution. For the purpose of this algorithm, we want to operate in the linear RGB color space. Most common file formats provide values in sRGB space [Stokes 96]. While being internally more complex, this representation can be approximated with gamma 2.2, i.e., after raising RGB values to power of 2.2 we obtain approximately linear light stimuli for red, green, and blue. We can approximate this with a gamma value of 2, which allows a simple use of multiplication and square root for conversion between sRGB and approximate linear RGB spaces. Strictly speaking, we will then be operating in a RGB space with a gamma of 1.1. While this slight nonlinearity will have only a minor impact on the estimation and the encoding, it is important to use the same simplified gamma value of 2 during the conversion back to the sRGB space after decoding for the final presentation to avoid change in the luminance levels.

After (approximately) converting color values to the linear RGB space, the other thing we have to remember is the fact that the hue perception is a result of the relation between the RGB components and is not linear. To correctly match hues as closely as possible, we could ideally use a perceptually linear color space (e.g., L*a*b*, explained in [Hoffmann 03]). However, this results in a much more costly decoding stage and thus we will limit ourselves to the linear RGB color space, accepting potential minor hue errors. Still, to minimize the impact of not operating in a perceptually correct linear RGB space, we can apply non-uniform scaling to the space before estimating the plane. This affects the error distribution across the RGB channels, allowing some hues to be represented more closely at the cost of others. The result of this non-uniform scaling is that as RGB components shrink, their influence on the color plane shrinks, because distances along the shrunk axis are shortened. Due to the hue perception's nonlinearity, it is not easy to define the scaling factors once for all potential textures, and in our tests they were set experimentally based on the sample texture set. First we tried the RGB component weights used in the luminance computation (putting most importance on G and barely any on B), but experiments showed that some material textures are better represented when the estimation is done with more balanced weighting. To achieve acceptable results for various textures, we used an experimentally chosen weight set of 1/2 for red, 1 for green and 1/4 for blue, which lies between the classic luminance component weights and the equally weighted component average. Fortunately, the perceived difference in pixel hues after the encoding changes is barely noticeable with these scaling factors. Still, the scaling factors may be used to improve texture representation by fine tuning them separately for each texture.

With the two above operations, the whole initial pixel color processing can be expressed as

$$r'_i = r_i^\gamma w_r,$$
$$g'_i = g_i^\gamma w_g,$$
$$b'_i = b_i^\gamma w_b,$$

where γ is the gamma value used to transition from the input color space to the linear color space, and w_r, w_g and w_b are the color component importance weights.

Having taken into account the above considerations, the color of every texel represents a single point in 3D space. The optimal approximating color plane will be the plane that minimizes the sum of squared distances between the plane and each point. Because the plane is assumed to be passing by the point (0,0,0), we can express it by its normal. In effect, the point-plane distance computation reduces to a dot product. Note that since we are using the RGB space, the vector components are labeled r, g, and b instead of the usual x, y, and z:

$$d_i = N \cdot P_i = n_r r'_i + n_g g'_i + n_b b'_i.$$

The optimal plane normal vector is the vector, which minimizes the point-plane distances. Such problems can be solved using least squared fit method that aims to minimize sum of squared distances. The approximation error we want to minimize is expressed as

$$err = \sum_i d_i^2 = \sum_i (N \cdot P_i)^2 = \sum_i (n_r r'_i + n_g g'_i + n_b b'_i)^2,$$

which after simple transformations becomes

$$err = n_r^2 \left(\sum_i r_i'^2 \right) + n_g^2 \left(\sum_i g_i'^2 \right) + n_b^2 \left(\sum_i b_i'^2 \right)$$
$$+ 2 n_r n_g \left(\sum_i r_i' g_i' \right) + 2 n_r n_b \left(\sum_i r_i' b_i' \right) + 2 n_g n_b \left(\sum_i g_i' b_i' \right).$$

For minimalistic implementation, we can use the above equation to compute all six partial sums depending only on the texel colors. Then we can use a brute force approach to test a predefined set of potential normal vectors to find the one minimizing the total approximation error. Because each test is carried out in linear time, costing only several multiplications and additions, this approach is still tolerably fast.

The final step after finding the optimal color plane is to revert the color space distortion caused by the color component weighting by scaling using the reciprocal weights. Because the plane normal is a surface normal vector, the usual rule of non-uniform space scaling for normals applies and we have to multiply the normal by the inverse transpose of the matrix we would use otherwise. While the transposition does not affect the scaling matrix, the matrix inversion does and the final scaling operation is using non-reciprocal weights again:

$$N' = N \left(\begin{bmatrix} 1/w_r & 0 & 0 \\ 0 & 1/w_g & 0 \\ 0 & 0 & 1/w_b \end{bmatrix}^{-1} \right)^T = N \begin{bmatrix} w_r & 0 & 0 \\ 0 & w_g & 0 \\ 0 & 0 & w_b \end{bmatrix}.$$

As all subsequent computation is typically done in the linear RGB space, we do not have to convert into sRGB (which would be nonlinear transform anyway).

22.2.2　Computing Base Colors

The important parameters for the encoding and the decoding process are the two base colors. The color plane cutting through the RGB unit cube forms a triangle or a quadrilateral, with one of the corners placed at the point (0,0,0). The two corners neighboring the point (0,0,0) in this shape are defined as the base colors for the planar color space, as shown on Figure 22.2. Every other color available on the plane lies within the angle formed by the point (0,0,0) and the two base color points. Because the color plane starts at (0,0,0) and enters the unit cube, the base color points will always lie on the silhouette of the unit cube, as seen from the point (0,0,0). To find the base colors, we can simply compute the plane intersection with the silhouette edges, resulting in the desired pair of points. We have to bear in mind that the plane can slice through the silhouette vertices, or even embed a pair of silhouette edges. Therefore, to compute the points we can

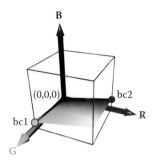

Figure 22.2. Base colors on the color plane.

use an algorithm, which walks around the silhouette computing the two points in which the silhouette crosses the plane.

The key observation now is that we can represent a hue value as the angle to the vectors spanning the plane or, alternatively, using a linear interpolation between the two base colors. In order to compute the final color, we only have to adjust the luminance and perform any required final color space conversions.

22.2.3 Luminance Encoding

The luminance of the color being encoded is stored directly. After colors have been transformed into the linear RGB space, we can use a classic equation for obtaining perceived luminance value derived from the sRGB to XYZ color space transformation in [Stokes 96]:

$$L = 0.2126 \cdot R + 0.7152 \cdot G + 0.0722 \cdot B.$$

Because the weighting coefficients sum up to 1, the luminance value ranges from zero to one. Since the luminance has its own dedicated channel in the 2-channel format, it can now be stored directly. However, as luminance perception is not linear, we are using a gamma value of 2 for the luminance storage. This is close enough to the standard gamma 2.2 and gives the same benefits—dark colors have improved luminance resolution at the cost of unnoticeably reduced quality of highlights. Also the gamma value of 2 means that luminance can simply have its square root computed while encoding and will simply be squared while decoding.

22.2.4 Hue Estimation and Encoding

To encode the hue of the color, we have to find the closest suitable color on the approximating plane and then find the proportion with which we should mix the base colors to obtain the proper hue. The hue encoding process is demonstrated

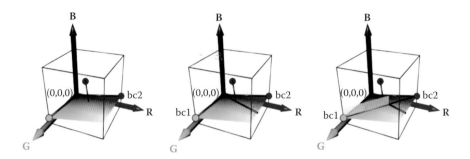

Figure 22.3. Hue encoding process.

in Figure 22.3 and can be outlined as follows:

1. Project the color point in the linear RGB space onto the color plane.

2. Compute the 2D coordinates of the point on the plane.

3. Find a 2D line on plane passing through (0,0,0) and the point.

4. Find the proportion in which the line crosses the 2D line between the base color points, i.e., determine the blend factor for the base colors.

The first step is a simple geometric operation. From the second step on, we have to perform geometric operations on 2D coordinates embedded within the plane. Having the two base color points A and B, we can compute the 2D coordinate frame of the plane as

$$F_x = \frac{A}{\|A\|} \quad F_y = \frac{B - (F_x \cdot B)F_x}{\|B - (F_x \cdot B)F_x\|}$$

and then compute 2D coordinates of any point within the plane using the dot product:

$$(x_i, y_i) = (P_i \cdot F_x, P_i \cdot F_y).$$

Please note that we do not actually need the explicit RGB coordinates of the point on the plane nearest to the color being encoded, but only its 2D coordinates within the plane, x_i and y_i. As both the original point and the point projected onto the plane will have the same 2D coordinates, we can skip step 1 in the outlined algorithm completely. The projection onto the plane is a side effect of the reduction to only two dimensions.

The problem of computing the base color blend factor for hue, when considering the points embedded within the color plane, is now reduced to the problem of intersection of two lines: a line connecting both base color points and a line

```
float3 texture_decode( float2 data, float3 bc1, float3 bc2 )
{
  float3 color = lerp( bc1, bc2, data.y );
  float color_lum = dot( color, float3(0.2126,0.7152,0.0722) );
  float target_lum = data.x * data.x;

  color *= target_lum / color_lum;
  return color;
}
```

Listing 22.1. Two-channel texture decoding algorithm.

passing through the origin and the point on the plane being encoded. This gives us the following line-line intersection equation:

$$A + t(B - A) = sP.$$

Solving this linear equation for t gives us the result—the base color blend factor resulting in a hue most closely matching the hue of the encoded point. This blend factor is then simply stored directly in the second channel, completing the 2-channel encoding process.

22.3 Decoding Algorithm

The decoding algorithm is simple and best described by the actual decoding shader code in Listing 22.1.

First, the base colors bc1 and bc2, which are passed as constant data, are blended with a blend factor coming from the second channel of data, resulting in a color having the desired hue, but wrong luminance. This luminance is computed as color_lum. Next, we compute the desired luminance target_lum as a value of first channel of data squared (because we stored the luminance with gamma 2). As the resulting color is in a linear color space, we can adjust the luminance by simply dividing the color by the current luminance and then multiplying it by the desired one. If needed, we can of course convert the computed color to a nonlinear color space for presentation purposes.

22.4 Encoded Image Quality

Figures 22.4, 22.5, and 22.6 show examples of the encoding and decoding process. The example textures are taken from the CGTextures texture library and were selected because of their relatively rich content and variety.

Figure 22.4 presents a 2-channel approximation result of a dirt texture with grass patches. Both dirt and grass are reproduced with slight, but mostly unnoticeable differences in color. As the method is designed with limited-color material

Figure 22.4. Grass and dirt texture example. Original image (left) and result after the encoding/decoding process (right).

textures in mind, the color probe added on the image is of course severely degraded, but clearly shows that the estimation algorithm picked the green-purple color plane as fitting the image best. These extreme colors may not be used directly on the texture, but we should remember that all colors resulting from blending green and purple are available at this stage and this includes colors with reduced saturation in the transition zone. Because of the separate treatment of pixel luminance, the luminance values are unaffected except for processing and storage rounding errors.

Figures 22.5 and 22.6 show two examples of textures with mixed materials. This time, the estimation process has chosen a blue-yellow for the first and a

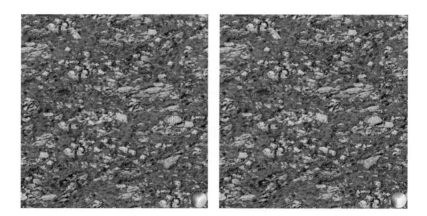

Figure 22.5. Rock and stone texture example. Original image (left) and result after the encoding/decoding process (right).

Figure 22.6. Sand, dead grass, and rocks texture example. Original image (left) and the decoded result after 2-channel compression (right).

teal-orange plane for the second image. While the stone and grass texture mostly remains unaffected, the sand, grass, and stones texture required finding a compromise resulting in some grass discoloration and smaller off-color elements changing color completely.

22.5 Conclusion

The encoding and decoding methods presented in this chapter allow storing textures with low color variety using only two texture channels. Apart from the obvious savings, this opens additional possibilities. For example, considering that most texture sampler implementations support 4-channel textures, the two remaining channels can be used for other purposes, e.g., storing x and y components of the material normal map, resulting in a compact material representation with just a single texture image. Even if not using this feature, the fact that the proposed 2-channel color encoding relies on a luminance-hue decomposition allows custom texture compression algorithms. We can assign higher priority to luminance information during texture compression, accumulating most of the compression error in hue, to changes to which the human eye is less sensitive, increasing the overall compressed image quality. We should also note that the proposed encoding scheme can be used directly with existing mip-mapping solutions, because averaging luminance-values and hue-blend factors is a good approximation of averaging color values. We should only be aware that the luminance values are stored with a gamma of 2 and may require a custom mip-map chain generation if we require fully linear color processing in the whole lighting pipeline.

Bibliography

[Hoffmann 03] Gernot Hoffmann. *CIELab Color Space.* http://docs-hoffmann.de/cielab03022003.pdf, 2003.

[Miro 10] Todd Miro. *Teal and Orange—Hollywood, Please Stop the Madness.* http://theabyssgazes.blogspot.com/2010/03/teal-and-orange-hollywood-please-stop.html, 2010.

[Mitton 09] Richard Mitton. *Two-Channel Framebuffers for Next-Gen Color Schemes.* http://www.codersnotes.com/notes/two-channel, 2009.

[Stokes 96] Michael Stokes, Matthew Anderson, Srinivasan Chandrasekar, and Ricardo Motta. *A Standard Default Color Space for the Internet—sRGB.* http://www.w3.org/Graphics/Color/sRGB, 1996.

23

Particle-Based Simulation of Material Aging

Tobias Günther, Kai Rohmer, and Thorsten Grosch

23.1   Introduction

The composition of detailed textures, facilitating weathered and aged looks, is an everyday task for content artists in game and movie production. Examples of aged scenes are shown in Figure 23.1. In the process of meticulously editing textures, each inaccuracy or later change in the scenery can cause implausibility and quickly break the immersion. Therefore, interactively steerable, automatic simulations that favor the plausibility of aging effects, caused by interacting objects, e.g., dripping of rust, are vitally needed. This chapter describes implementation details of a GPU-assisted material aging simulation, which is based on customizable aging rules and material transport through particles. The chapter is based on

Figure 23.1. Interactively aged scene, exported and rendered in a DCC tool.

our paper [Günther et al. 12], where further results and discussions can be found. The simulation machinery is partly CUDA-based and partly rasterization-based to exploit the advantages of both sides. In fact, it is driven by an interplay of a number of modern GPU features, including GPU ray tracing, dynamic shader linkage, tessellation, geometry shaders, rasterization-based splatting and transform feedback, which are described in the following.

23.2 Overview

Our simulation of weathering effects is based on material transporting particles— so-called gammatons, introduced in [Chen et al. 05]. Gammatons are emitted from sources, such as clouds or roof gutters, to drip and distribute material, as shown in Figure 23.2. On impact, material is deposited or taken away, and the gammaton either bounces, floats, or is absorbed (see Figure 23.3). Eventually, resting material is subject to aging rules, for instance, turning metal into rust or spreading lichen growth. For this, the resting material is stored in a texture atlas, which we call *material atlas*; see later in Section 23.3.1 for a detailed discription of its content.

The simulation pipeline is illustrated in Figure 23.4. The particle movement and collision detection are done in CUDA, using Nvidia's ray tracing engine OptiX [Parker et al. 10]. Thus, in the *simulation step* a CUDA kernel is called, which emits and traces gammatons (elaborated in Section 23.3.2). In the following two stages, the *surface update* and the *gammaton update*, the material is transferred

Figure 23.2. Patina and dirt being transported by gammatons. A subset of the gammatons are rendered as spheres. *[Appeared in [Günther et al. 12] and reproduced by kind permission of the Eurographics Association.]*

Figure 23.3. Depiction of collision responses, left to right: bounce, float, absorb. *[Appeared in [Günther et al. 12] and reproduced by kind permission of the Eurographics Association.]*

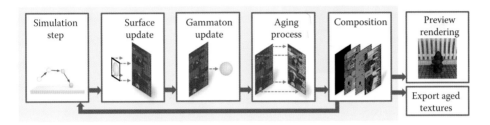

Figure 23.4. Illustration of the simulation pipeline. *[Appeared in [Günther et al. 12] and reproduced by kind permission of the Eurographics Association.]*

between the gammatons and the hit surfaces (detailed in Section 23.3.3). This happens in two consecutive steps: a rasterization pass to drop material into the *material atlas* and a transform feedback pass to update the gammaton material. Moreover, we determine the subsequent behavior of the gammatons by Russian Roulette (e.g., float, bounce, or absorb) and specify their velocity for the next iteration. In the following stage, the *aging process*, aging rules are applied, e.g., rusting in the presence of water and metal. To select the rule set, we use dynamic shader linkage, further explained in Section 23.3.4. Based on the material stored in the *material atlas* (Section 23.3.1) we compose texture maps for the aged diffuse color, shininess, surface normal, and height in the *composition stage* (Section 23.3.5). These maps can be used for preview rendering (Section 23.4) and can be exported (alongside all additional material atlas data), for instance, for external use in game engines or DCC tools.

23.3 Simulation

23.3.1 The Material Atlas

In order to decouple the weathering operations from the scene complexity, we maintain all simulation-relevant material, surface, and normalization data in a texture atlas, which we refer to as *material atlas*, depicted in Figure 23.5. Thereby, the amount of material carried by gammatons or resting on a surface—

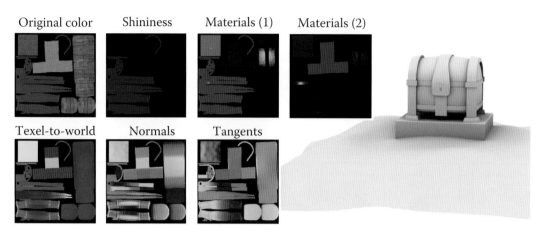

Figure 23.5. The material atlas contains all surface information. In this image a subset of the atlas textures is shown for the Chest scene.

the latter is stored in texels of the atlas—is assignable to eight available slots. In our examples, we needed only seven slots for water, dirt, metal, wood, organic, rust, and stone. All in all, the material atlas contains color + shininess (RGBA8), geometric normals and tangents ($2 \times$ RGB16F), shading normals (RGB16F), original and current height ($2 \times$ R16F), eight material amounts (ping-pong of $2 \times$ RGBA8), eight original material amounts ($2 \times$ RGBA8), and a texture-to-world scale (RG16F), used later for equally-sized splatting. Thus, a parameterization is required for a one-to-one relation between surface points and respective atlas coordinates, which we obtain semi-automatically using standard DCC tools. For this, UV maps already present in game and movie production can be reused.

The atlas resolution is the dominant factor in trading visual quality for performance. To decrease the memory consumption, we reduced the amounts of our materials to 256 discrete steps each, thus $2 \times$ RGBA8 textures are used for storage.

23.3.2 Gammaton Transport—The Simulation Step

To attain interactive frame rates, we only compute a fixed number of simulation steps each frame. Gammatons that are midair are marked as such and do not yet participate in material transport. The data stored for the gammatons is shown in Listing 23.1, including the payload carried by a gammaton during ray tracing, which is later passed into CUDA kernels as prd = payload record data, and the persistent data stored on the OptiX side alone (position) or shared with D3D (atlas texture coordinates of hit, material, etc.).

```
// Information a gammaton carries during tracing
struct GammaPayload
{
  uint ray_index;  // index in the hit buffers
  uint ray_depth;  // number of ray indirections
  float speed;     // speed (multiplied with direction)
};

// Hit buffer data that is used by OptiX only.
struct GammaHitOptix
{
  float3 position;  // position of the gammaton
};

// Hit buffer data that is shared between DirectX and OptiX
struct GammaHitShared
{
  float3 velocity;      // velocity vector
  int flags;            // midair (yes/no), active (yes/no)
  float2 texcoord;      // atlas coord at last hit surface
  uint2 carriedMaterial; // 8 bytes = 8 material slots
  int randomSeed;       // seed for random number generation
};
```

Listing 23.1. Data stored for the gammatons.

Recursive ray tracing. The CUDA entry program that launches the gammatons is shown in Listing 23.2 and works as follows: If a gammaton is active, i.e., it is currently midair or received a new direction in response to a collision, we continue the tracing from its last known position. Otherwise a gammaton is not active, i.e., it left the simulation domain, came to a halt on a nearly horizontal surface, or was absorbed. In that case, a new gammaton is emitted. This entry program is executed for each gammaton source in turn, using customizable emission parameters, e.g., position, direction, speed, and distribution. For the subsequent parallel processing of all gammatons, we assign each source an exclusive range of memory of a shared gammaton stream. Therefore, we set for each source a start offset g_SourceRayIndexOffset, as shown in Figure 23.6. The gammaton trajectory is traced as a recursive series of linear steps, each reporting a hit or miss. In OptiX, kernels are called for the respective events, as shown in Listings 23.3 and 23.4. In each step, we add gravity according to the traveled distance, which results in parabolic trajectories. For floating particles, gravity is acting tangentially. We trace a fixed number of linear steps per iteration until either a surface got hit, the gammaton left the domain, or the maximum recurrence depth is reached. In the latter case, we mark the gammaton as midair (flag). The material transport that is issued on impact of a gammaton is described later in Section 23.3.3. The collision response is selected by Russian Roulette on the events bouncing, floating, and absorbing (see Figure 23.3), according to their associated probabilities. Bouncing and floating particles are reflected by the tangent plane orthogonal to

```
void gammaton_entry_program()
{
  // initialize payload
  Ray ray;  GammaPayload prd;
  prd.ray_index = launch_index + g_SourceRayIndexOffset;
  prd.ray_depth = 0;  // counts recursions

  // get gammaton data (ping pong)
  GammaHitShared& hitshared_i = HitShared_In [prd.ray_index];
  GammaHitShared& hitshared_o = HitShared_Out[prd.ray_index];

  // if gammaton is alive, continue the ray
  if (IS_ALIVE(hitshared_i.flags))
  {
    // continue from last position
    ray.origin = HitOptix[prd.ray_index].position;
    ray.direction = normalize(hitshared_i.velocity);
    prd.speed = length(hitshared_i.velocity);
    hitshared_o.carriedMaterial = hitshared_i.carriedMaterial;
  }
  else // else emit a new ray
  {
    ray.origin = generateRandomPosition();
    ray.direction = generateRandomDirection()
    prd.speed = g_InitialVelocity;
    hitshared_o.carriedMaterial = g_StartMaterial;
  }

  SET_ALIVE(hitshared_o.flags)  // set alive
  SET_BOUNCE(hitshared_o.flags) // flying freely
  hitshared_o.randomSeed = hitshared_i.randomSeed; // pass seed
  float maxDist = prd.speed * g_IntegrationStepSize;
  optixTraceGammaton(ray, prd, maxDist);          // launch ray
}
```

Listing 23.2. OptiX/CUDA entry program for gammaton emission and continue.

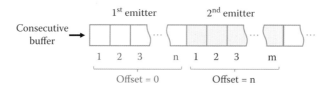

Figure 23.6. All gammaton emitters share an output gammaton stream. For each emitter a contiguous memory block is reserved to store the respective particles (here, n and m). Each gammaton keeps its address, even when inactive.

the estimated surface normal (see Section 23.3.5), and the outgoing direction is randomized by Phong lobe sampling for spreading material. For floating particles the resulting velocity vector is projected back into the tangent plane.

```
void gammaton_closest_hit()
{
   GammaHitShared& hitshared = HitShared_Out[prd.ray_index];

   float3 v = ray.direction * prd.speed;   // velocity
   float3 phit = ray.origin + t_hit * ray.direction:
   float3 pnew = phit + attr_normal * EPSILON;   // move up

   // pick up velocity by fallen distance
   float s = length(pnew - ray.origin);
   float dt = s / prd.speed; // time = distance / speed
   v += dt * gravity;

   if (isTooSlow(v))              // too slow?
     SET_DEAD(hitshared.flags);   // set inactive
   SET_HIT(hitshared.flags);      // we hit a surface

   hitshared.texcoord = attr_texcoord;
   hitshared.velocity = normalize(v) * prd.speed;

   // Remember position until next launch
   GammaHitOptix& gammaState = GammaHitOptixMap[prd.ray_index];
   gammaState.position = pnew;

   // plant with probability (explained later).
   plantletPlacement(hitshared.randomSeed, pnew, attr_texcoord);
}
```

Listing 23.3. OptiX/CUDA gammmaton closest hit program. Attributes, e.g., `attr_normal` and `attr_texcoord`, are passed by the intersection test program.

Numerical considerations of floating particles. We apply a numerical offset ϵ to the gammaton's position to avoid a self-intersection at the launch position. Since a floating particle moves tangentially to the surface, it virtually hovers above the surface. To create an intersection in the next iteration we let the ray aim at the surface by pulling the ray direction along the negated normal by the amount h (see Figure 23.7). The resulting speed of the floating gammatons depends on both

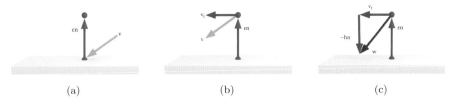

(a)   (b)   (c)

Figure 23.7. (a) Apply offset ϵ in normal direction to the hit position. (b) Project the velocity $\mathbf{v}$ (●) into the tangential plane giving $\mathbf{v_t}$. (c) Pull $\mathbf{v_t}$ in negated normal direction by the amount of h, which yields a new direction $\mathbf{w}$ (●). *[Appeared in [Günther et al. 12] and reproduced by kind permission of the Eurographics Association.]*

```
void gammaton_miss()
{
  // compute position of gammaton
  float dt = g_IntegrationStepSize;
  float3 vold = ray.direction * prd.speed;

  float3 pnew = ray.origin + dt * vold;
  float3 vnew = vold + dt * gravity;

  GammaHitShared& hitshared = HitShared_Out[prd.ray_index];

  if (leftDomain(pnew)) {  // if outside bounding box
    SET_DEAD(hitshared.flags);
    return;
  }

  // Floating particle moved over edge
  if (IS_FLOAT(hitshared.flags)) {  // float
    vnew = make_float3(0,0,0);       // let gammaton fall
    SET_BOUNCE(hitshared.flags);     // free fall
  }

  // gammaton still alive after maximum depth
  prd.ray_depth++;
  if (prd.ray_depth >= MAX__GAMMATON__DEPTH) {
    HitOptix[prd.ray_index].position = pnew;
    hitshared.velocity = vnew;
    SET_ALIVE(hitshared.flags);
    SET_MIDAIR(hitshared.flags);
    return;
  }

  prd.speed = length(vnew);
  Ray ray(pnew, normalize(vnew));
  float maxDist = dt * prd.speed;
  optixTraceGammaton(ray, prd, maxDist);  // launch ray
}
```

Listing 23.4. OptiX/CUDA gammaton miss program.

the numerical offset ϵ as well as h. Floating particles can flow bottom up and around overhangs (see Figure 23.8). If a bounce event occurs or no intersection is found at an overhang, we let the gammaton fall down. On impact the resulting velocity typically acts only tangentially, but to further speed up the distribution of material, we allow the artist to alter the loss of energy of impacting particles. To approximate friction, both bouncing and floating gammatons are slowed down by a specific rate.

23.3.3 Material Transport

Our approach is based on the transport of materials by floating and bouncing gammatons. Thus, we let gammatons that hit a surface issue material transfer, for which both the material on the surface as well as the material carried by the

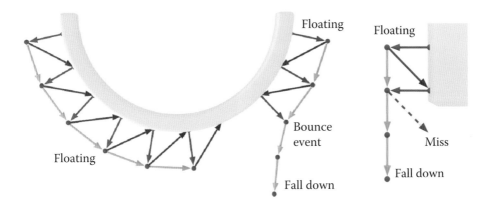

Figure 23.8. The visible course (●) of a gammaton floating around an overhang (left) and when dripping off a cliff (right). In the first, the gammaton on the right falls due to a bounce event. In the latter, the blue dashed ray misses and in response the gammaton falls down.

gammaton are sequentially updated. First, the gammatons are splatted into the material atlas to deposit material. Afterwards, a separate transform feedback pass is executed to update the material of the gammatons. (Modern graphics APIs allow for unordered access from all shader stages, making it possible to implement both update procedures in one pass. Legacy implementations require two separate steps.)

Determining transfer rates. The amount of material that is picked up depends first on the material type, for instance, to accommodate that water is more volatile than stone, and second on the material already present on the surface. The initial material on the surfaces is assigned by presets. The coefficients required for modeling volatileness `g_volatileness` are stored per material and can be part of an asset library. They are set once prior to the simulation for each material and can be stored and reused in other scenes. At runtime one degree of freedom remains: the pick-up ratio `g_pickUpRatio` between the amount of material picked up from the surface and added to the gammaton (and vice versa). A ratio of zero means that material is only picked up, whereas a ratio of one means all is dropped. Naturally, we obtain material preservation if this ratio is 1:1. Exposing this ratio to the artist allows both to speed up the aging process and to reverse it by washing away material, i.e., picking up more material than depositing (see Figure 23.9).

The amount of material to transfer is determined by the method in Listing 23.5.

Figure 23.9. Picking up more material than despositing allows for washing away material (left: before, right: after). *[Appeared in [Günther et al. 12] and reproduced by kind permission of the Eurographics Association.]*

```
float4 transferRate(float4 surfaceMat, float4 gammaMat)
{
   float4 delta =  surfaceMat * (1-g_pickUpRatio)
                 - gammaMat *     g_pickUpRatio;
   return delta * g_volatileness;
}
```

Listing 23.5. Determination of transfer rates for four materials at once.

Transport from gammaton to atlas.   In order to transfer material from the gammatons into the atlas, we expand all gammatons that hit a surface to quads and splat the transferred material into the material atlas textures, using multiple render targets. The procedure is outlined in Listing 23.6. An issue to deal with is the varying area covered by texels of the atlas texture, since more space is reserved for detailed areas. To ensure that splats are equally sized in world space, we scale the quads in the geometry shader by the aforementioned, precomputed *texel-to-world scale*. Note that the clamping to the original material (last line in Listing 23.6) preserves the original material on the surface. This prevents the material from being washed away completely and thus continuously provides material input to the aging simulation.

Transport from atlas to gammaton.   The gammaton material is updated afterwards in a separate transform feedback pass by feeding the gammatons into the ren-

```
void PS_SurfaceUpdate(
  in float4 gammaPos : SV_Position, // atlas pos of gammaton
  in float4 gammaMat : MATERIAL,    // material of gammaton
  out float4 newMat : SV_Target0)   // new surface material
{
  // get current and initial material on surface
  float4 curMat = g_TexMatCur.Load(gammaPos);
  float4 orgMat = g_TexMatOrg.Load(gammaPos);

  // calculate transfer rates and update material
  newMat = curMat - transferRate(curMat, gammaMat);
  newMat = max(orgMat, newMat); // clamp
}
```

Listing 23.6. Gammatons are expanded to quads in a geometry shader and are splatted into the atlas. This pixel shader removes material from the surface. Here, four material slots are updated at once.

dering pipeline as point list. In a geometry shader the material to transfer is calculated again and is added to the gammatons. Additionally, we chose this shader to handle collisions, i.e., to compute new bounce and float directions for the gammatons. Doing this in OptiX is possible as well. The respective geometry shader is outlined in Listing 23.7. We decided to keep inactive gammatons in the stream, as it eases launching of new gammatons.

23.3.4 Aging Rules

Aside from the transport of material by gammatons, the actual aging process is the other key aspect of our system. The idea is to model the temporal aging phenomena that take place if certain materials co-occur, by a set of generic rules. In our system, rules are implementations of a shader interface that alter a material set. In the simulation, we assign the chosen rule permutation by *dynamic shader linkage*. This concept is an advance from uber-shaders, for which registers are always allocated for the worst case branch, and sets of specialized shader files, which are hard to maintain due to their combinatorial growth. Dynamic shader linkage draws a profit from inlining selected functions (e.g., chosen rules) at bind time, thus enabling an optimal register allocation, while providing object-oriented aspects for the definition of rules. We chose to apply the rules to every material atlas texel by rendering a fullscreen quad, i.e., by using a pixel shader. The parameters of the rules are again stored in presets and are fetched at runtime from a single constant buffer. The interface, a sample implementation and the respective pixel shader are outlined in Listing 23.8. Practice showed that for many involved processes plausible approximations can be found by means of simple rules, as described next.

```
[maxvertexcount(1)]
void GS_GammatonUpdate( point GammaHitShared input[1],
  inout PointStream<GammaHitShared> PntStream )
{
  GammaHitShared output = input[0];
  if (IS_MIDAIR(input[0].Flags) || IS_DEAD(input[0].Flags)) {
    PntStream.Append(output);    // no need to act
    return;
  }
  // get material at surface and gammaton
  float4 surfMat = g_TexMatCur.SampleLevel(
                   g_Linear, gammaton.texcoord, 0);
  float4 gammaMat = unpackFromUint(gammaton.carriedMaterial);
  // calculate transfer rates and update material
  gammaMat += transferRate(surfMat, gammaMat);
  gammaMat = saturate(gammaMat);  // clamp
  gammaton.carriedMaterial = packToUint(gammaMat);

  float roulette = rnd(output.Seed);   // random value in [0..1]
  if (roulette < g_BounceProbability) {
    SET_BOUNCE(output.Flags);      // set bounce
    PhongLobeBounce(output);       // handles bounce
  }
  else if (roulette < g_BounceProbability+g_FloatProbability) {
    SET_FLOAT(output.Flags);       // set float
    PhongLobeBounce(output);       // handles float
  }
  else SET_DEAD(output.Flags);     // absorb

  PntStream.Append(output);
}
```

Listing 23.7. Geometry shader, used in the transform feedback loop to update both the gammaton material and the rebound direction. For simplicity, this listing shows the update of four materials. Note that both bouncing and floating gammatons are handled by the `PhongLobeBounce` method, depending on the value of `output.Flags`.

Rust. The first rule corrodes metal in the presence of water. We limit the corrosion speed by the rarer material. Therefore, we set the strength of the rust generation to the minimum of the amount of water and metal, as shown in Listing 23.8. An additional speed parameter provides user control to adjust aging processes relative to one another, e.g., to accommodate that corrosion is slower than lichen growth. Finally, the created amount of rust is added to the already existing rust on the surface.

Decay. The second rule is used to produce organic material and dirt. Here, the amount of created material depends on the currently present water and wood. The implementation is similar to the previous rule, with the difference that two materials are generated instead of one.

Evaporation. We added an additional rule that evaporates water over time; in part to model the phenomenon but also for a practical reason: as a gammaton

```
struct RuleParams {
  float Chance;
  float Speed;
  /* optional: further parameters */
};

interface IRule {
  MatProperty Apply(MatProperty mat, RuleParams p);
};

class IRust : IRule {
  MatProperty Apply(MatProperty mat, RuleParams p);
  {
    mat.Rust += min(mat.Water, mat.Metal) * p.Speed;
    return mat;
  }
};
IRust pRust;

/* other rules */

IRule pRules[NUM_RULES] = {pRust, /* other instances */ }

OUTPUT PS_AgingProcess(int3 atlasCoord)
{
  MatProperty mat = READ_SURFACE_MATERIAL(atlasCoord);
  uint seed = READ_RANDOM_SEED(atlasCoord);

  for(int r=0; r<NUM_RULES; r++)
    if (rnd(seed) < g_RuleParameters[r].Chance)
      mat = pRules[r].Apply(mat, g_RuleParameters[r]);

  OUTPUT.Material = mat;
  OUTPUT.RandomSeed = seed;
}
```

Listing 23.8. Aging rules are implementions of an interface and are bound using dynamic shader linkage. Rules are applied at a customizable probability.

source constantly emits water, we want to keep the amount of water in the scene limited to better control where aging takes place.

Since our material amounts are discretized to 256 steps each, we invoke the aging rules at a customizable probability to allow for slow corrosion speeds as well. The therefore required random numbers are generated by a linear congruence generator, thus the modified random seed is written on output to be input to the next iteration.

23.3.5   Composition

The composition stage is used to produce aged textures and is implemented in two subsequent rasterization passes. In the first pass, aged colors, shininess, and the height map are computed based on the amount of material resting on the ground. In the second pass, we estimate normals based on the height (see Figure 23.10).

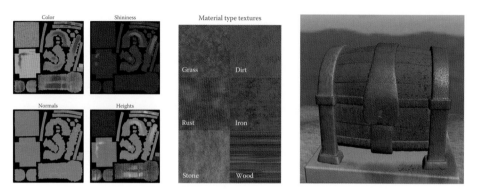

Figure 23.10. Composed textures (left), textures associated with the material types (center), composed aged chest (right). While the left side of the model is aged only slightly the amount of rust, dirt, and organic material increases to the right.

Depending on the needs of the artists or production standards, the composition processes might need to be adapted and further material information might need to be exported. For preview rendering purposes, we used the Phong reflection model and used the same output textures for a high-quality rendering in a DCC tool (see Figure 23.1). The initial material on the surface is already visually represented in the original diffuse texture. Thus, for compositing we only need to consider the amount of newly added material by taking the difference between the currently present material $\mathbf{m}_{curr}$ and the initial material $\mathbf{m}_{init}$. To assemble the resulting diffuse color, we blend the original surface texture with color textures $\mathbf{s}_i$ representing the individual material types (see Figure 23.10, center). The appearance pattern of the deposited material color $\mathbf{c}_{deposit}$ is controlled by a base strength b_i and a random variation v_i:

$$\mathbf{c}_{deposit} = \sum_i \max(0, \mathbf{m}_{curr,i} - \mathbf{m}_{init,i}) \cdot \mathbf{s}_i \cdot (b_i + v_i \cdot \xi_i),$$

whereas ξ_i denotes a uniformly distributed random number. This allows modeling a wider range of appearances, including homogeneous patina of copper or noisy rust stains on iron surfaces.

The resulting diffuse color is computed by the weighted sum of the deposited colors of all material types:

$$\mathbf{c}_{diffuse} = \mathrm{lerp}\left(\mathbf{c}_{org}, \mathbf{c}_{deposit}, \mathrm{saturate}\left(\sum_i (b_i + v_i \cdot \xi_i)\right)\right).$$

The shininess is estimated similarly, leaving out the color textures. The height map is computed based on the amount of material resting on the surface, which is then used in a second pass to estimate surface normals from neighboring texels. The parameters of the composition can be changed during or after the simulation.

23.4   Preview Rendering

Once the weathered textures are composed, we can start with the preview rendering, which serves two purposes: First, it is a preview for the eventually employed renderer, thus needs to resemble it closely. Ideally, the simulation system should be integrated into a content creation system, running on top of the eventually used rendering engine. For our demo, we render the scene with forward shading and apply the output textures from the composition stage, i.e., the aged color, normals, height, and shininess. Second, the preview rendering needs to make the amounts of material visible to give the content artist feedback. Therefore, we use distance-dependent tessellation and displacement mapping to display the height and place billboards to visualize lichen growth.

```
float dtf(float3 pos)   // distance-dependent tess factor
{
  return lerp(g_MinTessFactor, g_MaxTessFactor,
    smoothstep(g_MinTessDist, g_MaxTessDist, dist(g_Eye, pos)));
}

HS__CONSTANT__DATA ConstantHS(in InputPatch<float3, 3> Pos,
  out float Edges[3] : SV_TessFactor,
  out float Inside[1] : SV_InsideTessFactor)
{
  HS__CONSTANT__DATA output;
  // compute tessellation factors for each vertex
  float3 tess = float3(dtf(Pos[0]), dtf(Pos[1]), dtf(Pos[2]));

  // set factors for the edges and the interior
  Edges[0] = max(tess.y, tess.z);
  Edges[1] = max(tess.x, tess.z);
  Edges[2] = max(tess.x, tess.y);
  Inside[0] = max(tess.x, Edges[0]);
}

[domain("tri")]
PS_INPUT DomainShader( HS__CONSTANT__DATA input,
  float3 UV : SV_DomainLocation,
  const OutputPatch<DS_INPUT, 3> controlPnt )
{
  // Barycentric interpolation of control points
  float3 outPos = controlPnt[0].Pos * UV.x
                + controlPnt[1].Pos * UV.y
                + controlPnt[2].Pos * UV.z;

  /* Barycentric interpolation of normal, tangents, ... */
  /* Displace surface point outPos in normal direction ... */

  return PS_INPUT(outPos, normal, tangents, ...);
}
```

Listing 23.9. We employ distance-dependent tessellation in the preview rendering to display the amount of material on the surface by displacement mapping.

23.4.1   Displaying Height

Tessellation shaders allow for adaptive subdivision of the surface geometry by introducing two new shader stages after the vertex shader: a hull and a domain shader. The hull shader is typically used to perform calculations for each control point of a surface patch. In our case, both the vertex and hull shader by-pass positions, normals, and texture coordinates. The function `ConstantHS` in Listing 23.9 is executed once per control patch to compute the distance-dependent tessellation factors. Based on these factors, a fixed-function tessellation engine subdivides the patches. The domain shader is executed for each vertex of the refined mesh and is used to interpolate properties from the control points, i.e., positions, normals, tangents, and so on. Additionally, we apply a vertex displacement by the value in the height map, which originates in the amount of material on the surface. Eventually, the pixel shader shades the surface using normal mapping.

23.4.2   Displaying Lichen

To visualize the spread of lichen, we place and scale plantlet billboards according to the concentration of organic material, shown in Figure 23.11. To maintain a constant number of plantlets we randomly reseed them to adapt to the current organic distribution in the scene. Thereby, each gammaton is responsible for one plantlet, see function `plantletPlacement` in Listing 23.10, as called from the closest hit program in Listing 23.3. For the billboards we expand the quads in view space using a geometry shader.

 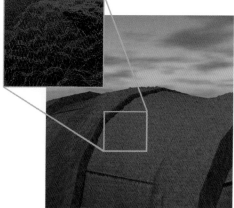

Figure 23.11. Depictions of the intermediate output. Left: plantlets distributed in regions of high lichen growth. Right: Distance-dependent tessellation with displacement mapping, depending on the amount of rust and organic material. *[Appeared in [Günther et al. 12] and reproduced by kind permission of the Eurographics Association.]*

```
// Data stored per plantlet (shared between DirectX and OptiX)
struct PlantletShared {
  float3 Position;     // Position of the plantlet.
  uint RayIndex;       // Used to select texture.
  float2 AtlasCoord;   // Atlas coordinate of the plantlet.
};

void plantletPlacement(int rndSeed, float3 pos, float2 texcoord)
{
  if (rnd(rndSeed) < g_SeedProbability) {
    PlantletShared& plantlet = PlantletShared[prd.ray_index];
    plantlet.Position = pos;
    plantlet.RayIndex = prd.ray_index;
    plantlet.AtlasCoord = texcoord;
  }
}
```

Listing 23.10. CUDA device function for placing plantlets.

23.5 Results

The polishing of textures to attain weathered looks is a building brick in most content creation pipelines, one that was previously subject to manual processing alone. In Figure 23.12, we show a time series of our aging simulation and for Figure 23.1 we exported the composed textures and rendered the scenes in a standard DCC tool.

Our system presents intermediate output and allows for interactive modification of parameters (simulation, aging rules, composition, etc.) and the interactive movement of gammaton sources. Timing results are given in Table 23.1 for an Intel Core i7-2600K CPU and an Nvidia GeForce GTX 560 Ti GPU. The composition is the slowest component, though optional to the simulation pipeline. It may be broken down, to be carried out over a span of multiple frames in order to adjust to the narrow time budget of real-time applications, e.g., modern games.

Step	Chest	Hydrant	Otto
Simulation Step	2.57	1.72	2.25
Surface Update	0.03	0.03	0.03
Gammaton Update	0.03	0.03	0.03
Aging Process	0.25	0.25	0.25
Composition	7.19	7.11	7.01
Preview Rendering	2.32	2.08	1.82
Total Time	12.39	11.22	11.39

Table 23.1. Timing breakdown in milliseconds for the pipeline stages at an atlas resolution of 1K × 1K, 5K gammatons per iteration and a screen resolution of 800 × 800 pixels.

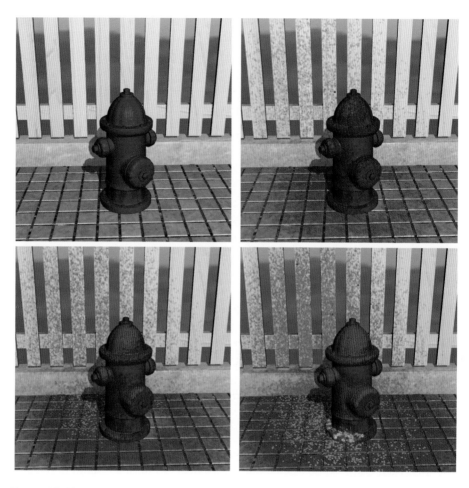

Figure 23.12. Aging of a selected part of the hydrant scene, shown at different time steps. *[Appeared in [Günther et al. 12] and reproduced by kind permission of the Euro-graphics Association.]*

Further discussions on user interface decisions, the impact of the atlas resolution on memory consumption and visual quality, as well as texture seam handling can be found in our paper [Günther et al. 12].

23.6   Conclusions

In this chapter, we presented an interactive material aging simulation based on gammaton tracing on the GPU. We used a simple yet powerful set of rules to obtain the most common aging effects, including dirt, rust, organic, and water precipitate, and displayed those in a few seconds in which the scene progressively and visibly ages. Open for further investigation is the simulation on large scenes. For now, our approach is limited to a few objects chosen by the content artist as a region of interest, since the memory consumption limits the material atlas size and thus the visual quality. A number of extensions to our approach are imaginable. If more memory was available, e.g., by compression, it would be possible to add multiple layers of material, not only one as we do now. Related to this is the gradual peeling of layers [Paquette et al. 02], possibly initiating a more distinctive deformation of the surface, which could go beyond the capabilities of a single-pass tessellation shader. Another direction to look into is the implementation of a more detailed temporal aging behavior, since many materials are subject to a nonlinear aging process [Gu et al. 06]. On the GPU, discrete time steps could be easily encoded in a 3D texture, whereas the third dimension is time.

Bibliography

[Chen et al. 05] Yanyun Chen, Lin Xia, Tien-Tsin Wong, Xin Tong, Hujun Bao, Baining Guo, and Heung-Yeung Shum. "Visual Simulation of Weathering by Gammaton tracing." *ACM Transactions on Graphics* 24:3 (2005), 1127–1133.

[Gu et al. 06] Jinwei Gu, Chien-I Tu, Ravi Ramamoorthi, Peter Belhumeur, Wojciech Matusik, and Shree Nayar. "Time-varying Surface Appearance: Acquisition, Modeling and Rendering." *ACM Transactions on Graphics* 25:3 (2006), 762–771.

[Günther et al. 12] Tobias Günther, Kai Rohmer, and Thorsten Grosch. "GPU-Accelerated Interactive Material Aging." In *Proceedings of the Vision, Modeling and Visualization Workshop 2012*, pp. 63–70. Genevea: Eurographics Association, 2012.

[Paquette et al. 02] Eric Paquette, Pierre Poulin, and George Drettakis. "The Simulation of Paint Cracking and Peeling." In *Graphics Interface 2002*, pp. 59–68. Natick, MA: Canadian Human-Computer Communications Society and A K Peters, Ltd., 2002.

[Parker et al. 10] Steven G Parker, James Bigler, Andreas Dietrich, Heiko Friedrich, Jared Hoberock, David Luebke, David McAllister, and Martin Stich. "OptiX: A General Purpose Ray Tracing Engine." *ACM Transactions on Graphics* 29:4 (2010), 1–13.

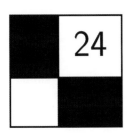

Simple
Rasterization-Based Liquids
Martin Guay

24.1 Overview

Rasterization pipelines are ubiquitous today. They can be found in most of our personal computers as well as in smaller, hand-held devices—like smart phones—with lower-end hardware. However, simulating particle-based liquids requires sorting the particles, which is cumbersome when using a rasterization pipeline.

In this chapter, we describe a method to simulate liquids *without* having to sort the particles. Our method was specifically designed for these architectures and low shader model specifications (starting from shader model 3 for 3D liquids). Instead of sorting the particles, we splat them onto a grid (i.e., a 3D or 2D texture) and solve the inter-particle dynamics *directly* on the grid. Splatting is simple to perform in a rasterization pipeline, but can also be costly. Thanks to the simplified pass on the grid, we only need to splat the particles once.

The grid also provides additional benefits: we can easily add artificial obstacles for the particles to interact with, we can ray cast the grid directly to render the liquid surface, and we can even gain a speed up over sort-based liquid solvers—such as the optimized solver found in the DirectX 11 SDK.

24.2 Introduction

Simulating liquids requires dealing with two phases of *fluid*—the liquid and the air—which can be tricky to model as special care may be required for the interface between the two phases depending on the fluid model. In computer graphics, there are mainly two popular formulations for *fluids*: strongly incompressible and weakly incompressible.

The strong formulation is usually more complex as it requires a hard constraint (e.g., solving a Poisson equation), but it is more accurate and therefore more visually pleasing. Because it is more complex, it is often used along simple, regular *grid* discretizations [Stam 99]. For liquids, several intermediate steps are required for the surface to behave adequately [Enright et al. 02]. Implementing these steps using rasterization APIs is challenging. For instance, [Crane et al. 07] only partially implements them and the fluid behaves more like a single phase fluid. Furthermore, the strong formulation requires a surface representation like a *level-set* density field, which requires its own set of specificities (re-initialization). Again, in [Crane et al. 07] the level-set method is only partially implemented and had to be hacked into staying at a certain height; preventing them from generating such scenarios as the water jet shown in Figure 24.3.

The weak formulation on the other hand, requires only a simple soft constraint to keep the fluid from compressing. It is much simpler, but also less accurate. It is often used along particle discretizations and *mesh-free* numerical schemes like *Smooth Particles Hydrodynamics* (SPH) [Desbrun and Cani 96]. The advantage of the weak formulation along particles is really for liquids. This combination allowed reproducing the behavior of liquids without computing any surface boundary conditions similar to [Enright et al. 02]. Additionally, the particles can be used directly to render the liquid surface and there is no need for a level-set. The drawback however, is that particles require finding their neighbors, in order to compute forces ensuring they keep at a minimal distance. Typically buckets or other spacial sorting algorithms are used to cluster the particles into groups [Amada et al. 04, Rozen et al. 08, Bayraktar et al. 08], which can be cumbersome to implement using rasterization APIs.

Instead of sorting the particles, our method makes use of rasterization capabilities. First, we rasterize, or splat, the particle density onto a grid. Then, we use simple finite difference to compute all the interacting forces—including the soft incompressibility constraint—on the grid, in a single pass. Some have considered splatting before [Kolb and Cuntz 05] but had to splat for each force (*pressure and viscosity*), while we only need to splat once—for all the forces. Finally, the particles are corrected and moved by sampling the grid—which in turn can also be used *directly* to render the liquid surface by ray casting the splatted *density*. Overall, our method allows treating each particle independently while making sure they automatically repulse one another and avoid rigid obstacles in the domain.

24.3   Simple Liquid Model

Our liquid model is best described as follows: particles are allowed to move freely in the domain while their mass and kinetic energy remains conserved. For instance, if we add gravity it should translate into velocity $\mathbf{u}$. To keep the particles from interpenetrating, we add a soft incompressibility constraint P derived from the density ρ of particles and the resulting force is the negative gradient of P:

$$\frac{D\rho}{Dt} = 0,$$

$$\frac{D\mathbf{u}}{Dt} = -\nabla P + \mathbf{g} + \mathbf{f}_{\text{ext}}, \tag{24.1}$$

where $\mathbf{g}$ gravity and $\mathbf{f}_{\text{ext}}$ accounts for external forces such as user interactions. The terms $\frac{D\rho}{Dt}$ and $\frac{D\mathbf{u}}{Dt}$ account for the transport of density and velocity. There is never any density added nor removed, it is only transported and held by the particles leading to $\frac{D\rho}{Dt} = 0$. Energy added to the velocity—like gravity—needs to be conserved as well, resulting in equation (24.1). Next we define the incompressibility constraint P and how to compute the density of particles ρ.

24.3.1 Pressure Constraint

To keep the fluid from compressing and the particles from inter-penetrating, we penalize high density: $P = k\rho$ [Desbrun and Cani 96], where k is a stiffness parameter that makes the particles repulse one another more strongly (but can also make the simulation unstable if too large). Hence, by minimizing the density, the particles will move in the direction that reduces density the most and thereby avoid each other. At the same time, gravity and boundary conditions, like the walls, will act to keep the particles from simply flying away.

Keeping the particles from inter-penetrating is crucial in particle-based liquid simulations. To give strict response to the particles that are close to colliding, we can make the density nonlinear leading to the pressure constraint [Becker and Teschner 07]: $P = k \left(\frac{\rho}{\rho_0} \right)^\gamma$, where γ is an integer (5 in our case). Dividing by the initial density ρ_0 comes in handy for stability; it becomes easier to control the magnitude of the force through the parameter k and thereby keep the simulation stable.

Setting the initial ρ_0 can be tricky. It should be a proportional evaluation of ρ at an initial rest configuration, i.e., with a uniform distribution of particles. In practice, however, we can set it manually. We approximate ρ by performing a convolution, which we pre-compute on a texture by rasterizing, or splatting the kernels of each particle.

24.4 Splatting

To evaluate the density of particles smoothly, we perform a convolution: the density is the weighted average of the surrounding discrete samples, in this case the particles. The weight is given by a kernel function, which falls off exponentially with distance, as shown in Figure 24.1. Instead of sampling the nearby particles,

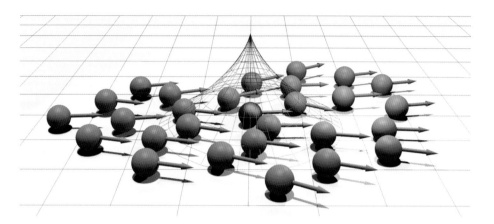

Figure 24.1. Splatting consists in *rasterizing* the smooth kernel function, the 2D case shown here in red. In Figure 24.2, we see the sum of all the kernel functions; a scalar field representing the density of particles.

Figure 24.2. Illustrating the scalar density field used to define the pressure constraint. The pressure force is proportional to the density gradient pushing the particles toward minimum density. For simplicity, we show the idea in 2D with density shown as a height field—which can also be used as the liquid surface in *Shallow Water* simulations (see Figure 24.4).

we rasterize the kernel function centered at each particle. The final result is a smooth density grid (texture)—like the one shown in Figure 24.2—that is equivalent to a convolution evaluation at each point on the texture. We could say also that we now have a virtual particle on each grid cell.

24.4.1 Rasterizing Kernel Functions

To update the velocity on the grid, we need to transfer both the density of the particles—to compute pressure—and their velocity. Hence, the first step in our algorithm is to rasterize the smooth kernel function (red in Figure 24.1) and the weighted velocity of each particle. We render the particles as points and create quad slices—spanning a cube—in the geometry shader. For each corner vertex $\mathbf{x}_i$, we write the distance $d = \|\mathbf{x}_i - \mathbf{x}_p\|$ to the center of the particle $\mathbf{x}_p$, and let the rasterizer perform the interpolation between vertices. Then, in a pixel shader, we render the smooth kernel value $w(d, r)$ to the alpha channel, and the weighted velocity $w(d, r)\mathbf{u}_p$ to the other three channels—in an additive fashion. Finally, the density on the grid can be sampled by multiplying the sum of kernel weights by the mass, and the velocity by dividing the sum of weighted velocities by the sum of weights:

$$\rho(\mathbf{x}_i) = m_i \sum_p w\left(\|\mathbf{x}_i - \mathbf{x}_p\|, r\right), \qquad \mathbf{u}(\mathbf{x}_i) = \frac{\sum_p w\left(\|\mathbf{x}_i - \mathbf{x}_p\|, r\right) \mathbf{u}_p}{\sum_p w\left(\|\mathbf{x}_i - \mathbf{x}_p\|, r\right)},$$

where i denotes texture indices, p particle indices, and r the kernel radius. We used the following convolution kernel:

$$w(d, r) = \left(1 - \frac{d^2}{r^2}\right)^3.$$

Next we update the velocity field on the grid to make the particles move in a direction that keeps them from compressing, by computing a pressure force from the density of particles and adding it to the velocity.

24.5 Grid Pass

In the grid pass, we update the splatted velocity field with the pressure force, gravity, and artificial pressure for obstacles (see Section 24.7). We compute the pressure gradient using a finite difference approximation and add forces to the velocity field using forward Euler integration:

$$\mathbf{u}^{n+1} = \mathbf{u}^n - \Delta t \left(\frac{P(x_{i+1}) - P(x_{i-1})}{\Delta x}, \frac{P(x_{j+1}) - P(x_{j-1})}{\Delta y}\right),$$

where Δt is the time step, Δx the spatial resolution of grid, and n the temporal state of the simulation.

While we update the velocity, we set the velocity on the boundary cells of the grid to a no-slip boundary condition by setting the component of the velocity that is normal to the boundary to 0. This is a simple boundary test; before writing the final velocity value, we check if the neighbor is a boundary and set the component of the velocity in that direction to 0.

24.6 Particle Update

We update the position and velocity of particles following the Particle-In-Cell (PIC) and Fluid-In-Particle (FLIP) approaches that mix particles and grids [Zhu and Bridson 05]. The main idea with these numerical schemes is that instead of sampling the grid to assign new values (e.g., velocities) to the particles, we can recover only the differences to their original values.

24.6.1 Particle Velocity

In PIC, the particle's velocity is taken directly from the grid, which tends to be very dissipative, viscous and leads to damped flow. For more lively features and better energy conservation, FLIP assigns only the *difference* in velocities; the difference between the splatted velocity and the updated splatted velocity discussed in Section 24.5.

By combining both PIC and FLIP, the liquid can be made very viscous like melting wax, or it can be made very energetic like water. A parameter r lets the user control the amount of each:

$$\mathbf{u}_p = r\mathbf{u}^{n+1}(\mathbf{x}_p) + (1 - r)(\mathbf{u}_p - \Delta\mathbf{u}), \quad \text{with} \quad \Delta\mathbf{u} = \mathbf{u}^n(\mathbf{x}_p) \quad \mathbf{u}^{n+1}(\mathbf{x}_p),$$

where $\mathbf{u}^n$ and $\mathbf{u}^{n+1}$ are grid velocities before and after the velocity update in Section 24.5, and $\mathbf{x}_p, \mathbf{u}_p$ are the particle's position and velocity. Using a bit of PIC ($r = 0.05$) is useful in stabilizing the simulation performed with explicit Euler integration, which can become unstable if the time step is too large.

24.6.2 Particle Position

While we update the particle velocity, we also update the particle positions. We integrate the particle position using two intermediate steps of Runge-Kutta 2 (RK2), each time sampling the velocity on the grid. The second-order scheme is only approximate in our case because the velocity field on the grid is kept constant during integration. At each intermediate step, we keep the particles from leaving the domain by clamping their positions near the box boundaries:

$$\mathbf{x}_p^{n+1} = \Delta t\mathbf{u}^{n+1}(\mathbf{x}_p^{n+\frac{1}{2}}), \quad \text{with} \quad \mathbf{x}_p^{n+\frac{1}{2}} = 0.5\Delta t\mathbf{u}^{n+1}(\mathbf{x}_p^n).$$

Note that we never modify the density value of the particles.

24.7 Rigid Obstacles

We can prevent the particles from penetrating rigid obstacles in the domain by adding an artificial pressure constraint where the objects are. This follows the same logic as with the particle density. We define a smooth distance field to the surface of the object, which can also be viewed as a density field. We can use analytical functions for primitives like spheres to approximate the shape of the objects. This avoids rasterizing volumes or voxelizing meshes on the GPU. Alternatively, one could approximate shapes using *Metaballs* [Blinn 82] and implicit surfaces that naturally provide a distance field. No matter which approach we choose, the gradient of these distance fields ρ_{Obstacle} can be computed analytically or numerically and plugged into the velocity update formula covered in Section 24.5.

When looking at the Shallow Water Equations (SWE), we find similarities with the equations outlined in this chapter. In fact, by looking at the density field as the height field of a liquid surface, we can imagine using our method directly for height field simulations shown in Figure 24.4. On the other hand, there is usually a ground height term in the SWE. This in turn can be interpreted in 3D as a distance field for rigid objects as we mentioned above.

24.8 Examples

We show a few simulation examples implemented with HLSL, compiled as level 4 shaders. They include a 3D liquid with rigid objects in the domain, a 2D shallow water height field simulation, and a 2D simulation comparing with the optimized Direct Compute implementation of SPH available in the DirectX 11 SDK. Measures include both simulation and rendering. We splat particles with a radius of 3 cells on 16-bit floating point textures without any significant loss in visual quality. In general we used a grid size close to $\sqrt[d]{N_{\text{P}}}$ texels per axis, where d is the domain dimension (2 or 3) and N_P is the total number of particles.

In Figure 24.3, we rendered the fluid surface by raycasting the density directly. We perform a fixed number of steps and finish with an FXAA antialiasing pass (framebuffer size 1024×768). We used 125k particles on a 96^3 texture and the

Figure 24.3. A 3D liquid simulation with obstacles in the domain implemented using the rasterization pipeline. The simulation runs at 35 FPS using 125k particles on a Quadro 2000M graphics card.

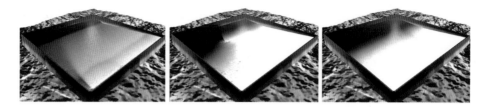

Figure 24.4. The shallow water equations describe the evolution of water height over time. By looking at the height as the density of a 2D fluid, we see the equations becoming similar. Hence, our method can be used directly to simulate height fields. This figure shows a SWE simulation with 42k particles using our method.

simulation performs at 35 frames per second (FPS) on a Quadro 2000M graphics card.

In Figure 24.4, we see a shallow water simulation using 42k particles on a 256^2 grid. The simulation and rendering together run at 130 FPS using the same graphics card.

We compared our solver *qualitatively* with the SPH GPU implementation in the DirectX 11 SDK (Figure 24.5). Their solver is implemented using the Direct Compute API, has shared memory optimizations and particle neighbor search acceleration. Ours uses HLSL shaders only. In Table 24.1, we compare the performance of both methods with different particle quantities. We can see that our method scales better with the number of particles involved for a given grid size and splatting radius on the hardware we used.

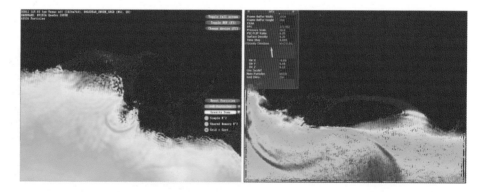

Figure 24.5. Comparison between an optimized SPH solver implemented with Compute Shaders on the left and our method implemented with rasterization APIs. Our method performs at 296 FPS using while the optimized SPH solver runs at 169 FPS.

Particle Amount	Grid Size Dim(ϕ, u)	Our Method (FPS)	DX SDK 11 (FPS)	Speedup Ratio
64,000	256^2	296	169	1.75
32,000	256^2	510	325	1.55
16,000	256^2	830	567	1.45

Table 24.1. Comparison between our method and the optimized SPH solver found in the DirectX 11 SDK.

24.9 Conclusion

In *GPU Pro 2*, we described the \$1 fluid solver: by combining the simplicity of weakly incompressible fluids with the simplicity of grids, we could simulate a single phase fluid (smoke or fire) in a single pass [Guay et al. 11]. In this chapter, we described the \$1 liquid solver for rasterization APIs by combining the simplicity of the particles for dealing with liquids with the simplicity of the grids to compute the forces. This is useful in getting a liquid solver running quickly on platforms that do not necessarily implement compute APIs.

Bibliography

[Amada et al. 04] T. Amada, M. Imura, Y. Yasumoto, Y. Yamabe, and K. Chihara. "Particle-Based Fluid Simulation on GPU." In *ACM Workshop on General-Purpose Computing on Graphics Processors*, pp. 228–235. New York: ACM, 2004.

[Bayraktar et al. 08] S. Bayraktar, U. Güdükbay, and B. Özgüç. "GPU-Based Neighbor-Search Algorithm for Particle Simulations." *Journal of Graphics, GPU, and Game Tools* 14:1 (2008), 31–42.

[Becker and Teschner 07] M. Becker and M. Teschner. "Weakly compressible SPH for free surface flows." In *Proceedings of the 2007 ACM SIGGRAPH/Eurographics Symposium on Computer Animation*, pp. 209–218. Aire-la-Ville, Switzerland: Eurographics Association, 2007.

[Blinn 82] J. F. Blinn. "A Generalization of Algebraic Surface Drawing." *ACM Transactions on Graphics (TOG)* 1:3 (1982), 235–256.

[Crane et al. 07] K. Crane, I. Llamas, and S. Tariq. "Real-Time Simulation and Rendering of 3D Fluids." In *GPU Gems 3*, edited by Hubert Nguyen. Upper Saddle River, NJ: Addison-Wesley, 2007.

[Desbrun and Cani 96] M. Desbrun and M.P. Cani. "Smoothed Particles: A New Paradigm for Animating Highly Deformable Bodies." In *Proceedings of*

Eurographics Workshop on Computer Animation and Simulation, pp. 61–76. New York: Springer, 1996.

[Enright et al. 02] D. Enright, S. Marschner, and R. Fedkiw. "Animation and Rendering of Complex Water Surfaces." In *Proceedings of the 29th Annual Conference on Computer Graphics and Interactive Techniques (SIGGRAPH '02)*, pp. 736–744. New York: ACM, 2002.

[Guay et al. 11] M. Guay, F. Colin, and R. Egli. "Simple and Fast Fluids." In *GPU Pro 2*, edited by Wolfgang Engel, pp. 433–444. Natick, MA: A K Peters, Ltd., 2011.

[Kolb and Cuntz 05] A. Kolb and N. Cuntz. "Dynamic Particle Coupling for GPU-Based Fluid Simulation." Presentation, Symposium on Simulation Technique, Wuppertal, Germany, March, 2005.

[Rozen et al. 08] T. Rozen, K. Boryczko, and W. Alda. "GPU Bucket Sort Algorithm with Applications to Nearest-Neighbour Search." *Journal of the 16th Int. Conf. in Central Europe on Computer Graphics, Visualization and Computer Vision* 16:1-3 (2008), 161–167.

[Stam 99] J. Stam. "Stable Fluids." In *Proceedings of the 26th ACM SIGGRAPH Conference*, pp. 121–128. New York: ACM Press, 1999.

[Zhu and Bridson 05] Y. Zhu and R. Bridson. "Animating Sand as a Fluid." In *Proceedings of ACM SIGGRAPH 2005*, pp. 965–972. New York: ACM, 2005.

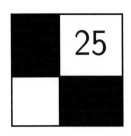

Next-Generation Rendering
in Thief
Peter Sikachev, Samuel Delmont, Uriel Doyon, and
Jean-Normand Bucci

25.1 Introduction

In this chapter we present the rendering techniques used in *Thief*, which was developed by Eidos Montreal for PC, Playstation 3, Playstation 4, Xbox 360, and Xbox One. Furthermore, we concentrate solely on techniques, developed exclusively for the next-generation platforms, i.e., PC, Playstation 4, and Xbox One.

We provide the reader with implementation details and our experience on a range of rendering methods. In Section 25.2, we discuss our reflection rendering system. We describe each tier of our render strategy as well as final blending and postprocessing.

In Section 25.3, we present a novel contact-hardening shadow (CHS) approach based on the AMD CHS sample. Our method is optimized for Shader Model 5.0 and is capable of rendering high-quality large shadow penumbras at a relatively low cost. Section 25.4 describes our approach toward lit transparent particles rendering.

Compute shaders (CSs) are a relatively new feature in graphics APIs, introduced first in the DirectX 11 API. We have been able to gain substantial benefits for postprocessing using CSs. We expound upon our experience with CSs in Section 25.5.

Performance results are presented in the end of each section. Finally, we conclude and indicate further research directions in Section 25.6.

25.2   Reflections

Reflections rendering has always been a tricky subject for game engines. As long as the majority of games are rasterization based, there is no cheap way to get correct reflections rendered in the most general case. That being said, several methods for real-time reflection rendering produce plausible results in special cases.

25.2.1   Related Methods

One of the first reflection algorithms used for real-time applications, was real-time planar reflection (RTPR) rendering [Lengyel 11]. This method yields an accurate solution for geometry reflected over a plane and is typically used for water or mirror reflections. The method involves rendering objects, or proxies of them, as seen through the reflection plane. Depending on the number of things rendered in the reflection scene, it is possible to balance performance and quality, but the technique is generally considered to be expensive. The main drawback of this method is that in practice, several planes of different heights and orientations would be required to model correctly the environment view surrounding the player, which would be unacceptably expensive to process. This prevents the technique from being used across a wide range of environments.

Cube map reflections are another approach that has been used for many years [NVIDIA Corporation 99]. Though they are very fast and they can handle nonplanar objects, cube maps have their limitations, too. They usually lack resolution and locality compared to other techniques. One also usually needs to precompute cube maps in advance, as it is usually prohibitively expensive to generate cube maps dynamically at runtime. This could additionally complicate an asset pipeline. Precomputed cube maps will not reflect a change in lighting or dynamic objects. Moreover, cube maps do not produce high-quality reflections when applied to planar surfaces, which was one of our main scenarios.

Screen-space reflection (SSR) is a relatively new technique that has grown quickly in popularity [Uludag 14]. It has a moderate performance cost and is easy to integrate. Moreover, it provides great contact reflections (i.e., reflections that occur when an object stands on a reflecting surface; these reflections "ground" an object) hardly achieved by other techniques. However, SSR is prone to numerous artifacts and fails to reflect invisible (or offscreen) parts of a scene. Therefore, it is usually used in combination with some backup technique.

Image-based reflection (IBR) is a method that utilizes planar proxies in order to approximate complex geometries to accelerate ray tracing [Wright 11]. It was developed and shown off in the Unreal Engine 3 *Samaritan* demo. IBR can achieve good results in reflection locality and allows an arbitrary orientation of a reflector. However, the complexity grows linearly with the number of proxies, which could become prohibitive for large scenes.

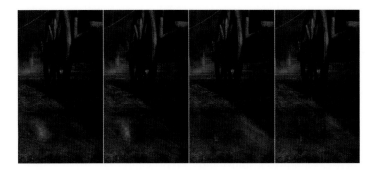

Figure 25.1. From left to right: cube map reflections only, SSR + cube maps, IBR + cube maps, and SSR + IBR + cube maps. [Image courtesy Square Enix Ltd.]

Numerous variations of the methods discussed above have been proposed and used in real-time rendering. For instance, localized, or parallax-corrected cube maps [Lagarde and Zanuttini 13] are arguably becoming an industry standard. In the next sections, we will describe the reflection system we used in *Thief*.

25.2.2   Thief Reflection System Overview

Creating a reflection system that perfectly handles every surface type, in real time, is a very difficult problem. Therefore, together with the art department, we developed a specification of requirements and limitations for the *Thief* reflection system. Given that *Thief* was originally designed for the Xbox 360 and Playstation 3 generation of platforms, we had quite a generous performance budget for the reflection system on the next-generation platforms: 5 ms. Beforehand, we implemented the real-time planar reflection method, which ran at 10 ms. This running time was obviously unacceptable; moreover, this technique could render reflections for only one plane.

The majority of reflections in the game world come from the ground (wet spots, tile, etc.), therefore we limited ourselves to quasi-horizontal surfaces. However, since *Thief* is a multilevel game (e.g., you can make your way across rooftops instead of streets), unlike [Lagarde and Zanuttini 13], we could not be limited to a single reflection plane. As mentioned above, we performed tests with PRTR and the single reflection plane limitation was insufficient for our assets.

The target was to accurately capture human-sized objects and contact reflections. In addition, we also wanted to capture principal landmarks (e.g., large buildings). Finally, as torches and bonfires are a typical light source in the world of *Thief*, we needed a way to render reflection from certain transparent geometry as well.

To achieve these goals, we came up with a multitier reflection system, outlined in Figure 25.1. The reflection system of *Thief* consists of the following tiers:

- screen-space reflections (SSR) for opaque objects, dynamic and static, within a human height of a reflecting surface;

- image-based reflections (IBR) for walls and far away landmarks;

- localized cube map reflections to fill the gaps between IBR proxies;

- global cube map reflections, which are mostly for view-independent sky-boxes.

Each tier serves as a fallback solution to the previous one. First, SSR ray-marches the depth buffer. If it does not have sufficient information to shade a fragment (i.e., the reflected ray is obscured by some foreground object), it falls back to image-based reflection. If none of the IBR proxies are intersected by the reflection ray, the localized cube map reflection system comes into play. Finally, if no appropriate localized cube map is in proximity, the global cube map is fetched. Transition between different tiers is done via smooth blending, as described in Section 25.2.6.

25.2.3   Screen-Space Reflections

SSR is an image-based reflection technique based on ray-marching through the depth buffer [Kasyan et al. 11]. We use the lit color buffer, the normal buffer, and the depth buffer from the current frame. SSR is applied before rendering translucent geometry in order to avoid perspective artifacts.

At each fragment we reconstruct the camera-space position, using the screen uv-coordinates, the fetched depth, and the projection matrix. Afterward, we ray-march with a constant step along the reflected ray until the analytical depth of the fetch along the ray is more than the depth buffer fetch from the same screen-space position. Finally, the intersection location is refined with several binary search steps, as shown in Figure 25.2.

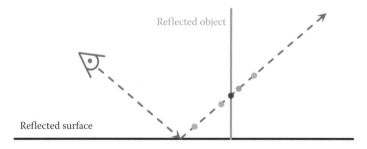

Figure 25.2. Screen-space reflections linear steps (green) and binary search steps (orange and then red).

This method yields very accurate reflections at the contact of a reflective surface and a reflected object. There are, however, several major issues with SSR. First, this method is very expensive: at each fragment we need to make several potentially uncoalesced (due to the discrepancy of reflection rays) texture fetches, some of which are even view-dependent (binary search). Second, reflected information is often missing: it's either out of screen or obscured by a closer object.

We address the first issue with several optimization techniques, described below in this subsection. The second issue is addressed by falling back to the subsequent tier of the reflection system.

We decrease the memory traffic by approximating the normal at the fragment with a normal pointing vertically up. This dramatically increases the number of texture fetches at neighboring fragments that might be coalesced and processed within a single dynamic random-access memory (DRAM) burst. However, this naturally results in ideal mirror-like reflections without any normal perturbation. We address this issue further in Section 25.2.7.

Moreover, we use dynamic branching to employ early exit for the constant step loop when the first intersection with the depth buffer is found. Although it might result in false ray-depth buffer collision detection, we compromise on accuracy in order to further save on bandwidth.

Another optimization is decreasing the number of samples for the distant fragments. We came up with an empirical formula that decreases the number of steps proportional to the exponent of the distance:

$$N_{\text{linear samples}} = \max(1, k_1 e^{-k_2 d}),$$

where depth is denoted with d, k_1 is the linear factor, and k_2 is the exponential factor.

Additionally, we use a bunch of early-outs for the whole shader. We check if the surface has a reflective component and if a reflection vector points to the camera. The latter optimization does not significantly deteriorate visual quality, as in these situations SSR rarely yields high-quality results anyway and the reflection factor due to the Fresnel equation is already low. Moreover, this reduces the SSR GPU time in the case when IBR GPU time is high, thus balancing the total.

However, one should be very careful when implementing such an optimization. All fetches inside the `if`-clause should be done with a forced mipmap level; all variables used after should be initialized with a meaningful default value, and the `if`-clause should be preceded with a `[branch]` directive. The reason is that a shader compiler might otherwise try to generate a gradient-requiring instruction (i.e., `tex2D`) and, therefore, flatten a branch, making the optimizations useless.

25.2.4 Image-Based Reflections

Image-based reflections are a reflection technique implemented in [Wright 11]. The key idea is to introduce one or more planar quad reflection proxies and pre-render an object of interest into it. During fragment shading, we just ray-trace the reflected ray against an array of proxies in the pixel shader. A similar idea is utilized in [Lagarde and Zanuttini 13]. However, in the latter, the reflections are rendered only for planes at a single height. Therefore, we were unable to use optimizations proposed in [Lagarde and Zanuttini 13].

In *Thief*, our ambition was to have around 50 IBR proxies per scene. IBR back-face culling effectively reduces the visible proxy count by half. A straightforward approach resulted in well over 8 ms of GPU time at the target configuration, which was totally unacceptable. Therefore, we employed a series of acceleration techniques, described below.

First, we utilized the same approach for normal approximation as for SSR to increase memory coalescing. This allowed the following optimizations:

- rejecting planes not facing the player,

- rejecting planes behind the player,

- tile-based IBR rendering (discussed below).

Bump perturbation was then performed for SSR and IBR together.

Second, we introduced tile-based IBR. Because we have limited ourselves to quasi-horizontal reflections, we divided the entire screen space into a number of vertical tiles. Our experiments have proven 16 tiles to be an optimal number. After that, for each reflection proxy, we calculate the screen-space coordinates for each vertex. If a vertex is in front of the near clip plane, we flip the w sign before perspective divide in order to handle close proxies. Then x-coordinates of the transformed vertices might be used as minimum and maximum values to determine the tiles covered by the proxy's reflection.

However, due to perspective projection, this method would result in reflections being cut, especially when a proxy approaches the screen borders. To fix that, we introduce the following workaround. For each of two vertical sides of the proxy, we extend them to the intersections with top and bottom screen borders as shown in Figure 25.3. The resultant x-coordinates are used to decrease the minimum and/or increase the maximum. The pseudocode of this method is shown in Algorithm 25.1.

The above mentioned optimization decreases GPU time dramatically; however, if a player looks straight down, all the proxies start occupying almost all tiles due to high perspective distortions. To alleviate performance drops in this case, we use a bounding sphere test in the pixel shader for an early-out before the actual high-cost tracing. While this check deteriorates the performance in the most common cases, it increases GPU performance in the worst cases, resulting in a more consistent frame rate.

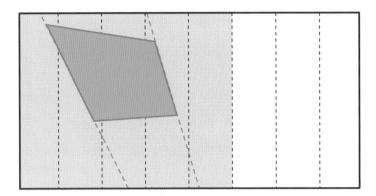

Figure 25.3. IBR tile-based rendering optimization. IBR proxy is shown in orange. Tiles are shown in dotted blue lines, and vertical sides extensions are shown in orange dotted lines. The affected tiles are shaded with thin red diagonal lines.

1: $x_{min} = 1$
2: $x_{max} = -1$
3: **for all** IBR proxies in front of player and facing player **do**
4:     find AABB of the current proxy
5:     **for all** vertices of AABB **do**
6:         calculate vertex coordinate in homogeneous clip space
7:         $w := |w|$
8:         calculate vertex coordinate in screen clip space
9:         $x_{min} := min(x, x_{min})$
10:         $x_{max} := max(x, x_{max})$
11:     **end for**
12:     **for all** vertical edges of AABB in screen space **do**
13:         calculate intersections x_1 and x_2 with top and bottom of the screen
14:         $x_{min} := min(x_1, x_2, x_{min})$
15:         $x_{max} := max(x_1, x_2, x_{max})$
16:     **end for**
17:     **for all** IBR tiles **do**
18:         **if** the tile overlaps with $[x_{min}, x_{max}]$ **then**
19:             add the proxy to the tile
20:         **end if**
21:     **end for**
22: **end for**

Algorithm 25.1. Algorithm for finding affected tiles for an IBR proxy.

Additionally, in order to limit the number of active IBR proxies in the frame, we introduced the notion of *IBR rooms*. Essentially, an IBR room defines an AABB so that a player can see IBR reflections only from the IBR proxies in

Figure 25.4. Non-glossy reflection rendering (left) and CHGR (right). [Image courtesy Square Enix Ltd.]

the same room. Moreover, the lower plane of an IBR room's AABB defines the maximum *reflection extension* of each of the proxies inside it. This allowed us to drastically limit the number of reflections when a player is looking down.

As a side note, *Thief* has a very dynamic lighting environment. In order to keep the IBR reflection in sync with the dynamic lights, IBR had to be scaled down based on the light intensity. This makes the IBR planes disappear from reflection when lights are turned off. Although this is inaccurate since the IBR textures are generated from the default lighting setup, it was not possible to know which parts of the plane were actually affected by dynamic lighting.

Also, IBRs were captured with particles and fog disabled. Important particles, like fire effects, were simulated with their own IBRs. Fog was added accordingly to the fog settings and the reflection distance after blending SSR and IBR.

25.2.5 Contact-Hardening Glossy Reflections

Because the majority of the reflecting surfaces in *Thief* are not perfect mirror reflectors, we decided to simulate glossy reflections. Glossy SSR reflections are not a new feature, having been first implemented in [Andreev 13]. We decided to take SSR a step further and render contact-hardening glossy reflections (CHGRs). An example of a CHGR is shown in Figure 25.4.

The main phenomena we wish to capture is that a reflection is sharpest near the contact point of the reflected object and the reflecting surface. The reflection grows more blurry as these two surfaces get farther away from each other.

The algorithm for CHGR rendering is as follows. First, we output the distance between the reflecting surface and the point where the reflected ray hits the reflected object. Because we want to limit the size of the render targets, we

```
//World-space unit is 1 centimeter
int distanceLo = int(worldSpaceDistance) % 256;
int distanceHi = int(worldSpaceDistance) / 256;

packedDistance = float2(float(distanceLo) / 255.0f,
                        float(distanceHi) / 255.0f);
```

Listing 25.1. Reflection distance packing.

```
float3 reflectedCameraToWorld =
    reflect(cameraToWorld, worldSpaceNormal);
float reflectionVectorLength =
    max(length(reflectedCameraToWorld), FP_EPSILON);
float worldSpaceDistance = 255.0f * (packedDistance.x +
                           256.0f * packedDistance.y) /
                           reflectionVectorLength;
...
//Reflection sorting and blending
...
float4 screenSpaceReflectedPosition =
    mul(float4(reflectedPosition, 1), worldToScreen);
screenSpaceReflectedPosition /= screenSpaceReflectedPosition.w;

ReflectionDistance = length(screenSpaceReflectedPosition.xy -
                           screenSpaceFragmentPosition.xy);
```

Listing 25.2. Reflection distance unpacking.

utilize R8G8B8A8 textures for color and depth information. As 8 bits does not provide enough precision for distance, we pack the distance in two 8-bit channels during the SSR pass, as shown in Listing 25.1.

The IBR pass unpacks the depth, performs blending, and then converts this world-space distance into screen-space distance as shown in Listing 25.2. The reason for this is twofold. First, the screen-space distance fits naturally into the [0, 1] domain. As we do not need much precision for the blurring itself, we can re-pack it into a single 8-bit value, ensuring a natural blending. Second, the screen-space distance provides a better cue for blur ratio: the fragments farther away from the viewer should be blurred less than closer ones, if both have the same reflection distance.

The second step is to dilate the distance information. For each region, we select the maximum distance of all the pixels covered by the area of our blur kernel. The reason for this is that the distance value can change suddenly from one pixel to the next (e.g., when a close reflection proxy meets a distant background pixel). We wish to blur these areas with the maximum blur coefficient from the corresponding area. This helps avoid sharp silhouettes of otherwise blurry objects. This problem is very similar to issues encountered with common depth-of-field rendering algorithms. In order to save on memory bandwidth, we apply a two-pass, separable dilation maximum filter. This provides us with an acceptable approximation.

Finally, we perform the blur with the adjustable separable kernel. In addition to selecting the Gaussian parameters based on the distance value, we also apply the following tricks. First, we ignore the samples with zero specular intensity in order to avoid bleeding at the silhouette of an object. This requires on-the-fly adjustment of the kernel in the shader. Second, we follow the same heuristic as in [Andersson 13], so we blur the image more in the vertical direction than in the horizontal direction, achieving more plausible visual results.

25.2.6   Reflection Blending

As our reflection system consists of several tiers, we need to define how we blend between them. In addition to the distance factor, our SSR pass also outputs a blending factor. This factor depends on the following:

- height (the longer we cast a reflection ray, the less contribution it makes),

- tracing accuracy (depth delta between the ray coordinate and the fetched depth),

- surface tilt (the more the surface normal diverges from vertical, the less SSR should contribute),

- Reflection ray going toward camera or out of screen.

Afterward, IBR is merged on top, outputting a cumulative blending factor. Finally, the cube map is applied. Figure 25.5 shows seamless blending between SSR and IBR.

Figure 25.5. SSR only (left) and SSR blended with IBR (right). [Image courtesy Square Enix Ltd.]

Figure 25.6. Reflection blending without sorting (left) and with sorting (right). [Image courtesy Square Enix Ltd.]

However, this approach causes certain problems in cases when a transparent IBR proxy is in front of the object that could be potentially reflected with SSR. Figure 25.6 shows the issue. To address this problem, instead of simply blending SSR and IBR, we perform layer sorting beforehand. We create a small (three to four entries) array of reflection layers in the IBR shader and inject SSR results into it as the first element. The array is kept sorted when we add every subsequent IBR trace result. Thus, we end up with the closest intersections only.

25.2.7 Bump as a Postprocess

As mentioned above, we assume that the normal is pointing up for SSR and IBR rendering in order to apply acceleration techniques. Furthermore, in order to reduce memory bandwidth, we render reflection at half resolution. Together, this diminishes high-frequency details, which are crucial for reflections, especially on highly bumped surfaces. To alleviate this, we apply a *bump* effect as a postprocess when upscaling the reflection buffer to full resolution.

The main idea is very similar to the generic refraction approach [Sousa 05]. We use the difference between the vertical normal and the per-pixel normal to offset the UV in the rendered reflection texture. To fight reflection leaking, we revert to the original fetch if the new fetch is significantly closer than the old one. Figure 25.7 shows the benefits of applying reflection bump.

25.2.8 Localized Cube Map Reflections

In the SSR, IBR, and cube map reflection strategies, the cube map would ideally only contain the skybox and some far away geometry since the playable environment would be mapped by IBR planes. In this situation, only one cube map would be required. In practice, the IBR planes have many holes and do not connect perfectly to each other. This is a consequence of how our IBR planes are generated using renderable textures.

Figure 25.7. Reflection without bump (left) and with bump as a postprocess (right). [Image courtesy Square Enix Ltd.]

When a reflected ray enters into one of these cracks and hits the skybox, it results in a bright contrast pixel because most *Thief* scenes typically use a skybox that is much brighter than the rest of the environment. To fix this, we used localized cube maps taken along the playable path. Any primitive within reach of a localized cube map would then use it in the main render pass as the reflected environment color.

Technically, the cube map could be mapped and applied in screen space using cube map render volumes, but we chose to simply output the cube map sample into a dedicated render target. This made the cube map material-bound and removed its dependency with the localized cube map mapping system.

The main render pass in *Thief* would output the following data for reflective primitives:

- material lit color (sRGB8),

- environment reflection color + diffuse lighting intensity (sRGB8),

- world normal + reflectivity (RGB8).

After generating the IBR and SSR half-resolution reflection texture, the final color is computed by adding SSR, IBR, and finally the environment reflection color (i.e., cube map color). If the material or platform does not support IBR/SSR, the color would simply be added to the material-lit color and the extra render targets are not needed.

Figure 25.8. Creation of the multiple volumes for covering the whole environment. [Image courtesy Square Enix Ltd.]

Note here that we needed the diffuse lighting intensity to additionally scale down the IBR and cube map color because they were captured with the default lighting setup, which could be very different from the current in-game lighting setup. This scale was not required for the SSR because it is real-time and accurate, while the IBR proxies and cube maps are precomputed offline.

25.2.9 Art Pipeline Implications

For each level in *Thief*, we set a default cube map. This one is used by all the geometry that has reflective materials. This cube map is pretty generic and reflects the most common area of the level.

We then identify the areas where we require a more precise cube map definition. The decision is often based on lighting conditions or the presence of water puddles. For an area that could benefit from a more precise cube map, artists add a localized cube map, which comes with its own scene capture preview sphere. This is shown in the Figure 25.8.

We then built our entire environment using these volumes that enhance the look of the level. After using a build process, we generated all the cube maps for the volumes created. Figure 25.9 shows the additional build process created with the different resources generated.

Thief's reflection systems strongly enhanced the visual quality and next-generation look of the game. It was deeply embedded into the artistic direction of the title. The water puddles, in particular, helped create the unique look our artists wanted for the game. This also contributed to the gameplay of *Thief*. Because light and shadows are so important to our gameplay, the reflective water puddles became an additional challenge the player must manage when trying to stay hidden in the shadows.

For *Thief*, we dedicated a budget of 5 ms for the reflection pipeline. Given the allocated budget and the production stage at which we pushed the data in, we had to make clever choices, sometimes using all available techniques and other times

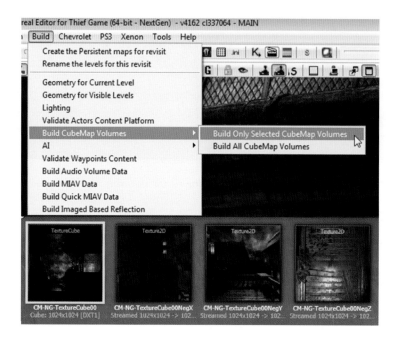

Figure 25.9. Build process generating the individual cube map captures. [Image courtesy Square Enix Ltd.]

using only one, given the rendering stresses of an environment. For example, certain environment condition might force us to use only one technique. Poor lighting condition could be a good example where you do not want to pay the extra cost of an expensive cube map or IBR planes.

We found that screen-space reflections were very easy for our art team to integrate. For this reason, we used SSR as our base tool for most of our reflection needs. This would then dictate where some of our IBR planes should go; it was a fallback solution when SSR failed.

25.2.10   Results

We came up with a robust and fast reflection system that is ready for the next-generation consoles. Both SSR and IBR steps take around 1–1.5 ms on Playstation 4 (1080p) and Xbox One (900p). However, these are worst case results, i.e., taken on a synthetic scene with an SSR surface taking up the whole screen and 50 IBR proxies visible. For a typical game scene, the numbers are usually lower than that. Reflection postprocessing is fairly expensive (around 2 ms). However, we did not have time to implement it using compute shaders, which could potentially save a lot of bandwidth.

Figure 25.10. Shadow with ordinary filtering (left) and with contact-hardening shadows (right). [Image courtesy Square Enix Ltd.]

Our reflection system does not support rough reflections. Taking into account the emerging interest in physically based rendering solutions, we are looking into removing this limitation. Reprojection techniques also look appealing both for quality enhancement and bandwidth reduction.

25.3 Contact-Hardening Shadows

Contact-hardening shadows (CHSs), similar to percentage-closer soft shadows (PCSSs) [Fernando 05], are a shadow-mapping method to simulate the dynamic shadows from area lights. The achieved effect is a sharper shadow as the shadow caster and the receiver are closer to each other and a blurrier (softer) shadow as the caster and the receiver are farther from each other (see Figure 25.10). The implementation in *Thief* is based on the method from the AMD SDK [Gruen 10].

This method is easy to integrate because it uses the shadow map generated by a single light source and can just replace ordinary shadow filtering. One of the main drawbacks in this technique is the extensive texture fetching, and in *Thief* we implemented an optimized method for Shader Model 5.0 that drastically limits the access to the shadow map. The CHS process is divided into three steps, which are the blocker search, the penumbra estimation, and the filtering.

25.3.1 Blocker Search

The first step consists of computing the average depth of the blockers inside a search region around the shaded point (that we will reference as *average blocker depth*). A kernel grid of $N \times N$ texels centered at the shaded point covers this search region. A blocker is a texel in the shadow map representing a point closer to the light than the currently computed fragment, as shown in Figure 25.11. This average-blocker-depth value will be used in the penumbra estimation.

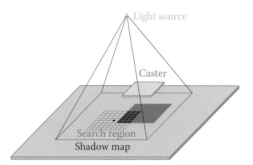

Figure 25.11. Blockers in a 8×8 search grid.

Shader Model 5.0's new intrinsic `GatherRed()` accelerates this step by sampling four values at once. In *Thief*, we decided to use a 8×8 kernel size, which actually performs 16 samples instead of 64 for a Shader Model 4.0 implementation (see Listing 25.4). Increasing the size of the kernel will allow a larger penumbra, since points that are farther from the shaded one can be tested, but it obviously increases the cost as the number of texture fetches grows.

Because the penumbra width (or blurriness) is tightly related to the size of the kernel, which depends on the shadow map resolution and its projection in world space, this leads to inconsistent and variable penumbra width when the shadow map resolution or the shadow frustum's FOV changes for the same light caster/receiver setup. Figure 25.12 shows the issue.

To fix this issue in *Thief*, we extended the CHS by generating mips for the shadow map in a prepass before the CHS application by downsizing it iteratively. Those downsizing operations are accelerated with the use of the `GatherRed()` intrinsic as well. Then, in the CHS step, we dynamically chose the mip that gives

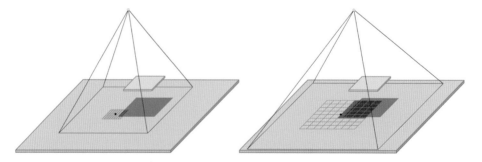

Figure 25.12. For the same 8×8 search grid, a smaller search region due to higher resolution shadow map (left) and a bigger search region due to wider shadow frustum (right).

```
#define KERNEL_SIZE 8
float wantedTexelSizeAt1UnitDist =
  wantedPenumbraWidthAt1UnitDist / KERNEL_SIZE;
float texelSizeAt1UnitDist =
  2*TanFOVSemiAngle/shadowMapResolution;
float MaxShadowMip =
  -log(texelSizeAt1UnitDist/wantedTexelSizeAt1UnitDist)/log(2);
MaxShadowMip = min(float(MIPS_COUNT-1),max(MaxShadowMip,0.0));
// both BlkSearchShadowMipIndex and MaxShadowMip are passed
// to the shader as parameters
int BlkSearchShadowMipIndex = ceil(MaxShadowMip);
```

Listing 25.3. Algorithm for choosing a mip from a user-defined penumbra width, the shadow map resolution, and the FOV angle of the shadow frustum.

Figure 25.13. Shadow-map mips layout. [Image courtesy Square Enix Ltd.]

a kernel size in world space that is closer to a user-defined parameter. Listing 25.3 shows how the mip index is computed from this user-defined parameter, the shadow map resolution, and the FOV angle of the shadow frustum. This process can be done on the CPU and the result is passed to a shader as a parameter.

Unfortunately, the GatherRed() intrinsic does not allow mip selection. Therefore, the mips are stored in an atlas, as shown in Figure 25.13, and we offset the texture coordinates to sample the desired mip. This is achieved by applying a simple offset scale to the coordinates in texture space (see Listing 25.4).

In order to save on fragment instructions, the function returns, as an early out, a value of 0.0 (fully shadowed) if the average blocker depth is equal to 1.0 (found a blocker for all samples in the search region) or returns 1.0 (fully lit) if the average blocker depth is equal to 0.0 (no blocker found). Listing 25.4 shows the details of the average-blocker-depth compute.

```
#define KERNEL_SIZE 8
#define BFS2 (KERNEL_SIZE - 1) / 2

float3 blkTc = float3(inTc.xy, inDepth);
// TcBiasScale is a static array holding the offset-scale
in the shadow map for every mips.
float4 blkTcBS = TcBiasScale[BlkSearchShadowMipIndex];
blkTc.xy = blkTcBS.xy + blkTc.xy * blkTcBS.zw;
// g_vShadowMapDims.xy is the shadow map resolution
// g_vShadowMapDims.zw is the shadow map texel size
float2 blkAbsTc = ( g_vShadowMapDims.xy * blkTc.xy );
float2 fc = blkAbsTc - floor( blkAbsTc );
blkTc.xy  = blkTc.xy - ( fc * g_vShadowMapDims.zw );
float blkCount = 0; float avgBlockerDepth = 0;
[loop]for( int row = -BFS2; row <= BFS2; row += 2 )
{
  float2 tc = blkTc.xy + float2(-BFS2*g_vShadowMapDims.z,
            row*g_vShadowMapDimensions.w);
  [unroll]for( int col = -BFS2; col <= BFS2; col += 2 )
  {
    float4 depth4 = shadowTex.GatherRed(pointSampler, tc.xy);
    float4 blk4 = (blkTc.zzzz <= depth4)?(0).xxxx:(1).xxxx;
    float4 fcVec = 0;
    if (row == -BFS2)
    {
      if (col == -BFS2)
        fcVec = float4((1.0-fc.y) * (1.0-fc.x),
                       (1.0-fc.y), 1, (1.0-fc.x));
      else if (col == BFS2)
        fcVec = float4((1.0-fc.y), (1.0-fc.y) * fc.x, fc.x, 1);
      else
        fcVec = float4((1.0-fc.y), (1.0-fc.y), 1, 1);
    }
    else if (row == BFS2)
    {
      if (col == -BFS2)
        fcVec = float4((1.0-fc.x), 1, fc.y, (1.0-fc.x) * fc.y);
      else if (col == BFS2)
        fcVec = float4(1, fc.x, fc.x * fc.y, fc.y);
      else
        fcVec = float4(1, 1, fc.y, fc.y);
    }
    else
    {
      if (col == -BFS2)
        fcVec = float4((1.0-fc.x), 1, 1, (1.0-fc.x));
      else if (col == BFS2)
        fcVec = float4(1, fc.x, fc.x, 1);
      else
        fcVec = float4(1,1,1,1);
    }
    blkCount += dot(blk4, fcVec.xyzw);
    avgBlockerDepth += dot(depth4, fcVec.xyzw*blk4);
    tc.x += 2.0*g_vShadowMapDims.z;
  }
}
if( blkCount == 0.0 ) // Early out - fully lit
  return 1.0f;
else if (blkCount == KERNEL_SIZE*KERNEL_SIZE) // Fully shadowed
  return 0.0f;
avgBlockerDepth /= blkCount;
```

Listing 25.4. Average-blocker-depth compute.

$$\text{width}_{\text{penumbra}} = \frac{(\text{depth}_{\text{receiver}} - \texttt{avgBlockerDepth}) \cdot \text{width}_{\text{light}}}{\texttt{avgBlockerDepth}}$$

Algorithm 25.2. Algorithm for computing the penumbra estimation.

25.3.2 Penumbra Estimation

Based on the average-blocker-depth value from the previous step and the user-defined light width, a factor (the penumbra estimation) is computed. Algorithm 25.2 is pretty straightforward and is the same as many other PCSS implementation.

25.3.3 Filtering

The final CHS step consists of applying a dynamic filter to the shadow map to obtain the light attenuation term. In this step, we also take advantage of the shadow-map mips. The main idea is to use higher-resolution mips for the sharp area of the shadow and lower-resolution mips for the blurry area. In order to have a continuous and unnoticeable transition between the different mips, we use two mips selected from the penumbra estimation and perform one filter operation for each mip before linearly blending the two results (see Figure 25.14). Doing

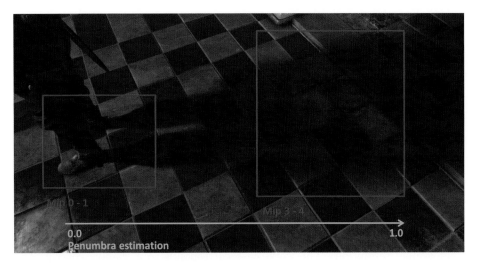

Figure 25.14. Mips used for the filtering, depending on the user-defined region search width and the penumbra estimation. [Image courtesy Square Enix Ltd.]

```
#define KERNEL_SIZE 8
#define FS2 (KERNEL_SIZE - 1) / 2

float Ratio = penumbraWidth;
float clampedTexRatio = max(MaxShadowMip - 0.001, 0.0);
float texRatio = min(MaxShadowMip * Ratio, clampedTexRatio);
float texRatioFc = texRatio - floor(texRatio);
uint textureIndex = min(uint(texRatio), MIPS_COUNT-2);
float4 highMipTcBS = TcBiasScale[textureIndex]; // higher res
float4 lowMipTcBS  = TcBiasScale[textureIndex+1]; // lower res
// Pack mips Tc into a float4, xy for high mip, zw for low mip
float4 MipsTc = float4(highMipTcBS.xy + inTc.xy*highMipTcBS.zw,
                       lowMipTcBS.xy + inTc.xy*lowMipTcBS.zw);
float4 MipsAbsTc = (g_vShadowMapDims.xyxy * MipsTc);
float4 MipsFc = MipsAbsTc - floor(MipsAbsTc);
MipsTc  = MipsTc - (MipsFc * g_vShadowMapDims.zwzw);
...
//Apply the same dynamic weight matrix to both mips
//using ratio along with the corresponding MipsTc and MipsFc
...
return lerp(highMipTerm, lowMipTerm, texRatioFc);
```

Listing 25.5. Shadow mips filtering and blending.

so gives a realistic effect with variable levels of blurriness, using the same kernel size (8×8 in *Thief*) through the whole filtering. The highest mip index possible (which corresponds to a penumbra estimation of 1.0) is the same one used in the blocker search step.

As described above, we need to get the attenuation terms for both selected mips before blending them. A dynamic weight matrix is computed by feeding four matrices into a cubic Bézier function, depending only on the penumbra estimation, and used to filter each mip (not covered here; see [Gruen 10] for the details). Like the previous steps, this is accelerated using the GatherCmpRed() intrinsic [Gruen and Story 09]. Listing 25.5 shows how to blend the filtered mips to obtain the final shadow attenuation term.

The number of shadow map accesses for the blocker search is 16 (8×8 kernel with the use of GatherCmpRed()) and 2×16 for the filter step (8×8 kernel for each mip with the use of GatherCmpRed()), for a total of 48 texture fetches, producing very large penumbras that are independent from the shadow resolution (though the sharp areas still are dependent). A classic implementation in Shader Model 4.0 using a 8×8 kernel with no shadow mipmapping would perform 128 accesses for smaller penumbras, depending on the shadow resolution.

Performance-wise, on an NVIDIA 770 GTX and for a 1080p resolution, the CHS takes 1–2 ms depending on the shadow exposure on the screen and the shadow map resolution. The worst case corresponds to a shadow covering the whole screen.

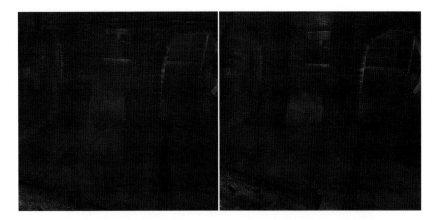

Figure 25.15. Old-generation *Thief* particles rendering (left) and next-generation version (right). Notice the color variation of the fog due to different lighting. [Image courtesy Square Enix Ltd.]

25.4 Lit Particles

Another addition made for the next-generation version of *Thief* was the support for lit particles. Prior to this, our particle system colors had to be tweaked by hand, and this meant that particles could not react to lighting changes. With lighting support, particles look much more integrated into the environment and they appear to react more dynamically to changes in lighting.

The lighting feature set for particles included static light maps, static shadow maps, projected textures, and up to four dynamic lights. We experimented with having dynamic shadow maps, but it revealed too much about the geometry used to render the visual effects (it made it obvious that we were using camera-aligned sprites). Each sprite would have a well-defined shadow mapped as a plane, while the texture used for the particle is usually meant to fake a cloud-like shape. This issue was not visible with static light maps and shadow maps because they were mapped as 3D textures across the particle bounds. Figure 25.15 shows a comparison between old- and next-generation versions of particle rendering in *Thief*.

25.5 Compute-Shader-Based Postprocessing

One of the major novelties of the DirectX 11 API and the next-generation consoles' hardware is the support of compute shaders. One particular feature of compute shaders is the introduction of local data storage (LDS), a.k.a. thread group shared memory (TGSM). LDS is a cache-like on-chip memory, which is generally faster than VRAM but slower than register memory. One can use LDS to exchange data between shader threads running within the same thread group.

Figure 25.16. Gaussian-based DoF with circular bokeh (top) and DoF with hexagonal bokeh (bottom). [Image courtesy Square Enix Ltd.]

This functionality can be used for numerous applications. One obvious use case is decreasing bandwidth for postprocesses, which computes a convolution of a fairly large radius. In *Thief*, we used this feature for depth-of-field (DoF) computations, as will be described below.

25.5.1 Depth-of-Field Rendering

For our DoF algorithm we used two approaches: Gaussian blur for the round-shaped bokeh and [White and Barré-Brisebois 11] for hexagonal bokeh. Figure 25.16 shows examples of these techniques. Both approaches result in two separable filter passes. DoF is texture-fetch limited, as kernels take a big number of samples to accommodate a large radius bokeh.

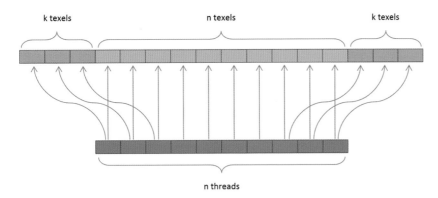

Figure 25.17. Fetching of texels with a filter kernel using local data storage.

25.5.2 Improving Bandwidth by Using Local Data Storage

In order to reduce the texture bandwidth for the DoF pass, we use LDS. The main idea is for a filter of radius k and n threads to prefetch $2k + n$ samples as shown in Figure 25.17. Each of the n threads loads a texel; additionally, every thread close to the thread group boundaries loads another texel. Then, each thread stores the values it loaded into LDS. Finally, to compute the kernel, each thread reads values from LDS instead of DRAM, hence the bandwidth reduction.

Initially, we used the code from Listing 25.6 to load and store from LDS. However, this resulted in even worse performance than not using LDS at all. The reason for this is a four-way LDS memory bank conflict, which we introduced. As bank size on the majority of the video cards is 32-bits wide, each thread will make a strided access with $stride = 4$. To fix that, we needed to de-vectorize our code, as shown in Listing 25.7.

25.5.3 Results

To understand the LDS win, we tested different implementations of the DoF kernel filters. For a DoF pass using a kernel with $radius = 15$ for a FP16 render target, we got 0.15 ms without LDS, 0.26 with vectorized LDS structure, and 0.1 ms for de-vectorized LDS on AMD HD7970. Both next-generation consoles have shown a speedup with a similar factor. In contrast, using LDS on NVIDIA GPUs (GeForce 660 GTX) resulted in no speedup at all in the best case. As a result, on AMD GPUs (which include next-generation consoles), using compute shaders with LDS can result in a significant (33%) speedup if low-level performance considerations (e.g., banked memory) are taken into account.

```
groupshared float4 fCache[NR_THREADS + 2 * KERNEL_RADIUS];

Texture2D inputTexture : register(t0);
RWTexture2D<float4> outputTexture : register(u0);

[numthreads(NR_THREADS, 1, 1)]
void main(uint3 groupThreadID : SV_GroupThreadID,
        uint3 dispatchThreadID : SV_DispatchThreadID)
{
    //Read texture to LDS
    int counter = 0;
    for (int t = groupThreadID.x;
              t < NR_THREADS + 2 * KERNEL_RADIUS;
              t += NR_THREADS, counter += NR_THREADS)
    {
        int x = clamp(
            dispatchThreadID.x + counter - KERNEL_RADIUS,
            0, inputTexture.Length.x - 1);
        fCache[t] = inputTexture[int2(x, dispatchThreadID.y)];
    }
    GroupMemoryBarrierWithGroupSync();

    ...
    //Do the actual blur
    ...

    outputTexture[dispatchThreadID.xy] = vOutColor;
}
```

Listing 25.6. Initial kernel implementation. Notice a single LDS allocation.

25.6   Conclusion

In this chapter, we gave a comprehensive walkthrough for the rendering techniques we implemented for the next-generation versions of *Thief*. We presented our reflection system, the contact-hardening shadow algorithm, particles lighting approach, and compute shader postprocesses. Most of these techniques were integrated during the later stages of *Thief* production, therefore they were used less extensively in the game than we wished. However, we hope that this postmortem will help game developers to start using the techniques, which were not practical on the previous console generation.

25.7   Acknowledgments

We would like to thank Robbert-Jan Brems, David Gallardo, Nicolas Longchamps, Francis Maheux, and the entire *Thief* team.

```
groupshared float fCacheR[NR_THREADS + 2 * KERNEL_RADIUS];
groupshared float fCacheG[NR_THREADS + 2 * KERNEL_RADIUS];
groupshared float fCacheB[NR_THREADS + 2 * KERNEL_RADIUS];
groupshared float fCacheA[NR_THREADS + 2 * KERNEL_RADIUS];

Texture2D inputTexture : register(t0);
RWTexture2D<float4> outputTexture : register(u0);

[numthreads(NR_THREADS, 1, 1)]
void main(uint3 groupThreadID : SV_GroupThreadID,
        uint3 dispatchThreadID : SV_DispatchThreadID)
{
    //Read texture to LDS
    int counter = 0;
    for (int t = groupThreadID.x;
            t < NR_THREADS + 2 * KERNEL_RADIUS;
            t += NR_THREADS, counter += NR_THREADS)
    {
        int x = clamp(
            dispatchThreadID.x + counter - KERNEL_RADIUS,
            0, inputTexture.Length.x - 1);
        float4 tex = inputTexture[int2(x, dispatchThreadID.y)];
        fCacheR[t] = tex.r;
        fCacheG[t] = tex.g;
        fCacheB[t] = tex.b;
        fCacheA[t] = tex.a;
    }
    GroupMemoryBarrierWithGroupSync();

    ...
    //Do the actual blur
    ...

    outputTexture[dispatchThreadID.xy] = vOutColor;
}
```

Listing 25.7. Final kernel implementation. Notice that we make a separate LDS allocation for each channel.

Bibliography

[Andersson 13] Zap Andersson. "Everything You Always Wanted to Know About mia_material." Presented in Physically Based Shading in Theory and Practice, SIGGRAPH Course, Anaheim, CA, July 21–25, 2013.

[Andreev 13] Dmitry Andreev. "Rendering Tricks in Dead Space 3." Game Developers Conference course, San Francisco, CA, March 25–29, 2013.

[Fernando 05] Randima Fernando. "Percentage-Closer Soft Shadows." In *ACM SIGGRAPH 2005 Sketches*, p. article 35. New York: ACM, 2005.

[Gruen and Story 09] Holger Gruen and Jon Story. "Taking Advantage of Direct3D 10.1 Features to Accelerate Performance and Enhance Quality." Presented at AMD sponsored session, Eurographics, Munich, Germany, March 30–April 3, 2009.

[Gruen 10] Holger Gruen. "Contact Hardening Shadows 11." AMD Radeon SDK, http://developer.amd.com/tools-and-sdks/graphics-development/ amd-radeon-sdk/archive/, 2010.

[Kasyan et al. 11] Nick Kasyan, Nicolas Schulz, and Tiago Sousa. "Secrets of CryENGINE 3 Graphics Technology." SIGGRAPH course, Vancouver, Canada, August 8, 2011.

[Lagarde and Zanuttini 13] Sébastien Lagarde and Antoine Zanuttini. "Practical Planar Reflections Using Cubemaps and Image Proxies." In *GPU Pro 4: Advanced Rendering Techniques*, edited by Wolfgang Engel, pp. 51–68. Boca Raton, FL: CRC Press, 2013.

[Lengyel 11] Eric Lengyel. *Mathematics for 3D Game Programming and Computer Graphics*, Third edition. Boston: Cengage Learning PTR, 2011.

[NVIDIA Corporation 99] NVIDIA Corporation. "Cube Map OpenGL Tutorial." http://www.nvidia.com/object/cube_map_ogl_tutorial.html, 1999.

[Sousa 05] Tiago Sousa. "Generic Refraction Simulation." In *GPU Gems 2*, edited by Matt Farr, pp. 295–305. Reading, MA: Addison-Wesley Professional, 2005.

[Uludag 14] Yasin Uludag. "Hi-Z Screen-Space Cone-Traced Reflections." In *GPU Pro 5: Advanced Rendering Techniques*, edited by Wolfgang Engel, pp. 149–192. Boca Raton, FL: CRC Press, 2014.

[White and Barré-Brisebois 11] John White and Colin Barré-Brisebois. "More Performance! Five Rendering Ideas from *Battlefield 3* and *Need For Speed: The Run*." Presented in Advances in Real-Time Rendering in Games, SIGGRAPH Course, Vancouver, August 7–11, 2011.

[Wright 11] Daniel Wright. "Image Based Reflections." http://udn.epicgames. com/Three/ImageBasedReflections.html, 2011.

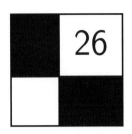

26

Grass Rendering and Simulation with LOD

Dongsoo Han and Hongwei Li

26.1 Introduction

Grass rendering and simulation are challenging topics for video games because grass can cover large open areas and require heavy computation for simulation. As an extension of our previous hair technology, TressFX [Tre 13], we chose grass because it has unique challenges. (See Figure 26.1.) Our initial plan was to support rendering many individual grass blades covering a wide terrain and simulating their interactions using rigid bodies and wind.

To satisfy our requirements, we developed an efficient and scalable level-of-detail (LOD) system for grass using DirectX 11. In addition to LOD, a master-and-slave system reduces simulation computation dramatically but still preserves the quality of the simulation.

Figure 26.1. Grass rendering and simulation with balls.

Figure 26.2. Five grass blade types generated by an in-house tool.

26.2 Render Grass Blades

To make the grass look natural, it is vital to acquire a natural shape for the grass blades. We first adopted the method described in [Bouatouch et al. 06], where they generate grass blade in a procedural manner. For each grass blade, its stem is defined as a parabolic curve formed by tracking the motion of a point, shooting from the root vertex, with a random initial speed and angle. This method is simple yet effective, but cannot provide a rich variance in the grass blade geometric appearance as they are always parabolic curves, tall or low, curved or straight. It is difficult to generate complex and natural-looking grass blades using this approach since the blades are poorly described by a quadratic curve alone.

We find instancing can tackle this variance problem very well. First, we generate a few grass blade types, each of which has a fixed number of knots. In our application, the number of knots is 16, which balances the efficiency of simulation and the smoothness of blade shape. Also, we have experimented with different numbers of types and find five is good enough to create a grass lawn with rich variance. More types do not hurt the performance but do not increase the visual quality much either. Figure 26.2 shows five blade types that we created using an in-house tool.

To further increase the variance, when we instantiate these blade types and plant them in the scene (we call it the growing process), we randomize orientations, lengths, widths, and textures of instantiated blades. For example, for the fifth blade type, its length can vary between 0.1 m and 0.15 m. When it is instantiated, its length will be set to a number between 0.1 m and 0.15 m with regards to the normal distribution. Each knot on the blade is linearly scaled to this new length. The range of length for each blade type is hard coded. The variance is further enhanced by distributing blade types unevenly. Some of them will be used more often than others. The probability of instantiating one particular blade type is tweaked for the best look in the final scene.

The grass blade created by hand or tool only describes the blade stem. The stem is expanded to a blade in the runtime so that we can set the width of each blade separately. Each line segment in the stem becomes a quad, i.e., two triangles. There are 16 knots and thus there are 15 quads or 30 triangles. The

Figure 26.3. Expand the stem to grass blade in vertex shader. The two overlapping vertices from two triangles are dragged to opposite positions in the vertex shader.

expansion direction follows the binormal of the grass blade, and the expansion width is chosen by the user. Moreover, we reduce the expansion width gradually from bottom knots to top in order to make a sharp blade tip. This geometry expansion was firstly implemented in a geometry shader, but the performance was not satisfying. We then adopted the approach presented in TressFX, where they do the geometry expansion in the vertex shader by expanding two degraded triangles to normal, nondegenerate triangles. Figure 26.3 illustrates the process of expanding the degenerate triangles. We also modified our in-house blade modeling tool so that its output became a triangle strip: each knot in the stem is duplicated into two vertices at the same coordinate as the knot, and one line segment becomes two triangles. At runtime, we upgrade triangles by translating two overlapping vertices at the knot position in opposite directions determined by the modulo 2 result of the vertex ID, e.g., `SV_VertexID`.

Regarding the rendering, we do not have much freedom in choosing a shading model for the grass blade for there are thousands of blades to be rendered in one frame. It must be a lightweight shading model that still can create a promising, natural appearance for the grass blade. Under this constraint, we adopt the conventional Phong model and replace its ambient component with Hemispherical Ambient Light [Wilhelmsen 09]. Hemispherical ambient light is a good approximation of the true ambient color of grass in lieu of the more precise ambient occlusion and color, which can be very expensive to generate. It is computed as the sum of sky light and earth light as shown in following equation:

$$ambient = skylight \times ratio + earthlight \times (1 - ratio),$$

where *ratio* is defined by the dot product between the hemisphere's "up" direction and the vertex normal.

We also investigated screen-space translucency [Jimenez and Gutierrez 10], but the increase in the visual quality is minor, and it added an extra 50 shader instructions, so we did not use it.

Besides the lighting model, a grass blade has both a front and a back face, and thus we cannot disable face culling on the GPU. We rely on DirectX's semantic

`SV_IsFrontFace` to tell us whether the current pixel is now facing forward or backward. If it is the back face, we invert the normal and use the back surface texture in the shading computation.

26.3 Simulation

Like hair simulation in TressFX, each grass blade is represented as vertices and edges. We usually use 16 vertices for each blade and 64 for the thread group size for compute shaders, but it is possible to change the thread group size to 32 or 128.

For hair simulation in TressFX, three constraints (edge length, global shape, and local shape) are applied after integrating gravity. The TressFX hair simulation includes a "head"I transform. This is required in a hair simulation since the character's head can change its position and orientation, but we do not require this transform for grass. We can also skip applying the global shape constraint because grass gets much less force due to the absence of head movement. For the edge length constraint and the local shape constraint, two to three iterations are usually good enough.

The last step of simulation before going to LOD is to run a kernel to prevent grass blades from going under the ground. This can be done simply by moving each vertex position above the position of the blade root vertex position.

26.3.1 Master-and-Slave System

Master blades are the grass blades that are actively simulated. During the process of growing blades procedurally, we arrange master blade vertex positions followed by slave vertex positions. In our demo, we typically use a 1:4 ratio of master to slave blades, but that ratio can be easily changed during the growing process.

After simulating master blades, we copy the master vertex positions to their slaves. The important part of this process is that we should add perturbations so that slave blades are not exactly showing the same motion of their master. The perturbations become larger along the vertices toward the tip so that blades can be separated wider between tips and avoid parallel patterns. It is also possible to increase or decrease the perturbations based on the master blade's velocity so that if the master moves faster, the slaves will be farther behind.

26.3.2 Distance-Based Sorting

For LOD, two new read/write buffers (`QuantizedLODDistance` and `LODSortedStrand Index`) were added to TressFX. `QuantizedLODDistance` is to store the distances from the camera to each blade. `LODSortedStrandIndex` is to store the blade index for `QuantizedLODDistance`. Basically, these two buffers make key and value pairs for sorting.

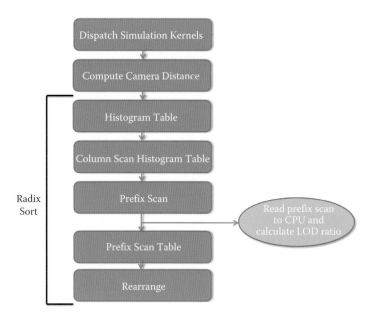

Figure 26.4. Kernel execution flow chart of radix sort.

The sorting algorithm we choose must run on the GPU efficiently and support key and value pairs. Also, we need to count how many keys are less than a given distance threshold so that we can determine the work item size for dispatch. Choosing radix sort could give us an extra benefit that, if we quantize the distance value in 8 bits, we need only one pass. Normally, radix sort needs four passes to sort 32-bit keys with an 8-bit radix; see Figure 26.4.

After simulating master blades and updating slave vertices, `ComputeCamera Distance` in Listing 26.1 calculates the distance from the camera position to each blade. Also, frustum culling is performed here, and a negative distance value will be assigned if the blade is outside of the camera's frustum. We quantize the distance values to 8 bits using the maximum distance given as user input.

Listings 26.2, 26.3, and 26.4 show the full code of radix sort. The inputs of radix sort are `QuantizedLODDistance` and `LODSortedStrandIndex`. `PrefixScan` performs a prefix scan of all the elements of `QuantizedLODDistance`. Before running the next kernels of radix sort, we read the prefix scan data on the CPU and compute the LOD ratio, which is a ratio of the number of valid blades to the number of total blades. We use this LOD ratio to compute the thread group size for simulation during the next frame.

Listing 26.5 shows how we can use a prefix scan to get the LOD ratio. We first calculate the quantized distance threshold and simply read the value of the prefix-scan array using the quantized distance threshold as an index; the prefix scan stores counts of values.

```
#define THREAD_GROUP_SIZE 64

RWStructuredBuffer<uint> QuantizedLODDistance : register(u6);
RWStructuredBuffer<uint> LODSortedStrandIndex : register(u7);

// cameraPos, cameraDir, and maxDist are given through
// const buffer.

[numthreads(THREAD_GROUP_SIZE, 1, 1)]
void ComputeCameraDistance(uint GIndex : SV_GroupIndex,
                uint3 GId : SV_GroupID,
                uint3 DTid : SV_DispatchThreadID)
{
  uint globalBladedIndex, globalRootVertexIndex;

  // Calculate indices above here.

  float4 pos = g_HairVertexPositions[globalRootVertexIndex+1];
  float dist = dot((pos.xyz - cameraPos.xyz), cameraDir.xyz);

  // Perform frustum culling and assign negative distance
  // if this blade is out of frustum here.

  // Quantize distance into 8 bits (0 ~ 2^8-1)
  // so that radix sort can sort it in one pass.
  if ( dist < 0 || dist > maxDist )
    dist = maxDist;

  uint quantizedDist = (uint)((dist/maxDist) * 255.f);

  QuantizedLODDistance[globalBladedIndex] = quantizedDist;
  LODSortedStrandIndex[globalBladedIndex] = globalBladedIndex;
}
```

Listing 26.1. Compute camera distance kernel.

```
#define RADIX 8                   // 8 bit
#define RADICES (1 << RADIX)    // 256 or 0x100
#define RADIX_MASK (RADICES - 1) // 255 or 0xFF
#define THREAD_GROUP_SIZE RADICES

cbuffer CBRadixSort : register( b0 )
{
  int numElement;
  int bits;
  float dummy[2];
}

// UAVs
RWStructuredBuffer<uint> QuantizedLODDistance : register(u0);
RWStructuredBuffer<uint> histogramTable : register(u1);
RWStructuredBuffer<uint> particiallySortedData : register(u2);
RWStructuredBuffer<uint> prefixScan : register(u3);
RWStructuredBuffer<uint> LODSortedStrandIndex : register(u4);
RWStructuredBuffer<uint> particiallySortedValue : register(u5);

groupshared uint sharedMem[RADICES];
groupshared uint sharedMemPrefixScan[RADICES];
```

```
uint pow2(uint a)
{
  return ( ((uint)1) << a);
}

// Each thread (work item) works on one element.
[numthreads(THREAD_GROUP_SIZE, 1, 1)]
void HistogramTable(uint GIndex : SV_GroupIndex,
                    uint3 GId : SV_GroupID,
                    uint3 DTid : SV_DispatchThreadID)
{
  uint localId = GIndex;
  uint groupId = GId.x;
  uint groupSize = RADICES;
  uint globalId = groupSize * groupId + localId;

  // Initialize shared memory.
  sharedMem[localId] = 0;
  GroupMemoryBarrierWithGroupSync();

  particiallySortedData[globalId]
                     = QuantizedLODDistance[globalId];
  particiallySortedValue[globalId]
                     = LODSortedStrandIndex[globalId];

  uint value = particiallySortedData[globalId];
  value = (value >> bits) & RADIX_MASK;
  InterlockedAdd(sharedMem[value], 1);
    GroupMemoryBarrierWithGroupSync();

  uint index = RADICES * groupId + localId;
  histogramTable[index] = sharedMem[localId];
}
```

Listing 26.2. Constant buffer, UAVs, and histogram table kernels in radix sort.

```
// There is only one thread group and the each thread
// (work item) works on each column on histogram table.
[numthreads(THREAD_GROUP_SIZE, 1, 1)]
void ColumnScanHistogramTable(uint GIndex : SV_GroupIndex,
                uint3 GId : SV_GroupID,
                uint3 DTid : SV_DispatchThreadID)
{
  uint localId = GIndex;
  uint numHistograms = numElement / THREAD_GROUP_SIZE;
  uint sum = 0;

  for ( uint i = 0; i < numHistograms; i++ )
  {
    sum += histogramTable[RADICES * i + localId];
    histogramTable[RADICES * i + localId] = sum;
  }
}

// There is only one thread group.
[numthreads(THREAD_GROUP_SIZE, 1, 1)]
void PrefixScan(uint GIndex : SV_GroupIndex,
                uint3 GId : SV_GroupID,
```

```
                        uint3 DTid : SV_DispatchThreadID)
{
  uint localId = GIndex;

  uint numHistograms = numElement / THREAD_GROUP_SIZE;
  sharedMemPrefixScan[localId]
      = histogramTable[RADICES * (numHistograms - 1) + localId];
  sharedMem[localId] = sharedMemPrefixScan[localId];
  GroupMemoryBarrierWithGroupSync();

  uint iter = (uint)(log2(256));
  uint k = localId;

  for ( uint i = 0; i < iter; i++ )
  {
    if ( k >= pow2(i) )
      sharedMem[k] = sharedMemPrefixScan[k]
                     + sharedMemPrefixScan[k-pow2(i)];

    GroupMemoryBarrierWithGroupSync();
    sharedMemPrefixScan[k] = sharedMem[k];
    GroupMemoryBarrierWithGroupSync();
  }

  if ( localId > 0 )
    prefixScan[localId] = sharedMemPrefixScan[localId-1];
  else
    prefixScan[localId] = 0;
}
```

Listing 26.3. Column scan histogram table and prefix scan kernels in radix sort.

```
// Each thread (work item) works on one element.
[numthreads(THREAD_GROUP_SIZE, 1, 1)]
void PrefixScanTable(uint GIndex : SV_GroupIndex,
              uint3 GId : SV_GroupID,
              uint3 DTid : SV_DispatchThreadID)
{
  uint localId = GIndex;
  uint groupId = GId.x;

  uint index = RADICES * groupId + localId;
  sharedMem[localId] = histogramTable[index];
  GroupMemoryBarrierWithGroupSync();

  sharedMem[localId] += prefixScan[localId];
  histogramTable[index] = sharedMem[localId];
}

// One thread (work item) works on one element.
[numthreads(THREAD_GROUP_SIZE, 1, 1)]
void Rearrange(uint GIndex : SV_GroupIndex,
              uint3 GId : SV_GroupID,
              uint3 DTid : SV_DispatchThreadID)
{
  uint localId = GIndex;
  uint groupId = GId.x;

  if ( localId == 0 )
```

```
{
  for ( int i = 0; i < RADICES; i++ )
  {
    uint element = particiallySortedData[groupId
                                    * RADICES + i];
    uint value = (element >> bits) & RADIX_MASK;
    uint index;

    if ( groupId == 0 )
    {
      index = prefixScan[value];
      prefixScan[value]++;
    }
    else
    {
      index = histogramTable[RADICES * (groupId-1) + value];
      histogramTable[RADICES * (groupId-1) + value]++;
    }

    QuantizedLODDistance[index] =
                particiallySortedData[groupId * RADICES + i];
    LODSortedStrandIndex[index] =
                particiallySortedValue[groupId * RADICES + i];
  }
 }
}
```

Listing 26.4. Prefix scan table and rearrange kernels in radix sort.

```
// distThresholdLOD is a distance threshold for LOD
// and maxDistanceLOD is the maximum distance for quantization.
unsigned int quantizedDistThresholdLod =
    (unsigned int)((distThresholdLOD/maxDistanceLOD) * 255.f);

int count = prefixScan[quantizedDistThresholdLod+1];
LODRatio = (float)count / (float)numMasterBlades;
```

Listing 26.5. Calulating the LOD ratio.

26.3.3 Wind

There are two kinds of wind motions: local ambient and global tidal motions. Local ambient motion is small scale and is independent of neighboring blades. In TressFX, wind was applied to each vertex by calculating the force from the wind and edge vectors. In grass, we simplified this by grabbing the tip vertex and moving it along the wind vector. This simple method works as well as the force-based approach. The amount of displacement is controlled by the magnitude of the wind. To prevent a visible directional pattern, perturbations are added into the wind directions and magnitudes.

Global tidal motion is also simple. This is wavy motion and neighbor blades should work together. In our grass, we simply sweep the grass field with large cylindrical bars and the collision handling system generates the nice wave motion.

26.4   Conclusion

With 32,768 master blades and 131,072 slave blades, simulating an entire grass field takes around 2.3 ms without LODs. Because radix sort takes around 0.3 ms, we see that simulation time can easily drop by more than 50% with LODs using reasonable distance thresholds.

In our test, we applied only one distance threshold. However, it is also possible to use multiple distance thresholds. This would allow us to smoothly change between LOD regions and reduce popping problems during camera movement.

Bibliography

[Bouatouch et al. 06] Kadi Bouatouch, Kévin Boulanger, and Sumanta Pattanaik. "Rendering Grass in Real Time with Dynamic Light Sources." Rapport de recherche RR-5960, INRIA, 2006.

[Jimenez and Gutierrez 10] Jorge Jimenez and Diego Gutierrez. "Screen-Space Subsurface Scattering." In *GPU Pro: Advanced Rendering Techniques*, edited by Wolfgang Engel, pp. 335–351. Natick, MA: A K Peters, Ltd., 2010.

[Tre 13] "TressFX 2.0." http://developer.amd.com/tools-and-sdks/graphics -development/amd-radeon-sdk/, accessed November 13, 2013.

[Wilhelmsen 09] Petri Wilhelmsen. "Hemispheric Ambient Light." http:// digitalerr0r.wordpress.com/2009/05/09/xna-shader-programming-tutorial -19-hemispheric-ambient-light/, accessed May 9, 2009.

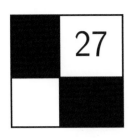

27

Hybrid Reconstruction
Antialiasing
Michał Drobot

27.1 Introduction

In this article, we present the antialiasing (AA) solution used in the Xbox One and Playstation 4 versions of *Far Cry 4*, developed by Ubisoft Montreal: hybrid reconstruction antialiasing (HRAA). We present a novel framework that utilizes multiple approaches to mitigate aliasing issues with a tight performance budget in mind.

The Xbox One, Playstation 4, and most AMD graphics cards based on the GCN architecture share a similar subset of rasterizer and data interpolation features. We propose several new algorithms, or modern implementations of known ones, making use of the aforementioned hardware features. Each solution is tackling a single aliasing issue: efficient spatial super-sampling, high-quality edge antialiasing, and temporal stability. All are based around the principle of data reconstruction. We discuss each one separately, identifying potential problems, benefits, and performance considerations. Finally, we present a combined solution used in an actual production environment. The framework we demonstrate was fully integrated into the Dunia engine's deferred renderer. Our goal was to render a temporarily stable image, with quality surpassing $4\times$ rotated-grid super-sampling, at a cost of 1 ms at a resolution of 1080p on the Xbox One and Playstation 4 (see Figure 27.1).

27.2 Overview

Antialiasing is a crucial element in high-quality rendering. We can divide most aliasing artifacts in rasterization-based rendering into two main categories: temporal and spatial. Temporal artifacts occur as flickering under motion when details fail to get properly rendered due to missing the rasterization grid on certain

Figure 27.1. The crops on the right show no AA (top), SMAA (middle), and the presented HRAA (bottom) results. Only HRAA is capable of reconstructing additional details while providing high-quality antialiasing.

frames. Spatial artifacts result from signal under-sampling when dealing with a single, static image. Details that we try to render are just too fine to be properly resolved at the desired resolution, which mostly manifests itself as jagged edges.

Both sources of aliasing are directly connected with errors of signal under-sampling and occur together. However, there are multiple approaches targeting different aliasing artifacts that vary in both performance and quality. We can divide these solutions into analytical, temporal, and super-sampling–based approaches.

In this article, we present a novel algorithm that builds upon all these approaches. By exploring the new hardware capabilities of modern GPUs (we will base our findings on AMD's GCN architecture), we optimize each approach and provide a robust framework that shares the benefits of each algorithm while minimizing their shortcomings.

27.3   Related Work

A typical antialiasing solution used in offline rendering is to super-sample (SSAA) the image; render at a higher resolution and then perform a resolve step, which is a down-sampling filter into the desired final resolution [Burley 07]. If enough samples are used, then this type of antialiasing tackles all the aliasing problems mentioned earlier. Unfortunately, it requires effectively rendering the image multiple times and is of limited usefulness for real-time rendering.

An optimized version of super-sampling is provided by graphics hardware in the form of multi-sampled antialiasing (MSAA) [Kirkland et al. 99]. Instead of shading all pixels at higher resolution, only samples along triangle edges are rasterized multiple times (but only shaded once), which is followed by an optimized resolve. MSAA proves to be a valid solution to spatial aliasing issues, but is strictly limited to triangle edges. All samples need to be stored in an additional framebuffer until they are resolved, therefore making this method very expensive in terms of memory consumption. As a result, not many games use it as the main antialiasing solution on performance-limited platforms.

It is worth noting that the number of gradient steps on antialiased edges is strictly correlated to the number of samples that MSAA or SSAA uses (i.e., 4×MSAA can provide a maximum of five gradients depending on the sampling pattern and edge orientation).

On the previous generation of consoles (Xbox 360 and Playstation 3), we observed a rise in popularity of image-based, postprocessing, morphological antialiasing solutions such as FXAA [Lottes 09], MLAA [Reshetov 09], and SMAA [Jimenez et al. 11]. These algorithms provided excellent results, with perceptual quality comparable to extremely high levels of MSAA rendering at a fraction of the cost of MSAA. A typical morphological filter derives visually perceivable edges from the current image and performs edge re-vectorization. Unfortunately the result still relies only on the final rasterized image data, which can suffer from temporal and spatial aliasing. In practice, static images that are processed with these algorithms look much better than what the hardware-based MSAA can achieve. Unfortunately the quality degrades dramatically under motion, where spatial and temporal under-sampling result in "wobbly" edges and temporal flicker of high-contrast details.

It is clear that morphological methods alone will not achieve the high-quality spatio-temporal results of super-sampling. This sparked research in two different directions: analytical- and temporal-based antialiasing. Several researchers experimented with postprocessing methods, augmented by additional information, derived from actual triangle-edge equation. Probably the most well known is GBAA [Persson 11], which calculates per-pixel signed distance to the closest triangle edge. This information is stored in an additional buffer and is used later during a postprocessing pass to effectively rerasterize triangle edge-pixel intersections analytically. This method can provide a high level of quality and perfect temporal stability of triangle edges. Unfortunately, due to its use of a geometry shader pass to gather triangle information, it exhibits poor performance and thus never gained widespread adoption. It is also hindered by multiple other issues that we will discuss in-depth in Section 27.5.

Another approach gaining popularity is based on temporal algorithms that try to perform filtering using previously rendered frames utilizing image temporal coherency [Nehab et al. 07]. This effectively allows multi-sampled algorithms to be amortized over time [Yang et al. 09]. Several titles use temporal resolves to augment SSAO [Bavoil and Andersson 12, Drobot 11] or to stabilize the final image in motion [Sousa 13]. Some engines experiment with temporal super-sampling [Malan 12]; however, due to a lack of robust sample rejection methods, those approaches are rather conservative, i.e., accumulating only two frames using a limited subset of visible pixels [Sousa 11].

Recently *Killzone: Shadow Fall* used a robust temporal up-sampling method, effectively rendering images with 2× super-sampling. It also used previously re-constructed frames to stabilize images in motion in order to avoid image flickering [Valient 14].

Several researchers have tried to combine the benefits of hardware-based MSAA, temporal sampling and morphological filtering into one combined so-lution. This resulted in 4×SMAA [Jimenez et al. 12], which combines the quality of SMAA edge gradients with the temporal stability of 2×MSAA and 2×temporal super-sampling. Unfortunately, not many console titles can afford this due to the use of expensive 2×MSAA.

One more research direction has been toward optimizing sampling patterns for multi-sampled approaches [Akenine-Möller 03]. Unfortunately, this approach didn't get much traction in the real-time rendering field due to a lack of hard-ware and software support for custom sampling patterns. Only a few predefined sampling patterns are supported in hardware-based MSAA modes.

Another hardware-based solution involves augmenting the standard MSAA pipeline with coverage samples that can be evaluated with minimal performance and memory overhead. This solution was, up to this point, a part of the fixed GPU pipeline in the form of EQAA [AMD 11] and CSAA [Young 06].

27.4   Hybrid Antialiasing Overview

Our antialiasing solution can be divided into several components. Each one can stand on its own and can be freely mixed with any other approach.

The aim of each component is to tackle a different source of aliasing, so each algorithm can be used to its best effect in limited use-case scenarios.

Our framework is built around the following components:

- temporally stable edge antialiasing,

- temporal super-sampling,

- temporal antialiasing.

27.5   Temporally Stable Edge Antialiasing

The aim of this component is to provide perceptually plausible gradients, for geometric edges, that remain stable under motion. We do not need to worry about pixel discontinuities that come from texture data or lighting, as that source of aliasing will be taken care of by a different framework component.

In Section 27.3, we briefly discussed potential algorithms that would suit our needs for high-quality edge rendering: morphological and analytical. However, only the latter can provide temporally stable antialiasing. Unfortunately, all purely analytical methods exhibit problems, including performance issues.

We would like to propose a new implementation based on AMD's GCN architecture that makes analytical edge antialiasing virtually free. In Section 27.5.1, we propose several extensions as well as real production issues connected with the method itself. Section 27.5.2 offers a brief introduction to EQAA's inner workings. It also introduces a new algorithm—coverage reconstruction antialiasing—that uses coverage samples from hardware-based EQAA to analytically estimate the edge orientation as well as triangle spatial coverage, building upon previous analytical-only algorithms.

27.5.1   Analytical Edge Antialiasing (AEAA)

The original GBAA algorithm relies on a geometry shader to pass down geometry information to the pixel shader. Interpolators are used to store the distance to the edge in the major direction. Then, the pixel shader selects the closest signed distance to the currently rasterized pixel and outputs it into an additional offscreen buffer. Distance data needs to contain the major axis and the actual signed distance value in range $[-1, 1]$, where 0 is considered to be at the rasterized pixel center. Later, a fullscreen postprocessing pass searches for each pixel's immediate neighbor's closest edges. After an edge crossing the pixel is found, we use its orientation and distance to blend the two nearest pixels accordingly (see Figure 27.2).

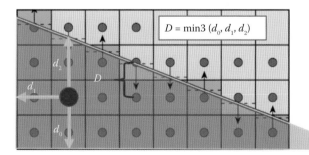

Figure 27.2. In analytical distance-to-edge techniques, every triangle writes out the distance to the closest edge used to antialias pixels in a postprocessing pass.

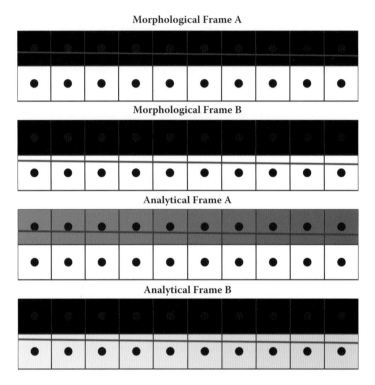

Figure 27.3. Antialiased edge changes in motion when using analytical data. Note that every morphological solution will fail as no gradient change will be detected due to the same results of rasterization. This gets more problematic with shorter feature search distance.

Such methods provide temporally stable edge antialiasing, as the blend factor relies on continuous triangle information rather than discrete rasterization results (see Figure 27.3).

Gradient length is limited only by storage. In practice, it is enough to store additional data in 8 bits: 1 bit for the major axis and 7 bits for signed distance, providing 64 effective gradient steps.

This algorithm also deals efficiently with alpha-tested silhouettes, if a meaningful distance to an edge can be estimated. This proves to be relatively easy with nonbinary alpha channels. Alpha test derivatives can be used to estimate the distance to a cutout edge. A better solution would be to use signed distance fields for alpha testing and directly output the real distance to the edge.

Both methods are fast and easy to implement in practice. It is worth noting that the final distance to the edge should be the minimum of the geometric distance to the triangle edge and the edge derived from the alpha channel.

We implemented GBAA and optimized it to take advantage of the benefits of the new hardware features found in modern GPUs. AMD's GCN architecture allows pixel shaders to sample vertex data from the triangle descriptors used to rasterize the current pixel. This means that we no longer need the expensive geometry-shader stage to access vertex data in order to calculate the distance to the edge as shown by [Drobot 14].

The snippet in Listing 27.1 shows the improved GBAA algorithm with offsets directly evaluated in the pixel shader. The final postprocess resolve step remains unchanged from the original algorithm.

```
// Calculate closest axis distance between point X
// and line AB. Check against known distance and direction
float ComputeAxisClosestDist(float2 inX,
float2 inA,
float2 inB,
inout uint     ioMajorDir,
inout float    ioAxisDist)
{
float2 AB          = normalize(inB - inA);
float2 normalAB = float2(-AB.y, AB.x);
float dist         = dot(inA, normalAB) - dot(inX, normalAB);
bool majorDir      = (abs(normalAB.x) > abs(normalAB.y));
float axisDist     = dist * rcp(majorDir? normalAB.x : normalAB.y);

if(axisDist < ioAxisDist) ioAxisDist = axisDist;
if(axisDist < ioAxisDist) ioMajorDir = majorDir;
}

void GetGeometricDistance(float2 inScreenCoord,
out float oDistance,
out bool oMajorDir)
    {
    // GetParameterX are HW implementation dependant
float2 sc = GetParameterInterpolated( inScreenCoord );
    float2 sc0 = GetParameterP0( inScreenCoord )
    float2 sc1 = GetParameterP1( inScreenCoord );
    float2 sc2 = GetParameterP2( inScreenCoord );
oDistance = FLT_MAX;

ComputeAxisClosestDist(sc, sc0, sc1, oMajorDir, oDistance);
ComputeAxisClosestDist(sc, sc1, sc2, oMajorDir, oDistance);
ComputeAxisClosestDist(sc, sc2, sc0, oMajorDir, oDistance);
}

// inAlpha is result of AlphaTest,
// i.e., Alpha - AlphaRef
// We assume alpha is a distance field
void GetSignedDistanceFromAlpha(float inAlpha,
out float oDistance,
out bool oGradientDir)
{
    // Find alpha test gradient
float xGradient = ddx_fine(inAlpha);
float yGradient = ddy_fine(inAlpha);
oGradientDir = abs(xGradient) > abs(yGradient);
// Compute signed distance to where alpha reaches zero
oDistance = -inAlpha * rcp(oGradientDir ? xGradient : yGradient);
    }
```

```
void GetAnalyticalDistanceToEdge(float inAlpha,
float2 inScreenCoord,
out float oDistance,
out bool oMajorDir )
{
bool alphaMajorAxis; float alphaDistance;
GetSignedDistanceFromAlpha(inAlpha,
alphaDistance,
alphaMajorAxis)
GetGeometricDistance(inScreenCoord,
oDistance,
oMajorDir);
if(alphaDistance < oDistance) oDistance = alphaDistance;
if(alphaDistance < oDistance) alphaMajorAxis = alphaMajorAxis;
}
```

Listing 27.1. Optimized GBAA distance to edge shader. This uses direct access to vertex data from within the pixel shader.

In terms of quality, the analytical methods beat any morphological approach. Unfortunately, this method proves to be very problematic in many real-world scenarios. Malan developed a very similar antialiasing solution and researched further into the practical issues [Malan 10].

The main problem stems from subpixel triangles, which are unavoidable in a real game production environment. If an actual silhouette edge is composed of multiple small or thin triangles, then only one of them will get rasterized per pixel. Therefore, its distance to the edge might not be the actual distance to the silhouette that we want to antialias. In this case, the resulting artifact will show up as several improperly smoothed pixels on an otherwise antialiased edge, which tends to be very visually distracting (see Figure 27.4 and Figure 27.5).

Malan proposed several ways of dealing with this problem [Malan 10]. However, none of these solutions are very practical if not introduced at the very beginning of the project, due to complex mesh processing and manual tweaking.

Another issue comes again from the actual data source. Hints for antialiasing come from a single triangle, therefore it is impossible to correctly detect and process intersections between triangles. Many assets in a real production scenario have intersecting triangles (i.e., a statue put into the ground will have side triangles intersecting with the terrain mesh). GPU rasterization solves intersections by depth testing before and after rendering a triangle's pixels. Therefore, there is no analytical information about the edge created due to intersection. In effect, the distance to the closest edge does not represent the distance to the intersection edge, which results in a lack of antialiasing.

27.5.2   Coverage Reconstruction Antialiasing (CRAA)

In order to improve upon the techniques and results shared in Section 27.5.1, we would like to find a way to determine more information about a triangle's actual

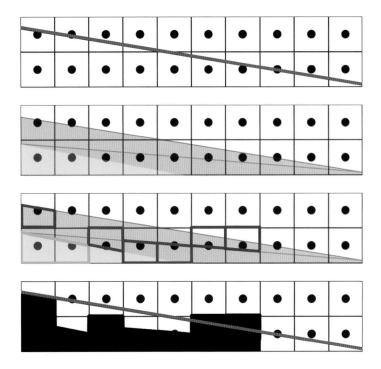

Figure 27.4. False distance to a silhouette edge due to subpixel triangles. Taking a single triangle into account would result in rerasterization of a false edge (blue) instead of the real silhouette edge (red).

Figure 27.5. Top to bottom: a visualization of analytical distance to edge, rasterized edge, analytically antialiased edge, an edge using 5-bit gradients, and an edge showing minor artifacts when multiple triangles intersect one pixel.

intersections and edges within a pixel. With this information, we could partially address most of the aforementioned issues. Fortunately, EQAA provides exactly the information we are interested in by using AMD's hardware EQAA.

EQAA overview. The enhanced quality antialiasing (EQAA) framework augments the standard MSAA color/depth resolve with coverage samples. The rasterizer, while processing triangles, can do cheap analytical sample coverage tests within a triangle. The results of such tests are saved into a compressed buffer called a *fragment mask* (FMask). The FMask acts as an indirection table that associates sample locations with color fragments that were rasterized and stored in the fragment buffer (as in normal MSAA). The number of samples can be higher than the number of stored fragments. In order to accomidate this, a sample in FMask may be marked as "unknown" if it is associated with a fragment that cannot be stored in the fragment buffer (see Figure 27.6).

An important aspect of coverage rendering is correct depth testing. Normally, incoming coverage samples need to be tested against depth fragments stored in the MSAA depth buffer. In order to get correct coverage information, normal MSAA would require a depth buffer that stores of the same number of depth fragments as the number of coverage samples (we can get away with storing fewer color fragments because FMask allows us to associate a single fragment with multiple samples). Fortunately, one feature of AMD's GCN architecture is an ability to work with a compressed depth buffer, which is stored as a set of plane equations. When this mode is enabled, EQAA uses these plane equations to do correct depth testing by analytically deriving depth values for all coverage samples. This means that it is possible to get correct coverage information, even if depth and color information is evaluated and stored as a single fragment (thus MSAA is effectively turned off for all render targets).

Another important requirement for correctly resolving coverage is to sort triangles from front to back. Otherwise, due to the rules of rasterization, it is possible for a triangle to partially overlap a pixel and not get rasterized. If that happens, then that pixel's coverage value might not get updated. Therefore, it is essential to sort objects from front to back (which most rendering engines do already). Fragment sorting is mostly taken care of by GCN hardware. Unfortunately, it is still possible to get incorrect results due to subpixel triangles that won't get rasterized and therefore can't correctly update pixel coverage information.

The memory footprint of FMask is directly proportional to number of unique fragments and samples used. For every sample, we need enough bits to index any of the fragment stored for that pixel and also an additional flag for an unknown value. For the sake of this article, we will focus on use cases with one fragment and eight samples (1F8S)—which require 1 bit per sample, thus 8 bits per pixel total (see Figure 27.7). Such a setup proved to be optimal with regard to EQAA performance as well as the FMask's memory footprint.

CRAA setup. Our goal is to use part of the EQAA pipeline to acquire coverage information at a high resolution (8 samples per pixel) without paying the computational and memory overhead of full MSAA rendering. We would like to use

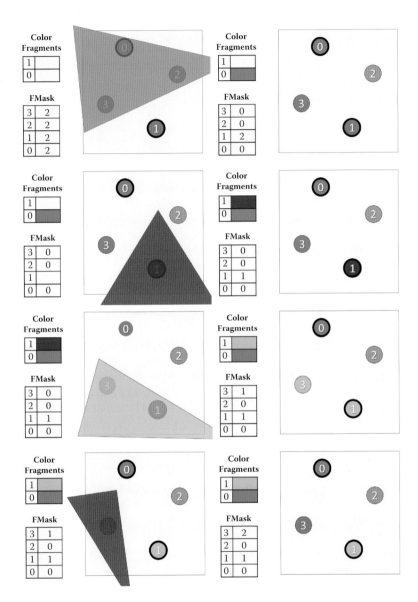

Figure 27.6. The steps here illustrate an updated FMask as new triangles are rasterized. Important note: in the last step, the red triangle does not need to evict Sample 3 if it would fail a Z-test against the sample. (This, however, depends on the particular hardware setup and is beyond the scope of this article.)

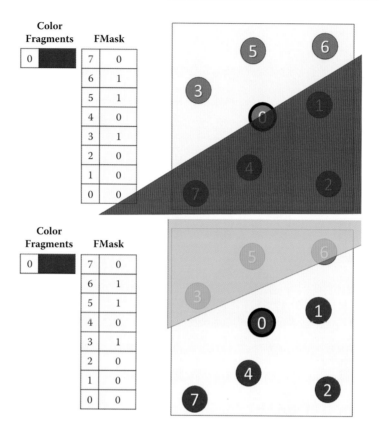

Figure 27.7. Simple rasterization case and corresponding FMask.

information recovered from the coverage data to derive blending hints in a similar fashion to AEAA.

In our simplified case of 1F8S we know that FMask will be an 8-bit value, where the nth bit being set to 0 represents the nth sample being associated with the rasterized fragment (therefore it belongs to the current pixel's triangle and would pass depth testing), while 1 informs us that this sample is unknown—i.e., it was occluded by another triangle.

We can think of FMask as a subset of points that share the same color. If we were to rasterize the current pixel with this newly acquired information, we would need to blend the current pixel's fragment weighted by the number of its known coverage samples, with the other fragment represented by "unknown" coverage samples. Without adding any additional rendering costs, we could infer the unknown color fragments from neighboring pixels. We assume that the depth buffer is working in a compressed mode and that EQAA is using analytical depth testing, thus providing perfectly accurate coverage information.

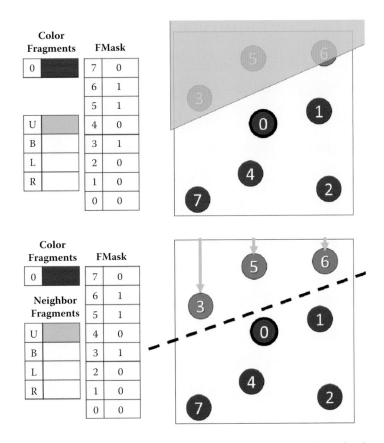

Figure 27.8. Here we illustrate the process of finding an edge that divides a set of samples into "known" and "unknown" samples. Later, this half plane is used to find an appropriate neighboring pixel for deriving the unknown color value.

Single edge scenario. We can apply the same strategy behind AEAA to a simple case in which only a single edge has crossed the pixel. In this case, the pixel's FMask provides a clear division of coverage samples: those that passed will be on one side of the edge, while failed samples will be on the other side. Using a simple line-fitting algorithm, we can find an edge that splits our set of samples into two subsets—passed and failed. This edge approximates the real geometric edge of the triangle that crossed the pixel. In the same spirit of the GBAA algorithm, we find the major axis of the edge as well as its distance from the pixel's center. Then we just need to blend the nearest neighboring pixel color with the current fragment using the edge distance as a weight. Thus, this technique infers the unknown samples from the pixel closest to the derived half plane (see Figure 27.8).

```
float4 CRAA( Texture2DMS<float4> inColor,
             Texture2D<uint2> inFMask,
             uint2 inTexcord )
{
  // Read FMask / HW dependant
  uint iFMask = inFMask.Load( uint3( viTexcoord, 0 ) );
  uint unknownCov = 0;
  float2 hP = 0.0;

  // Average all directions to unknown samples
  // to approximate edge halfplane
  for( uint iSample = 0; iSample < NUM_SAMPLES; ++iSample )
    if( getFMaskValueForSample(iFMask, iSample) == UNKNOWN_CODE )
    {
        hP += TexColorMS.GetSamplePosition(iSample);
        unknownCoverage++;
    }

  // Find fragment offset to pixel on the other side of edge
  int2 fOff = int2( 1, 0);
  if(abs(hP.x) > abs(hP.y) && hP.x <= 0.0) fOff = int2(-1, 0);
  if(abs(hP.x) <= abs(hP.y) && hP.x > 0.0) fOff = int2( 0, 1);
  if(abs(hP.x) <= abs(hP.y) && hP.x <= 0.0) fOff = int2( 0,-1);

  // Blend in inferred sample
  float knownCov = NUM_SAMPLES -- unknownCoverage;
  float4 color = inColor.Load( viToxcoord, 0 ) * knownCov;
  color += inColor.Load( viTexcoord + fOff, 0 ) * unknownCov;
  return color /= NUM_SAMPLES;
}
```

Listing 27.2. A simple shader for finding the half plane that approximates the orientation of the "unknown" subset of samples. The half plane is then used to find the closest pixel on the other side of the edge in order to infer the unknown sample's color.

The resolve we have described is akin to GBAA with a limited number of gradient steps (the number of steps is equal to the number of samples used by EQAA). An important thing to note is that our resolve does not need to know anything about the neighboring geometric data (all the information that is needed for reconstruction is contained within the pixel). This is an important difference, because we can reconstruct an edge that was created as the result of rasterizating multiple overlapping triangles; GBAA can only recreate the edge of a single triangle.

Our resolve can be efficiently implemented at runtime by approximating the half plane (see Listing 27.2) while still providing quality comparable to MSAA with the same sampling ratio (see Figure 27.9).

Complex scenario. Following what we learned about resolving simple edges using FMask, we would now like to apply similar ideas to resolving more complex situations in which multiple edges cross a given pixel. In order to achieve this, we would like to be able to group together "failed" samples from different triangles

Figure 27.9. A challenging rendering scenario for antialiasing (top left). Rasterization grid and edge layout (top right). Simple 8×CRAA resulting in edge antialiasing comparable to 8×MSAA apart from pixels that are intersected by multiple triangles (bottom left). The results of 8×MSAA (bottom right).

into multiple disconnected sets. For every disconnected set, we find edges (up to two edges in our implementation) that split it off from other sets. Then we use the acquired edges to find major directions that should be used for subset blending. For every subset of unknown fragments, we blend in a color from the neighboring fragment associated with that subset and weighted by the subset's area coverage within the pixel. Finally, we sum all the color values for each subset and blend this with the current fragment's known color weighted by the percentage of passing coverage samples. This way, we can partially reconstruct the subpixel data using the current pixel's surrounding neighborhood (see Figure 27.10).

Using precomputed LUT. Clearly, our algorithm could be rewritten to provide a set of weights for blending colors from the surrounding 3×3 pixel neighborhood. The blend weights rely only on the data present in FMask, and thus our blend weights can be precomputed and stored in a look up table (LUT), which is indexed directly by a pixel's FMask bit pattern.

In our 1F8S case, the LUT would only need 256 entries. Our implementation uses only top, bottom, left, and right neighboring pixels and uses only 4-bit gradients or blend weights. Therefore, the whole LUT requires $256 \times 4 \times 4 = 512$-byte array, which easily fits entirely within the cache.

We also experimented with more complex LUT creation logic. FMask can be evaluated in a morphological fashion to distinguish shapes, thus calculating more accurate and visually plausible gradients. Unfortunately, due to our project's time constraints, we did not have time to properly pursue this direction of research. We believe that a significant quality improvement can be gained from smarter

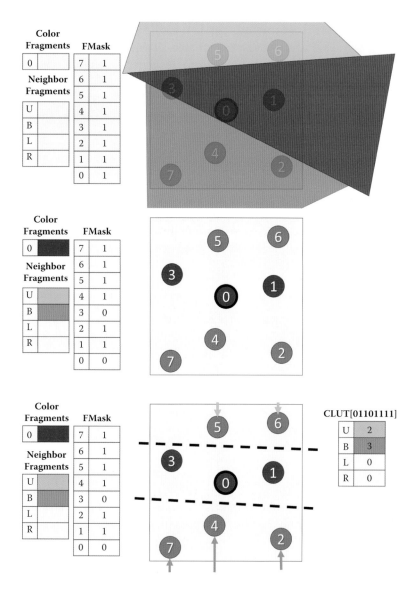

Figure 27.10. One of the possible methods for finding blend weights for sample subsets. The bottom image illustrates a blend weight resolve using a lookup table.

FMask analysis. Using 1F16S would also provide significantly better precision and subpixel handling.

It is worth noting that even the simple logic presented in this section allows for significant aliasing artifact reduction on thin triangles. Figure 27.11 illustrates a

Figure 27.11. Top to bottom: edge layout, rasterized edge, simple 8×CRAA resolve, and 8×CRAA LUT correctly resolving subpixel artifacts.

problematic case for AEAA, where our simple CRAA resolve correctly antialiased the edge. Unfortunately, when there are too many subpixel triangles that don't pass rasterization, CRAA may also fail due to incorrect coverage information. In practice, this heavily depends on the exact rendering situation, and still CRAA has much more relaxed restrictions than AEAA.

The code snippet in Listing 27.3 illustrates the CRAA LUT resolve properly resolving minor subpixel details (see Figure 27.10).

```
float4 CRAA_LUT( Texture2DMS<float4> inColor,
                 Texture2D<uint2> inFMask,
                 Texture1D<uint> inCRAALUT,
                 uint2 inTexcord )
{
  // Read FMask / HW dependant
  uint iFMask     = inFMask.Load( uint3( viTexcoord, 0 ) );
  uint LUTResult  = inCRAALUT[iFMask];
  float wC, wN, wE, wS, wW;

  // LUT is packed as 8bit integer weights
  // North 8b | West 8b | South 8b | East 8b
  // Can also pack whole neighborhood weights in 4 bits
  ExctractLUTWeights(LUTResult, wC, wN, wE, wS, wW);

  float4 color = inColor.Load( viTexcoord + int2( 0, 0) * wC;
          color += inColor.Load( viTexcoord + int2( 0,-1) * wN;
          color += inColor.Load( viTexcoord + int2( 0, 1) * wE;
          color += inColor.Load( viTexcoord + int2( 0, 1) * wS;
          color += inColor.Load( viTexcoord + int2(-1, 0) * wW;
          return color;
}
```

Listing 27.3. CRAA LUT implementation.

27.6   Temporal Super-Sampling

27.6.1   Overview

Temporal super-sampling can be succinctly described by the following simple algorithm:

1. Every frame, offset the projection matrix by a subpixel offset.

2. Use the current frame's N motion vectors to reproject data from frame $N - k$ to time step N.

3. Test if the reprojected data is valid:

   - No occlusion occurred.
   - The data comes from the same source (i.e., object or triangle).
   - The data is not stale (i.e., due to lighting changes).

4. Accumulate data from frame N with data reprojected from frame $N - k$.

5. Repeat steps 2–4 for k frames back in time.

The number k dictates the number of unique subpixel offsets used for jitter in order to get spatially unbiased results after converging by accumulation of all the k samples. However, it is easy to see that by increasing the number k of frames of history, the algorithm has a much higher complexity and therefore a much higher chance of failure.

  The most proper (and expensive) approach would be to hold the last k frames in memory along with their motion vectors and additional data required to verify sample validity. Then we would need to evaluate a series of dependent reads and checks to verify if reprojected pixels were valid back in both the spatial and temporal domains. For a given pixel, we could only accumulate as many samples as managed to pass these checks until we encountered the first failure. This approach would guarantee a very high-quality result [Yang et al. 09], however the cost when $k > 1$ is prohibitively expensive for real-time, performance-oriented scenarios, such as games.

  Other solutions rely on a so-called *history buffer* that holds all the accumulated samples, thus simplifying the previously described method to the $k = 1$ case. Unfortunately, this solution can't guarantee convergence as it is impossible to remove stale samples from the history buffer without discarding it totally. Also, the validation functions need to be much more conservative in order to prevent incoherent samples from entering the history buffer. This approach, when used for super-sampling, results in a somewhat unstable image with possible "fizzing" high-contrast pixels since they can't converge [Malan 12]. Very similar approaches can be used to stabilize the image over time (instead of super-sampling), as shown in [Sousa 13] and [Valient 14]. We will be discussing this more in Section 27.7.

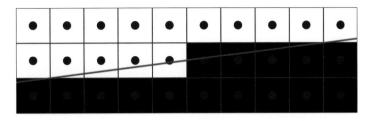

Figure 27.12. One sample centroid rasterization pattern.

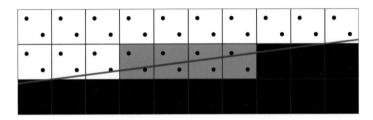

Figure 27.13. Two rotated samples from a standard 2×MSAA pattern.

Taking all pros and cons into account, we decided to pursue the highest possible quality with $k = 1$. This means that we are only dealing with one frame of history, and for every single frame we have two unique samples at our disposal (assuming that our history sample was accepted as valid); we would like to get as much data from them as possible.

27.6.2 Sampling Patterns

A single sample resolve can't provide any gradients (see Figure 27.12 for a baseline reference).

As discussed in Section 27.6.1, we want to maximize the resolve quality while using only two unique samples. One possible way to achieve this is through a more complex resolve and sampling pattern. Currently, common implementations of 2× super-sampling use the 2×MSAA sampling pattern (see Figure 27.13).

One possible improvement upon this is to use a quincunx sampling pattern [NVIDIA 01]. This pattern relies on sharing a noncentral sample with adjacent pixels; thus, the resolve kernel needs to sample corner data from neighboring pixels (see Figure 27.14).

In practice, quincunx sample positions are not very beneficial. Having sampling points on regular pixel rows and columns minimizes the number of potential edges that can be caught. In general, a good pattern should be optimized for maximum pixel row and column coverage. The 4× rotated-grid pattern is a good example (see Figure 27.15).

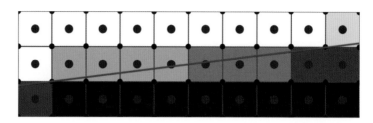

Figure 27.14. Quincunx sampling and resolve pattern guarantees higher-quality results than 2×MSAA while still keeping the sample count at 2.

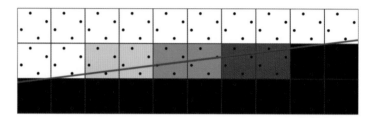

Figure 27.15. The 4× rotated-grid super-sampling pattern maximizes row and column coverage.

27.6.3 FLIPQUAD

[Akenine-Möller 03] proposed several other low-sample-cost patterns such as FLIP-TRI and FLIPQUAD. We will focus on FLIPQUAD as it perfectly matches our goal of using just two unique samples. This sampling pattern is similar to quincunx in its reuse of samples between pixels. However, a massive quality improvement comes from putting sampling points on pixel edges in a fashion similar to the rotated-grid sampling patterns. This provides unique rows and columns for each sample, therefore guaranteeing the maximum possible quality.

The FLIPQUAD pattern requires a custom per-pixel resolve kernel as well as custom per-pixel sampling positions (see Figure 27.16). An important observation is that the pattern is mirrored, therefore every single pixel quad is actually the same.

The article [Laine and Aila 06] introduced a unified metric for sampling pattern evaluation and proved FLIPQUAD to be superior to quincunx, even surpassing the 4× rotated-grid pattern when dealing with geometric edges (see Figure 27.17 and Table 27.1).

We can clearly see that the resolve kernel is possible in a typical pixel shader. However, the per-pixel sampling offsets within a quad were not supported in hardware until modern AMD graphic cards exposed the EQAA rasterization pipeline extensions. This feature is exposed on Xbox One and Playstation 4, as well as through an OpenGL extension on PC [Alnasser 11].

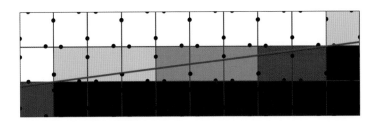

Figure 27.16. FLIPQUAD provides optimal usage of two samples matching quality of 4× rotated-grid resolve.

Figure 27.17. Left to right: single sample, FLIPQUAD, and quincunx. [Image courtesy [Akenine 03].]

The implementation of the FLIPQUAD pattern is fairly straightforward using 2×MSAA. The snippets in Listings 27.4 and 27.5 give sampling positions for pixels within a quad and the reconstruction kernel.

27.6.4 Temporal FLIPQUAD

In Section 27.6.3 we discussed implementing FLIPQUAD sampling and reconstruction on modern hardware. However, in the context of temporal supersampling, we need to adapt our pattern and resolve kernel. We decided to split the pattern into two subsets—one that will be used to render even frames (blue) and one used on odd frames (red) (see Figure 27.18).

Pattern	E
1× Centroid	> 1.0
2 × 2 Uniform Grid	0.698
2 × 2 Rotated Grid	0.439
Quincunx	0.518
FLIPQUAD	0.364

Table 27.1. Error metric (E) comparison against a 1024-sample reference image as reported by [Laine and Aila 06] (lower is better).

```
// Indexed [SAMPLES LOCATIONS] in n/16 pixel offsets
int2 gFQ_Q00[2] = { int2 (-8,-2), int2 ( 2,-8) };
int2 gFQ_Q10[2] = { int2 (-8, 2), int2 (-2,-8) };
int2 gFQ_Q01[2] = { int2 (-8, 2), int2 (-2,-8) };
int2 gFQ_Q11[2] = { int2 (-8,-2), int2 ( 2,-8) };
```

Listing 27.4. FLIPQUAD sample array.

```
s0 = CurrentFrameMS.Sample(PointSampler, UV, 0);
s1 = CurrentFrameMS.Sample(PointSampler, UV, 1);
s2 = CurrentFrameMS.Sample(PointSampler, int2( 1, 0), 0);
s3 = CurrentFrameMS.Sample(PointSampler, int2( 0, 1), 1);

return 0.25 * (s0 + s1 + s2 + s3);}
```

Listing 27.5. FLIPQUAD reconstruction kernel.

To resolve this sampling scheme properly, we need two resolve kernels—one for even and one for odd frames (see Listings 27.6 and 27.7). Due to the alternating patterns, in each frame the kernel will be guaranteed to properly resolve horizontal or vertical edges. If data from the previous frame is accepted, a full pattern will be properly reconstructed.

It is worth noting that an incorrect (or missing) FLIPQUAD reconstruction pass will result in jigsaw edges, which are a direct result of a nonuniform sampling grid (see Figure 27.19).

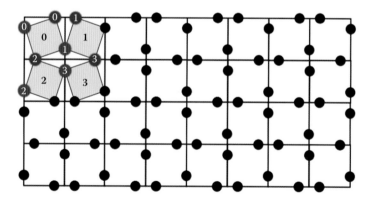

Figure 27.18. Temporal FLIPQUAD pattern. Red samples are rendered on even frames. Blue samples are rendered on odd frames.

```
// Indexed[FRAME][SAMPLES LOCATIONS] in n/16 pixel offsets
// BLUE RED
int2 gTempFQ_Q0[2][1]   = { int2 (-8,-2), int2 ( 2,-8) };
int2 gTempFQ_Q1[2][1]   = { int2 (-8, 2), int2 (-2,-8) };
int2 gTempFQ_Q2[2][1]   = { int2 (-8, 2), int2 (-2,-8) };
int2 gTempFQ_Q3[2][1]   = { int2 (-8,-2), int2 ( 2,-8) };
```

Listing 27.6. Temporal FLIPQUAD sample array.

```
#if defined(ODD_FRAME) // RED
// Horizontal pattern for frame [1]
int2 offset0 = int2(0, 1);
int2 offset1 = int2(1, 0);
#else if defined(EVEN_FRAME) // BLUE
int2 offset0 = int2(1, 0);
int2 offset1 = int2(0, 1);
#endif

s0 = CurrentFrame.Sample(PointSampler, UV);
s1 = CurrentFrame.Sample(PointSampler, UV, offset0);
s2 = PreviousFrame.Sample(LinearSampler, previousUV);
s3 = PreviousFrame.Sample(LinearSampler, previousUV, offset1);

return 0.25 * (s0 + s1 + s2 + s3);}
```

Listing 27.7. Temporal FLIPQUAD reconstruction kernel.

Rasterization should happen at sample locations in order to take full advantage of FLIPQUAD. This can be easily achieved by using the `sample` prefix in HLSL's interpolator definition. This way, texture data will be offset properly, resulting in a correctly super-sampled image.

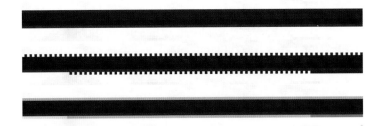

Figure 27.19. Top to bottom: edge rasterized on an even frame and then an odd frame and the final edge after temporal FLIPQUAD reconstruction kernel.

```
// Quad defined as (sample positions within quad)
// s00 s10
// s01 s11
DDX[f(s00)] = [f(s00) -- f(s10)]/dx, dx = |s00 -- s10|
DDY[f(s00)] = [f(s00) -- f(s01)]/dy, dy = |s00 -- s01|

// Hardware assumes dx = dy = 1
// In case of sampling pattern from Listing 6. dx != dy
// Footprint-based sampling picks base mip level
// Based on max(ddx, ddy)
// Frame A max(ddx, ddy) != Frame B max(ddx, ddy)
// Implies non temporarily coherent mip selection

// Calculated in 1/16th of pixel
// Frame A (BLUE)
dx = |-8 -- (16 + (-8))| = 16
dy = |-2 -- (16 + ( 2))| = 20
baseMip ~ max(dx, dy) = 20

// Frame B (RED)
dx = | 2 -- (16 + (-2))| = 12
dy = |-8 -- (16 + (-8))| = 16
baseMip ~ max(dx, dy) = 16}
```

Listing 27.8. Default method for derivative calculation.

27.6.5   Temporal FLIPQUAD and Gradients

One side effect of using the temporal FLIPQUAD pattern is a nonuniform distance between samples within a quad. This causes problems for the gradient calculation and mipmap selection. Graphics cards rely on calculating per-pixel (or per-quad) derivatives using differentials within a quad. This process is fairly straightforward (see Listing 27.8).

As an optimization, spatial distances, used to normalize the differential, are assumed to be 1. However, if we look at our temporal FLIPQUAD pattern, we clearly see that distances between samples are different between the x- and y-axes, and we alternate from frame to frame (see Listing 27.8).

Nonuniform distances will result in a biased mipmap level-of-detail calculation, as $ddx(uv)$ or $ddy(uv)$ will be increasing faster than it should. In effect, the textures will appear sharper or blurrier than they should be. In the worst case, a single texture can select different mipmap levels, under the same viewing direction, when rendering even and odd frames. This would lead to temporal instability since bilinear filtering picks the mipmap based on $\max(ddx, ddy)$, which, in this case, would result in differences between frames (see Figure 27.20).

One way to solve this issue would be to switch all texture samples to a gradient-based texture read (i.e., `tex2Dgrad` in HLSL) and to calculate the gradients analytically taking sample distance into account. Unfortunately, this complicates all shaders and can have significant performance overhead.

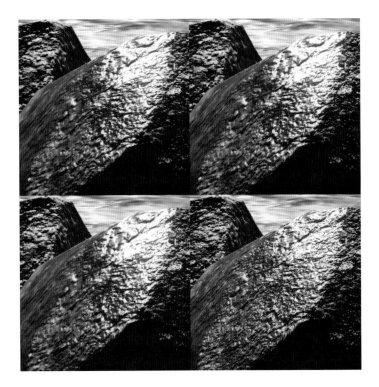

Figure 27.20. The top row shows even and odd frames of the reordered Temporal FLIPQUAD pattern. The bottom row shows the default temporal FLIPQUAD pattern clearly suffering from mipmap level mismatches. (The bottom right represents an oversharpened odd frame.)

Another option is to change the pattern in order to minimize frame-to-frame sample distance variance. While this will not provide correct results, the error may not be noticeable in practice as long as it is temporarily stable (see Figure 27.20). Please note that this also requires different offsets (kernel and projection matrix offsets) to shift samples outside the pixel window (see Listings 27.9 and 27.10 for details).

```
// Indexed[FRAME][SAMPLES LOCATIONS] in n/16 pixel offsets
int2 gTempFQ_Q0[2][1] = { int2 ( 0,-2), int2 (-2, 0) };
int2 gTempFQ_Q1[2][1] = { int2 ( 0, 2), int2 ( 2, 0) };
int2 gTempFQ_Q2[2][1] = { int2 ( 0, 2), int2 ( 2, 0) };
int2 gTempFQ_Q3[2][1] = { int2 ( 0,-2), int2 (-2, 0) };
int2 gProjMatOff[2][1] = { int2 (-8, 0), int2 ( 0, 8) };}
```

Listing 27.9. Reordered temporal FLIPQUAD with additional projection matrix offsets.

```
#if defined(ODD_FRAME) // RED
// Horizontal pattern for frame [1]
int2 offset0 = int2(0,-1);
int2 offset1 = int2(1, 0);
#else if defined(EVEN_FRAME) // BLUE
int2 offset0 = int2(1, 0);
int2 offset1 = int2(0,-1);
#endif

s0 = CurrentFrame.Sample(PointSampler, UV);
s1 = CurrentFrame.Sample(PointSampler, UV, offset0);
s2 = PreviousFrame.Sample(LinearSampler, previousUV);
s3 = PreviousFrame.Sample(LinearSampler, previousUV, offset1);

return 0.25 * (s0 + s1 + s2 + s3);}
```

Listing 27.10. Reordered temporal FLIPQUAD reconstruction kernel.

27.6.6   History Sample Acceptance Method

Our acceptance method for history samples is based on the algorithm used in *Killzone: Shadow Fall* [Valient 14].

The history sample from frame $N - 1$ is valid only if

- the motion flow between frame N and $N - 1$ is coherent,

- the color flow between frames N and $N - 2$ is coherent. (Note that $N - 2$ and N have the same subpixel jitter.)

The first constraint guarantees that a sample was not occluded and was moving in a similar direction. The second constraint guarantees that there was no major change in lighting conditions between frames with the same subpixel jitter. Both tests use a 3×3 neighborhood using the sum of absolute differences to estimate the degree of similarity between frames. It is possible to achieve reasonable results using a smaller neighborhood, however, testing might need to be more conservative.

If any constraint fails, then we fall back to clamping history samples to the current frame color bounding box, as described in Section 27.7. This guarantees no ghosting and enhanced temporal stability. It is worth noting that the color flow constraint is very important in a real production environment. It enables the unrestricted usage of animated textures and particle effects as well as lighting changes. Another important benefit is that it grants convergence in the event that the viewport becomes fixed.

27.6.7   Resampling

Any reprojection method is prone to numerical diffusion errors. When a frame is reprojected using motion vectors and newly acquired sampling coordinates do not land exactly on a pixel, a resampling scheme must be used. Typically, most methods resort to simple bilinear sampling. However, bilinear sampling will result in over-smoothing. If we would like to use a history buffer in order to accumulate multiple samples, we will also accumulate resampling errors, which can lead to serious image quality degradation (see Figure 27.22). Fortunately, this problem is very similar to well-researched fluid simulation advection optimization problems.

In fluid simulation, the advection step is very similar to our problem of image reprojection. A data field of certain quantities (i.e., pressure and temperature) has to be advected forward in time by a motion field. In practice, both fields are stored in discretized forms; thus, the advection step needs to use resampling. Assuming that the operation is a linear transform, this situation is equal to the problem of reprojection.

Under these circumstances, a typical semi-Lagrangian advection step would be equal to reprojection using bilinear resampling. A well-known method to prevent over-smoothing is to use second order methods for advection. There are several known methods to optimize this process, assuming that the advection operator is reversible. One of them is the MacCormack scheme and its derivation: back and forth error compensation and correction (BFECC). This method enables one to closely approximate the second order accuracy using only two semi-Lagrangian steps [Dupont and Liu 03].

BFECC is very intuitive. In short, we advect the solution forward and backward in time using advection operator A and its reverse, A^R. Operator error is estimated by comparing the original value against the newly acquired one. The original value is corrected by error $(\frac{\varphi^n - \widehat{\varphi}^n}{2})$ and finally advected forward into the next step of the solution (see Algorithm 27.1 and Figure 27.21 for an illustration).

In the context of reprojection, our advection operator is simply a bilinear sample using a motion vector offset. It is worth noting that the function described by the motion vector texture is not reversible (i.e., multiple pixels might move to same discretized position).

A correct way to acquire a reversible motion vector offset would be through a depth-buffer–based reprojection using an inverse camera matrix. Unfortunately, this would limit the operator to pixels subject to camera motion only. Also, the operator would be invalid on pixels that were occluded during the previous time step.

1: $\widehat{\varphi}^{n+1} = A(\varphi^n)$.
2: $\widehat{\varphi}^n = A^R(\widehat{\varphi}^{n+1})$.
3: $\bar{\varphi} = \varphi^n + \dfrac{\varphi^n - \widehat{\varphi}^n}{2}$.
4: $\varphi^{n+1} = A(\bar{\varphi})$.

Algorithm 27.1. Original BFECC method.

$$1: \widehat{\varphi}^{n+1} = A(\varphi^n).$$
$$2: \widehat{\varphi}^n = A^R(.\widehat{\varphi}^{n+1}).$$
$$3: \varphi^{n+1} = \widehat{\varphi}^{n+1} + \frac{\varphi^n - \widehat{\varphi}^n}{2}.$$

Algorithm 27.2. Simplified BFECC method.

Another option is to assume a high-coherency motion vector field (texture) and just use a negative motion vector for the reverse operator. However, this approach would break under perspective correction (i.e., high slopes) as well as with complex motion.

In practice, we used a mix of both approaches. The reverse operator is acquired through depth-based reprojection for static pixels and reversing motion vectors for pixels from dynamic objects. For us, this proved to be both efficient and visually plausible (even if not always mathematically correct).

Another important optimization we used was inspired by the simplified BFECC method by [Selle et al. 08]. In this approach, it is proven that the error is not time dependent; therefore the results from frame $n + 1$ can be directly compensated by an error estimate. This simplifies the original BFECC by one full semi-Lagrangian (see Algorithm 27.2).

Unfortunately, the proposed method requires reading $\widehat{\varphi}^n$, φ^n, and $\widehat{\varphi}^{n+1}$ in order to evaluate φ^{n+1}. However, as we already assumed that the error estimate is time invariant, we can as use the values from step $n + 1$ to estimate the error. Therefore, we can calculate φ^{n+1} using only $\widehat{\varphi}^{n+1}$ and $\widehat{\widehat{\varphi}}^{n+1}$, where $\widehat{\widehat{\varphi}}^{n+1}$ is easy to acquire in a shader (see Algorithm 27.3, Listing 27.11, and Figure 27.21 for details).

One last thing worth mentioning is that BFECC, by default, is not unconditionally stable. There are multiple ways of dealing with this problem, but we found bounding by local minima and maxima to be the most practical [Dupont and Liu 03, Selle et al. 08]. Listing 27.11 presents the simplest implementation of our optimized BFECC, and Figure 27.22 demonstrates the results.

$$1: \widehat{\varphi}^{n+1} = A(\varphi^n).$$
$$2: \widehat{\varphi}^n = A^R(\widehat{\varphi}^{n+1}).$$
$$3: \widehat{\widehat{\varphi}}^{n+1} = A(\widehat{\varphi}^n).$$
$$4: \varphi^{n+1} = \widehat{\varphi}^{n+1} + \frac{\widehat{\varphi}^{n+1} - \widehat{\widehat{\varphi}}^{n+1}}{2}.$$

Algorithm 27.3. Shader optimized simplified BFECC method.

```
// Pass outputs phiHatN1Texture
// A() operator uses motion vector texture
void GetPhiHatN1(float2 inUV, int2 inVPOS)
{
  float2 motionVector = MotionVectorsT.Load(int3(inVPOS, 0)).xy;
  float2 forwardProj = inUV + motionVector;
  // Perform advection by operator A()

  return PreviousFrameT.SampleLevel(Linear, forwardProj, 0).rgb;
}

// Pass outputs phiHatTexture
// AR() operator uses negative value from motion vector texture
// phiHatN1 texture is generated by previous pass GetPhiHatN1()
void GetPhiHatN(float2 inUV, int2 inVPOS)
{
  float2 motionVector = MotionVectorsT.Load(int3(inVPOS, 0)).xy;
  float2 backwardProj = inUV - motionVector;

  // Perform reverse advection by operator AR()
  return phiHatN1T.SampleLevel(Linear, backwardProj, 0).rgb;
}

// Final operation to get correctly resampled phiN1
// A() operator uses motion vector texture
// phiHatN1 and phiHatN textures are generated by previous passes
void GetResampledValueBFECC(float2 inUV, int2 inVPOS)
{
  float3 phiHatN1 = phiHatN1T.Load(int3(inVPOS, 0)).rgb;

  // Find local minima and maxima
  float3 minima, maxima;
  GetLimitsRGB(phiHatN1Texture, inUV, minima, maxima);

  float2 motionVector = MotionVectors.Load(int3(inVPOS, 0)).xy;
  float2 A = inUV + motionVector;

  // Perform advection by operator A()
  float3 phiHatHatN1 = phiHatT.SampleLevel(Linear, A, 0).rgb;

  // Perform BFECC
  float3 phiN1         = 1.5 * phiHatN1 - 0.5 * phiHatHatN1;

  // Limit the result to minima and maxima
  phiN1                = clamp(phiN1, minima, maxima);
  return phiN1;
}
```

Listing 27.11. Reordered temporal FLIPQUAD reconstruction kernel.

27.7 Temporal Antialiasing (TAA)

27.7.1 Overview

In Sections 27.5 and 27.6, we presented methods for improving spatial and temporal stability and resolution of antialiased images. However, even when using $4\times$ rotated-grid super-sampling and dedicated edge antialiasing, disturbing tem-

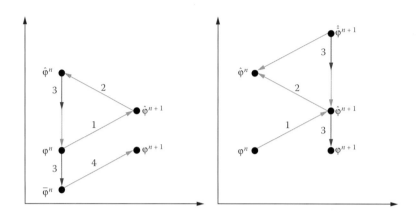

Figure 27.21. Conceptual scheme of the original BFCE method (left) and of the shader optimized BFCE used for texture resampling (right).

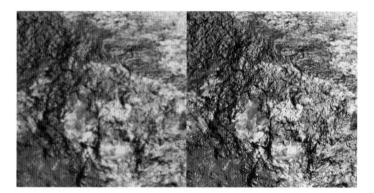

Figure 27.22. Continuous resampling of 30 frames using a history buffer. The camera is in motion, panning from left to right. Using bilinear sampling shows numerical diffusion errors resulting in a blurry image (left). Using optimized linear BFCE helps to minimizes blurring (right).

poral artifacts may occur. Ideally we would like to accumulate more frames over time to further improve image quality. Unfortunately, as described in Sections 27.6.1 and 27.6.6, it is very hard to provide a robust method that will work in real-world situations, while also using multiple history samples, without other artifacts. Therefore, several methods rely on super-sampling only in certain local contrast regions of an image [Malan 12, Sousa 13, Valient 14]. These approaches rely on visually plausible temporal stabilization (rather than super-sampling). We would like to build upon these approaches to further improve our results.

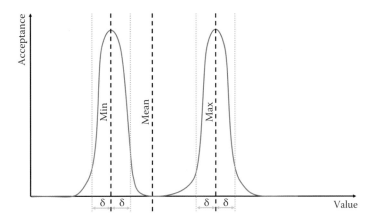

Figure 27.23. Frequency-based acceptance function plot.

27.7.2 Frequency-Based Acceptance Metric

A simple temporal antialiasing scheme can be described as a cumulative blend between the current frame and an accumulation buffer of previous frames (history data). However, finding the correct blend factor is difficult. We would like to stabilize the data such that we avoid fluctuations over time and enhance the image quality by accumulating new information. On the other hand, we need to detect when data becomes stale or invalid.

We build a color bounding box of fresh data by sampling the 3×3 spatial neighborhood from the current frame. From this data we evaluate the local minima, maxima, and mean value per RGB channel.

We follow a reasoning grounded in signal frequency analysis. If our history data is too similar to the local mean, it does not bring much new information to the current frame and might even diffuse the result if it contains accumulated errors (i.e., due to sampling errors). The more "different" the data is from mean, the more important it is. However, certain information might just be a fluctuation that skews the data. With all of this in mind, we can treat information that is in close proximity to fresh data's local minima and maxima as valid (to a degree). Therefore, we could plot our function of history data acceptance as two peaks centered at a local minima and maxima, with a slope curve steered by a user controlled δ value (see Figure 27.23).

To reduce incorrectly accepted samples even further, we utilize motion-based constraints as described in Section 27.6.6. This combination method minimizes the possible reprojection artifacts to a 3×3 pixel neighborhood (i.e., ghosting) while still guaranteeing a very high level of temporal stabilization. It's worth noting that this method can't provide convergence in the context of super-sampling (or jittered rendering), as sample acceptance relies on local data changes. See Listing 27.12 for details.

```
// curMin, curMax, curMean are estimated from 3x3 neighborhood
float3 getTAA(float2 inCurtMotionVec,
              float2 inPrevMotionVec,
              float3 inCurtMean,
              float3 inCurtMin,
              float3 inCurtMax,
              float3 inCurtValue,
              float3 inPrevValue)
{

  // Motion coherency weight
  float motionDelta = length(inCurMotionVec - inPrevMotionVec);
  float motionCoherence = saturate(c_motionSens * motionDelta));

  // Calculate color window range
  float3 range = inCutMin - inCurMax;

  // Offset the window bounds by delta percentage
  float3 extOffset = c_deltaColorWindowOffset * range;
  float3 extBoxMin = max(inCurMin - extOffset.rgb, 0.0);
  float3 extdBoxMax = inCurMax + extOffset;

  // Calculate deltas between previous and current color window
  float3 valDiff = saturate(extBoxMin - inPrevValue);
  valDiff += saturate(inPreviousValue - extBoxMax);
  float3 clampedPrevVal = clamp(inPrevValue, extBoxMin, extBoxMax);

  // Calculate deltas for current pixel against previous
  float3 meanWeight = abs(inCurValue - inPreValue);
  float loContrast = length(meanWeight)* c_loWeight;
  float hiContrast = length(valDiff) * c_hiWeight;

  // Calculate final weights
  float denom = max((loContrast - hiContrast), 0.0);
  float finalWeight = saturate(rcp(denom + epsilon));

  // Check blend weight against minimum bound
  // Prevents the algorithm from stalling
  // in a 'saddle' due to numerical imprecision
  // Regulates minimum blend of current data
  finalWeight= max(c_minLimiter, w);

  // Correct previous samples according to motion coherency weights
  finalWeight = saturate(finalWeight - motionCoherence);
  // Final value blend
  return lerp(inCurValue, clampedPrevVal, finalWeight);
}
```

Listing 27.12. Temporal antialiasing using our frequency-based acceptance metric.

27.8 Final Implementation

Our final framework's implementation can be split into two main stages:

- temporally stable edge antialiasing, which includes

  ○ SMAA,

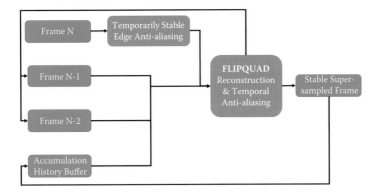

Figure 27.24. Data flow graph in our implementation of the HRAA pipeline.

    ○ CRAA,

    ○ AEAA (GBAA);

- Temporal FLIPQUAD reconstruction combined with temporal antialiasing (TAA) (see Listing 27.13).

Figure 27.24 illustrates the data flow inside the framework.

During production, we implemented and optimized all three approaches to temporarily stable edge antialiasing.

SMAA was implemented with geometric edge detection based on depth and normal buffers. Edges were refined by a predicated threshold based on the luminescence contrast. Our edge-detection algorithm choice was dictated by making the resolve as temporally stable as possible.

CRAA and AEAA used the implementations described in Sections 27.5.1 and 27.5.2. Our EQAA setup used a 1F8S configuration, while our AEAA offset buffer was compressed down to 5 bits (utilizing the last remaining space in our tightly packed G-buffer).

The results of either edge antialiasing pass were used as N, $N-1$, and $N-2$ frame sources in the last pass. The history buffer used by TAA at frame N was the output buffer of TAA from frame $N-1$.

27.9 Results Discussion

Our packing/performance scheme resulted in fairly low-quality gradients coming out of edge antialiasing (only 3 bits for steps). However, FLIPQUAD reconstruction provided two to four times the edge gradients virtually for free. In practice, the whole system provided excellent results, matching a 4× rotated-grid super-sampled reference while providing much higher-quality edge antialiasing and temporal stability at minimal cost.

```
// Unoptimized pseudocode for final
// Temporal FLIPQUAD reconstruction & TAA
// Frames N & N-2 are assumed
// To have same jitter offsets
float3 getFLIPQUADTaa()
{
  float3 curMin, currMax, curMean;
  GetLimits(currentValueTexture, curMin, curMax, curMean);

  float3 prevVal = Resample(prevValueTexture);
  float3 prevPrevVal = Resample(prevPrevValueTexture);

  // Get sums of absolute difference
  float3 curSAD = GetSAD(curValueTexture);
  float3 prevPrevSAD = GetSAD(prevPrevValueTexture);

  // Motion coherency weight
  float moCoherence = GetMotionCoherency(curMotionTexture,
                                         prevMotionTexture);

  // Color coherency weight
  float colCoherence = GetColorCoherency(curSAD, prevPrevSAD);

  // FLIPQUAD parts
  float3 FQCurPart = GetCurFLIPQUAD(curValueTexture);
  float3 FQPrevPart = GetPrevFLIPQUAD(prevValueTexture);
  float FQCoherency = motionCoherence + colorCoherence;
  float3 clampFQPrev = clamp(FQPrevPart, curMin, curMax);

  // This lerp allows full convergance
  // If color flow (N-2 to N) is coherent
  FQPrevPart = lerp(FQPrevPart, clampFQPrev, colCoherence);

  // Final reconstruction blend
  float3 FLIPQUAD = lerp(FQCurPart, FQPrevPart,0.5*moCoherence);

  float3 historyVal = Resample(historyValueTexture);

  return getTAA(curMotionTexture, prevMotionTexture,
                curMin, curMax, curMean,
                FLIPQUAD, historyVal)
}
```

Listing 27.13. Pseudocode for the combined temporal FLIPQUAD reconstruction and temporal antialiasing.

While temporal FLIPQUAD and TAA remained stable and reliable components of the framework, the choice of the edge antialiasing solution proved to be problematic.

SMAA provided the most visually plausible results on static pixels under any circumstances. The gradients were always smooth and no edge was left without antialiasing. Unfortunately, it sometimes produced distracting gradient wobble while in motion. The wobble was partially mitigated by the FLIPQUAD and TAA resolves. Unfortunately, SMAA had the highest runtime cost out of the whole framework.

AEAA provided excellent stability and quality, even in close-ups where triangles are very large on screen. Unfortunately, objects with very high levels of tessellation resulted in very objectionable visual noise or even a total loss of antialiasing on some edges. Even though this was the fastest method for edge antialiasing, it proved too unreliable for our open world game. It is worth noting that our AEAA implementation required us to modify every single shader that writes out to the G-buffer. This might be prohibitively expensive in terms of developer maintainability and runtime performance.

CRAA mitigated most of the issues seen with AEAA and was also the easiest technique to implement. Unfortunately, on the current generation of hardware, there is a measurable cost for using even a simple EQAA setup and the cost scales with the number of rendered triangles and their shader complexity. However, in our scenario, it was still faster than SMAA alone. Even though we were able to solve multiple issues, we still found some finely tessellated content that was problematic with this technique and resulted in noisy artifacts on edges. These artifacts could be effectively filtered by temporal FLIPQUAD and TAA. Unfortunately the cost of outputting coverage data from pixel shaders was too high for our vegetation-heavy scenarios. We did not experiment with manual coverage output (i.e., not hardware based).

At the time of writing, we have decided to focus on two main approaches for our game: SMAA with AEAA used for alpha-tested geometry or CRAA with AEAA used for alpha-tested geometry. SMAA with AEAA is the most expensive and most reliable while also providing the lowest temporal stability. CRAA with AEAA provides excellent stability and performance with medium quality and medium reliability. The use of AEAA for alpha-tested objects seems to provide the highest quality, performance, and stability in both use cases; therefore, we integrated its resolve filter into the SMAA and CRAA resolves. See the performance and image quality comparisons of the full HRAA framework in Figure 27.25 and Table 27.2.

27.10 Conclusion

We provided a production proven hybrid reconstruction antialiasing framework along with several new algorithms, as well as modern implementations of well-known algorithms. We believe that the temporal FLIPQUAD super-sampling as well as temporal antialiasing will gain wider adoption due to their low cost, simplicity, and quality. Our improvements to distance-to-edge–based methods might prove useful for some projects. Meanwhile, CRAA is another addition to the temporally stable antialiasing toolbox. Considering its simplicity of implementation and its good performance, we believe that with additional research it might prove to be a viable, widely adopted edge antialiasing solution. We hope that the ideas presented here will inspire other researchers and developers and provide readers with valuable tools for achieving greater image quality in their projects.

Figure 27.25. Comparison of different HRAA setups showing different scenarios based on actual game content. From left to right: centroid sampling (no antialiasing), temporal FLIPQUAD (TFQ), AEAA + TFQ, CRAA + TFQ, and SMAA + TFQ.

Single Pass	Timing (ms)	G-Buffer Overhead (%)
BFECC single value	0.3	N/A
Temporal FLIPQUAD (TFQ)	0.2	N/A
AEAA	0.25	< 1% C
8×CRAA	0.25	< 8% HW/C
SMAA	0.9	N/A
TAA	0.6	N/A
TFQ + TAA	0.62	N/A
AEAA(alpha test) + 8×CRAA + TFQ + TAA	0.9	< 3% HW/C
SMAA + TFQ + TAA	1.4	N/A

Table 27.2. Different HRAA passes and timings measured on an AMD Radeon HD 7950 at 1080p resolution, operating on 32-bit image buffers. "C" means content dependent and "HW" means hardware type or setup dependent.

Bibliography

[Akenine-Möller 03] T. Akenine-Möller. "An Extremely Inexpensive Multisampling Scheme." Technical Report No. 03-14, Ericsson Mobile Platforms AB, 2003.

[AMD 11] AMD Developer Relations. "EQAA Modes for AMD 6900 Series Graphics Cards." http://developer.amd.com/wordpress/media/2012/10/EQAAModesforAMDHD6900SeriesCards.pdf, 2011.

[Alnasser 11] M. Alnasser, G. Sellers, and N. Haemel. "AMD Sample Positions." *OpenGL Extension Registry*, https://www.opengl.org/registry/specs/AMD/sample_positions.txt, 2011.

[Bavoil and Andersson 12] L. Bavoil and J. Andersson. "Stable SSAO in Battlefield 3 with Selective Temporal Filtering." Game Developer Conference Course, San Francisco, CA, March 5–9, 2012.

[Burley 07] B. Burley. "Filtering in PRMan." *Renderman Repository*, https://web.archive.org/web/20130915064937/http:/www.renderman.org/RMR/st/PRMan_Filtering/Filtering_In_PRMan.html, 2007. (Original URL no longer available.)

[Drobot 11] M. Drobot. "A Spatial and Temporal Coherence Framework for Real-Time Graphics." In *Game Engine Gems 2*, edited by Eric Lengyel, pp. 97–118. Boca Raton, FL: CRC Press, 2011.

[Drobot 14] M. Drobot. "Low Level Optimizations for AMD GCN Architecture." Presented at Digital Dragons Conference, Kraków, Poland, May 8–9, 2014.

[Dupont and Liu 03] T. Dupont and Y. Liu. "Back and Forth Error Compensation and Correction Methods for Removing Errors Induced by Uneven Gradients of the Level Set Function." *J. Comput. Phys.* 190:1 (2003), 311–324.

[Jimenez et al. 11] J. Jimenez, B. Masia, J. Echevarria, F. Navarro, and D. Gutierrez. "Practical Morphological Antialiasing." In *GPU Pro 2: Advanced Rendering Techniques*, edited by Wolfgang Engel, pp. 95–114. Natick, MA: A K Peters, 2011.

[Jimenez et al. 12] J. Jimenez, J. Echevarria, D. Gutierrez, and T. Sousa. "SMAA: Enhanced Subpixel Morphological Antialiasing." *Computer Graphics Forum: Proc. EUROGRAPHICS 2012* 31:2 (2012), 355–364.

[Kirkland et al. 99] Dale Kirkland, Bill Armstrong, Michael Gold, Jon Leech, and Paula Womack. "ARB Multisample." *OpenGL Extension Registry*, https://www.opengl.org/registry/specs/ARB/multisample.txt, 1999.

[Laine and Aila 06] S. Laine and T. Aila. "A Weighted Error Metric and Optimization Method for Antialiasing Patterns." *Computer Graphics Forum* 25:1 (2006), 83–94.

[Lottes 09] T. Lottes. "FXAA." NVIDIA white paper, 2009.

[Malan 10] H. Malan. "Edge Anti-aliasing by Post-Processing." In *GPU Pro: Advanced Rendering Techniques*, edited by Wolfgang Engel, pp. 265–290. Natick, MA: A K Peters, 2010.

[Malan 12] H. Malan. "Realtime global illumination and reflections in Dust 514." Advances in Real-Time Rendering in Games: Part 1, SIGGRAPH Course, Los Angeles, CA, August 5–9, 2012.

[NVIDIA 01] NVIDIA Corporation. "HRAA: High-Resolution Antialiasing Through Multisampling". Technical report, 2001.

[Nehab et al. 07] D. Nehab, P. V. Sander, J. Lawrence, N. Tararchuk, and J. R. Isidoro. "Accelerating Real-Time Shading with Reverse Reprojection Caching." In *Proceedings of the 22nd ACM SIGGRAPH/EUROGRAPHICS Symposium on Graphics Hardware*, edited by Dieter Fellner and Stephen Spencer, pp. 25–35. Aire-la-Ville, Switzerland: Eurographics Association, 2007.

[Persson 11] E. Persson. "Geometric Buffer Antialiasing." Presented at SIGGRAPH, Vancouver, Canada, August 7–11, 2011.

[Reshetov 09] A. Reshetov. "Morphological Antialiasing." In *Proceedings of the Conference on High Performance Graphics*, edited by S. N. Spencer, David McAllister, Matt Pharr, and Ingo Wald, pp. 109–116. New York: ACM, 2009.

[Selle et al. 08] A. Selle, R. Fedkiw, B. Kim, Y. Liu, and J. Rossignac. "An Unconditionally Stable MacCormack Method." *J. Scientific Computing* 35:2–3 (2008), 350–371.

[Sousa 11] T. Sousa. "Anti-aliasing Methods in CryENGINE3." Presented at SIGGRAPH 2011, Vancouver, Canada, August 7–11, 2011.

[Sousa 13] T. Sousa T. "CryENGINE 3 Graphics Gems." Presented at SIGGRAPH 2013, Anaheim, CA, July 21–25, 2013.

[Valient 14] M. Valient. "Taking *Killzone Shadow Fall* Image Quality into the Next Generation." Presented at Game Developers Conference, San Francisco, CA, March 17–21, 2014.

[Yang et al. 09] L. Yang, D. Nehab, P. V. Sander, P. Sitthi-Amorn, J. Lawrence, and H. Hoppe. "Amortized Supersampling." Presented at SIGGRAPH Asia, Yokohama, Japan, December 17–19, 2009.

[Young 06] P. Young. "Coverage Sampled Antialiasing." Technical report, NVIDIA, 2006.

28

Real-Time Rendering of Physically Based Clouds Using Precomputed Scattering

Egor Yusov

28.1 Introduction

Rendering realistic clouds has always been a desired feature for a variety of applications, from computer games to flight simulators. Clouds consist of innumerable tiny water droplets that scatter light. Rendering clouds is challenging because photons are typically scattered multiple times before they leave the cloud. Despite the impressive performance of today's GPUs, accurately modeling multiple scattering effects is prohibitively expensive, even for offline renderers. Thus, real-time methods rely on greatly simplified models.

Using camera-facing billboards is probably the most common real-time method [Dobashi et al. 00, Wang 04, Harris and Lastra 01, Harris 03]. However, billboards are flat, which breaks the volumetric experience under certain conditions. These methods have other limitations: lighting is precomputed resulting in static clouds [Harris and Lastra 01], multiple scattering is ignored [Dobashi et al. 00], or lighting is not physically based and requires tweaking by artists [Wang 04]. Volume rendering techniques are another approach to render clouds [Schpok et al. 03, Miyazaki et al. 04, Riley et al. 04]. To avoid aliasing artifacts, many slices usually need to be rendered, which can create a bottleneck, especially on high-resolution displays. More physically accurate methods exist [Bouthors et al. 06, Bouthors et al. 08], which generate plausible visual results, but are difficult to reproduce and computationally expensive.

We present a new physically based method to efficiently render realistic animated clouds. The clouds are comprised of scaled and rotated copies of a single particle called the *reference particle*. During the preprocessing stage, we precompute optical depth as well as single and multiple scattering integrals describing the light transport in the reference particle for all possible camera positions and view directions and store the results in lookup tables. At runtime, we load the data from the lookup tables to approximate the light transport in the cloud in order to avoid costly ray marching or slicing. In this chapter, we elaborate upon our previous work [Yusov 14b]. In particular, the following improvements have been implemented:

- a better real-time shading model based on precomputed lookup tables,

- an improved method to calculate light attenuation in the body of the cloud using a 3D grid,

- a new particle generation algorithm,

- performance optimization, including GPU-based particle sorting.

We briefly review the main concepts of this method, but we will concentrate on implementation details and improvements. Additional information can be found in the original paper [Yusov 14b].

28.2   Light Transport Theory

Now we will briefly introduce the main concepts of the light transport in a participating medium. More information can be found in [Riley et al. 04, Bouthors 08]. There are three phenomena that can be found in a participating medium: scattering, absorption, and emission. Scattering only changes the direction of a photon traveling through the medium. Absorption eliminates the photon by transforming its energy into other forms, while emission does the opposite. The intensity of these processes is described by scattering, absorption, and emission coefficients β_{Sc}, β_{Ab}, and β_{Em}, respectively. Absorption and scattering both reduce the intensity of light traveling through the medium. The extinction coefficient $\beta_{Ex} = \beta_{Ab} + \beta_{Sc}$ describes the net attenuation. In the cloud body, emission and absorption are negligible: $\beta_{Em} = \beta_{Ab} = 0$. As a result, both scattering and extinction can be described by the same coefficient: $\beta_{Sc} = \beta_{Ex} = \beta$.

The intensity of light traveling from point $\mathbf{A}$ to point $\mathbf{B}$ inside the cloud is reduced by a factor of $e^{-\tau(\mathbf{A}, \mathbf{B})}$. $\tau(\mathbf{A}, \mathbf{B})$, called *optical depth*, is the integral of the extinction coefficient over the path from $\mathbf{A}$ to $\mathbf{B}$:

$$\tau(\mathbf{A}, \mathbf{B}) = \int_{\mathbf{A}}^{\mathbf{B}} \beta(\mathbf{P}) \cdot ds, \qquad (28.1)$$

where $\mathbf{P} = \mathbf{A} + \frac{\mathbf{B} - \mathbf{A}}{||\mathbf{B} - \mathbf{A}||} \cdot s$ is the current integration point.

To determine the intensity of single scattered light, we need to step along the view ray and accumulate all the differential amounts of sunlight scattered at

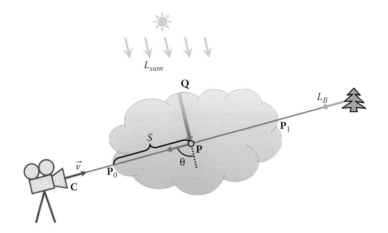

Figure 28.1. Single scattering.

every point toward the camera:

$$L_{In}^{(1)}(\mathbf{C}, \vec{v}) = \int_{\mathbf{P}_0}^{\mathbf{P}_1} \beta(\mathbf{P}) \cdot L_{Sun} \cdot e^{-\tau(\mathbf{Q},\mathbf{P})} \cdot e^{-\tau(\mathbf{P},\mathbf{P}_0)} \cdot P(\theta) \cdot ds. \qquad (28.2)$$

In this equation, $\mathbf{C}$ is the camera position and $\vec{v}$ is the view direction. $\mathbf{P}_0$ and $\mathbf{P}_1$ are the points where the view ray enters and leaves the cloud body, L_{Sun} is the intensity of sunlight outside the cloud, and $\mathbf{Q}$ is the point through which the sunlight reaches the current integration point $\mathbf{P}$ (Figure 28.1). $P(\theta)$ is the phase function that defines how much energy is scattered from the incident direction to the outgoing direction, with θ being the angle between the two. Note that the sunlight is attenuated twice before it reaches the camera: by the factor of $e^{-\tau(\mathbf{Q},\mathbf{P})}$ on the way from the entry point $\mathbf{Q}$ to the scattering point $\mathbf{P}$, and by the factor of $e^{-\tau(\mathbf{P},\mathbf{P}_0)}$ on the way from the scattering point to the camera.

The phase function for cloud droplets is very complex [Bohren and Huffman 98]. In real-time methods, it is common to approximate it using the Cornette-Shanks function [Cornette and Shanks 92]:

$$P(\theta) \approx \frac{1}{4\pi} \frac{3(1-g^2)}{2(2+g^2)} \frac{(1+\cos^2(\theta))}{(1+g^2-2g\cos(\theta))^{3/2}}. \qquad (28.3)$$

Using the intensity $L_{In}^{(1)}$ of single scattering, we can compute secondary scattering $L_{In}^{(2)}$, then third-order scattering $L_{In}^{(3)}$, and so on. The nth-order scattering intensity measured at point $\mathbf{C}$ when viewing in direction $\vec{v}$ is given by the following integral:

$$L_{In}^{(n)}(\mathbf{C}, \vec{v}) = \int_{\mathbf{P}_0}^{\mathbf{P}_1} J^{(n)}(\mathbf{P}, \vec{v}) \cdot e^{-\tau(\mathbf{P},\mathbf{P}_0)} \cdot ds. \qquad (28.4)$$

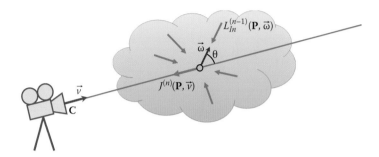

Figure 28.2. Multiple scattering.

In Equation (28.4), $J^{(n)}(\mathbf{C}, \vec{v})$ is the net intensity of order $n-1$ light $L_{In}^{(n-1)}(\mathbf{C}, \vec{v})$ that is scattered in the view direction:

$$J^{(n)}(\mathbf{P}, \vec{v}) = \beta(\mathbf{P}) \cdot \int_{\Omega} L_{In}^{(n-1)}(\mathbf{P}, \vec{\omega}) \cdot P(\theta) \cdot d\omega, \qquad (28.5)$$

where integration is performed over the whole sphere of directions Ω, and θ is the angle between $\vec{\omega}$ and $\vec{v}$ (see Figure 28.2).[1]

The total in-scattering intensity is found by calculating the sum of all scattering orders:

$$L_{In}(\mathbf{C}, \vec{v}) = \sum_{n=1}^{\infty} L_{In}^{(n)}(\mathbf{C}, \vec{v}). \qquad (28.6)$$

The final radiance measured at the camera is the sum of in-scattered intensity and background radiance L_B (see Figure 28.1) attenuated in the cloud:

$$L(\mathbf{C}, \vec{v}) = L_{In}(\mathbf{C}, \vec{v}) + e^{-\tau(\mathbf{P}_0, \mathbf{P}_1)} \cdot L_B. \qquad (28.7)$$

28.3   Precomputed Solutions

Equations (28.1)–(28.7) are very complex and cannot be solved at runtime. Our solution to this problem is to model the light transport in a reference volumetric particle at preprocess time and to solve all the equations for that particle. We store the resulting information in lookup tables and use it at runtime to compute shading.

28.3.1   Optical Depth

Consider some inhomogeneous volumetric particle with known density distribution (Figure 28.3 (left)). Our goal is to precompute the optical depth integral in

---

[1]Strictly speaking, θ is the angle between the incident direction $-\vec{\omega}$ and the outgoing direction $-\vec{v}$, which is the same.

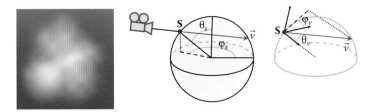

Figure 28.3. Volumetric particle (left) and 4D parameterization (middle and right).

Equation (28.1) through the particle for every camera position and view direction. To describe every ray piercing the particle, we need 4D parameterization.[2] The first two parameters are the azimuth $\varphi_S \in [0, 2\pi]$ and zenith $\theta_S \in [0, \pi]$ angles of the point $\mathbf{S}$ where the view ray enters the particle's bounding sphere (Figure 28.3 (middle)). The other two parameters are the azimuth $\varphi_v \in [0, 2\pi]$ and zenith $\theta_v \in [0, \pi/2]$ angles of the view ray in the tangent frame constructed at the entry point $\mathbf{S}$ (Figure 28.3 (right)). The z-axis of this frame is pointing toward the sphere center. Note that we only need to consider the rays going inside the sphere; thus, the maximum value for θ_v is $\pi/2$.

To precompute the optical depth integral, we go through all possible values of φ_S, θ_S, φ_v, and θ_v and numerically evaluate the integral in Equation (28.1). Section 28.5.1 provides additional details.

28.3.2 Single Scattering

In contrast to optical depth, we cannot precompute scattering inside the inhomogeneous particle. The reason for this is that we also need to account for the light direction, and this would require five parameters, which is impractical. So we precompute scattering in a homogeneous spherical particle. We assume that the light is shining in the positive z direction. Due to the symmetry of the problem, the light field is symmetrical with respect to the light direction, so the φ_S parameter can be dropped. On the other hand, to compute Equation (28.5), we need to know the light field in the entire volume, not only on the sphere's surface. We thus use the distance from the sphere center to the start point as the fourth parameter. Our parameterization for computing single scattering is then $\theta_S \in [0, \pi]$, $\varphi_v \in [0, 2\pi]$, $\theta_v \in [0, \pi]$, $r \in [0, 1]$. Note that because we now need to cover the entire sphere of directions, the maximum value for θ_v is π.

Precomputing single scattering is then implemented by going through all the parameter values and numerically evaluating Equation (28.2). Since the particle is assumed to be homogeneous, $\beta(\mathbf{P}) \equiv \beta$. Sun intensity, L_{Sun}, and phase function, $P(\theta)$, are factored out and evaluated separately. Additional details can be found in Section 28.5.1.

---

[2]We assume that the camera is always located outside the particle's bounding sphere.

28.3.3 Multiple Scattering

We use the same parameterization for the multiple scattering lookup table as for the single scattering. To precompute multiple scattering, we process scattering orders one by one, and for every order we perform three steps:

1. compute the $J^{(n)}$ term using the previous order $L^{(n-1)}$ for all parameter values according to Equation (28.5);

2. compute the current order $L^{(n)}$ according to Equation (28.4);

3. accumulate the current scattering order.

Implementation details are given in Section 28.5.1.

After each scattering order is processed, we retain only the light field on the surface, discarding the rest of the data. It must be noted that in contrast to optical depth, scattering is not linear with respect to density and particle radius. In our original method, we precomputed scattering for a number of densities and encoded the resulting information in a 4D lookup table with the fourth parameter being the particle density scale. This, however, required additional storage and two fetches from a 3D texture. We found out that using just one density still works reasonably well and simplifies the algorithm.

Computing cloud shading using the precomputed lookup tables is discussed in Section 28.5.3.

28.4 Volume-Aware Blending

Our clouds consists of a collection of individual particles and we need to merge them together into a continuous medium. A typical way to achieve this would be using alpha blending. This method, however, is primarily intended for blending "thin" objects such as glass or tree leaves. Our particles are volumetric entities, and there is no way to account for their intersections using standard alpha blending. To solve the problem, we propose a new technique, which we call *volume-aware blending*. The key idea of this technique is to keep track of the volumetric element closest to the camera, for each pixel, and blend every new particle against this representation.

The algorithm starts by clearing the closest element buffer and the back buffer. It then renders all volumetric particles back to front. Each particle's extent is tested against the current closest element. If the particle is closer to the camera, then the closest element's color is written into the back buffer using alpha blending and the new particle replaces the closest element (see Figure 28.4). If the particle is located farther from the camera, then its color is blended into the back buffer and the closest element is retained.

If the particle extent intersects the current closest element, then things become a bit more involved. First, the tail is alpha-blended into the back buffer

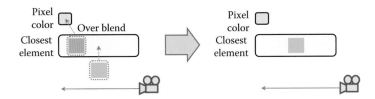

Figure 28.4. Volume-aware blending when the new particle does not intersect the closest element.

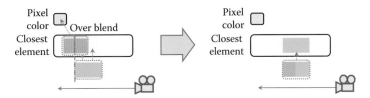

Figure 28.5. Volume-aware blending when the new particle intersects the closest element.

(Figure 28.5). Next, the color of the intersection is computed using the density-weighted average:

$$T_i = e^{-(\rho_0 + \rho_1) \cdot d_i \cdot \beta}, \tag{28.8}$$

$$C_i = \frac{C_0 \cdot \rho_0 + C_1 \cdot \rho_1}{\rho_0 + \rho_1} \cdot (1 - T_i), \tag{28.9}$$

where C_0, C_1, ρ_0, and ρ_1 are non–alpha-premultiplied colors and densities, and d_i is the intersection length. The color of the front part is then alpha-blended with the resulting color C_i, and the new merged element is written back as shown in Figure 28.5 (right). Section 28.5.4 provides additional details.

28.5 Implementation

We implemented our method in C++ using the Direct3D 11 API. The full source code can be found in the supplemental materials to this book. It is also available at https://github.com/GameTechDev/CloudsGPUPro6.

28.5.1 Precomputing Light Transport

Our precomputed data constitute a 4D and a 3D lookup table. The optical depth integral is stored in a $32 \times 16 \times 32 \times 16$ ($N_{\varphi_S} = 32$, $N_{\theta_S} = 16$, $N_{\varphi_v} = 32$, $N_{\theta_v} = 16$) 8-bit lookup table. Multiple scattering is stored in a $32 \times 64 \times 16$ ($N_{\theta_S} = 32$, $N_{\varphi_v} = 64$, $N_{\theta_v} = 16$) 16-bit float lookup table. The first table requires 0.25 MB of storage, while the latter requires 64 KB. Note that in contrast to our base method, we use a different approach to approximate single scattering that does not rely on a precomputed lookup table.

Because current graphics hardware does not natively support 4D textures, we implement them with 3D textures, such that a $X \times Y \times Z \times W$ 4D texture is stored as a $X \times Y \times Z \cdot W$ 3D texture. We perform manual filtering for the fourth coordinate as shown below:

```
#define SAMPLE_4D(tex3DLUT, LUT_DIM, f4LUTCoords, fLOD, Result) \
{                                                               \
  float3 f3UVW0;                                                \
  f3UVW0.xy = f4LUTCoords.xy;                                   \
  float fQSlice = f4LUTCoords.w * LUT_DIM.w - 0.5;             \
  float fQ0Slice = floor(fQSlice);                             \
  float fQWeight = fQSlice - fQ0Slice;                        \
  f3UVW0.z = (fQ0Slice + f4LUTCoords.z) / LUT_DIM.w;          \
  /* frac() assures wraparound filtering of w coordinate*/    \
  float3 f3UVW1 = frac(f3UVW0 + float3(0,0,1/LUT_DIM.w));      \
  Result = lerp(                                               \
    tex3DLUT.SampleLevel(samLinearWrap, f3UVW0, fLOD),        \
    tex3DLUT.SampleLevel(samLinearWrap, f3UVW1, fLOD),        \
    fQWeight);                                                 \
}
```

Note that φ_S and φ_v coordinates require wraparound filtering to avoid artifacts. We use the `frac()` function to achieve this for the fourth coordinate. Also note that the z-coordinate cannot be filtered with wraparound mode.

The precomputation process can be summarized as follows:

1. Precompute the optical depth integral.

2. Precompute single scattering in the whole volume and store the data in the temporary 32-bit float lookup table.

3. For scattering order n from 2 to N,

   (a) evaluate the $J^{(n)}$ term in the whole volume,

   (b) evaluate $L_{In}^{(n)}$ in the whole volume,

   (c) accumulate $L_{In}^{(n)}$ in the multiple scattering lookup table.

4. Copy multiple scattering radiance on the sphere's surface from the temporary lookup table into the final 16-bit float table

The rest of this subsection gives details on each step.

Optical depth.   Precomputing the optical depth integral as discussed in Section 28.3.1 is implemented by a shader that renders slices of the lookup table one by one. The shader code is shown in Listing 28.1.

The shader first computes the start position and the ray direction from the input 4D coordinates using the `OpticalDepthLUTCoordsToWorldParams()` function

```
1 float2 PrecomputeOpticalDepthPS(SQuadVSOutput In) : SV_Target
2 {
3   float3 f3StartPos, f3RayDir;
4   // Convert lookup table 4D coordinates into the start
5   // position and view direction
6   OpticalDepthLUTCoordsToWorldParams(
7       float4(ProjToUV(In.m_f2PosPS), g_Attribs.f4Param.xy),
8       f3StartPos, f3RayDir );
9
10  // Intersect the view ray with the unit sphere
11  float2 f2RayIsecs;
12  // f3StartPos is located exactly on the surface; slightly
13  // move it inside the sphere to avoid precision issues
14  GetRaySphereIntersection(f3StartPos + f3RayDir*1e-4, f3RayDir,
15                           0, 1.f, f2RayIsecs);
16
17  float3 f3EndPos = f3StartPos + f3RayDir * f2RayIsecs.y;
18  float fNumSteps = NUM_INTEGRATION_STEPS;
19  float3 f3Step = (f3EndPos - f3StartPos) / fNumSteps;
20  float fTotalDensity = 0;
21  for(float fStepNum=0.5; fStepNum < fNumSteps; ++fStepNum)
22  {
23    float3 f3CurrPos = f3StartPos + f3Step * fStepNum;
24    float fDensity = ComputeDensity(f3CurrPos);
25    fTotalDensity += fDensity;
26  }
27
28  return fTotalDensity/fNumSteps;
29 }
```

Listing 28.1. Precomputing optical depth integral.

(lines 3–8). The first two components come from the pixel position, the other two are stored in the `g_Attribs.f4Param.xy` uniform variable. The shader then intersects the ray with the unit sphere (lines 11–15) and finds the ray exit point (line 17). The `GetRaySphereIntersection()` function takes the ray start position and direction, sphere center (which is 0), and radius (which is 1) as inputs and returns the distances from the start point to the intersections in its fifth argument (the smallest value always go first). Finally, the shader performs numerical integration of Equation (28.1). Instead of storing the integral itself, we store the normalized average density along the ray, which always lies in the range $[0, 1]$ and can be sufficiently represented with an 8-bit UNorm value. Optical depth is reconstructed by multiplying that value by the ray length and extinction coefficient. The `ComputeDensity()` function combines several 3D noises to evaluate density at the current point.

Single scattering. Precomputing single scattering (Section 28.3.2) is performed by a pixel shader as presented in Listing 28.2. Note that single scattering is computed inside the entire volume, not only on the surface, and a temporary 4D lookup table is used to store it. The fourth coordinate of this table encodes the distance from the sphere center and is provided by the uniform variable `g_Attribs.f4Param.y`.

```
 1 float PrecomputeSingleSctrPS(SQuadVSOutput In) : SV_Target
 2 {
 3   float3 f3EntryPoint, f3ViewRay, f3LightDir;
 4   ScatteringLUTToWorldParams(
 5     float4(ProjToUV(In.m_f2PosPS), g_Attribs.f4Param.xy),
 6     g_Attribs.f4Param.z, f3EntryPoint, f3ViewRay, f3LightDir);
 7
 8   // Intersect the view ray with the unit sphere
 9   float2 f2RayIsecs;
10   GetRaySphereIntersection(f3EntryPoint, f3ViewRay,
11                            0, 1.f, f2RayIsecs);
12   float3 f3EndPos = f3EntryPoint + f3ViewRay * f2RayIsecs.y;
13
14   float fNumSteps = NUM_INTEGRATION_STEPS;
15   float3 f3Step = (f3EndPos - f3EntryPoint) / fNumSteps;
16   float fStepLen = length(f3Step);
17   float fCloudMassToCamera = 0;
18   float fParticleRadius = g_Attribs.RefParticleRadius;
19   float fInscattering = 0;
20   for(float fStepNum=0.5; fStepNum < fNumSteps; ++fStepNum)
21   {
22     float3 f3CurrPos = f3EntryPoint + f3Step * fStepNum;
23     GetRaySphereIntersection(f3CurrPos, f3LightDir,
24                              0, 1.f, f2RayIsecs);
25     float fCloudMassToLight = f2RayIsecs.x * fParticleRadius;
26     float fAttenuation = exp(
27       -g_Attribs.fAttenuationCoeff *
28       (fCloudMassToLight + fCloudMassToCamera) );
29
30     fInscattering += fAttenuation * g_Attribs.fScatteringCoeff;
31     fCloudMassToCamera += fStepLen * fParticleRadius;
32   }
33
34   return fInscattering * fStepLen * fParticleRadius;
35 }
```

Listing 28.2. Precomputing single scattering.

The shader numerically integrates Equation (28.2). Note that the phase function $P(\theta)$ and the sun intensity L_{Sun} are omitted. Thus, at every step, the shader needs to compute the following integrand: $\beta(\mathbf{P}) \cdot e^{-\tau(\mathbf{Q},\mathbf{P})} \cdot e^{-\tau(\mathbf{P},\mathbf{P}_0)}$. The scattering/extinction coefficient $\beta(\mathbf{P})$ is assumed to be constant and is provided by the g_Attribs.fScatteringCoeff variable. We use $\beta = 0.07$ as the scattering/extinction coefficient and a reference particle radius of 200 meters. Extinction $e^{-\tau(\mathbf{Q},\mathbf{P})}$ from the current point to the light entry point is evaluated by intersecting the ray going from the current point toward the light with the sphere (lines 23–25). Extinction $e^{-\tau(\mathbf{P},\mathbf{P}_0)}$ toward the camera is computed by maintaining the total cloud mass from the camera to the current point in the fCloudMassToCamera variable (line 31).

Multiple scattering. After single scattering, we compute up to $N = 18$ scattering orders. During this process, we use three temporary 4D 32-bit float lookup tables:

one to store the $J^{(n)}$ term, the other to store the current order scattering $L_{In}^{(n)}$, and the third to accumulate higher-order scattering. Note that these intermediate tables cover the entire volume.

Computing every scattering order consists of three steps, as discussed in Section 28.3.3. The first step is evaluating the $J^{(n)}$ term according to Equation (28.5). This step is implemented by the shader shown in Listing 28.3.

The first step in this shader, like the prior shaders, retrieves the world-space parameters from the 4D texture coordinates (lines 3–6). In the next step, the shader constructs local frame for the ray starting point by calling the `ConstructLocalFrameXYZ()` function (lines 8–10). The function gets two directions as inputs and constructs orthonormal basis. The first direction is used as the z-axis. Note that the resulting z-axis points toward the sphere center (which is 0).

The shader then runs two loops going through the series of zenith θ and azimuth φ angles (lines 18–19), which sample the entire sphere of directions. On every step, the shader constructs a sample direction using the (θ, φ) angles (lines 23–25), computes lookup coordinates for this direction (lines 26–28), and loads the order $n-1$ scattering using these coordinates (lines 29–31). Remember that the precomputed single scattering does not comprise the phase function and we need to apply it now, if necessary (lines 32–34). `g_Attribs.f4Param.w` equals 1 if we are processing the second-order scattering and 0 otherwise. After that, we need to account for the phase function $P(\theta)$ in Equation (28.5) (line 35). For single scattering, we use anisotropy factor $g = 0.9$, and for multiple scattering we use $g = 0.7$ to account for light diffusion in the cloud. Finally, we need to compute the $d\omega = d\theta \cdot d\varphi \cdot sin(\theta)$ term (lines 37–40).

After the $J^{(n)}$ term is evaluated, we can compute nth scattering order according to Equation (28.4). The corresponding shader performing this task is very similar to the shader computing single scattering (Listing 28.4). The difference is that in the integration loop we load $J^{(n)}$ from the lookup table (lines 19–23) instead of computing sunlight attenuation in the particle. We also use trapezoidal integration to improve accuracy.

In the third stage, the simple shader accumulates the current scattering order in the net multiple scattering lookup table by rendering every slice with additive blending.

28.5.2 Particle Generation

We wanted to efficiently control the level of detail and provide high fidelity for close clouds, while still being able to render distant clouds. To do this, we use a nested grid structure inspired by the geometry clipmaps method [Losasso and Hoppe 04]. The grid consists of a number of rings. Particles in each next outer ring are twice the size of particles in the inner ring and have twice the spacing interval. We refer to this structure as a *cell grid* (Figure 28.6 (left)). Each cell

```
 1 float GatherScatteringPS(SQuadVSOutput In) : SV_Target
 2 {
 3   float3 f3StartPos, f3ViewRay, f3LightDir;
 4   ScatteringLUTToWorldParams(
 5     float4(ProjToUV(In.m_f2PosPS), g_Attribs.f4Param.xy),
 6           f3StartPos, f3ViewRay, f3LightDir);
 7
 8   float3 f3LocalX, f3LocalY, f3LocalZ;
 9   ConstructLocalFrameXYZ(-normalize(f3StartPos), f3LightDir,
10                          f3LocalX, f3LocalY, f3LocalZ);
11
12   float fJ = 0;
13   float fTotalSolidAngle = 0;
14   const float fNumZenithAngles = SCTR_LUT_DIM.z;
15   const float fNumAzimuthAngles = SCTR_LUT_DIM.y;
16   const float fZenithSpan = PI;
17   const float fAzimuthSpan = 2*PI;
18   for(float Zen = 0.5; Zen < fNumZenithAngles; ++Zen)
19     for(float Az = 0.5; Az < fNumAzimuthAngles; ++Az)
20     {
21       float fZenith = Zen/fNumZenithAngles * fZenithSpan;
22       float fAzimuth = (Az/fNumAzimuthAngles - 0.5) * fAzimuthSpan;
23       float3 f3CurrDir =
24         GetDirectionInLocalFrameXYZ(f3LocalX, f3LocalY, f3LocalZ,
25                                     fZenith, fAzimuth);
26       float4 f4CurrDirLUTCoords =
27         WorldParamsToScatteringLUT(f3StartPos, f3CurrDir,
28                                    f3LightDir);
29       float fCurrDirSctr = 0;
30       SAMPLE_4D(g_tex3DPrevSctrOrder, SCTR_LUT_DIM,
31                 f4CurrDirLUTCoords, 0, fCurrDirSctr);
32       if( g_Attribs.f4Param.w == 1 )
33         fCurrDirSctr *= HGPhaseFunc( dot(-f3CurrDir, f3LightDir),
34                                      0.9 );
35       fCurrDirSctr *= HGPhaseFunc( dot(f3CurrDir, f3ViewRay), 0.7 );
36
37       float fdZenithAngle = fZenithSpan / fNumZenithAngles;
38       float fdAzimuthAngle = fAzimuthSpan / fNumAzimuthAngles *
39                              sin(ZenithAngle);
40       float fDiffSolidAngle = fdZenithAngle * fdAzimuthAngle;
41       fTotalSolidAngle += fDiffSolidAngle;
42       fJ += fCurrDirSctr * fDiffSolidAngle;
43     }
44
45   // Total solid angle should be 4*PI. Renormalize to fix
46   // discretization issues
47   fJ *= 4*PI / fTotalSolidAngle;
48
49   return fJ;
50 }
```

Listing 28.3. Computing J term.

in the grid contains a predefined number of layers. Each voxel of a resulting 3D structure can potentially contain a particle. We refer to this structure as a *particle lattice* (Figure 28.6 (right)). To facilitate particle generation and lighting,

```
 1 float ComputeScatteringOrderPS(SQuadVSOutput In) : SV_Target
 2 {
 3    // Transform lookup coordinates into the world parameters
 4    // Intersect the ray with the sphere, compute
 5    // start and end points
 6    ...
 7
 8    float fPrevJ = 0;
 9    SAMPLE_4D(g_tex3DGatheredScattering, SCTR_LUT_DIM,
10              f4StartPointLUTCoords, 0, fPrevJ);
11    for(float fStepNum=1; fStepNum <= fNumSteps; ++fStepNum)
12    {
13      float3 f3CurrPos = f3StartPos + f3Step * fStepNum;
14
15      fCloudMassToCamera += fStepLen * fParticleRadius;
16      float fAttenuationToCamera = exp( -g_Attribs.fAttenuationCoeff *
17                                    fCloudMassToCamera );
18
19      float4 f4CurrDirLUTCoords =
20        WorldParamsToScatteringLUT(f3CurrPos, f3ViewRay, f3LightDir);
21      float fJ = 0;
22      SAMPLE_4D(g_tex3DGatheredScattering, SCTR_LUT_DIM,
23                f4CurrDirLUTCoords, 0, fJ);
24      fJ *= fAttenuationToCamera;
25
26      fInscattering += (fJ + fPrevJ) / 2;
27      fPrevJ = fJ;
28    }
29
30    return fInscattering * fStepLen * fParticleRadius *
31           g_Attribs.fScatteringCoeff;
32 }
```

Listing 28.4. Computing order-n scattering.

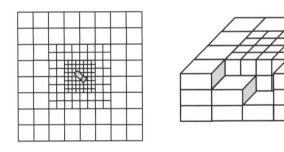

Figure 28.6. Cell grid (left) and 3D lattice (right).

we maintain two additional 3D structures: *cloud density 3D lattice* and *light attenuation 3D lattice*. These two structures have twice the resolution of the particle lattice in each dimension and are implemented as 3D textures.

The steps for particle generation and processing are as follows:

1. Process the 2D cell grid to build a list of valid nonempty cells, and compute the cell attributes.

2. Compute the density for each voxel of the cloud density lattice located in the nonempty cells.

3. Process the visible voxels of the light attenuation lattice located in the nonempty cells and compute attenuation for each voxel.

4. Process the particle lattice and generate particles for visible cells whose density is above the threshold.

5. Process the particles and store lighting information.

6. Sort the particles.

Every step mentioned above is implemented by a compute shader. We use a GPU-based implementation, thus the CPU does not know how many GPU threads need to be executed for each compute kernel. We use the Dispatch Indirect() function to let the GPU assign work to itself. This function takes the same arguments as the regular Dispatch() function, but these arguments are stored in a GPU buffer. What is important is that other compute kernels can write data to that buffer, thus allowing the GPU to control itself. We discuss each step in detail below.

Processing cell grid. The processing cell grid is performed by a compute shader that executes one thread for every cell. It computes the cell center and size based on the camera world position and the location of the cell in the grid. Using the cell center, the shader then computes the base cell density by combining two 2D noise functions. If the resulting value is above the threshold, the cell is said to be *valid* (Figure 28.7). The shader adds indices of all valid cells to the append buffer (g_ValidCellsAppendBuf), which at the end of the stage contains an unordered list of all valid cells. If a cell is also visible in the camera frustum, the shader also adds the cell to another buffer (g_VisibleCellsAppendBuf) that collects valid visible cells.

Processing cloud density lattice. In the next stage, we need to process only those voxels of the lattice that are located within the valid cells of the cloud grid. To compute the required number of GPU threads, we execute a simple one-thread compute shader:

```
RWBuffer<uint> g_DispatchArgsRW : register( u0 );
[numthreads(1, 1, 1)]
void ComputeDispatchArgsCS()
```

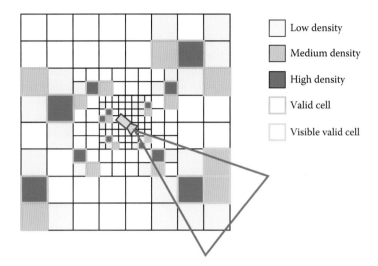

Figure 28.7. Valid cells.

```
{
  uint s = g_GlobalCloudAttribs.uiDensityBufferScale;
  g_DispatchArgsRW[0] = (g_ValidCellsCounter.Load(0) * s*s*s *
    g_GlobalCloudAttribs.uiMaxLayers + THREAD_GROUP_SIZE-1) /
    THREAD_GROUP_SIZE;
}
```

The number of elements previously written into the append buffer can be copied into a resource suitable for reading (g_ValidCellsCounter) with the CopyStructure Count() function. The buffer previously bound as UAV to g_DispatchArgsRW is then passed to the DispatchIndirect() function to generate the required number of threads. Each thread then reads the index of the valid cell it belongs to from g_ValidCellsUnorderedList, populated at the previous stage, and finds out its location within that cell. Then the shader combines two 3D noise functions with the cell base density to create volumetric noise. The noise amplitude decreases with altitude to create typical cumulus cloud shapes with wider bottoms and narrower tops.

Light attenuation. Light attenuation is computed for every voxel inside the *visible* grid cells. To compute the required number of threads, we use the same simple compute shader used in the previous stage, but this time provide the number of valid *and* visible cells in the g_ValidCellsCounter variable. Light attenuation is then computed by casting a ray from the voxel center toward the light and ray marching through the density lattice. We perform a fixed number of 16 steps. Instead of storing light attenuation, we opt to store the attenuating cloud mass because it can be properly interpolated.

Particle generation. The next stage consists of processing valid and visible voxels of the cloud lattice and generating particles for some of them. To generate the required number of threads, we again use the simple one-thread compute shader. The particle generation shader loads the cloud density from the density lattice and, if it is not zero, it creates a particle. The shader randomly displaces the particle from the voxel center and adds a random rotation and scale to eliminate repeating patterns. The shader writes the particle attributes, such as position, density, and size, into the particle info buffer and adds the particle index into another append buffer (`g_VisibleParticlesAppendBuf`).

Processing visible particles. This is required to compute lighting information. In particular, we compute the color of the sunlight reaching the center of the particle, ignoring occlusion by the cloud and the intensity of ambient skylight. We also sample the light-attenuating mass texture to compute the light occlusion. We use the value on the particle surface to compute attenuation for multiple scattering and the value in the particle center for single scattering. Moreover, we scale the light-attenuating mass by a factor of 0.25 to account for strong forward scattering when computing attenuation for multiple scattering.

Sorting. Sorting particles back to front is the final stage before they can be rendered and is necessary for correct blending. In our original work, we sorted all the voxels of the particle lattice on the CPU and then streamed out only valid visible voxels on the GPU. This approach had a number of drawbacks. First, it required active CPU–GPU communication. Second, due to random offsets, particle order could slightly differ from voxel order. But the main problem was that all voxels were always sorted even though many of them were actually empty, which resulted in significant CPU overhead.

We now sort particles entirely on the GPU using the merge sort algorithm by Satish et al. [Satish et al. 09] with a simplified merge procedure. We begin by subdividing the visible particle list into subsequences of 128 particles and sorting each subsequence with a bitonic sort implemented in a compute shader. Then we perform a number of merge stages to get the single sorted list. When executing the binary search of an element to find its rank, we directly access global memory. Because the number of particles that need to be sorted is relatively small (usually not greater than 50,000), the entire list can fit into the cache and merging is still very efficient even though we do not use shared memory.

An important aspect is that we do not know how many particles were generated on the GPU and how many merge passes we need to execute. Thus, we perform enough passes to sort the maximum possible number of particles. The compute shader performs an early exit, with very little performance cost, when no more work needs to be done.

28.5.3 Rendering

After visible particles are generated, processed, and sorted, they are ready for rendering. Since only the GPU knows how many particles were generated, we use the `DrawInstancedIndirect()` function. It is similar to `DrawInstanced()`, but reads its arguments from a GPU buffer. We render one point primitive per visible particle. The geometry shader reads the particle attributes and generates the particle bounding box, which is then sent to the rasterizer.

In the pixel shader, we reconstruct the view ray and intersect it with the ellipsoid enclosed in the particle's bounding box. If the ray misses the ellipsoid, we discard the pixel. Otherwise, we apply our shading model based on the precomputed lookup tables, as shown in Listing 28.5.

Our first step is to compute the normalized density along the view ray using the optical depth lookup table (lines 2–10). We randomly rotate the particle around the vertical axis to eliminate repetitive patterns (line 6). `f3EntryPoint USSpace` and `f3ViewRayUSSpace` are the coordinates of the entry point and the view ray direction transformed into the particle space (which is unit sphere space, thus the US suffix). Next, we compute the transparency (lines 14–17).

Our real-time model consists of three components: single scattering, multiple scattering, and ambient light. We compute single scattering in lines 20–27. It is a product of a phase function, sunlight attenuation (computed as discussed in Section 28.5.2), and the sunlight intensity. Because single scattering is most noticeable where cloud density is low, we multiply the value by the transparency.

Next, we evaluate multiple scattering by performing a lookup into the precomputed table (lines 30–39). We multiply the intensity with the light attenuation. Since multiple scattering happens in dense parts of the cloud, we also multiply the intensity with the opacity (`1-fTransparency`).

Finally, we use an ad hoc approximation for ambient light (lines 42–52). We use the following observation: ambient light intensity is stronger on the top boundary of the cloud and decreases toward the bottom. Figure 28.8 shows different components and the final result.

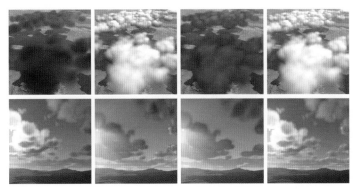

Figure 28.8. From left to right, single scattering, multiple scattering, ambient, and all components.

```
 1 // Compute lookup coordinates
 2 float4 f4LUTCoords;
 3 WorldParamsToOpticalDepthLUTCoords(f3EntryPointUSSpace,
 4                                    f3ViewRayUSSpace, f4LUTCoords);
 5 // Randomly rotate the sphere
 6 f4LUTCoords.y += ParticleAttrs.fRndAzimuthBias;
 7 // Get the normalized density along the view ray
 8 float fNormalizedDensity = 1.f;
 9 SAMPLE_4D_LUT(g_tex3DParticleDensityLUT, OPTICAL_DEPTH_LUT_DIM,
10               f4LUTCoords, 0, fNormalizedDensity);
11
12 // Compute actual cloud mass by multiplying the normalized
13 // density with ray length
14 fCloudMass = fNormalizedDensity * fRayLength;
15 fCloudMass *= ParticleAttrs.fDensity;
16 // Compute transparency
17 fTransparency = exp( -fCloudMass * g_Attribs.fAttenuationCoeff );
18
19 // Evaluate phase function for single scattering
20 float fCosTheta = dot(-f3ViewRayUSSpace, f3LightDirUSSpace);
21 float PhaseFunc = HGPhaseFunc(fCosTheta, 0.8);
22
23 float2 f2Attenuation = ParticleLighting.f2SunLightAttenuation;
24 // Compute intensity of single scattering
25 float3 f3SingleScattering =
26   fTransparency *  ParticleLighting.f4SunLight.rgb *
27   f2Attenuation.x * PhaseFunc;
28
29 // Compute lookup coordinates for multiple scattering
30 float4 f4MultSctrLUTCoords =
31   WorldParamsToScatteringLUT(f3EntryPointUSSpace,
32   f3ViewRayUSSpace, f3LightDirUSSpace);
33 // Load multiple scattering from the lookup table
34 float fMultipleScattering =
35   g_tex3DScatteringLUT.SampleLevel(samLinearWrap,
36   f4MultSctrLUTCoords.xyz, 0);
37 float3 f3MultipleScattering =
38   (1-fTransparency) * fMultipleScattering *
39   f2Attenuation.y * ParticleLighting.f4SunLight.rgb;
40
41 // Compute ambient light
42 float3 f3EarthCentre = float3(0, -g_Attribs.fEarthRadius, 0);
43 float fEnttryPointAltitude = length(f3EntryPointWS - f3EarthCentre);
44 float fCloudBottomBoundary =
45   g_Attribs.fEarthRadius + g_Attribs.fCloudAltitude -
46   g_Attribs.fCloudThickness/2.f;
47 float fAmbientStrength =
48     (fEnttryPointAltitude - fCloudBottomBoundary) /
49     g_Attribs.fCloudThickness;
50 fAmbientStrength = clamp(fAmbientStrength, 0.3, 1);
51 float3 f3Ambient = (1-fTransparency) * fAmbientStrength *
52                    ParticleLighting.f4AmbientLight.rgb;
```

Listing 28.5. Real-time shading.

28.5.4   Volume-Aware Blending

Blending is the final stage after all particle shading attributes are computed. To implement the volume-aware blending technique described in Section 28.4, we use an unordered access view, which enables the pixel shader to read and write to arbitrary memory locations. For each pixel on the screen, we store the following information about the closest element: minimal/maximal distance along the view ray, optical mass (which is the cloud mass times the scattering coefficient), and color:

```
struct SParticleLayer
{
  float2 f2MinMaxDist;
  float fOpticalMass;
  float3 f3Color;
};
```

The pixel shader implements the merging scheme described in Section 28.4 and is shown in the code snippet given in Listing 28.6. The shader creates an array of two layers. The properties of one layer are taken from the attributes of the current particle (lines 8–10). The other layer is read from the appropriate position in the buffer (lines 12–17). Then the layers are merged (lines 20–23), and the merged layer is written back (line 26) while color f4OutColor is passed to the output merger unit to be blended with the back buffer.

```
1 // Init extensions
2 IntelExt_Init();
3 ...
4 // Process current particle and compute its color f3NewColor,
5 // mass fCloudMass, and extents fNewMinDist/fNewMaxDist
6
7 SParticleLayer Layers[2];
8 Layers[1].f2MinMaxDist = float2(fNewMinDist, fNewMaxDist);
9 Layers[1].fOpticalMass = fCloudMass * g_Attribs.fAttenuationCoeff;
10 Layers[1].f3Color = f3NewColor;
11
12 uint2 ui2PixelIJ = In.f4Pos.xy;
13 uint uiLayerDataInd =
14   (ui2PixelIJ.x + ui2PixelIJ.y * g_Attribs.uiBackBufferWidth);
15 // Enable pixel shader ordering
16 IntelExt_BeginPixelShaderOrdering();
17 Layers[0] = g_rwbufParticleLayers[uiLayerDataInd];
18
19 // Merge two layers
20 SParticleLayer MergedLayer;
21 float4 f4OutColor;
22 MergeParticleLayers(Layers[0], Layers[1], MergedLayer,
23                     f4OutColor.rgb, f4OutColor.a);
24
25 // Store updated layers
26 g_rwbufParticleLayers[uiLayerDataInd] = MergedLayer;
```

Listing 28.6. Volume-aware blending.

Particle info buffer `g_rwbufParticleLayers` is declared as a read/write buffer:

```
RWStructuredBuffer<SParticleLayer> g_rwbufParticleLayers;
```

It must be noted that the algorithm described above would not work as expected on standard DirectX 11–class graphics hardware. The reason is that we are trying to read from the same memory in parallel from different pixel shader threads, modify data, and write it back. There is no efficient way on DirectX 11 to serialize such operations. Intel graphics chips, starting with the Intel HD Graphics 5000, can solve this problem. They contain a special extension, called *pixel shader ordering*. When it is enabled, it guarantees that all read–modify–write operations from different pixel shader instances, which map to the same pixel, are performed atomically. Moreover, the pixel shader instances are executed in the same order in which primitives were submitted for rasterization. The second condition is very important to ensure temporally stable results. In DirectX 11, the extensions are exposed through two functions. `IntelExt_Init()` tells the compiler that the shader is going to use extensions, and after the call to `IntelExt_BeginPixelShaderOrdering()`, all instructions that access UAVs get appropriately ordered. It is worth mentioning that this capability will be a standard feature of DirectX 12, where it will be called rasterizer ordered views.

After all particles are rendered, the closest volume buffer needs to be merged with the back buffer. We render a screen-size quad and perform the required operations in the pixel shader.

During rendering, we generate three buffers: cloud color, transparency, and the distance to the closest cloud. To improve performance, we render the clouds to a quarter resolution buffers $(1/2 \times 1/2)$ and then upscale to the original resolution using a bilateral filter.

28.5.5   Integration with Atmospheric Effects

To render the earth's atmosphere, we use the method described in our earlier work [Yusov 14a]. To create the effect of light shafts, we employ a light-space cloud transparency buffer. This buffer is populated by projecting the 2D noise (Section 28.5.2) onto the light projection plane. The buffer has the same structure as a cascaded shadow map. We use this buffer to attenuate the sunlight. We assume that the cloud altitude is fixed. Then, at each step, we check if the current sample on the ray is below or above this altitude. If it is, we sample the light-space attenuation texture to get the amount of light that reaches the point through the cloud. We use the same minimum–maximum structure to accelerate the ray traversal. To eliminate artifacts, we reduce the step size to one texel when crossing the cloud altitude. We also use screen-space cloud transparency

Figure 28.9. Sample refinement takes cloud transparency into account.

and distance to the cloud to attenuate the light samples along the view ray (please refer to [Yusov 14b] for more details).

One important missing detail is sample refinement (see [Yusov 14a]), which needs to account for screen-space cloud transparency. When computing coarse unoccluded in-scattering, we take the screen-space cloud transparency and distance to attenuate the current sample. This automatically gives the desired effect (Figure 28.9) with a minimal increase in performance cost.

28.6 Results and Discussion

Figure 28.10 shows some images generated using our method under different lighting conditions. To evaluate the performance, we used two test platforms. The first platform is an Ultrabook powered by an Intel Core i5 CPU and an Intel HD Graphics 5200 GPU (47 W shared between CPU and GPU). Our second test platform is a desktop workstation powered by an Intel Core i7 CPU and an NVIDIA GeForce GTX 680 GPU (195 W TDP). The viewport resolution was set to 1280×720 on the first platform and to 1920×1080 on the second. Note also that the NVIDIA GPU does not support pixel shader ordering, so images were rendered with volume-aware blending disabled. Also note that this feature is going to be exposed in DirectX 12, so it will soon be available on a wide range of graphics hardware.

We used four quality settings: low, medium, high, and highest (Table 28.1). Figure 28.11 compares images rendered by our algorithm in each setting.

Table 28.2 summarizes the performance of different stages of the algorithm on our first test platform.

Rendering particles takes the most time, about 70% of the rendering time, in all cases. The main sticking point is sampling the precomputed optical depth texture. Reducing its resolution can significantly improve performance at the

Figure 28.10. Images generated by our algorithm.

Profile	Num. rings	Ring dimension	Num. layers	Num. particles
Low	4	120	3	2919
Medium	5	136	4	7103
High	5	168	6	15,725
Highest	5	216	8	33,702

Table 28.1. Quality profiles.

Profile	Clearing	Processing	Sorting	Rendering	Total
Low	0.62	0.63	0.24	4.22	5.71
Medium	1.31	1.00	0.31	8.72	11.34
High	2.98	2.07	0.48	15.73	21.26
Highest	6.53	4.62	0.83	26.5	28.48

Table 28.2. Performance of the algorithm on Intel HD Graphics 5200, 1280 × 720 resolution (times in ms).

Figure 28.11. Test scene rendered in different quality profiles: highest (top left), high (top right), medium (bottom left), and low (bottom right).

Profile	Processing	Sorting	Rendering	Total
Low	0.38	0.1	1.74	2.22
Medium	0.65	0.11	3.73	4.49
High	1.39	0.14	6.53	8.06
Highest	2.97	0.24	10.72	13.93

Table 28.3. Performance of the algorithm on NVIDIA GeForce GTX 680, 1920 × 1080 resolution (times in ms).

cost of lower quality. The processing stage includes all the steps discussed in Section 28.5.2 except sorting, which is shown in a separate column. The clearing column shows the amount of time required to clear the cloud density and light attenuation 3D textures to initial values. This step takes almost the same time as processing itself. This is because of the low memory bandwidth of the GPU. Rendering light scattering effects takes an additional 5.8 ms. In the medium-quality profile, the total required time is less than 20 ms, which guarantees real-time frame rates.

Performance results on our high-end test platform are given in Table 28.3. Because our second GPU has much higher memory bandwidth, the performance of the algorithm is significantly better. It takes less than 2.3 ms to render the clouds in low profile and less than 4.5 ms to render in medium profile at full HD resolution. Since clearing the 3D textures takes much less time, we do not separate this step in Table 28.3. Computing atmospheric light scattering takes an additional 3.0 ms of processing time. Also note that the GTX 680 is a relatively old GPU. Recent graphics hardware provides higher memory bandwidth, which will improve the performance of our method.

28.6.1 Limitations

Our method is physically based, not physically accurate. We make two main simplifications when approximating shading: scattering is precomputed in a homogeneous spherical particle, and energy exchange between particles is ignored. Precomputing the scattering inside an inhomogeneous particle would require a 5D table. It is possible that some degrees of that table can allow point sampling, which would reduce the lookup into the table to two fetches from a 3D texture. This is an interesting direction for future research.

The other limitation of our method is that our volume-aware blending can precisely handle the intersection of only two particles. When more than three particles intersect, the method can fail. However, visual results are acceptable in most cases. We also believe that our method gives a good use-case example for the capabilities of upcoming GPUs.

28.7 Conclusion

In this chapter we presented a new method for rendering realistic clouds. The key idea of our approach is to precompute optical depth and single and multiple scattering for a reference particle at preprocess time and to store the resulting information in lookup tables. The data is then used at runtime to compute cloud shading without the need for ray marching or slicing. We also presented a new technique for controlling the level of detail as well as a method to blend the particles accounting for their volumetric intersection. We believe that our idea of precomputing scattering is promising and can be further improved in future research. The idea of precomputing transparency can also be used for rendering different kinds of objects such as distant trees in forests.

Bibliography

[Bohren and Huffman 98] C. Bohren and D. R. Huffman. *Absorption and Scattering of Light by Small Particles.* Berlin: Wiley-VCH, 1998.

[Bouthors et al. 06] Antoine Bouthors, Fabrice Neyret, and Sylvain Lefebvre. "Real-Time Realistic Illumination and Shading of Stratiform Clouds." In *Proceedings of the Second Eurographics Conference on Natural Phenomena*, pp. 41–50. Aire-la-Ville, Switzerland: Eurographics Association, 2006.

[Bouthors et al. 08] Antoine Bouthors, Fabrice Neyret, Nelson Max, Eric Bruneton, and Cyril Crassin. "Interactive Multiple Anisotropic Scattering in Clouds." In *SI3D*, edited by Eric Haines and Morgan McGuire, pp. 173–182. New York: ACM, 2008.

[Bouthors 08] Antoine Bouthors. "Real-Time Realistic Rendering of Clouds." PhD thesis, Université Joseph Fourier, 2008.

[Cornette and Shanks 92] W.M. Cornette and J.G. Shanks. "Physical Reasonable Analytic Expression for the Single-Scattering Phase Function." *Applied Optics* 31:16 (1992), 3152–3160.

[Dobashi et al. 00] Yoshinori Dobashi, Kazufumi Kaneda, Hideo Yamashita, Tsuyoshi Okita, and Tomoyuki Nishita. "A Simple, Efficient Method for Realistic Animation of Clouds." In *Proceedings of the 27th Annual Conference on Computer Graphics and Interactive Techniques*, pp. 19–28. New York: ACM Press/Addison-Wesley, 2000.

[Harris and Lastra 01] Mark J. Harris and Anselmo Lastra. "Real-Time Cloud Rendering." *Comput. Graph. Forum* 20:3 (2001), 76–85.

[Harris 03] Mark Jason Harris. "Real-Time Cloud Simulation and Rendering." Ph.D. thesis, The University of North Carolina at Chapel Hill, 2003.

[Losasso and Hoppe 04] Frank Losasso and Hugues Hoppe. "Geometry Clipmaps: Terrain Rendering Using Nested Regular Grids." *ACM Trans. Graph.* 23:3 (2004), 769–776.

[Miyazaki et al. 04] Ryo Miyazaki, Yoshinori Dobashi, and Tomoyuki Nishita. "A Fast Rendering Method of Clouds Using Shadow-View Slices." In *Proceeding of Computer Graphics and Imaging 2004, August 17–19, 2004, Kauai, Hawaii, USA*, pp. 93–98. Calgary: ACTA Press, 2004.

[Riley et al. 04] Kirk Riley, David S. Ebert, Martin Kraus, Jerry Tessendorf, and Charles Hansen. "Efficient Rendering of Atmospheric Phenomena." In *Proceedings of the Fifteenth Eurographics Conference on Rendering Techniques*, pp. 375–386. Aire-la-Ville, Switzerland: Eurographics Association, 2004.

[Satish et al. 09] Nadathur Satish, Mark Harris, and Michael Garland. "Designing Efficient Sorting Algorithms for Manycore GPUs." In *Proceedings of the 2009 IEEE International Symposium on Parallel&Distributed Processing, IPDPS '09*, pp. 1–10. Washington, DC: IEEE Computer Society, 2009.

[Schpok et al. 03] Joshua Schpok, Joseph Simons, David S. Ebert, and Charles Hansen. "A Real-time Cloud Modeling, Rendering, and Animation System." In *Proceedings of the 2003 ACM SIGGRAPH/Eurographics Symposium on*

Computer Animation, pp. 160–166. Aire-la-Ville, Switzerland: Eurographics Association, 2003.

[Wang 04] Niniane Wang. "Realistic and Fast Cloud Rendering." *J. Graphics, GPU, and Game Tools* 9:3 (2004), 21–40.

[Yusov 14a] Egor Yusov. "High Performance Outdoor Light Scattering using Epipolar Sampling." In *GPU Pro 5: Advanced Rendering Techniques*, edited by Wolfgang Engel, pp. 101–126. Boca Raton, FL: CRC Press, 2014.

[Yusov 14b] Egor Yusov. "High-Performance Rendering of Realistic Cumulus Clouds Using Pre-computed Lighting." In *Proceedings of High-Performance Graphics 2014*, edited by Ingo Wald and Jonathan Ragan-Kelley, pp. 127–136. Lyon, France: Eurographics Association, 2014.

29

Sparse Procedural
Volume Rendering
Doug McNabb

29.1 Introduction

The capabilities and visual quality of real-time rendered volumetric effects disproportionately lag those of film. Many other real-time rendering categories have seen recent dramatic improvements. Lighting, shadowing, and postprocessing have come a long way in just the past few years. Now, volumetric rendering is ripe for a transformation. We now have enough compute to build practical implementations that approximate film-style effects in real time. This chapter presents one such approach.

29.2 Overview of Current Techniques

There are many different kinds of volumetric effects, and games render them with several different techniques. We cover a few of them here.

Many games render volumetric effects with 2D billboard sprites. Sprites can produce a wide range of effects, from smoke and fire to water splashes, froth, and foam. They have been around for years, and talented artists are constantly getting better at using them. But, the sprite techniques have limits and are beginning to show their age. The growing excitement for virtual reality's stereoscopic rendering is particularly difficult because the billboard trick is more apparent when viewed in stereo, challenging the illusion. We need a better approximation. The techniques presented here help improve the illusion. (See the example in Figure 29.1.)

There have been several recent advancements in rendering light scattering in homogeneous media, enabling effects like skies, uniform smoke, and fog. These techniques leverage the volume's uniformity to simplify the light-scattering approximations. They're now fast enough to approximate multiple scattering in

Figure 29.1. Sparse procedural volume rendering example.

real time with amazing visual quality [Yusov 14]. Light scattering in heterogeneous participating media is the more-general problem, and correspondingly is more expensive. Our technique approximates single scattering in heterogeneous media and can look very good. It is worth noting that our scattering model is simpler than the typical homogeneous counterparts to accommodate the added complexity from heterogeneous media.

Fluid simulation is another mechanism for generating volumetric effects. The results are often stunning, particularly where accuracy and realism are required. But, the costs can be high in both performance and memory. Developers typically use these simulations to fill a volume with "stuff" (e.g., smoke, fire, water, etc.), and then render that volume by marching rays originating from the eye's point of view. They periodically (e.g., every frame) update a 3D voxel array of properties. Each voxel has properties like pressure, mass, velocity, color, temperature, etc. Our technique fills the volume differently, avoiding most of the traditional simulation's computation and memory costs. We can use less memory than typical fluid simulations by directly populating the volume from a small set of data. We can further reduce the memory requirements by filling the volume on demand, processing only the parts of the volume that are covered by volume primitives. This volume-primitive approach is also attractive to some artists as it gives good control over sculpting the final effect.

29.3 Overview

Our goal for rendering the volume is to approximate efficiently how much light propagates through the volume and reaches the eye. We perform a three-step process to produce our results:

1. Fill a volume with procedural volume primitives.

2. Propagate lighting through the volume.

3. Ray-march the volume from the eye's point of view.

Before we compute how much light propagates through a volume, we need to know the volume's contents; we need to fill the volume with interesting stuff. Volume primitives are an inexpensive, expressive option for describing a volume's contents [Wrennige and Zafar 11]. Different volume primitive types are characterized by their different mechanisms for describing and controlling the contents. Procedural volume primitives describe the contents with algorithms controlled by a set of parameters (e.g., size, position, radius, etc.). We can populate a volume with multiple primitives, sculpting more-complex results. There are many possible volume primitive types. Our system implements a single "displaced sphere" procedural volume primitive. We often refer to them interchangeably as *particles* and *displaced spheres*.

Rendering a single volume primitive is interesting, but a system that can render many and varied overlapping volume primitives is much more useful. We need to render many volume primitives within a unified volume; they need to correctly shadow and occlude each other. Supporting translucent volume primitives is particularly useful. We satisfy these requirements by decoupling the volume "filling" step from the light propagation step. We fill a metavoxel with all relevant volume primitives before we propagate lighting by ray-marching through the volume. We simplify light propagation by supporting only a single directional light (e.g., the sun), allowing us to orient the volume to align with the light's direction. This enables us to traverse trivially the volume one voxel at a time along the light's direction. Each light propagation step illuminates the current voxel with the current light intensity. At each step, the intensity is attenuated to account for absorption and scattering. Note that we propagate only the light intensity. This process can be extended (at additional cost) to accommodate colored light by independently propagating each of the red, green, and blue wavelength intensities.

We capture the volume's lit color and density (or opacity) at each voxel. Note that our model doesn't include light scattered from the neighboring volume. This could presumably be added at additional cost in time and complexity. Our model does account for shadows cast by the rest of the scene onto the volume, and for casting the volume's shadow onto the rest of the scene.

When the eye sees the lit volume, the amount of light it sees at each voxel is reduced by any other voxels between the lit volume and the eye. This is similar to propagating light through the volume with a couple of important differences. The eye view is a perspective view, in contrast to the directional light's orthographic view. And, each voxel along the eye ray can both occlude more-distant voxels and contribute light (if the voxel is emissive, or lit by the light).

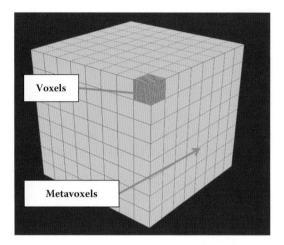

Figure 29.2. A large volume composed of metavoxels, which are composed of voxels.

The volume may also occlude the background; the amount of light from the background that reaches the eye can be absorbed and scattered by the volume. Our approach separates these two eye-view contributions. We determine the lit volume's contribution with a pixel shader and attenuate the background's contribution with alpha blending.

29.4 Metavoxels

The key point of our approach is that we can gain efficiency by avoiding unoccupied parts of the volume. Each of our tasks can be made significantly less expensive: we can fill fewer voxels, propagate light through fewer voxels, and ray-march fewer voxels. We accomplish this by logically subdividing the volume into a uniform grid of smaller volumes. Each of these smaller volumes is in turn a collection of voxels, which we call a *metavoxel*. (See Figure 29.2.)

The metavoxel enables us to efficiently fill and light the volume. Most importantly, it allows us to avoid working on empty metavoxels. It also allows processing multiple metavoxels in parallel (filling can be parallel; lighting has some dependencies). It allows us to switch back and forth between filling metavoxels and ray-marching them, choosing our working set size to balance performance against memory size and bandwidth. Using a small set improves locality. Reusing the same memory over many metavoxels can reduce the total memory required and may reduce bandwidth (depending on the hardware). It also improves ray-marching efficiency, as many rays encounter the same voxels.

Figure 29.3 shows a few variations of a simple scene and the related metavoxels. The first pane shows a few stand-in spheres, a camera, and a light. The

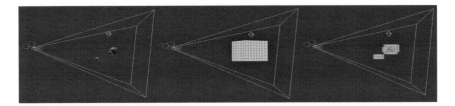

Figure 29.3. A simple scene (left), with all metavoxels (middle) and with only interesting/occupied metavoxels (right).

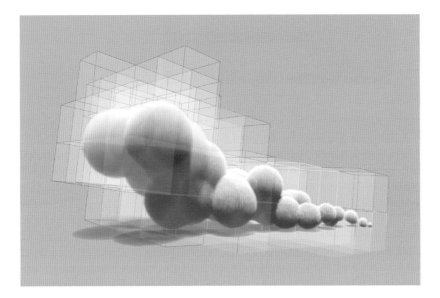

Figure 29.4. Multiple spheres and the metavoxels they cover.

second pane shows a complete volume containing the spheres. The third pane shows the scene with only those metavoxels covered by one or more spheres. This simplified example shows a total volume of $512(8^3)$ metavoxels. It requires processing only 64 of them, culling 7/8 of the volume.

Figure 29.4 shows a stream of simple spheres and a visualization of the metavoxels they cover. Note how the metavoxels are tilted toward the light. Orienting the volume this way allows for independently propagating light along each voxel column. The lighting for any individual voxel depends only on the voxel above it in the column (i.e., the next voxel closer to the light) and is unrelated to voxels in neighboring columns.

Computers get more efficient every year. But memory bandwidth isn't progressing as rapidly as compute efficiency. Operating on cache-friendly metavoxels

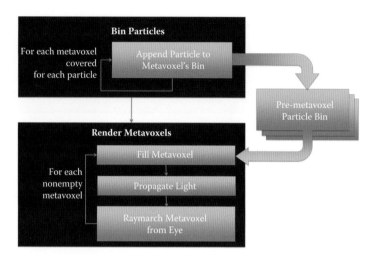

Figure 29.5. High-level algorithm.

may be more useful in the coming years as compute efficiency will almost certainly continue to outpace bandwidth efficiency. Ray-marching multiple metavoxels one at a time can be more efficient than ray-marching a larger volume. The metavoxel localizes the sample points to a relatively small volume, potentially improving cache hit rates and minimizing expensive off-chip bandwidth.

We fill a metavoxel by testing its voxels against the set of particles that cover the metavoxel. For each of the voxels covered by a particle, we compute the particle's color and density at the covered location. Limiting this test to the metavoxel's set of voxels is more efficient than filling a much larger volume; choosing a metavoxel size such that it fits in the cache(s) can reduce expensive off-chip bandwidth. Processing a single voxel multiple times, e.g., once for each particle, can also be more efficient if the voxel's intermediate values are in the cache. Populating the metavoxel with one particle type at a time allows us to maintain separate shaders, which each process different particle types. Note that we currently populate the volume with only a single particle type (displaced sphere). But, composing an effect from multiple particle types is a desirable feature and may be simplified through sharing intermediate results versus a system that requires that a single shader support every particle type.

29.5 Algorithm

Our goal is to render the visible, nonempty metavoxels. Figure 29.5 shows that we loop over each of these interesting metavoxels, filling them with particles (i.e., our displaced sphere volume primitive), and then ray-marching them from the

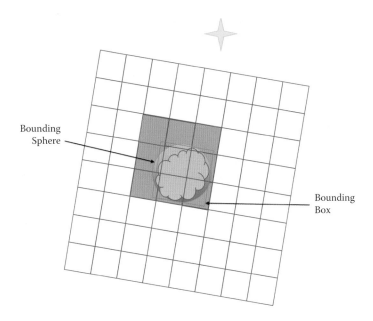

Figure 29.6. Visualization of binning rules.

eye. It's worth noting that "visible" here means visible either from the eye's view or the light's view. We consider the light's view when culling because even if a metavoxel lies outside the eye view, it may still lie between the light and the eye's view such that the metavoxels that are within the eye's view may receive its shadows. We need to propagate lighting through all parts of the volume that contribute to the final scene.

29.5.1 Binning

We determine the interesting metavoxels using a binning process. Binning adds a small amount of extra work but it reduces the overall workload. We can quickly generate a list for each metavoxel containing the indices for the particles that cover the metavoxel, and only those particles. It also allows us to completely avoid metavoxels that aren't covered by any particles.

Each bin holds a list of particle indices. We populate the bin with an index for every particle that covers the metavoxel. We maintain an array of bins—one bin for every metavoxel. (For example, were we to subdivide our total volume into $32 \times 32 \times 32$ metavoxels, then we would have a $32 \times 32 \times 32$ array of bins.) A typical sparsely populated volume will involve a small fraction of these, though the algorithm does not inherently impose a limit.

We bin a particle by looping over the metavoxels covered by the particle's bounding box. (See Figure 29.6.) We refine the approximation and improve over-

```
// Determine the particle's extents
min = particleCenter - particleRadius
max = particleCenter + particleRadius

// Loop over each metavoxel within the extents
// Append the particle to those bins for the
// metavoxels also covered by the bounding sphere
for Z in min.Z to max.Z
    for Y in min.Y to max.Y
        for X in min.X to max.X
            if particleBoundingSphere covers metavoxel[Z,Y,X]
                append particle to metavoxelBin[Z,Y,X]}
```

Listing 29.1. Binning pseudocode.

all efficiency by testing each of these metavoxels against the particle's bounding sphere. If the particle's bounding sphere covers the metavoxels, then we append the particle to the metavoxel's bin.

Listing 29.1 shows simple pseudocode for binning a particle.

29.5.2 Filling Metavoxels

Our goal is to ray-march the metavoxels from the eye's point of view. Before we can do that, we need a metavoxel through which to march rays. We populate a metavoxel by testing each of its voxels against each volume-primitive particle. We say the voxel is covered by the particle if and only if the voxel is inside the volume primitive.

We reduce the number of tests by testing each metavoxel only against the particles that cover it; many more particles may participate in the system, but they may cover only other metavoxels. There are many more potential optimizations for reducing the total number of tests (e.g., progressive/hierarchical traversal). Some of these strategies can be explored within this framework, but some of them encourage fundamental changes. We look forward to future improvements.

Our task for filling the metavoxel has two goals:

1. a final density value for every voxel,

2. a final color value for every voxel.

We use a simple model for combining particle densities and colors:

$$\text{density}_{\text{final}} = \sum_1^n \text{density}_n,$$

$$\text{color}_{\text{final}} = \max(\text{color}_0 \ldots \text{color}_n).$$

The final density is given by a simple sum of the densities for every particle that covers the voxel. Color is more complex. We could blend colors together

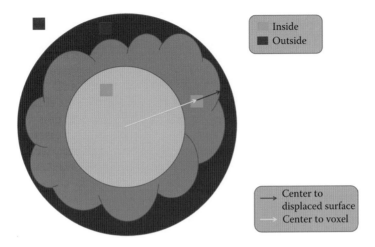

Figure 29.7. Determining coverage.

proportionally to particle density (i.e., a dense particle affects the final color more than a less-dense particle). In practice, simply accepting the maximum between two colors produces plausible results and is computationally inexpensive. This won't work for every effect, but it efficiently produces good results for some.

Different color components may be required for different effects. For example, fire is emissive with color ranging from white through yellow and orange to red, then black as the intensity drops. Smoke is often constant color and not emissive. The diffuse color is modulated by light and shadow, while the emissive color is not.

We compute the density by performing a coverage test. Figure 29.7 shows our approach. We determine the particle's density at each voxel's position. If a voxel is inside the displaced sphere, then we continue and compute the particle's color and density. Voxels outside the displaced sphere are unmodified. Note that the displacement has a limited range; there are two potentially interesting radii—inner and outer. If the voxel is inside the inner radius, then we can be sure it's inside the displaced sphere. If the voxel is outside the outer radius, then we can be sure that it's outside the displaced sphere. Coverage for voxels that lie between these two points is defined by the displacement amount.

We radially displace the sphere. The position of each point on the displaced sphere's surface is given by the length of the vector from the sphere's center to the surface. If the vector from the sphere's center to the voxel is shorter than this displacement, then the voxel is inside the sphere; otherwise it's outside.

Note a couple of optimizations. First, the dot product inexpensively computes length^2: $\mathbf{A} \cdot \mathbf{A} = \text{length}^2(\mathbf{A})$. Using distance^2 allows us to avoid the potentially expensive square-root operations. The second optimization comes from storing

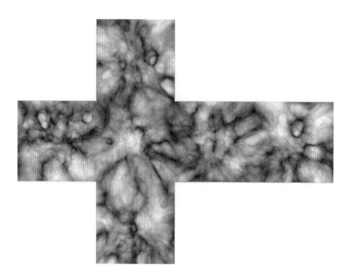

Figure 29.8. Example cube map: 3D noise sampled at sphere surface, projected to cube map faces.

our displacement values in a cube map. The cube map, like the displacement is defined over the sphere's surface. Given a voxel at position (X, Y, Z) and the sphere's center at $(0, 0, 0)$, the displacement is given by cubeMap$[X, Y, Z]$.

We don't currently support dynamically computed noise. We suspect that a dynamic solutions would benefit from using a cube map for intermediate storage as an optimization; the volume is 3D while the cube map is 2D (cube map locations are given by three coordinates, but they project to a flat, 2D surface as seen in Figure 29.8). The number of expensive dynamic-noise calculations can be reduced this way.

We determine each voxel's lit color by determining how much light reaches it and multiplying by the unlit color. We propagate the lighting through the volume to determine how much light reaches each voxel. (See Figure 29.9.)

There are many possible ways to compute the color: constant, radial gradient, polynomial, texture gradient, cube map, noise, etc. We leave this choice to the reader. We note a couple of useful approximations: Figure 29.10 shows the results of using the displacement map as an ambient occlusion approximation and using the radial distance as a color ramp (from very bright red-ish at the center to dark gray further out). The ambient occlusion approximation can help a lot to provide form to the shadowed side.

Many of the displaced sphere's properties can be animated over time: position, orientation, scale, opacity, color, etc. This is a similar paradigm to 2D billboards, only with 3D volume primitives.

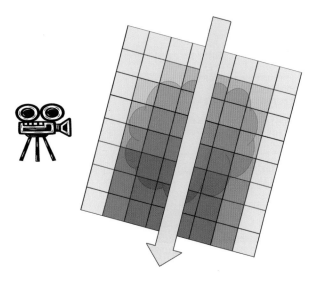

Figure 29.9. Propagating light through a metavoxel's voxels.

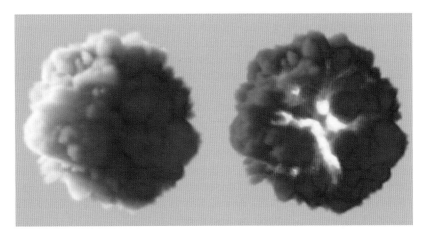

Figure 29.10. Procedural colors.

29.5.3 Light Propagation

We propagate light through the metavoxel with a simple loop. We use the rasterizer and pixel shader to perform the work. We draw one pixel for each of the metavoxel's voxel columns—i.e., a two-triangle quad covering one pixel for each of our voxel columns (e.g., for a $32 \times 32 \times 32$ metavoxel, we draw a 32×32 pixel square). Our pixel/fragment shader loops over each voxel in the corresponding voxel column.

```
// 100% light propagates to start
propagatedLight = 1

// Loop over all voxels in the column
for Z in 0 to METAVOXEL_HEIGHT
    // Light this voxel
    color[Z] *= propagatedLight

    // Attenuate the light leaving this voxel
    propagatedLight /= (1 + density[Z])
```

Listing 29.2. Light propagation pseudocode.

Listing 29.2 shows pseudocode for propagating lighting through the metavoxel. At each step, we light the current voxel and attenuate the light for subsequent voxels.

29.5.4   Eye-View Ray March

We march along the eye rays, through the metavoxel, accumulating color from the metavoxel's lit voxels and attenuating according to the voxel's density.

We implement the eye-view ray march by drawing a cube (i.e., 6 quads = 12 triangles) with the rasterizer from the eye's point of view. The pixel shader executes once for each pixel covered by the cube. Listing 29.3 gives pseudocode for the pixel shader. It loops along a ray from the eye through the pixel, sampling

```
// The ray starts at the eye and goes through the
// near plane at the current pixel
ray = pixelPosition - eyePosition

// Compute the start and end points where the ray
// enters and exits this metavoxel
start = intersectFar( ray, metavoxel )
end = intersectNear( ray, metavoxel )

// Clamp the ray to the eye position
end = max( eyePosition, end )

// Start assuming volume is empty
// == black, and 100% transmittance
resultColor = 0
resultTransmittance = 1

// step along the ray, accumulating and attenuating
for step in start to end
    color = volume[step].rgb
    density = volume[step].a
    blendFactor = 1/(1 + density)
    resultColor = lerp( color, resultColor, blendFactor )
    resultTransmittance *= blendFactor
```

Listing 29.3. Ray march pseudocode.

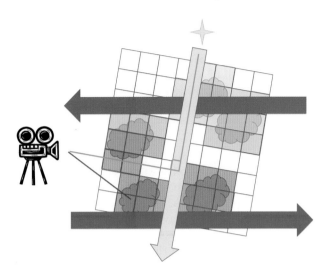

Figure 29.11. Metavoxel sort order.

the volume as a 3D texture at each step. It accumulates lighting from the sample's color and attenuates it by the sample's alpha (i.e., density). The end result is a color and an alpha we can use with alpha blending to composite with our back buffer.

Note that we draw this box with front-face culling. If the eye is inside the box, then it sees only back faces. If we were to use back-face culling, then the pixels wouldn't draw and no ray marching would occur. We also don't want to draw without culling because that would potentially cause our pixels to unnecessarily draw twice.

29.5.5 Metavoxel Sort Order

Lastly, we need to render the metavoxels in the correct order for the alpha blending to be correct. We render the metavoxels one at a time, propagating light and ray-marching each one. The results blend to a shared render target. Because the metavoxels can contain semitransparent voxels, order matters.

Figure 29.11 demonstrates why we need to process our metavoxels from the top to bottom (with respect to the light) and back to front (with respect to the eye). Light propagation dictates the top-to-bottom order because an individual metavoxel's final colors depend on how much light propagates through any metavoxels nearer the light. Similarly, we need to blend each metavoxel's eye-view ray march results with those of previously rendered metavoxels.

There's a twist, however. Rendering from top to bottom and back to front can produce incorrect results for those metavoxels below the perpendicular (the green line from the camera). The eye is looking down on those metavoxels. So, the eye can see through some previously rendered metavoxels. In this case, we need to render the more-recent metavoxel behind the previously rendered metavoxel. The solution is to process all of the metavoxels above the perpendicular before processing those below. We also switch sort order and render those metavoxels below the line sorted front to back.

The different sort orders require different alpha-blending modes. We render back to front with *over blending*. We render front to back with *under blending* [Ikits et al. 04].

It is possible to render all metavoxels sorted front to back with under blending. That requires maintaining at least one column of metavoxels. Light propagation requires processing from top to bottom. Sorting front to back can require rendering a metavoxel before those above it have been processed. In that case, we would still propagate the lighting through the entire column before ray-marching them. Consistently sorting front to back like this could potentially allow us to "early out," avoiding future work populating and ray-marching fully occluded voxels.

29.6   Conclusion

Computers are now fast enough for games to include true volumetric effects. One way is to fill a sparse volume with volume primitives and ray-march it from the eye. Efficiently processing a large volume can be achieved by breaking it into smaller metavoxels in which we process only the occupied metavoxels that contribute to the final image. Filling the metavoxels with volume primitives allows us to efficiently populate the volume with visually interesting contents. Finally, sampling the metavoxels from a pixel shader as 3D textures delivers an efficient ray-marching technique.

Bibliography

[Ikits et al. 04] Milan Ikits, Joe Kniss, Aaron Lefohn, and Charles Hansen. "Volume Rendering Techniques." In *GPU Gems*, edited by Randima Fernando, Chapter 39. Reading, MA: Addison-Wesley Professional, 2004.

[Wrennige and Zafar 11] Magnus Wrennige and Nafees Bin Zafar "Production Volume Rendering Fundamentals." SIGGRAPH Course, Vancouver, Canada, August 7–11, 2011.

[Yusov 14] Egor Yusov. "High Performance Outdoor Light Scattering using Epipolar Sampling" In *GPU Pro 5: Advanced Rendering Techniques*, edited by Wolfgang Engel, pp. 101–126. Boca Raton, FL: CRC Press, 2014.

30

Adaptive Virtual Textures
Ka Chen

30.1 Introduction

Adaptive Virtual Textures (AVT) are an improvement upon Procedural Virtual Textures. This technique can be applied to a large open world and can achieve a much higher texture resolution when needed. With AVT, the artist can place thousands of projected decals with high-resolution textures on the terrain surface These decals will be baked together with terrain materials into virtual textures at runtime. Once baked, the rendering engine will directly display the virtual textures instead of rendering terrain materials and decals. Thus, the render performance is greatly improved.

30.2 Procedural Virtual Textures Basics

Procedural Virtual Textures are mipmapped texture caches that store the recent rendering result of terrain material blending and projected decals. In a deferred rendering engine, these virtual textures store the composite using the G-buffer's format, which can then be used directly when rendering subsequent frames. It is a powerful optimization technique because the rendering engine can simply skip the expensive terrain material blending once it has been cached in the virtual textures. (See [Widmark 12] for more details.)

30.3 Adaptive Virtual Textures

30.3.1 Goals

The standard virtual textures technique allocates a large mipmapped texture, which is then uniformly applied onto the whole terrain world. The actual texture resolution can be calculated as

$$\text{texel ratio} = \frac{\texttt{TextureSize.xy}}{\texttt{WorldSize.xy}}.$$

Although usually a very large virtual texture (such as $512K \times 512K$) is allocated, sometimes the texture resolution is not high enough when it is applied on a large open world such as a $10KM \times 10KM$ world. In this case the texel ratio is only 0.5 texels/cm. Such a low texture resolution limits the potential usage of procedural virtual textures in next-generation games. In order to prevent the look of low-resolution terrain, an additional detail material layer has to be applied on top of procedural virtual textured terrain.

In this chapter, we will present Adaptive Virtual Textures (AVT), which greatly improve the texture resolution in a very large world. We will discuss the practical implementation of AVT and how we overcame those challenges in our game.

30.3.2 Overview

By using a $512K \times 512K$ resolution virtual texture, we would like to achieve a high texture resolution such as 10 texels/cm in a $10KM \times 10KM$ world. Such a high texel ratio is only needed for terrain surfaces that may appear very close to the camera. For terrain surfaces that are a bit farther away, a lower texel ratio such as 5 texels/cm is sufficient. We would require even less texture resolution for surfaces that are much farther away. The key is to find a solution to apply the virtual texture based on the distance from the camera to the terrain surface.

We divide the game world into multiple sectors and each sector has a pre-defined size (such as 64×64 meters), as shown in Figure 30.1. Every sector is allocated with a virtual image inside the virtual texture. The size of the virtual image is calculated based on the distance from the camera. The closest sectors are allocated with the maximum virtual image size, for example $64K \times 64K$. Farther sectors are allocated with smaller sizes, such as $32K \times 32K$ or $16K \times 16K$. The minimum size can be $1K \times 1K$.

After allocating all the sectors in the world, our virtual texture becomes a texture atlas for all the virtual images with different sizes The closest sector has the maximum resolution of 10 texels/cm calculated as

$$\text{texel ratio} = \frac{64K}{64 \text{ meters}} = 10 \text{ texels/cm}.$$

Farther sectors have lower resolutions such as 5 texels/cm and so on. It is important to note that these virtual image sizes will be adjusted dynamically at runtime based on camera distance whenever the camera moves.

30.3.3 Allocate Virtual Texture Atlas

As mentioned at the end of Section 30.3.2, we need to adjust the size of each virtual image dynamically at runtime. It is important to have a good texture atlasing algorithm so that the performance of AVT is maximized and space fragmentation is kept to a minimum. We use a quad-tree scheme to allocate the

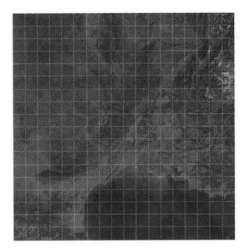

Figure 30.1. World divided into multiple sectors.

virtual images. This scheme makes sure that the image is always allocated at the location where the UV address is aligned with image size. Figure 30.2 shows the allocation of three virtual images inside the virtual texture atlas.

30.3.4 Adjust Virtual Image Size at Runtime

In each frame we calculate a target virtual image size based on its distance from the camera. If the target size is different than the current size of the sector, we will insert a new image with the target size into the atlas and remove the old one. Listings 30.1 and 30.2 show the code to calculate and adjust, respectively, the size of virtual images for sectors in the world.

For example, as shown in Figure 30.3, when the camera moves and Sector B becomes farther away from the camera, it will be allocated using a smaller image size of 32K × 32K. Sector C becomes closer to the camera, so it will be allocated with a larger image size of 64K × 64K.

30.3.5 Remap the Indirection Texture

Indirection texture Our virtual texture system uses an indirection texture to translate from the virtual UV address to the physical UV address. (For the basic virtual texture technique and information about indirection textures, please refer to [Mittring 08].) When virtual image are moved and scaled, we have to update the indirection texture so that the new virtual UV address will reuse the existing pages in the physical texture caches. The format of our indirection texture is 32 bit and it is defined as in Figure 30.4.

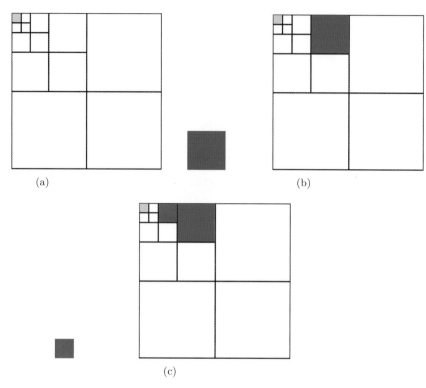

Figure 30.2. (a) First, insert a virtual image of size 16×16 for Sector A. (b) Then, insert a virtual image of size 64×64 for Sector B. (c) Then, insert a virtual image of size 32×32 for Sector C.

```
typedef unsigned int U32;
const U32 highestResolution = 64 * 1024;
U32 CalculateTargetImageSize(const SectorInfo& sectorInfo, const
Vector3& cameraPosition)
{
    //Get sectorPosition.
    ......
    // Distance between sector and camera in top-down view.
    float distance = - (sectorPosition - cameraPosition).GetLength2();
    U32 t = (U32)(distance / switchDistance);
    // Calculate the LOD of virtual image.
    U32 lodImage = 0;
    if(t >= 1)
    {
        lodImage = std::log2(t) + 1;
    }
    U32 virtualImageSize = highestResolution >> lodImage;
    return virtualImageSize;
}
```

Listing 30.1. Calculating the virtual image size.

```
std::vector<SectorInfo> delayedRemoveSectors;
for (auto& sectorInfo : m_AllSectors)
{
    virtualImageSize = CalculateTargetImageSize(sectorInfo,
                          cameraPosition);
    If (virtualImageSize != sectorInfo.m_VirtualImageSize)
    {
        m_Atlas.InsertImage(sectorInfo, virtualImageSize);
        delayedRemoveSectors.push_back(sectorInfo);
    }
}
for (auto& removingSector : delayedRemoveSectors)
{
    m_Atlas.RemoveImage(removingSector);
}
delayedRemoveSectors.clear();
```

Listing 30.2. Adjusting the virtual image size.

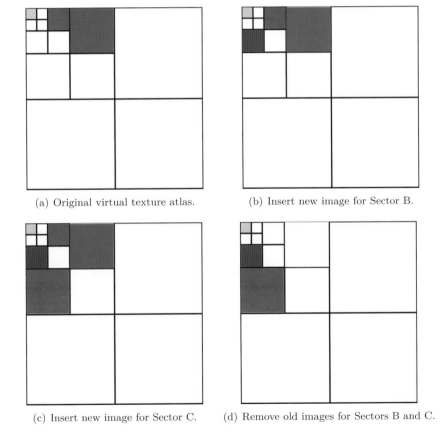

(a) Original virtual texture atlas.   (b) Insert new image for Sector B.

(c) Insert new image for Sector C.   (d) Remove old images for Sectors B and C.

Figure 30.3. Adjusting the size of two virtual images.

PageOffsetX : 8	PageOffsetY : 8	Mip : 8	Debug : 8

Figure 30.4. Indirection texture format.

```
scale = (virtual texture size / physical texture size) >> mip;
bias = physical page offset - virtual page offset * scale;
physical uv = virtual uv * scale + bias;
```

Listing 30.3. Calculating the physical texture UV address from the indirection texture and the virtual UV address.

`PageOffsetX` and `PageOffsetY` are the UV offsets of the physical page pointed to by the current virtual page. `Mip` describes the available mipmap level for the current virtual page. The final physical texture UV address is calculated as shown in Listing 30.3.

Remap the indirection texture when the image is up-scaled The update of the indirection texture for Sector B is shown in Figure 30.5.

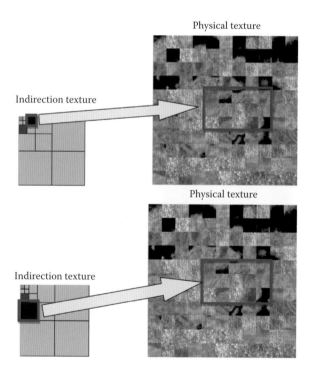

Figure 30.5. Indirection texture (left) and physical texture cache (right) before update (top) and after update (bottom).

```
For every mipmap level of the indirection texture,
{
    //The following part is executed by a compute shader going
    //through all indirection texture entries, with the number of
    //threads set as the number of entries in the X and Y
    //dimensions.
    For every entry enclosed by new image in that mipmap level,
    {
        If (current mipmap level is greater than 0)
        {
            Copy the content from 1 mip level higher old image
            (PageOffsetX, PageOffsetY, Mip) and increase Mip by 1
            The new entry content becomes (PageOffsetX,
            PageOffsetY, Mip + 1);
        }
        else
        {
            Copy the content from 1 mip level higher old image,
            The new entry content becomes (PageOffsetX,
            PageOffsetY, Mip);
        }
    }
}
```

Listing 30.4. Pseudocode to update the indirection texture for a newly allocated virtual image.

The work involved in updating the indirection texture is shown in Listing 30.4.

The remapping of an up-scaled virtual image can be viewed in Figure 30.6. In this case the image size is up-scaled from 32K to 64K. We can conclude that the indirection entries for the new image should point to the exact same entries of one mip level higher in the old image, as shown by the red arrows. As the mip level 0 of the new image doesn't exist in the old image, we will set the entries of mip level 0 in the new image to lower mip level physical texture pages to prevent visual popping in the current frame.

Remap the indirection texture when image is down-scaled Remapping a down-scaled virtual image is just to reverse the steps of up-scaling a virtual image, as shown in Figure 30.7.

30.4 Virtual Texture Best Practices

In the previous section we discussed the key features of AVT and how to handle updating the virtual texture atlas and indirection texture when dynamic adjustments of the image size happens in real time. In this section we will talk about some practical implementation details of AVT.

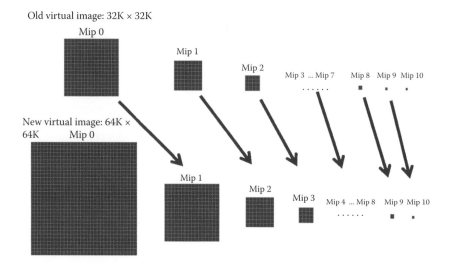

Figure 30.6. Remapping of an up-scaled virtual image.

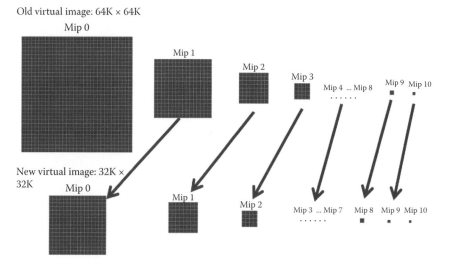

Figure 30.7. Remapping a down-scaled virtual image.

30.4.1   Output Page IDs

Virtual textures are divided into multiple 256×256 sized virtual pages. For every pixel on the screen, we calculate to which virtual page it is related and output the page information into a read/write buffer during the G-buffer rendering pass. We call this buffer the *Page ID buffer*.

PageID X : 12	PageID Y : 12	Mip : 4	Size : 4

Figure 30.8. The format of the page ID.

```
#define PAGEID_DOWNSCALE 8
void OutputPageID(VTextureArgs vArgs, float2 screenPos)
{
    //Write to page ID read/write buffer
    uint2 vpos = (uint2)screenPos;
    uint2 vpos2 = ((uint2) vpos) % PAGEID_DOWNSCALE;
    uint virtualPageID = pack_pageid(vArgs);
    if(vpos2.x == (uint)g_VirtualSectorsInfo.VirtualDither.x &&
       vpos2.y == (uint)g_VirtualSectorsInfo.VirtualDither.y)
            PageIDOutputTexture[((uint2) vpos) / PAGEID_DOWNSCALE] =
                virtualPageID;
}
```

Listing 30.5. Writing to $1/8 \times 1/8$ Page ID buffer in the G-buffer rendering shader.

The page information for every pixel is written as a 32-bit integer as shown in Figure 30.8.

`PageID` and `Size` are calculated as

$$PageID.xy = \frac{Virtual\ UV.xy}{virtual\ page\ size},$$

$$Size = \log_2(virtual\ page\ size).$$

The size of the Page ID buffer is $1/8$ of the G-buffer texture in both directions in order to reduce the memory overhead. Listing 30.5 is the fragment shader used to output the page ID to the small read/write buffer.

Note that `g_VirtualSectorsInfo.VirtualDither.xy` is the shader parameter passed in from the rendering engine, and its value ranges from 0 to 7 and changes according to a predefined pattern in every frame. Since we only pick one pixel out of 64 to output, if a page ID is missed in one frame, it will be processed during a subsequent frame.

30.4.2 Physical Textures and Compressing

We allocate three physical textures for deferred rendering purposes. These are the albedo texture, normal map texture, and specular texture. Table 30.1 provides the color channel information for these textures.

Every physical texture page is compressed at runtime by a compute shader on the GPU. We modified the sample code provided by Microsoft for the Xbox One to compress three different types of physical texture pages in one pass. For the normal map texture, we choose the BC5 format to compress only the X and Y

Physical Texture	Channels	Representation	Compress Format
Albedo Texture	RGB	Albedo Color	BC1
Normal Map Texture	RG	Tangent Space Normal	BC5
Specular Texture	RGB	Glossness, Specular Intensity, Normal Map Scale	BC1

Table 30.1. Physical textures' channel information.

```
//Output terrain G-buffer color by fetching physical texture cache.
gbuffer.albedo = DiffusePhysicalTexture.SampleGrad(
        TextureSampler, physical_uv, dx, dy).xyz;
gbuffer.normal.xy = NormalPhysicalTexture.SampleGrad(
        TextureSampler, physical_uv, dx, dy).xy;
gbuffer.normal.xy = gbuffer.normal.xy * 2 - 1;
gbuffer.normal.z = sqrt(saturate(1 - dot(gbuffer.normal.xy,
                gbuffer.normal.xy)));
float3 GlossnessSpecularIntensity =
    SpecularPhysicalTexture.SampleGrad(TextureSampler,
                physical_uv, dx, dy).xyz;
gbuffer.normal.xyz *= GlossnessSpecularIntensity.z;
gbuffer.glossness_specularIntensity =
    GlossnessSpecularIntensity.xy;
```

Listing 30.6. Calculating the final G-buffer colors from virtual textures.

channels of the normal map into a separated 4 bits-per-pixel block. This gives a much less blocky result than with the BC1 format. In some situations the normal vector saved in the virtual texture is not unit length. For example, when the pixel is on a big slope on the terrain surface, the final normal vector might be scaled by the slope angle or a mask texture. We save the scale of the normal vector in the Z channel of the Specular Physical Texture during compression. Later on, when we fetch the virtual textures, we reapply the scale to the normal vector coming from the physical texture. Listing 30.6 shows the HLSL shader for calculating the final G-buffer colors.

30.4.3 Improve Performance by Distributed Rendering

The performance of virtual texture rendering may vary depending on how many virtual pages are visible in a given frame. When the camera is moving or turning very fast, it could take significant time to cache the physical textures. We can spread the rendering of virtual pages into multiple frames to alleviate this problem. We call this method *distributed rendering.*

On the CPU we read the Page ID buffer that is output from the GPU, collect the visible virtual pages, and remove the duplicated pages. We then sort the

```
struct PageIDSortPredicate
{
    bool operator()(const unsigned id0, const unsigned id1) const
    {
        VTexturePageID key0(id0);
        VTexturePageID key1(id1);

        //key.size is saved in Log2 space, so it is in the same
        //space as the mipmap level.
        return (key0.size - key0.mip) < (key1.size - key1.mip);
    }
};

std::sort(pageIDs.Begin(),pageIDs.End(), PageKeySortPredicate());
```

Listing 30.7. Sorting the visible pages.

visible pages according to their image sizes scaled by mipmap level, as shown in
Listing 30.7.

For each sorted virtual page starting from the first page, we first search for
its physical page in the physical texture cache and allocate one if it is not already
there; then, we render the fully composited terrain material into the page. At
the same time we record the actual rendering time for virtual textures. If the
accumulated rendering time for the current frame is longer than a threshold, we
skip the rendering of the remaining pages in the list. The skipped pages will be
rendered during the next frame.

We always sort the virtual pages such that we render the page with the smallest image size first. This guarantees that the terrain is always displayed on
screen even if some pages have been skipped. Some parts of the image may appear blurry in the current frame if they have been skipped, but these areas will
become sharper later, once they are updated. In practice this is generally not
noticeable because it happens very quickly from one frame to the next.

30.4.4 Virtual Texture Filtering

Anisotropic filtering Our Adaptive Virtual Texutres support 8X anisotropic filtering. This means that the pixel shader may access neighboring pixels up to
4 pixels away If the shader accesses a pixel lying on the border of the page, its
neighboring pixel could reside in another physical page and it might not be the
correct neighboring pixel in the world space. This would cause color bleeding
problems between pages.

To fix this problem, we allocate a 4-pixel-wide border on each side of the
physical texture page. For a 256×256 virtual page, its physical page size becomes
264×264. When rendering into the physical page, the viewport is also enlarged
to 264×264 so that the neighboring pixels at the border are rendered. (See
Figure 30.9.)

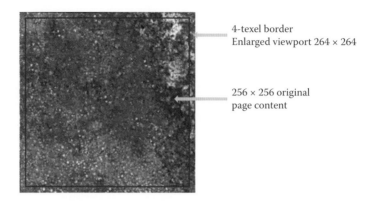

Figure 30.9. A 4-pixel border on a physical page.

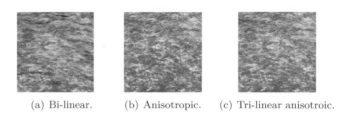

(a) Bi-linear.   (b) Anisotropic.   (c) Tri-linear anisotroic.

Figure 30.10. Comparison of three filtering methods.

Tri-linear filtering Software tri-linear filtering is also supported by simply fetching the indirection texture twice with a higher mipmap level and a lower mipmap level to get two sets of physical UV addresses, then fetching from the physical textures twice and blending between them according to the calculated ratio between the mipmap levels.

Another approach is to use hardware tri-linear filtering with virtual textures. For every physical texture we have, we can create an additional quarter size physical texture as mipmap level 1 and render into this mipmap level 1 page whenever the mipmap 0 page is rendered. This method requires 25% more video memory for the physical texture caches. It also increases the GPU overhead because the mipmap level 1 cache must be synced with the mipmap level 0 all the time.

Figure 30.10 shows a comparison between bi-linear filtering, anisotropic filtering, and tri-linear anisotropic filtering when looking at the ground with a sharp view angle. The image looks blurred with bi-linear filtering. With anisotropic filtering alone, the image looks much sharper but there is a visible seam where mipmap levels change. With tri-linear anisotropic filtering, both problems are solved.

(a) Render terrain materials.   (b) Render a decal on top of terrain.   (c) Render next decal.   (d) Render the third decal.

Figure 30.11. Rendering terrain and decals into a virtual texture page.

30.4.5 Combine with Projected Decals

Adaptive Virtual Textures become very powerful when they are combined with projected decals on terrain. The G-buffer properties (albedo, normal, and specular) of the decals can be baked into the same virtual page where terrain surfaces are rendered. Thus rendering of projected decals becomes almost free with Adaptive Virtual Textures. Since AVT supports very high virtual texture resolutions (10 texels/cm), level artists can put thousands of high-detail projected decals on the ground, and this vastly improves the visual appearance for next-generation games.

The rendering pipeline for projected decals in adaptive virtual textures is quite straight forward:

For every visible page collected and sorted from the Page ID buffer,

1. find or allocate a physical texture page,

2. render terrain surface materials into the physical page,

3. find decals belonging to this page in the world space,

4. render decals into the physical page by projecting them into the virtual texture.

Figure 30.11 shows the steps to render terrain materials and decals into a virtual texture page.

30.5 Conclusion

This chapter described a new technique called Adaptive Virtual Textures for rendering terrain and decals with a high resolution in an open world. AVT is an improvement upon Procedural Virtual Textures. The main contribution of this technique is that it supports a very high virtual texture resolution at close range and can be used to render thousands of decals very efficiently.

Bibliography

[Mittring 08] Martin Mittring. "Advanced Virtual Texture Topics." In *ACM SIG-GRAPH 2008 Games*, pp. 23–51. New York: ACM, 2008.

[Widmark 12] Mattias Widmark. "Terrain in Battlefield 3." Paper presented at Game Developers Conference, San Francisco, CA, March 5–9, 2012.

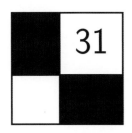

31

Deferred Coarse Pixel Shading
Rahul P. Sathe and Tomasz Janczak

31.1 Overview

Deferred shading has become a popular rendering technique in the games industry to avoid redundant shading of occluded pixels. With increasing screen resolutions and DPI, one can reduce the frequency of slowly varying components of the rendering equation to something lower than once per pixel without a perceivable difference in visual quality. Recent research addresses this issue and proposes hardware solutions like Coarse Pixel Shading [Vaidyanathan et al. 14]. Although an elegant solution, the Coarse Pixel Shader does not fit well into the deferred shading pipeline. Lauritzen proposed a solution for deferred shading engines that identifies the pixels where pixel rate shading is not enough and shades them at the sample rate using a compute shader [Lauritzen 10]. We extend the later idea further, but in the reverse direction by identifying the regions of the screen where one can reduce the shading to a rate lower than pixel frequency (e.g., 2×2 pixel sized blocks). With our technique we are able show about 40–50% reduction in shading time with a slight increase in the G-buffer generation time.

31.2 Introduction and Background

Shading calculations often involve multiple components, e.g., ambient occlusion, diffused lighting, and specular highlights. Some of these components have a lower spatial frequency than others. When these slowly changing components are evaluated at a rate lower than once per pixel, the image artifacts are hardly noticeable on a high DPI screen. A large percentage of the power consumed by the graphics processors is due to pixel shading [Pool 12]. As a result, reducing the pixel shader usage directly translates to a power savings. Vaidyanathan et al. proposed a solution that is well suited for the forward rendering pipeline [Vaidyanathan et al. 14]. In their approach, one shades primitives in screen space at different rates: coarse pixels (e.g., 2×2 block of pixels), pixels, and then samples. But this does not extend well to the deferred shading or postprocessing passes because at the time of deferred shading, the notion of primitive is not present. Moreover, the primitive might have been partly occluded with one or more additional primitives.

Lauretzen proposed a compute shader-based solution for deferred shading that works well with multisample antialiasing (MSAA) [Lauritzen 10]. In his approach, the G-buffer is rendered at the MSAA resolution and contains the view-space derivatives and the normal, in addition to other surface data used for shading. He then analyzes the G-buffer samples within a pixel to find if that pixel needs to be shaded at the sample frequency. He uses the triangle inequality of the view-space depth derivatives along with the normal variation to find out which pixels need to be shaded at the sample rate. We expand upon his idea, but in the opposite direction.

31.3 Algorithm

31.3.1 G-Buffer Generation

Just like in a normal deferred shading engine, our algorithm starts off by generating a G-buffer by writing out shading inputs at the pixel center. The G-buffer stores derivatives of the view-space Z values in addition to the other surface data (position, normal, UVs, TBN basis, etc.) required for evaluating the BRDF during the shading pass. View-space Z derivatives are calculated by first multiplying the position with the camera-world-view matrix and evaluating `ddx_coarse` and `ddy_coarse` instructions. We use the spherical encoding to encode the surface normal into `float2` to save some G-buffer space and bandwidth. Other types of encoding [Pranckevičius 09] are possible, but we chose a spherical encoding because that works well with the optimization discussed at the end of Section 31.3.2. We pack the specular intensity and the specular power in the other two components to occupy a full `float4`. The G-buffer layout is as follows:

```
struct GBuffer
{
    float4 normal_specular : SV_Target0; // Encoded normal and
                                         // specular power/intensity.
    float4 albedo          : SV_Target1; // Albedo.
    float4 biased_albedo   : SV_Target2; // Albedo sampled with
                                         // the biased sampler.
    float2 positionZGrad   : SV_Target3; // ddx, ddy of view-space Z.
    float  positionZ       : SV_Target4; // View-space Z.
};
```

31.3.2 Shading Pass

For the shading pass, we use a tiled compute shader similar to the one proposed by Lauritzen [Lauritzen 10]. Our compute shader is launched such that one thread processes one coarse region of the screen (e.g., 2×2 or 4×4 pixels region, henceforth referred to as a *coarse pixel*). One thread group works on a larger screen-space region containing multiple coarse regions (henceforth referred to as a *tile*). Our compute shader is conceptually divided in multiple phases:

1. light tiling phase,

2. analysis phase,

3. coarse pixel shading phase,

4. pixel shading phase.

At the end of each phase, the threads within the thread group synchronize. Listing 31.1 shows the pseudocode for the shading pass. Figure 31.1 shows the flowchart for the same.

We will now describe each of the phases in detail.

Light tiling phase When the renderer has a large number of lights to deal with, the bandwidth required to read the light data structures can be a substantial. To alleviate this problem, it is common practice to find the lights that intersect a particular tile. Once found, the indices to the lights that intersect a particular tile are maintained in the shared local memory. Subsequent portions of the shading pass deal with only the lights that hit at least one pixel in that tile. Further details about light culling can be found in [Lauritzen 10].

Analysis phase The goal of this phase is to determine the coarse pixels at which the shading rate can be lowered. To that end, each thread reads the normals and the view-space depth derivatives for all the pixels within the coarse pixel. We then analyze the G-buffer data at each of the pixels in the coarse pixel with respect to a reference pixel (e.g., the top-left pixel in each region). During the analysis, similar to that of Lauritzen [Lauritzen 10], we use the triangle inequality to check if the shading rate can be reduced to once per coarse pixel. The underlying principle in using this criterion is to check if the entire region belongs to the same triangle. The maximum possible range of Z in a given region is calculated as the region's span (e.g., $\sqrt{2}N$ for $N \times N$ pixels) times the sum of the absolute values of the view-space derivatives of the reference sample. We use the triangle inequality to see if the absolute difference of the view-space Z is greater than the maximum possible Z range over that region. Alternatively, one could store a 3-tuple (`DrawcallId`, `InstanceId`, `PrimitiveId`) to identify if the coarse pixel belongs to a single primitive, but this consumes more memory and bandwidth.

Having the coarse pixel belong to one triangle is necessary, but it is not a sufficient condition for us to be able to reduce the shading rate. We also check if the maximum variation of the surface normal with respect to the reference pixel is under some predefined threshold (e.g., 2 degrees). If other G-buffer components contribute to BRDF in any meaningful way, we check to see if their variance from a reference sample is within the acceptable threshold.

```
#define GROUP_DIM   16
#define GROUP_SIZE (GROUP_DIM * GROUP_DIM)
groupshared uint sMinZ, sMaxZ; // Z-min and -max for the tile.

// Light list for the tile.
groupshared uint sTileLightIndices[MAX_LIGHTS];
groupshared uint sTileNumLights;

// List of coarse-pixels that require per-pixel shading.
// We encode two 16-bit x/y coordinates in one uint to save shared memory space.
groupshared uint sPerPixelCPs [GROUP_SIZE/(N*N)];
groupshared uint sNumPerPixelCPs;

[numthreads(GROUP_DIM/N,   GROUP_DIM/N, 1)] // Coarse pixel is NxN.
void ComputeShaderTileCS(...)

{
    // Load the surface data for all the pixels within NxN.
    // Calculate the Z-bounds within the coarse pixel.
    // Calculate min and max for the entire tile and store it in sMinZ, sMaxZ.

    // One thread processes one light.
    for (lightIndex = groupIndex..totalLights){
    // If the light intersects the tile, append it to sTileLightIndices[].
    }
    Groupsync();

    // Read the lights that touch this tile from the groupshared memory.
    // Evaluate and accumulate the lighting for every light for the top-left pixel.
    // Check to see if per-pixel lighting is required.
    bool perPixelShading = IsPerPixelShading(surfaceSamples);
    if (perPixelShading) {
       // Atomically increment sNumPerPixelCPs with the read back.
       // Append the pixel to sPerPixelCPs[].
    } else {
       // Store the results in the intermediate buffer in groupshared or
       // global memory,
       // OR if no per-pixel component, splat the top-left pixel's color to other
       // pixels in NxN.
    }
    GroupSync();

    uint globalSamples = sNumPerSamplePixels * (N*N -1);
    for (sample = groupIndex..globalSamples..sample += GROUP_SIZE/(N*N))
    {
       // Read the lights that touch this tile from the groupshared memory.
       // Accumulate the lighting for the sample.
       // Write out the results.
    }
    GroupSync();

    // Process the per-pixel component for every pixel in NxN, and add the results
    // to the intermediate results calculated for the top-left pixel.
}
```

Listing 31.1. Pseudocode for the shading pass. It has four phases: light culling phase, analysis phase, coarse pixel shading phase, and pixel shading phase. Phases are separated by a groupsync().

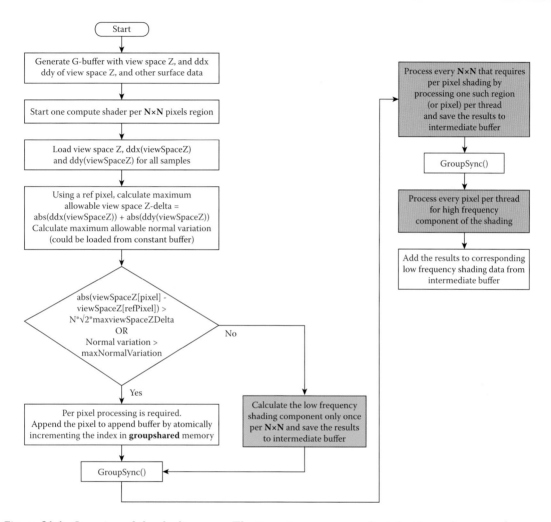

Figure 31.1. Overview of the shading pass. The items in green are evaluated at lower frequency (once per $N \times N$ pixels) and the items in orange are executed at once-per-pixel frequency.

Coarse pixel shading phase Regardless of whether we are able to reduce the shading frequency of the slowly varying shading term to the coarse rate or not, we evaluate it at the top-left pixel. Using the analysis described for the analysis phase, we find out where a shading term can be evaluated at the coarse rate and we store its results in memory (groupshared or global). If the DPI is high enough and there is no shading term that must be evaluated at the pixel rate, we can splat the intermediate results to the other pixels in that coarse pixel. For the other threads, we append their thread IDs to an append buffer in the groupshared memory, indicating that the shading term needs to be evaluated at the other pixels in that coarse pixel. All threads within the group wait at the synchronization point. By structuring the code this way, we have moved the shading term evaluation (often expensive) out of the control flow and reduced the control flow divergence.

For the regions where we could not lower the shading rate, we change the axis of parallelism from one thread per coarse pixel to one thread per pixel and evaluate the shading term. The threads that evaluated the shading term at the coarse rate wait at the group synchronization point. If the DPI is high enough, there may be no need to do per-pixel shading. In this situation, the next phase can be skipped altogether.

Pixel shading phase If there is a shading component that must be evaluated at the pixel rate (or if the DPI is not high enough), we change the axis of parallelism to one thread per coarse pixel again but now each thread processes all the pixels in that coarse pixel and adds the results to the ones calculated in the previous step.

31.3.3   Biasing the Sampler

Texturing is typically done in the forward passes and is not deferred. The G-buffer was generated at a pixel frequency (with the assumption that shading will be done once per pixel). However, we try to reduce the shading rate to once per coarse pixel wherever possible during the shading pass. This introduces temporal artifacts like shimmering. Possible solutions to this are

1. to sample the textures using a biased sampler (biased by $\log_2 N$) during the forward pass for the regions where the shading rate will be lowered;

2. to filter the texture data on the fly during the rendering pass.

The latter can increase the bandwidth significantly (depending on the size of N). So, we propose to introduce an additional G-buffer component per texture that uses a biased sampler. This does add some cost to the G-buffer generation.

The DirectX 11.2 Tier 2 specifications introduced minimum/maximum filtering along with tiled resources. One way to optimize this algorithm even further is to offload the minimum/maximum bounds calculation of the $N \times N$ region of the G-buffer to a texture sampling unit. This frees the shader cores from loading all the values and calculating the minimum/maximum. Shader cores reduce the shading rate when the difference in the minimum and maximum is less than some acceptable threshold. This technique might invoke some false positives because it is more conservative than the one proposed in the shader-based solution.

Loop Count	Power Plant			Sponza		
	Pixel (ms)	Coarse Pixel (ms)	Savings (%)	Pixel (ms)	Coarse Pixel (ms)	Savings (%)
0	22.7	11.2	50.7	12.5	9.4	24.9
100	50.3	21.1	58.1	26.8	17.6	34.3
500	87.7	34.9	60.2	43.6	27.7	36.5

Table 31.1. Shading time (ms) when shading was reduced to 2×2 pixel blocks wherever possible compared to when shading was performed every pixel.

31.4 Performance

We measured our performance on a system with Windows 8.1, running with an Intel HD 5500 integrated GPU. We used scenes that we felt were representative of game assets. We used two scenes, the power plant scene and the Sponza scene. Each scene was lit with 1024 colored point lights. Our rendering equation consists of the diffuse and the specular terms. We tried to reduce the frequency at which the entire rendering equation is evaluated to once per coarse pixel of the size 2×2 pixels. We could do that because our DPI was high enough at 1920×1080 pixels. At this DPI, we did not have a shading term that had to be evaluated at the pixel rate. To mimic how the performance would change for more expensive shaders, such as AO cone tracing, we added a dummy loop inside our shader to make it more compute intensive and varied the loop length as a parameter. In some cases, users may want to evaluate certain coefficients in the rendering equation at the lower rate, but the actual rendering equation could be evaluated at the higher rate. The algorithm proposed here is fully generic and one can lower the frequency of only some parts of the rendering equation.

Table 31.1 summarizes the performance benefits of reducing the shading rate as a function of shader length. We see anywhere from 25% to 60% improvement in the shading time depending upon the shader complexity. For a given scene, we see higher gains if the shader is more complex. However, sampling the albedo texture using a biased sampler and storing that as an extra G-buffer component increases the G-buffer generation time only by 2.2 ms and 1.9 ms for the power plant and the Sponza scenes, respectively. (See Figure 31.2.) As a result, we see this technique as a net win.

31.5 Conclusion

We have presented a technique to reduce the shading costs during deferred shading. The same technique is applicable to postprocessing passes, too. With this technique developers can apply their postprocessing effects at a reduced rate with minimal impact to image quality.

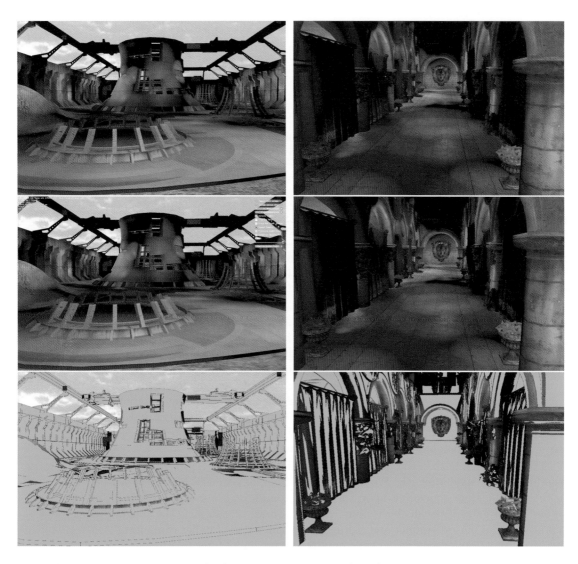

Figure 31.2. The power plant scene (left) and the Sponza scene (right). Coarse pixel size was 2×2 pixels. Top row images were rendered at the full pixel resolution. Middle row images were rendered with coarse pixel shading wherever possible. Bottom row shows in green the regions where shading was reduced to coarse pixel rate.

Demo

A real-time demo implemented using DirectX shader Model 5.0 will be available on the Intel Developer Zone (https://software.intel.com/en-us).

Bibliography

[Lauritzen 10] A. Lauritzen. "Deferred Rendering for Current and Future Rendering Pipelines." SIGGRAPH Course: Beyond Programmable Shading, Los Angeles, CA, July 29, 2010.

[Pool 12] J. Pool. "Energy-Precision Tradeoffs in the Graphics Pipeline." PhD thesis, Univeristy of North Carolina, Chapel Hill, NC, 2012.

[Pranckevičius 09] A. Pranckevičius. "Compact Normal Storage for Small G-Buffers." http://aras-p.info/texts/CompactNormalStorage.html, 2009.

[Vaidyanathan et al. 14] K. Vaidyanathan, M. Salvi, R. Toth, T. Foley, T. Akenine-Moller, J. Nilsson, J., et al. "Coarse Pixel Shading." Paper presented at High Performance Graphics, Lyon, France, June 23–25, 2014.

Progressive Rendering Using Multi-frame Sampling

Daniel Limberger, Karsten Tausche, Johannes Linke, and Jürgen Döllner

32.1   Introduction

This chapter presents an approach that distributes sampling over multiple, consecutive frames and, thereby, enables sampling-based, real-time rendering techniques to be implemented for most graphics hardware and systems in a less complex, straightforward way. This systematic, extensible schema allows developers to effectively handle the increasing implementation complexity of advanced, sophisticated, real-time rendering techniques, while improving responsiveness and reducing required hardware resources.

The approach is motivated by the following observations related to 3D system and application development:

- Creating advanced rendering techniques and computer graphics systems is intriguing in the case of target platforms equipped with the latest graphics hardware. Business and industry applications, however, are often strongly constrained in terms of both hardware and API support: software and hardware adapt slowly to new APIs and are often limited in terms of available processing power and video memory, e.g., with regards to high-resolution image generation. Thus, it sometimes takes years for state-of-the-art, real-time rendering techniques to become a core part of 3D systems and applications in business and industry.

- Many 3D systems and applications do not require a strictly continuous stream of high-quality images. For example, in interactive visualization of static data, which is common for digital-content-creation tools, the rendering process can be partially paused as user interactions and data changes occur less frequently. Thus, strict real-time, high-quality imaging constraints can sometimes be lessened.

- The adoption of the latest rendering techniques in 3D systems and applications is faced with increasing software complexity and increasing hardware requirements due to their single-frame design, e.g., designing, implementing, and testing complex, shader-based, multi-platform rendering techniques. In particular, this phenomenon increases financial and technical risks in system and application development.

The key idea of our approach, *multi-frame sampling*, is based on, technically speaking, the following idea: Instead of rendering a single frame in response to an update request, multiple frames are rendered and accumulated. Thereby, every accumulation result can be immediately displayed while the frame quality progressively increases. We demonstrate our approach for a variety of rendering techniques, i.e., antialiasing (AA), depth of field (DoF), soft shadows, and screen-space ambient occlusion (SSAO), as well as order-independent transparency (OIT). Progressive rendering using multi-frame sampling allows us to use rather simple implementations of rendering techniques to produce state-of-the-art effects. Furthermore, the multi-frame approach usually reduces memory usage, decreases rendering cost per frame (lower response time), allows for better maintainable implementations, and provides more comprehensible parameterizations.

32.2   Approach

An integral part of today's hardware-accelerated, real-time rendering technologies is built on *sampling*, as the "process of rendering images is inherently a sampling task" [Akenine-Möller et al. 08]. Sampling is generally used to approximate continuous characteristics and signals, e.g., reducing aliasing artifacts caused by insufficient depictions of continuous domains. For single-frame rendering, sampling is limited to a single frame. Increasing the number of samples improves the resulting image quality but also increases the rendering costs per frame in terms of time and memory.

Our multi-frame sampling approach distributes samples over a well-defined number n_{MF} of consecutive frames. With each frame we progressively increase image quality while having reduced cost per frame and still being able to process massive amounts of samples. Each frame generated during multi-frame sampling uses a unique subset of samples of a well-defined set of samples called the *kernel*. Consecutive frames are accumulated until n_{MF} frames are generated and the rendering finally pauses. On any update request, the accumulation process is restarted.

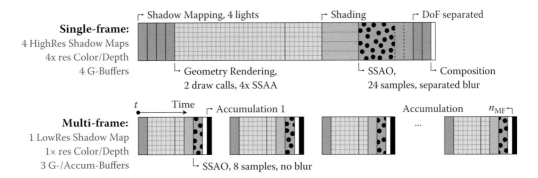

Figure 32.1. Conceptual illustration of a typical single-frame rendering structure transformed into a multi-frame rendering structure: Only one shadow pass instead of four, and 8 SSAO samples instead of 24, are used. DoF and AA are inherently available due to camera and NDC (normalized device coordinate) space shifting. The required resources are reduced, and to increase quality, more frames can be rendered and accumulated.

Assumptions The application of multi-frame sampling in 3D systems and applications is based on the following assumptions:

- The underlying rendering uses sampling as one of its elements.

- Rendering update requests are less frequent, and responsiveness in terms of frames per second is favored over intermediate frame quality.

- The converging image quality is not disruptive to the use cases or usability of 3D systems and applications.

Implementation To transform a given single-frame, sampling-based technique into a multi-frame technique, we proceed as follows:

1. We identify segments within the technique that are processed repeatedly. A parameterization that controls an iteration per frame (e.g., number of samples) often indicates such segments. These iterations are unrolled, which causes samples to be distributed over consecutive frames (Figure 32.1).

2. We have to verify that (a) an increase in number of executions of a segment results in better quality and (b) each segment's result can be accumulated throughout multiple consecutive frames.

3. We adapt the original technique such that it supports an appropriate sampling characteristic: the sampling type (single or multiple samples per frame) and the spatio-temporal distribution of samples.

When multi-frame sampling is used with multiple techniques simultaneously, depending on their assembly, there might be combinations that require special attention, for example, stochastic per-fragment discarding combined with screen-space ambient occlusion.

The remainder of this chapter describes sampling strategies and frame accumulation. For a variety of rendering techniques, associated multi-frame approaches are discussed (Section 32.3). Within each of these sections, results are discussed and brief performance remarks are given. All code snippets are based on GLSL and C++ using the OpenGL API.

32.2.1 Sampling Strategies

For multi-frame sampling we distinguish between techniques processing either one or multiple samples per frame. A single sample per frame is taken from a kernel, which is precomputed on the CPU and provided as a *uniform* (usually `float`, `vec2`, or `vec3`). For every subsequent frame, the uniform is updated (per technique). When using multiple samples per frame, the kernel is precomputed on the CPU as well but then uploaded to the GPU encoded as a uniform buffer, texture, or buffer (depending on kernel's size and shader capability). Since the rendering can unfold over multiple frames, most rendering techniques can be reduced to their core concept. Neither performance-related caching nor other optimization strategies are required. Furthermore, some techniques are virtually for free because they are inherent to multi-frame rendering (e.g., AA, DoF).

Nevertheless, the final rendering quality and especially the convergence speed and its "temporal tranquility" strongly depend on a well-designed kernel. The kernel's characteristics include

- required number of samples for targeted quality,

- spatial distribution or value-based distribution,

- sample regularity and completeness for finite accumulation,

- temporal convergence constraints regarding the sequence of samples,

- additional per-fragment randomization.

Since we do not use GPU-based pseudo-randomness and all samples are typically precomputed and designed for a specific multi-frame number n_{MF}, accumulating additional frames on top of that is futile. Especially when passing low multi-frame numbers, this may lead to temporal clustering. The presented techniques have been implemented based on the open-source, header-only libraries `glm` [Riccio 15] and `glkernel` [Limberger 15] used for dynamic computation of kernels of required characteristics at runtime.

```
1  // weight = 1.0 / n, with n enumerating the current multi-frame.
2  uniform float weight;
3  ...
4  {
5      ...
6      vec3 a = texture(accumBuffer, v_uv).rgb;
7      vec3 c = texture(frameBuffer, v_uv).rgb;

9      // average is pointing to the accumulation target.
10     average = mix(a, c, weight);
11 }
```

Listing 32.1. Example of an accumulation GLSL fragment shader adding the last frame to the overall average; `frameBuffer` contains the nth frame's color and `accumBuffer` the last average. Texture filtering is set to nearest filtering for both texture objects.

32.2.2   Frame Accumulation

The accumulation of consecutive frames can be implemented using hardware-accelerated blending. Alternatively, the accumulation can be executed as an additional postprocessing pass. Either a screen-aligned triangle with a fragment shader or, if available, a compute shader can be used to average all existing frames. For this, the accumulation buffer is set up as an input texture and a color attachment of the target framebuffer object simultaneously. The current frame is provided as a second input texture. The color c of the nth frame is read and added to the previous average a: $a = c/n + a(1 - 1/n)$. This works with a single accumulation buffer (no ping pong; reduced memory footprint) as long as no adjacent fragments are processed (Listing 32.1).

On update requests, multi-frame rendering is reset to a multi-frame number of 1 and accumulation is just blitting this frame; accumulation is skipped and the frame is rendered into the accumulation buffer directly. The accumulation buffer's texture format should support sufficient accuracy (16I or 32F) because the weight for frame averaging gets subsequently smaller (Figure 32.2).

Since the scene and its underlying data is assumed to be static during accumulation, the time per frame is roughly constant for subsequent frames. Thus, individual sampling characteristics can be adapted ad hoc for the second and all subsequent frames to approach the constrained frame time (e.g., decrease or increase number of samples per frame). Alternatively, vertical synchronization can be turned off during accumulation. In our tests we experienced no tearing artifacts because the expected, consecutive differences converge to zero. Apart from that, extensions for application-controlled synchronization could be used to exclude artifacts entirely.

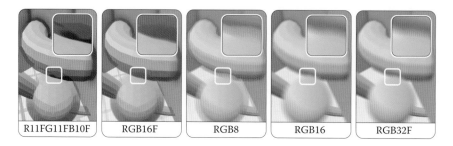

Figure 32.2. Accumulation results (test scene, AA and DoF) for 1024 frames using various texture formats. From left to right, the quality is (obviously) increasing.

32.3 Multi-frame Rendering Techniques

One motivation for multi-frame sampling is to have better control of the adjustment of the rendering quality, while implementing against older, limited APIs and conserving as many GPU resources as possible. Even though the techniques discussed in this section do not always reflect state-of-the-art techniques, they have been picked to express the required (re)thinking when creating multi-frame rendering techniques. They are intended as blueprints for the transformation of other sampling-based techniques.

32.3.1 Multi-frame Antialiasing

Without taking specific countermeasures, image synthesis based on rasterization depicts a continuous domain and, thus, usually contains aliasing artifacts like jagged edges and moiré patterns. Antialiasing is commonly applied to mitigate these artifacts, e.g., super-sampling and multi-sampling: Color or depth buffers are rendered at a higher resolution than the output resolution. While these buffers provide good results for single-frame-constrained applications, they use a lot of processing power and memory. Alternatively, several sampling strategies for post-processing have been created, e.g., AMD's MLAA, NVIDIA's FXAA, and Intel's CMAA. Varying in their performance and quality, these all provide a comparably low memory footprint. With temporal antialiasing, another type of antialiasing was introduced recently: NVIDIA's TXAA and subsequently MFAA [NVIDIA 15] claim to result in better quality and increased performance in comparison to MSAA. Temporal antialiasing already uses varying sampling patterns and information from multiple consecutive frames, albeit limited (two subsequent frames) as they are still designed for single-frame rendering.

Approach   For our implementation, a sampling offset in $[-0.5, +0.5]$ is semi-randomly chosen per frame. The offset is then transformed into a subpixel offset and added to the vertices' xy-coordinates in normalized device coordinates

```
1  in vec3 a_vertex;
2  uniform mat4 mvp; // Model view projection
3  // Per-frame offset in [-0.5,+0.5], pre-multiplied by
4  // 1.0 / viewport size.
5  uniform vec2 ndcOffset;
6    ...
7      vec4 ndcVertex = mvp * vec4(a_vertex, 1.0);

9      // Shift the view frustum within the subpixel extent.
10     ndcVertex.xy  += ndcOffset * ndcVertex.w;
11     gl_Position = ndcVertex;
```

Listing 32.2. A GLSL vertex shader for progressive multi-frame antialiasing.

(NDC), effectively shifting the complete NDC space (Listing 32.2). Note that shifting the camera's position and center in world space does not work due to the parallax effect.

Sampling characteristics Pseudo-randomly chosen offsets within a square work surprisingly well. The convergence can be speed up by using uniform, shuffled samples or common sampling patterns [Akenine-Möller et al. 08]. For our implementation we use shuffled Poisson-disk sampling to generate a uniform distribution of offsets for a specific number of frames (Listing 32.3). This prevents clustering of "pure" random sampling and provides better convergence than regular patterns for a large number of samples (e.g., eight or more), which are nontrivial to calculate for an arbitrary number of samples. Due to the random distance between consecutive offsets, the image tends to shift noticeably by up to one pixel during the first few frames. This can be almost eliminated by constraining the first sample to the center of the pixel (offset $[0.0, 0.0]$). Sorting all offsets by their length (i.e., the distance to the pixel center) is not recommended: Although it reduces the subtle shifting further, it also results in temporal clustering. Finally, to avoid clustering at pixel edges and corners of adjacent pixels, we use a tile-based Poisson-disk sampling (Figure 32.3).

Performance and remarks Accumulation of only a few frames usually results in decent antialiasing. With Poisson-disk sampling, it takes about 16 frames for a result that appears optimal and about 64 frames until subsequent frames yield no visual improvements anymore. In comparison, pseudo-random sampling takes about 1.3 times longer to yield comparable quality and, additionally, is less predictable due to clustering. As an addition, blurring can be applied by increasing the offsets and using an appropriate distribution.

```
1  // 3D array of glm::vec2 values with extent: 64x1x1 (glkernel)
2  auto aaSamples = glkernel::kernel2{ 64 };
3  glkernel::sample::poisson_square(aaSamples, -.5f, .5f);
4  glkernel::shuffle::random(aaSamples, 1); // From index 1 to last

6  while(rendering)
7  {
8      ...
9      const auto ndcOffset = aaSamples[accumCount] / viewport;
10     program.setUniform("ndcOffset", ndcOffset);
11     ...
12 }
```

Listing 32.3. C++ example for an AA sample computation using `glkernel`.

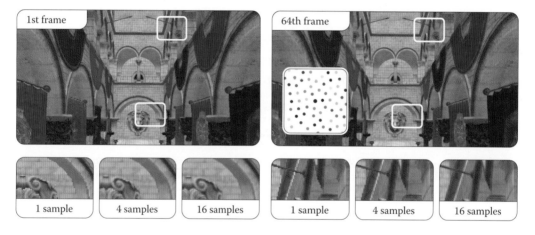

Figure 32.3. Sponza scene rendered with multi-frame AA (shuffled Poisson). The dots depict a 64-sample kernel, encoding its sequence from dark to light gray, starting at the center (big circle).

32.3.2 Multi-frame Depth of Field

Depth of field is an effect that can be used to guide a users attention to a certain region within a scene. The effect blurs objects depending on their distance to a chosen focal plane or point, which usually lies on an object or region of interest. DoF is often implemented at postprocessing, mixing the sharp focus field with one or two (near and far field) blurry color buffers per fragment, based on the fragment's distance to the focal point or plane [Bukowski et al. 13]. More advanced techniques are also available, usually reducing boundary discontinuities and intensity leakage artifacts as well as accounting for partial occlusion by using

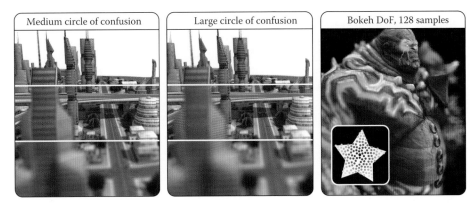

Figure 32.4. Multi-frame DoF with (top to bottom) 4, 16, and 64 samples for medium and large CoC. The sequence of 128 samples is depicted from dark to light gray.

multiple focus layers [Schedl and Michael 13, Selgrad et al. 15]. Even though multi-layer approaches can be adapted to multi-frame rendering, we present a minimal approach favoring rendering speed over convergence time and enabling high-quality DoF.

Approach For DoF we use a random two-dimensional vector on a unit disc as per-frame sample. This vector indicates for each point in a scene, where on its circle of confusion (CoC) it should be rendered on the image plane. With subsequent sampling, each point gradually covers its circle of confusion. Similar to our AA approach, the sample vector is added to the vertices' xy-coordinates in a vertex shader, this time, however, in view space before applying the projection matrix. It is scaled with the vertices' z-distance to the chosen focal plane. Additional postprocessing passes per frame, e.g., separated blurring, are not required. (See Figure 32.4.)

```glsl
1  // z-distance to the camera at which objects are sharp
2  uniform float focalDist;
3  // Point in circle of confusion (opt. pre-multiplied by scale)
4  uniform vec2 cocPoint;
5  ...
6  {
7      ...
8      vec4 viewVertex = modelView * vec4(a_vertex, 1.0);
9      viewVertex.xy  += cocPoint * (viewVertex.z + focalDist);
10     gl_Position = projection * viewVertex;
11 }
```

Sampling characteristics Similar to multi-frame antialiasing, random sampling works but results in comparatively long convergence times. Furthermore, fragments of points distant from the focal plane are spread widely on the screen, causing substantially unsteady output in the first few frames. To prevent this, Poisson-disk samples are sorted by the distance to the center. The center is used as the initial sample again, omitting shifting for consecutive update requests. By that, the effect gradually increases until all samples have been processed. Arbitrary Bokeh shapes can be easily accounted for by masking the samples with the desired shape:

```
1  auto dofSamples = glkernel::kernel2{ 128 };
2  glkernel::sample::poisson_square(dofSamples, -1.f, 1.f);
3  // Opt. mask every sample by its position using a bitfield
4  glkernel::mask::by_value(dofSamples, bitmask);
5  // Sort by dist to ref
6  glkernel::sort::distance(dofSamples, 0.f, 0.f);
```

Performance and remarks The number of required samples to produce an "artifact-free" image depends on the largest CoC any point in the scene has, which in turn is proportional to the desired effect scale as well as the point's distance to the focal plane. Although it may seem counterintuitive, scaling the number of required samples linearly with the CoC's radius, at least for reasonably large CoCs, results in sufficient image quality. We found a sample count (and thus, frame count) about ten times the radius in pixels to be sufficient. While this can mean a few seconds to full convergence in extreme cases, keep in mind that the effect's strength gradually increases over time.

For implementing a focal point instead of a focal area, one can scale the sample by the vertices' distance to that point. If a strong blurriness for out-of-focus objects in combination with a large focal area is desired, the vertex shader could be extended accordingly.

32.3.3 Multi-frame Soft Shadows

Shadow mapping is an omnipresent technique in real-time computer graphics. The original approach renders distances as seen from a light. Advanced variations improve on problems like heavy aliasing and hard edges at the cost of additional texture lookups per fragment, more computations, or additional passes. While soft shadows cast by occluders of large distance to the receiver can be handled well, correctly and efficiently modeling shadow casting of area lights is still a problem for single-frame techniques.

Approach For our approach, we use the most-basic shadow mapping and take only a small number of lights into account per frame. For multi-frame shadow mapping, the lights' surfaces are randomly sampled: For each frame, a random position on each of the selected lights is used for shadow map rendering as well as scene lighting and shading. Accumulating multiple frames results in realistic and aliasing-free soft shadows with large penumbras.

Sampling characteristics Good convergence is achieved by uniformly sampling the surfaces of all lights. For very large area or volumetric lights, we used an approach similar to the previously described multi-frame DoF, starting with sampling the light in its center and slowly progressing toward its edges, gradually increasing the penumbras. If multiple light sources of various areas/volumes are used, each light should be accounted for at least once per frame. Lights of larger surfaces should be sampled preferentially.

Performance and remarks The convergence time depends on the maximum penumbra width, which in turn depends on the size of the area lights and their relation to occluding and receiving scene objects. Similar to DoF, we experienced that the number of samples required for a completely banding-free result correlates to the largest penumbra width in the screen space. Convergence can be greatly improved, e.g., by applying variance shadow mapping [Donnelly and Lauritzen 06] combined with perspective shadow maps [Stamminger and Drettakis 02]. We also found that surprisingly low shadow map resolutions can provide visually pleasing shadows: A resolution of 128×128 pixels, for example, does not result in any distracting artifacts, although smaller objects and scene details were not captured and contact shadows were inadequate (Figure 32.5).

Since our approach relies on sampling light surfaces, all lights should show at least a certain surface (larger for lower shadow map resolutions). Even for hard cases (imagine a large TV illuminating a room with nearby occluders), the presented approach is able to provide correct shadows of high quality, albeit with increased convergence times. For a correct illumination induced by large numbers of local lights, our basic frame accumulation of non-HDR lights currently conflicts with partial light sampling.

32.3.4   Multi-frame Screen-Space Ambient Occlusion

The complex interactions of real-world objects and lights pose a significant challenge even for today's most sophisticated real-time rendering engines. SSAO is typically used to capture local effects of real-world lighting. Since Crytek's initial concept, numerous variants and enhancements have been proposed (e.g., HBAO+, SSDO). Due to the performance-intensive nature of these effects, they use different optimizations at the cost of quality: e.g., blurring the occlusion map to mask the noise (and its resulting shower-door artifacts) is usually suggested. Multi-frame approaches can also be found: For example, using reverse reprojection provides higher temporal coherence but introduces additional complexity and resource requirements (history buffers) and utilizes only the previous frame.

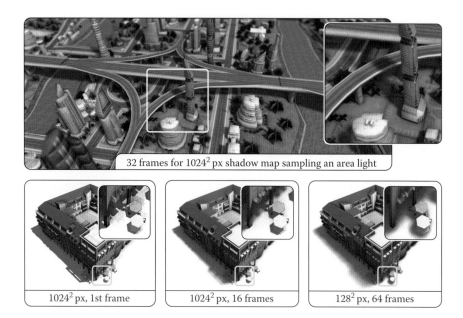

Figure 32.5. Soft shadows using area light sampling and basic shadow mapping.

Approach We use the original SSAO as the basis for our multi-frame approach. In order to mitigate banding artifacts produced by using the same sampling kernel for all pixels, the original implementation randomly rotates the kernel per pixel. This in turn introduces noise to the image, which is masked by blurring. When using multi-frame sampling, the noise is mitigated within a few frames even without blurring. In fact, removing the blur pass results in a better final image quality. The random rotation can also be removed, although the banding artifacts are more noticeable and result in a more unsteady image during the first few frames.

Sampling characteristics We use Poisson-disk sampling with best-candidate optimization to uniformly distribute points in a unit sphere that are used as sampling offsets. Compared to a single-frame approach, a lower sample count per frame can be used to accommodate for low-end devices. If desired, all samples can be assigned a random length within the unit sphere and can be sorted by this to account for local ambient occlusion effects for early frames. As for DoF, this reduces noise and banding artifacts resulting in a less disruptive effect.

Performance and remarks For this effect the number of frames required for a converging image is again dependent on its desired parameters, more specifically its radius. For moderate settings we found that about 480 samples provided a nearly artifact-free result, i.e., 60 frames when using 8 samples per frame. For small radii, removing the random rotation actually improves convergence times, reducing the adequate number of samples by two thirds. Since the more recent screen-space ambient occlusion and obscurance approaches rely on sampling the depth buffer multiple times per frame as well, they should be similarly easy to adapt to multi-frame sampling.

32.3.5 Multi-frame Transparency

Rendering transparent objects is often avoided in real-time rendering systems. Most approaches either achieve high performance by neglecting correctness and thus quality, or produce credible results by using many rendering passes or super-sampling while lowering rendering performance. Additionally, they are hard to integrate into deferred rendering systems (except that k-buffer rendering is available).

Screen-door transparency [Mulder et al. 98] applies a threshold pattern to small groups of fragments; within each group, fragments with an opacity value lower than their threshold are discarded. Drawbacks comprise highly visible patterns and insufficient accuracy. Stochastic transparency [Enderton et al. 10] improves on that by applying random patterns per pixel using multi-sampling, but still produces slightly noisy output for a single frame. The suggested multiple passes per frame can be transformed to a 1:1 frame mapping for multi-frame rendering of fast converging transparency.

Approach We discard super-sampling (color and coverage sampling) due to the heavy resource implications. Instead, transparent fragments are discarded based on a single random opacity threshold per fragment or object at a time. (See Figure 32.6.) Thus, using per-fragment thresholding with back-face culling disabled, we achieve correct order-independent transparency.

Sampling characteristics The technique's implementation is straightforward, but special care must be taken to generate "good" per-fragment randomness. Based on stochastic transparency, a mapping of n distinct opacity values in the range $[0, 1]$ to associated bitmasks is precomputed on the CPU and provided to the GPU (Figure 32.7). For example, for an opacity of 0.8 and bitmask size of 1024, a bitmask of about $0.8 \cdot 1024 = 819$ uniformly distributed (avoiding clusters) bits is computed. Additionally, random, fragment-specific offsets can be used to shuffle the threshold access between adjacent fragments over time. For object-based transparency, no objects should be discarded within the first frame. Thus, all objects are initially opaque and gradually converge toward their individual opacity (limiting minimal opacity to $1/n$ for n frames). For all consecutive frames, the object-based bit masking skips the draw call or discards fragments based on an object ID (Figure 32.7).

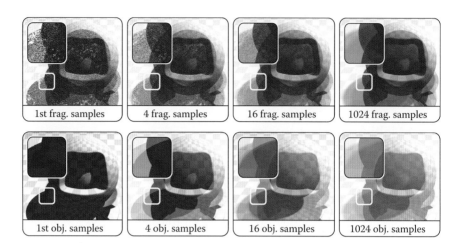

Figure 32.6. Convergence for per-fragment (top row) and per-object (bottom row) transparency thresholding. For per-fragment thresholding, back-face culling is on. Note the two distinct shadows resulting from the inner and out sphere.

Figure 32.7. Kernel used for transparency masking. Left: For 128 opacity values from 0 (top) to 1 (bottom), 128 uniformly distributed bits (left to right) are computed. Right: This kernel can be used for per-fragment as well as per-object discarding, the latter shown here, but with 1024 instead of 128 bits per mask.

Performance and remarks Stochastic transparency usually requires full multi-sampling within a single pass with up to 16 coverage samples per fragment, requiring extreme amounts of memory. In contrast, multi-frame transparency requires no additional memory at all. The amount of frames required for a low-noise transparency is dependent on the depth complexity of the current scene and camera angle. While direct use of more advanced techniques like stochastic transparency might lead to shorter convergence times, we prefer the more basic

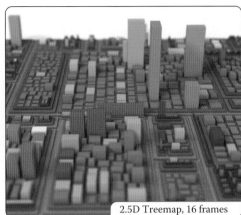

Sponza, 16 frames

2.5D Treemap, 16 frames

Figure 32.8. Multi-frame sampling applying the presented techniques all together.

approach for its low memory footprint, minimal performance overhead per frame, and implementation simplicity.

A major drawback for pixel-based transparency is that it can hardly be combined with some postprocessing techniques, e.g., SSAO, as the G-buffers of individual frames are highly noisy and do not show coherent surfaces. In contrast, though still not completely accurate, object-based transparency shows SSAO results on transparent objects and even on objects overlaid by them; this is usually difficult to achieve in conventional real-time rendering. Using object-based transparency, however, (1) opacity cannot be determined via texturing anymore, and (2) back-faces as well as concave objects cannot be rendered adequately (at least, not without additional draw calls) and might result in inaccuracies.

32.4 Conclusion and Future Work

We have presented an approach to transform and integrate sampling-based rendering techniques into a progressive multi-frame rendering system (Figure 32.8). It allows us to focus on sampling and its characteristics instead of optimizations necessary for satisfying single-frame limitations. It favors low response times and low-level APIs over per-frame quality. Furthermore, at least for the discussed techniques, a better maintainability and simpler, easy-to-understand parameterization in terms of target quality and effect characteristics is derived. From a software-engineering perspective, our approach reduces the implementation complexity of 3D systems and applications that need to combine independent, real-time rendering techniques.

The current limitations and future challenges include the following topics: When using multiple multi-frame techniques simultaneously, sampling parameterization of all effects is to be coordinated for the targeted number of frames. In addition, some techniques might not be used in combination (e.g., pixel-based transparency with SSAO), and interaction issues arise for, e.g., picking or coordinate retrieval because depth and ID buffers cannot be accumulated in a meaningful way.

For future work, automatically adapting kernel parameterization to hardware and frame rendering times is desirable. Additional research comprises strategies for optimal convergence, a generic multi-frame rendering template for sampling-based rendering techniques, and finally, the evaluation of other techniques' applicability (e.g., image-based reflections, translucency, massive lighting, subsurface scattering).

32.5 Acknowledgment

This work was funded by the Federal Ministry of Education and Research (BMBF), Germany, within the InnoProfile Transfer research group "4DnDVis" (www.4dndvis.de).

Bibliography

[Akenine-Möller et al. 08] Tomas Akenine-Möller, Eric Heines, and Naty Hoffman. *Real-Time Rendering*, Third edition. Natick, MA: A K Peters, Ltd., 2008.

[Bukowski et al. 13] Mike Bukowski, Padraic Hennessy, Brian Osman, and Morgan McGuire. "The Skylanders SWAP Force Depth-of-Field Shader." In *GPU Pro 4*, edited by Wolfgang Engel, pp. 175–184. Boca Raton, FL: A K Peters/CRC Press, 2013.

[Donnelly and Lauritzen 06] William Donnelly and Andrew Lauritzen. "Variance Shadow Maps." In *Proceedings of the 2006 Symposium on Interactive 3D Graphics and Games, I3D '06*, pp. 161–165. New York: ACM, 2006.

[Enderton et al. 10] Eric Enderton, Erik Sintorn, Peter Shirley, and David Luebke. "Stochastic Transparency." In *Proc. of the 2010 ACM SIGGRAPH Symposium on Interactive 3D Graphics and Games, I3D '10*, pp. 157–164. ACM, 2010.

[Limberger 15] Daniel Limberger. "Kernel Utilities for OpenGL (glkernel)." https://github.com/cginternals/glkernel, 2015.

[Mulder et al. 98] Jurriaan D. Mulder, Frans C. A. Groen, and Jarke J. van Wijk. "Pixel Masks for Screen-Door Transparency." In *Proceedings of the Conference on Visualization '98, VIS '98*, pp. 351–358. Los Alamitos, CA: IEEE Computer Society Press, 1998.

[NVIDIA 15] NVIDIA. "Multi-frame Sampled Anti-aliasing (MFAA)." http://www.geforce.com/hardware/technology/mfaa/technology, 2015.

[Riccio 15] Christophe Riccio. "OpenGL Mathematics (GLM)." http://glm.g-truc.net/, 2015.

[Schedl and Michael 13] David Schedl and Wimmer Michael. "Simulating Partial Occlusion in Post-Processing Depth-of-Field Methods." In *GPU Pro 4*, edited by Wolfgang Engel, pp. 187–200. Boca Raton, FL: A K Peters/CRC Press, 2013.

[Selgrad et al. 15] Kai Selgrad, Christian Reintges, Dominik Penk, Pascal Wagner, and Marc Stamminger. "Real-time Depth of Field Using Multi-layer Filtering." In *Proceedings of the 19th Symposium on Interactive 3D Graphics and Games, i3D '15*, pp. 121–127. New York: ACM, 2015.

[Stamminger and Drettakis 02] Marc Stamminger and George Drettakis. "Perspective Shadow Maps." In *Proceedings of the 29th Annual Conference on Computer Graphics and Interactive Techniques, SIGGRAPH '02*, pp. 557–562. New York: ACM, 2002.

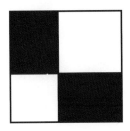

About the Contributors

Ulf Assarsson is an associate professor at Chalmers University of Technology. His main research interests are real-time shading, hard and soft shadows—including shadows in hair, fur, smoke, and volumetric participating media—GPGPU algorithms, GPU ray tracing, and real-time global illumination. He is also coauthor of the book *Real-Time Shadows* (2011).

Florian Bagar is a Rendering Software Engineer at Havok Inc., in Southern Germany. He previously worked as a Senior Programmer at Sproing Interactive Media GmbH. He studied computer graphics and digital image processing at the Vienna University of Technology, where he received an MSc degree in 2010. His current interests include real-time rendering, game development, multi-platform development, optimization, and engine design.

Markus Billeter holds an MSc degree in physics and complex adaptive systems. He is currently completing his PhD in the computer graphics research group at Chalmers University of Technology (Gothenburg, Sweden), where he participates in research in real-time rendering and high-performance and highly-parallel algorithms for GPGPU applications. In late 2012 and early 2013, he interned at the Robert Bosch Research and Technology Center in Palo Alto, California.

George Borshukov is CTO of embodee, a technology company that helps anyone find, select, and personalize apparel using a fun yet useful process. He holds an MS from the University of California, Berkeley, where he was one of the creators of *The Campanile Movie* and real-time demo (1997). He was technical designer for the "bullet time" sequences in *The Matrix* (1999) and received an Academy Scientific and Technical Achievement Award for the image-based rendering technology used in the film. Borshukov led the development of photoreal digital actors for *The Matrix* sequels (2003) and received a Visual Effects Society Award for the design and application of the universal capture system in those films. He is also a co-inventor of the UV pelting approach for parameterization and seamless texturing of polygonal or subdivision surfaces. He joined Electronic Arts in 2004 to focus on setting a new standard for facial capture, animation, and rendering in next-generation interactive entertainment. As director of creative R&D for EA

SPORTS he led a team focused on expanding the label's brand and its interactive entertainment offerings through innovation in hi-fidelity graphics and new forms of interactivity, including 3D camera devices.

Jean-Normand Bucci is managing a multi-disciplinary team of seven engineers and two technical artists as the director of Labs, Eidos-Montrèal's research-and-development department. The team's mandate is to work on innovation for the portfolio of all the western studios of Square-Enix Europe: Eidos-Montrèal, Io Interactive, and Crystal Dynamics. Prior to Labs, Jean-Normand, technical art director at the time, shipped *Thief* for both past and present generations of consoles. He worked in close collaboration with the lead 3D and programming director in finding the best visual improvements for the game given the constraints. With ten years of experience working on major AAA games at both Ubisoft Montrèal and Eidos-Montrèal, Jean-Normand feels comfortable and performs well in pipeline, feature, and tool brainstorming/creation roles.

Matthäus G. Chajdas is a starting PhD student at TU MÃijnchen. He recently graduated from the University of Erlangen, having worked on virtual texture mapping and automatic texturing methods, the latter in cooperation with REVES/INRIA. He is mainly interested in improving the quality of real-time graphics through novel rendering algorithms and simplified content generation.

Ka Chen started his career as a 3D programmer at Ubisoft Shanghai in 1998. In 2006 he moved to Ubisoft Montreal and continued his game developing effort, focusing on graphics rendering. He has helped develop multiple games such as *F1 Championship 2000, Splinter Cell: Pandora Tomorrow, Splint Cell: Double Agent, Rainbow Six: Vegas*, and *Ghost Recon*. From 2011 to 2015, he took a new role as central technique architect and focused on identifying and researching advanced rendering technologies for his company. His work includes Adaptive Virtual Texturing in *Far Cry 4* and Temporal Re-Projection Rendering in *Rainbow Six: Siege*. He is currently working at EA Motive.

Carsten Dachsbacher is a full professor at the Karlsruhe Institute of Technology. His research focuses on real-time computer graphics, global illumination, scientific visualization, and perceptual rendering, on which he published articles at various conferences and journals including SIGGRAPH, IEEE VIS, EG, and EGSR. He has been a tutorial speaker at SIGGRAPH, Eurographics, and the Game Developers Conference.

Samuel Delmont is a graphics programmer at Eidos Montrèal. He graduated in computer science at ESIEE Paris in 2007, and he worked in the game industry on several engines as an R&D programmer. In 2013 he joined Eidos Montrèal to work on *Thief* and is now a research programmer in Eidos Montrèal's Labs, an R&D group dedicated to new graphic technologies.

Hawar Doghramachi studied dental medicine at the Semmelweis University in Budapest and received in 2003 the doctor of dental medicine (DMD) title. After working for a while as a dentist, he decided to turn his lifetime passion for programming into his profession. After he studied 3D programming at the Games Academy in Frankfurt, from 2010 he worked as an Engine-Programmer in the Vision team of Havok. Currently he is working as a Graphics-Programmer in the R&D team of Eidos Montreal. He is particularly interested in finding solutions for common real-time rendering problems in modern computer games.

Jürgen Döllner is a full professor at the Hasso Plattner Institute at the University of Potsdam, where he is leading the computer graphics and visualization department. He studied mathematics and computer science at the University of Siegen, Germany and got his PhD in computer science from the University of Münster, Germany, in 1996. He also received there his habilitation degree in 2001. His major research areas are in information visualization, software visual analytics, and geospatial visual analytics. In particular, his research is focused on concepts, tools, and techniques for complex software systems and graphics-based systems. He is an author of more than 200 papers in computer graphics and visualization (for an overview of publications, see http://www.hpi3d.de). He serves as a reviewer to a number of international and national journals, conferences, and workshops.

Uriel Doyon is a 3D programmer at Eidos Montreal. He studied computer engineering at Ecole Polytechnique de Montreal, during which he made several internships at Matrox Graphics. He joined Ubisoft Montreal in 2004 as a 3D programmer and worked on several titles on the GameCube, Wii, and Playstation 3. In 2009, he started working at Eidos Montreal as the lead 3D programmer on *Thief.* He is currently working in Labs, which is an R&D group dedicated to new graphic technologies.

Michał Drobot is a principal rendering engineer at Infinity Ward, Activision. He most recently helped design and optimize the 3D renderer in *Far Cry 4* at Ubisoft Montreal. Prior to that, he worked at Guerrilla Games, designing and optimizing the rendering pipeline for the Playstation 4 launch title *Killzone: Shadow Fall.* He likes sharing his work at conferences as well as spending time writing publications about art and technology. He finds fast and pretty pixels exciting.

Jose I. Echevarria received his MS degree in computer science from the Universidad de Zaragoza, Spain, where he is currently doing research in computer graphics. His research fields range from real-time to off-line rendering, including appearance acquisition techniques.

Athanasios Gaitatzes received his PhD in 2012 from the University of Cyprus. He received his master of science in computer science, with a specialization in computer graphics, in 1989 from Purdue University. He has developed virtual reality exhibits at the cultural center of the Foundation of the Hellenic World (FHW) in Greece, worked as a project manager of the virtual reality stereoscopic production "The Battle of Chaeronia," and worked as a software engineer at the Advanced Systems Division of IBM. Based on his extensive experience in the design and development of software, he has taken part in several European research projects. His research interests include real-time computer graphics, photorealistic visualization, and real-time rendering techniques.

Mark Gjøl is a systems developer at Zylinc, with a focus on mobipe platforms. This interest has initially been realized as the spare-time project *Floating Image* for Android, which has achieved a rating of 4.3/5.0 with more than 950,000 downloads. He received an MS degree in computer graphics from the Danish Technical University in 2007.

Mikkel Gjøl is a graphics programmer at Splash Damage, a UK-based company that recently released the game *Brink* on the Xbox360, Playstation3, and PC. He received an MS degree in computer graphics from the Danish Technical University in 2005.

Thorsten Grosch is a junior professor of computational visualistics at the University of Magdeburg, Germany. Prior to this appointment he worked as a post-doctoral fellow at MPI Informatik in Saarbruecken. Thorsten received his PhD at the University of Koblenz-Landau; his main research interest is in both the areas of physically accurate and real-time global illumination.

Martin Guay is a PhD student at INRIA Grenoble where he is conducting research on computer animation. His work includes techniques for physically based simulation as well as character control. Before graduate school, Martin worked as a graphics programmer at the game studio Cyanide in Montreal.

Tobias Günther received his master's degree in computer science at the University of Magdeburg in 2013. He is currently a scientific researcher at the Department of Simulation and Graphics in Magdeburg, working on his PhD. His research interests include scientific visualization, real-time rendering, and physically-based global illumination.

Diego Gutierrez is a tenured associate professor at the Universidad de Zaragoza, where he got his PhD in computer graphics in 2005. He now leads his group's research on graphics, perception, and computational photography. He is an associate editor of three journals, has chaired and organized several conferences, and has served on numerous committees, including the SIGGRAPH and Eurographics conferences.

Dongsoo Han works as a researcher in AMD's GPU Tech Initiatives Group. At AMD, he focuses on developing physics simulations such as rigid body, fluid, cloth, hair, and grass for real-time applications. His research focuses on parallelizing physics simulation algorithms on GPUs. His hair simulation technique is a part of TressFX and has been used for several games and demos. He earned his master's degree in computer science at University of Pennsylvania, where he focused on various fluid simulation methods.

Takahiro Harada is a researcher and the architect of a GPU global illumination renderer called Firerender at AMD. He developed Forward+ and the GPU rigid body simulation solver that is used as a base of Bullet 3.0. Before joining AMD, he engaged in research and development on real-time physics simulation on PC and game consoles at Havok. Before coming to the industry, he was in academia as an assistant professor at the University of Tokyo, where he also earned his PhD in engineering.

Benjamin Hathaway is an experienced graphics programmer who has programmed everything from the Spectrum to the mighty PS3. He began his career as a frustrated artist who was unable to draw objects that rotated and who set about writing something that could... he has never looked back since. With over 14 years of industry experience, Benjamin has worked for the likes of Bits Studios (engine/lead Xbox programmer), Criterion (RenderWare core graphics engineer), Criterion Games (post processing: *Burnout Paradise*), Electronic Arts (Core Tech), and Rockstar. He can currently be found at Black Rock Studio, specializing in low-level optimization, post-processing, and generally achieving parity between the PS3 and Xbox 360 (*Pure* and *Split/Second*).

Pedro Hermosilla is an MS student at Universitat Politècnica de Catalunya in Barcelona. He worked at McNeel during 2008 and now works with the Moving Graphics Group. He is interested in real-time rendering, non-photorealistic rendering, and illumination techniques.

Karl Hillesland creates GPU product demos and graphics research for AMD. Prior to AMD, Karl worked in physics middleware (Pixelux's Digital Molecular Matter or DMM) and game development (Maxis, Electronic Arts). His PhD in computer science is from the University of North Carolina at Chapel Hill.

Samuel Hornus is a researcher at Inria in Nancy, France. He is interested in geometric problems that arise in computer graphics.

Tomasz Janczak is a principal engineer working at the Intel Corporation site located in Gdansk, Poland. His professional work focuses on analyzing and modeling new 3D rendering features for the upcoming processor graphics products, covering both software and hardware aspects. He received his PhD in 2004 and has authored a number of technical papers, as well as several patent applications. In his private life, he enjoys traveling around the world with his family and visiting places of diverse cultures and climates.

Jorge Jimenez is a real-time graphics researcher at the Universidad de Zaragoza, in Spain, where he received his BSc and MSc degrees, and where he is pursuing a PhD in real-time graphics. His passion for graphics started after watching old school demos in his brother's Amiga A1000. His interests include real-time photorealistic rendering, special effects, and squeezing rendering algorithms to be practical in game environments. He has numerous contributions in books and journals, including *Transactions on Graphics*, where his skin renderings made the front cover of the SIGGRAPH Asia 2010 issue. He loves challenges, playing games, working out in the gym, and more than anything, breaking in the street.

Krzysztof Kluczek Krzysztof got his Masters degree in Computer Science at Gdansk University of Technology. Then, having worked for 5 years at Intel as a Graphics Software Engineer he set off to become a self-employed indie game developer. He is also currently pursuing his PhD degree at Gdansk University of Technology and doing graphics research. In his free time he is enjoying learning new technologies, making games, being a part of gamedev.pl community and Polish Demoscene.

Sébastien Lagarde is a senior engine/graphics programmer who has been in the game industry for ten years. He has been credited on several games including casual and AAA titles on different platforms (PS2, GameCube, Nintendo DS, Xbox 360, PS3, PC), and he developed the 3D stereoscopic Trioviz SDK technology that has been integrated in several games (*Batman Arkham Asylum, Batman Arkham City, Assassin's Creed 2* and *3, Gear of War 3*, etc.). He has worked for several companies—Neko entertainment (video game), Dark-Works (video game), Piranese (architecture), Trioviz (stereoscopy middleware)—and now, he is using his expertise at DONTNOD entertainment in France on *Remember Me*, edited by Capcom. Passionate about rendering technologies, he has a blog (http://seblagarde.wordpress.com/) where he publishes some graphics articles.

Anass Lasram received his PhD in computer science from INRIA in 2012 then joined Advanced Micro Devices, Inc. (AMD), where he develops software to interact with future GPUs. He is interested in hardware-accelerated rendering and animation.

Sylvain Lefebvre is a researcher at INRIA, France. He completed his PhD in 2004, on the topic of texturing and procedural texture generation using GPUs. He joined Microsoft Research (Redmond, WA) as a postdoctoral researcher in 2005. In 2006 he was recruited by INRIA as a permanent researcher. He is currently a member of the team ALICE in the Nancy Grand-Est INRIA center.

His main research focuses are in procedural content generation—often starting from examples—end-user content manipulation, and compact GPU-friendly data structures for interactive applications, games, and 3D printing.

Hongwei Li received his PhD in computer science from Hong Kong University of Science and Technology. He was a researcher in AMD advanced graphics research group, focusing on real-time rendering and GPGPU applications. He is also very active in the open source community and is the main contributor of a rendering engine for mobile platforms.

Gábor Liktor is a PhD student at the Karlsruhe Institute of Technology (KIT), Germany. He received his diploma in computer science from the Budapest University of Technology and Economics (BUTE), Hungary. As a member of the computer graphics research group first at VISUS, University of Stuttgart, then at KIT, he is working in collaboration with Crytek GmbH. His primary areas of interest are real-time rendering architectures, volume rendering, adaptive shading, and geometry subdivision.

Daniel Limberger is a PhD student at the Hasso Plattner Institute at the University of Potsdam. His research interests include interactive image processing and stylization, rendering system design and architecture, and visualization of massive, multi-dimensional data in real time. He has been involved as a graphics engineer in the industry for over ten years and lately manages the development of various open-source graphics libraries, applications, and services (https://github.com/cginternals).

Johannes Linke received his BA in IT systems engineering in 2014 at the Hasso Plattner Institute in Potsdam, Germany. After interning at the rendering department of Unity Technologies, he joined the Master program at said institute, specializing in real-time rendering and GPU computing.

Belen Masia received her MS degree in computer science and systems engineering from the Universidad de Zaragoza, Spain, where she is currently a PhD student. Her research interests lie somewhere between the fields of computer graphics and computer vision, currently focusing on image processing and computational photography. Her work has already been published in several venues, including *Transactions on Graphics*.

Oliver Mattausch is currently employed as a post doctorate in the VMML Lab of the University of Zurich, working on processing and visualizing large datasets. Previously he worked as a computer graphics researcher at the Vienna University of Technology and at the University of Tokyo/ERATO. He received his MSc in 2004 and his PhD in 2010 from Vienna University of Technology. His research interests are real-time rendering, visibility and shadows, global illumination, and geometry processing.

Pavlos Mavridis is a software engineer at the Foundation of the Hellenic World, where he is working on the design and implementation of real-time rendering techniques for virtual reality installations. He received his BSc and MSc degrees in computer science from the University of Athens, Greece. He is currently pursuing his PhD in real-time computer graphics at the Department of Informatics of the Athens University of Economics and Business. His current research interests include real-time photorealistic rendering, global illumination algorithms, texture compression, and texture filtering techniques.

Jay McKee is a senior engineer in the Advanced Technology Initiatives group at AMD. There he conducts research on real-time rendering techniques and develops graphics-related tools and demos. He was the technical lead for AMD's 2012 "Leo" demo. He received a BS in computer science from the University of West Florida.

Doug McNabb is currently a game developer's voice inside Intel. He's currently creating new technologies to help advance the state of the art in visual computing. He was previously the CTO and rendering system architect at 2XL Games and the rendering system architect at Rainbow Studios. He contributed to more than a dozen games, with the most-recent being *Baja: Edge of Control.* You can find him on twitter @mcnabbd.

Fernando Navarro works as lead technical artist for Lionhead Studios (Microsoft Games Studios). Prior to that he directed the R&D departments of different production houses. His experience covers vfx, feature films, commercials, and games. He has a MSc from the Universidad de Zaragoza and is currently pursuing a PhD in computer science, focused on advanced rendering algorithms.

Ola Olsson is currently a PhD student at Chalmers University of Technology in Gothenburg, Sweden. He's a member of the computer graphics group and spends most of his time these days forcing pixels into boxes of various shapes and sizes. His primary research focus is algorithms for managing and shading thousands of lights in real time, resulting in several influential publications on tiled and, later, clustered shading. Before becoming a PhD student, Ola was a game programmer for around ten years with roles ranging from game-play programmer on *Ty the Tasmanian Tiger* to lead rendering programmer on *Race Pro.*

Georgios Papaioannou is currently an assistant professor of computer graphics at the Department of Informatics of the Athens University of Economics and Business. He received a BSc in computer science and a PhD in computer graphics and pattern recognition, both from the University of Athens, Greece. In the past, he has worked as a research fellow in many research and development projects, and as a virtual reality software engineer at the Foundation of the Hellenic World. His research is focused on real-time computer graphics algorithms, photorealistic rendering, virtual reality systems, and three-dimensional pattern recognition. He has contributed many scientific papers in the above fields and has coauthored one international and two Greek computer graphics textbooks. He is also a member of IEEE, ACM, SIGGRAPH, and Eurographics Association and has been a member of the program committees of many computer graphics conferences.

Eric Penner is a rendering engineer at Electronic Arts and a research associate at the Hotchkiss Brain Institute Imaging Informatics lab at the University of Calgary. He holds a MSc degree from the University of Calgary, Alberta, where he worked on GPU-accelerated medical volume rendering algorithms. Eric's MSc work is being commercialized by Calgary Scientific Inc. At Electronic Arts Eric has filled the roles of lead programmer on a Creative R&D team focused on cutting edge rendering and new forms of controller free interaction, as well as rendering engineer on the NHL series of games. Prior to working at Electronic Arts, Eric was a rendering engineer on the Advanced Technology group at Radical Entertainment and worked on the popular games *Prototype* and *Scarface*.

Emil Persson is the Head of Research at Avalanche Studios, where he is conducting forward-looking research, with the aim to be relevant and practical for game development, as well as setting the future direction for the Avalanche Engine. Previously, he was an ISV Engineer in the Developer Relations team at ATI/AMD. He assisted tier-one game developers with the latest rendering techniques, identifying performance problems and applying optimizations. He also made major contributions to SDK samples and technical documentation.

Ferenc Pintér is an engine programmer at Digital Reality's Technology Team. After working on network congestion control systems for Ericsson, he joined Eidos Hungary to create *Battlestations: Pacific* for PC and X360. His passion for outdoor rendering, procedurally aided content creation, and artist-friendly graphics tools has only been getting more fueled ever since.

Donald Revie graduated from the University of Abertay with a BSc (Hons) in computer games technology before joining Cohort Studios in late 2006. He worked on Cohort's Praetorian Tech platform from its inception, designing and implementing much of its renderer and core scene representation. He also worked individually and with others to develop shaders and graphics techniques across many of the company's projects. Since leaving Cohort Studios in early 2011 he has continued refining his ideas on engine architecture and pursuing his wider interests in game design and writing.

Kai Rohmer works as a scientific researcher at the Department of Simulation and Graphics at the University of Magdeburg, Germany. His research interests include physically based real-time rendering as well as augmented reality on mobile devices. He received his MSc in computer science with distinction in 2012.

Rahul P. Sathe works as a senior software engineer at Intel Corporation. His current role involves defining and prototyping the next-generation technologies in Intel Graphics Performance Analyzer. Prior to this role, he worked in various capacities in research and product groups at Intel. He is passionate about all aspects of 3D graphics and its hardware underpinnings. He holds several patents in rendering and game physics. Prior to joining Intel, he studied at Clemson University and University of Mumbai. While not working on the rendering-related things, he likes running and enjoying good food with his family and friends.

Daniel Scherzer is professor of visual computing at the University of Applied Sciences Ravensburg-Weingarten. He has also worked at MPI, KAUST, the University of Applied Sciences Hagenberg, the Ludwig Boltzmann Institute for Archaeological Prospection and Virtual Archaeology, and the Institute of Computer Graphics and Algorithms of the Vienna University of Technology, where he received an MSc in 2005, an MSocEcSc in 2008, and a PhD in 2009. His current research interests include global illumination, temporal coherence methods, shadow algorithms, modeling, and level-of-detail approaches for real-time rendering. He has authored and coauthored several papers in these fields.

Christian Schüler has been in the games industry since 2001 in various roles as engine programmer, technical lead, and consultant, contributing to a total of seven shipped games. He has an interest in 3D and shading algorithms as well as in sound synthesis. He is currently self-employed, doing serious games and simulation for naval training at the time of this writing.

Peter Sikachev graduated from Lomonosov Moscow State University in 2009, majoring in applied mathematics and computer science. He started his career game development in 2011 at Mail.Ru Games as a graphics programmer. He contributed to a range of rendering features of the *Skyforge* next-generation MMORPG. In 2013 he joined Eidos Montreal as a research-and-development graphics programmer. He helped ship *Thief* and *Rise of the Tomb Raider* and contributed to *Deus Ex: Universe*. Peter has been an author of multiple entries in the *GPU Pro* series and a speaker at ACM SIGGRAPH courses. He now holds a senior graphics programmer position at Rockstar Toronto.

Marc Stamminger is a professor for computer graphics at the University of Erlangen-Nuremberg, Germany, since 2002. After finishing his PhD thesis on finite element methods for global illumination in 1999, he was a post doctorate at MPI Informatics in Saarbrücken, Germany, and at the INRIA Sophia-Antipolis, France. In his research he investigates novel algorithms to exploit the power of current graphics hardware for rendering, geometry processing, and medical visualization. He participates in the program committees of all major computer graphics conferences and was program co-chair of Eurographics 2009 and the Eurographics Rendering Symposium 2010. Since 2012, he is head of the DFG-funded Research Training Group "Heterogeneous Image Systems."

Karsten Tausche is a student at the Hasso Plattner Institute, enrolled in the Master program of IT systems engineering, focusing on visualization techniques and GPU computing.

Pere-Pau Vázquez is an associate professor at the Universitat Politècnica de Catalunya in Barcelona. His research interests are illustrative visualization, GPU-accelerated rendering, and the applications of information theory to computer graphics.

Jason C. Yang is senior manager of the Advanced Technology Initiatives group at AMD, which develops new graphics algorithms, real-time physics technologies, and GPU demos. He received his BS and PhD in electrical engineering and computer science from MIT.

Egor Yusov is a senior graphics software engineer in Visual Computing Engineering group at Intel, where he has worked on a variety of 3D technologies including deformable terrain, physically based water rendering, shadows, and volumetric and postprocess effects. He received his PhD in computer science from Nizhny Novgorod State Technical University, Russia, in 2011. His research interests include real-time visualization and rendering, data compression, GPU-based algorithms, and shader programming.

Antoine Zanuttini works for DONTNOD Entertainment as a software engineer. He received his PhD in 2012 from the Arts and Technologies of Image Department of Université Paris 8. His research interests include material lighting, fluids simulation, depth of field, and expressive rendering.